# Child Development Observation Video CD-ROM

This CD-ROM brings to life more than 30 key concepts discussed in the text. After reading about one of the developmental concepts, you can see and hear the behavior in action on the CD-ROM and then assess your understanding of it on-line. Look for the video icons in the margin, and then go to the CD-ROM to see these concepts come to life.

**VIDEO 12.2**
Imaginary Audience

---

**VIDEO 1.1**
Little Albert
CLASSIC MODULE

**VIDEO 7.4**
Deductive Reasoning

**VIDEO 12.3**
Invincibility Fable

**VIDEO 4.1**
Prenatal Development

**VIDEO 7.5**
Theory of Mind

**VIDEO 13.1**
Bullying

**VIDEO 4.2**
Reflexes

**VIDEO 7.6**
Scaffolding

**VIDEO 13.2**
Reactive Aggression

**VIDEO 5.1**
Physical Growth

**VIDEO 9.1**
Mental Age Testing
CLASSIC MODULE

**VIDEO 13.3**
Relational Aggression

**VIDEO 5.2**
Synaptic Development

**VIDEO 10.1**
Teaching Sign Language to the Chimpanzee Washoe
CLASSIC MODULE
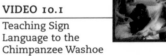

**VIDEO 13.4**
Human Aggression: Bandura's Bobo Doll
CLASSIC MODULE

**VIDEO 6.1**
Gibson's Visual Cliff
CLASSIC MODULE

**VIDEO 11.1**
Stranger Anxiety

**VIDEO 14.1**
Gender Consistency

**VIDEO 6.2**
Habituation/ Dishabituation

**VIDEO 11.2**
Social Referencing

**VIDEO 16.1**
Parten's Play Categories

**VIDEO 7.1**
Object Permanence

**VIDEO 11.3**
Nature and Development of Affection: Harlow's Monkeys
CLASSIC MODULE

**VIDEO 16.2**
Sociodramatic Play (social pretend play)

**VIDEO 7.2**
Egocentrism

**VIDEO 11.4**
Separation Anxiety

**VIDEO 16.3**
Rough and Tumble Play

**VIDEO 7.3**
Conservation

**VIDEO 12.1**
Self Awareness

**VIDEO 16.4**
Neglected Child

# Children
## and Their
# Development

### third edition

## Robert V. Kail
**Purdue University**

Upper Saddle River, NJ 07458

**Library of Congress Cataloging-in-Pubblication Data**

Kail, Robert V.
    Children and their development / Robert V. Kail.--3rd ed.
      p. cm.
    Includes bibliographical references and indexes.
    ISBN 0-13-182976-9
    1. Child development.    I. Title.

HQ767.9.K345 2003
305.231--dc21

2003048082

To Laura, Matt, and Ben

*VP, Editor-in-Chief:* Leah Jewell
*Executive Editor:* Jennifer Gilliland
*Editorial Assistant:* Blythe Ferguson
*Editor-in-Chief, Development:* Rochelle Diogenes
*Developmental Editor:* Susan Moss
*Senior Media Editor:* David Nusspickel
*Director of Marketing:* Beth Mejia
*Marketing Manager:* Sheryl Adams
*Marketing Assistant:* Jeanette Laforet
*VP, Director Production and Manufacturing:* Barbara Kittle
*Managing Editor:* Joanne Riker
*Production Editor:* Kathy Sleys
*Manufacturing Manager:* Nick Sklitsis
*Manufacturing Buyer:* Tricia Kenny
*Creative Design Director:* Leslie Osher

*Interior and Cover Design:* Anne Demarinis
*Manager, Production/Formatting and Art:* Guy Ruggiero
*Illustrators (Interior):* Mirella Signoretto; Steve Mannion
*Director, Image Resource Center:* Melinda Reo
*Manager, Rights and Permissions:* Zina Arabia
*Interior Image Specialist:* Beth Brenzel
*Cover Image Specialist:* Karen Sanatar
*Image Permission Coordinator:* Frances Toepfer
*Photo Researcher:* Francelle Carapetyan
*Composition:* This book was set in 10.5/13 Minion
    by Preparé, Inc.
*Printer/Binder:* This book was printed and bound
    by Courier Companies, Inc. The cover was printed
    by Phoenix Color Corp.

Credits and acknowledgments for material borrowed from other sources
and reproduced, with permission, in this textbook appear on page 520-521.

**Pearson Prentice Hall™** is a trademark of Pearson Education, Inc.
**Pearson®** is a registered trademark of Pearson plc
**Prentice Hall®** is a registered trademark of Pearson Education, Inc.

Pearson Education LTD.
Pearson Education Australia PTY, Limited
Pearson Education Singapore, Pte. Ltd
Pearson Education North Asia Ltd.

Pearson Education Canada, Ltd
Pearson Educación de Mexico, S.A. de C.V.
Pearson Education—Japan
Pearson Education Malaysia, Pte. Ltd

10 9 8 7 6 5 4 3 2 1
ISBN 0-13-182976-9

# BRIEF CONTENTS

# CONTENTS

## CULTURAL INFLUENCES

## IMPROVING CHILDREN'S LIVES

## FOCUS ON RESEARCH

## REAL CHILDREN

CHILD DEVELOPMENT AND FAMILY POLICY

# PREFACE

Like many professors turned textbook authors, I began this book because none of the texts available met the aims of the child-development classes that I taught at Purdue. What were those aims? I wanted a book that would:

- provide a solid, research oriented overview of child-development science but would also use effective pedagogy to enhance students' learning;

- use fundamental developmental issues as a foundation for integrating the many discoveries that make child-development science a dynamic and exciting field;

- explain the many different methods used by researchers, then illustrate them repeatedly to drive home the lesson that science progresses when complementary methods converge; *and*

- demonstrate that the results of child-development research can be used to enhance the lives of children and their families.

*Children and Their Development*, first published in 1998, is my effort to meet these goals. In the next few pages, I want to explain how the book works to achieve the goals I just described.

**Goal 1: Use effective pedagogy to promote students' learning.** The focus on a student–friendly book begins with the structure of the chapters, which is designed to promote students' learning. Each chapter consists of three or four modules that provide a clear and well–defined organization to the chapter. Each module begins with a set of learning objectives and a vignette that introduces the topic to be covered. Within each module, all figures, tables, and photos are fully integrated with the exposition, eliminating the need for students to search for a graphic. Similarly, special topics that are set off in other textbooks as feature boxes are, by contrast, fully integrated with the main text and identified by a distinctive icon. Each module ends with several questions intended to help students check their understanding of the major ideas in the module.

The end of each chapter includes several additional study aids. "Unifying Themes" links the ideas in the chapter to a major developmental theme (more about this in a minute. ...). "See for Yourself" suggests activities that allow students to observe topics in child development firsthand. "Resources" includes books and Web sites where students can learn more about child development. "Key Terms" is a list of all of the important boldface terms appearing in the chapter. The "Summary" is organized by module and the primary headings within each module; it reviews the entire chapter.

These different pedagogical elements *do* work; students using previous editions frequently comment that the book is easy to read and presents complex topics in an understandable way.

**Goal 2: Use fundamental developmental issues as a foundation for students' learning of research and theory in child development.** The child-development course sometimes overwhelms students because of the sheer number of topics and studies that don't "hang together"—students see only the trees and never the forest. Of course, today's child-development science is really propelled by a concern with a handful of fundamental developmental issues, such as the continuity of development and the roles of nature and nurture in development. In *Children and Their Development*, four of these foundational issues are introduced in Chapter 1, then reappear in subsequent chapters to scaffold students' understanding. The "Check Your Learning" questions at the end of each module include one thought question that is aligned with one of the four issues. Then, as I mentioned already, the end of the chapter includes "Unifying Themes" in which the ideas from the chapter are used to illustrate one of the foundational themes. By occurring repeatedly throughout the text, the themes remind students that all child-development science ultimately addresses a set of core issues.

**Goal 3: Teach students that child-development science draws on many complementary research methods, each of which contributes uniquely to scientific progress.** In Module 2.1, I portray child development research as a dynamic process in which scientists make a series of decisions as they plan their work. In the process, they create a study that has both strengths and weaknesses. Each of the remaining chapters of the book contains a "Focus on Research" feature that illustrates this process by showing— in an easy-to-read question–and–answer format—the different decisions that investigators made in designing a particular study. I trace each of the steps and explain the decisions that were made. Then the results are shown, usually with an annotated figure, so that students can learn how to interpret graphs. The investigators' conclusions are described, and I then end each "Focus on Research" by mentioning the kind of converging evidence that would strengthen the author's conclusions. Thus, the research methods introduced in Chapter 2 reappear in every chapter, depicting research as a collaborative enterprise that depends on the contributions of many scientists using different methods.

**Goal 4: Show students how the findings from child-development research can improve children's lives.** Child-development scientists and students alike want to know how the findings of research can be use to promote children's development. In Chapter 2 of *Children and Their Development*, I describe the different means by which researchers can use their work to improve children's lives. In the chapters that follow, these ideas come alive in two special features. "Improving Children's Lives" provides research-based solutions to common problems in children's lives. "Child Development and Family Policy" demonstrates how research has inspired change in social policies that affect children and families. From these features, students see that child-development research really matters—parents, teachers, and policy-makers can use research to foster children's development.

## New to the Third Edition

The third edition of *Children and Their Development* has several improvements designed to make the book more useful to students and instructors.

- **Expanded Coverage of Research Methods and Application of Findings.** In previous editions, theory and research were both covered in Chapter 1. In the third edition, theories and themes are included in Chapter 1 while additional information on research methods and the application of research findings to family policy is presented in Chapter 2. The new "converging evidence" paragraph in the "Focus on Research" sections in each chapter illustrates and reinforces my emphasis on this dynamic process.

- **New Pedagogical Features**. In most chapters, one or more new "Summary Tables" provides a capsule review of a topic (e.g., different theoretical perspectives; different influences on child maltreatment). In addition, key terms now appear in color at first mention in the text to promote students' recognition and recall.

- **More Explicit Integration of Developmental Themes**. One of the four child development research themes introduced in Chapter 1 is emphasized at the end of every module in a theme-based reflective question. In addition, one theme per chapter is exemplified in the end-of-chapter "Unifying Themes."

- **Enhanced Illustration Program**. More than $\frac{1}{3}$ of the photos in this edition are new. In addition, a number of new figures have been added, updated, or otherwise revised.

- **Updated Research Coverage**. In updating the coverage of research, I have added hundreds of new citations to research published since 2000.

- **Substantive Content Additions**. I have also added significant new content to every chapter. Of particular note:

  **Chapter 1** has additional information on the history of child-development research and now describes evolutionary developmental psychology.

  **Chapter 2** describes important new research tools (e.g., microgenetic studies, longitudinal-sequential designs, and meta-analysis) and includes a brand-new module on child development and family policy.

  **Chapter 3** provides information on the history of screening infants for PKU and has a new "Focus on Research" feature on behavioral genetics.

  **Chapter 4** has expanded coverage on risks to older mothers, principles of teratogenic action, "crack babies," and adjustments to parenthood.

  **Chapter 5** now covers nutritional needs of older children, dealing with picky eaters, keys for healthy bone growth in adolescents, and the impact of disease and accidents on development.

  **Chapter 6** includes new material on sensory integration, object perception, ADHD (including the MTA study), and physical fitness.

  **Chapter 7** has a completely rewritten description of sensory-motor development (one that emphasizes the major accomplishments instead of the six stages), more on the historical contributions of Piaget's work, and expanded coverage of "theory theory."

  **Chapter 8** now describes Siegler's overlapping waves model, executive functioning, and metacognition (including cognitive self-regulation).

  **Chapter 9** contains new material on emotional intelligence and on historical change in IQ scores.

  **Chapter 10** has information on language development in children with cochlear implants as well as information on the social-interactionist perspective on the acquisition of grammar.

  **Chapter 11** now begins with a description of the functional approach to emotion, includes expanded coverage of emotional regulation and father-infant relationships, and contains a reorganized presentation of the domains of temperament.

  **Chapter 12** has information on teens' increased risk for depression and contains expanded coverage of the early stage of self-awareness and of prejudice.

Chapter 13 describes Turiel's work on domains of social judgment and has expanded coverage of victims of aggression.

Chapter 14 includes new material on sex differences in depression and on gender-role development in children with congenital adrenal hyperplagia.

Chapter 15 has expanded coverage of grandparents and new material on adopted children.

Chapter 16 contains expanded coverage of romantic relationships, a reorganized section on the influence of computers, and new material on the impact of neighborhoods on children's development.

# Support Materials

*Children and Their Development* is accompanied by a superb set of ancillary materials. They include the following:

## Instructor and Student Supplements to accompany

*Children and Their Development, Third Edition* The Third Edition's supplements package has gone through extensive revision and refinement to provide you and your students with the best teaching and learning materials, both in print and media formats.

## Print and Media Supplements for the Instructor

**NEW Prentice Hall's** *Observations in Child Development,* **by David Daniel. Packaged** *FREE* with every new text, this CD-ROM brings to life more than 30 key concepts discussed in the narrative of the text. Students get to view each video twice: once with an introduction to the concept being illustrated and again with commentary describing what is taking place at crucial points in the video. Whether your course has an observation component or not, this CDROM provides your students the opportunity to see children in action.

*Instructor's Resource Manual* Created by Dale Grubb of Baldwin Wallace College, each chapter in the manual includes the following resources: Learning Objectives; Lecture Suggestions and Discussion Topics; Classroom Activities, Demonstrations, and Exercises; Out-of-Class Assignments and Projects; Multimedia Resources; Video Resources; Transparencies Masters; and Handouts. Designed to make your lectures more effective and to save you preparation time, this extensive resource gathers together the most effective activities and strategies for teaching your Child Development course.

*Test Item File* Created by Terri Combs of Indiana University, this test bank contains over 3,500 multiple choice, true/false, and short answer essay questions. Each question references the section and page number in the text, provides an easy, moderate or difficult key for level of difficulty, and lists the question type of factual, conceptual or applied.

**NEW** *Prentice Hall's TestGen* Available on one dual-platform CD-ROM, this test generator program provides instructors "best in class" features in an easy to use program. Create tests using the *TestGen* Wizard and easily select questions with drag-and-drop or point and click functionality. Add or modify test questions using the built in Question Editor and print tests in a variety of formats. The program comes with full technical support and telephone "Request a Test" service.

**NEW** *Instructor's Resource CD-ROM* This valuable, time-saving supplement provides you with electronic version of a variety of teaching resources all in one place so that you may customize your lecture notes and media presentations. This CD-ROM includes PowerPoint Slides customized to the Third Edition, electronic versions of the artwork in the text chapters, electronic version of the Overhead Transparencies, electronic files for the Instructor Resource Manual and the Test Item File as well as clips from Prentice Hall's *Observations in Child Development* CDROM formatted for in class presentation.

*PowerPoint Slides for Children and Their Development*, Third Edition Each chapter's presentations highlight the key points covered in the text. Provided in two versions—one with the Chapter Graphics and one without—to give you flexibility in preparing your lectures. Available on the Instructor's Resource CD-ROM or on Prentice Hall's *PsychologyCentral* website described below.

**NEW** *Prentice Hall's Child Development Transparencies, 2004* Designed to be used in large lecture settings, this set of over 130 full-color transparencies includes illustrations from the text as well of images from a variety of other sources. Available in acetate form, online at *PsychologyCentral* or on the Instructor's Resource CDROM.

**NEW** *PsychologyCentral Website at* **www.prenhall.com/psychology** Password protected for instructor's use only, this site allows you online access to all of Prentice Hall's Psychology supplements. You'll find a multitude of resources for teaching Developmental Psychology. From this site you can download any of the key supplements available for *Children and Their Development*, Third Edition including the following: Instructor's Resource Manual, Test Item File, PowerPoint Slides, Chapter Graphics and electronic versions of the Child Development Transparencies, 2004. Contact your Prentice Hall representative for the User ID and Password to access this site.

Online Course Management with *WebCT, BlackBoard or CourseCompass* **FREE** upon adoption of the text, instructors interested in using online course management have their choice of options. Each course comes preloaded with text specific quizzing and testing material and can be fully customized for your course. Contact your Prentice Hall representative or visit **www.prenhall.com/demo** for more information.

## Video Support for *Children and Their Development*

**Films for the Humanities and Sciences.** A wealth of full-length videos from the extensive library of Films for the Humanities and Sciences, on a variety of topics in developmental psychology, are available to qualified adopters. Contact your Prentice Hall representative for a list of videos.

**ABC News/Prentice Hall Video Libraries.** Consisting of brief segments from award-winning news programs such as *Good Morning America, Nightline, 20/20* and

*World News Tonight*, these videos discuss current issues and are a great way to launch your lectures.

> **NEW** *Developmental Psychology, 2004*
> **NEW** *Issues in Child and Adolescent Development, 2002*
> *Human Development, Series IV*

**NEW** *Lecture Launcher Video for Developmental Psychology* from *Films for Humanities and Sciences*. Adopters can receive this new videotape that includes short clips covering all major topics in developmental psychology. The videos have been carefully selected from the *Films for Humanities and Sciences* library, and edited to provide brief and compelling video content for enhancing your lectures. Contact your local representative for a full list of video clips on this tape.

## Print and Media Supplements for the Student

**NEW Prentice Hall's** *Observations in Child Development*, **by David Daniel Packaged FREE** with every new text, this CD-ROM brings to life more than 30 key concepts discussed in the narrative of the text. Students get to view each video twice: once with an introduction to the concept being illustrated and again with commentary describing what is taking place at crucial points in the video. Whether your course has an observation component or not, this CDROM provides your students the opportunity to see children in action.

**Study Guide** Written by Dea DeWolff, Purdue University, this student study guide helps students master the core concepts presented in each chapter. For each chapter, this study guide provides an outline, learning objectives, key terms and concepts review, a guided review, practice multiple choice and essay questions.

**Companion Website at www.prenhall.com/kail** Authored by Pamela Anderson and Deborah Bobek of Tufts University, this online study guide allows students to review each chapter's material, take practice tests, research topics for course projects and more! The third edition's companion website includes the following resources for each chapter: Chapter Objectives, Interactive Lectures, five different types of quizzes that provide immediate, text-specific feedback and coaching comments, WebEssays, WebDestinations, NetSearch, and **NEW** FlashCards Access to the website is free and unrestricted to all students.

**NEW** *The Prentice Hall Guide to Evaluating Online Resources with Research Navigator: Psychology, 2004* This guide provides students with a hands-on introduction to the Internet, teaches students how to critically evaluate online resources and guides students through the research process for three different types of research projects using *Research Navigator*. Access to *Research Navigator*, a customized research database for students of psychology described below, comes **FREE** with this guide!

**Research Navigator**™ Research Navigator features three exclusive databases full of source material, including:

- *EBSCO's ContentSelect Academic Journal Database* organized by subject. Each subject contains 50-100 of the leading academic journals for that discipline. Instructors and students can search the online journals by keyword, topic, or multiple topics. Articles include abstract and citation information and can be cut, pasted, emailed, or saved for later use.

- *The New York Times Search-by-Subject One Year Archive* organized by subject and searchable by keyword, or multiple keywords. Instructors and students can view the full text of the article.

- *Link Library,* organized by subject, offers editorially selected "best of the web" sites. Link Libraries are continually scanned and kept up to date providing the most relevant and accurate links for research assignments.

To see for yourself how this resource works, take a tour at **www.researchnavigator.com**, or ask your local Prentice Hall representative for more details.

## Supplementary Texts

Contact your Prentice Hall representative to package any of these supplementary texts with *Children and Their Development,* **Third Edition:**

*Twenty Studies that Revolutionized Child Psychology* by Wallace E. Dixon, Jr. Presenting the seminal research studies that have shaped modern developmental psychology, this brief text provides an overview of the environment that gave rise to each study, its experimental design, its findings, and its impact on current thinking in the discipline.

*Human Development in Multicultural Context: A Book of Readings* by Michele A. Paludi. This compilation of readings highlights cultural influences in developmental psychology.

*The Psychology Major: Careers and Strategies for Success* by Eric Landrum (Idaho State University), Stephen Davis (Emporia State University), and Terri Landrum (Idaho State University). This 160-page paperback provides valuable information on career options available to psychology majors, tips for improving academic performance, and a guide to the APA style of research reporting.

# Acknowledgments

Textbook authors do not produce books on their own. I want to thank the many reviewers who generously gave their time and effort to help sharpen my thinking about child development and shape the development of this text. I am especially grateful to the following people who reviewed various aspects of the manuscript: William Holt, UMASS Dartmouth; Dennis A. Lichty, Wayne State College; Monica L. McCoy, Converse College; Robert Pasnak, George Mason University; Christopher Radi, University of New Mexico; Lesa Rae Varjanian, Indiana University—Purdue University Fort Wayne; John Bates, Indiana University; Lisabeth DiLalla, Southern University School of Medicine; Marta Laupa, University of Nevada; Jane E. Clark, University of Maryland; Maureen Callanan, University of California—Santa Cruz; Malinda Colwell, Texas Tech University; Erika Hoff, Florida Atlantic University.

Thanks, as well, to those who reviewed the previous editions of this book: Susan McClure, Westmoreland County Community College; Rebecca Bigler, University of Texas–Austin; Kathleen Fox, Salisbury State University; Rick Medlin, Stetson University; Joan Cook, County College of Morris; Elizabeth Lemerise, Western

Kentucky University; Jim Dannemiller, University of Wisconsin–Madison; Mark B. Alcorn, University of Northern Colorado; Vernon C. Hall, Syracuse University; May X. Wang, Metropolitan State College of Denver, Jack Meacham, University of Buffalo; Lesa Rae Vartanian, Purdue University; Adam Winsler, George Mason University; Tony Simon, Furman University; K. Robert Bridges, Pennsylvania State University; Frank Manis, University of Southern California; Marianne Taylor, University of Puget Sound; Karen Rudolph, University of Illinois; Cynthia Stifter, Pennsylvania State University; James Black, University of Illinois; Laura Hess, Purdue University; Lisa Oakes, University of Iowa; Jacquelyn Mice, Auburn University; Amy Weiss, University of Iowa; Brad Pillow, Northern Illinois University; Janet DiPietro, Johns Hopkins University; Lee Ann Thompson, Case Western Reserve University; Gary Ladd, University of Illinois. Without their thoughtful comments, this book would be less complete, less accurate, and less interesting.

I also owe a debt of thanks to many people who helped take this project from a first draft to a bound book. As she did for the second edition, Anne Demarinis designed a book that is both beautiful and functional. Kathy Sleys skillfully orchestrated the many activities that were involved in actually producing the book. Francelle Carapetyan found the marvelous photographs that appear throughout the book. Tessa Mui helped to compile the many new references that were added to this edition.

I am particularly grateful to three people whose contributions to *Children and Their Development* are especially noteworthy. Jennifer Gilliland has long supported this book enthusiastically and served as a savvy guide to its revision. On the first and second editions, Harriett Prentiss labored long to make my writing clear and inviting. This task fell to Susan Moss on the third edition and she did a superb job of making sure that topics were covered thoroughly and clearly. To all these individuals, many, many thanks.

—Robert V. Kail

# ABOUT THE AUTHOR

**Robert V. Kail** is Professor of Psychological Sciences at Purdue University. His undergraduate degree is from Ohio Wesleyan University, and he received his Ph. D. from the University of Michigan. Kail is currently Editor of the *Journal of Experimental Child Psychology* and of *Advances in Child Development and Behavior*. He received the McCandless Young Scientist Award from the American Psychological Association, was named the Distinguished Sesquicentennial Alumnus in Psychology by Ohio Wesleyan University, and is a fellow in the American Psychological Society. His research interests are in the area of cognitive development and focus on the causes and consequences of developmental change in the speed of information processing. Away from the office, he enjoys working out and watching his children grow.

# .1

Beginning as a microscopic cell, every person takes a fascinating journey designed to lead to adulthood. This trip is filled with remarkable events that make it both interesting and challenging. In this book, we'll trace this journey as we learn about the science of child development, a multidisciplinary study of all aspects of growth from conception to adulthood. As an adult, you've lived the years that are the heart of this book. I hope you enjoy reviewing your developmental journey from the perspective of child-development research and that this perspective will lead you to new insights into the developmental forces that made you the person you are today.

Chapter 1 sets the stage for our study of child development. We begin, in Module 1.1, by learning how to use this book. In Module 1.2, we'll examine theories that are central to the science of child development. Finally, in Module 1.3, we explore themes that guide much research in child development.

# The Science of Child Development

**1.1** Using This Book

**1.2** Theories of Child Development

**1.3** Themes in Child-Development Research

# 1.1

## Using This Book

In most textbooks, the material on the next few pages appears in a preface entitled "To the Student." But I'm afraid that most students never read this material, so I'm including it here at the beginning of Chapter 1. Please don't skip it now; read on to learn how to use this book. It will save you time in the long run.

In this book, we'll trace children's development from conception through adolescence. Given this goal, you may expect to find chapters devoted to early childhood, middle childhood, and the like. Instead, if you look at the table of contents, you'll see that this book is organized differently—around topics. Chapters 3 through 6 are devoted to the genetic and biological bases of human development, and the growth of perceptual and motor skills. Chapters 7 through 10 cover intellectual development—how children learn, think, reason, and solve problems. Chapters 11 through 16 concern social and emotional development—how children acquire the customs of their society and learn to play the social roles expected of them.

This organization reflects the fact that when scientists conduct research on children's development, they usually study how some specific aspect of a child develops. For example, a researcher might study how memory changes as children grow or how friendship in childhood differs from that in adolescence. Thus, the organization of this book reflects the way researchers actually study child development.

Each of the chapters follows the same format, one that is designed to help you understand the material within the chapter. This format is explained in the next section.

## Organization of Chapters

Each of the 16 chapters in the book includes two to four modules that are listed at the beginning of each chapter. As you can see in the inset page below, each module begins with a set of learning objectives phrased as questions.

---

### 2.1

## Doing Child-Development Research

**Measurement in Child-Development Research**

**General Designs for Research**

**Designs for Studying Development**

**Ethical Responsibilities**

**Communicating Research Results**

**LEARNING OBJECTIVES**

- How do scientists measure topics of interest in children's development?
- What general research designs are used in child-development research? What designs are unique to child-development research?
- What ethical procedures must researchers follow?
- How do researchers communicate results to other scientists?

*Leah and Joan are both mothers of 10-year-old boys. Their sons have many friends, but the basis for the friendships are not obvious to the mothers. Leah believes that "opposites attract"—children form friendships with peers who have complementary interests and abilities. Joan doubts this; her son seems to seek out other boys who are near clones of himself in their interests and abilities.*

Suppose Leah and Joan know you're taking a course in child development, so they ask you to settle their argument. You know, from Module 1.2, that Leah and

---

Next is a brief vignette that introduces the topic to be covered in the module by describing an issue or problem like the kind faced by real people. In the margin is a mini-outline listing the major subheadings of the module—a kind of road map for reading. The learning objectives, vignette, and mini-outline tell you what to expect in the module.

Each module typically examines three to four major topics that are listed in the mini-outline. In addition, each module in Chapters 2 through 16 includes at least one special feature that expands or highlights a topic. There are five different kinds of features; you can recognize each one by its distinctive icon:

*Focus on Research* provides details on the design and methods used in a particular research study. Closely examining specific studies demystifies research and shows that scientific work is a series of logical steps conducted by real people.

*Improving Children's Lives* shows how research and theory can be applied to improve children's development. These practical solutions to everyday problems show the relevance of research and theory to real life.

*Cultural Influences* shows how culture influences children and illustrates that developmental journeys are diverse. All children share the biological aspects of development, but their cultural contexts differ. This feature celebrates the developmental experiences of children from different backgrounds.

*Real Children* provides a case study that illustrates an issue in child development in the life of a real child. These authentic accounts make the study of child development come alive.

*Child Development and Family Policy* shows how results from research are used to create social policy that is designed to improve the lives of children and their families.

The inset below shows another important element of each module: All illustrations and tables are integrated with the text.

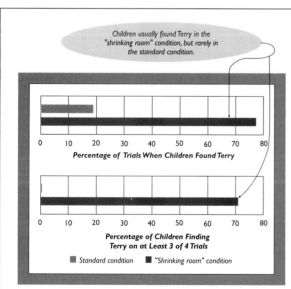

Children usually found Terry in the "shrinking room" condition, but rarely in the standard condition.

Percentage of Trials When Children Found Terry

Percentage of Children Finding Terry on at Least 3 of 4 Trials

■ Standard condition   ■ "Shrinking room" condition

FIG. 7–3

*What were the results?* The top part of the graph shows the percentage of trials in which children found the toy. Children rarely found the toy in the standard condition, but they frequently found it in the "shrinking machine" condition. The bottom part of the graph shows the percentage of children who found Terry on at least three of the four trials. No children in the standard condition were this accurate, but most children in the "shrinking machine" condition were.

*What did the investigators conclude?* When $2\frac{1}{2}$-year-olds must think of the model as an object and as a symbol—so that appearance conflicts with reality—they find this very difficult and, consequently, cannot find the hidden toy, even though the model is an exact replica of the full-size room. In contrast, when children can think of the model as the room, but much smaller—thereby avoiding the conflict between appearance and reality—they readily find the toy.

*What converging evidence would strengthen these conclusions?* Because the changes observed by DeLoache and her colleagues appeared across a fairly narrow age range, this would be an ideal opportunity to conduct a microgenetic study: The goal would be to show, for individual children, the age at which they understand that the model is a symbol of something else. Additional useful research would be to compare the results with other situations in which an object also serves a symbolic function (e.g., children's understanding that a map is a colorful piece of paper as well as a symbol of a much larger physical space). ●

You won't need to turn pages searching for a picture or table that is described in the text; instead, pictures, tables, and words are linked to tell a unified story.

Three other elements are designed to help you focus on the main points of the text. First, whenever a key term is introduced in the text, it appears in **red bold** like these and the definition appears in **black boldface type**. This format should make key terms easier for you to find and learn. Second, about half the pages in the book include a sentence in large type that extends into the margin. This sentence summarizes a key point that is made in the surrounding text. When you see one of these sentences, take a moment to think about it—it captures an important idea; and reviewing these sentences later will help you prepare for exams. Third, summary tables throughout the book review key ideas and provide a capsule account of each. For example, the Summary Table shows the many study aids that I've included in the book.

> A sentence in the margin like this summarizes the surrounding text. Use these sentences to help preview the text before you read.

**SUMMARY TABLE**

| STUDY AIDS USED IN CHILDREN AND THEIR DEVELOPMENT | |
|---|---|
| **Study Aid** | **Key Features** |
| Module-opening material | Learning objectives, vignette, mini-outline |
| Special features | Focus on Research, Improving Children's Lives, Cultural Influences, Real Children, Child Development and Family Policy |
| Design elements that promote learning | Integrated art and text, boldface key terms defined in text, key concepts in margin, Summary Table (like this one) |
| Check Your Learning | Fill-in-the-blank questions, critical-thinking questions linked to developmental themes |
| End-of-chapter material | Unifying Themes, See for Yourself, Resources, Key Terms, Summary |

Each module concludes with "Check Your Learning" questions to help you review the major ideas in the module. As you can see in the inset, there are two kinds of questions: fill-in-the-blank and critical-thinking questions.

---

**CHECK YOUR LEARNING**

1. The _____ perspective emphasizes the role of conflict in child development.

2. _____ proposes that children learn about the world through reinforcement, punishment, and imitation.

3. According to _____, development is linked to changes in mental hardware and mental software.

4. Vygotsky believed that a fundamental task for all cultures is _____.

5. The influence of multiple levels of the environment is central in _____ theory.

**CONNECTIONS**
Erikson and Piaget both proposed stage theories of children's development. Although the theories differed in emphasis—Erikson was concerned with psychosocial growth and Piaget was concerned with cognitive growth—can you see similarities in their approach to development?

**Answers:** (1) psychodynamic, (2) Albert Bandura's social cognitive theory, (3) the information-processing approach, (4) to pass along beliefs, customs, and skills to children, (5) Bronfenbrenner's contextual

To help you make connections, these critical-thinking questions are linked to one of four developmental themes that will be introduced later in this chapter. If you can answer the questions in "Check Your Learning" correctly, you are on your way to mastering the material in the module. However, do not rely exclusively on "Check Your Learning" as you study for exams. The questions are designed to give you a quick spot check of your understanding, not a comprehensive assessment of your knowledge of the entire module.

At the very end of each chapter are several additional study aids. "Unifying Themes" links the contents of the chapter to the developmental themes that I'll introduce in Module 1.3. "See for Yourself" suggests some simple activities for exploring issues in child development on your own. "Resources" includes books and Web sites where you can learn more about children and their development. "Key Terms" is a list of all the important terms that appear in the chapter, along with the page where each term is defined. Finally, drawing the chapter to a close is a "Summary"—a review of the entire chapter, organized by module and the primary headings within the module.

## How to Use This Book

I strongly encourage you to take advantage of these learning and study aids as you read the book. In the next few paragraphs, I'm going to suggest how you could do this. Obviously, I can't know exactly how your course is organized, but my suggestions should work well with most courses, sometimes with a few changes.

Your instructor will probably assign about one chapter per week. Don't try to read an entire chapter in one sitting. Instead, on the first day, preview the chapter. Read the introduction and notice how the chapter fits into the scheme of the whole book. Then page through the chapter, reading the learning objectives, vignettes, mini-outlines, and major headings to see the general framework of the material. Also read the sentences in the margins and the boldface sentences. Your goal is to get a general overview of the entire chapter—a sense of what it's all about.

Now you're ready to begin reading. Return to the first module and preview it again, reminding yourself of the topics covered. Then start to read. As you do, think about what you're reading. Make predictions about what will come next; make mental images that depict what you've read. Every few paragraphs, stop briefly. Try to summarize the main ideas in your own words; ask yourself if the ideas remind you of something in your own childhood or that of others that you know; tell a roommate about something interesting in the material. In other words, *read actively*—get involved in what you're reading. Don't just stare glassy-eyed at the page!

Continue this process—reading, summarizing, relating, and reviewing—until you finish the module. Then answer the questions in "Check Your Learning" to determine how well you've learned what you've read. If you've followed the read-summarize-think cycle as you worked your way through the module, you should be able to answer most of the questions. If you can't answer the questions, then skim the module again until you can find the correct answer.

The next time you sit down to read—preferably the next day—start by previewing the second module and then tackle it with the read-summarize-think cycle. Repeat this procedure for all the modules.

After you've finished the last module, wait a day or two and then review each module, paying careful attention to the sentences in the margins, the boldface terms, and the "Check Your Learning" questions. Reread confusing or complex passages. Also, use the study aids at the end of the chapter to help you integrate the ideas in the chapter.

With this approach, you should need several 30 to 45 minute study sessions to complete each chapter. Don't be tempted to blast through an entire chapter in a single session. Research consistently shows that you learn more effectively by having daily (or nearly daily) study sessions devoted to both reviewing familiar material *and* taking on a relatively small amount of new material.

Finally, *Children and Their Development* has its own Web site (**www.prenhall.com/kail/**) that includes much additional material that should be useful to you. In particular, as you begin to prepare for exams, the Web site has questions that you can use to see how well you've mastered the material in the book.

## Terminology

Every field has its own terminology, and child development is no exception. I will be using several terms to refer to different periods of infancy, childhood, and adolescence. Although these terms are familiar, I will use each to refer to a specific range of ages:

| | |
|---|---|
| Newborn | Birth to 1 month |
| Infant | 1 month to 1 year |
| Toddler | 1 to 2 years |
| Preschooler | 2 to 6 years |
| School-age child | 6 to 12 years |
| Adolescent | 12 to 18 years |
| Adult | 18 years and older |

Sometimes for the sake of variety I will use other terms that are less tied to specific ages, such as *babies, youngsters,* and *elementary-school children*. When I do, you will be able to tell from the context what groups are being described.

I will also use very specific terminology in describing research findings from different cultural and ethnic groups. The appropriate terms to describe different cultural, racial, and ethnic groups change over time. For example, the terms *colored people, Negroes, Black Americans,* and *African Americans* have all been used to describe Americans who trace their ancestry to the individuals who emigrated from Africa. In this book, I will use the term *African American* because it emphasizes the unique cultural heritage of this group of people. Following this same line of reasoning, I will use the terms *European American* (instead of *Caucasian* or *white*), *Native American* (instead of *Indian* or *American Indian*), *Asian American,* and *Hispanic American*.

These labels are not perfect. Sometimes, they blur distinctions within ethnic groups. For example, the term *Hispanic American* ignores differences between individuals who came to the United States from Puerto Rico, Mexico, and Guatemala; the term *Asian American* blurs variations among people whose heritage is Japanese, Chinese, or Korean. Whenever researchers identified the subgroups in their research sample, I will use the more specific terms in describing results. When you see the more general terms, remember that conclusions may not apply to all subgroups within the group.

## A Final Word

I wrote this book to make child development come alive for my students at Purdue. Although I can't teach you directly, I hope this book sparks your interest in children and their development. Please let me know what you like and dislike about the book so that I can improve it in later editions. You can send e-mail to me at **rkail@sla.purdue.edu**— I'd love to hear from you.

The many topics described in the rest of this book all draw on the same developmental theories, which I describe next.

# Theories of Child Development

## 1.2

### LEARNING OBJECTIVES

- What are the major tenets of the biological perspective?

- How do psychodynamic theories account for development?

- What is the focus of learning theories?

- How do cognitive-developmental theories explain changes in children's thinking?

- What are the main points of the contextual approach?

> *Marcus has just graduated from high school, first in his class. For his proud mother, Betty, this is a time to reflect on Marcus's past and ponder his future. Marcus has always been a happy, easygoing child—a joy to rear. And he's always been interested in learning. Betty wonders why he is so perpetually good-natured and so curious. If she knew the secret, she laughed, she could write a best-selling book and be a guest on Oprah!*

Betty is not the first person to ask these questions about children. In fact, such questions have occupied the minds of some of the greatest philosophers in history. Nearly 400 years ago, the English philosopher John Locke (1632–1704) claimed that the human infant is a *tabula rasa*, or "blank slate." Experience then molds the infant, child, adolescent, and adult into a unique individual. Locke's view was challenged by the French philosopher, Jean Jacques Rousseau (1712–1778), who believed that newborns were endowed with an innate sense of justice and morality that unfolds naturally as children grow.

By the middle of the 19th century, progress in science had merged with growing concerns about children's welfare to bring about a new field: child development. The impetus for the new science came from many sources. **One source was baby biographies, detailed, systematic observations of individual children.** Beginning in the 19th century, many scientists (including Charles Darwin, the founder of evolutionary theory) kept such diaries. The observations in the biographies were often subjective and conclusions were sometimes reached on minimal evidence. Nevertheless, the systematic and extensive records in baby biographies paved the way for objective, analytic research.

Taking the lead in the new science at the dawn of the 20th century was G. Stanley Hall (1844–1924), who developed theories of child development based on evolutionary theory and conducted many studies to determine age trends in children's beliefs and feelings about a range of topics. More importantly, Hall founded the first scientific journal in English where scientists could publish findings from child-development research. Hall also founded a child-study institute at Clark University and was the first president of the American Psychological Association.

Meanwhile, in France Alfred Binet (1857–1911) had begun to devise the first mental tests, which we'll examine in Module 9.2; Sigmund Freud (1856–1939) had startled the world with his suggestion that the experiences of early childhood seemed

**Philosophers have long asked questions about child development but only since the 19th century have scientists studied child development.**

to account for patterns of behavior in adulthood. And John B. Watson (1878–1958), the founder of behaviorism, had begun to write and lecture on the importance of reward and punishment for child-rearing practices.

All these events led to enormous interest in child-development research. Infancy, childhood, and adolescence were seen as important waypoints on the journey to adulthood. The first child-development scientists began to conduct studies and create new theories. Their work provided the foundation for modern theories of child development that I'll describe in this module.

Before we consider individual theories, it's important to discuss the role of theories in general in child-development research. **In child development, a theory is an organized set of ideas that is designed to explain and make predictions about development.** For example, suppose friends of yours have a baby who cries often. You could imagine several explanations for her crying. Maybe the baby cries because she's hungry; maybe she cries to get her parents to hold her; maybe she cries because she's simply a cranky, unhappy baby. Each of these explanations is a very simple theory: It tries to explain why the baby cries so much. Of course, real developmental theories are much more complicated, but the purpose is the same—to explain behavior and development.

> Five major theoretical perspectives have guided most research on children and their development.

Theories lead to predictions that we can test in research; in the process, the theory is supported or not. Think about the different explanations for the crying baby. Each one leads to unique predictions. If, for example, the baby is crying because she's hungry, we predict that feeding her more often should stop the crying. When results of research match the predictions, the theory gains support. When results differ from the predictions, the theory is incorrect and is revised.

Perhaps now you see why theories are essential for child-development research: They are the source of predictions for research, which often lead to changes in the theories. These revised theories then provide the basis for new predictions, which lead to new research, and the cycle continues.

Over the 100-year history of child development as a science, many theories have guided research and thinking about children's development. The earliest developmental theories were useful in generating research, but findings from that research led child-development scientists to newer, improved theories. In this module, I describe both the earlier theories and the modern ones, because newer theories are best understood in terms of their historical roots. Some theories share assumptions and ideas about children and development; grouped together they form five major theoretical perspectives in child-development research: the biological, psychodynamic, learning, cognitive-developmental, and contextual. As you read about each perspective in the next few pages, think about how it differs from the others in its view of development.

## The Biological Perspective

According to the biological perspective, intellectual and personality development, as well as physical and motor development, proceed according to a biological plan. One of the first biological theories, maturational theory, was proposed by Arnold Gesell (1880–1961). **According to maturational theory, child development reflects a specific and prearranged scheme or plan within the body.** In Gesell's view, development is simply a natural unfolding of a biological plan; experience matters little. Like Jean Jacques Rousseau 200 years before him, Gesell encouraged parents to let their children develop naturally. Without interference from adults, Gesell claimed, such behaviors as speech, play, and reasoning would emerge spontaneously according to a predetermined developmental timetable.

Maturational theory was discarded because it had little to say about the impact of the environment on children's development. However, other biological theories give greater weight to experience. **Ethological theory views development from an evolutionary perspective.** In this theory, many behaviors are adaptive—they have survival value. For example, clinging, grasping, and crying are adaptive for infants because they elicit caregiving from adults. Ethological theorists assume that people inherit many of these adaptive behaviors.

So far, ethological theory seems like maturational theory, with a dash of evolution for taste. How does experience fit in? Ethologists believe that all animals are biologically programmed so that some kinds of learning occur only at certain ages. **A critical period is the time in development when a specific type of learning can take place; before or after the critical period, the same learning is difficult or even impossible.**

One of the best-known examples of a critical period comes from the work of Konrad Lorenz (1903–1989), a Nobel-prize-winning Austrian zoologist. Lorenz noticed that newly hatched chicks follow their mother about. He theorized that chicks are biologically programmed to follow the first moving object that they see after hatching. **Usually this was the mother, so following her was the first step in imprinting, creating an emotional bond with the mother.** Lorenz tested his theory by showing that if he removed the mother immediately after the chicks hatched and replaced it with another moving object, the chicks would follow that object and treat it as "mother." As the photo shows, this included Lorenz himself!

Lorenz also discovered that the chick had to see the moving object within about a day of hatching. Otherwise, the chick would not imprint on the moving object. In other words, the critical period for imprinting lasts about a day; when chicks experience the moving object outside of the critical period, imprinting does not take place. Even though the underlying mechanism is biological, experience is essential for triggering programmed, adaptive behaviors.

In recent years, child-development researchers have embraced the notion of adaptation that is central to ethology. **According to evolutionary psychology, many human behaviors represent successful adaptation to the environment.** That is, over human history, some behaviors have made it more likely that people will reproduce and pass on their genes to following generations. For example, you probably take it for granted that most people enjoy being with other people. We occasionally enjoy being alone but dread the prospect of complete isolation (which is why solitary confinement is considered such a severe punishment). According to evolutionary psychologists, our "social nature" is a product of evolution: For early humans, being in a group offered protection from predators and made it easier to locate food. Thus, early humans who were social were more likely than their asocial peers to live long enough to reproduce, passing on their social orientation to their offspring (Gaulin & McBurney, 2001). Over many, many generations, "being social" had such a survival advantage that nearly all people are socially oriented (though in varying amounts, as we'll see later).

Applied to child development, evolutionary psychology highlights the adaptive value of children's behavior at different points in development (Bjorklund & Pellegrini, 2000). For example, as we'll explore in detail in Module 4.4, infants are born with an assortment of reflexes that speed their adjustment to life outside the uterus. A newborn

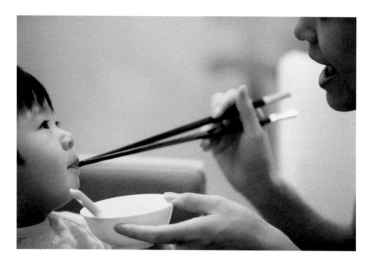

spontaneously sucks any object placed in its mouth, simplifying the task of getting adequate nutrition. Another example of a successful adaptation is the time and energy that parents like the mother in the photo invest in child rearing. Without such effort, infants and young children would die before they were sexually mature, which means that a parent's genes could not be passed along to grandchildren (Geary, 2002). Here, too, parenting just seems "natural" but really represents an adaptation to the problem of guaranteeing that one's helpless offspring can survive until they're sexually mature.

The evolutionary approach to child development is relatively recent but is already becoming influential. As you'll see on several occasions in this book, the evolutionary approach forces us to remember that children's (and their parents') behavior often has "… evolved over the past several million years to handle the problems faced by our…ancestors" (Bjorklund & Pellegrini, 2000, p. 1696).

Evolutionary psychology and maturational theory both highlight the biological bases of child development. Biological theorists remind us that children's genes, which are the product of a long evolutionary history, influence virtually every aspect of children's development. Consequently, a biological theorist would tell Betty, the mother of the high-school graduate in the module-opening vignette, that her son's good nature and his outstanding academic record are both largely products of heredity.

## The Psychodynamic Perspective

The psychodynamic perspective is the oldest scientific perspective on child development, tracing its roots to the work of Sigmund Freud (1856–1939) in the late 19th and early 20th centuries. Freud was a physician who specialized in diseases of the nervous system. Many of his patients were adults who suffered from ailments that seemed to have no obvious biological causes. As Freud listened to his patients describe their problems and their lives, he became convinced that early experiences establish patterns that endure throughout a person's life. **Using his patients' case histories, Freud created the first psychodynamic theory, which holds that development is largely determined by how well people resolve conflicts they face at different ages.**

As part of his theory, Freud argued that personality includes three primary components that emerge at distinct ages. **The id is a reservoir of primitive instincts and drives.** Present at birth, the id presses for immediate gratification of bodily needs and wants. A hungry baby crying illustrates the id in action. **The ego is the practical, rational component of personality.** The ego begins to emerge during the first year of life, as infants learn that they cannot always have what they want. The ego tries to resolve conflicts that occur when the instinctive desires of the id encounter the obstacles of the real world. The ego often tries to channel the id's impulsive demands into socially more acceptable channels. For example, the child in the photo without the toy is obviously envious of the child who has the toy. According to Freud, the id would urge the child to grab the toy, but the ego would encourage the child to play with the peer and, in the process, the attractive toy.

**The third component of personality, the superego, is the "moral agent" in the child's personality.** It emerges during the preschool years as children begin to internalize adult standards of right and wrong. If the peer in the previous example left the attractive toy unattended, the id might tell the child to grab the toy and run; the superego would remind the child that taking another's toy would be wrong.

Subsequently, scientists criticized many aspects of Freud's work. They argued that his views of development were based on adults recalling the past, not from observing children directly. Although these and other shortcomings have undermined much of Freud's theory, two of his insights have had lasting impact on child-development research and theory. First, he noted that early experiences can have enduring effects on children's development. Second, he suggested that children often experience conflict between what they want to do and what they know they should do.

**ERIKSON'S PSYCHOSOCIAL THEORY.** Erik Erikson (1902–1994), Freud's student, embraced Freud's idea of conflict, but he emphasized the psychological and social aspects of conflict rather than the biological and physical aspects. **In Erikson's psychosocial theory, development consists of a sequence of stages, each defined by a unique crisis or challenge.** The complete theory includes the eight stages shown in the table below. The name of each stage reflects the challenge that individuals face at a particular age. For example, the challenge for young adults is to become involved in a loving relationship. Adults who establish this relationship experience intimacy; those who don't, experience isolation.

> Psychodynamic theories emphasize that development is a product of the child's responses to life's challenges.

### Erikson's Eight Stages of Psychosocial Development

| Psychosocial Stage | Age | Challenge |
| --- | --- | --- |
| Basic trust versus mistrust | Birth to 1 year | To develop a sense that the world is safe, a "good place" |
| Autonomy versus shame and doubt | 1 to 3 years | To realize that one is an independent person who can make decisions |
| Initiative versus guilt | 3 to 6 years | To develop a willingness to try new things and to handle failure |
| Industry versus inferiority | 6 years to adolescence | To learn basic skills and to work with others |
| Identity versus identity confusion | Adolescence | To develop a lasting, integrated sense of self |
| Intimacy versus isolation | Young adulthood | To commit to another in a loving relationship |
| Generativity versus stagnation | Middle adulthood | To contribute to younger people, through child rearing, child care, or other productive work |
| Integrity versus despair | Late life | To view one's life as satisfactory and worth living |

TABLE 1–1

Erikson also argued that the earlier stages of psychosocial development provide the foundation for the later stages. For example, adolescents who do not meet the challenge of developing an identity will not establish truly intimate relationships; instead, they will become overly dependent on their partners as a source of identity.

Whether we call them conflicts, challenges, or crises, the psychodynamic perspective emphasizes that the trek to adulthood is difficult because the path is strewn with obstacles. Outcomes of development reflect the manner and ease with which children surmount life's barriers. When children overcome early obstacles easily, they are better able to handle the later ones. Returning to our opening vignette, a psychodynamic theorist would tell Betty that her son's cheerful disposition and his academic record suggest that he handled life's early obstacles well, which is a good sign for his future development.

## The Learning Perspective

**VIDEO 1.1**
Little Albert
CLASSIC MODULE

Learning theorists endorse John Locke's view that the infant's mind is a blank slate on which experience writes. John Watson (1878–1958) was the first theorist to apply this approach to child development. Watson argued that learning determines what children will be. He assumed that with the correct techniques anything could be learned by almost anyone. In other words, in Watson's view, experience was just about all that mattered in determining the course of development.

**EARLY LEARNING THEORIES.** Watson did little research to support his claims, but B. F. Skinner (1904–1990) filled this gap. **Skinner studied operant conditioning, in which the consequences of a behavior determine whether a behavior is repeated in the future.** Skinner showed that two kinds of consequences were especially influential. **A reinforcement is a consequence that increases the future likelihood of the behavior that it follows.** Positive reinforcement consists of giving a reward—such as chocolate, gold stars, or paychecks—to increase the likelihood of repeating a previous behavior. The parents of the child whose room is shown in the photograph could use positive reinforcement to encourage her to clean her room. Every time she cleaned her room, they could reinforce her with praise, food, or money. Negative reinforcement consists of rewarding people by taking away unpleasant things. The same parents could use negative reinforcement by saying that whenever she cleaned her room, she wouldn't have to wash the dishes or fold laundry.

**A punishment is a consequence that decreases the future likelihood of the behavior that it follows.** Punishment suppresses a behavior by either adding something aversive or by withholding a pleasant event. When the child failed to clean her room, the parents could punish her by making her do extra chores (adding something aversive) or by not allowing her to watch television (withholding a pleasant event).

Skinner's research was done primarily with animals, but child-development researchers soon showed that the principles of operant conditioning could be extended readily to children's behavior (Baer & Wolf, 1968). Applied properly, reinforcement and punishment are indeed powerful influences on children. However, researchers discovered that children sometimes learn without reinforcement or punishment. **Children learn much simply by watching those around them, which is known as imitation or observational learning.** For example, imitation occurs when one toddler throws a toy after seeing a peer do so or when a school-age child offers to help an older adult carry groceries because she's seen her parents do the same.

The learning perspective emphasizes the role of experience in children's development.

**SOCIAL COGNITIVE THEORY.** Perhaps imitation makes you think of "monkey-see, monkey-do," or simple mimicking. Early investigators had this view, too, but research quickly showed that this was wrong. Children do not always imitate what they see around them. Children are more likely to imitate if the person they see is popular, smart, or talented. They're also more likely to imitate when the behavior they see is rewarded than when it is punished. Findings like these imply that imitation is more complex than sheer mimicry. Children do not mechanically copy what they see and hear; instead, they look to others for information about appropriate behavior. When popular, smart peers are reinforced for behaving in a particular way, it makes sense to imitate them.

**Albert Bandura (1925– ) based his social cognitive theory on this more complex view of reward, punishment, and imitation.** Bandura calls his theory "cognitive" because he believes that children are actively trying to understand what goes on in their world; the theory is "social" because, along with reinforcement and punishment, what other people do is an important source of information about the world (Bandura, 2000).

**Bandura also argues that experience gives children a sense of self-efficacy, beliefs about their own abilities and talents.** Self-efficacy beliefs help determine when children will imitate others. A child who sees himself as athletically untalented, for example, will not try to imitate Tiger Woods driving a golf ball, despite the fact that he is obviously talented and popular. But the youngster in the photo is likely to imitate Tiger, because he believes he's talented and thus it makes sense to try to imitate him. Thus, whether children imitate others depends on who the other person is, whether that person's behavior is rewarded, and the children's beliefs about their own talents.

Bandura's social cognitive theory is a far cry from Skinner's operant conditioning. The social cognitive child, who actively interprets events, has replaced the operant conditioning child, who responds mechanically to reinforcement and punishment. Nevertheless, Skinner, Bandura, and all learning theorists share the view that experience propels children along their developmental journeys. Returning to our opening scenario, they would tell Betty that she can thank experience for making Marcus both happy and successful academically.

## The Cognitive-Developmental Perspective

**The cognitive-developmental perspective focuses on how children think and on how their thinking changes over time.** Jean Piaget (1896–1980) proposed the best known of these theories. He believed that children naturally try to make sense of their world. Throughout infancy, childhood, and adolescence, youngsters want to understand the workings of both the physical and the social world. For example, infants want to know about objects: "What happens when I push this toy off the table?" And babies want to know about people: "Who is this person who feeds and cares for me?"

Piaget argued that in their efforts to comprehend their world, children act like scientists in creating theories about the physical and social worlds. They try to weave all that they know about objects and people into a complete theory. Children's theories are tested daily by experience because their theories lead them to expect certain things to happen. As with real scientific theories, when the predicted events do occur, a child's belief in her theory grows stronger. When the predicted events do not occur, the child must revise her theory. For example, think about the baby in the photo and her theory of objects like the rattle she's holding. Her theory of objects might include the idea that "If I let go, the rattle will fall to the floor." If the infant drops

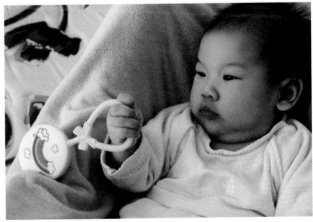

some other object—a plate or an article of clothing—she will find that it, too, falls to the floor and can make the theory more general: Objects that are dropped fall to the floor.

Piaget also believed that at a few critical points in development, children realize their theories have basic flaws. When this happens, they revise their theories radically. These changes are so fundamental that the revised theory is, in many respects, a brand-new theory. Piaget claimed that radical revisions occur three times in development: once at about age 2, a second time at about age 7, and a third time just before adolescence. These radical changes mean children go through four distinct stages in cognitive development. Each stage represents a fundamental change in how children understand and organize their environment, and each stage is characterized by more sophisticated types of reasoning. For example, the sensorimotor stage begins at birth and lasts until about age 2. As the name implies, sensorimotor thinking is closely linked to the infant's sensory and motor skills. This stage and the three later stages are shown in the table.

> In Piaget's theory, children are like scientists in that they are constantly trying to understand their world.

### Piaget's Four Stages of Cognitive Development

| Stage | Approximate Age | Characteristics |
| --- | --- | --- |
| Sensorimotor | Birth to 2 years | Infant's knowledge of the world is based on senses and motor skills. By the end of the period, infant uses mental representations. |
| Preoperational thought | 2 to 6 years | Child learns how to use symbols such as words and numbers to represent aspects of the world, but relates to the world only through his or her perspective. |
| Concrete operational thought | 7 to 11 years | Child understands and applies logical operations to experiences, provided they are focused on the here and now. |
| Formal operational thought | Adolescence and beyond | Adolescent or adult thinks abstractly, speculates on hypothetical situations, and reasons deductively about what may be possible. |

TABLE 1–2

Not all cognitive-developmental theorists view development as a sequence of stages. Information-processing theorists, for example, draw heavily on how computers work to explain thinking and how it develops through childhood and adolescence. **Just as computers consist of both hardware (disk drives, random-access memory, and a central processing unit) and software (the programs we use), information-processing theory proposes that human cognition consists of mental hardware and mental software.** *Mental hardware* refers to cognitive structures, including different memories where information is stored. *Mental software* includes organized sets of cognitive processes that allow children to complete specific tasks, such as reading a sentence, playing a video game, or hitting a baseball.

How do information-processing psychologists explain developmental change in thinking? To answer this question, think about improvements in personal computers. Modern personal computers can accomplish much more than a computer that was built even a few years ago. Why? Because a state-of-the-art computer has better hardware (for example, more memory and a faster central processing unit) and because it has more sophisticated software that takes advantage of the better hardware. Like modern computers, older children and adolescents have better hardware and software than younger children, who are more like last year's out-of-date model. For example, older children typically can solve math word problems better than younger children because they have greater memory capacity to store the facts in the problem and because their methods for performing arithmetic operations are more efficient.

For both Piaget and information-processing theorists, children's thinking becomes more sophisticated as they develop. Piaget explains this change in terms of more sophisticated theories that children create; information-processing psychologists attribute it to more sophisticated mental hardware and mental software. Returning to our opening scenario, neither approach would have much to say to Betty about Marcus's good nature. As for his academic success, Piaget would explain that all children naturally want to understand their worlds; Marcus is simply unusually skilled in this regard. An information-processing psychologist would point to superior cognitive structures and processes as the keys to his academic success.

## The Contextual Perspective

Most developmentalists agree that the environment is an important force in development. Traditionally, however, most theories of child development have emphasized environmental forces that affect children directly. Examples of direct environmental influences would be a parent praising a child, an older sibling teasing a younger one, and a nursery-school teacher discouraging girls from playing with trucks. These direct influences are important in children's lives, but in the contextual perspective they are simply one part of a much larger system, where each element of the system influences all other elements. This larger system includes one's parents and siblings as well as important individuals outside of the family, such as extended family, friends, and teachers. The system also includes institutions that influence development, such as schools, television, the workplace, and a church, temple, or mosque.

**All these people and institutions fit together to form a person's culture—the knowledge, attitudes, and behavior associated with a group of people.** Culture can refer to a particular country or people (e.g., French culture), to a specific point in time (e.g., popular culture of the 1990s), or to groups of individuals who maintain specific, identifiable cultural traditions, like this African American family celebrating Kwanzaa. A culture provides the context in which a child develops and thus is a source of many important influences on development throughout childhood and adolescence.

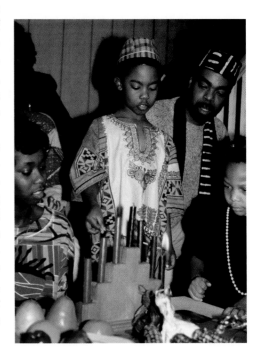

One of the first theorists to emphasize cultural context in children's development was Lev Vygotsky (1896–1934). A Russian psychologist, Vygotsky focused on ways that adults convey to children the beliefs, customs, and skills of their culture. Vygotsky believed that because a fundamental aim of all societies is to enable children to acquire essential cultural values and skills, every aspect of a child's development must be considered against this backdrop. For example, most parents in the United States want their children to work hard in school and be admitted to college, because earning a degree is one of the keys to getting a good job. In the same way, parents in Efe (a developing nation in Africa) want their children to learn to hunt, build houses, and gather food, because these skills are key to survival in their environment.

FIG. 1–1

The contextual approach emphasizes the many different elements of culture that affect children's development.

Vygotsky was the first proponent of the contextual view, but Urie Bronfenbrenner (1917– ) is its best proponent today. Bronfenbrenner views the developing child as embedded in a series of complex and interactive systems. As the diagram shows, Bronfenbrenner (1979, 1995) divides the environment into four levels: the microsystem, the mesosystem, the exosystem, and the macrosystem. **At any point in life, the microsystem consists of the people and objects in an individual's immediate environment.** These are the people closest to a child, such as parents or siblings. Some children have more than one microsystem; for example, a young child might have the microsystems of the family and of the day-care setting. As you can imagine, microsystems strongly influence development.

**Microsystems themselves are connected to create the mesosystem.** The mesosystem represents the fact that what happens in one microsystem is likely to influence others. Perhaps you've found that if you have a stressful day at work or school, you're grouchy at home. This indicates that your mesosystem is alive and well; your microsystems of home and work are interconnected emotionally for you.

**The exosystem refers to social settings that a person may not experience firsthand but that still influence development.** For example, a mother's work environment is part of her child's exosystem, because she may pay more attention to her child when her work is going well and less attention when she's under a great deal of work-related stress. Although the influence of the exosystem is at least secondhand, its effects on the developing child can be quite strong. Think about the woman in the photo, who doesn't look as if she's having a good day at work; do you think she'll do her best mothering when she gets home? Probably not, which means that the workplace has affected her child's development.

**The broadest environmental context is the macrosystem, the subcultures and cultures in which the microsystem, mesosystem, and exosystem are embedded.** A mother, her workplace, her child, and the child's school are part of a larger cultural setting, such as Asian Americans living in Southern California or Italian Americans living in large cities on the East Coast. Members of these cultural groups share a common identity, a common heritage, and common values. The macrosystem evolves over time; what is true about a particular culture today may or may not have been true in the past and may or may not be true in the future. Thus, each successive generation of children develops in a unique macrosystem.

Returning to our opening vignette, Bronfenbrenner and other contextual theorists would agree with learning theorists in telling Betty that the environment has been pivotal in her son's amiable disposition and his academic achievements. However, the contextual theorist would insist that "environment" means much more than the reinforcements, punishments, and observations that are central to learning theory. The contextual theorist would emphasize the different levels of environmental influence on Marcus. Betty's ability to balance home and work so skillfully (which means that she is usually in a good mood herself) contributed positively to Marcus's development, as does Betty's membership in a cultural group that values doing well in school.

**THE BIG PICTURE.**   Comparing five major perspectives in 11 pages is like trying to see all the major sights of a large city in a day: It can be done, but it's demanding and, after a while, everything blurs together. Relax. The Summary Table gives a capsule account of all five perspectives and their important theories.

**SUMMARY TABLE**

### CHARACTERISTICS OF DEVELOPMENTAL PERSPECTIVES

| Perspective | Key Assumptions | Specific Theories |
|---|---|---|
| Biological | Development is determined primarily by biological forces. | *Maturational theory*: emphasizes development as a natural unfolding of a biological plan<br><br>*Evolutionary theory*: emphasizes that children's and parents' behavior has adapted over generations to meet specific environmental challenges |
| Psychodynamic | Development is determined primarily by how a child resolves conflicts at different ages. | *Freud's theory*: emphasizes the conflict between primitive biological forces and societal standards for right and wrong<br><br>*Erikson's theory*: emphasizes the challenges posed by the formation of trust, autonomy, initiative, industry, and identity |
| Learning | Development is determined primarily by a child's environment. | *Skinner's operant conditioning*: emphasizes the role of reinforcement and punishment<br><br>*Bandura's social cognitive theory*: emphasizes children's efforts to understand their world, using reinforcement, punishment, and others' behavior |
| Cognitive-Developmental | Development reflects children's efforts to understand the world. | *Piaget's theory*: emphasizes the different stages of thinking that result from children's changing theories of the world<br><br>*Information-processing theory*: emphasizes changes in thinking that reflect changes in mental hardware and mental software |
| Contextual | Development is influenced by immediate and more distant environments, which typically influence each other. | *Vygotsky's theory*: emphasizes the role of parents (and other adults) in conveying culture to the next generation<br><br>*Bronfenbrenner's theory*: emphasizes the influences of the microsystem, mesosystem, exosystem, and macrosystem |

As I mentioned at the beginning of this module, many of these theories are no longer considered valid. Nevertheless, they have been invaluable in fostering research that has led scientists to formulate modern theories. For example, today few child-development scientists believe that Piaget's theory provides the definitive account of changes in children's thinking. Yet this theory is the forerunner of a number of modern theories, including those of infants' understanding of objects (described in Module 7.2) and of preschoolers' theory of mind (see Module 7.4). Similarly, Erikson's theory has been largely abandoned, yet it contributed to work on mother-infant attachment (see Module 11.3) and formation of identity during adolescence (see Module 12.1).

These examples reflect a common trend in theories of child development. Classic developmental theories were very broad; they attempted to account for the

> Classic developmental theories tend to be very broad; modern theories are more precise but often narrow.

development of many different facets of behavior across infancy, childhood, and adolescence. For the most part, this approach has given way to theories that account for much more restricted phenomena, usually across a narrower age range (e.g., understanding of objects in infancy, identity formation in adolescence). In general, this shift produces theories that are more precise, in the sense that they are more likely to produce specific, testable hypotheses. What's lost in the change, of course, is breadth: Modern theories are less likely to make connections between different phenomena.

Throughout this book, I describe modern theories that are derived from all five perspectives listed in the Summary Table on page 19. Why? Because no single perspective provides a truly complete explanation of all aspects of children's development. Theories from the cognitive-developmental perspective are useful for understanding how children's thinking changes as children grow older. By contrast, theories from the contextual and learning perspectives are particularly valuable in explaining how environmental forces such as parents, peers, schools, and culture influence children's development. By drawing on all the perspectives, we'll be better able to understand the different forces that contribute to children's development. Just as you can better appreciate a beautiful painting by examining it from different viewpoints, child-development researchers often rely on multiple perspectives to understand why children develop as they do.

Another way to understand the forces that shape development is to consider several themes of development—themes that cut across different theoretical perspectives and specific research topics. We'll look at these themes in Module 1.3.

### CHECK YOUR LEARNING

1. The _____ perspective emphasizes the role of conflict in child development.

2. _____ proposes that children learn about the world through reinforcement, punishment, and imitation.

3. According to _____, development is linked to changes in mental hardware and mental software.

4. Vygotsky believed that a fundamental task for all cultures is _____.

5. The influence of multiple levels of the environment is central in _____ theory.

**CONNECTIONS**
Erikson and Piaget both proposed stage theories of children's development. Although the theories differed in emphasis—Erikson was concerned with psychosocial growth and Piaget was concerned with cognitive growth—can you see similarities in their approach to development?

**Answers:** (1) psychodynamic, (2) Albert Bandura's social cognitive theory, (3) the information-processing approach, (4) to pass along beliefs, customs, and skills to children, (5) Bronfenbrenner's contextual

# Themes in Child-Development Research    1.3

## LEARNING OBJECTIVES

● How well can developmental outcomes be predicted from early life?

● How do heredity and environment influence development?

● What role do children have in their own development?

● Is development in different domains connected?

Early Development Is Related to Later Development but Not Perfectly

Development Is Always Jointly Influenced by Heredity and Environment

Children Influence Their Own Development

Development in Different Domains Is Connected

*Javier Suarez smiled broadly as he held his newborn grandson for the first time. So many thoughts rushed into his mind—What would Ricardo experience growing up? Would the poor neighborhood they live in prevent him from reaching his potential? Would the family genes for good health be passed on? How would Ricardo's life growing up as a Chicano in the United States be different from Javier's own experiences in Mexico?*

Like many grandparents, Javier wonders what the future holds for his grandson. And his questions actually reflect several fundamental themes in development that are the focus of this module. These four themes will provide you with a foundation to understand and organize the many specific facts about child development that fill the rest of this book. In fact, to help you do this, "Check Your Learning" questions at the end of each module always include a question about one of these themes. Also, at the end of Chapters 2 through 16, "Unifying Themes" links the contents of the chapter to one of the themes.

Here are the four unifying themes.

## Early Development Is Related to Later Development but Not Perfectly

This theme concerns the "predictability" of development. Do you believe that happy, cheerful 5-year-olds remain outgoing and friendly throughout their lives? If you do, this shows that you believe development is a continuous process: According to this view, once a child begins down a particular developmental path, he or she stays on that path throughout life. In other words, if Ricardo is friendly and smart as a 5-year-old, he should be friendly and smart as a 15- and 25-year-old. The other view, that development is not continuous, is shown in the cartoon. Sweet, cooperative Trixie has become a demanding, assertive child. According to this view, Ricardo might be friendly and smart as a 5-year-old but obnoxious and foolish at 15 and quiet but wise at 25! **Thus, the continuity-versus-discontinuity issue is really about the "relatedness" of development: Are early aspects of development consistently related to later aspects?**

In reality, neither of these views is accurate. Development is not perfectly predictable. A friendly, smart 5-year-old does not guarantee a friendly, smart 15- or 25-year-old, but the chances of a friendly, smart adult are greater than if the child were obnoxious and foolish. There are many ways to become a friendly and smart 15-year-old; being a friendly and smart 5-year-old is not a required step, but it is probably the most direct route!

## Development Is Always Jointly Influenced by Heredity and Environment

I want to introduce this theme with a story about my sons. Ben, my first son, was a delightful baby and toddler. He awoke each morning with a smile on his face, eager to start another fun-filled day. When Ben was upset, which occurred infrequently, he was quickly consoled by being held or rocked. I presumed that his cheerful disposition must reflect fabulous parenting. Consequently, I was stunned when my second son, Matt, spent much of the first year of his life being fussy and cranky. He was easily irritated and hard to soothe. Why wasn't the all-star parenting that had been so effective with Ben working with Matt? The answer, of course, is that Ben's parenting wasn't the sole cause of his happiness. I thought environmental influences accounted for his amiable disposition, but in fact, biological influences also played an important role.

> Virtually all aspects of development are determined by the combined forces of heredity and environment.

**This anecdote illustrates the nature-nurture issue: What roles do biology (nature) and environment (nurture) play in child development?** If Ricardo is outgoing and friendly, is it due to his heredity or his experiences? Scientists once hoped to answer questions like this by identifying either heredity or environment as *the* cause. Their goal was to be able to say, for example, that intelligence was due to heredity or that personality was due to experience. Today, we know that virtually no aspects of child development are due exclusively to either heredity or environment. Instead, development is always shaped by both—nature and nurture interact. In fact, a major goal of child-development research is to understand how heredity and environment jointly determine children's development. Biology will be more influential in some areas and environment will prevail in others.

## Children Influence Their Own Development

Whenever I teach child development, I ask students their plans for when they have children. How will they rear them? What do they want them to grow up to be? It's interesting to hear students' responses. Many have big plans for their future children. It's just as interesting, though, to watch students who already have children roll their eyes in a "You don't have a clue" way at what the others say. The parent-students in class admit that they, too, once had grand designs about child rearing. What they quickly learned, however, was that their children shaped the way in which they parented.

**These two points of view illustrate the active-passive child issue: Are children simply at the mercy of the environment (passive child) or do children actively influence their own development through their own unique individual characteristics (active child)?** The passive view corresponds to Locke's description of the child as a blank slate on which experience writes, whereas the active view corresponds to

Rousseau's view of development as a natural unfolding that takes place within the child. Today, we know that experiences are indeed crucial but not always in the way Locke envisioned. Often, it's a child's interpretation of experiences that shapes his or her development. From birth, children like Ricardo are trying to make sense of their world; and in the process, they help shape their own destinies.

Also, a child's unique characteristics may cause him or her to have some experiences but not others. Think about the child in the photo, who is responding defiantly to her parent's discipline. Do you think this child's defiance will affect the way her parents discipline her in the future? You might predict that they will punish her more harshly the next time, showing the impact of the girl's behavior on her parents' behavior.

## Development in Different Domains Is Connected

Child-development researchers usually examine different domains or areas of development, such as physical growth, cognition, language, personality, and social relationships. One researcher might study how children learn to speak grammatically; another might explore children's reasoning about moral issues. Of course, you should *not* think of each aspect of development as an independent entity, one that is completely separate from the others. To the contrary, development in different domains is always intertwined. Cognitive and social development, for example, are not independent; advances in one area affect advances in the other. Ricardo's cognitive growth (e.g., he becomes an excellent student) will influence his social development (e.g., he becomes friends with peers who share his zeal for school).

Having introduced the themes, let's see them together once before we move on.

- *Continuity:* Early development is related to later development but not perfectly.
- *Nature and nurture:* Development is always jointly influenced by heredity and environment.
- *Active children:* Children influence their own development.
- *Connections:* Development in different domains is connected.

Most child-development scientists would agree that these are important general themes in children's development. However, just as lumber, bricks, pipe, and wiring can be used to assemble an incredible assortment of homes, these themes show up in different ways in the major theories of child development. Think, for example, about the nature–nurture issue. Of the five perspectives, the biological perspective is at one extreme in emphasizing the impact of nature; at the other extreme are the learning and contextual perspectives, which emphasize nurture.

The perspectives also see different degrees of connectedness across different domains of development. Piaget's cognitive-developmental theory takes the hardest line: Because children strive to have a single integrated theory to explain the world, cognitive and social growth are closely interconnected. That is, because children interpret all aspects of their lives with the same unified view of the world, everything is linked. The learning perspective, in contrast, holds that the degree of connectedness depends entirely on the nature of environmental influences. Similar environmental influences in different domains of children's lives produce many connections; dissimilar environmental influences would produce few connections.

## CHECK YOUR LEARNING

**1.** The _____ issue concerns how early development relates to later development.

**2.** In determining the importance of nature and nurture, today scientists believe that _____.

**3.** The extent to which children help to shape their own development is central to the _____ issue.

 **ACTIVE CHILDREN**
How might parents respond differently to a very active child compared to a very quiet child?

**Answers:** (1) continuity–discontinuity; (2) heredity and environment jointly influence most aspects of development, (3) active–passive child

## See for Yourself

One good way to see how children influence their own development is to interview parents who have more than one child. Ask them if they used the same child-rearing methods with each child or if they used different techniques with each. If they used different techniques, find out why. You should see that, although parents try to be consistent in a general philosophy for rearing their children, many of the specific parenting techniques will vary from one child to the next, reflecting the children's influence on the parents. See for yourself!

## Resources

For more information about...

the different theories described in Module 1.2, I recommend Patricia H. Miller's *Theories of Developmental Psychology* (Worth, 2001) for its comprehensive account of each of the theoretical perspectives.

the history of childhood, visit the Web site of the Philosophy and History of Education Institute at the University of Nijmegen, in the Netherlands

http://www.socsci.kun.nl/ped/whp/histeduc/index.html

where you can find some fascinating paintings and photographs depicting children of centuries past as well as an on-line edition of an education manual written by philosopher John Locke in 1693.

## Key Terms

active–passive child issue  22
baby biographies  9
cognitive-developmental perspective  15
continuity–discontinuity issue  22
critical period  11
culture  17
ego  12
ethological theory  11
evolutionary psychology  11
exosystem  18
id  12
imitation (observational learning)  14
imprinting  11
information-processing theory  16

macrosystem  18
maturational theory  10
mesosystem  18
microsystem  18
nature–nurture issue  22
operant conditioning  14
psychodynamic theory  12
psychosocial theory  13
punishment  14
reinforcement  14
self-efficacy  15
social cognitive theory  15
superego  13
theory  10

# 1.1 Using This Book

### Organization of Chapters

Each chapter includes three or four modules that begin with learning objectives, a vignette, and a mini-outline. In the text, key terms and their definitions appear in boldface type. Each module includes a special feature that examines a specific topic in depth. The module ends with questions that allow you to check your learning. Each chapter ends with several elements that should encourage you to think about the information in the chapter as well as a summary like the one you're reading now.

### How to Use This Book

Preview the entire chapter, then read one module daily. As you read, try to summarize the main ideas; ask yourself questions. When you've finished the chapter, review each module and use the study aids at the end of the chapter.

### Terminology

I use specific terms to refer to people of different ages: newborn, infant, toddler, preschooler, school-age child, adolescent, and adult. Also, when describing different ethnic groups, I use terms that identify the unique cultural heritage of each: African American, Asian American, European American, Hispanic American, and Native American.

### A Final Word

Enjoy the book! Let me know what you like and dislike!

# 1.2 Theories of Child Development

Theories are important because they provide the explanations for development and provide hypotheses for research. Traditionally, five broad theoretical perspectives have guided researchers.

### The Biological Perspective

According to this perspective, biological factors are critical in shaping development. In maturational theory, child development reflects a natural unfolding of a prearranged biological plan. Ethological theory states that children's and parents' behavior is often adaptive—it has survival value. This idea has been expanded to represent an evolutionary perspective on child development.

### The Psychodynamic Perspective

This perspective emphasizes the role of conflict or crises in development. Freud proposed a theory of personality that included the id, ego, and superego. However, the lasting contribution of Freud's work is an emphasis on the roles of early experience and conflict in children's development.

Erikson proposed a life-span theory of psychosocial development consisting of eight universal stages, each characterized by a particular struggle.

### The Learning Perspective

Learning theory focuses on the development of observable behavior. Operant conditioning is based on the notions of reinforcement, punishment, and environmental control of behavior. Social learning theory proposes that people learn by observing others. Social cognitive theory emphasizes that children actively interpret the events they observe.

### The Cognitive-Developmental Perspective

The cognitive-developmental perspective focuses on thought processes. Piaget proposed a four-stage universal sequence based on the notion that, throughout development, people create their own theories to explain how the world works. According to information-processing theory, people deal with information like a computer does; development consists of increased efficiency in handling information.

### The Contextual Perspective

Vygotsky emphasized the role of culture in children's development, and Bronfenbrenner proposed that development occurs in the context of interconnected systems. These range from the microsystem (people and objects in the child's immediate environment) to the macrosystem (the cultures and subcultures in which all the other systems are embedded).

# 1.3 Themes in Child-Development Research

Four themes help unify the findings from child-development research that are presented throughout this book.

### Early Development is Related to Later Development but Not Perfectly

According to the view that development is continuous, children stay on the same path throughout development; according to the view that development is discontinuous, children can change paths at virtually any point in development. Research supports an intermediate view: Development is not completely rigid as in the continuous view, nor is it completely flexible as in the discontinuous view.

### Development Is Always Jointly Influenced by Heredity and Environment

The nature–nurture issue involves the extent to which heredity and the environment influence children's development. Today scientists view heredity and environment as interactive forces that work together to chart the course of development.

### Children Influence Their Own Development

Scientists once viewed children primarily as passive recipients of experience who are at the mercy of their environments. The modern view, however, is that children constantly interpret their experiences and, by their individual characteristics, often influence the experiences they have.

### Development in Different Domains Is Connected

Although researchers usually study separate aspects of children's development, in reality development in different domains of children's lives is always connected. Cognitive development affects social development and vice versa.

# .2

When you think of research, what comes to mind? Maybe the chemicals and test tubes of a chemistry lab? Perhaps the telescope of an observatory? Or maybe the particle accelerator of a high-energy physics lab? Test tubes, telescopes, and particle accelerators are indeed important tools for chemists, astronomers, and physicists. Like research conducted in these other sciences, child-development scientists depend on important research tools, which I'll describe in this chapter. We begin, in Module 2.1, by exploring the techniques that researchers use to study children and their development. Then in Module 2.2, we'll see how child-development research can be used to create more-informed public policies concerning children and their families.

# Research in Child Development

# 2.1

# Doing Child-Development Research

## LEARNING OBJECTIVES

- How do scientists measure topics of interest in children's development?

- What general research designs are used in child-development research? What designs are unique to child-development research?

- What ethical procedures must researchers follow?

- How do researchers communicate results to other scientists?

> *Leah and Joan are both mothers of 10-year-old boys. Their sons have many friends, but the basis for the friendships is not obvious to the mothers. Leah believes that "opposites attract"—children form friendships with peers who have complementary interests and abilities. Joan doubts this; her son seems to seek out other boys who are near clones of himself in their interests and abilities.*

Suppose Leah and Joan know you're taking a course in child development, so they ask you to settle their argument. You know, from Module 1.2, that Leah and Joan each have simple theories about children's friendships. Leah's theory is that complementary children are more often friends, whereas Joan's theory is that similar children are more often friends. And you know that these theories should be tested with research. But how? In fact, child-development researchers must make several important decisions as they prepare to study a topic. They need to decide how to measure the topic; they must design their study; they must be sure their proposed research respects the rights of the individuals participating; and, once the study is complete, they must communicate their results to other researchers.

Child-development researchers do not always stick to this sequence of steps. For example, researchers usually consider the rights of research participants as they make each of the other decisions, perhaps rejecting a procedure because it violates those rights. Nevertheless, for simplicity, I will use this sequence to describe the steps in doing developmental research.

## Measurement in Child-Development Research

Research usually begins by deciding how to measure the topic or behavior of interest. For example, the first step toward answering Leah and Joan's question about friendships would be to decide how to measure friendships. Child-development researchers typically use one of three approaches: observing systematically, using tasks to sample behavior, and asking children for self reports.

SYSTEMATIC OBSERVATION.   **As the name implies, systematic observation involves watching children and carefully recording what they do or say.** Two forms of systematic observation are common. **In naturalistic observation, children are observed as they behave spontaneously in some real-life situation.** Of course, researchers can't keep track of everything that a child does. **Beforehand they must decide which variables—factors subject to change—to record.** Researchers studying friendship, for example, might decide to observe children in a school lunchroom like the one in the photo. They would record where each child sits and who talks to whom. They might also decide to observe children at the start of the first year in a middle school, because many children make new friends at this time.

**In structured observation, the researcher creates a setting likely to elicit the behavior of interest.** Structured observations are particularly useful for studying behaviors that are difficult to observe naturally. Some phenomena occur rarely, such as emergencies. An investigator using natural observations to study children's responses to emergencies wouldn't make much progress because, by definition, emergencies don't occur at predetermined times and locations. However, using structured observation, an investigator might stage an emergency, perhaps by having a nearby adult cry for help and then observing children's responses.

Other behaviors are difficult for researchers to observe because they occur in private settings, not public ones. For example, much interaction between friends takes place at home, where it would be difficult for investigators to observe unobtrusively. However, children who are friends could be asked to come to the researcher's laboratory, which might be furnished with comfortable chairs and tables. They would be asked to perform some activity typical of friends, such as playing a game or deciding what movie to see. By observing friends' interactions in a setting like the one in the photo (perhaps through a one-way mirror), researchers could learn more about how friends interact.

Though structured observations allow researchers to observe behaviors that would otherwise be difficult to study, investigators must be careful that the settings they create do not disturb the behavior of interest. For instance, observing friends as they play a game in a mock family room has many artificial aspects to it: The friends are not in their own homes, they were told (in general terms) what to do, and they know they're being observed. Any or all of these factors may cause children to behave differently than they would in the real world. Researchers must be careful that their method does not distort the behavior they are observing.

**SAMPLING BEHAVIOR WITH TASKS.** When investigators can't observe a behavior directly, an alternative is to create tasks that are thought to sample the behavior of interest. For example, to measure memory, investigators sometimes use a digit span task: Children listen as a sequence of numbers is presented aloud. After the last digit is presented, children try to repeat the digits in the exact order in which they heard them. To measure children's ability to recognize different emotions, investigators sometimes use the task shown in the diagram. The child has been asked to look at the facial expressions and point to the person who is happy.

Sampling behavior with tasks is popular with child-development researchers because it is so convenient. A major

FIG. 2–1

problem with this approach, however, is whether the task really samples the behavior of interest. For example, asking children to judge emotions from photographs may not be valid, because it underestimates what children do in real life. Can you think of reasons why this might be the case? I mention several reasons on page 41, just before "Check Your Learning."

**SELF REPORTS.**     The last approach to measurement, using self reports, is actually a special case of using tasks to measure children's behavior. **Self reports are simply children's answers to questions about the topic of interest.** When questions are posed in written form, the report is a questionnaire; when questions are posed orally, the report is an interview. In either format, questions are created that probe different aspects of the topic of interest. For example, if you believe that children more often become friends when they have interests in common, then research participants might be told the following:

> *Tom and Dave just met each other at school. Tom likes to read, plays the clarinet in the school orchestra, and is not interested in sports; Dave likes to watch videos on MTV, plays video games, and is a star on the soccer team. Do you think Tom and Dave will become friends?*

Children would decide, perhaps using a rating scale, if the boys are likely to become friends.

Child development researchers use systematic observation, sampling behavior with tasks, and self reports to study children's development.

Self reports are useful because they can lead directly to information on the topic of interest. They are also relatively convenient (particularly when they can be administered to groups of children or adolescents). However, self reports are not always valid measures of children's behavior, because children's answers are sometimes inaccurate. Why? When asked about past events, children may not remember them accurately. For example, an adolescent asked about childhood friends may not remember those friendships well. Also, children sometimes answer incorrectly due to response bias. That is, some responses may be more socially acceptable than others, and children are more likely to select those than socially unacceptable answers. For example, many children would be reluctant to admit that they have no friends at all. But, as long as investigators keep these weaknesses in mind, self reports are a valuable tool for child-development research.

The three approaches to measurement are summarized in the table on page 31.

**EVALUATING MEASURES.**     After researchers choose a method of measurement, they must show that it is both reliable and valid. **A measure is reliable if the results are consistent over time.** A measure of friendship, for example, would be reliable if it yields the same results about friendship each time it is administered. All measures used in child-development research must be shown to be reliable, or they cannot be used. **A measure is valid if it really measures what researchers think it measures.** For example, a measure of friendship is only valid if it can be shown to actually measure friendship (and not, for example, popularity). Validity is often established by showing that the measure in question is closely related to another measure known to be valid. We could show the validity of a questionnaire that claims to measure friendship by showing that scores on the questionnaire are related to peers' and parents' measures of friendship.

Throughout this book, you'll come across many studies using these different methods. You'll also see that studies of the same topic or behavior often use different methods. This is very desirable: Because the approaches to measurement have different strengths

## WAYS OF MEASURING BEHAVIOR IN CHILD-DEVELOPMENT RESEARCH

| Method | Strength | Weakness |
| --- | --- | --- |
| Systematic observation | | |
| Naturalistic observation | Captures children's behavior in its natural setting | Difficult to use with behaviors that are rare or that typically occur in private settings |
| Structured observation | Can be used to study behaviors that are rare or that typically occur in private settings | May be invalid if the structured setting distorts the behavior |
| Sampling behavior with tasks | Convenient—can be used to study most behaviors | May be invalid if the task does not sample behavior as it occurs naturally |
| Self reports (questionnaires and interviews) | Convenient—can be used to study most behaviors | May be invalid because children answer incorrectly due to forgetting or response bias |

and weaknesses, finding the same results regardless of the approach leads to particularly strong conclusions. Suppose, for example, that a researcher using self reports claims that arguments, like the one shown in the photo, are more common in boys' friendships than in girls' friendships. It would be reassuring that other investigators have found the same result from systematic observation and from sampling behavior with tasks.

**REPRESENTATIVE SAMPLING.** Valid measures depend not only on the method of measurement, but also on the children who are tested. **Researchers are usually interested in broad groups of children called populations.** Examples of populations would be all American 7-year-olds or all African American adolescents. However, it would be extremely difficult for researchers to study every member of such large groups. **Virtually all studies include only a sample of children, a subset of the population.** Researchers must take care that their sample really represents the population of interest. An unrepresentative sample can lead to invalid research. For example, what would you think of a study of children's friendship if you learned that the sample consisted entirely of 8-year-olds whose friends were primarily preschool children? You would decide quite correctly that this sample is not representative of the population of 8-year-olds, and you would hesitate to generalize the results from this sample back to the population at large.

As you read on, you'll discover that much of the research I describe was conducted with samples of middle-class European American youngsters. Are these samples representative of all children in the United States? Of children like those in the photo who grow up in developing countries? Sometimes, but not always. Be careful not to assume that findings from this group necessarily apply to people in other groups.

## General Designs for Research

Having selected a way to measure the topic or behavior of interest, researchers must then put this measure into a research design. Child-development researchers usually use one of two designs: correlational or experimental studies.

CORRELATIONAL STUDIES.    **In a correlational study, investigators look at relations between variables as they exist naturally in the world.** In the simplest possible correlational study, a researcher measures two variables, then sees how they are related. Imagine a researcher who wants to test the idea that smarter children have more friends. To test this claim, the researcher would measure two variables for each child in the sample: the number of friends the child has and the child's intelligence.

**The results of a correlational study are usually expressed as a correlation coefficient, abbreviated $r$, which stands for the direction and strength of a relation between two variables.** Correlations can range from $-1.0$ to $+1.0$:

- *When r equals 0, two variables are completely unrelated:* Children's intelligence is unrelated to the number of friends they have.

- *When r is greater than 0, scores are related positively:* Children who are smart tend to have more friends than children who are not as smart. That is, more intelligence is associated with having more friends.

- *When r is less than 0, scores are related, but inversely:* Children who are smart tend to have fewer friends than children who are not as smart. That is, more intelligence is associated with having fewer friends.

In interpreting a correlation coefficient, you need to consider both the sign *and* the size of the correlation. The sign indicates the *direction* of the relation between variables: a positive sign means that larger values on one variable are associated with larger values on the second variable, whereas a negative sign means that larger values on one variable are associated with smaller values on a second variable.

> Unlike correlational studies, experimental studies allow conclusions about cause and effect.

The *strength* of a relation is measured by how much the correlation differs from 0, either positively or negatively. If the correlation between intelligence and number of friends were .9, the relation between these variables would be very strong: Knowing a child's intelligence, you could accurately predict how many friends the child has. If, instead, the correlation were .3, the link between intelligence and number of friends would be relatively weak: Although more intelligent children would have more friends on the average, there would be many exceptions to this rule. Similarly, a correlation of $-.9$ would indicate a strong negative relation between intelligence and number of friends, but a correlation of $-.3$ would indicate a weak negative relation.

The results of a correlational study tell whether variables are related, but this design doesn't address the question of cause and effect between the variables. In other words, suppose a researcher finds that the correlation between intelligence and number of friends is .7. This means that children who are smarter have more friends than children who are not as smart. How would you interpret this correlation? The diagram at the top of page 33 shows that three interpretations are possible. Maybe being smart causes children to have more friends. Another interpretation is that having more friends causes children to be smarter. A third interpretation is that neither variable causes the other; instead, intelligence and number of friends are caused by a third variable that was not measured in the study. Perhaps parents who are warm and

**Three Interpretations of a Correlation Coefficient**

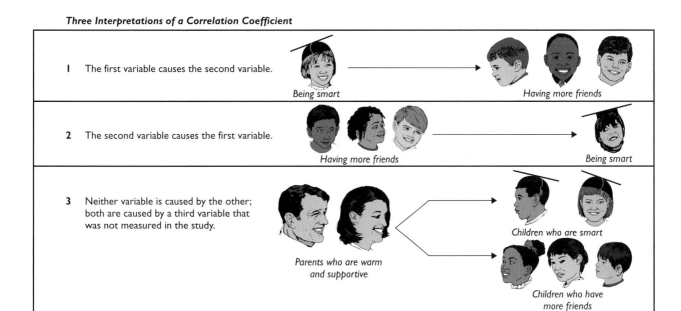

| | | |
|---|---|---|
| 1 | The first variable causes the second variable. | *Being smart* → *Having more friends* |
| 2 | The second variable causes the first variable. | *Having more friends* → *Being smart* |
| 3 | Neither variable is caused by the other; both are caused by a third variable that was not measured in the study. | *Parents who are warm and supportive* → *Children who are smart* / *Children who have more friends* |

FIG. 2–2

supportive tend to have children who are smart and who also have many friends. Any of these interpretations could be true. Cause and effect cannot be distinguished in a correlational study. When investigators want to track down causes, they must use a different design, an experimental study.

EXPERIMENTAL STUDIES.   **An experiment is a systematic way of manipulating the key factor(s) that an investigator thinks causes a particular behavior. The factor that is manipulated is called the independent variable; the behavior that is measured is called the dependent variable.** In an experiment, the investigator begins with one or more treatments, circumstances, or events (independent variables) that are thought to affect a particular behavior. Children are then assigned randomly to different groups. Next, the dependent variable is measured in all groups. Because each child has an equal chance of being assigned to any group (due to random assignment), the groups should be the same except in the treatment they receive. Any differences between the groups can then be attributed to the differential treatment the children received in the experiment, rather than to other factors.

Suppose, for example, that an investigator believes children share more with friends than with children they do not know. The diagram shows how the investigator might test this hypothesis. Based on random assignment, some fifth-grade children would be asked to come to the investigator's laboratory with a good friend. Other fifth graders would come to the laboratory site without a friend and would be paired with a child they don't know. The laboratory itself would be

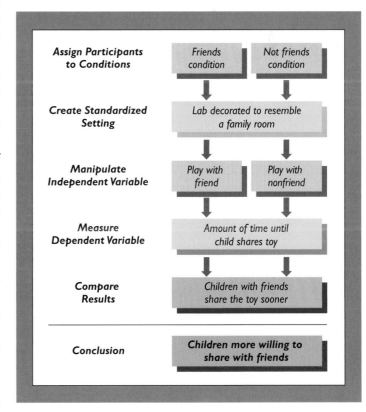

| | |
|---|---|
| **Assign Participants to Conditions** | Friends condition / Not friends condition |
| **Create Standardized Setting** | Lab decorated to resemble a family room |
| **Manipulate Independent Variable** | Play with friend / Play with nonfriend |
| **Measure Dependent Variable** | Amount of time until child shares toy |
| **Compare Results** | Children with friends share the toy sooner |
| **Conclusion** | *Children more willing to share with friends* |

FIG. 2–3

decorated to look like a family room in a house. The investigator creates a task in which one child is given an interesting object to play with—perhaps a Game Boy—but the other child receives nothing. The experimenter explains the task to the children and then claims that she needs to leaves the room briefly. Actually, the experimenter goes to a room with a one-way mirror and observes whether the child with the Game Boy offers to share it with the other child.

This same scenario would be used with all pairs of children: The room and toy would be the same and the experimenter would always be away for the same amount of time. The circumstances would be held as constant as possible for all children, except that some children participate with friends but others do not. If children who participated with friends gave the toy more quickly or more readily to the other child, the investigator could say with confidence that children are more likely to share with their friends than with children they don't know. Conclusions about cause and effect are possible because there was a direct manipulation of an independent variable (participating with a friend or with an unknown child) under controlled conditions.

Child-development researchers usually conduct their experiments in laboratory-like settings to control all the variables that might influence the outcome of the research. A shortcoming of laboratory work is that the behavior of interest is not studied in its natural setting. Consequently, the results may be invalid because they are artificial—specific to the laboratory setting and not representative of the behavior in the natural environment.

> **Field experiments allow strong conclusions about cause and effect because they are conducted in natural settings.**

To avoid this limit, researchers sometimes rely on a special type of experiment. **In a field experiment, the researcher manipulates independent variables in a natural setting so that the results are more likely to be representative of behavior in real-world settings.** To illustrate a field experiment, let's return to the hypothesis that children share more with friends. We might conduct the research in a classroom where students must complete a group assignment. In collaboration with teachers, we place the children in groups of three—in some groups, all three children are good friends; in others, the three children are acquaintances but not friends. When the assignment is complete, the teacher gives each group leader many stickers and tells the leader to distribute them to group members based on how much each child contributed. We predict that leaders will share more (i.e., distribute the stickers more evenly) when group members are friends than when they are not.

Field experiments allow investigators to draw strong conclusions about cause and effect because they embed manipulation of an independent variable in a natural setting. However, field experiments are often impractical because of logistical problems. In most natural settings, children are supervised by adults (e.g., parents and teachers) who must be willing to become allies in the proposed research. Adults may not want to change their routines to fit a researcher's needs. In addition, researchers usually sacrifice some control in field experiments. In the example of distributing stickers to group members, some children no doubt actually worked harder than others, which means children's sharing will *not* be based simply on whether the other children are friends.

Both research designs used by developmentalists—correlational and experimental—have strengths and weaknesses. No method is perfect. Consequently, no single investigation can definitely answer a question, and researchers rarely rely on one study or even one method to reach conclusions. Instead, they prefer to find converging evidence from as many different kinds of studies as possible. Suppose, for example, our hypothetical laboratory and field experiments showed that children did, indeed, share more readily with their friends. One way to be more confident of this conclusion would be to do correlational research, perhaps by observing children during lunch and measuring how often they share food with different people.

## Designs for Studying Development

Sometimes child-development research is directed at a single age group, such as fifth-grade children in the experiment on sharing between friends and nonfriends, memory in preschool-age children, or mother–infant relationships in 1-year-olds, like the one shown in the photo. When this is the case, after deciding how to measure the behavior of interest and whether the study will be correlational or experimental, the investigator could skip directly to the last step and determine whether the study is ethical. However, much research in child development concerns changes that occur as children develop. In these cases, investigators must make one further decision: Will they do a longitudinal study or a cross-sectional study?

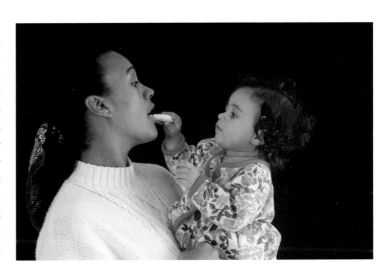

**LONGITUDINAL STUDIES.** **In a longitudinal study, the same individuals are observed or tested repeatedly at different points in their lives.** As the name implies, the longitudinal approach takes a lengthwise view of development and is the most direct way to watch growth occur. As the diagram shows, in a longitudinal study, children might be tested first at age 6 and then again at ages 9 and 12. The longitudinal approach is well suited to studying almost any aspect of development. More important, it is the only way to answer questions about the continuity or discontinuity of behavior: Will characteristics such as aggression, dependency, or mistrust observed in infancy or early childhood persist into adulthood? Will a traumatic event, such as being abandoned by one's parents, influence later social and intellectual development? Such questions can be explored only by testing children early in development and then retesting them later.

Usually the repeated testing of longitudinal studies extends over years, but not always. **In a microgenetic study, a special type of**

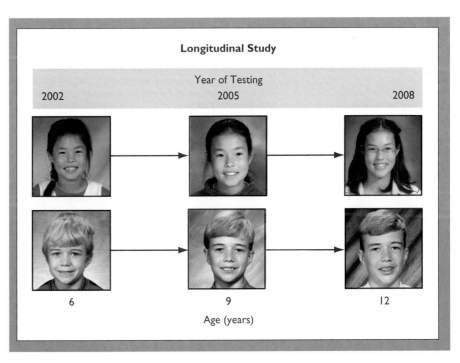

FIG. 2–4

**longitudinal study, children are tested repeatedly over a span of days or weeks, typically with the aim of observing change directly as it occurs.** For example, researchers might test children every week, starting when they are 12 months old and continuing until 18 months. Microgenetic studies are particularly useful when investigators have hypotheses about a specific period when developmental change should occur. In this case, researchers arrange to test children frequently before, during, and after this period, hoping to see change as it happens.

> Cross-sectional studies are more convenient but only longitudinal studies can answer questions about continuity of development.

The longitudinal approach, however, has disadvantages that frequently offset its strengths. An obvious one is cost: The expense of merely keeping up with a large sample of people can be staggering. Other problems are not so obvious:

*Practice effects:* When children are given the same test many times, they may become "test-wise." Improvement over time that is attributed to development may actually stem from practice with a particular test. Changing the test from one session to the next solves the practice problem but makes it difficult to compare responses to different tests.

*Selective attrition:* Another problem is the constancy of the sample over the course of research. Some children may drop out because they move away. Others may simply lose interest and choose not to continue. These "dropouts" are often significantly different from their more research-minded peers, and this fact alone may distort the outcome. For example, a study might find that memory improves between 8 and 11 years. What has actually happened, however, is that 8-year-olds who found the testing too difficult quit the study, thereby raising the group average for the 11-year-olds.

*Cohort effects:* When children in a longitudinal study are observed over a period of several years, the developmental change may be specific to that particular generation. For example, the results of a 10-year longitudinal study of infants born in 1975 may be general (i.e., apply to infants born in 1950 as well as infants born in 2000), but they may reflect experiences that were unique to members of Generation X.

Because of these and other problems with the longitudinal method, child-development researchers often use cross-sectional studies instead.

**CROSS-SECTIONAL STUDIES. In a cross-sectional study, developmental changes are identified by testing children of different ages at one point in their development.** In other words, as shown in the diagram, a researcher might chart the differences in some attribute between, say, 6-, 9-, and 12-year-olds.

**Cross-Sectional Study**

Year of Testing

| 2005 | 2005 | 2005 |

| 6 | 9 | 12 |

Age (years)

FIG. 2–5

The cross-sectional approach avoids many of the problems associated with repeated testing, including practice effects and selective attrition. But cohort effects are still a problem: The results may apply to children who are 6, 9, and 12 years old at the time of testing (in the example, 2005) and not generalize to previous or future generations. And cross-sectional studies have a unique shortcoming: Because children are tested at only one point in their development, we learn nothing about the continuity of development. Consequently, we cannot tell whether an aggressive 6-year-old remains aggressive at age 9 and 12, because an individual child would be tested at age 6, 9, or 12, but not at all three ages.

**LONGITUDINAL-SEQUENTIAL STUDIES.** Neither longitudinal nor cross-sectional studies are foolproof; each has weaknesses. Consequently, sometimes investigators use a design that is a hybrid of the traditional designs. A longitudinal-sequential study includes sequences of samples, each studied longitudinally. For example, researchers might start with 6- and 9-year-olds. As shown in the graph, each group is tested twice— at the beginning of the study and again, three years later. As in a pure longitudinal study, the longitudinal-sequential design provides some information about continuity of development: Researchers can determine whether aggressive 6-year-olds become aggressive 9-year-olds and whether aggressive

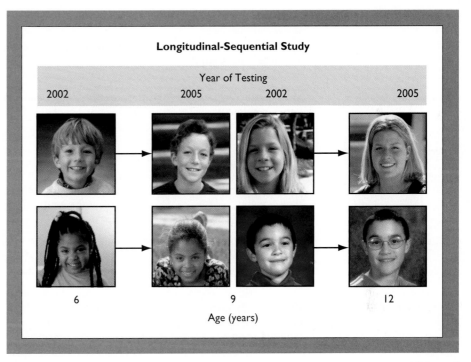

FIG. 2–6

9-year-olds become aggressive 12-year-olds. Of course, to determine whether aggressive 6-year-olds become aggressive 12-year-olds would require a full-blown longitudinal study.

Another advantage of the longitudinal-sequential study is that researchers can determine whether their study is plagued by practice effects or cohort effects: The key is to compare the results for the age common to both sequences (in the example in the figure, 9-year-olds). Practice and cohort effects tend to make scores different for the two groups of 9-year-olds, so if scores are the same, a researcher can be confident that practice and cohort effects are not a problem in the study.

Each of the three designs for studying development (longitudinal, cross-sectional, longitudinal-sequential) can be combined with the two general research designs (observational, experimental), resulting in six prototypic designs. To illustrate the different possibilities, think back to our hypothetical laboratory experiment on children's sharing with friends and nonfriends (described on pages 33-34). If we tested 7- and 11-year-olds with either friends or nonfriends, this would be a cross-sectional experimental study. If instead we observed 7-year-olds' spontaneous sharing at lunch, then observed the same children four years later, this would be a longitudinal correlational study.

The different designs are summarized in the table. In this book, you'll read about studies using these various designs, although the two cross-sectional designs will show up more frequently than the other designs. Why? For most developmentalists, the ease of cross-sectional studies compared to longitudinal studies more than compensates for the limitations of cross-sectional studies.

SUMMARY TABLE

## DESIGNS USED IN CHILD-DEVELOPMENT RESEARCH

| Type of Design | Definition | Strengths | Weaknesses |
|---|---|---|---|
| *General Designs* | | | |
| Correlational | Observe variables as they exist in the world and determine their relations | Behavior is measured as it occurs naturally | Cannot determine cause and effect |
| Experimental | Manipulate independent and dependent variables | Control of variables allows conclusions about cause and effect | Work is often laboratory-based, which can be artificial |
| *Developmental Designs* | | | |
| Longitudinal | One group of children is tested repeatedly as they develop | Only way to chart an individual's development and look at the continuity of behavior over time | Expensive, participants drop out, and repeated testing can distort performance |
| Cross-sectional | Children of different ages are tested at the same time | Convenient—solves most problems associated with longitudinal studies | Cannot study continuity of behavior; cohort effects complicate interpretation of differences between groups |
| Longitudinal-sequential | Different sequences of children are tested longitudinally | Provides information about continuity; researchers can determine the presence of practice and cohort effects | Provides less information about continuity than a full longitudinal study and is more time consuming than a cross-sectional study |

**INTEGRATING FINDINGS FROM DIFFERENT STUDIES.** Several times in this module, I've emphasized the value of conducting multiple studies on a topic using different methods. The advantage of this approach, of course, is that conclusions are most convincing when the results are the same regardless of method.

In reality, though, findings are often inconsistent. Suppose, for example, many researchers find that children often share with friends, some researchers find that children share occasionally with friends, and a few researchers find that children never share with friends. What results should we believe? What should we conclude? **Meta-analysis is a tool that allows researchers to synthesize the results of many studies to estimate relations between variables** (Rosenthal, Rosnow, & Rubin, 2000). In conducting a meta-analysis, investigators find all studies published on a topic over a substantial period of time (e.g., 10 to 20 years), then record and analyze the results and important methodological variables.

The usefulness of meta-analysis is illustrated in a study by McClure (2000), who asked whether boys and girls differ in their ability to recognize emotions in facial expressions. She found 60 studies, published between 1931 and 1999, that included nearly 10,000 children and adults. In each study, participants were administered some sort of task like the one shown on page 29, in which the aim is to select a face expressing a particular emotion. Analyzing across the results of all 60 studies, McClure found that overall girls recognized emotions in facial expressions more accurately than boys. The sex difference was constant from 4 to 16 years of age and was the same when the faces were shown as photos and as drawings. However, the sex difference was larger when participants judged emotions in children's faces than when they judged emotions in adults' faces.

Thus, meta-analysis is a particularly powerful tool because it allows scientists to determine whether a finding generalizes across many studies that used different methods. In addition, meta-analysis can reveal the impact of those different methods on results.

## Ethical Responsibilities

Having selected a way of measuring the behavior of interest and having chosen appropriate general and developmental designs, researchers must confront one very important remaining step: They must determine whether their research is ethical, that it does not violate the rights of the children who participate in it. Of course, scientists must always consider the ethics of research with humans, but especially for children who are vulnerable and sensitive. Professional organizations and government agencies have codes of conduct that specify the rights of research participants and procedures to protect those participants. The following guidelines are included in all those codes:

> **Ethical research minimizes risk and deception, allows individuals to decide if they want to participate, and keeps results confidential.**

*Minimize risks to research participants:* Use methods that have the least potential for harm or stress for research participants. During the research, monitor the procedures to be sure to avoid any unforeseen stress or harm.

*Describe the research to potential participants so they can determine whether they wish to participate:* Prospective research participants should be told all details of the research so they can make an informed decision about participating. Children are minors and are not legally capable of giving consent; consequently, as shown in the photograph, researchers must describe the study to parents and ask them for permission for their children to participate.

*Avoid deception; if participants must be deceived, provide a thorough explanation of the true nature of the research as soon as possible:* Providing complete information about a study in advance can sometimes bias or distort participants' responses. Consequently, investigators sometimes provide only partial information or even mislead participants about the true purpose of the study. As soon as it is feasible—typically just after the experiment—any false information must be corrected and the reasons for the deception must be provided.

*Keep results anonymous or confidential:* Research results should be anonymous, which means that participants' data cannot be linked to their name. When anonymity is not possible, research results should be confidential, which means that only the investigator conducting the study knows the identities of the individuals.

Before researchers can conduct a study, they must convince review boards consisting of scientists from many disciplines that they have carefully addressed each of these ethical points. If the review board objects to some aspects of the proposed study, the researcher must revise those aspects and present them anew for the review board's approval.

Much child-development research does not raise ethical red flags because the methods are harmless and avoid deception. Some methods, however, involve risk or deception; in these cases, review boards must balance the rights of children against the value of the research for contributing to knowledge and thereby improving children's lives. For example, in Module 11.3 we'll see that one tool for studying mother–infant relationships involves separating mothers and infants briefly, then watching infants' responses. Many infants are upset when the mother leaves and some are difficult to console when she returns. Obviously, this method is not pleasant for infants. But scientists have determined that it produces no lasting harm and therefore is suitable as long as parents receive a thorough description of the study beforehand and they consent to participate.

## Communicating Research Results

When the study is complete and the data have been analyzed, researchers write a report of their work. This report uses a standard format in which the authors describe the problem they studied, the methods they used, the results they obtained, and the meaning(s) of their results. The researchers submit the report to one of several scientific journals that specialize in child-development research. Some of these are *Child Development, Developmental Psychology,* and the *Journal of Experimental Child Psychology.* The editor of the journal asks other scientists to evaluate the report, to decide whether the work was well done and the findings represent a substantial advance in scientific understanding of a topic. If the scientists recommend that the report be published, it will appear in the journal, where other child-development researchers can learn of the results.

> Scientists communicate their results to other researchers by publishing them in scientific journals.

These reports of research are the basis for virtually all the information I present in this book. As you read, you'll see names in parentheses, followed by a date, like this:

(Levine, 1983).

This indicates the person who did the research and the year it was published. By looking in the References, which begin on page 503 and are organized alphabetically, you can find the title of the article and the journal where it was published.

Maybe all these different steps in research seem tedious and involved to you. For a child-development researcher, however, much of the fun of doing research is planning a novel study that will provide useful information to other specialists. This is one of the most creative and challenging parts of child-development research.

The "Focus on Research" features that appear in the remaining chapters of this book (listed on page xiii) are designed to convey both the creativity and the challenge of doing child-development research. Each feature focuses on a specific study. Some are studies that have just recently been published; others are classics that defined a new area of investigation or provided definitive results in some area. In each "Focus" feature, I trace the decisions that researchers made as they planned their study. In the process, you'll see the ingenuity of researchers as they pursue questions of child development. You'll also see that any individual study has limitations. Only when converging evidence from many studies—each using a unique combination of measurement methods and designs—points to the same conclusion can we feel confident about research results.

From studies like those described in the "Focus on Research" feature, we now know much about children and their development. Many scientists, practitioners, and elected officials are eager to use this knowledge to create policies that benefit children. We'll look at this connection between research and policy in Module 2.2.

*Responses to question on page 30 about using photographs to measure children's understanding of emotions*: Children's understanding of emotions depicted in photographs may be less accurate than in real life because (1) in real life, facial features are usually moving—not still as in the photographs—and movement may be one of the clues that children naturally use to judge emotions; (2) in real life, facial expressions are often accompanied by sounds, and children use both sight and sound to understand emotion; and (3) in real life, children most often judge facial expressions of people they know (parents, siblings, peers, teachers), and knowing the "usual" appearance of a face may help children determine emotions accurately.

## CHECK YOUR LEARNING

1. In _____, children are observed as they behave spontaneously in a real-life setting.

2. A problem with _____ is that children may give distorted answers due to response bias.

3. A _____ is a group of individuals considered representative of some larger population.

4. In a _____, investigators look at relations between variables as they exist naturally.

5. The _____ variable is measured in an experiment in order to evaluate the impact of the variable that was manipulated.

6. Problems of longitudinal studies include the amount of time and money required to complete the work, cohort effects, loss of research participants over time, and _____.

7. _____ is a procedure used to synthesize the results of different studies on the same topic.

**8.** Researchers must submit their plans for research to a review board that determines whether the research _____.

**9.** Child-development scientists report the findings of their research by _____.

 **CONNECTIONS**

Suppose you wanted to determine the impact of divorce on children's academic achievement. What would be the merits of correlational versus experimental research on this topic? How would a longitudinal study differ from a cross-sectional study?

**Answers:** (1) naturalistic observation, (2) self report, (3) sample, (4) correlational study, (5) dependent, (6) influence of repeated testing on children's performance, (7) Meta-analysis, (8) preserves the rights of research participants, (9) publishing them in a scientific journal.

# 2.2

# Child-Development Research and Family Policy

**LEARNING OBJECTIVES**

● Why have child-development researchers recently become more involved in designing family policy?

● How do child-development researchers influence family policy?

● How has concern for family policy improved child-development research?

> Kendra loved her 12-month-old son Roosevelt, but she was eager to return to her job as a loan officer at a local bank. Kendra knew a woman in her neighborhood who had cared for some of her friends' children and they all thought she was wonderful. But down deep Kendra wished she knew more about whether this type of care was really best for Roosevelt. She also wished that her neighbor's day-care center had a "stamp of approval" from someone who knew how to evaluate these facilities.

This vignette introduces the topics that form the title of this module: child-development research and family policy. **Family policy refers to laws and regulations that directly or indirectly affect families with children.** Kendra wishes that experts could tell her more about the impact of day care on her son's development, had used child-development research to create policies for child-care facilities, and had certified that the neighbor's facility met those standards. In the rest of this module, we'll explore how research is used to foster children's development through sound family policies.

## Why Link Research to Policy?

Child-development researchers have long been interested in applying their work to improving children's lives. After all, when a child-development researcher does an experiment and discovers that one set of conditions enhances children's growth but a second set does not, it would seem natural to use that knowledge to form standards and policies (Rutter, 2002).

Links between child development and family policy have become much stronger in recent years. One reason for the stronger link is that families are changing in America (Zigler, 1998). The "traditional" family, in which children are cared for by a stay-at-home mom and a dad who works outside of the home, has given way to families with a single parent, families in which both parents are employed outside the home, and "blended" families with stepparents and half-siblings. Researchers and parents alike have been concerned about the potential impact of changing family arrangements (NICHD Early Child Care Research Network, 2002). These changes in family life raise questions that trouble child-development professionals, parents, and policymakers alike. For example, when parents divorce, who should receive custody of the children? When children like the one in the photo spend most days at a child-care facility, what are the effects? Child-development researchers now work to provide evidence-based answers to questions like these.

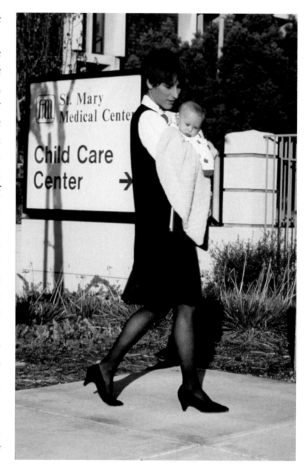

Child-development researchers have also been prompted by evidence showing that many American youngsters—particularly those who are members of minority groups—face many hurdles on the road to healthy development (Duncan & Brooks-Gunn, 2000). These hurdles are expressed numerically in the Index of Social Health for Children and Youth (ISHCY). Just as the Consumer Price Index or the Gross Domestic Product integrate several sources of data to serve as a barometer of the nation's economic health, the ISHCY integrates different kinds of evidence to assess the well-being of the nation's children (Miringoff, Miringoff, & Opdycke, 1996). Contributing to the ISHCY are variables such as infant mortality, child abuse, family poverty, teenage suicide, and teenage drug use. The graph, which depicts annual changes in the ISHCY, shows that America's children and youth faced ever-greater challenges at the end of the 20th century.

Because of these factors, many child-development researchers now participate actively in designing and implementing social policy concerning children and their families. In fact, a new orientation to child-development research has emerged. **Applied developmental science uses developmental research to promote healthy development, particularly for vulnerable children and families** (Lerner, Fisher, & Weinberg, 2000). As the name implies,

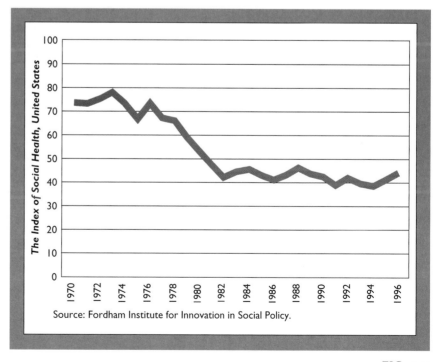

Source: Fordham Institute for Innovation in Social Policy.

FIG. 2–7

scientists with this orientation are interested in applied research that has direct implications for family policy. They rely on theories and methods of developmental science to guide their work on children and families.

In the next section, we'll look at the many different roles that child-development researchers play in formulating family policy.

## Ways to Influence Family Policy

Child-development researchers contribute to sound family policy through a number of distinct pathways (White, 1996): by building understanding of children, by serving as their advocates, by evaluating health-promoting policies and programs, and by developing model programs.

**BUILD UNDERSTANDING OF CHILDREN AND THEIR DEVELOPMENT.** When city officials must alleviate traffic congestion during rush hour, they consult with transportation experts for background information and potential solutions. Similarly, when government officials need to address problems affecting children, child-development experts can provide useful information about children and their development (Fasig, 2002). That is, sound policies should be based on accurate understanding of the key factors involved, rather than on stereotypes or assumptions about children and youth. For example, policymaking concerning adolescents is often unduly influenced by stereotypes of teenagers as irresponsible and defiant. In fact, as we'll see later in this book, most adolescents have neither of these negative qualities; and family policy for teens that is based on such stereotypes will be ineffective. Thus, child-development researchers contribute to policymaking by ensuring that the general consideration of policy issues and options is based on factual knowledge derived from child-development research.

> Researchers influence policy by providing needed knowledge, acting as advocates for children, by evaluating programs, and by devising model programs.

**SERVE AS AN ADVOCATE FOR CHILDREN.** Children are ill prepared to represent their own interests. They cannot vote and do not have the financial resources to hire lobbyists or prepare media campaigns. Often parents like to serve as advocates for their children, but individual parents usually lack the expertise and resources to represent children adequately. However, child-development researchers—typically in conjunction with a child advocacy group—can alert policymakers to children's needs and can argue for family policy that addresses those needs.

One well-known advocacy group for children was Action for Children's Television (ACT). From 1968 until 1992, ACT worked to ensure quality television for children and to regulate the kinds of commercials aimed at children. With strong backing from ACT (and despite stiff opposition from the television industry), the U.S. Congress passed the Children's Television Act of 1990. This law requires that the Federal Communications Commission, as it determines whether to renew a station's broadcast license, consider whether the station's programming meets children's needs. Child-development scientists were key players in ACT's efforts because their research demonstrated both the harmful effects of bad TV programs and the beneficial effects of good ones.

**EVALUATE POLICIES AND PROGRAMS.** Sometimes policies and programs affect families and children even though they are not the primary targets of the policy. In this case, child-development experts may be called to evaluate aspects of policy that affect families and children. For example, the goals of welfare reform historically have been to reduce the amount of money spent on welfare and to encourage people to be economically self-sufficient (i.e., to have more people support themselves through work rather than depending primarily on welfare payments). Consequently, most evaluations of welfare reform focus on changes in spending and employment. Yet changes in welfare programs may also affect families and children (Chase-Lansdale et al., Morris, 2002).

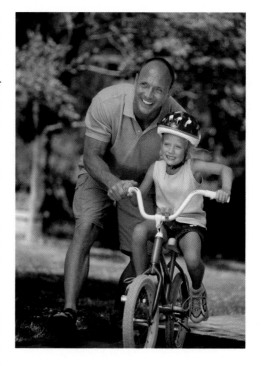

In evaluating the impact of policies on families and children, child-development researchers have two important tools. One is existing theory and research in child development, which can indicate how policy features are likely to affect families and children. For example, welfare reform includes mechanisms to encourage parents to pay child support. Research suggests that noncustodial parents, like the father in the photo, stay more involved with their children when they pay child support. Not surprisingly, their children benefit from this involvement. Thus, in this respect, welfare reform might benefit children.

A second important tool that child-development researchers can provide is a large catalog of methods to assess family functioning and child development. If, for example, policymakers are concerned that welfare reform may cause mothers to parent less effectively, a child-development researcher can provide methods to measure parental skill, such as questionnaires or structured observations that are known to be valid. Thus, by using existing findings to indicate the likely impact of policies and by providing proven methods to measure impact, child-development researchers can help judge how families and children are affected by policies.

**DEVELOP A MODEL PROGRAM.**   Elected officials usually like results, so one of the best ways to sway policymakers is to create an actual program that works. In other words, researchers could first develop a program to combat "X"—where X could be teenage pregnancy, drug abuse, or infant mortality, for example. Next, they implement the program on a small scale to show that it does indeed reduce X. This task is more complicated than some of the others because it requires obtaining resources to start the untested program as well as convincing families they should be "guinea pigs" in a program that may not work. Nevertheless, when this approach works, the outcome is powerful ammunition for influencing policymakers.

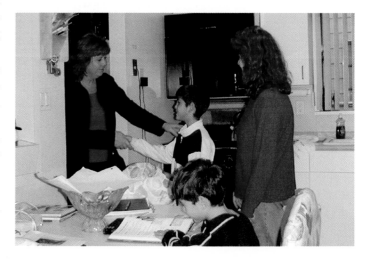

The School of the 21st Century (21C) illustrates this approach (Zigler & Gilman, 1996). Devised in the mid 1980s to meet the dual needs for improved child care and more successful schools, 21C includes year-round all-day care for preschool children as well as before-school, after-school, and vacation care for school-age children. The program also includes guidance for parents through home visits by parent educators like the one in the photo. Other components are a referral service that provides information about community services available to families and their children, health care, and training for child-care providers. Participation in the different program elements is voluntary; if, for example, a parent is home to care for a preschool child, that child is not forced to attend day care.

The 21C program was launched in 1988 in one city and has now spread to more than 500 schools across the United States. Research shows that children attending 21C schools learn more and have fewer behavioral problems; in addition, their parents are more involved in school and report less stress associated with arranging adequate child care (e.g., Finn-Stevenson, Desimone, & Chung, 1998). Based on this success, legislatures in Connecticut and Kentucky have made 21C the model for schools statewide. And 21C is a textbook example of first showing that a program effectively addresses a problem, then letting that success convince policymakers on a wider scale.

## An Emphasis on Policy Implications Improves Research

Child-development research undoubtedly can lead to more informed policies toward children and their families. Less obvious at first glance is that the converse is also true: When child-development scientists conduct their work with one eye focused on the family policy implications, the usual result is improved theory and research. One improvement is more emphasis on broader, inclusive models of children and their development. When doing basic research, a common tactic is for scientists to simplify the problem, often by examining certain aspects of children's development to the exclusion of others. One researcher might study how reading improves as children grow; a second researcher might look at how children benefit from having friends; and a third might examine parents' influence on children's self-control. In contrast, when formulating programs for children, policymakers cannot use the basic researcher's "slice and dice" approach, because in real children these different elements—their reading skills, their friendships, their parents' influence—are all interconnected. Change in one element can often lead to change in another. Consequently, a focus on family policy forces researchers to take a much broader perspective on child development than they might otherwise, often crossing traditional disciplinary lines between psychology, sociology, and economics (McCall & Groak, 2000).

> Emphasizing policy improves research by making scientists take a broader perspective and use more sophisticated research designs

A concern for family policy has also improved the methods used by researchers. As I described in Module 2.1, the strongest claims about cause and effect come from experiments in which participants are assigned randomly to various experimental conditions. Unfortunately, random assignment is often impossible in policy-oriented research, for pragmatic or ethical reasons. Obviously, we cannot randomly assign children to high-school-educated versus college-educated parents or to single- versus dual-parent families. Consequently, child-development researchers and statisticians have devised more powerful correlational methods that permit some statements about causality (West, Biesanz, & Pitts, 2000). **A quasi-experimental design includes multiple groups that were not formed by random assignment.** For example, researchers might want to compare children's reading level at the end of a school year in two schools, one using a traditional reading curriculum and another using an innovative curriculum. Because children were not assigned randomly to the two schools, this is a quasi-experiment. Children in the two schools might differ in reading or reading-related skills at the beginning of the year, before the onset of reading instruction. New methods allow researchers to account for such possible differences—using statistics to equate the groups of children at the beginning of the year—thereby making it easier to compare them at the end of the year and make conclusions about causality.

The message here should be clear: Closer links between child-development research and family policy produces better policy and better research. To emphasize this connection, many of the other chapters in this book have a feature called "Child Development and Family Policy." Each of these features, listed on page xiv, provides a concrete example of the close ties between research and policy.

## CHECK YOUR LEARNING

1. Links between child-development research and family have become stronger because of changes in the family and because _____.

2. Child-development researchers contribute to policymaking by ensuring that discussion of issues is based on factual knowledge of children, by _____, by evaluating existing policies, and by developing model programs.

3. Concern for public policy has improved research by forcing researchers to take a broader perspective on children's development and to _____.

 **CONNECTIONS**

Suppose a child-development researcher was an expert on the impact of nutrition on children's physical and cognitive development. Describe several different ways in which the researcher might help to form public policy concerning children's nutrition.

**Answers:** (1) measures of social health suggest that many children face numerous obstacles on the road to healthy development, (2) acting as an advocate for children, (3) develop more sophisticated research methods

# Unifying Themes: **Connections**

In this first "Unifying Themes," I want to underscore the theme that *development in different domains is connected*. With the research methods introduced in Module 2.1 (and used in many of the studies described throughout the book), researchers often look at separate elements of children's development—memory, physical growth, or peer relations, for example. This strategy makes sense because the elements are easier to understand in isolation. But effective family policy—described in Module 2.2—reminds us that these elements are interconnected in real children. For example, the School of the 21st Century program is built on the idea that children's achievement in school depends on children having effective learning strategies, being healthy, and having safe, reliable care before and after school. Physical, cognitive, social, and emotional development are linked: Change in one area almost always leads to change in another.

## See for Yourself

A good first step toward learning about child-development research is to read the reports of research that scientists publish in journals. Visit your library and locate some of the child-development journals mentioned on page 40. Look at the contents of an issue to get an idea of the many different topics that child-development researchers study. When you find an article on a topic that interests you, skim the contents and try to determine what design the investigator(s) used. See for yourself!

## Resources

For more information about...

**conducting research with children**, I recommend Scott A. Miller's *Developmental Research Methods*, 2nd edition (Prentice Hall, 1998), for a clear description of all phases of doing developmental research, beginning with measurement and ending with a written report of the project.

**research in child development**, visit the Society for Research in Child Development (SRCD) Web site: **http://www.srcd.org**

## Key Terms

applied developmental science  43
correlation coefficient  32
correlational study  32
cross-sectional study  36
dependent variable  33
experiment  33
family policy  42
field experiment  34
independent variable  33
longitudinal study  35
meta-analysis  38

microgenetic study  35
naturalistic observation  28
quasi-experimental design  46
population  31
reliability  30
sample  31
self reports  30
structured observation  29
systematic observation  28
validity  30
variable  28

## 2.1 Doing Child-Development Research

**Measurement in Child-Development Research**
Research typically begins by determining how to measure the topic of interest. Systematic observation involves recording children's behavior as it takes place, either in a natural environment (naturalistic observation) or in a structured setting (structured observation). Researchers sometimes create tasks to obtain samples of children's behavior. In self reports, children answer questions posed by the experimenter. Researchers must also obtain a sample that is representative of some larger population.

**General Designs for Research**
In correlational studies, investigators examine relations between variables as they occur naturally. This relation is measured by a correlation coefficient, $r$, which can vary from $-1$ (strong negative relation) to 0 (no relation) to $+1$ (strong positive relation). Correlational studies cannot determine cause and effect, so researchers do experimental studies in which they manipulate an independent variable to determine the impact on a dependent variable. Experimental studies allow conclusions about cause and effect, but the strict control of all possible variables often makes the situation artificial. Field studies involve manipulation of independent variables in a natural setting. The best approach is to use both experimental and correlational studies to provide converging evidence.

**Designs for Studying Development**
To study development, some researchers use a longitudinal design in which the same children are observed repeatedly as they grow. This approach provides evidence of actual patterns of individual growth but has shortcomings: Repeated testing can affect performance and some children drop out of the project. The cross-sectional design involves testing children in different age groups.

This design avoids the problems of the longitudinal design but provides no information about individual growth. Because neither design is problem-free, some investigators use a longitudinal-sequential method that consists of separate small-scale longitudinal studies. Meta-analysis is used to synthesize the results of different studies on the same topic.

**Ethical Responsibilities**
Planning research also involves selecting methods that preserve the rights of research participants. Experimenters must minimize the risks to potential research participants, describe the research so that potential participants can decide whether they want to participate, avoid deception, and keep results anonymous or confidential.

**Communicating Research Results**
Once research data are collected and analyzed, investigators publish the results in scientific journals where they can be read and scrutinized by others. Such results form the foundation of scientific knowledge about child development.

## 2.2 Child-Development Research and Family Policy

**Why Link Research to Policy?**
Child-development researchers have become increasingly interested in applying the results of their work to family policy because of many changes in the American family and because changes in infant mortality, child abuse, and other variables indicate that American children and youth face many challenges to healthy development.

**Ways to Influence Family Policy**
Child-development researchers help to shape family policy by providing useful knowledge about children and their development so that policies can be based on accurate information. They also contribute by serving as advocates for children, by evaluating the impact of programs on families and children, and by developing effective programs that can be implemented elsewhere.

**An Emphasis on Policy Implications Improves Research**
Focusing on public policy implications improves research because researchers must take a broader perspective on children's development than they would otherwise. Also, policy-related research has produced more sophisticated research methods, such as the quasi-experimental design.

# 3

I wish I had a dollar for every time my parents or in-laws said about one of my children, "He (or she) comes by that naturally." The usual prompt for their comment is that the child has just done something exactly as I or my wife did at the same age. By their remarks, grandparents are reminding us that some behavioral characteristics are inherited from parents just as physical characteristics like height and hair color are inherited.

In this chapter, we'll see how heredity influences children and their development. We'll start, in Module 3.1, by examining the basic mechanisms of heredity. In Module 3.2, we'll focus on disorders that some children inherit. Finally, in Module 3.3, we'll see how the environment is crucial in determining how heredity influences development.

# Genetic Bases
# of Child Development

**3.1**  Mechanisms of Heredity

**3.2**  Genetic Disorders

**3.3**  Heredity Is Not Destiny

# 3.1

# Mechanisms of Heredity

## LEARNING OBJECTIVES

● What are chromosomes and genes?

● What are dominant and recessive traits? How are they inherited?

● How does heredity influence behavioral and psychological development?

*Leslie and Glenn have decided to try to have a baby. They are thrilled at the thought of starting their own family but also worried because Leslie's grandfather had sickle cell disease and died when he was just 20 years old. Leslie is terrified that their baby could inherit the disease that killed her grandfather. Leslie and Glenn wish someone could reassure them that their baby will be okay.*

How could we reassure Leslie and Glenn? For starters, we need to know more about sickle cell disease. Red blood cells like the ones in the left photo carry oxygen and carbon dioxide to and from the body. When a person has sickle cell disease, the red blood cells look like those in the right photo—long and curved like a sickle:

These stiff, misshapen cells can't pass through small capillaries, so oxygen can't reach all parts of the body. The trapped sickle cells also block the way of white blood cells that are the body's natural defense against bacteria. As a result, people with sickle cell disease—including Leslie's grandfather and many other African Americans, who are more prone to this painful disease than other groups—often die from infections before age 20.

Sickle cell disease is inherited. Because Leslie's grandfather had the disorder, it apparently runs in her family. Would Leslie's baby inherit the disease? To answer this question, we need to examine the mechanisms of heredity.

## The Biology of Heredity

The teaspoon of semen released into the vagina during an ejaculation contains from 200 million to 500 million sperm. Only a few hundred of these actually complete the 6- or 7-inch journey to the fallopian tubes. If an egg is present, many sperm simultaneously begin to burrow their way through the cluster of nurturing cells that surround the egg. When a sperm like the one in the photo penetrates the cellular wall of the egg, chemical changes that occur immediately block out all other sperm. **Each egg and sperm cell contains 23 chromosomes, tiny structures in the nucleus that contain genetic material.** When a sperm penetrates an egg, their chromosomes combine to produce 23 pairs of chromosomes. The development of a new human being is under way.

For most of history, the merging of sperm and egg took place only after sexual intercourse. No longer. In 1978, Louise Brown captured the world's attention as the first test-tube baby conceived in a laboratory dish instead of in her mother's body. Today, this reproductive technology is no longer experimental; it is a multibillion-dollar business in the United States (Winter, 1997). Many new techniques are available to couples who cannot conceive a child through sexual intercourse. **The best known, in vitro fertilization, involves mixing sperm and egg together in a laboratory dish and then placing several fertilized eggs in the mother's uterus.** The photo shows this laboratory version of conception, with the sperm in the dropper being placed in the dish containing the eggs. If the eggs are fertilized, in about 24 hours they are placed in the mother's uterus, with the hope that they will become implanted in the wall of her uterus.

The sperm and egg usually come from the prospective parents, but sometimes they are provided by donors. Occasionally the fertilized egg is placed in the uterus of a surrogate mother who carries the baby throughout pregnancy. Thus, a baby could have as many as five "parents": the man and woman who provide the sperm and egg, the surrogate mother who carries the baby, and the mother and father who rear the child.

New reproductive techniques offer hope for couples who have long wanted a child, and studies of the first generation of children conceived via in vitro fertilization indicates that their social and emotional development is perfectly normal (Golombok, MacCallum, & Goodman, 2001). But there are difficulties as well. Only about 20 percent of attempts at in vitro fertilization succeed. Moreover, when a woman becomes pregnant, she is more likely to have twins or triplets because multiple eggs are transferred to increase the odds that at least one fertilized egg will implant in the mother's uterus. And her risk of giving birth to a baby with low birth weight or birth defects doubles (Hansen et al., 2002; Shieve et al., 2002). These problems emphasize that, although technology has increased the alternatives for infertile couples, pregnancy on demand is still in the realm of science fiction.

Whatever the source of the egg and sperm, and wherever they meet, their merger is a momentous event: The resulting 23 pairs of chromosomes define a child's heredity—what he or she "will do naturally." For Leslie and Glenn, this moment also determines whether their child inherits sickle cell disease.

To understand how heredity influences child development, let's begin by taking a closer look at chromosomes. The photo shows all 46 chromosomes, organized in pairs ranging from the largest to the smallest. **The first 22 pairs of chromosomes are called autosomes; the chromosomes in each pair are about the same size.** In the 23rd pair, however, the chromosome labeled X is much larger than the chromosome labeled Y. **The 23rd pair determines the sex of the child; hence, these two are known as the sex chromosomes.** An egg always contains an X 23rd chromosome, but a sperm contains either an X or a Y. When an X-carrying sperm fertilizes the egg, the 23rd pair is XX and the result is a girl. When a Y-carrying sperm fertilizes the egg, the 23rd pair is XY and the result is a boy.

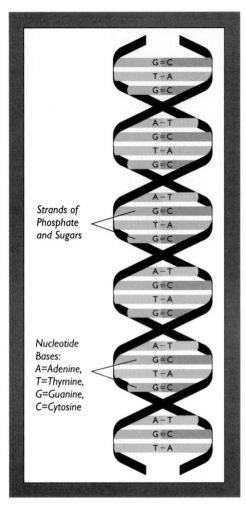

*Strands of Phosphate and Sugars*

*Nucleotide Bases:*
*A=Adenine,*
*T=Thymine,*
*G=Guanine,*
*C=Cytosine*

FIG. 3–1

**Each chromosome actually consists of one molecule of deoxyribonucleic acid—DNA for short.** The DNA molecule resembles a spiral staircase. As you can see in the diagram on the left, the rungs of the staircase carry the genetic code, which consists of pairs of nucleotide bases: Adenine is paired with thymine, and guanine is paired with cytosine. The order of the nucleotide pairs is the code that causes the cell to create specific amino acids, proteins, and enzymes—important biological building blocks. **Each group of nucleotide bases that provides a specific set of biochemical instructions is a gene.** For example, three consecutive thymine nucleotides is the instruction to create the amino acid phenylalanine.

The diagram below summarizes these links between chromosomes, genes, and DNA. Each cell contains chromosomes that carry genes made up of DNA.

Altogether, a child's 46 chromosomes include roughly 30,000 genes. Through biochemical instructions that are coded in DNA, genes regulate the

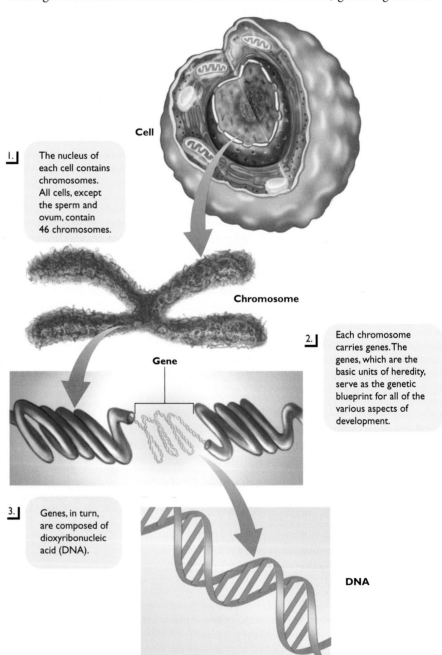

**Cell**

1. The nucleus of each cell contains chromosomes. All cells, except the sperm and ovum, contain 46 chromosomes.

**Chromosome**

2. Each chromosome carries genes. The genes, which are the basic units of heredity, serve as the genetic blueprint for all of the various aspects of development.

**Gene**

3. Genes, in turn, are composed of dioxyribonucleic acid (DNA).

**DNA**

FIG. 3–2

development of all human characteristics and abilities. **The complete set of genes makes up a person's heredity and is known as the person's genotype. Genetic instructions, in conjunction with environmental influences, produce a phenotype, an individual's physical, behavioral, and psychological features.**

In the rest of this module, we'll see the different ways that instructions contained in genes produce different phenotypes.

## Single Gene Inheritance

How do genetic instructions produce the misshapen red blood cells of sickle cell disease? **Genes come in different forms that are known as alleles.** In the case of red blood cells, for example, one of two alleles can be present on chromosome 11. One allele has instructions for normal red blood cells; the other allele has instructions for sickle-shaped red blood cells. **The alleles in the pair of chromosomes are sometimes the same, which makes them homozygous. The alleles sometimes differ, which makes them heterozygous.** In Leslie's case, her baby could be homozygous, in which case it would have two alleles for normal cells or two alleles for sickle-shaped cells. Leslie's baby might also be heterozygous, which means that it would have one allele for normal cells and one for sickle-shaped cells.

How does a genotype produce a phenotype? The answer is simple if a person is homozygous. When both alleles are the same and therefore have chemical instructions for the same phenotype, that phenotype results. If Leslie's baby had alleles for normal red blood cells on both of the chromosomes in its 11th pair, the baby would be almost guaranteed to have normal cells. If, instead, the baby had two alleles for sickle-shaped cells, her baby would almost certainly suffer from the disease.

When a person is heterozygous, the process is more complex. **Often one allele is dominant, which means that its chemical instructions are followed whereas instructions of the other, the recessive allele, are ignored.** In the case of sickle cell disease, the allele for normal cells is dominant and the allele for sickle-shaped cells is recessive. This is good news for Leslie: As long as either she or Glenn contribute the allele for normal red blood cells, her baby will not develop sickle cell disease.

The diagram summarizes what we've learned about sickle cell disease. The letter *A* denotes the allele for normal blood cells, and *a* denotes the allele for sickle-shaped cells. In the diagram, Glenn's genotype is homozygous dominant because he's positive that no one in his family has had sickle cell disease. From Leslie's family history, she could be homozygous dominant or heterozygous; in the diagram, I've assumed the latter. You can see that Leslie and Glenn cannot have a baby with sickle cell disease. However, their baby might be affected in another way. **Sometimes one allele does not dominate another completely, a situation known as incomplete dominance.** In incomplete dominance, the phenotype that results often falls between the phenotype associated with either allele. This is the case for the genes that control red blood cells. **Individuals with one dominant and one recessive allele have sickle cell trait: In most situations they have no problems, but when they are seriously short of oxygen they suffer a temporary, relatively mild form of the disease.** Thus, sickle cell trait is likely to appear when the person exercises vigorously or is at high altitudes (Sullivan, 1987). Leslie and Glenn's baby would have sickle cell trait if it inherited a recessive gene from Leslie and a dominant gene from Glenn.

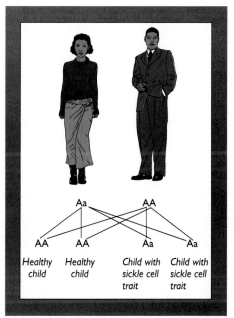

FIG. 3–3

One aspect of sickle cell disease that we haven't considered so far is why this disorder primarily affects African American children. The "Cultural Influences" feature addresses this point and, in the process, tells more about how heredity operates.

## CULTURAL INFLUENCES

### Why Do African Americans Inherit Sickle Cell Disease?

Sickle cell disease affects about 1 in 400 African American children. In contrast, virtually no European American children have the disorder. Why? Surprisingly, because the sickle cell allele has a benefit: Individuals with this allele are more resistant to malaria, an infectious disease that is one of the leading causes of childhood death worldwide. Malaria is transmitted by mosquitos, so it is most common in warm climates, including many parts of Africa. Compared to Africans who have alleles for normal blood cells, Africans with the sickle cell allele are less likely to die from malaria, which means that the sickle cell allele is passed along to the next generation.

This explanation of sickle cell disease has two implications. First, sickle cell disease should be found in any group of people living where malaria is common. In fact, sickle cell disease affects Hispanic Americans who trace their roots to malaria-prone regions of the Caribbean, Central America, and South America. Second, malaria is rare in the United States, which means that the sickle cell allele has no survival value to African Americans. Accordingly, the sickle cell allele should become less common in successive generations of African Americans, and research indicates that this is happening.

There is an important general lesson here. The impact of heredity depends on the environment. An allele may have survival value in one environment but not in others.

The simple genetic mechanism responsible for sickle cell disease, involving a single gene pair with one dominant allele and one recessive allele, is also responsible for many other common traits, as shown in the table. In each case, individuals with the recessive phenotype have two recessive alleles, one from each parent. Individuals with the dominant phenotype have at least one dominant allele.

You'll notice that the table includes many biological and medical phenotypes but lacks behavioral and psychological phenotypes. Behavioral and psychological characteristics can be inherited, but the genetic mechanism is more elaborate, as we'll see in the next section.

## Behavioral Genetics

**Behavioral genetics is the branch of genetics that deals with inheritance of behavioral and psychological traits.** Behavioral genetics is complex, in part because behavioral and psychological phenotypes are complex. The traits controlled by single genes usually represent "either-or" phenotypes. That is, the genotypes are usually associated with two (or sometimes three) well-defined phenotypes. For example, a person either has normal color vision or has red-green color blindness; a person has blood that clots normally, has sickle cell trait, or has sickle cell disease.

### Some Common Phenotypes Associated with Single Pairs of Genes

| Dominant Phenotype | Recessive Phenotype |
|---|---|
| Curly hair | Straight hair |
| Normal hair | Pattern baldness (men) |
| Dark hair | Blond hair |
| Thick lips | Thin lips |
| Cheek dimples | No dimples |
| Normal hearing | Some types of deafness |
| Normal vision | Nearsightedness |
| Farsightedness | Normal vision |
| Normal color vision | Red-green color blindness |
| Type A blood | Type O blood |
| Type B blood | Type O blood |
| Rh-positive blood | Rh-negative blood |

Source: McKusick, 1995.

TABLE 3–1

Most important behavioral and psychological characteristics are not either-or cases but represent an entire range of different outcomes. Take extroversion as an example. You probably know a few extremely outgoing individuals and a few intensely shy persons, but most of your friends and acquaintances are somewhere in between. Classifying your friends would produce a distribution of individuals across a continuum, from extreme extroversion at one end to extreme introversion at the other.

Many behavioral and psychological characteristics are distributed in this fashion, including intelligence and many aspects of personality. **When phenotypes reflect the combined activity of many separate genes, the pattern is known as polygenic inheritance.** Because so many genes are involved in polygenic inheritance, we usually cannot trace the effects of each gene. But we can use a hypothetical example to show how many genes work together to produce a behavioral phenotype that spans a continuum. Let's suppose that four pairs of genes contribute to extroversion, that the allele for extroversion is dominant, and that the total amount of extroversion is simply the sum of the dominant alleles. If we continue to use upper-case letters to represent dominant alleles and lower-case letters to represent the recessive allele, the four gene pairs would be *Aa*, *Bb*, *Cc*, and *Dd*.

These four pairs of genes produce 81 different genotypes and 9 distinct phenotypes. For example, a person with the genotype *AABBCCDD* has 8 alleles for extroversion (a party animal). A person with the genotype *aabbccdd* has no alleles for extroversion (a wallflower). All other genotypes involve some combinations of dominant and recessive alleles, so these are associated with phenotypes representing intermediate levels of extroversion. In fact, the diagram shows that the most common outcome is for people to inherit exactly 4 dominant and 4 recessive alleles: 19 of the 81 genotypes produce this pattern (e.g., *AABbccDd*, *AaBbcCDd*). A few extreme cases (very outgoing or

> **Behavioral characteristics often reflect polygenic inheritance in which a phenotype depends on the combined actions of many genes.**

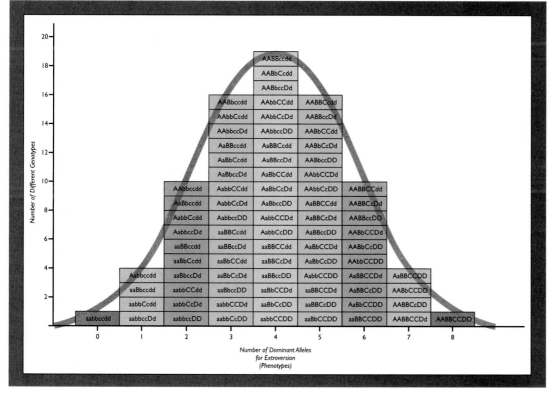

FIG. 3–4

very shy), when coupled with many intermediate cases, produce the familiar bell-shaped distribution that characterizes many behavioral and psychological traits.

Remember, this example is completely hypothetical. Extroversion is *not* based on the combined influence of eight pairs of genes. I merely want to show how several genes working together could produce a continuum of phenotypes. Something like our example is probably involved in the inheritance of numerous human behavioral traits, except that many more pairs of genes are involved and the environment also influences the phenotype (Plomin et al., 1997).

**METHODS OF BEHAVIORAL GENETICS.** If many behavioral phenotypes involve countless genes, how can we hope to unravel the influence of heredity? Traditionally, behavior geneticists have relied on statistical methods in which they compare groups of people known to differ in their genetic similarity. Twins, for example, provide important clues about the influence of heredity. **Identical twins are called monozygotic twins because they come from a single fertilized egg that splits in two.** Because identical twins come from the same fertilized egg, they have the same genes that control body structure, height, and facial features, which explains why identical twins like those in the photo look alike. **In contrast, fraternal or dizygotic twins come from two separate eggs fertilized by two separate sperm.** Genetically, fraternal twins are just like any other siblings; on average, about half their genes are the same. In twin studies, scientists compare identical and fraternal twins to measure the influence of heredity. If identical twins are more alike than fraternal twins, this implicates heredity.

An example will help illustrate the logic underlying comparisons of identical and fraternal twins. Suppose we want to determine whether extroversion is inherited. We would first measure extroversion in a large number of identical and fraternal twins. We might use a questionnaire with scores ranging from 0 to 100 (100 indicating maximal extroversion). Some of the hypothetical results are shown in the table.

### Twins' Hypothetical Scores on a Measure of Extroversion

| | Fraternal Twins | | | | Identical Twins | | |
|---|---|---|---|---|---|---|---|
| Family | One Twin | Other Twin | Difference between Twins | Family | One Twin | Other Twin | Difference between Twins |
| Aikman | 80 | 95 | 15 | Bettis | 100 | 95 | 5 |
| Fernandez | 70 | 50 | 20 | Harbaugh | 32 | 30 | 2 |
| Herrod | 10 | 35 | 25 | Park | 18 | 15 | 3 |
| Stewart | 25 | 5 | 20 | Ramirez | 55 | 60 | 5 |
| Tomczak | 40 | 65 | 25 | Robinson | 70 | 62 | 8 |
| ⋮ | ⋮ | ⋮ | | ⋮ | ⋮ | ⋮ | |

TABLE 3–2

Look first at the results for the fraternal twins. Most have similar scores: The Aikman twins both have high scores but the Herrod twins have low scores. Looking at the identical twins, their scores are even more alike, typically differing by no more than five points. This greater similarity among identical twins than among fraternal twins would be evidence that extroversion is inherited, just as the fact that identical twins look more alike than fraternal twins is evidence that facial appearance is inherited.

Adopted children are another important source of information about heredity. In this case, adopted children are compared with their biological parents and their adoptive parents. The idea is that biological parents provide the child's genes but adoptive parents provide the child's environment. Consequently, if a behavior has genetic roots, then adopted children should resemble their biological parents even though they have never met them. But if the adopted children resemble their adoptive parents, we know that family environment affects behavior.

> Heredity is implicated when identical twins are more alike than fraternal twins and when adopted children resemble their biological parents more than their adoptive parents.

If we wanted to use an adoption study to determine whether extroversion is inherited, we would measure extroversion in a large sample of adopted children, their biological mothers, and their adoptive mothers. (Why just mothers? Obtaining data from biological fathers of adopted children is often difficult.) The results of this hypothetical study are shown in the table.

First, compare children's scores with their biological mothers' scores. Overall, they are related: Extroverted children like Michael tend to have extroverted biological mothers. Introverted children like Troy tend to have introverted biological mothers. In contrast, children's scores don't show any clear relation to their adoptive mothers' scores. For example, although Michael has the highest score and Troy has the lowest, their adoptive mothers have very similar scores. Children's greater similarity to biological than to adoptive parents would be evidence that extroversion is inherited.

Twin studies and adoption studies, which are summarized in the table on page 60, are powerful tools. They are not foolproof, however. Maybe you thought of a potential flaw in twin studies: Parents and other people may treat identical twins more similarly than they treat fraternal twins. This would make identical twins more similar than fraternal twins in their experiences as well as in their genes. Adoption studies have their own Achilles' heel. Adoption agencies sometimes try to place youngsters in homes like those of their biological parents. For example, if an agency believes that the biological parents are bright, the agency may try harder to have the child adopted by parents that the agency believes are bright. This can bias adoption studies because biological and adoptive parents end up being similar.

### Hypothetical Scores from an Adoption Study on a Measure of Extroversion

| Child's Name | Child's Score | Biological Mother's Score | Adoptive Mother's Score |
|---|---|---|---|
| Anila | 60 | 70 | 35 |
| Jerome | 45 | 50 | 25 |
| Kerri | 40 | 30 | 80 |
| Michael | 90 | 80 | 50 |
| Troy | 25 | 5 | 55 |
| ⋮ | ⋮ | ⋮ | ⋮ |

TABLE 3–3

| PRIMARY RESEARCH METHODS FOR BEHAVIORAL GENETICS | | | |
| --- | --- | --- | --- |
| Method | Defined | Evidence for Heredity | Main Weakness |
| Twin study | Compare monozygotic and dizygotic twins | Monozygotic twins more alike than dizygotic twins | Others may treat monozygotic twins more similarly than they treat dizygotic twins |
| Adoption study | Compare children with biological and adoptive parents | Children more like biological parents than adoptive parents | Selective placement: Children's adoptive parents may resemble their biological parents |

The problems associated with twin and adoption studies are not insurmountable. Because twin and adoption studies have different faults, if the two kinds of studies produce similar results on the influence of heredity, we can be confident of those results. In addition, behavioral geneticists are moving beyond traditional methods such as twin and adoption studies to connect behavior to molecular genetics (Dick & Rose, 2002; Plomin & Crabbe, 2000). Today, researchers are able to isolate particular segments of DNA in human chromosomes. These segments then serve as markers for identifying specific alleles. The procedure is complicated, but the basic approach often begins by identifying people who differ in the behavior or psychological trait of interest. For example, researchers might identify children who are outgoing and children who are shy. Or they might identify children who read well and children who read poorly. The children rub the inside of their mouth with a cotton swab, which yields cheek cells that contain DNA. The cells are analyzed in a lab, and the DNA markers for the two groups are compared. If the markers differ consistently, then the alleles near the marker probably contribute to the differences between the groups.

Techniques like these have the potential to identify the many different genes that contribute to complex behavioral and psychological traits. Of course, these new methods have limits. Some require very large samples of children, which can be hard to obtain with rare disorders. Also, some require that an investigator have an idea, before even beginning the study, about which chromosomes to search and where. These can be major hurdles. But, when used with traditional methods of behavioral genetics (e.g., adoption studies), the new methods promise much greater understanding of how genes influence behavior and development (Plomin & Crabbe, 2000).

WHICH PSYCHOLOGICAL CHARACTERISTICS ARE AFFECTED BY HEREDITY? Research reveals consistent genetic influence in many psychological areas, including cognitive abilities and school achievement, psychological disorders, personality, and substance abuse (Plomin et al., 2001). **To illustrate, let's consider depression, a disorder in which individuals have pervasive feelings of sadness, are irritable, and have low self-esteem.** In twin studies, identical twins show remarkable similarity for depression: If one identical twin is depressed, the other twin has roughly a 50 percent chance of being depressed. For fraternal twins, the odds are much lower—approximately 25 percent (Plomin & Crabbe, 2000).

Cognitive abilities, psychological disorders, and personality are all strongly influenced by heredity.

Research that demonstrates the influence of heredity on cognitive development is the topic of the "Focus on Research" feature.

## FOCUS ON RESEARCH

### Hereditary and Environmental Bases of Cognitive Development

*Who were the investigators, and what was the aim of the study?* Children and adolescents differ in their cognitive skills. Some are quite skilled cognitively—they remember accurately and solve problems easily. Other children and adolescents are less skilled in remembering and solving problems. Robert Plomin and his colleagues (1997) measured cognitive skills in children, their biological parents, and their adoptive parents to understand the influence of heredity on the development of cognitive skill.

*How did the investigators measure the topic of interest?* The parents completed a comprehensive battery of standardized tests that assessed a broad range of cognitive skills. Biological mothers were tested in the last few months of pregnancy. Adoptive parents were tested in the first year after the adoption. Every few years, the children took an intelligence test. (The test varied depending on the child's age.)

*Who were the children in the study?* The sample included 245 children whose mothers relinquished them at birth. The children were approximately 1 month old when they were adopted.

*What was the design of the study?* This study was correlational because Plomin and his colleagues examined how children's cognitive skill was related to their biological parents' cognitive skill and their adoptive parents' cognitive skill. The study was longitudinal because children were tested repeatedly, every year or two.

*Were there ethical concerns with the study?* No. The tests were ones used commonly by psychologists. Biological and adoptive parents provided written consent for their own and their children's participation.

*What were the results?* The primary results, correlations between children's skills and their parents' skills, are shown in the graph. At every age, the correlation between children's skill and their biological parents' skill (shown by the blue line) is greater than the correlation between children's skill and their adoptive parents' skill (shown by the red line). In fact, children's scores are essentially unrelated to their adoptive parents' scores. Notice, too, that the relation between children's scores and their biological parents' scores actually gets stronger as children get older. In other words, as adopted children grow, their test scores increasingly resemble their biological parents' scores despite the fact that these adopted children have had no contact with their biological parents for 16 years.

*What did the investigators conclude?* Children's cognitive skill reflects heredity and the impact of heredity actually is stronger in adolescence than in childhood. However, the correlations between children's scores and their biological parents' scores are not very large, which says that heredity is not the sole influence on cognitive growth; the environment must contribute, too.

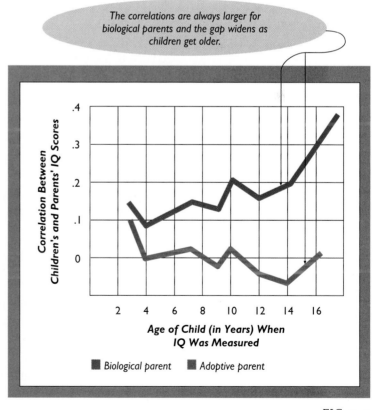

The correlations are always larger for biological parents and the gap widens as children get older.

FIG. 3–5

*What converging evidence would strengthen these conclusions?* As I described on page 59, selective placement can weaken adoption studies. But this was not a problem in the study by Plomin and his colleagues: Biological parents' cognitive scores were unrelated to adoptive parents' scores. However, there is another problem: The adoptive parents were not representative of all parents—they tended to be somewhat older, smarter, and more affluent than the national average. Of course, this is often true of adoptive parents (they tend to be older and financially more secure), so it would be difficult to redo the study with adoptive parents who are more representative of average parents. A different approach would be to conduct a longitudinal study of twins, with the expectation that identical twins' cognitive skills would be more alike as they grew. ◉

We will look at intelligence in greater detail later in this book. For now, keep in mind two conclusions from twin studies and adoption studies like the one described in the "Focus on Research" feature. On the one hand, the impact of heredity on behavioral development is substantial and widespread. Heredity has a sizable influence on such different aspects of development as intelligence and personality. In understanding children and their development, we must always think about how heredity may contribute. On the other hand, heredity is never the sole determinant of behavioral development. For example, roughly 50 percent of the differences among children's scores on intelligence tests is due to heredity. But the remaining 50 percent is due to environment. Throughout this book, we'll see that the course of development is controlled by both heredity and environment.

## CHECK YOUR LEARNING

1. In _____, an egg is fertilized by a sperm in a laboratory dish, then placed in the uterus.
2. The first 22 pairs of chromosomes are called _____.
3. A person is _____ when the alleles in a pair of chromosomes differ.
4. In _____, the phenotype often falls between the dominant and recessive phenotype.
5. _____ reflects the combined activity of a number of distinct genes.
6. Traditionally, behavioral geneticists relied on twin and _____ studies.
7. Cognitive skills and school achievement, _____, personality, and substance abuse are among the psychological characteristics known to be influenced by heredity.

Φ **NATURE AND NURTURE**
The goal of twin and adoption studies is to reveal the contributions of heredity and environment to development. However, a problem in twin studies is that identical twins may be treated more similarly than fraternal twins; a problem in adoption studies is that children's biological parents may resemble their adoptive parents. How could an investigator determine whether these problems were present in his or her research?

**Answers:** (1) in vitro fertilization, (2) autosomes, (3) heterozygous, (4) incomplete dominance, (5) Polygenic inheritance, (6) adoption, (7) psychological disorders

# Genetic Disorders

# 3.2

## LEARNING OBJECTIVES

- What disorders are inherited?

- What disorders are caused by too many or too few chromosomes?

Inherited Disorders ─

Abnormal Chromosomes ─

> *Carolyn and Doug, both 46, hadn't planned to have a baby, but Carolyn soon discovered that her lingering case of the flu was actually morning sickness. She and Doug both knew that with Carolyn's age they risked having a baby with Down syndrome, but they decided not to worry about this. When Carolyn gave birth to a baby boy, they learned that he did have Down syndrome. Carolyn and Doug were startled by the news, but it didn't change their joy at being parents. They did want to know more about the special challenges their son would face.*

Like Carolyn and Doug's baby, some children are affected by heredity in a special way: They have genetic disorders that disrupt the usual pattern of development. Genetics can derail development in two ways. First, some disorders are inherited. Sickle cell disease is one example of an inherited disorder. Second, sometimes eggs or sperm have more or fewer than the usual 23 chromosomes. In this module, we'll see how inherited disorders and abnormal numbers of chromosomes can alter a child's development. **We'll also learn more about Down syndrome, a genetic disorder caused by an extra 21st chromosome that results in mental retardation\*.**

## Inherited Disorders

In Module 3.1, we saw that sickle cell disease is a disorder that affects people who inherit two recessive alleles. In fact, sickle cell disease is one of many disorders that are homozygous recessive—triggered when a child inherits recessive alleles from both parents. The table lists four more disorders that are commonly inherited in this manner.

### Common Disorders Associated with Recessive Alleles

| Disorder | Frequency | Characteristics |
|---|---|---|
| Albinism | 1 in 10,000 to 1 in 20,000 births | Skin lacks melanin, which causes visual problems and extreme sensitivity to light. |
| Cystic fibrosis | 1 in 2,500 births among European Americans; less common in African and Asian Americans | Excess mucus clogs digestive and respiratory tracts. Lung infections common. |
| Phenylketonuria (PKU) | 1 in 10,000 births | Phenylalanine, an amino acid, accumulates in the body and damages the nervous system, causing mental retardation. |
| Tay-Sachs disease | 1 in 3,000 births among Jews of European descent | The nervous system degenerates in infancy, causing deafness blindness, mental retardation, and, during the preschool years, death. |

Source: Based on Committee on Genetics, 1998; McKusick, 1995.

TABLE 3–4

---

\*The scientific name is Trisomy 21, reflecting the fact that a person with the disorder has a trio of 21st chromosomes instead of a pair. But most people refer to the disorder as Down syndrome, reflecting the name of the English physician, John Langdon Down, who identified the disorder in the 1860s.

Relatively few serious disorders are caused by dominant alleles. Why? If the allele for the disorder is dominant, every person with at least one of these alleles will have the disorder. But individuals affected with these disorders typically do not live long enough to reproduce, so dominant alleles that produce fatal disorders soon vanish from the species. **An exception is Huntington's disease, a fatal disease characterized by progressive degeneration of the nervous system.** Huntington's disease is caused by a dominant allele found on chromosome 4. Individuals who inherit this disorder develop normally through childhood, adolescence, and young adulthood. However, during middle age, nerve cells begin to deteriorate, causing muscle spasms, depression, and significant changes in personality (Shiwach, 1994). By the time symptoms of Huntington's disease appear, adults who are affected may already have produced children, many of whom go on to develop the disease themselves.

Fortunately, most inherited disorders are rare. PKU, for example, occurs once in every 10,000 births, and Huntington's disease occurs even less frequently. Nevertheless, adults who believe that these disorders run in their family want to know whether their children are likely to inherit the disorder. The "Improving Children's Lives" feature shows how these couples can get help in deciding whether to have children.

## IMPROVING CHILDREN'S LIVES

### Genetic Counseling

Family planning is not easy for couples who fear that children they have may inherit serious or even fatal diseases. The best advice, though, is to seek the help of a genetic counselor before the woman becomes pregnant. With the couple's help, a genetic counselor constructs a detailed family history that can be used to decide whether it's likely that either the man or the woman has the allele for the disorder that concerns them.

A family tree for Leslie and Glenn, the couple from Module 3.1, would confirm that Leslie is likely to carry the recessive allele for sickle cell disease. The genetic counselor would then take the next step, obtaining a sample of Leslie's cells (probably from a blood test). The cells would be analyzed to determine if the 11th chromosome carries the recessive allele for sickle cell disease. If Leslie learns she is homozygous—has two dominant alleles for healthy blood cells—then she and Glenn can be assured their children will not have sickle cell disease. If Leslie learns that she has one recessive allele, then she and Glenn will know they have a 50 percent risk of having a baby with sickle cell trait. Tests can also be administered after a woman is pregnant to determine whether the child she is carrying has an inherited disorder. We'll learn about these tests in Chapter 4.

More common than inherited diseases are disorders caused by the wrong number of chromosomes, as we'll see in the next section.

## Abnormal Chromosomes

Sometimes individuals do not receive the normal complement of 46 chromosomes. If they are born with extra, missing, or damaged chromosomes, development is always disturbed. The best example is Down syndrome, the disorder that affects Carolyn and Doug's son and occurs in about 1 out of every 1,000 births. Like the child in the photo, persons with Down syndrome have almond-shaped eyes and a fold over the eyelid. The head, neck, and nose of a child with this disorder are usually smaller than normal. During the first several months, babies with Down syndrome seem to develop normally.

Thereafter, though, their mental and behavioral development begins to lag behind the average child's. For example, a child with Down syndrome might not sit up without help until about 1 year, not walk until 2, or not talk until 3—months or even years behind children without Down syndrome. By childhood, mental retardation is apparent.

Carolyn and Doug are right in believing that rearing a child with Down syndrome presents special challenges. During the preschool years, children with Down syndrome need special programs to prepare them for school. Educational achievements of children with Down syndrome are likely to be limited and their life expectancy ranges from 25 to 60 years (Yang, Rasmussen, & Friedman, 2002). Nevertheless, as we'll see in Chapter 9, many persons with Down syndrome lead fulfilling lives.

> Damaged autosomes always affect development because autosomes contain so much genetic material.

What causes Down syndrome? Individuals with Down syndrome typically have an extra 21st chromosome that is usually provided by the egg (Antonarakis & the Down Syndrome Collaborative Group, 1991). Why the mother provides two 21st chromosomes is unknown. However, the odds that a woman will bear a child with Down syndrome increase markedly as she gets older. For a woman in her late 20s, the risk of giving birth to a baby with Down syndrome is about 1 in 1,000; for a woman in her early 40s, the risk is about 1 in 50. The increased risk may be because a woman's eggs have been in her ovaries since her own prenatal development. Eggs may deteriorate over time as part of aging, or eggs may become damaged because an older woman has a longer history of exposure to hazards in the environment, such as X rays.

An extra autosome (as in Down syndrome), a missing autosome, or a damaged autosome always has far-reaching consequences for development because the autosomes contain huge amounts of genetic material. In fact, nearly half of all fertilized eggs abort spontaneously within 2 weeks, primarily because of abnormal autosomes. Thus, most eggs that could not develop normally are removed naturally (Moore & Persaud, 1993).

Abnormal sex chromosomes can also disrupt development. The table lists four of the more frequent disorders associated with atypical numbers of X and Y

| Common Disorders Associated with the Sex Chromosomes | | | |
| --- | --- | --- | --- |
| Disorder | Sex Chromosomes | Frequency | Characteristics |
| Klinefelters syndrome | XXY | 1 in 500 male births | Tall, small testicles, sterile, below-normal intelligence, passive |
| XYY complement | XYY | 1 in 1,000 male births | Tall, some cases apparently have below-normal intelligence |
| Turner's syndrome | X | 1 in 2,500 to 5,000 female births | Short, limited development of secondary sex characteristics, problems perceiving spatial relations |
| XXX syndrome | XXX | 1 in 500 to 1,200 female births | Normal stature but delayed motor and language development |

Source: Based on Bancroft et al., 1982; Downey et al., 1991; Linden et al., 1988; Plomin et al., 1990.

TABLE 3–5

chromosomes. Keep in mind that *frequent* is a relative term; although these disorders occur more frequently than PKU or Huntington's disease, the table shows that most are rare. Notice that no disorders consist solely of Y chromosomes. The presence of an X chromosome appears to be necessary for life. These genetic disorders demonstrate the remarkable power of heredity. Nevertheless, to fully understand how heredity influences development, we need to consider the environment, which we'll do in Module 3.3.

## CHECK YOUR LEARNING

1. _____ is an inherited disorder caused by the accumulation of a particular amino acid, resulting in mental retardation.

2. Genetic disorders involving dominant alleles are rare because _____.

3. Down syndrome usually is caused by _____.

4. Many fertilized eggs are aborted spontaneously, primarily because of _____.

5. Disorders involving abnormal numbers of sex chromosomes suggests that the presence of _____ is necessary for life.

### CONNECTIONS

Children with Down syndrome are slow in their mental development. How might this delayed mental development affect their social relationships with parents, siblings, and peers?

**Answers:** (1) PKU, (2) individuals with these disorders often do not live long enough to have children, (3) an extra 21st chromosome, (4) abnormal autosomes, (5) an X chromosome

# 3.3 Heredity Is Not Destiny

## LEARNING OBJECTIVES

● How do genes affect behavior?

● Does a genotype always lead to the same phenotype?

● How does the relation between heredity and environment change as children develop?

● How do family environments influence children's development?

*Sadie and Molly are fraternal twins. As babies, Sadie was calm and easily comforted, but Molly was fussy and hard to soothe. Their parents wondered if they'd always differ or if they'd become more alike as they grew older.*

Many people mistakenly view heredity as a set of phenotypes that unfold automatically from the genotypes that are set at conception. Nothing could be further from the truth. Although genotypes are fixed when the sperm fertilizes the egg, phenotypes are not fixed. Instead, heredity and environment combine to direct a child's behavioral and psychological development. In this module, we'll look at links between heredity and environment. In the process, we'll learn whether Sadie and Molly became more alike as they grew.

## Paths from Genes to Behavior

You know, from Module 3.1, that there is no single intelligence gene and no one shyness gene; instead, many genes work together to influence these and other aspects of behavioral development. But how do genes work together to make some children brighter than others and some children more outgoing than others? That is, how does the information in strands of DNA influence a child's behavioral and psychological development?

The specific paths from genes to behavior are largely uncharted, but some of their general properties are known. The most important is that genes never cause behavior directly; instead, they influence behavior indirectly, by making behaviors more or less likely. For example, there is no gene for dunking a basketball, but genes do regulate bone length. Consequently, some people grow taller than others and they are therefore more capable of dunking. Similarly, there is no gene for alcoholism, but genes do regulate how the body breaks down alcohol that is consumed. Consequently, some people become nauseated because their bodies cannot break down alcohol and they are therefore less likely to become alcoholics. These examples show that genes for height and breaking down alcohol affect behavior indirectly, by changing the odds that a person can dunk a basketball or become an alcoholic.

> The influence of genes on behavior is always indirect and depends on the environment in which the genetic instructions are carried out.

Another important property of gene-behavior paths is that the behavioral consequences of genetic instructions depend on environments. In a world without basketball, the gene for height would still produce taller people, but they would no longer be more likely to dunk. In other words, to understand how heredity affects behavior, we must consider the environment in which genetic instructions are carried out.

In the remaining sections of this module, we'll look at other aspects of links between heredity and environment.

## Reaction Range

If you read the fine print on a can of diet soda (and some other food products), you'll see the following warning:

"Phenylketonurics: contains phenylalanine."

Children with phenylketonuria (PKU) are missing an enzyme that breaks down phenylalanine. When phenylalanine accumulates, it damages the nervous system. Today, most American hospitals check for PKU at birth—with a blood or urine test. Newborns who have the disease are immediately placed on a diet that limits intake of phenylalanine, and mental retardation is avoided. Thus, an individual who has the genotype for PKU but not exposed to phenylalanine has normal intelligence. PKU illustrates that development depends on heredity and environmental factors—in this case, diet. And, as you'll see in the "Child Development and Family Policy" feature, PKU represents an exciting example of how research has influenced family policy.

## CHILD DEVELOPMENT AND FAMILY POLICY

### Screening for PKU

PKU was first discovered in 1934 when a Norwegian mother asked a physician, Dr. Asbjørn Fjølling, to help her two children, both of whom suffered from mental retardation. Dr. Fjølling discovered that the children had large amounts of phenylpyruvic acid in their urine and phenylalanine in their blood. By the 1950s, other scientists had determined that the build-up of phenylalanine damaged the nervous system and had shown that a low-protein diet would leave the nervous system unharmed. The missing link was an effective way to diagnose PKU in newborns, before phenylalanine had a chance to accumulate and cause damage. In 1959, Dr. Robert Guthrie devised a quick and inexpensive way to determine levels of phenylalanine in a newborn's blood. Studies soon proved that the test was effective. Armed with this information and aided by a complimentary story in *Life* magazine, Dr. Guthrie and the National Association for Retarded Children lobbied vigorously for laws that required newborns to be screened for PKU. In 1965, New York became the first state to require mandatory screening; by the end of the 1960s, most U.S. states required screening. Today, all states require PKU screening and require health insurance providers to cover the cost of low-protein formula for infants with PKU. Thus, research revealed the mechanisms of PKU and led to a simple screening test; public policy that required mandatory screening and low-protein diets means that hundreds of children who are born each year with PKU can lead healthy, normal lives.

In general, heredity and environment jointly determine the direction of development. **Reaction range refers to the fact that the same genotype can produce a range of phenotypes, in reaction to the environment where development takes place.** For example, imagine two children with the same genotype for "average intelligence." The children's phenotypic intelligence would depend on the environments in which they develop. If one child is brought up in an impoverished, unstimulating environment, his or her phenotypic intelligence may be below average. In contrast, if the second child is brought up in an enriched environment filled with stimulation, this child's phenotypic intelligence may be above average. Thus the same genotype for intelligence can lead to a range of phenotypes, depending on the quality of the rearing environment. Of course, what makes a "good" or "rich" environment is not the same for all facets of behavioral or psychological development. Throughout this book, you will see how specific kinds of environments influence very particular aspects of development (Wachs, 1983).

> The same genotype can lead to a range of phenotypes, depending on the environment in which development occurs.

### Changing Relations Between Nature and Nurture

How nature (genetics) and nurture (environment) work together partly depends on a child's age. Sandra Scarr (1992; Scarr & McCartney, 1983) describes three types of relations between heredity and environment. **In the first, a passive gene-environment relation, parents pass on genotypes to their children and provide much of the early environment for their young children.**

For example, bright parents are likely to transmit genes that make for bright children. Bright parents are also likely to provide books, museum visits, and discussions that are intellectually stimulating. In this case, heredity and environment are positively related: Both foster brighter children. In both respects, children are passive recipients of heredity and environment. This passive type of relation is most common with infants and young children.

In the second type of relation, an **evocative gene-environment relation, different genotypes evoke different responses from the environment.** For example, children who are bright (due in part to their genes) may pay greater attention to their teachers and ask more questions and, in turn, receive greater positive attention in school than children who are not as bright. Or, children who are friendly and outgoing (again, due in part to their genes) may elicit more interactions with others (and, in particular, more satisfying interactions) than children who are not as friendly and outgoing. In the evocative relation, which is common in young children, a child's genotype evokes or prompts people to respond differently to the child.

In the third type of relation, an **active gene-environment relation, individuals actively seek environments related to their genetic makeup.** Children who are bright (due in part to heredity) may actively seek peers, adults, and activities that strengthen their intellectual development. Similarly, children like the one in the photo, who are outgoing (due in part to heredity), seek the company of other people, particularly extroverts like themselves. **This process of deliberately seeking environments that fit one's heredity is called niche-picking.** Niche-picking is first seen in childhood and becomes more common as children get older and can control their environments. The "Real Children" feature shows niche-picking in action.

## REAL CHILDREN

### Sadie and Molly Pick Their Niches

Did Sadie and Molly, the twins in the module-opening vignette, become more alike as they grew? No. Even as a young baby, Sadie was always a "people person." She relished contact with other people and preferred play that involved others. Molly was more withdrawn and was quite happy to play alone. When they entered school, Sadie enjoyed making friends, while Molly looked forward to the new activities and barely noticed the new faces. These differences reveal heredity in action because sociability is known to have important genetic components (Braungart et al., 1992).

As adolescents, Sadie and Molly continued to seek environments that fit their differing needs for social stimulation. Sadie was in school plays and sang in the school choir. Molly developed a serious interest in crafts, which she pursued by herself. Sadie was always doing something with friends. Molly enjoyed the company of some long-time friends, but she was just as happy to be working alone on some new craft project. Sadie and Molly chose distinctive and very different niches, choices that were influenced by the genes that regulate sociability.

The description of Sadie and Molly illustrates that genes and environment rarely influence development alone. Instead, nature and nurture interact. Experiences determine which phenotypes emerge, and genotypes influence the nature of children's experiences. The story of Sadie and Molly also makes it clear that, to understand how genes influence development, we need to look carefully at how environments work, our next topic.

## The Nature of Nurture

For each of their children, parents provide a unique set of genes and a unique environment.

Traditionally, psychologists have considered some environments beneficial for children and others detrimental. This view has been especially strong in regard to family environments. Some parenting practices are thought to be more effective than others, and parents who use these effective practices are believed to have children who are, on average, better off than children of parents who don't use these practices. This view leads to a simple prediction: Children within a family should be similar because they all receive the same type of effective (or ineffective) parenting. However, dozens of behavioral genetic studies show that, in reality, siblings are not very much alike in their cognitive and social development (Dunn & Plomin, 1990).

Does this mean that family environment is not important? No. **These findings point to the importance of nonshared environmental influences, the forces within a family that make children different from one another.** Although the family environment is important, it usually affects each child in a unique way, which makes siblings differ. For example, parents may be more affectionate with one child than another, they may use more physical punishment with one child than another, or they may have higher expectations for school achievement for one child than another. All these contrasting parental influences tend to make siblings different, not alike (Tyrkheimer & Waldron, 2000). Family environments are important, but, as I describe their influence throughout this book, you should remember that families really create multiple unique environments, one for each child.

Much of what I have said about genes, environment, and development is summarized in the diagram. Parents are the source of children's genes and, at least for young children, the primary source of children's experiences. Children's genes also influence the experiences they have and the impact of those experiences on them. However, to capture the idea of nonshared environmental influences, we would need a separate diagram for each child, reflecting the fact that parents provide unique genes and a unique family environment for each of their offspring.

Most of this book is devoted to explaining the links between nature, nurture, and development. We can first see the interaction of nature and nurture during prenatal development, which is the topic of Chapter 4.

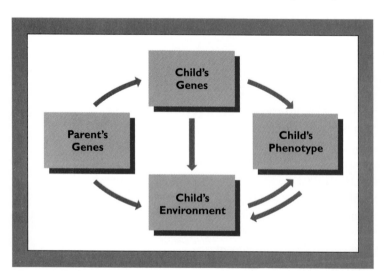

FIG. 3–6

## CHECK YOUR LEARNING

**1.** The path from genes to environment is always _____.

**2.** _____ refers to the fact that the same genotype can be associated with many different phenotypes.

**3.** In _____ gene-environment relations, children's genotypes cause others to respond differently to them.

**4.** Nonshared environmental influences tend to make siblings _____.

**ACTIVE CHILDREN**

Leslie and Glenn, the couple from Module 3.1 who were concerned that their baby could have sickle cell disease, are already charting their baby's life course. Leslie, who has always loved to sing, is confident that her baby will be a fantastic musician and easily imagines a regular routine of music lessons, rehearsals, and concerts. Glenn, a pilot, is just as confident that his child will share his love of flying; he is already planning trips the two of them can take together. Are Leslie's and Glenn's ideas more consistent with the active or passive views of children? What advice might you give to Leslie and Glenn about factors they are ignoring?

**Answers:** (1) indirect, by making some behaviors more or less likely, (2) Reaction range, (3) evocative, (4) different rather than similar

# Unifying Themes: Nature and Nurture

This entire chapter is devoted to a single theme: *Development is always jointly influenced by heredity and environment.* We have seen, again and again, how heredity and environment are essential ingredients in all developmental recipes, though not always in equal parts. In sickle cell disease, an allele has survival value in malaria-prone environments but not in environments where malaria has been eradicated. In PKU, persons who inherit the disorder experience retarded development when their dietary environment includes foods with phenylalanine but not when they avoid phenylalanine. And children with genes for normal intelligence develop below-average, average, or above-average intelligence, depending on the environment in which they grow. Nature and nurture . . . development always depends on both.

## See for Yourself

The Human Genome Project, launched in the late 1980s by U.S. scientists, aims to identify the exact location of all 30,000 human genes. It is a vast undertaking that first requires determining the sequence of roughly 3 billion pairs of nucleotides like those shown in the diagram on page 54. The project has produced maps of each chromosome showing the location of known genes. You can see these maps at a Web site maintained by the Human Genome Project. The address is:

**http://www.ornl.gov/hgmis/posters/chromosome/**

At this site, you can select a "favorite" chromosome and see which genes have been located on it. See for yourself!

## Resources

For more information about...

**human heredity**, try Matt Ridley's *Genome: The Autobiography of a Species in 23 Chapters* (HarperCollins, 2000), which describes progress in genetics research by telling fascinating stories about the impact of chromosomes on intelligence, language, cancer, and sex, to name just a few.

**children with Down syndrome**, visit the Down syndrome Web site:
**http://www.nas.com/downsyn**

## Key Terms

active gene-environment relation  69
alleles  55
autosomes  53
behavioral genetics  56
chromosomes  52
deoxyribonucleic acid (DNA)  54
depression  60
dizygotic (fraternal) twins  58
dominant  55
Down syndrome  63
evocative gene-environment relation  69
gene  54
genotype  55
heterozygous  55

homozygous  55
Huntington's disease  64
in vitro fertilization  53
incomplete dominance  55
monozygotic (identical) twins  58
niche-picking  69
nonshared environmental influences  70
passive gene-environment relation  68
phenotype  55
polygenic inheritance  57
reaction range  68
recessive  55
sex chromosomes  53
sickle cell trait  55

## SUMMARY

## 3.1 Mechanisms of Heredity

### The Biology of Heredity

At conception, the 23 chromosomes in the sperm merge with the 23 chromosomes in the egg. The 46 chromosomes that result include 22 pairs of autosomes plus 2 sex chromosomes. Each chromosome is one molecule of DNA, which consists of nucleotides organized in a structure that resembles a spiral staircase. A section of DNA that provides specific biochemical instructions is called a gene. All of a person's genes make up a genotype; phenotype refers to the physical, behavioral, and psychological characteristics that develop when the genotype is exposed to a specific environment.

### Single Gene Inheritance

Different forms of the same gene are called alleles. A person who inherits the same allele on a pair of chromosomes is homozygous; in this case, the biochemical instructions on the allele are followed. A person who inherits different alleles is heterozygous; in this case, the instructions of the dominant allele are followed whereas those of the recessive allele are ignored. In incomplete dominance, the person is heterozygous but the phenotype is midway between the dominant and recessive phenotypes.

### Behavioral Genetics

Behavioral and psychological phenotypes that reflect an underlying continuum (such as intelligence) often involve polygenic inheritance. In polygenic inheritance, the phenotype reflects the combined activity of many distinct genes. Polygenic inheritance has been examined traditionally by studying twins and adopted children, and more recently, by identifying DNA markers. These studies indicate substantial influence of heredity in three areas: intelligence, psychological disorders, and personality.

## 3.2 Genetic Disorders

### Inherited Disorders

Most inherited disorders are carried by recessive alleles. Examples include sickle cell disease, albinism, cystic fibrosis, phenylketonuria, and Tay-Sachs disease. Inherited disorders are rarely carried by dominant alleles because individuals with such a disorder usually don't live long enough to have children. An exception is Huntington's disease, which doesn't become symptomatic until middle age.

### Abnormal Chromosomes

Most fertilized eggs that do not have 46 chromosomes are aborted spontaneously soon after conception. One exception is Down syndrome, caused by an extra 21st chromosome. Down syndrome individuals have a distinctive appearance and are mentally retarded. Disorders of the sex chromosomes, which are more common because these chromosomes contain less genetic material than autosomes, include Klinefelter's syndrome, XYY complement, Turner's syndrome, and XXX syndrome.

## 3.3 Heredity Is Not Destiny

### Paths from Genes to Behavior

Genes never influence behavior directly. Instead, they affect behavior indirectly by increasing the odds that a child will behave in a particular way. Also, the impact of a gene on behavior depends on the environment in which the genetic instructions are carried out.

### Reaction Range

PKU does not lead to mental retardation when individuals with the disorder maintain a diet low in phenylalanine. This demonstrates the concept of reaction range—the same genotype can lead to different phenotypes. The outcome of heredity depends on the environment in which development occurs.

### Changing Relations Between Nature and Nurture

In infants and young children, the gene-environment relation is passive: parents pass on genotypes to their children and provide much of the early environment for their young children. An evocative gene-environment relation increasingly occurs during development as the child's genotype evokes responses from the environment. In older children and adolescents, an active gene-environment relation is common: Individuals actively seek environments related to their genetic makeup.

### The Nature of Nurture

Family environments affect siblings differently, which is known as nonshared environmental influences. Parents provide a unique environment for each child in the family as well as providing a unique genotype for each child.

4

If you ask parents to name some of the most memorable experiences of their lives, many mention events associated with pregnancy and childbirth. From the exciting news that a woman is pregnant through birth 9 months later, the entire experience evokes awe and wonder. The events of pregnancy and birth provide the foundation on which all child development is built. In Module 4.1, we'll trace the events of prenatal development that transform sperm and egg into a living, breathing human being. In Module 4.2, we'll learn about some developmental problems that can occur before birth. In Module 4.3, we'll turn to birth. We'll see what happens during labor and delivery, and we'll consider some problems that can arise. In Module 4.4, we'll discover what newborn babies are like.

# Prenatal Development, Birth, and the Newborn

# 4.1

## From Conception to Birth

- **Period of the Zygote**
- **Period of the Embryo**
- **Period of the Fetus**

### LEARNING OBJECTIVES

- What happens to a fertilized egg in the first 2 weeks after conception?
- When do body structures and internal organs emerge in prenatal development?
- When do body systems begin to function well enough to support life?

*Eun Jung has just learned that she is pregnant with her first child. Like many other parents-to-be, she and her husband, Kinam, are ecstatic. But they also soon realize how little they know about "what happens when" during pregnancy. Eun Jung is eager to visit her obstetrician to learn more about the normal timetable of events during pregnancy.*

VIDEO 4.1
Prenatal Development

**The changes that transform a fertilized egg into a newborn human make up prenatal development.** Prenatal development takes an average of 38 weeks, which are divided into three stages: the period of the zygote, the period of the embryo, and the period of the fetus. Each period gets its name from the term used to describe the baby-to-be at that point in prenatal development.

In this module, we'll trace the major developments during each period. As we go, you'll learn the answer to the "what happens when" question that intrigues Eun Jung.

### Period of the Zygote (Weeks 1–2)

The diagram traces the major events of the first period of prenatal development, which begins with fertilization and lasts about 2 weeks. **It ends when the fertil-**

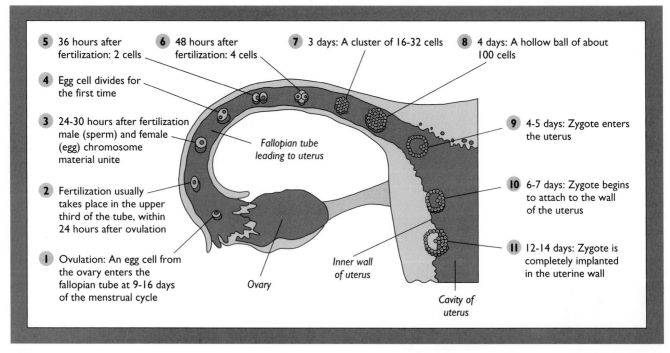

**5** 36 hours after fertilization: 2 cells

**6** 48 hours after fertilization: 4 cells

**7** 3 days: A cluster of 16-32 cells

**8** 4 days: A hollow ball of about 100 cells

**4** Egg cell divides for the first time

**3** 24-30 hours after fertilization male (sperm) and female (egg) chromosome material unite

**2** Fertilization usually takes place in the upper third of the tube, within 24 hours after ovulation

**1** Ovulation: An egg cell from the ovary enters the fallopian tube at 9-16 days of the menstrual cycle

*Fallopian tube leading to uterus*

*Ovary*

*Inner wall of uterus*

*Cavity of uterus*

**9** 4-5 days: Zygote enters the uterus

**10** 6-7 days: Zygote begins to attach to the wall of the uterus

**11** 12-14 days: Zygote is completely implanted in the uterine wall

FIG. 4-1

ized egg, called a zygote, implants itself in the wall of the
uterus. During these 2 weeks, the zygote grows rapidly through
cell division and travels down the fallopian tube toward the
uterus. Within hours, the zygote divides for the first time; then
division occurs every 12 hours. Occasionally, the zygote sepa-
rates into two clusters that develop into identical twins. Fraternal twins, which are more common, are created when two eggs
are released and each is fertilized by a different sperm cell. **After
about 4 days, the zygote consists of about 100 cells, resembles a
hollow ball, and is called a blastocyst.**

By the end of the first week, the zygote reaches the uterus.
**The next step is implantation: The blastocyst burrows into the
uterine wall and establishes connections with the mother's
blood vessels.** Implantation takes about a week to complete and
triggers hormonal changes that prevent menstruation, letting the
woman know she has conceived.

The implanted blastocyst, shown in the photograph, is less
than a millimeter in diameter. Yet its cells have already begun to
differentiate. In the diagram, which shows a cross-section of the
blastocyst and the wall of the uterus, you can see different layers of cells. **A small cluster of cells near the
center of the blastocyst, the germ disc, eventually
develops into the baby.** The other cells are destined
to become structures that support, nourish, and protect the developing organism. **The layer of cells closest to the uterus becomes the placenta, a structure
for exchanging nutrients and wastes between the
mother and the developing organism.**

Implantation and differentiation of cells mark
the end of the period of the zygote. Comfortably
sheltered in the uterus, the blastocyst is well prepared
for the remaining 36 weeks of the marvelous journey
to birth.

FIG. 4–2

## Period of the Embryo (Weeks 3–8)

**Once the blastocyst is completely embedded in the
uterine wall, it is called an embryo.** This new period typically begins the third week after conception
and lasts until the end of the eighth week. During
the period of the embryo, body structures and inter-
nal organs develop. At the beginning of the period, three layers form in the embryo. **The outer layer or ectoderm will become hair, the outer layer of skin, and
the nervous system; the middle layer or mesoderm will form muscles, bones,
and the circulatory system; the inner layer or endoderm will form the digestive system and the lungs.**

One dramatic way to see the changes that occur during the embryonic period is to
compare a 3-week-old embryo with an 8-week-old embryo. The 3-week-old embryo

shown in the left photo is about 2 millimeters long. Cell specialization is under way, but the organism looks more like a salamander than a human being. But growth and specialization proceed so rapidly that the 8-week-old embryo shown in the photo on the right looks very different: You can see an eye, the jaw, an arm, and a leg. The brain and the nervous system are also developing rapidly, and the heart has been beating for nearly a month. Most of the organs found in a mature human are in place, in some form. (The sex organs are a notable exception.) Yet, being only an inch long and weighing a fraction of an ounce, the embryo is much too small for the mother to feel its presence.

The embryo's environment is shown in the diagram below. **The embryo rests in an amniotic sac, which is filled with amniotic fluid that cushions the embryo and maintains a constant temperature.** The embryo is linked to the mother by two structures. **The umbilical cord houses blood vessels that join the embryo to the placenta.** In the placenta, the blood vessels from the umbilical cord run close to the mother's blood vessels but aren't actually connected to them. **Instead, the blood flows through villi, finger-like projections from the umbilical blood vessels that are shown in the diagram.**

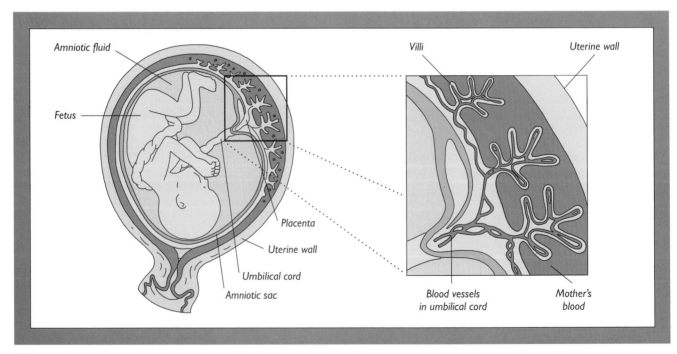

FIG. 4–3

As you can see, villi lie in close proximity to the mother's blood vessels and thus allow nutrients, oxygen, vitamins, and waste products to be exchanged between mother and embryo.

With body structures and internal organs in place, another major milestone passes in prenatal development. What's left is for these structures and organs to begin working properly. This is accomplished in the final period of prenatal development, as we'll see in the next section.

## Period of the Fetus (Weeks 9–38)

**The final and longest phase of prenatal development, the period of the fetus, extends from the ninth week after conception until birth.** During this period, the baby-to-be becomes much larger and its bodily systems begin to work. The increase in size is remarkable. At the beginning of this period, the fetus weighs less than an ounce. At about 4 months, the fetus weighs roughly 4 to 8 ounces, enough for the mother to feel its movements. During the last 5 months of pregnancy, the fetus gains an average of an additional 7 or 8 pounds before birth. The chart below, which depicts the fetus at one-eighth of its actual size, shows these incredible increases in size.

During the fetal period, the finishing touches are put on the body systems that are essential to human life, such as the nervous, respiratory, and digestive systems. Some highlights of this period include the following:

- At 4 weeks after conception, a flat set of cells curls to form a tube. One end of the tube swells to form the brain; the rest forms the spinal cord. By the start of the fetal period, the brain has distinct structures and has begun to regulate body functions. **During the period of the fetus, all regions of the brain grow, particularly**

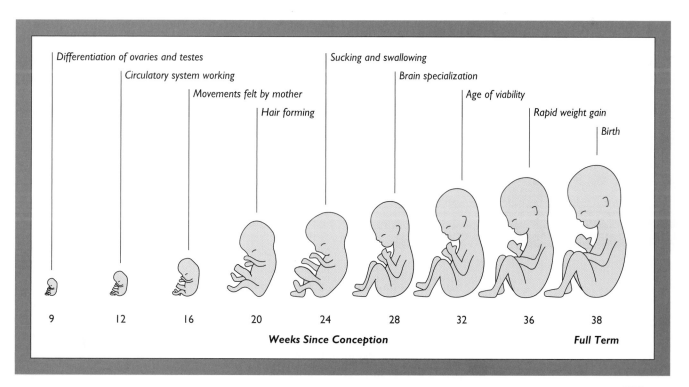

FIG. 4–4

Source: Moore and Persaud, 1993.

the cerebral cortex, the wrinkled surface of the brain that regulates many important human behaviors.

- Near the end of the embryonic period, male embryos develop testes and female embryos develop ovaries. In the third month, the testes in a male fetus secrete a hormone that causes a set of cells to become a penis and scrotum; in a female fetus, this hormone is absent, so the same cells become a vagina and labia.
- During the fifth and sixth months after conception, eyebrows, eyelashes, and scalp hair emerge. **The skin thickens and is covered with a thick greasy substance, vernix, that protects the fetus during its long bath in amniotic fluid.**

**With these and other rapid changes, by 22 to 28 weeks most systems function well enough that a fetus born at this time has a chance to survive, which is why this age range is called the age of viability.** By this age, the fetus has a distinctly baby-like look, as you can see in the photo. However, babies born this early have trouble breathing because their lungs are not yet mature. Also, they cannot regulate their body temperature very well because they lack the insulating layer of fat that appears in the eighth month after conception. With modern neonatal intensive care, infants born this early can survive, but they face other challenges, as I'll describe in Module 4.3.

The changes of the fetal period also mean that the fetus actually starts to behave (Joseph, 2000). The fetus responds to stimulation (Birnholz & Benacerraf, 1983; Kisilevsky & Low, 1998). For example, although we can't observe it directly, sounds from the guitar in the photo probably cause the fetal heart rate to increase and may cause the fetus to move. Also, the fetus develops regular periods of activity: Most mothers report times when the fetus is moving and other times when the fetus is still. Some fetuses are more active than others, and these differences predict infants' behavior: An active fetus is more likely than an inactive fetus to be an unhappy, difficult baby (DiPietro et al., 1996).

Remarkably, newborns apparently can recognize some of the sounds they hear during prenatal development. DeCasper and Spence (1986) had pregnant women read aloud the famous Dr. Seuss story *The Cat in the Hat* twice a day for the last $1\frac{1}{2}$ months of pregnancy. As newborns, then, these babies had heard *The Cat in the Hat* for more than 3 hours. The newborns were then allowed to suck on a mechanical nipple connected to a tape recorder so that the baby's sucking could turn the tape on or off. The investigators discovered that babies would suck to hear a tape of their mother reading *The Cat in the Hat* but not to hear her reading other stories. Evidently, newborns recognized the familiar, rhythmic quality of *The Cat in the Hat* from their prenatal story times.

These and other important prenatal changes are summarized in the table on page 81. The milestones listed in the table make it clear that prenatal development does a remarkable job of preparing the fetus for independent living as a newborn baby. But these astonishing prenatal changes can only take place when a woman provides a healthy environment for her baby-to-be. The "Improving Children's Lives" feature describes what pregnant women should do to provide the best foundation for prenatal development.

| Trimester | Period | Weeks | Size | Highlights |
|---|---|---|---|---|
| First | Zygote | 1–2 | | Fertilized egg becomes a blastocyst that is implanted in the uterine wall |
| | Embryo | 3–4 | 1/4 inch | Period of rapid growth; most body parts including nervous system (brain and spinal cord), heart, and limbs are formed |
| | Embryo | 5–8 | 1 inch, fraction of an ounce | |
| | Fetus | 9–12 | 3 inches, about an ounce | Rapid growth continues, most body systems begin to function |
| Second | Fetus | 13–24 | 12–15 inches, about 2 pounds | Continued growth; fetus is now large enough for a woman to feel its movements, fetus is covered with vernix |
| Third | Fetus | 25–38 | 20 inches, 7–8 pounds | Continued growth; body systems become mature in preparation for birth, layer of fat is acquired, reaches the age of viability |

# IMPROVING CHILDREN'S LIVES

## Five Steps Toward a Healthy Baby

1. Visit a health care provider for regular prenatal checkups. You should have monthly visits until you get close to your due date, when you will have a checkup every other week or maybe even weekly.

2. Eat healthy foods. Be sure your diet includes foods from each of the five major food groups (cereals, fruits, vegetables, dairy products, and meats and beans). Your health care provider may recommend that you supplement your diet with vitamins, minerals, and iron to be sure you are providing your baby with all the nutrients it needs.

3. Stop drinking alcohol and caffeinated beverages. Stop smoking. Consult your health care provider before taking any over-the-counter medications or prescription drugs.

4. Exercise throughout pregnancy. If you are physically fit, your body is better equipped to handle the needs of the baby.

5. Get enough rest, especially during the last 2 months of pregnancy. Also, attend childbirth education classes so that you'll be prepared for labor, delivery, and your new baby. ●

As critically important as these steps are, they unfortunately do not guarantee a healthy baby. In Module 4.2, we'll see how prenatal development can sometimes go awry.

## CHECK YOUR LEARNING

**1.** Fraternal twins develop when _____.

**2.** The period of the zygote ends _____.

**3.** Body structures and internal organs form during the period of the _____.

**4.** The embryo rests in a fluid within the _____.

**5.** _____ is called the age of viability because at this time most body systems function well enough to support life.

**6.** During the last few months of prenatal development, the fetus has regular periods of activity and _____, which are the first signs of fetal behavior.

**ACTIVE CHILDREN**
Suppose a fetus is extremely active before birth and is a fussy, demanding baby after birth. How might these behaviors affect the baby's parents and other family members?

**Answers:** (1) two eggs are fertilized by two sperm, (2) at 2 weeks after conception (when the zygote is completely implanted in the wall of the uterus), (3) embryo, (4) amniotic sac, (5) between 22 and 28 weeks, (6) the eyes and ears respond to stimulation

---

# 4.2    Influences on Prenatal Development

General Risk Factors

Teratogens: Diseases, Drugs, and Environmental Hazards

How Teratogens Influence Prenatal Development

Prenatal Diagnosis and Treatment

## LEARNING OBJECTIVES

● How is prenatal development influenced by a pregnant woman's nutrition, the stress she experiences while pregnant, and her age?

● What is a teratogen, and what specific diseases, drugs, and environmental hazards can be teratogens?

● How exactly do teratogens affect prenatal development?

● How can prenatal development be monitored? Can abnormal prenatal development be corrected?

*Chloe was barely 2 months pregnant at her first prenatal checkup. As she waited for her appointment, she looked at the list of questions that she wanted to ask her obstetrician. "I spend much of my workday at a computer. Is radiation from the monitor harmful to my baby?" "When my husband and I get home from work, we'll have a glass of wine to help unwind from the stress of the day. Is moderate drinking like this okay?" "I'm 38. I know older women more often give birth to mentally retarded babies. Is there any way I can know if my baby will be mentally retarded?"*

All of Chloe's questions concern potential harm to her baby-to-be. She worries about the safety of her computer monitor, about her nightly glass of wine, and about her age. Chloe's concerns are well founded. Beginning with conception, environmental factors influence the course of prenatal development, and they are the focus of this module. If you're sure you can answer all of Chloe's questions, skip this module and go directly to Module 4.3 on page 95. Otherwise, read on to learn about problems that sometimes arise in pregnancy.

## General Risk Factors

As the name implies, general risk factors can have widespread effects on prenatal development. Scientists have identified three general risk factors: nutrition, stress, and a mother's age.

**NUTRITION.**    The mother is the developing child's sole source of nutrition, so a balanced diet that includes foods from each of the five major food groups is vital. Most pregnant women need to increase their intake of calories by about 10 to 20 percent to meet the needs of prenatal development. A woman should expect to gain between 25 and 35 pounds during pregnancy, assuming that her weight was normal before pregnancy. A woman who was underweight before becoming pregnant may gain as much as 40 pounds; a woman who was overweight should gain at least 15 pounds (Institute of Medicine, 1990). Of this gain, about one-third reflects the weight of the baby, the placenta, and the fluid in the amniotic sac; another third comes from increases in a woman's fat stores; yet another third comes from the increased volume of blood and increases in the size of her breasts and uterus (Whitney & Hamilton, 1987).

> Adequate nutrition–in terms of calories as well as proteins, vitamins, and minerals–is essential for healthy prenatal development.

Sheer amount of food is only part of the equation for a healthy pregnancy. What a pregnant woman eats is also very important. Proteins, vitamins, and minerals are essential for normal prenatal development. For example, folic acid, one of the B vitamins, is important for the nervous system to develop properly (Shaw et al., 1995). **When mothers do not consume adequate amounts of folic acid, their babies are at risk for spina bifida, a disorder in which the embryo's neural tube does not close properly during the first month of pregnancy.** Since the neural tube develops into the brain and spinal cord, when it does not close properly, the result is permanent damage to the spinal cord and the nervous system. Many children with spina bifida need crutches, braces, or wheelchairs. Other prenatal problems have also been traced to inadequate proteins, vitamins, or minerals, so health care providers typically recommend that pregnant women supplement their diet with additional proteins, vitamins, and minerals.

When a pregnant woman does not provide adequate nourishment, the infant is likely to be born prematurely and to be underweight. Inadequate nourishment during the last few months of pregnancy can particularly affect the nervous system, because this is a time of rapid brain growth. Finally, babies who do not receive adequate nourishment are vulnerable to illness (Guttmacher & Kaiser, 1986).

**STRESS.**    Does a pregnant woman's mood affect the zygote, embryo, or fetus in her uterus? Is a woman who is happy during pregnancy more likely to give birth to a happy baby? Is a pregnant woman like the harried office worker in the photo more likely to give birth to an irritable baby? **These**

questions address the impact on prenatal development of chronic stress, which refers to a person's physical and psychological responses to threatening or challenging situations. We can answer these questions with some certainty for nonhumans. When pregnant female animals experience constant stress such as repeated electric shock or intense overcrowding, their offspring are often smaller than average and prone to other physical and behavioral problems (Schneider, 1992).

Determining the impact of stress on human pregnancy is more difficult because we must rely solely on correlational studies. (It would be unethical to do an experiment that assigned some pregnant women to a condition of extreme stress.) Studies typically show that women who report greater anxiety during pregnancy more often give birth early or have babies who weigh less than average (Copper et al., 1996; Paarlberg et al., 1995).

Increased stress can harm prenatal development in several ways. First, when a pregnant woman experiences stress, her body secretes hormones that reduce the flow of oxygen to the fetus while increasing its heart rate and activity level (Monk et al., 2000). Second, stress can weaken a pregnant woman's immune system, making her more susceptible to illness (Cohen & Williamson, 1991), which can, in turn, damage fetal development. Third, pregnant women under stress are more likely to smoke or drink alcohol and less likely to rest, exercise, and eat properly (Kolberg, 1999). All these behaviors endanger prenatal development.

> Problems during pregnancy are more common when a woman experiences chronic stress and when she is 35 or older.

I want to emphasize that the results described here apply to women who experience prolonged, extreme stress. Virtually all women sometimes become anxious or upset while pregnant. But occasional, relatively mild anxiety is not thought to have any harmful consequences for prenatal development.

**MOTHER'S AGE.** Traditionally, the 20s were thought to be the prime childbearing years. Teenage women as well as women who were 30 or older were considered less fit for the rigors of pregnancy. Is being a 20-something really important for a successful pregnancy? Let's answer this question separately for teenage and older women. Compared to women in their 20s, teenage women are more likely to have problems during pregnancy, labor, and delivery. This is largely because pregnant teenagers do not get good prenatal care, usually because they are unaware of the need and do not seek it out. For example, research done on African American adolescents suggests that when differences in prenatal care are taken into account, teenagers are just as likely as women in their 20s to have problem-free pregnancies and give birth to healthy babies (Goldenberg & Klerman, 1995).

Nevertheless, even when a teenager receives adequate prenatal care and gives birth to a healthy baby, all is not rosy. Children of teenage mothers generally do less well in school and more often have behavioral problems (Fergusson & Woodward, 2000). The problems of teenage motherhood—incomplete education, poverty, and marital difficulties—affect the child's later development (Moore & Brooks-Gunn, 2002).

Of course, not all teenage mothers and their infants follow this dismal life course. Some teenage mothers finish school, find good jobs, and have happy marriages; their children do well in school, academically and socially. However, teenage pregnancies with "happy endings" are definitely the exception; for most teenage mothers and their children, life is a struggle. Educating teenagers about the true consequences of teen pregnancy is crucial.

Are older women better suited for pregnancy? This is an important question because present-day American women typically are waiting longer than ever to become pregnant. Completing an education and beginning a career often delay childbearing. In fact, the birthrate in the early 2000s among 30- to 44-year-olds was nearly double what it was 1980 (Martin et al., 2002).

Today we know that older women like the one in the photo have more difficulty getting pregnant and are less likely to have successful pregnancies. Women in their 20s are twice as fertile as women in their 30s (Dunson et al., 2002). And, past 35 years of age, the risks of miscarriage and stillbirth increase rapidly. Among 40- to 45-year-olds, for example, nearly half of all pregnancies result in miscarriage (Andersen et al., 2000). What's more, women in their 40s are more liable to give birth to babies with Down syndrome.

In general, then, prenatal development is most likely to proceed normally when women are between the ages of 20 and 35, are healthy and eat right, get good health care, and lead lives that are free of chronic stress. But even in these optimal cases, prenatal development can be disrupted, as we'll see in the next section.

## Teratogens: Diseases, Drugs, and Environmental Hazards

In the late 1950s, many pregnant women in Germany took thalidomide, a drug to help them sleep. Soon, however, came reports that many of these women were giving birth to babies with deformed arms, legs, hands, or fingers. **Thalidomide was a powerful teratogen, an agent that causes abnormal prenatal development.** Ultimately, more than 10,000 babies worldwide were harmed before thalidomide was withdrawn from the market (Kolberg, 1999).

Prompted by the thalidomide disaster, scientists began to study teratogens extensively. Today, we know a great deal about the three primary types of teratogens: diseases, drugs, and environmental hazards. Let's look at each.

**DISEASES.**   Sometimes women become ill while pregnant. Most diseases, such as colds and many strains of flu, do not affect the developing organism. However, several bacterial and viral infections can be very harmful and, in some cases, fatal to the embryo or fetus; five of the most common of these are listed in the table.

### Teratogenic Diseases and Their Consequences

| Disease | Potential Consequences |
| --- | --- |
| AIDS | Frequent infections, neurological disorders, death |
| Cytomegalovirus | Deafness, blindness, abnormally small head, mental retardation |
| Genital herpes | Encephalitis, enlarged spleen, improper blood clotting |
| Rubella (German measles) | Mental retardation; damage to eyes, ears, and heart |
| Syphilis | Damage to the central nervous system, teeth, and bones |

TABLE 4–1

Some of these diseases pass from the mother through the placenta to attack the embryo or fetus directly. They include cytomegalovirus (a type of herpes), rubella, and syphilis. Other diseases attack at birth: The virus is present in the lining of the birth canal, and the baby is infected as it passes through to be born. Genital herpes is transmitted this way. AIDS is transmitted both ways—through the placenta and during passage through the birth canal.

The only way to guarantee that these diseases do not harm prenatal development is for a woman to not contract the disease before or during her pregnancy. Medication may help the woman, but does not prevent the disease from damaging the developing baby.

**DRUGS.**  Thalidomide illustrates the harm that drugs can cause during prenatal development. The table lists other drugs that are known teratogens.

## Teratogenic Drugs and Their Consequences

| Drug | Potential Consequences |
|------|------------------------|
| Alcohol | Fetal alcohol syndrome, cognitive deficits, heart damage, retarded growth |
| Aspirin | Deficits in intelligence, attention, and motor skill |
| Caffeine | Lower birth weight, decreased muscle tone |
| Cocaine and heroin | Retarded growth, irritability in newborns |
| Marijuana | Lower birth weight, less motor control |
| Nicotine | Retarded growth, possible cognitive impairments |

TABLE 4–2

Notice that most of the drugs in the list are substances that you may use routinely—alcohol, aspirin, caffeine, and nicotine. Nevertheless, when consumed by pregnant women, they present special dangers (Behnke & Eyler, 1993).

Cigarette smoking is typical of the potential harm from teratogenic drugs (Cornelius et al., 1995; Fried, O'Connell, & Watkinson, 1992). The nicotine in cigarette smoke constricts blood vessels and thus reduces the oxygen and nutrients that can reach the fetus through the placenta. Therefore, pregnant women who smoke are more likely to miscarry (abort the fetus spontaneously) and to bear children who are smaller than average at birth (Ernst et al., 2000). And, as children develop, they are more likely to show signs of impaired attention, language, and cognitive skills, along with behavioral problems (Brennan et al., 2002). Finally, even second-hand smoke harms the fetus: When pregnant women don't smoke but fathers do, babies tend to be smaller at birth (Friedman & Polifka, 1996). The message is clear and simple: Pregnant women shouldn't smoke and they should avoid others who do.

Alcohol also carries serious risk. **Pregnant women who consume large quantities of alcoholic beverages often give birth to babies with fetal alcohol syndrome (FAS).** Children with FAS usually grow more slowly than normal and have heart problems and misshapen faces. Like the child in the photo, youngsters with FAS often have a small head, a thin upper lip, a short nose, and widely spaced eyes. FAS is the leading cause of mental retardation in the United States, and children with FAS have serious attentional, cognitive, and behavioral problems. FAS is most common among pregnant women who are heavy recreational drinkers—that is, women who drink 5 or more ounces of alcohol a few times each week (Jacobson & Jacobson, 2000).

Does this mean that moderate drinking is safe? No. When women drink moderately throughout pregnancy, their children are often afflicted with alcohol-related neurodevelopmental disorder (ARND). Children with ARND are normal in appearance but have deficits in attention, memory, and intelligence (Jacobson et al., 1998).

Is there any amount of drinking that's safe during pregnancy? Maybe, but that amount is yet to be determined. Gathering definitive data is complicated by two factors: First, researchers usually determine the amount a woman drinks by her own responses to interviews or questionnaires. If for some reason she does not accurately report her consumption, it is impossible to accurately estimate the amount of harm associated with drinking. Second, any safe level of consumption is probably not the same for all women. Based on their health and heredity, some women may be able to consume more alcohol more safely than others.

These factors make it impossible to guarantee safe levels of alcohol or any of the other drugs listed in the table at the top of page 86. The best policy, therefore, is for a pregnant woman to avoid drugs if at all possible (including over-the-counter, prescription, and illegal drugs) and to consult a health care professional before using essential drugs.

**Whenever possible, woman should take no drugs while pregnant.**

ENVIRONMENTAL HAZARDS.   As a byproduct of life in an industrialized world, people are often exposed to toxins in food they eat, fluids they drink, and air they breathe. Chemicals associated with industrial waste are the most common environmental teratogens, and the quantities involved are usually minute. However, as is true for drugs, amounts that go unnoticed by an adult can cause serious damage to a developing fetus. Several environmental hazards that are known teratogens are listed in the table.

### Environmental Teratogens and Their Consequences

| Hazard | Potential Consequences |
| --- | --- |
| Lead | Mental retardation |
| Mercury | Retarded growth, mental retardation, cerebral palsy |
| PCBs | Impaired memory and verbal skill |
| X rays | Retarded growth, leukemia, mental retardation |

TABLE 4–3

You'll notice that although X rays are included in this table, radiation associated with computer monitors and video display terminals (VDTs) is not. Several major studies have examined the impact of exposure to the electromagnetic fields that are generated by VDTs, and they have found no negative results. For example, Schnorr and her colleagues (1991) compared the pregnancies in telephone operators who worked at VDTs at least 25 hours weekly with operators who never used VDTs. For both groups of women, about 15 percent of the pregnancies ended in miscarriage. Other investigators have found no relation between exposure to VDTs and birth defects (Parazzini et al., 1993; Shaw, 2001). Evidently, VDTs can be used safely by pregnant women.

In the "Focus on Research" feature, we look at one of the environmental teratogens in detail.

## FOCUS ON RESEARCH

### Impact of Prenatal Exposure to PCBs on Cognitive Functioning

*Who were the investigators, and what was the aim of the study?* For many years, polychlorinated biphenyls (PCBs) were used in electrical transformers and paints, but the U.S. government banned them in the 1970s. Like many industrial byproducts, they seeped into the waterways, where they contaminated fish and wildlife. The amount of PCBs in a typical contaminated fish does not affect adults, but Joseph Jacobson and Sandra Jacobson wanted to determine if this level of exposure was harmful to prenatal development. In particular, they knew from earlier work that substantial prenatal exposure to PCBs affected cognitive skills in infants and preschoolers; they hoped to determine if prenatal exposure similarly affected cognitive skills in school-age children.

*How did the investigators measure the topic of interest?* Jacobson and Jacobson needed to measure prenatal exposure to PCBs and cognitive skill. To measure prenatal exposure, they measured concentrations of PCBs in (a) blood obtained from the umbilical cord and (b) breast milk of mothers who were breast-feeding. To measure cognitive skill, they used a standardized test of intelligence (the WISC, described on page 252) and a standardized test of reading comprehension.

*Who were the children in the study?* The sample included 212 children who were born in western Michigan in 1980–1981. This region was chosen because, at the time, Lake Michigan contained many contaminated salmon and lake trout.

*What was the design of the study?* The study was correlational because the investigators were interested in the relation that existed naturally between two variables: exposure to PCBs and cognitive skill. The study was longitudinal because children were tested several times: Their exposure to PCBs was measured immediately after birth, and their cognitive skill was measured at three ages: 7 months, 4 years, and 11 years.

*Were there ethical concerns with the study?* No. The children had been exposed to PCBs naturally, prior to the start of the study. (Obviously, it would not have been ethical for researchers to do an experiment that involved asking pregnant women to eat contaminated fish.) The investigators obtained permission from the parents for the children to participate.

*What were the results?* PCB exposure affects intelligence and reading comprehension. However, as you can see in the graphs, lower levels of exposure to PCBs apparently had little effect on intelligence and reading comprehension. Only children with high levels of exposure to PCBs were affected.

*What did the investigators conclude?* Prenatal exposure to PCBs affects children's cognitive skills. Though children's scores were in the normal range, their reduced cognitive skills may create special hurdles in school.

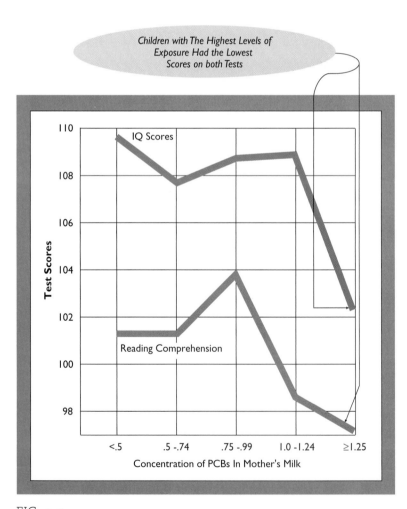

FIG. 4–5

*What converging evidence would strengthen these conclusions?* The results show that PCBs affect children's scores on standardized tests. More convincing would be longitudinal results showing that children exposed to PCBs were more likely to be diagnosed with a learning disability or language impairment, more likely to repeat a grade, or less likely to graduate from high school. ●

Environmental teratogens are treacherous because people are unaware of their presence in the environment. The women in the Jacobson and Jacobson (1996) study, for example, did not realize they were eating PCB-laden fish. This invisibility makes it more difficult for a pregnant woman to protect herself from environmental teratogens. Pregnant women need to be particularly careful of the foods they eat and the air they breathe. Be sure all foods are cleaned thoroughly to rid them of insecticides. Avoid convenience foods, which often contain many chemical additives. Stay away from air that's been contaminated by household products such as cleansers, paint strippers, and fertilizers. Women in jobs that require contact with potential teratogens (e.g., housecleaners, hairdressers) should switch to less potent chemicals. For example, they should use baking soda instead of more chemically laden cleansers. And they should wear protective gloves, aprons, and masks to reduce their contact with potential teratogens. Finally, because environmental teratogens continue to increase, check with a health care provider to learn if other materials should be avoided.

> Environmental teratogens are particularly dangerous because a pregnant woman may not know they are present in the environment.

## How Teratogens Influence Prenatal Development

By assembling all the evidence of harm caused by diseases, drugs, and environmental hazards, scientists have identified five important general principles about how teratogens usually work (Hogge, 1990; Jacobson & Jacobson, 2000; Vorhees & Mollnow, 1987).

1. *The impact of a teratogen depends on the genotype of the organism.* A substance may be harmful to one species but not to another. To determine thalidomide's safety, researchers had tested thalidomide in pregnant rats and rabbits, whose offspring had had normal limbs. Yet, when pregnant women took the same drug in comparable doses, many produced children with deformed limbs. Thalidomide was harmless to rats and rabbits but not to people. Moreover, some women who took thalidomide gave birth to babies with normal limbs, yet others who took comparable doses at the same time in their pregnancies gave birth to babies with deformities. Apparently, heredity makes some individuals more susceptible than others to a teratogen.

2. *The impact of teratogens changes over the course of prenatal development.* The timing of exposure to a teratogen is critical. The chart on page 90 shows how the consequences of teratogens differ for the periods of the zygote, embryo, and fetus. During the period of the zygote, exposure to teratogens usually results in spontaneous abortion of the fertilized egg. During the embryonic period, exposure produces major defects in body

structure. For example, women who took thalidomide during the embryonic period had babies with ill-formed or missing limbs. Women who contract rubella during the embryonic period have babies with heart defects. During the fetal period, exposure to teratogens either produces minor defects in body structure or causes body systems to function improperly. For example, when women drink large quantities of alcohol during the fetal period, the fetus develops fewer brain cells.

Even within the different periods of prenatal development, developing body parts and systems are more vulnerable at certain times. The blue shading in the chart indicates a time of maximum vulnerability; yellow shading indicates a time when the developing organism is less vulnerable. The heart, for example, is most sensitive to teratogens during the first two-thirds of the embryonic period. Exposure to teratogens before this time rarely produces heart damage; exposure after this time results in milder damage.

3. *Each teratogen affects a specific aspect (or aspects) of prenatal development.* Said another way, teratogens do not harm all body systems; instead, damage is selective. If a pregnant woman contracts rubella, her baby may have problems

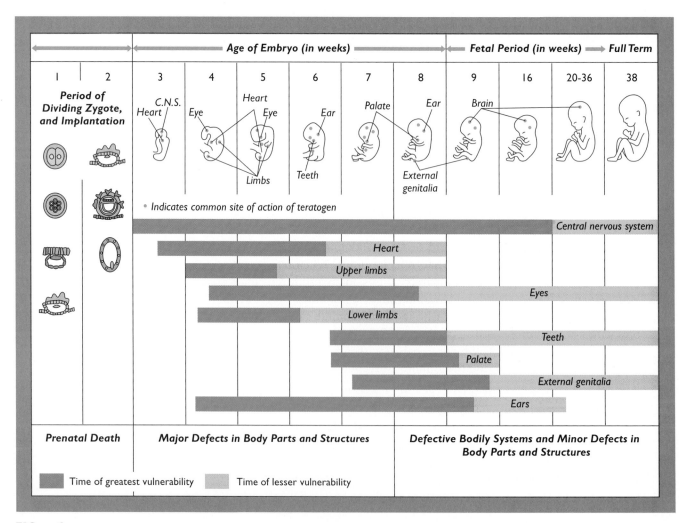

FIG. 4–6

with eyes, ears, and heart, but limbs will be normal. If a pregnant woman consumes PCB-contaminated fish, her baby typically has normal body parts and normal motor skills but below-average cognitive skills.

4. *The impact of teratogens depends on the dose.* Just as a single drop of oil won't pollute a lake, small doses of teratogens may not harm the fetus. In research on PCBs, for example, cognitive skills were affected only among children who had the greatest prenatal exposure to these byproducts. In general, the greater the exposure, the greater the risk for damage (Adams, 1999).

   An implication of this principle is that researchers should be able to determine safe levels for a teratogen. In reality, this is very difficult because sensitivity to teratogens will not be the same for all people (and it's not practical to establish separate safe amounts for each person). Hence, the safest rule is zero exposure to teratogens.

5. *Damage from teratogens is not always evident at birth but may appear later in life.* In the case of malformed infant limbs or babies born addicted to cocaine, the effects of a teratogen are obvious immediately. A cocaine baby goes through withdrawal shaking, crying, and being unable to sleep. Sometimes, however, the damage from a teratogen becomes evident only as the child develops. For example, between 1947 and 1971 many pregnant women in North America and Europe took the drug diethylstilbestrol (DES) to prevent miscarriages. The babies appeared normal at birth, but, as adults, they are more likely to have a rare cancer of the vagina and to have difficulty becoming pregnant themselves (Friedman & Polifka, 1996). Sons of women who took DES may be less fertile and at risk for cancer of the testes (Sharpe & Skakkebaek, 1993). Here is a case in which the impact of the teratogen is not evident until decades after birth.

> The impact of teratogens depends on the genotype of the organism and the timing and amount of exposure to the teratogen.

**THE REAL WORLD OF PRENATAL RISK.**   I have discussed risk factors individually, as if each were the only potential threat to prenatal development. In reality, many infants are exposed to multiple general risks and multiple teratogens (Giberson & Weinberg, 1992; Richardson, 1998). Pregnant women who drink alcohol often smoke and drink coffee. Pregnant women who are under stress often drink alcohol, and may self-medicate with aspirin or other over-the-counter drugs. Many of these same women live in poverty, which means they may have inadequate nutrition and receive minimal medical care during pregnancy. When all the risks are combined, prenatal development is rarely optimal.

This pattern explains why it's often challenging for child-development researchers to determine the harm associated with individual teratogens. Cocaine is a perfect example. You may remember stories in newspapers and magazines about "crack babies" and their developmental problems. In fact, the jury is still out on the issue of cocaine as a teratogen. Some investigators (e.g., Singer et al., 2002) find the harmful effects that made headlines in the 1990s, whereas others (e.g., Frank et al., 2001) argue that most of the effects attributed to cocaine actually stem from concurrent smoking and drinking.

From what I've said so far in this module, you may think that developing children have little chance of escaping harm. But most babies are born in good health. Of course, a good policy for pregnant women is to avoid diseases, drugs, and environmental hazards that are known teratogens. This, coupled with thorough prenatal medical care and adequate nutrition, is the best recipe for normal prenatal development.

## Prenatal Diagnosis and Treatment

"I really don't care whether I have a boy or girl, just as long as my baby's healthy." Legions of parents worldwide have felt this way, but until recently all they could do was hope for the best. Today, however, advances in technology give parents a much better idea whether their baby is developing normally.

Even before a woman becomes pregnant, a couple may go for genetic counseling, which I described in Module 3.2. A counselor constructs a family tree for each prospective parent to check for heritable disorders. If it turns out that one (or both) carries a disorder, further tests can determine the person's genotype. With this more detailed information, a genetic counselor can discuss choices with the prospective parents. They may choose to go ahead and conceive "naturally," taking their chances that the child will be healthy. Or they could decide to use sperm or eggs from other people. Yet another choice would be to adopt a child.

After a woman is pregnant, how can we know if prenatal development is progressing normally? Traditionally, obstetricians gauged development by feeling the size and position of the fetus through a woman's abdomen. This technique was not very precise and, of course, couldn't be done at all until the fetus was large enough to feel. Today, however, new techniques have revolutionized our ability to monitor prenatal growth and development. **A standard part of prenatal care in North America is ultrasound, a procedure using sound waves to generate a picture of the fetus.** As the photo shows, an instrument about the size of a hair dryer is rubbed over the woman's abdomen; the image is shown on a nearby TV monitor. The pictures that are generated are hardly portrait quality; they are grainy and it takes an expert's eye to distinguish what's what. Nevertheless, the procedure is painless and parents are thrilled to be able to see their babies and watch them move.

Ultrasound can be used as early as 4 or 5 weeks after conception; before this time the fetus is not large enough to generate an interpretable image. Ultrasound pictures are useful for determining the date of conception, which enables the physician to predict the due date more accurately. Ultrasound pictures are also valuable in showing the position of the fetus and placenta in the uterus, and they can be used to identify gross physical deformities, such as abnormal growth of the head. As shown in the photo, ultrasound can also help in detecting twins or other multiple pregnancies. Finally, beginning at about 20 weeks after conception, ultrasound images can reveal the child's sex.

When a genetic disorder is suspected, two other techniques are particularly valuable because they provide a sample of fetal cells that can be analyzed. **In amniocentesis, a needle is inserted through the mother's abdomen to obtain a sample of the amniotic fluid that surrounds the fetus.** Amniocentesis is typically performed at approximately 16 weeks after conception.

As you can see in the top diagram, ultrasound is used to guide the needle into the uterus. The fluid contains skin cells that can be grown in a laboratory dish and then analyzed to determine the genotype of the fetus.

**In chorionic villus sampling (CVS), a sample of tissue is obtained from the chorion (a part of the placenta) and analyzed.** The bottom diagram shows that a small tube, inserted through the vagina and into the uterus, is used to collect a small plug of cells from the placenta. CVS is often preferred over amniocentesis because it can be done about 10 to 12 weeks after conception, nearly 4 to 6 weeks earlier than amniocentesis. (Amniocentesis can't be performed until the amniotic sac is large enough to provide easy access to amniotic fluid.) In both procedures, results are returned from the lab within several days.

With samples obtained from either amniocentesis or CVS, about 200 different genetic disorders can be detected. For example, for pregnant women in their late 30s or 40s, either amniocentesis or CVS will often be used to determine if the fetus has Down syndrome. These procedures are virtually error-free, but they have a price: Miscarriages are slightly more likely after amniocentesis or CVS (Wilson, 2000). A woman must decide if the beneficial information gained from amniocentesis or CVS justifies the slight risk of a miscarriage. These procedures are summarized in the table at the bottom of the page.

Ultrasound, amniocentesis, and chorionic villus sampling have made it much easier to determine if prenatal development is progressing normally. But what happens when it is not? Until recently a woman's options were limited: She could continue the pregnancy or end it. But options are expanding. **A whole new field called fetal medicine is concerned with treating prenatal problems before birth.** One approach in fetal medicine is to treat disorders medically, by administering drugs or hormones to the fetus. In one case, when ultrasound pictures showed a fetus with an enlarged thyroid gland that would have made delivery difficult, a hormone was injected into the amniotic fluid to shrink the thyroid gland and allow normal delivery (Davidson et al., 1991). In another case, amniocentesis revealed that a fetus had inherited an immune system disorder that would leave the baby highly vulnerable to infections, so healthy immune cells were injected into the umbilical cord (Elmer-DeWitt, 1994).

Another way to correct prenatal problems is fetal surgery. For example, more than 200 cases of spina bifida have been corrected with fetal surgery in the seventh or eighth month of pregnancy. Surgeons cut through the mother's abdominal wall to expose the fetus, then cut through the fetal abdominal wall; the spinal cord is repaired, and the fetus is returned to the uterus (Okie, 2000).

Fetal surgery has also been used to treat a disorder affecting identical twins in which one twin—the "donor"—pumps blood through its own and the other twin's

FIG. 4–7

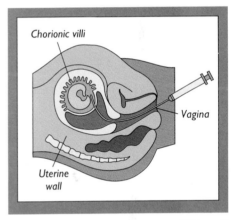

FIG. 4–8

**SUMMARY TABLE**

## METHODS OF PRENATAL DIAGNOSIS

| Procedure | Description | Primary Uses |
|---|---|---|
| Ultrasound | Sound waves used to generate an image of the fetus | Determine due date and position of fetus in uterus; check for physical deformities, multiple births, and child's sex |
| Amniocentesis | Sample of fetal cells are obtained from amniotic fluid | Screen for genetic disorders |
| Chorionic villus sampling (CVS) | Sample of tissue obtained from the chorion (part of the placenta) | Screen for genetic disorders |

circulatory system. The donor twin usually fails to grow; surgery corrects the problem by sealing off the unnecessary blood vessels between the twins (McCormick, 2000). Fetal surgery holds great promise, but it is still highly experimental and therefore considered as a last resort.

> The emerging field of fetal medicine treats prenatal problems medically, with surgery, or with genetic engineering.

**Yet another approach to treating prenatal problems is genetic engineering—replacing defective genes with synthetic normal genes.** Take PKU as an example. Remember, from Module 3.2, that if a baby inherits the recessive allele for PKU from both parents, toxins accumulate that cause mental retardation. In theory, it should be possible to take a sample of cells from the fetus, remove the recessive genes from the 12th pair of chromosomes, and replace them with the dominant genes. These "repaired" cells could then be injected into the fetus, where they would multiply and cause enough enzyme to be produced to break down phenylalanine, thereby avoiding PKU (Verma, 1990).

As with fetal surgery, however, translating idea into practice has been difficult, and there are many problems yet to be solved (Marshall, 1995). Nevertheless, gene therapy has been successful in a few cases.

Fetal medicine may sound like science fiction, but these techniques have been used with humans. Granted, they are highly experimental and failures occur, but prenatal treatment should progress rapidly in the 21st century.

*Answers to Chloe's questions:* Return to Chloe's questions in the module-opening vignette (page 82) and answer them for her. If you're not certain, I'll help by giving you the pages in this module where the answers appear:

- Question about her computer monitor—page 87
- Question about her nightly glass of wine—page 87
- Question about giving birth to a baby with mental retardation—page 85

### CHECK YOUR LEARNING

1. Important general risk factors in pregnancy include a woman's nutrition, _____, and her age.

2. Adolescent girls can have problem-free pregnancies and give birth to healthy babies if _____.

3. When it comes to drugs, the best advice for a pregnant woman is _____.

4. Some of the most dangerous teratogens are _____ because a pregnant woman is often unaware of their presence.

5. During the period of the zygote, exposure to a teratogen typically _____.

6. Cases of women who took DES during pregnancy show that _____.

7. Two techniques used to determine if a fetus has a hereditary disorder are amniocentesis and _____.

8. In fetal medicine, health care professionals treat problems of prenatal development with drugs and hormones, surgery, and _____.

**NATURE AND NURTURE**
Describe how the impact of teratogens on the fetus shows nature and nurture in action during prenatal development.

**Answers:** (1) prolonged stress, (2) they receive adequate prenatal care, (3) to avoid all drugs, including aspirin, caffeine, and nicotine, (4) environmental hazards, (5) results in miscarriage (spontaneous abortion of the fertilized egg), (6) the damage from some teratogens is not evident until later in life, (7) chorionic villus sampling (CVS), (8) genetic engineering.

# Happy Birthday!

# 4.3

## LEARNING OBJECTIVES

- What are the stages in labor and delivery?

- What are "natural" ways of coping with the pain of childbirth? Is childbirth at home safe?

- What are the effects of postpartum depression?

- What are some complications that can occur during birth?

Labor and Delivery

Approaches to Childbirth

Adjusting to Parenthood

Birth Complications

> *Marlena is about to begin classes to prepare for her baby's birth. She is relieved that the classes are finally starting because this means the end of pregnancy is in sight. But all the talk she has heard about "breathing exercises" and "coaching" sounds pretty silly to her. Marlena would prefer to get knocked out for the delivery and wake up when everything is over.*

As women like Marlena near the end of pregnancy, they find that sleeping and breathing become more difficult, they tire more rapidly, they become constipated, and their legs and feet swell. Women look forward to birth, both to relieve their discomfort and, of course, to see their baby. In this module, we'll see the different stages involved in birth, review various approaches to childbirth, and look at problems that can arise. We'll also look at childbirth classes like the one Marlena is taking.

## Labor and Delivery

In a typical pregnancy, a woman goes into labor about 38 weeks after conception. The timing of labor depends on the flow of hormonal signals between the placenta and the brain and adrenal glands of the fetus. When estrogen and other hormones reach critical levels, the muscles in the uterus begin to contract, the first sign of labor (Smith, 1999).

*Labor* is named appropriately, for it is the most intense, prolonged physical effort that humans experience. Labor is usually divided into

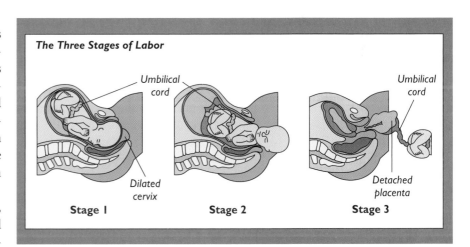

*The Three Stages of Labor*

Umbilical cord

Dilated cervix

**Stage 1**

Umbilical cord

**Stage 2**

Umbilical cord

Detached placenta

**Stage 3**

FIG. 4–9

the three stages shown in the diagram. The first stage begins when the muscles of the uterus start to contract. These contractions force amniotic fluid up against the cervix, the opening at the bottom of the uterus that is the entryway to the birth canal. The wavelike motion of the amniotic fluid with each contraction causes the cervix to enlarge gradually.

In the early phase of Stage 1, the contractions are weak and spaced irregularly. By the end of the early phase, the cervix is about 5 centimeters (2 inches) in diameter. In the late phase of Stage 1, contractions are stronger and occur at regular intervals. By the end of the late phase, the cervix is about 7 to 8 centimeters (3 inches) in diameter. In the transition phase of Stage 1, contractions are intense and sometimes occur without interruption. Women report that the transition phase is the most painful part of labor. At the end of transition, the cervix is about 10 centimeters (4 inches) in diameter.

Stage 1 lasts from 12 to 24 hours for the birth of a first child, and most of the time is spent in the relative tranquility of the early phase. Stage 1 is usually shorter for subsequent births, with 3 to 8 hours being common. However, as the wide ranges suggest, these times are only rough approximations; the actual times vary greatly among women and are virtually impossible to predict.

When the cervix is fully enlarged, the second stage of labor begins. Most women feel a strong urge to push the baby out, using their abdominal muscles. This pushing, along with uterine contractions, propels the baby down the birth canal. **Soon the top of the baby's head appears, an event known as crowning.** In about an hour for first births and less for later births, the baby passes through the birth canal and emerges from the mother's body. **Most babies arrive head first, but a small percentage come out feet or bottom first, which is known as a breech presentation.** (I was one of these rare bottom-first babies and have been the butt of bad jokes ever since.) The baby's birth marks the end of the second stage of labor.

With the baby born, you might think that labor is over, but it's not. There is a third stage, in which the placenta (also called, appropriately, the *afterbirth*) is expelled from the uterus. The placenta becomes detached from the wall of the uterus and contractions force it out through the birth canal. This stage is quite brief, typically lasting 10 to 15 minutes.

You can see the growing intensity of labor in this typical account. For Beth, a 27-year-old pregnant for the first time, the early phase of Stage 1 labor lasted $8\frac{1}{2}$ hours. For the first 4 hours, Beth averaged one 30-second contraction every 20 minutes. Then the contractions became longer—lasting 45 seconds. They came about every 15 minutes for 3 hours, and then every 8 to 10 minutes for another $11\frac{1}{2}$ hours. At this point, Beth's cervix was 5 centimeters in diameter—the early phase was over.

The late phase of Stage 1 lasted 3 hours. For 2 hours Beth had one 60-second contraction every 5 minutes. Then for 1 hour she had a 75-second contraction every 3 minutes. At this point, her cervix was 8 centimeters in diameter and she entered the transition phase. For the next 30 minutes she had a 90-second contraction every 2 minutes. Finally, her cervix was a full 10 centimeters and she could push. Thirty minutes later, David was born.

The stages of labor are summarized in the table.

**SUMMARY TABLE**

**STAGES OF LABOR**

| Stage | Duration | Primary Milestone |
|---|---|---|
| 1 | 12–24 hours | Cervix enlarges to 10 cm |
| 2 | 1 hour | Baby moves down the birth canal |
| 3 | 10–15 minutes | Placenta is expelled |

## Approaches to Childbirth

When my mother went into labor (with me), she was admitted to a nearby hospital, where she soon was administered a general anesthetic. My father went to a waiting room, where he and other fathers-to-be anxiously awaited news of their babies.

Some time later my mother recovered from anesthesia and learned that she had given birth to a healthy baby boy. My father, who had grown tired of waiting, had gone back to work, so he got the good news in a phone call.

These were standard hospital procedures in 1950, and virtually all American babies were born this way. No longer. In the middle of the 20th century, two European physicians—Grantly Dick-Read (1959) and Ferdinand Lamaze (1958)—criticized the traditional view in which labor and delivery had come to involve elaborate medical procedures that were often unnecessary and that often left women afraid of giving birth. Their fear led them to be tense, thereby increasing the pain they experienced during labor. These physicians argued for a more "natural" or prepared approach to childbirth, viewing labor and delivery as life events to be celebrated, rather than medical procedures to be endured.

> Prepared childbirth emphasizes education, relaxation, and the presence of a supportive coach.

Today many varieties of prepared childbirth are available to pregnant women. However, most share some fundamental beliefs. One is that birth is more likely to be problem-free and rewarding when mothers and fathers understand what's happening during pregnancy, labor, and delivery. Consequently, prepared childbirth means going to classes to learn basic facts about pregnancy and childbirth (like the material presented in this chapter).

A second common element is that natural methods of dealing with pain are emphasized over medication. Why? When a woman is anesthetized either with general anesthesia or regional anesthesia (in which only the lower body is numbed), she can't use her abdominal muscles to help push the baby through the birth canal. Without this pushing, the obstetrician may have to use mechanical devices to pull the baby through the birth canal, which involves some risk to the baby (Johanson et al., 1993). Also, drugs that reduce the pain of childbirth cross the placenta and can affect the baby. Consequently, when a woman receives large doses of pain-relieving medication, her baby is often withdrawn or irritable for days or even weeks (Brazelton, Nugent, & Lester, 1987; Ransjoe-Arvidson et al., 2001). These effects are temporary, but they may give the new mother the impression that she has a difficult baby. It is best, therefore, to minimize the use of pain-relieving drugs during birth.

Relaxation is the key to reducing birth pain without drugs. Because pain often feels greater when a person is tense, pregnant women learn to relax during labor, through deep breathing or by visualizing a reassuring, pleasant scene or experience. Whenever they begin to experience pain during labor, they use these methods to relax.

A third common element of prepared childbirth is to involve a supportive "coach." The father-to-be, a relative, or close friend attends childbirth classes with the mother-to-be. The coach learns the techniques for coping with pain and, like the man in the photo, practices them with the pregnant woman. During labor and delivery, the coach is present to help the woman use the techniques she has learned and to offer support and encouragement. **Sometimes the coach is accompanied by a doula, a person familiar with childbirth who is not part of the medical staff but instead provides emotional and physical support throughout labor and delivery.**

Although Marlena, the pregnant woman in our opening vignette, may have her doubts about prepared childbirth classes, they are beneficial. For example, prepared childbirth reduces the amount of drugs used to cope with the pain of labor. And mothers and fathers who attend childbirth classes feel more positive about labor and birth compared to mothers and fathers who do not attend classes (Hetherington, 1990).

Another basic premise of the trend toward natural childbirth is that birth need not always take place in a hospital. Nearly all babies in the United States are born in hospitals; only 1 percent are born at home (Curtain & Park, 1999). However, home birth is a common practice in some European countries. In the Netherlands, for example, about one-third of all births take place at home (Wiegers, Zee, & Keirse, 1998). Advocates note that home delivery is less expensive and that most women are more relaxed during labor in their homes. Many women also enjoy the greater control they have over labor and birth in a home delivery. A health care professional is present for home labor and delivery. Sometimes this is a doctor, but more often it is a trained nurse-midwife like the one in the photo.

For Americans accustomed to hospital delivery, home delivery can seem like a risky proposition. Is it safe? Yes, but with a very important catch. Birth problems are no more common in babies delivered at home than in babies delivered in a hospital if the woman is healthy, her pregnancy has been problem-free, the labor and delivery are expected to be problem-free, and a trained health care professional is there to assist (Olsen, 1997). If there is any reason to believe that problems requiring medical assistance might occur, labor and delivery should take place in the hospital, rather than at home.

Another alternative to home or hospital birth is the freestanding birth center. Birthing centers are typically small, independent clinics. A woman, her coach, and other family members and friends are assigned a birthing room that is often decorated to look homelike rather than institutional. A doctor or nurse-midwife assists in labor and delivery, which takes place entirely in the birthing room, where it can be observed by all. Like home deliveries, birthing centers are best for deliveries that are expected to be trouble-free.

## Adjusting to Parenthood

For parents, the time immediately after a trouble-free birth is full of excitement, pride, and joy—the much anticipated baby is finally here! But it is also a time of adjustments for parents. (And for siblings, as we'll see in Module 15.2). A woman experiences many physical changes after birth. Her breasts begin to produce milk and her uterus gradually becomes smaller, returning to its normal size in 5 or 6 weeks. And levels of female hormones (e.g., estrogen) drop.

*Mothers must adjust physically and psychologically to their newborn; some mothers experience postpartum depression, in which they are constantly irritable and apathetic.*

Parents must also adjust psychologically. They reorganize old routines, particularly for first-born children, to fit the young baby's sleep-wake cycle (which is described in Module 4.4). In the process, fathers sometimes feel left out when mothers devote most of their attention to the baby.

Researchers once believed that an important part of parents' adjustment involved forming an emotional bond to the infant. That is, the first few days of life were thought to be a critical period for close physical contact between parents and babies; without such contact, parents and babies would find it difficult to bond emotionally (Klaus & Kennell, 1976). Today, however, we know that such contact in the first few days after birth—although beneficial for babies and pleasurable for babies and parents alike—is not essential for normal development (Eyer, 1992). In Module 11.3, we'll learn what steps are essential to forge these emotional bonds.

Becoming a parent can be a huge adjustment, so it's not surprising that rough-ly half of all new mothers find that their initial excitement gives way to irritation, re-sentment, and crying spells. These feelings usually last a week or two and probably reflect both the stress of caring for a new baby and the physiological changes that take place as a woman's body returns to a nonpregnant state (Brockington, 1996).

**For 10 to 15 percent of new mothers, however, irritability continues for months and is often accompanied by feelings of low self-worth, disturbed sleep, poor appetite, and apathy—a condition known as postpartum depres-sion.** Postpartum depression does not strike randomly. Biology contributes: Par-ticularly high levels of hormones during the later phases of pregnancy place women at risk for postpartum depression (Harris et al., 1994). Experience also contributes: Women are more likely to experience postpartum depression when they were depressed before pregnancy, are coping with other life stresses (e.g., death of a loved one or moving to a new residence), did not plan to become preg-nant, and lack other adults (e.g., the father) to support their adjustment to moth-erhood (Brockington, 1996; Campbell et al., 1992).

Women who are lethargic and emotionless do not mother warmly and enthu-siastically. They don't touch and cuddle their new babies much or talk to them. If the depression lasts only a few weeks, babies are unaffected. However, if postpartum de-pression lasts for months and months, children of depressed mothers are more like-ly to become depressed themselves and are also at risk for other behavior problems (e.g., Brennan et al., 2000; Murray, Fiori-Cowley, & Hooper, 1996).

All new mothers need support from family and friends, but if depression doesn't lift after a few weeks, the mother should see a mental health professional.

## Birth Complications

Women who are healthy when they become pregnant usually have a normal preg-nancy, labor, and delivery. When women are not healthy or don't receive adequate prenatal care, problems can surface during labor and delivery. (Of course, even healthy women can have problems, but not as often.) The more common birth com-plications are listed in the table.

| Common Birth Complications | |
| --- | --- |
| **Complication** | **Features** |
| Cephalopelvic disproportion | The infant's head is larger than the pelvis, making it impossible for the baby to pass through the birth canal. |
| Irregular position | In shoulder presentation, the baby is lying crosswise in the uterus and the shoulder appears first; in breech presentation, the buttocks appear first. |
| Preeclampsia | A pregnant woman has high blood pressure, protein in her urine, and swelling in her extremities (due to fluid retention). |
| Prolapsed umbilical cord | The umbilical cord precedes the baby through the birth canal and is squeezed shut, cutting off oxygen to the baby. |

TABLE 4–4

Some of these complications, such as a prolapsed umbilical cord, are danger-ous because they can disrupt the flow of blood through the umbilical cord. **If this flow of blood is disrupted, infants do not receive adequate oxygen, a condition known as hypoxia.** Hypoxia sometimes occurs during labor and delivery because the umbilical cord is pinched or squeezed shut, cutting off the flow of blood. Hypoxia is very serious because it can lead to mental retardation or death (Petrie, 1991).

To guard against hypoxia, fetal heart rate is monitored during labor, either by ultrasound or with a tiny electrode that is passed through the vagina and attached to the scalp of the fetus. An abrupt change in heart rate can be a sign that the fetus is not receiving enough oxygen. If the heart rate does change suddenly, a health care professional will try to confirm that the fetus is in distress, perhaps by measuring fetal heart rate with a stethoscope on the mother's abdomen.

When a fetus is in distress or when the fetus is in an irregular position or is too large to pass through the birth canal, a physician may decide to remove it from the mother's uterus surgically (Guillemin, 1993). **In a cesarean section (or C-section) an incision is made in the abdomen to remove the baby from the uterus.** A C-section is riskier for mothers than a vaginal delivery because of increased bleeding and greater danger of infection. A C-section poses little risk for babies, although they are often briefly depressed from the anesthesia that the mother receives before the operation. And mother–infant interactions are much the same for babies delivered vaginally or by planned or unplanned C-sections (Durik, Hyde, & Clark, 2000).

Birth complications not only are hazardous for a newborn's health, but also have long-term effects. When babies experience many birth complications, they are at risk for becoming aggressive or violent and for developing schizophrenia (e.g., Cannon et al., 2000; Kandel & Mednick, 1991). This is particularly true for newborns with birth complications who later experience family adversity, such as living in poverty (Arseneault et al., 2002). These outcomes underscore the importance of excellent health care through pregnancy and labor and the need for a supportive environment throughout childhood.

PREMATURITY AND LOW BIRTH WEIGHT.    Normally, gestation takes 38 weeks from conception to birth. **Premature infants are born less than 38 weeks after conception. Small-for-date infants are substantially smaller than would be expected based on the length of time since conception.** Sometimes these two complications coincide, but not necessarily. Some, but not all, small-for-date infants are premature. And some, but not all, premature infants are small-for-date. In other words, an infant can go the full 9-month term and be under the average 7- to 8-pound birth weight of newborns; the child is therefore small-for-date but not premature. Similarly, an infant born at 7 months that weighs 3 pounds (the average weight of a 7-month fetus) is only premature. But if the baby born after 7 months weighs less than the average, it is both premature and small-for-date.

Of the two complications, prematurity is the less serious. In the first year or so, premature infants often lag behind full-term infants in many facets of development, but by age 2 or 3 years, differences vanish and most premature infants develop normally thereafter (Greenberg & Crnic, 1988).

Prospects are usually not so optimistic for small-for-date babies like the one shown in the photo. These infants are most often born to women who smoke or drink alcohol frequently during pregnancy or who do not eat enough nutritious food (Chomitz, Cheung, & Lieberman, 1995). Babies that weigh less than 1,500 grams (3.3 pounds) at birth often do not survive; when they do, they are usually delayed in their cognitive and motor development. For example, in one study

(Taylor et al., 2000), low birth weight babies as 11-year-olds were more likely to have low IQ, to be receiving special education, to have repeated a grade in school, and to have behavioral problems.

Small-for-date babies who weigh more than 1,500 grams have better prospects if they receive appropriate care. Like the infant in the photo on page 100, small-for-date babies are placed in special, sealed beds where temperature and air quality are regulated carefully. These beds effectively isolate infants, depriving them from environmental stimulation. You might think that stimulation is the last thing that these fragile creatures need, but, in fact, sensory stimulation helps small-for-date babies to develop. Consequently, they often receive auditory stimulation, such as a tape recording of soothing music or their mother's voice, or visual stimulation provided from a mobile placed over the bed. Infants also receive tactile stimulation — they are "massaged" several times daily. These forms of stimulation foster physical and cognitive development in small-for-date babies (Field, 2002; Marshall-Baker, Lickliter, & Cooper, 1998).

This special care should continue when infants leave the hospital for home. Consequently, intervention programs for small-for-date babies typically include training programs designed for infants' parents. In these programs, parents learn how to respond appropriately to their infant's behaviors. For example, they are taught the signs that a baby is in distress, overstimulated, or ready to interact, along with appropriate responses to these signs. This sensitive care promotes development in small-for-date babies; for example, sometimes they catch up to full-term infants in terms of cognitive development (Achenbach et al., 1990).

Long-term positive outcomes for these infants depends critically on providing a supportive and stimulating home environment. Unfortunately, not all at-risk babies have these optimal experiences. Many experience stress or disorder in their family life. In these cases, development is usually delayed. The importance of a supportive environment for at-risk babies was demonstrated dramatically in a longitudinal study of all children born in 1955 on the Hawaiian island of Kauai (Werner, 1995). At-risk newborns who grew up in stable homes were indistinguishable from children born without birth complications. ("Stable family environment" was defined as two supportive, mentally healthy parents present throughout childhood.) When at-risk newborns had an unstable family environment because of divorce, parental alcoholism, or mental illness, for example, they lagged behind their peers in intellectual and social development.

> Premature babies often develop normally, but small-for-date babies usually do not.

The Hawaiian study underscores a point I have made several times in this chapter: Development is best when pregnant women receive good prenatal care and children live in a supportive environment. The "Cultural Influences" feature makes the same point in a different way, by looking at infant mortality around the world.

## CULTURAL INFLUENCES

### Infant Mortality

In many respects, medical facilities in the United States are the finest in the world. Why, then, do American babies fare so poorly compared to infants from other countries? **Infant mortality is the number of infants out of 1,000 births who die before their first birthday.** In the United States, about 9 babies out of 1,000—roughly

1 percent—live less than a year. As you can see in the graph, the United States is near the bottom of the industrialized countries of the world (Wegman, 1994).

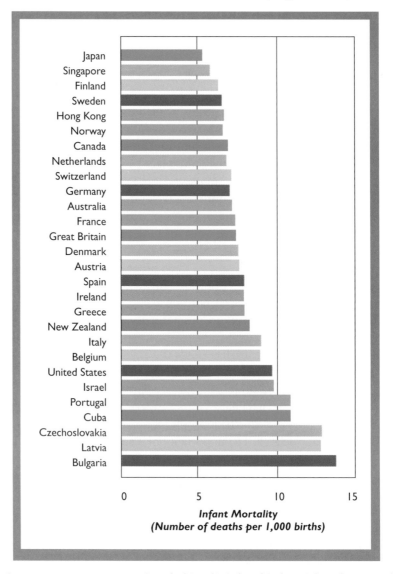

FIG. 4–10

One reason so many American babies die is low birth weight. The United States has more babies with low birth weight than virtually all other industrialized countries, and we've already seen that low birth weight places an infant at risk. Low birth weight can usually be prevented if a pregnant woman gets regular prenatal care, but many pregnant women in the United States receive inadequate or no prenatal care. Virtually all the countries that rank ahead of the United States provide complete prenatal care at little or no cost. Many of these countries also provide for paid leaves of absence for pregnant women (Kamerman, 1993).

Prenatal development is the foundation of all development, and only with regular prenatal checkups can we know if this foundation is being laid properly. Pregnant women and the children they carry need this care, and countries need to be sure that they receive it.

## CHECK YOUR LEARNING

**I.** The first (and longest) stage of labor includes early, late, and _____ phases.

**2.** The highlight of the third stage of labor is that _____.

3. Two problems with using anesthesia during labor are that a woman can't use her abdominal muscles to help push the baby down the birth canal and _____.

4. To help women cope with labor pain without drugs, childbirth classes emphasize the importance of relaxation, education, and _____.

5. Home delivery is safe when a pregnant woman is healthy, has had a problem-free pregnancy, expects to have a problem-free delivery, and _____.

6. After giving birth, women who suffer _____ often feel irritable, have poor appetite and disturbed sleep, and are apathetic.

7. When the fetus is in distress, is in an irregular position, or is too large, physicians will _____.

8. High infant mortality rates in the United States reflect low birth weight, which has been linked to _____.

**CONTINUITY**
Do studies on the long-term effects of prematurity and low birth weight provide evidence for continuity in development or discontinuity in development? Why?

**Answers:** (1) transition, (2) the placenta is expelled, (3) medication crosses the placenta and affects the baby, (4) a supportive coach, (5) a trained health care professional is present to deliver the baby, (6) postpartum depression, (7) perform a C-section, in which the fetus is removed surgically, (8) inadequate prenatal care

# The Newborn

# 4.4

## LEARNING OBJECTIVES

- How do we determine if a baby is healthy and adjusting to life outside the uterus?

- How do reflexes help newborns interact with the world?

- What behavioral states are observable in newborns?

- How well do newborns experience the world? Can they learn from experience?

Assessing the Newborn

The Newborn's Reflexes

Newborn States

Perception and Learning in the Newborn

*Lisa and Steve, the proud but exhausted parents, were astonished at how their lives revolved around 10-day-old Dan's eating and sleeping. Lisa felt as if she were feeding Dan around the clock. When Dan napped, Lisa would think of many things she should do but usually napped herself because she was so tired. Steve wondered when Dan would start sleeping through the night so that he and Lisa could get a good night's sleep themselves.*

The newborn baby that thrills parents like Lisa and Steve is actually rather homely, as this photo of my son Ben shows. I took it when he was 20 seconds old. Like other newborns, Ben is covered with blood and vernix, the white-colored "grease" that protects the fetus's skin during the many months of prenatal development. His head is temporarily distorted from coming through the birth canal, he has a beer belly, and he is bow-legged. Still, to us he was beautiful, and we were glad he'd finally arrived.

What can newborns like Dan and Ben do? We'll answer that question in this module and, as we do, learn when Lisa and Steve can expect to resume a full night's sleep.

## Assessing the Newborn

Imagine that a mother has just asked you if her newborn baby is healthy. How would you decide? **The Apgar score, a measure devised by Virginia Apgar, is used to evaluate the newborn baby's condition.** Health professionals look for five vital signs including breathing, heartbeat, muscle tone, presence of reflexes (e.g., coughing), and skin tone. As you can see in the table, each of the five vital signs receives a score of 0, 1, or 2, with 2 being optimal.

| **Five Signs Evaluated in the Apgar Score** | | | | | |
|---|---|---|---|---|---|
| Points | Activity (muscle tone) | Pulse | Grimace (response to irritating stimulus) | Appearance (skin color) | Respiration |
| 2 | Baby moves limbs actively | 100 beats per minute or more | Baby cries intensely | Normal color all over | Strong breathing and crying |
| 1 | Baby moves limbs slightly | Fewer than 100 beats per minute | Baby grimaces or cries | Normal color except for extremities | Slow, irregular breathing |
| 0 | No movement; muscles flaccid | Not detectable | Baby does not respond | Baby is blue-gray, pale all over | No breathing |

TABLE 4–5

The five scores are added together, with a score of 7 or more indicating a baby in good physical condition. A score of 4 to 6 means the newborn will need special attention and care. A score of 3 or less signals a life-threatening situation that requires emergency medical care (Apgar, 1953).

The Apgar score provides a quick, approximate assessment of the newborn's status by focusing on the body systems needed to sustain life. For a comprehensive evaluation of the newborn's well-being, pediatricians and child development specialists use the Neonatal Behavioral Assessment Scale, or NBAS (Brazelton, 1984). The NBAS evaluates a broad range of newborn abilities and behaviors that the infant needs to adjust to life outside the uterus. It measures reflexes, hearing, vision, alertness, irritability, and consolability (how easily the infant is soothed). The NBAS, along with a thorough physical examination, is particularly helpful in diagnosing disorders of the central nervous system (Brazelton et al., 1987).

> The Apgar score provides a quick assessment of a newborn's physical health.

## The Newborn's Reflexes

VIDEO 4.2
Reflexes

Most newborns are well prepared to begin interacting with their world. **The newborn is endowed with a rich set of reflexes, unlearned responses that are triggered by a specific form of stimulation.** The chart at the top of page 105 shows the many reflexes commonly found in newborn babies.

Some reflexes pave the way for newborns to get the nutrients they need to grow: Rooting and sucking ensure that the newborn is well prepared to begin a new diet of life-sustaining milk. Other reflexes protect the newborn from danger in the environment. The blink and withdrawal reflexes, for example, help newborns avoid unpleasant stimulation.

## Some Major Reflexes Found in Newborns

| Name | Response | Significance |
| --- | --- | --- |
| Babinski | A baby's toes fan out when the sole of the foot is stroked from heel to toe | Unknown |
| Blink | A baby's eyes close in response to bright light or loud noise | Protects the eyes |
| Moro | A baby throws its arms out and then inward (as if embracing) in response to loud noise or when its head falls | May help a baby cling to its mother |
| Palmar | A baby grasps an object placed in the palm of its hand | Precursor to voluntary walking |
| Rooting | When a baby's cheek is stroked, it turns its head toward the stroking and opens its mouth | Helps a baby find the nipple |
| Stepping | A baby who is held upright by an adult and is then moved forward begins to step rhythmically | Precursor to voluntary walking |
| Sucking | A baby sucks when an object is placed in its mouth | Permits feeding |
| Withdrawal | A baby withdraws its foot when the sole is pricked with a pin | Protects a baby from unpleasant stimulation |

TABLE 4–6

Yet other reflexes serve as the foundation for larger, voluntary patterns of motor activity. For example, the stepping reflex looks like a precursor to walking. In fact, we'll see in Module 6.3 that babies who practice the stepping reflex learn to walk earlier (Zelazo, 1983).

Reflexes indicate whether the newborn's nervous system is working properly. For example, infants with damage to their sciatic nerve, which is found in the spinal cord, do not show the withdrawal reflex; and infants who have problems with the lower part of the spine do not show the Babinski reflex. If these or other reflexes are weak or missing altogether, a thorough physical and behavioral assessment is called for.

## Newborn States

Newborns spend most of their day alternating among four states (St James-Roberts & Plewis, 1996; Wolff, 1987):

• *Alert inactivity.* The baby is calm with eyes open and attentive; the baby looks as if he is deliberately inspecting his environment.

• *Waking activity.* The baby's eyes are open, but they seem unfocused; the baby moves her arms or legs in bursts of uncoordinated motion.

• *Crying.* The baby cries vigorously, usually accompanying this with agitated but uncoordinated motion.

• *Sleeping.* The baby's eyes are closed and the baby drifts back and forth from periods of regular breathing and stillness to periods of irregular breathing and gentle arm and leg motion.

**CRYING.** Of these states, crying captures the attention of parents and researchers alike. Newborns spend 2 to 3 hours each day crying or on the verge of crying. If you've not spent much time around newborns, you might think that all crying is pretty much alike. In fact, scientists and parents can identify three distinctive types of cries (Snow, 1998). **A basic cry starts softly, then gradually becomes more intense and usually occurs when a baby is hungry or tired; a mad cry is a more intense version of a basic cry; and a pain cry begins with a sudden, long burst of crying, followed by a long pause and gasping.**

Crying is actually the newborn's first attempt to communicate with others. When a baby like the one in the photo cries, it's telling parents that it's hungry, tired, angry, or hurt. By responding, parents encourage their newborn's efforts to communicate.

Parents are naturally concerned when their baby cries, and if they can't quiet a crying baby, their concern mounts and can easily give way to frustration and annoyance. It's no surprise, then, that parents develop little tricks for soothing their babies. The "Real Children" feature shows what one mother did when her baby cried.

## REAL CHILDREN

### Calming Jake

Whenever 4-week-old Jake cried, Peggy's first reaction was to try to figure out why he was crying. Was he hungry? Was his diaper wet? Simply addressing the needs that caused Jake to cry in the first place usually worked. If he continued to cry, she found that the best way to quiet Jake was to lift him to her shoulder and rock him or walk with him. The combination of being upright, restrained, in physical contact with her, and moving all helped to calm him. Sometimes Peggy would swaddle Jake—wrap him tightly in a blanket—and then rock him in a cradle or take him for a ride in a stroller. Another method Peggy used sometimes was to give Jake a pacifier to suck; sucking seemed to allow Jake to calm himself. Sometimes, as a last resort, she'd strap Jake in his car seat and go for a drive. The motion of the car seemed to soothe him.

Peggy's techniques weren't foolproof. Some would work one day but not another. Sometimes Peggy combined these techniques, for example, taking a swaddled Jake to her shoulder. Sometimes nothing seemed to work, so she'd just put Jake in his crib. And sometimes, as if he were teasing Peggy, Jake would stop crying spontaneously and go right to sleep! 

**SLEEPING.** Crying may get parents' attention, but sleep is what newborns do more than anything else. They sleep 16 to 18 hours daily. The problem for tired parents—like the mom in the photo and Lisa and Steve from the vignette—is that newborns sleep in naps taken round the clock. Newborns typically go through a cycle of wakefulness and sleep about every four hours. That is, they will be awake for about an hour, sleep for three hours, then start the cycle anew. During the hour when newborns are awake, they regularly move between the different waking states several times. Cycles of alert inactivity, waking activity, and crying are common.

As babies grow older, the sleep-wake cycle gradually begins to correspond to the day-night cycle (St James-Roberts & Plewis, 1996). Most babies begin sleeping through the night at about 3 or 4 months, a major milestone for bleary-eyed parents like Lisa and Steve.

**Roughly half of newborns' sleep is irregular or rapid-eye-movement (REM) sleep, a time when the body is quite active.** During REM sleep, newborns move their arms and legs, they may grimace, and their eyes may dart beneath their eyelids. Brain waves register fast activity, the heart beats more rapidly, and breathing is more rapid. **In regular or non-REM sleep, breathing, heart rate, and brain activity are steady and newborns lie quietly without the twitching associated with REM sleep.** REM sleep becomes less frequent as infants grow. By 4 months, only 40 percent of sleep is REM sleep. By the first birthday, REM sleep drops to 25 percent, not far from the adult average of 20 percent (Halpern, MacLean, & Baumeister, 1995).

The function of REM sleep is still debated. Older children and adults dream during REM sleep, and brain waves during REM sleep resemble those of an alert, awake person. Consequently, many scientists believe that REM sleep stimulates the brain in some way that helps foster growth in the nervous system (Halpern et al., 1995; Roffwarg, Muzio, & Dement, 1966).

SUDDEN INFANT DEATH SYNDROME.   For many parents of young babies, sleep is sometimes a cause of concern. **In sudden infant death syndrome (SIDS), a healthy baby dies suddenly, for no apparent reason.** Approximately 1 to 3 of every 1,000 American babies dies from SIDS. Most of them are between 2 and 4 months old.

Scientists don't know the exact causes of SIDS, but they do know several contributing factors. Babies are more vulnerable to SIDS if they were born prematurely or with low birth weight. They are also more vulnerable if their parents smoke. SIDS is more likely when a baby sleeps on its stomach (face down) than when it sleeps on its back (face up). Finally, SIDS is more likely during winter, when babies sometimes become overheated from too many blankets and too heavy sleepwear (Carroll & Loughlin, 1994). Evidently, SIDS infants, many of whom were born prematurely or with low birth weight, are less able to withstand physiological stresses and imbalances that are brought on by cigarette smoke, breathing that is temporarily interrupted, or overheating.

> Infants are at greater risk for SIDS when they are born prematurely or with low birth weight and then are exposed to physiological stresses such as overheating.

As evidence about causes of SIDS accumulated, child advocates called for action. The result is described in the "Child Development and Family Policy" feature.

## CHILD DEVELOPMENT AND FAMILY POLICY

### Back to Sleep!

In 1992, based on mounting evidence that SIDS more often occurred when infants slept on their stomachs, the American Academy of Pediatrics (AAP) began advising parents to put babies to sleep on their backs or sides. In 1994, the AAP joined forces with the U.S. Public Health Service to launch a national program to educate parents about the dangers of SIDS and the importance of

FIG. 4–11

Perceptual systems function at birth, allowing the baby to experience the world.

putting babies to sleep on their backs. The "Back to Sleep" campaign was widely publicized through brochures, posters like the one shown here, and videos. Since the "Back to Sleep" campaign began, research shows that far more infants are now sleeping on their backs and that the incidence of SIDS has dropped (National Institutes of Health, 2000). The best advice for parents—particularly if their babies were premature or small-for-date—is to keep their babies away from smoke, to put them on their backs to sleep, and don't overdress them or wrap them too tightly in blankets (Willinger, 1995). ●

## Perception and Learning in the Newborn

Do you believe it is important to talk to newborns and give them fuzzy little toys? Should their rooms be bright and colorful? If you do, you really believe two things about newborns. First, you believe that newborns can perceive experiences—they can see, smell, hear, taste, and feel. Second, you believe that sensory experiences are somehow registered in the newborn through learning and memory, because unless experiences are registered, they can't influence later behavior. You'll be happy to know that research confirms your beliefs. All the basic perceptual systems are operating at some level at birth. The world outside the uterus can be seen, smelled, heard, tasted, and felt (Aslin, 1987). Moreover, newborns show the capacity to learn and remember. They change their behavior based on their experiences (Rovee-Collier, 1987).

We'll discuss these perceptual changes in more detail in Chapter 6, and we'll discuss learning and memory in Chapter 8. For now, the important point is that newborns are remarkably prepared to interact with the world. Adaptive reflexes coupled with perceptual and learning skills provide a solid foundation for the rest of child development.

### CHECK YOUR LEARNING

1. The _____ is based on five vital functions and provides a quick indication of a newborn's physical health.

2. Some reflexes help infants get necessary nutrients; other reflexes protect infants from danger; and still other reflexes _____.

3. A baby lying calmly with its eyes open and focused is in a state of _____.

4. Common among infants are the basic cry, the mad cry, and the _____ cry.

5. Newborns spend more time asleep than awake and about half of this time asleep is spent in _____, a time thought to foster central nervous system growth.

6. The campaign to reduce SIDS emphasizes that infants should _____.

7. The newborn's basic perceptual systems, such as vision and hearing, are _____.

**NATURE AND NURTURE**

How do the newborn's reflexes demonstrate the interaction of nature and nurture?

**Answers:** (1) Apgar score, (2) serve as the basis for later motor behavior, (3) alert inactivity, (4) pain, (5) REM sleep, (6) sleep on their backs, (7) working, allowing the newborn to perceive and experience the world

# Unifying Themes: Continuity

This chapter is a good opportunity to highlight the theme that *early development is related to later development but not perfectly*. Remember the Hawaiian study? This study showed that outcomes for at-risk infants are not uniform. When at-risk infants grow up in a stable, supportive environment, they become quite normal children. But when they grow up in stressful environments, they lag intellectually and socially. Similarly, SIDS is more likely to affect babies born prematurely and with low birth weight, yet not all of these babies die of SIDS. When premature and low-birth-weight babies sleep on their backs, are not overheated, and do not inhale smoke, they're unlikely to die from SIDS. Traumatic events early in development, such as being born early or underweight, do not predetermine the rest of a child's life, but they do make some developmental paths easier to follow than others.

## See for Yourself

Words can hardly capture the miracle of a newborn baby. If you have never seen a newborn, you need to see one, or even better, a roomful. Arrange to visit the maternity ward of a local hospital, which will include a nursery for newborns. Through a large viewing window, you will be able to observe a few or as many as 15 to 20 newborns. These babies will no longer be covered with blood or vernix, but you will be able to see how the newborn's head is often distorted by its journey from the birth canal. As you watch the babies, look for reflexive behavior and changes in states. Watch while a baby sucks its fingers. Find a baby who seems to be awake and alert, then note how long the baby stays this way. When alertness wanes, watch for the behaviors that replace it. Finally, observe how different the newborns look and act from each other. The wonderful variety and diversity found among human beings is already evident in those who are hours or days old. See for yourself!

## Resources

For more information about...

**babies**, try T. Berry Brazelton's *Infants and Mothers: Differences in Development* (Delacorte, 1994). This classic book, written by the famous pediatrician and scientist, traces the early development of three very different babies. In the process, it shows the wide range of normal patterns of development.

**prenatal development**, visit the Web site of the Multi-Dimensional Human Embryo, which has images and animations depicting the fetus at various stages of prenatal development:
**http://embryo.soad.umich.edu/**

## Key Terms

age of viability  80

amniocentesis  92

amniotic fluid  78

amniotic sac  78

Apgar score  104

basic cry  106

blastocyst  77

breech presentation  96

cerebral cortex  80

cesarean section (C-section)  100

chorionic villus sampling (CVS)  93

crowning  96

doula  97

ectoderm  77

embryo  77

endoderm  77

fetal alcohol syndrome (FAS)  86

fetal medicine  93

genetic engineering  94

germ disc  77

hypoxia  99

implantation  77

infant mortality  101

mad cry  106

mesoderm  77

non-REM (regular) sleep  107

pain cry  106

period of the fetus  79

placenta  77

postpartum depression  99

premature infants  100

prenatal development  76

rapid-eye-movement (REM) sleep (irregular sleep)  107

reflexes  104

small-for-date infants  100

spina bifida  83

stress  84

sudden infant death syndrome (SIDS)  107

teratogen  85

ultrasound  92

umbilical cord  78

villi  78

vernix  80

zygote  77

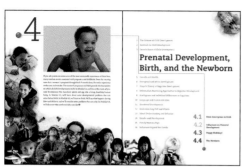

# 4.1 From Conception to Birth

**Period of the Zygote**
The first period of prenatal development lasts 2 weeks. It begins when the egg is fertilized by the sperm and ends when the fertilized egg has implanted in the wall of the uterus.

**Period of the Embryo**
The second period of prenatal development begins 2 weeks after conception and ends 8 weeks after. This is a period when most major body structures are formed.

**Period of the Fetus**
The third period of prenatal development begins 9 weeks after conception and lasts until birth. In this period, the fetus becomes much larger and body systems begin to function.

# 4.2 Influences on Prenatal Development

**General Risk Factors**
Prenatal development can be harmed if a pregnant woman does not provide adequate nutrition for the developing organism or experiences considerable stress. Teenagers often have problem pregnancies because they rarely receive adequate prenatal care. After age 35, women are less fertile and more likely to have problem pregnancies.

**Teratogens: Diseases, Drugs, and Environmental Hazards**
Teratogens are agents that can cause abnormal prenatal development. Several diseases are teratogens. Only by avoiding these diseases entirely can a pregnant woman escape their harmful consequences. Many drugs that adults take are teratogens. Environmental teratogens are particularly dangerous because a pregnant woman may not know when these substances are present.

**How Teratogens Influence Prenatal Development**
The effect of teratogens depends on the genotype of the organism, when during prenatal development the organism is exposed to the teratogen, and the amount of exposure. The impact of a teratogen may not be evident until later in life.

**Prenatal Diagnosis and Treatment**
Ultrasound uses sound waves to generate a picture of the fetus that reveals the position of the fetus, its sex, and any gross physical deformities. When genetic disorders are suspected, amniocentesis or chorionic villus sampling is used to determine the genotype of the fetus. Fetal medicine corrects problems of prenatal development medically, surgically, or through genetic engineering.

# 4.3 Happy Birthday!

**Labor and Delivery**
Labor consists of three stages. In Stage 1, the muscles of the uterus contract. The contractions, which are weak at first and gradually become stronger, cause the cervix to enlarge. In Stage 2, the baby moves through the birth canal. In Stage 3, the placenta is delivered.

**Approaches to Childbirth**
Prepared childbirth assumes that parents should understand what takes place during pregnancy and birth. In prepared childbirth, women learn to cope with pain through relaxation and the help of a supportive coach.

Although most American babies are born in hospitals, home birth is safe when the mother is healthy, the delivery is expected to be trouble-free, and a health care professional is present.

**Adjusting to Parenthood**
Following the birth of a child, a woman's body undergoes several changes: her breasts become filled with milk, her uterus becomes smaller, and hormone levels drop. Both parents also adjust psychologically and sometimes fathers feel left out. After giving birth, some women experience postpartum depression: they are irritable, have poor appetite and disturbed sleep, and are apathetic.

**Birth Complications**
During labor and delivery, the flow of blood to the fetus can be disrupted, causing hypoxia, a lack of oxygen to the fetus. If the fetus is endangered, the doctor may do a cesarean section, removing it from the uterus surgically. Babies with many birth complications are at risk for becoming aggressive and developing schizophrenia.

Premature babies develop more slowly at first but catch up in a few years. Small-for-date babies who weigh less than 1,500 grams often do not develop normally; larger small-for-date babies fare well when their environment is stimulating and stress-free.

Infant mortality is relatively high in the United States, primarily because of low birth weight and inadequate prenatal care.

# 4.4 The Newborn

**Assessing the Newborn**
The Apgar score measures five vital signs to determine a newborn's physical well-being. The Neonatal Behavioral Assessment Scale provides a comprehensive evaluation of a baby's behavioral and physical status.

**The Newborn's Reflexes**
Some reflexes help infants to adjust to life outside the uterus, some protect them, and some are the basis for later motor behavior.

**Newborn States**
Newborns spend their day in one of four states: alert inactivity, waking activity, crying, and sleeping. A newborn's crying includes a basic cry, a mad cry, and a pain cry.

Newborns spend approximately two-thirds of every day asleep and go through a complete sleep-wake cycle once every 4 hours. Newborns spend about half their time in REM sleep, characterized by active brain waves and frequent movements of the eyes and limbs. REM sleep may stimulate nervous system growth.

Some healthy babies die from sudden infant death syndrome (SIDS). Babies are vulnerable to SIDS when they are premature, have low birth weight, sleep on their stomachs, are overheated, and are exposed to cigarette smoke. Encouraging parents to have babies sleep on their backs has reduced the number of SIDS cases.

**Perception and Learning in the Newborn**
Newborns' perceptual and learning skills function reasonably well, which allows them to experience the world.

# 5

Humans take longer to become physically mature than any other animal. We spend about 20 percent of our lives—all of childhood and adolescence—growing physically. This slow journey to physical maturity is an interesting story in itself. But physical growth is just as important for its impact on other aspects of children's development, including cognition, social behavior, and personality. As children grow physically, they become less dependent on others for care, they're treated differently by adults, and they come to view themselves as older and more mature. By knowing more about children's physical growth, you'll be better prepared to understand other aspects of development that we'll study in the rest of the book.

In this chapter, we'll learn how children grow physically. In Module 5.1, we'll look at different facets of physical growth and some of the reasons why people differ in their physical growth and stature. Then, in Module 5.2, we'll explore problems that can disrupt physical growth. In Module 5.3, we'll look at physical growth that's not so obvious—the development of the brain.

# Growth and Health

**5.1**  Physical Growth

**5.2**  Challenges to Healthy Growth

**5.3**  The Developing Nervous System

# 5.1

## Physical Growth

### LEARNING OBJECTIVES

- What are the important features of physical growth during childhood? How do they vary from child to child?

- How do sleep and nutrition contribute to healthy growth?

- What are the physical changes associated with puberty, and what are their consequences?

> *Pete has just had his 15th birthday, but, as far as he is concerned, there is no reason to celebrate. Although most of his friends have grown about 6 inches in the past year or so, have a much larger penis and larger testicles, and have mounds of pubic hair, Pete looks just as he did when he was 10 years old. He is embarrassed by his appearance, particularly in the locker room, where he looks like a little boy among men. "Won't I ever change?" he wonders.*

For parents and children alike, physical growth is a topic of great interest. Parents marvel at how quickly babies add pounds and inches; 2-year-olds proudly proclaim, "I bigger now!" Many adolescents take great satisfaction in finally becoming taller than a parent; others, like Pete, suffer through their teenage years as they wait for the physical signs of maturity.

In this module, we'll examine some of the basic features of physical growth and variations in growth patterns. We'll also consider the mechanisms responsible for growth. Finally, we'll end the module with puberty—a phase of physical growth that is so special it needs to be considered separately.

## Features of Human Growth

VIDEO 5.1
Physical Growth

**Growth is particularly rapid in infancy and early adolescence.**

**DESCRIBING GROWTH.**   Probably the most obvious way to measure physical growth is in terms of sheer size—height and weight. The growth charts at the top of page 115 show the average changes in height and weight that take place as children grow from birth to age 20. Between birth and 2 years, for example, average height increases from 19 to 32 inches; average weight increases from 7 to 22 pounds. (An interesting rule of thumb is that boys achieve half their adult height by 2 years, and girls by 18 months.)

What is not so obvious in growth charts is that increases in height and weight are not steady. Looking at the average increase in weight and height annually—as opposed to the average total weight and height for each year—gives quite a different picture of the pattern of physical growth. The graphs at the bottom of page 115 show that growth is extraordinarily rapid during the first year, when the average baby gains about 10 inches and 15 pounds. Growth is fairly steady through the preschool and elementary-school years, about 3 inches and 7 to 8 pounds each year. In early adolescence, growth is rapid again. During this growth spurt, which corresponds to the peaks in the middle of the charts, teenagers typically grow 4 inches and gain 16 to 17 pounds each year. After this spurt, which begins 1 to 2 years earlier in girls, growth again slows as children reach adulthood.

FIG. 5–1

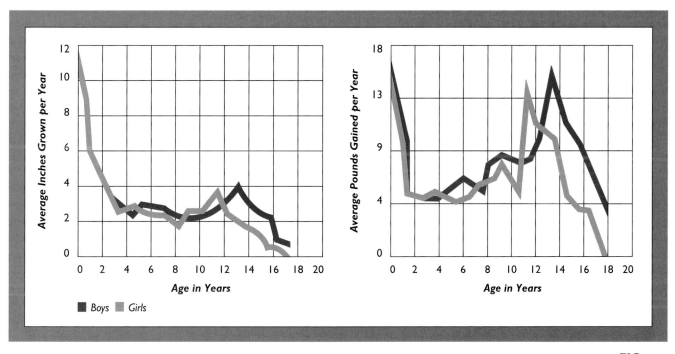

FIG. 5–2

As children grow, their body parts develop at different rates, which means that infants and young children are not simply scaled-down versions of adults. The head and trunk grow faster than the legs. As you can see in the diagram on page 116, infants and toddlers have disproportionately large heads and trunks, making them look top-heavy compared to older children and adolescents. As growth of the hips,

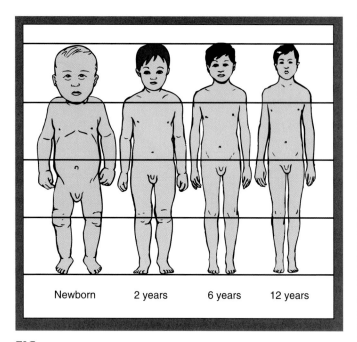

Newborn    2 years    6 years    12 years

FIG. 5-3

legs, and feet catches up later in childhood, bodies take on proportions that are more adultlike.

**MUSCLE, FAT, AND BONES.**    Other important features of physical growth take place inside the body, with the development of muscle, fat, and bones. Virtually all of the body's muscle fibers are present at birth. During childhood, muscles become longer and thicker as individual fibers fuse together. This process accelerates during adolescence, particularly for boys.

A layer of fat appears under the skin near the end of the fetal period of prenatal development; its purpose is to help the fetus and infant regulate body temperature (just as insulation in walls stabilizes the temperature inside a house). Fat continues to accumulate rapidly during the first year after birth, producing the familiar look we call *baby fat*. During the preschool years, children actually become leaner, but in the early elementary-school years they begin to acquire more fat again. This happens gradually at first, then more rapidly during adolescence. The increase in fat in adolescence is more pronounced in girls than in boys.

Bone begins to form during prenatal development. What will become bone starts as *cartilage*, a soft, flexible tissue. During the embryonic period, the center of the tissue turns to bone. **Then, shortly before birth, the ends of the cartilage structures, known as epiphyses, turn to bone.** Now the structure is hard at each end and in the center. Working from the center, cartilage turns to bone until finally the enlarging center section reaches the epiphyses, ending skeletal growth.

If you combine the changes in muscle, fat, and bone with changes in body size and shape, you have a fairly complete picture of physical growth during childhood. What's missing? The central nervous system, which we cover separately in Module 5.3.

**VARIATIONS ON THE AVERAGE PROFILE.**    Of course, the picture of children's physical growth that I have described so far is a typical profile; there are important variations on this prototype. For example, when the University of Oregon Ducks won the first NCAA men's basketball tournament in 1939, the average height of their starting lineup was 6 feet, 2 inches. When the University of Maryland Terrapins won the tournament in 2002, the average height of their starting lineup was 6 feet, 6 inches, a difference of 4 inches. Of course, the changing heights of basketball players simply correspond to changes in the U.S. population at large. Today, adults and children are taller and heavier than previous generations, due largely to improved health and nutrition. **Changes in physical development from one generation to the next are known as secular growth trends.** Secular trends have been quite large. A medieval knight's armor would fit today's 10- to 12-year-old boy; the average height of American sailors in the War of 1812 was 5 feet 2 inches!

"Average" physical growth varies not only from one generation to the next, but also from one country to another. The graph at the top of page 117 shows the average height of 8-year-old boys and girls in several countries around the world. Youngsters from the United States, Western European countries, Japan, and China are about the same height, approximately 49 inches. Children in Africa and India are shorter, averaging just under 46 inches. And 8-year-olds in Polynesia are shorter still, averaging 43 inches.

We also need to remember that "average" and "normal" are not the same. Many children are much taller or shorter than average and perfectly normal, of course. For example, among American 8-year-old boys, normal weights range from approximately 44 pounds to 76 pounds. In other words, an extremely light but normal 8-year-old boy would weigh only slightly more than half as much as his extremely heavy but normal peer. What is "normal" can vary greatly, and this applies not only to height and other aspects of physical growth, but also to all aspects of development. Whenever a "typical" or "average" age is given for a developmental milestone, you should remember that the normal range for passing the milestone is much wider. Some children pass the milestone sooner than the stated age and some later, but all are normal.

We've seen that children's heights vary within a culture, across time, and between cultures. What accounts for these differences? To answer this question, we need to look at the mechanisms that are responsible for human growth.

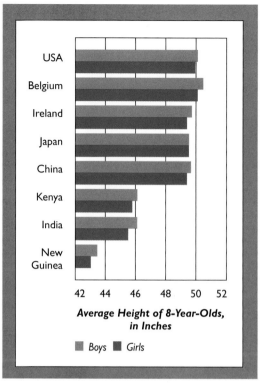

FIG. 5-4

## Mechanisms of Physical Growth

Physical growth is easily taken for granted. Compared to other milestones of child development, such as learning to read, physical growth seems to come so easily. Children, like weeds, seem to sprout without any effort at all. In reality, of course, physical growth is complicated. Of course, heredity is involved: As a general rule, two tall parents will have tall children; two short parents will have short children; and one tall parent and one short parent will have average-height offspring.

How are genetic instructions translated into actual growth? Sleep and nutrition are both involved.

**SLEEP.**   In Module 4.4, we saw that infants spend more time asleep than awake. The amount of time that children spend asleep drops gradually, from roughly 12 hours at age 3 to 10 hours at age 7 and 8 hours at age 12 (Sadeh, Raviv, & Gruber, 2000). **Sleep is essential for normal growth because about 80 percent of the hormone that stimulates growth—named, appropriately, growth hormone—is secreted while children and adolescents sleep** (Smock, 1998). Growth hormone is secreted during sleep by the pituitary gland in the brain; from the brain, growth hormone travels to the liver, where it triggers the release of another hormone, somatomedin, which causes muscles and bones to grow (Tanner, 1990).

Sleep also affects children's development in a less direct but no less important manner. Children's sleep affects their cognitive processes and their adjustment to school. When children do not sleep well—they wake frequently during the night or they do not sleep a consistent amount each night—they often are unable to pay attention in school (Sadeh, Gruber, & Raviv, 2002). And they're more likely to disregard teachers' requests, and they're often aggressive (Bates et al., 2002).

The key to avoiding sleep-related problems is a bedtime routine that helps children to "wind down" from busy daytime activities. This routine should start at about the same time every night ("It's time to get ready for bed . . .") and end at about the same time (when the parent leaves the child and the child tries to fall asleep). By following the routine consistently, children will find it easier to fall asleep and are more likely to get a restful night's sleep.

Sleep is essential because most growth hormone is secreted when children are asleep and because when children don't sleep well, they do poorly in school.

**NUTRITION.** The fuel for growth comes from the foods children eat and the liquids they drink. Nutrition is particularly important during infancy, when physical growth is so rapid. In a 2-month-old, roughly 40 percent of the body's energy is devoted to growth. Most of the remaining energy fuels basic bodily functions, such as digestion and respiration.

Because growth requires so much high energy, young babies must consume an enormous number of calories in relation to their body weight. An adult needs to consume only 15 to 20 calories per pound, depending on level of activity (National Research Council, 1989), but a 12-pound 3-month-old should eat about 50 calories per pound of body weight, or 600 calories. What's the best way for babies to receive the calories they need? The "Improving Children's Lives" feature has some answers.

## IMPROVING CHILDREN'S LIVES

### What's the Best Food for Babies?

Breast-feeding is the best way to ensure that babies get the nourishment they need. Human milk contains the proper amounts of carbohydrates, fats, protein, vitamins, and minerals for babies. Breast-feeding also has several other advantages compared to bottle-feeding (Shelov, 1993; Sullivan & Birch, 1990). First, breast-fed babies are ill less often because a mother's breast milk contains antibodies that kill bacteria and viruses. Second, breast-fed babies are less prone to diarrhea and constipation. Third, breast-fed babies typically make the transition to solid foods more easily, apparently because they are accustomed to changes in the taste of breast milk that reflect a mother's diet. Fourth, breast milk cannot be contaminated (as long as a nursing mother avoids certain drugs, such as cocaine); in contrast, contamination is often a significant problem when formula is used in developing countries to bottle-feed babies.

> When babies are breast-fed, they get proper nourishment, are ill less often, and adjust more rapidly to solid food.

The many benefits of breast-feeding do not mean that bottle-feeding is harmful. Formula, when prepared in sanitary conditions, provides generally the same nutrients as human milk, but infants are more prone to develop allergies from formula, and formula does not protect infants from disease. However, bottle-feeding does have advantages. A mother who cannot readily breast-feed can still enjoy the intimacy of feeding her baby, and other family members can participate in feeding. In fact, long-term longitudinal studies typically find that breast- and bottle-fed babies are similar in physical and psychological development (Fergusson, Horwood, & Shannon, 1987), so women in industrialized countries can choose either method and know that their babies' dietary needs will be met.

In the United States and Canada, newborns and very young babies are often breast-fed exclusively. Beginning at about 4 to 6 months, breast-feeding is supplemented by cereal and strained fruits and vegetables. Strained meats are introduced at 7 to 9 months and finely chopped table foods are introduced at 10 to 12 months (IFICF, 2000).

A good rule is to introduce only one new food at a time. A 7-month-old having cheese for the first time, for instance, should have no other new foods for a few days. In this way, allergies that may develop—manifested as skin rash or diarrhea—can be linked to a particular food, making it easier to prevent recurrences.

Preschoolers grow more slowly than infants and toddlers, so they need to eat less per pound than before. One rule of thumb is that preschoolers should consume about 40 calories per pound of body weight, which works out to be roughly 1,500 to 1,700 calories daily for many preschool children.

More important than the sheer number of calories, however, is a balanced diet that includes all five major food groups. The table shows a healthy diet that provides adequate calories and nutrients for preschool children. The servings listed in the

| Eating to Meet Preschoolers' Nutritional Needs | | |
|---|---|---|
| Group | Number of Servings | What Counts as a Serving? |
| Grains | 6 | 1 slice of bread, 1 cup of cereal |
| Vegetables | 3 | 1 cup of raw leafy vegetables, $\frac{3}{4}$ cup of vegetable juice |
| Fruits | 2 | 1 medium apple, $\frac{1}{2}$ cup of canned fruit |
| Milk | 2 | 1 cup of milk, $1\frac{1}{2}$ ounces of natural cheese |
| Meat and beans | 2 (5 ounces total) | 2 to 3 ounces of cooked lean meat, 2 tablespoons of peanut butter |

Source: USDA, 2000.

TABLE 5–1

table are definitely not a complete a list of the foods good for young children; they simply are examples of healthy choices (and quantities) for children. Many, many other foods could have been listed, too. A healthy diet doesn't mean that children must eat the same foods over and over again.

A healthy diet not only draws on all five food groups, but also avoids too much sugar and, especially, too much fat. For preschool children, no more than approximately 30 percent of the daily caloric intake should come from fat, which works out to be roughly 500 calories from fat. Unfortunately, too many preschool children like the ones in the photo become hooked on fast-food meals, which are notoriously high in fat. A Whopper®, fries, and shake have nearly 600 calories from fat, 100 more than children should consume all day! Excessive fat intake is the first step toward obesity (which I'll discuss later in this chapter), so parents need to limit their preschool children's fat intake (Whitaker et al., 1997).

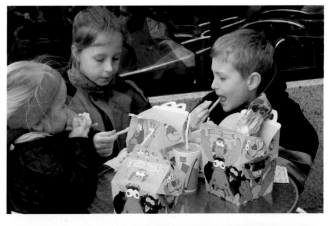

Encouraging preschool children to eat healthy foods is tough for parents because some preschoolers become notoriously picky eaters. Like the little girl in the photo, toddlers and preschool children find foods that they once ate willingly "yucky." As a toddler, my daughter loved green beans. When she reached 2, she decided that green beans were awful and refused to eat them. Though such finickiness can be annoying, it may actually be adaptive for increasingly independent preschoolers. Because preschoolers don't know what is safe to eat and what isn't, eating only familiar foods protects them from potential harm (Birch & Fisher, 1995).

Parents should not be overly concerned about this finicky period. Although some children do eat less than before (in terms of calories per pound), virtually all picky eaters get adequate food for growth. Nevertheless, picky-eating children can make mealtime miserable for all. What's a parent to do? Experts (Leach, 1991; American Academy of Pediatrics, 1992) recommend several guidelines for encouraging children to be more open-minded about foods and for dealing with them when they aren't:

- When possible, allow children to pick among different healthy foods (e.g., milk versus yogurt).
- Allow children to eat foods in any order they want.
- Offer children new foods one at a time and in small amounts; encourage but don't force children to eat new foods.
- Don't force children to "clean their plates."
- Don't spend mealtimes talking about what the child is or is not eating; instead, talk about other topics that interest the child.
- Never use food to reward or punish children.

By following these guidelines, mealtimes can be pleasant and children can receive the nutrition they need to grow.

> Children and adolescents need a well balanced diet that represents each of the five primary food groups.

As children enter elementary school, they need to eat more to support growth and to provide energy for their active lives. Although preschool children need only consume about 1,500 to 1,700 calories per day, the average 7- to 10-year-old needs about 2,400 calories each day. During adolescence, a typical girl should consume about 2,200 calories per day; a typical boy should consume about 2,700 calories. Of course, the exact levels depend on a number of factors, including body composition, growth rate, and activity level.

School-age children and adolescents also need a well-balanced diet. They should eat regularly from each of the five food groups shown in the table on page 119, but with larger servings. Teenagers also need calcium for growth and iron to make extra hemoglobin, the matter in red blood cells that carries oxygen. Boys need additional hemoglobin because of their increased muscle mass; girls need hemoglobin to replace that lost during menstruation. Unfortunately, children and adolescents too often consume calories from sweet foods and beverages, which are "empty"—they have very little nutritional value; this can lead to obesity, as we'll see in Module 5.2.

## The Adolescent Growth Spurt and Puberty

**For many child-development researchers, adolescence begins officially with puberty, which refers to the adolescent growth spurt and sexual maturation.** The adolescent growth spurt is easy to see in the graphs on page 115. Physical growth is slow during the elementary-school years: In an average year, a 6- to 10-year-old girl or boy gains about 5 to 7 pounds and grows 2 to 3 inches. But during the peak of the adolescent growth spurt, a girl may gain as many as 20 pounds in a year and a boy, 25 (Tanner, 1970). This growth spurt lasts a few years.

The figure on page 115 also shows that girls typically begin their growth spurt about 2 years before boys do. That is, girls typically start the growth spurt at about age 11, reach their peak rate of growth at about 12, and achieve their mature stature at about age 15. In contrast, boys start the growth spurt at 13, hit peak growth at 14, and reach mature stature at 17. This 2-year difference in the growth spurt can lead to awkward social interactions between 11- and 12-year-old boys and girls because during those years, as the photo shows, girls are often taller and much more mature-looking than boys.

During the growth spurt, bones become longer (which, of course, is why adolescents grow taller) and become more dense. Bone growth is accompanied by several other changes that differ for boys and girls. Muscle fibers become thicker and denser during adolescence, producing substantial increases in strength. However, muscle growth is much more pronounced in boys than in girls (Smoll & Schutz, 1990). Body fat also increases during adolescence, but much more rapidly in girls than boys. Finally, heart and lung capacities increase more in adolescent boys than in adolescent girls. Together, these changes help to explain why the typical adolescent boy has more strength, is quicker, and has greater endurance than the typical adolescent girl.

In the "Child Development and Family Policy" feature, you'll see how healthy bone growth in adolescence is also an essential defense against a disease that strikes during middle age.

## CHILD DEVELOPMENT AND FAMILY POLICY

### Preventing Osteoporosis

**Osteoporosis is a disease in which a person's bones become thin and brittle, and, as a consequence, sometimes break.** Although osteoporosis can strike at any age, people over 50 are at greatest risk because bone tissue starts to break down more rapidly than new bone can be formed. About 10 million Americans have osteoporosis. Approximately 80 percent are women because after menopause the ovaries no longer produce as much estrogen, which guards against bone deterioration.

Osteoporosis often has its roots in childhood and adolescence, for this is when bones acquire nearly all their mass. For bones to develop properly, children and adolescents need to consume approximately 1,300 milligrams of calcium daily. This is the equivalent of about 3 cups of milk, half an ounce of cheese, and a cup of spinach. In addition, children and adolescents should engage in weight-bearing exercise for 30 minutes daily, for at least 5 days a week. Weight-bearing exercises cause bones to carry the body weight, strengthening them. Walking briskly, running, playing tennis, climbing stairs, aerobic dancing, and cross-country skiing are all good forms of weight-bearing exercise. Swimming, cycling, and rowing do not require the bones to support body weight, so they are not good weight-bearing exercises (although, of course, they do benefit the heart, lungs, and muscles).

Unfortunately, many adolescents do not get enough calcium or exercise for healthy bone growth. Consequently, the U.S. Centers for Disease Control and Prevention, the U.S. Department of Health and Human Services' Office of Women's Health, and the National Osteoporosis Foundation have collaborated to create the National Bone Health Campaign (NBHC). This multiyear program is designed to encourage 9- to 12-year-olds (girls, especially) to consume more calcium and to exercise more often. Launched in 2001, the NBHC uses several media to communicate with adolescents. Ads appearing in magazines and newspapers and on radio and TV emphasize the importance of healthy bone growth. The Web site shown in the figure—Powerful Girls. Powerful Bones.™—includes information about bone health along with games that allow adolescents to learn more about how diet and exercise contribute to healthy growth. Working with partners in the public and private sectors, the NBHC establishes links with local communities, such as providing lesson plans on bone health for science and health teachers.

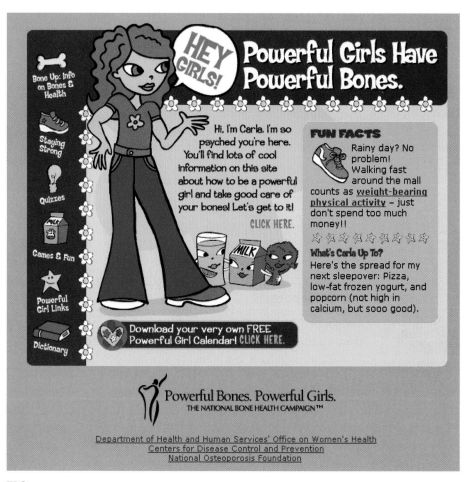

FIG. 5–5

**The best defence against osteoporosis is for adolescents to develop healthy bones, which requires calcium and exercise.**

The NBHC is too new for us to know its effectiveness. (After all, the real test won't come for another 35 to 40 years when the girls in the target audience reach the age when they'll be at risk for osteoporosis.) However, the hope is that by communicating effectively with adolescents and their parents (emphasizing that healthy bones are an essential part of overall healthy, positive growth), adolescents will get more calcium and become more active physically, thereby forging the strong bones that are the best defense against osteoporosis. ◉

Adolescents not only become taller and heavier, but also become mature sexually. **Sexual maturation includes change in primary sex characteristics, which refer to organs that are directly involved in reproduction.** These include the ovaries, uterus, and vagina in girls and the scrotum, testes, and penis in boys. **Sexual maturation also includes change in secondary sex characteristics, which are physical signs of maturity that are not linked directly to the reproductive organs.**

These include the growth of breasts and the widening of the pelvis in girls, the appearance of facial hair and the broadening of shoulders in boys, and the appearance of body hair and changes in voice and skin in both boys and girls.

Changes in primary and secondary sexual characteristics occur in a predictable sequence for boys and for girls. The chart shows these changes and the ages when they typically occur for boys and girls. For girls, puberty begins with growth of the breasts and the growth spurt, followed by the appearance of pubic hair. **Menarche, the onset of menstruation, typically occurs at about age 13.** Early menstrual cycles are usually irregular and without ovulation.

For boys, puberty usually commences with the growth of the testes and scrotum, followed by the appearance of pubic hair, the start of the growth spurt, and growth of the penis. **At about age 13, most boys reach spermarche, the first spontaneous ejaculation of sperm-laden fluid.** Initial ejaculations often contain relatively few sperm; only months or sometimes years later are there sufficient sperm to fertilize an egg (Chilman, 1983).

The onset of sexual maturity is one of the first signs that an adolescent is on the threshold of adulthood. This achievement is celebrated in many societies, including the Native American culture described in the "Cultural Influences" feature.

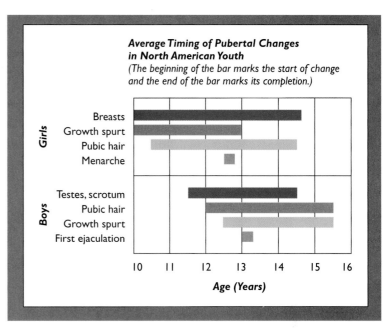

FIG. 5–6
Source: Tanner 1978.

## CULTURAL INFLUENCES

### How the Apache Celebrate Menarche

The Western Apache, who live in the southwest portion of the United States, traditionally have a spectacular ceremony to celebrate a girl's menarche (Basso, 1970). After a girl's first menstrual period, a group of older adults decide when the ceremony will be held and select a sponsor—a woman of good character and wealth (she helps to pay for the ceremony) who is unrelated to the initiate. On the day before the ceremony, the sponsor serves a large feast for the girl and her family; at the end of the ceremony, the family reciprocates, symbolizing that the sponsor is now a member of their family.

The ceremony itself begins at sunrise and lasts a few hours. As shown in the photo, the initiate dresses in ceremonial attire. The ceremony includes eight distinct phases in which the initiate dances or chants, sometimes accompanied by her sponsor or a medicine man. The intent of these actions is to transform the girl into "Changing Woman," a heroic figure in Apache myth. With this transformation comes longevity and perpetual strength.

The ceremony is a signal to all in the community that the initiate is now an adult. And it tells the initiate herself that her community now has adultlike expectations for her.

**MECHANISMS OF MATURATION.**   What causes the many physical changes that occur during puberty? The pituitary gland in the brain is the key player. As I mentioned on page 117, the pituitary helps to regulate physical development by releasing growth hormone. In addition, the pituitary regulates pubertal changes by signaling other glands to secrete hormones. During the early elementary-school years—long before there are any outward signs of puberty—the pituitary signals the adrenal glands to release androgens, initiating the biochemical changes that will produce body hair. A few years later, in girls the pituitary signals the ovaries to release estrogen, which causes the breasts to enlarge, the female genitals to mature, and fat to accumulate. In boys the pituitary signals the testes to release the androgen testosterone, which causes the male genitals to mature and muscle mass to increase.

The timing of pubertal events is regulated, in part, by genetics. For example, a mother's age at menarche is related to her daughter's age at menarche (Graber, Brooks-Gunn, & Warren, 1995). However, these genetic forces are strongly influenced by the environment, particularly an adolescent's nutrition and health. In general, puberty occurs earlier in adolescents who are well nourished and healthy than in adolescents who are not. For example, puberty occurs earlier in girls who are heavier and taller but later in girls who are afflicted with chronic illnesses or who receive inadequate nutrition (St. George et al., 1994).

*The timing of menarche is determined by genetics, nutrition, health, and social environment.*

Two other findings underscore the importance of nutrition and health in the onset of puberty. Cross-cultural comparisons reveal that menarche occurs earlier in areas of the world where nutrition and health care are adequate. For example, menarche occurs an average of 2 to 3 years earlier in Western European and North American countries than in African countries. And, within regions, socioeconomic status matters: Girls from affluent homes are more likely to receive adequate nutrition and health care and, consequently, they reach menarche earlier (Steinberg, 1999).

Historical data point to the same conclusion concerning the importance of nutrition and health care. In many industrialized countries around the world, the average age of menarche has declined steadily over the past 150 years. For example, in Europe the average age of menarche was 17 in 1840, compared to about 13 today. This drop reflects improvements and better health care over this period. In these countries, age of menarche is no longer dropping, which suggests that with adequate nutrition the biological lower limit for menarche is, on average, about 13 years.

What may surprise you is that the social environment also influences the onset of puberty, at least for girls. Menarche occurs at younger ages in girls who experience chronic stress or who are depressed (Belsky, Steinberg, & Draper, 1991; Moffit et al., 1992). For example, Ellis and Garber (2000) found that girls entered puberty at a younger age when their mothers' romantic relationships were stressful and when their mothers had remarried or had a boyfriend. The underlying nature of these links is not known, although repeated exposure to stress may affect the hormones that trigger menstruation (Graber et al., 1995).

**PSYCHOLOGICAL IMPACT OF PUBERTY.**   Of course, teenagers are well aware of the changes taking places in their bodies. Not surprisingly, some of these changes affect adolescents' psychological development. For example, compared to children and adults, adolescents are much more concerned about their overall appearance. Like the girl in the photo, many teenagers look in the mirror regularly, checking for signs of additional physical change. Generally, girls worry more than boys about appearance and are more likely to be dissatisfied with their appearance (Unger & Crawford, 1996; Vander Wal & Thelen, 2000).

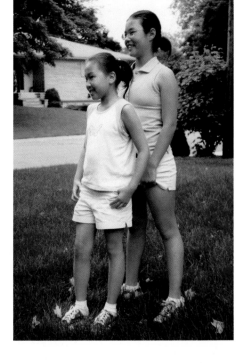

In addition, adolescents are affected by the timing of maturation: Many children begin puberty years before or after these norms. An early-maturing boy might begin puberty at age 11, whereas a late-maturing boy might start at 15 or 16. An early-maturing girl might start puberty at 9, a late-maturing girl, at 14 or 15. For example, the girls shown in the photo are the same age, but only one has reached puberty.

Maturing early or late has psychological consequences that differ for boys and girls. Several longitudinal studies show that early maturation benefits boys but, most often, not girls. Boys who mature early tend to be more independent and self-confident. They're also more popular with peers. In contrast, girls who mature early often lack self-confidence, are less popular, are more likely to be depressed and have behavior problems, and more likely to smoke and drink (Dick et al., 2000; Ge, Conger, & Elder, 2001; Stice, Presnell, & Bearman, 2001).

The differing consequences of early maturation on boys and girls are shown in the results of an extensive longitudinal study of adolescents growing up in Milwaukee during the 1970s (Simmons & Blyth, 1987). The early-maturing boys in this study dated more often and had more positive feelings about their physical development and athletic abilities. The early-maturing girls had more negative feelings about their physical development, received poorer grades, and were more often in trouble in school.

Why does rate of maturation have these consequences? Early maturation may benefit boys like the one in the photo because others perceive them as more mature and may be more willing to give them adultlike responsibilities. Late-maturing boys, like Pete in the vignette at the beginning of this section, are often frustrated because others treat them like little boys instead of like young men. Early maturation may hamper girls' development by leading them to associate with older adolescents who apparently encourage them to engage in age-inappropriate activities, such as drinking, smoking, and sex, for which they are ill-prepared (Ge, Conger, & Elder, 1996).

By young adulthood, many of the effects associated with rate of maturation vanish. When Pete, for example, finally matures, others will treat him like an adult and the few extra years of being treated like a child will not be harmful. But for some adolescents, particularly early-maturing girls, rate of maturation can have long-lasting effects. An early-maturing girl who is pressured into sex and becomes pregnant ends up with a different life course than a girl who matures later and is better prepared to resist pressures for sex. Thus, sometimes rate of maturation can lead to events that pick the path that development follows through the rest of life.

## CHECK YOUR LEARNING

**1.** Physical growth is most rapid during the first year and during _____.

**2.** Physical growth involves increases in height and weight, changes in _____, and changes in bone, muscle, and fat.

**3.** Changes in physical development from one generation to the next are called _____.

**4.** Sleep influences development directly because _____ and indirectly because, when children sleep poorly, they are inattentive and don't adjust well to school.

**5.** Compared to bottle-fed babies, breast-fed babies are ill less often, _____, and make the transition to solid foods more readily.

**6.** By allowing children to pick from different foods, to eat in any order they want, and to eat new foods in small amounts, parents can _____.

**7.** During adolescent physical growth, boys have greater muscle growth than girls, acquire less _____, and have greater increases in heart and lung capacities.

**8.** We know that nutrition and health determine the timing of puberty because puberty is earlier in girls who are taller and heavier, in regions of the world where nutrition and health care are adequate, and _____.

**9.** Early maturation often benefits boys because _____.

**NATURE AND NURTURE**
At first blush, the onset of puberty would seem to be due entirely to biology. In fact, the child's environment influences the onset of puberty. Summarize the ways in which biology and experience interact to trigger the onset of puberty.

**Answers:** (1) the adolescent growth spurt, (2) body proportions, (3) secular growth trends, (4) most growth hormone is secreted while children are asleep, (5) are less prone to diarrhea and constipation, (6) make it less likely that their children will become picky eaters, (7) fat, (8) in families that have higher socioeconomic status, (9) others are more likely to give them adult responsibilities.

# 5.2 Challenges to Healthy Growth

- Malnutrition
- Eating Disorders: Anorexia and Bulimia
- Obesity
- Disease
- Accidents

**LEARNING OBJECTIVES**

- What is malnutrition? What are its consequences? What is the solution to malnutrition?
- How do nature and nurture lead some adolescent girls to diet excessively?
- Why do some children become obese? How can they lose weight permanently?
- How do diseases and accidents threaten children's development?

*Ricardo, 12, has been overweight for most of his life. He dislikes the playground games that entertain most of his classmates during recess, preferring to stay indoors. He has relatively few friends and is not particularly happy with his lot in life. Many times Ricardo has lost weight from dieting, but he's always regained it quickly. His parents know that being overweight is a health hazard, and they wonder if there is anything that will help their son.*

Compared to many childhood tasks, physical growth seems easy. To paraphrase a famous line from the movie *Field of Dreams,* "If you feed them, they will grow." Of course, it's not this simple, in part because many children face obstacles on the path of healthy physical growth. Some obstacles concern nutrition. Growth requires enormous reserves of energy, and many children do not eat enough food to provide this energy. Other children and adolescents eat too much. Other problems are diseases and accidents, which affect millions of children worldwide. We'll look at these problems in this module, and as we do, we'll understand some of the reasons why Ricardo is overweight and what he can do about it.

## Malnutrition

An adequate diet is only a dream to many of the world's children. **Worldwide, about one in three children under age 5 suffers from malnutrition, as indicated by being small for his or her age** (Grantham-McGregor, Ani, & Fernald, 2001). Many, like the children in the photo, are from third-world countries. But malnutrition is regrettably common in industrialized countries, too. Many American children growing up homeless and in poverty are malnourished. Approximately 20 percent of American children receive inadequate amounts of iron, and 10 percent go to bed hungry (Children's Defense Fund, 1996; Pollitt, 1994).

Malnourishment is especially damaging during infancy because growth is so rapid during these years. A longitudinal study conducted in Barbados in the West Indies (Galler & Ramsey, 1989; Galler, Ramsey, & Forde, 1986) followed a group of children who were severely malnourished as infants and a group from similar family environments who had adequate nutrition as infants. As older children, the two groups were indistinguishable physically: Children who were malnourished as infants were just as tall and weighed just as much as their peers. However, the children with a history of infant malnutrition had much lower scores on intelligence tests. They also had difficulty maintaining attention in school; they were easily distracted. Malnutrition during rapid periods of growth apparently damages the brain, affecting a child's intelligence and ability to pay attention (Morgane et al., 1993).

Malnutrition would seem to have a simple cure—an adequate diet. But the solution is more complex than that. Malnourished children are frequently listless and inactive (Ricciuti, 1993), behaviors that are useful because they conserve energy. At the same time, when children are routinely unresponsive and lethargic, parents may provide fewer and fewer experiences that foster their children's development. For example, parents who start out reading to their children at night may stop because their malnourished children seem uninterested and inattentive. The result is a self-perpetuating cycle in which malnourished children are forsaken by parents, who feel that nothing they do gets a response, so they quit trying. A biological influence—lethargy stemming from insufficient nourishment—causes a profound change in the experiences— parental teaching—that shape a child's development.

Treating malnutrition requires improving children's diet and teaching parents to stimulate their children's development.

To break the vicious cycle, children need more than an improved diet. Their parents must also be taught how to foster their children's development. Programs that combine dietary supplements with parent training offer promise in treating malnutrition (Grantham-McGregor et al., 2001). Children in these programs often catch up with their peers in physical and intellectual growth, showing that the best way to treat malnutrition is by addressing both biological and sociocultural factors (Super, Herrera, & Mora, 1990).

**SHORT-TERM HUNGER.**    Breakfast should provide about one-fourth of a child's daily calories. Yet, many children—in developed and developing countries—do not eat breakfast (Grantham-McGregor et al., 2001). When children don't eat breakfast, they often have difficulty paying attention or remembering in school (Pollitt, 1995).

One strategy to attack this problem is to provide free and reduced-price meals for children at school. Lunch programs are the most common, but breakfast and dinner are sometimes available, too. These programs have a tremendous positive impact on children. Because they are better fed, they are absent from school less often and their achievement scores improve (Grantham-McGregor et al., 2001).

## Eating Disorders: Anorexia and Bulimia

Tracey Gold, an actress on the TV program *Growing Pains*, had to leave the show in the early 1990s. She had begun dieting compulsively, had withered away to a mere 90 pounds, and had to be hospitalized (Sporkin, Wagner, & Tomashoff, 1992). Tracey suffered from an eating disorder. **Anorexia nervosa is a disorder marked by a persistent refusal to eat and an irrational fear of being overweight.** Individuals with anorexia nervosa have a grossly distorted image of their own body. Like the girl in the photo, they claim to be overweight despite being painfully thin (Wilson, Heffernan, & Black, 1996).

Anorexia is a very serious disorder, often leading to heart damage. Without treatment, as many as 15 percent of adolescents with anorexia die (Wicks-Nelson & Israel, 1991). The "Real Children" feature describes a teenage girl with anorexia.

### REAL CHILDREN

#### Layla's Battle with Anorexia

Layla had always been a pleasant and obedient child. She was an above-average student in school, though she could never quite make the honor roll as her older brothers always did. At 15, Layla was 5 feet, $4\frac{1}{2}$ inches tall and weighed 120 pounds. Her weight was perfectly normal for her height, but she decided she was fat and began to diet. Over the next year, Layla lost 35 pounds. She looked pale, tired, and wasted, and she no longer menstruated. Layla insisted she looked fine and that nothing was wrong with her, but her parents and family doctor were so concerned they insisted she be hospitalized. Forced to eat regular meals in the hospital, Layla gained some weight and was sent home. But this cycle was repeated several times over the next two years: Layla would diet to the point that she looked like a skeleton draped in skin, and then she would be hospitalized. In her generally weakened condition, Layla developed mononucleosis and hepatitis; ultimately her liver and kidneys failed. Three days before her 18th birthday, Layla had a heart attack and died.

A related eating disorder is bulimia nervosa. **Individuals with bulimia nervosa alternate between binge eating periods when they eat uncontrollably and purging through self-induced vomiting or with laxatives.** The frequency of binge eating varies remarkably among people with bulimia nervosa, from a few times a week to more than 30 times. What's common to all is the feeling that they cannot stop eating (Mizes et al., 1995).

Anorexia and bulimia are alike in many respects. Both disorders primarily affect females and emerge in adolescence (Tyrka, Graber, & Brooks-Gunn, 2000). And both disorders have their origins in cultural ideals of the female body. In many industrialized cultures and certainly in the United States, the ideal female body is tall and slender. As girls enter adolescence (and as they begin to date), these cultural norms become particularly influential. Also during adolescence, girls experience a "fat spurt," gaining about 25 pounds—most of it fat. Though this pattern of growth is normal, many girls internalize the "thin-body" ideal; they become dissatisfied with their appearance and begin to diet. Most diets fail, leading girls to be even more unhappy with their appearance and leading some to the drastic dieting (sometimes accompanied by binge eating) that characterizes eating disorders (Stice, 2001).

> Anorexia and bulimia, eating disorders that affect teenage girls, can be linked to cultural ideals concerning the female body and to family dynamics.

Family dynamics may also contribute to anorexia. Adolescent girls are more prone to anorexia if their parents are overprotective, autocratic, and leave their adolescent daughters with little sense of self-control. Dieting allows the girls to assert their autonomy and achieve an individual identity (Tyrka et al., 2000).

## Obesity

Ricardo, the boy in the module-opening vignette, is overweight; he is very heavy for his height. **The technical definition for overweight is based on the body mass index (BMI), which is an adjusted ratio of weight to height.** Children and adolescents who are in the upper 5 percent (very heavy for their height) are defined as being overweight. Using these standards, in 2001 the U.S. Surgeon General announced that childhood obesity had reached epidemic proportions. In the past 25 to 30 years, the number of overweight children has doubled and the number of overweight adolescents has tripled, so that today roughly one child or adolescent out of seven is overweight (U.S. Department of Health and Human Services, 2001).

Like the boy in the photo, overweight youngsters are often unpopular and have low self-esteem (Braet, Mervielde, & Vandereycken, 1997). Furthermore, throughout life they are at risk for many medical problems, including high blood pressure and diabetes, because the vast majority of overweight children and adolescents become overweight adults (Serdula et al., 1993).

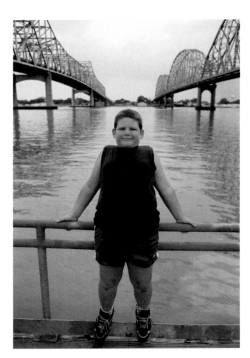

Heredity plays an important role in juvenile obesity. In adoption studies, children and adolescents' weight is related to the weight of their biological parents, rather than the weight of their adoptive parents (Stunkard et al., 1986). Genes may influence obesity by influencing a person's activity level. In other words, being genetically more prone to inactivity makes it more difficult to burn off calories and easier to gain weight. **Heredity may also help set basal metabolic rate, the speed at which the body consumes calories.** Children and adolescents with a slower basal metabolic rate burn off calories less rapidly, making it easier for them to gain weight (Epstein & Cluss, 1986).

The environment is also influential. Television advertising, for example, encourages youth to eat tasty but fattening foods. Parents play a role, too. They may inadvertently encourage obesity by emphasizing external rather than internal eating signals. Infants eat primarily because of internal signals: They eat when they experience hunger and stop eating when they feel full. During the preschool years, this internal control of eating is often gradually replaced by external signals. Parents who urge their children to "clean their plates" even when they are no longer hungry are teaching their children to ignore internal cues to eating. Thus, obese children and adolescents may overeat because they rely on external cues and disregard internal cues to stop (Birch, 1991).

Obese youth can lose weight. The most effective weight-loss programs have several features in common (Epstein et al., 1995; Foreyt & Goodrick, 1995; Israel et al., 1994):

- The focus of the program is to change obese children's eating habits, encourage them to become more active, and discourage sedentary behavior.

- As part of the treatment, children learn to monitor their eating, exercise, and sedentary behavior. Goals are established in each area, and rewards are earned when the goals are met.

- Parents are trained to help children set realistic goals and to use behavioral principles to help children meet these goals. Parents also monitor their own lifestyles to be sure they aren't accidentally fostering their child's obesity.

When programs incorporate these features, obese children do lose weight. However, even after losing weight, many of these children remain overweight. Consequently, it is best to avoid overweight and obesity in the first place; the *Surgeon General's Call for Action* emphasizes the role of increased physical activity and good eating habits in warding off overweight and obesity (U.S. Department of Health and Human Services, 2001).

## Disease

Around the world an estimated 11 million children aged 4 years and younger die every year. These are staggering numbers—roughly the equivalent of *all* U.S. 1-, 2-, and 3-year-olds dying in a single year. The leading killers of young children worldwide are infectious diseases—acute respiratory infections (including pneumonia and influenza) and diarrheal diseases each kill 2 million children annually (World Health Organization, 1999). The majority of these deaths can be prevented with proven, cost-effective treatments. For example, measles kills nearly 1 million children annually but can be prevented with vaccinations. Similarly, diarrhea kills by dehydrating youngsters, yet children can avert death by promptly drinking water that contains salt and potassium.

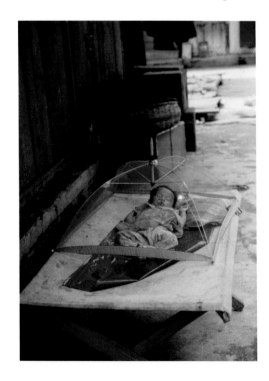

As part of a vigorous effort to prevent childhood illness, for the past two decades, the World Health Organization (WHO) has worked to vaccinate children worldwide. Due to these efforts, vaccination rates have skyrocketed in many developing countries. More recently, WHO has joined with the United Nations Children's Fund (UNICEF) to create Integrated Management of Childhood Illness (IMCI), a program to combat the five conditions that account for the vast majority of childhood deaths: pneumonia, diarrhea, measles, malaria, and malnutrition (World Health Organization, 1997). Because many children who are ill have symptoms related to two or more of these five conditions, IMCI takes an integrated strategy that focuses on the overall health of the child. One component of IMCI is training health care professionals to become more skilled in dealing with childhood illnesses. A second component is improving health care systems so that they are better able to respond to childhood illness (e.g., ensuring that required medicines are available). A third component involves changing family and community practices to make them more conducive to healthy growth. For example, to protect children from mosquitoes that carry malaria, children are encouraged to sleep in netting, as the child in the photo is doing. Integrated Management of Childhood Illness has been adopted in more than 60 countries and is playing a pivotal role in improving children's health worldwide.

## Accidents

During the first year of life, the most common causes of infant mortality in the United States are medical conditions associated with birth defects or low birth weight. From age 1 on, however, children are more likely to die from accidents than from any other single cause (Center for Disease Control and Prevention, 2000). Motor vehicle accidents are the most common cause of accidental death in children. Regrettably, many of these deaths could have been prevented had children and adolescents been wearing seat belts, or had infants been restrained properly in an approved infant car seat like the one shown in the photo. Without such restraint, children and adolescents typically suffer massive head injuries when thrown through the windshield or onto the road.

Many infants and toddlers also drown, die from burns, or suffocate. Often these deaths result because young children are supervised inadequately. All too common, for example, are reports of young children who wander away, jump or fall into a swimming pool that lacks protective fencing, then drown. Parents need to remember that children are often eager to explore their environs yet they are unable to recognize many hazards. Parents must constantly keep a protective eye on their young children. And, with older children, parents must be careful that they don't overestimate their children's skills. Some accidents happen because parents have too much confidence in their children's cognitive and motor skills. They may allow a child like the boy in the photo to ride to school in a bike lane adjacent to a street filled with commuters, even though children may not consistently pay attention while biking or may be unable to maneuver their bike around unexpected hazards, such as a pothole.*

For adolescents, motor vehicle accidents remain the leading cause of death. The difference, of course, is that adolescents are no longer passengers but are driving. And, sadly, far too many adolescents are killed because they drive too fast, drive while drunk, and drive without wearing a seatbelt (U.S. Department of Health and Human Services, 1997). Among teen-age boys, firearms represent a leading cause of death. In fact, firearms kill more 15- to 19-year-old African American boys and Hispanic American boys than any other single cause (Federal Interagency Forum on Child and Family Statistics, 2000).

---

*As a 10-year-old, my son Matt crashed his new bike right into the back of a parked car because he was too busy watching the gears shift. Fortunately, he escaped with just a few scrapes, but this illustrates how easily a childhood lapse in concentration can lead to a cycling accident.

Although the term *accident* implies that the event happened by chance and no one was to blame, in reality most accidents involving children and adolescents can be foreseen and either prevented or steps taken to reduce injury. In the case of automobile accidents, for example, the simple step of wearing a seat belt enhances safety immensely. Accidents involving firearms can be reduced by making guns less accessible to children and adolescents (e.g., storing guns and ammunition separately and locking each). School-based safety programs can also help to reduce childhood accidents. Children can learn safe ways of walking or riding their bikes to school, then be allowed to practice these skills, supervised by an adult. With programs like these, children readily learn behaviors that foster safety (Zins et al., 1994).

## CHECK YOUR LEARNING

1. Malnourishment is particularly damaging during infancy because _____.
2. Malnourished children need an adequate diet and _____.
3. Individuals with _____ alternate between binge eating and purging.
4. Parents may inadvertently contribute to their children's obesity by _____.
5. Effective programs for childhood obesity focus on changing eating habits, encouraging children to become more active, and discouraging _____.
6. IMCI includes training health care professionals, improving health care systems, and _____.
7. Parents can help their children avoid accidents by watching them closely and by making sure that they don't _____.

### ACTIVE CHILDREN
How does malnutrition show the impact that children can have on their own development?

**Answers:** (1) growth is so rapid during this period, (2) parents who foster their development, (3) bulimia nervosa, (4) encouraging them to ignore internal cues to eating, (5) sedentary behavior, (6) changing family and community practices to make them more conducive to healthy growth, (7) overestimate their children's abilities

# 5.3 The Developing Nervous System

- Organization of the Mature Brain
- The Developing Brain

## LEARNING OBJECTIVES

- What are the parts of a nerve cell? How is the brain organized?
- When is the brain formed in prenatal development? When do different regions of the brain begin to function?

*While crossing the street, 10-year-old Martin was struck by a passing car. He was in a coma for a week, but then gradually became more alert, and now he seems to be aware of his surroundings. Needless to say, Martin's mother is grateful that he survived the accident, but she wonders what the future holds for her son.*

The physical changes that we see as children grow are impressive, but even more awe-inspiring are the changes we cannot see, those involving the brain and the nervous system. An infant's feelings of hunger, a child's laugh, and an adolescent's efforts to learn algebra all reflect the functioning brain and the rest of the nervous system. All the information that children learn, including language and other cognitive skills, is stored in the brain.

How does the brain accomplish these many tasks? How is the brain affected by an injury like the one that Martin suffered? To begin to answer these questions, let's look at how the brain is organized in adults.

## Organization of the Mature Brain

**The basic unit of the brain and the rest of the nervous system is the neuron, a cell that specializes in receiving and transmitting information.** Neurons come in many different shapes, as you can see in the different photos. The diagram below makes it easier to understand the basic parts found in all neurons. **The cell body at the center of the neuron contains the basic biological machinery that keeps the neuron alive. The receiving end of the neuron, the dendrite, looks like a tree with many branches.** The highly branched dendrite allows one neuron to receive input from many thousands of other neurons (Morgan & Gibson, 1991). **The tubelike structure at the other end of the cell body is the axon, which sends information to other neurons. The axon is wrapped in myelin, a fatty sheath that allows it to transmit information more rapidly.** The boost in neural speed from myelin is like the difference between driving and flying: from about 6 feet per second to 50 feet per second. **At the end of the axon are small knobs called terminal buttons, which release neurotransmitters, chemicals that carry information to nearby neurons.** Finally, you'll see that the terminal buttons of one axon don't actually touch the dendrites of other neurons. **The gap between one neuron and the next is a synapse.** Neurotransmitters cross synapses to carry information between neurons.

Take 50 to 100 billion neurons like these and you have the beginnings of a human brain. An adult's brain weighs a little less than 3 pounds, and it easily fits into your hands. **The wrinkled surface of the brain is the cerebral cortex; made up of about 10 billion neurons, the cortex regulates many of the functions that we think of as distinctly human. The cortex consists of left and right halves, called hemispheres, that are linked by millions of axons in a thick bundle called the corpus callosum.** The characteristics that you value most—your engaging personality, your "way with words," your uncanny knack for reading others—are all controlled by specific regions of the cortex, many of which are shown in the diagram at the top of page 134.

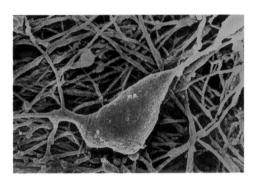

**Personality and your ability to make and carry out plans are largely functions of an area at the front of the cortex that is called, appropriately, the frontal cortex.** For most people, the ability to produce and understand language, to reason, and to compute is largely due to neurons in the cortex of the left hemisphere. Also for most people, artistic and musical abilities, perception of spatial relationships, and the ability to recognize faces and emotions come from neurons in the right hemisphere.

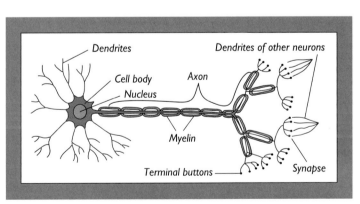

FIG. 5–7

Now that we know a bit of the organization of the mature brain, let's look at how the brain develops and begins to function.

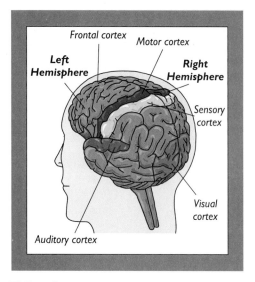

FIG. 5–8

## The Developing Brain

Scientists who study the brain's development are guided by several key questions: How and when do brain structures develop? When do different brain regions begin to function? Why do brain regions take on different functions? In this section, we'll see how research has answered each question.

**EMERGING BRAIN STRUCTURES.** We know from Module 4.1 that the beginnings of the brain can be traced to the period of the zygote. **At roughly 3 weeks after conception, a group of cells form a flat structure known as the neural plate.** At four weeks, the neural plate folds to form a tube that ultimately becomes the brain and spinal cord. When the ends of the tube fuse shut, neurons are produced in one small region of the neural tube. Production of neurons begins about 10 weeks after conception, and by 28 weeks the developing brain has virtually all the neurons it will ever have. During these weeks, neurons form at the incredible rate of more than 4,000 per second (Kolb, 1989).

From the neuron-manufacturing site in the neural tube, neurons migrate to their final positions in the brain. The brain is built in stages, beginning with the innermost layers. Neurons in the deepest layer are positioned first, followed by neurons in the second layer, and so on. This layering process continues until all six layers of the mature brain are in place, which occurs about 7 months after conception (Rakic, 1995). As you can see in the diagram, the nerve cells move to the top by wrapping themselves around supporting cells, just as a snake might climb a pole.

In the fourth month of prenatal development, axons begin to acquire myelin—the fatty wrap that speeds neural transmission. This process continues through infancy and into childhood and adolescence (Casaer, 1993). Neurons that carry sensory information are the first to acquire myelin; neurons in the cortex are among the last. You can see the effect of more myelin in improved coordination and reaction times. The older the infant and, later, the child, the more rapid and coordinated are his or her reactions. (We'll talk more about this phenomenon when we discuss fine-motor skills in Module 6.3.)

In the months after birth, the brain grows rapidly. Axons and dendrites grow longer, and, like a maturing tree, dendrites quickly sprout new limbs. As the number of dendrites increases, so does the number of synapses, reaching a peak at about the first birthday. This rapid neural growth is shown in the diagram on page 135. **Soon after, synapses begin to disappear gradually, a phenomenon known as synaptic pruning.** Thus, beginning in infancy and continuing into early

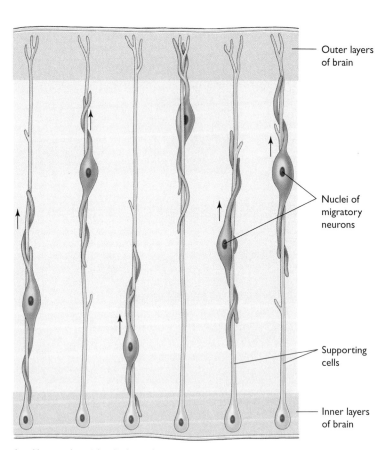

Just like a snake might climb a pole, neurons migrate to their final location in the brain by wrapping themselves around supporting cells.

FIG. 5–9

| At birth | I month | 3 months | I5 months | 24 months |

FIG. 5–10

adolescence, the brain goes through its own version of "downsizing," weeding out unnecessary connections between neurons. This pruning depends on the activity of the neural circuits—synapses that are active are preserved but those that aren't active are eliminated (Webb, Monk, & Nelson, 2001).

VIDEO 5.2
Synaptic
Development

**STRUCTURE AND FUNCTION.**   Because the mature brain is specialized, with different psychological functions localized in particular regions, a natural question for developmental researchers is, "How early in development does brain functioning become localized?" To answer this question, scientists have used many different methods to map functions onto particular brain regions.

- *Studies of children with brain damage*: Children who suffer brain injuries provide valuable insights into brain structure and function. If a region of the brain regulates a particular function (e.g., understanding speech), then damage to that region should impair the function.

- *Studies of electrical activity*: **Metal electrodes placed on an infant's scalp, as shown in the photo, produce an electroencephalogram (EEG), a pattern of brain waves.** If a region of the brain regulates a function, then the region should show distinctive EEG patterns while a child is using that function.

- *Studies using imaging techniques*: **One method, functional magnetic resonance imaging (F-MRI), uses magnetic fields to track the flow of blood in the brain.**

With this method, shown in the photo, the research participant's brain is literally wrapped in an incredibly powerful magnet that can track blood flow as participants perform different cognitive tasks (Casey, Giedd, & Thomas, 2000). **Another method, positron emission tomography (PET) scan, traces use of glucose in the brain.** If a region of the brain helps to regulate a function, then blood flow and use of glucose (a sugar that is a source of energy) should be higher in that region when a child is performing that function.

None of these methods is perfect; each has drawbacks. In cases of brain injury, for example, multiple areas of the brain may be damaged, making it hard to link impaired functioning to a particular brain region. Most imaging techniques are used sparingly because they're very expensive, because they usually require participants to lie still for several minutes at a time, and, in the case of PET scan, because they are potentially hazardous (i.e., PET scan requires injecting children with a radioactive form of glucose, so it's used more often in clinical work to help diagnose suspected brain damage).

Despite these limitations, the combined outcome of research using these different approaches indicates that many areas of the cortex begin to function in infancy. Early specialization of the frontal cortex is shown by the finding that damage to this region in infancy results in impaired decision making and abnormal emotional responses (Anderson et al., 2001). Similarly, EEG studies show that a newborn infant's left hemisphere generates more electrical activity in response to speech than the right hemisphere (Molfese & Burger-Judisch, 1991). Thus, by birth, the cortex of the left hemisphere is already specialized for language processing. As we'll see in Chapter 10, this specialization allows language to develop rapidly during infancy.

Is the right hemisphere also specialized early? A study designed to answer this question is described in the "Focus on Research" feature.

## FOCUS ON RESEARCH

### Right-hemisphere Specialization for Spatial Ability

*Who were the investigators, and what was the aim of the study?* Regions of the brain's right hemisphere are critical in understanding spatial relations. For example, if you were shown the arch in the drawing and then were asked to make one from a pile of blocks, understanding the spatial relations among the blocks—one block placed horizontally on two vertical blocks—would depend primarily on the right hemisphere. Joan Stiles and her colleagues (1996) wanted to determine whether the right hemisphere is specialized for this sort of processing during the preschool years.

*How did the investigators measure the topic of interest?* Stiles and her colleagues showed block models like the one in the drawing to children, who were asked to make a duplicate using eight rectangular blocks. Some models were simple (e.g., six blocks in a line) but others were complex (e.g., two connected arches).

*Who were the children in the study?* The researchers tested two groups of 4-year-olds who had suffered damage to either the left or the right hemisphere of the brain

FIG. 5–11

before 8 months of age. They also tested two groups of 3- and 4-year-old children who were developing normally and who had no known brain damage.

*What was the design of the study?* This study was correlational because Stiles and her colleagues were interested in the natural relation between two variables: brain functioning (damage to the left hemisphere, damage to the right hemisphere, no known damage) and children's ability to construct models (as a measure of their spatial ability). The part of the study involving children with brain damage was not developmental. However, the other part was cross-sectional because the study included one group of 3-year-olds and a separate group of 4-year-olds.

*Were there ethical concerns with the study?* No. Most young children love playing with blocks!

*What were the results?* The graph shows the percentage of the models that were constructed accurately. Looking first at the results for 3- and 4-year-olds, you can see that performance improves rapidly within a year: 4-year-olds constructed the models much more ac-

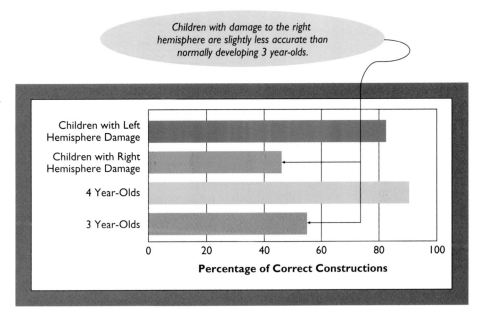

FIG. 5–12

curately than 3-year-olds did. Looking next at the results of the two groups of children with brain damage, it's obvious that children with damage to the left hemisphere perform nearly at the same level as normally developing 4-year-olds. In contrast, children with damage to the right hemisphere performed much less accurately—in fact, their constructions tended to be slightly less accurate than those of normally developing 3-year-olds.

*What did the investigators conclude?* When the left hemisphere is damaged in infancy, children's spatial processing is unharmed. In contrast, similar damage to the right hemisphere in infancy impairs children's spatial processing. Evidently, by 4 years of age, the right hemisphere has already begun to specialize in the processing of spatial information that is tapped in the blocks task.

*What converging evidence would strengthen these conclusions?* This work could be extended naturally in two directions. First, the investigators could examine children's performance on a wider range of tasks to identify, more precisely, which functions are impaired by early damage to the brain's right hemisphere. Second, the researchers could continue to study the children with brain damage to determine how their skills improve with age in comparison to children without brain damage. (In fact, Stiles and her colleagues have extended this work in both directions already!) ⊙

The "Focus on Research" highlights an important point in this module: *The brain begins to specialize early in life.* Language processing is associated primarily with the left hemisphere; recognizing nonspeech sounds, emotions, and faces is associated with the right hemisphere; and regulating emotions and intentional behavior is a function of the frontal cortex. Of course, this early specialization does not mean that the brain is functionally mature. During the remainder of childhood and into adulthood, these and other regions of the brain continue to become more specialized.

How do certain functions come to be localized in brain regions? How readily are they transferred to other regions? The next section will address these questions.

BRAIN PLASTICITY AND THE ROLE OF ENVIRONMENTAL INPUT.    **Plasticity refers to the extent to which brain organization is flexible.** How plastic is the human brain? Answers to this question reflect the familiar views on the nature–nurture issue (Nelson, 1999; Stiles, 2001). Some theorists believe that organization of brain function is predetermined genetically; it's simply in most children's biological makeup that, for example, the left hemisphere will specialize in language processing. According to this view, the brain is like a house—a structure that's specialized from the very beginning, with some rooms designed for cooking, others for sleeping, and others for bathing. In contrast, other theorists believe that few functions are rigidly assigned to specific brain sites at conception. Instead, experience helps determine the functional organization of the brain. According to this view, the brain is more like an office building—an all-purpose structure with rooms designed to be used flexibly to meet the different business needs of the companies with offices in the building.

Research designed to test these views shows that the brain has some plasticity. Remember Martin, the child in the vignette whose brain was damaged when he was struck by a car? His language skills were impaired after the accident. This was not surprising, because the left hemisphere of Martin's brain had absorbed most of the force of the collision. But within several months, Martin had completely recovered his language skills. Apparently other neurons took over language-related processing from the damaged neurons. This recovery of function is not uncommon—particularly for young children—and shows that the brain is plastic. In other words, young children often recover more skills after brain injury than older children and adults, apparently because functions are more easily reassigned in the young brain (Stiles, 2001).

> When children suffer brain damage, cognitive processes are usually impaired; over time, these processes, often recover, showing the brain's plasticity.

However, the brain is not completely plastic—brains have a similar structure and similar mapping of functions on those structures. The visual cortex, for example, is always near the back of the brain. The sensory cortex and motor cortex always run across the middle of the brain. But if a neuron's function is not specified at conception, how do different neurons take on different functions and in much the same pattern for most people? Researchers are trying to answer this question and many details still need to be worked out. The answer probably lies in complex biochemical processes (Barinaga, 1997; Kunzig, 1998). You can get an idea of what's involved by imagining people arriving for a football game at a stadium where there are no reserved seats. As fans enter the stadium, they see others wearing their own school colors and move in that direction. Of course, not everyone does this. Some fans sit with friends from the other team. Some pick seats based on other factors (e.g., to avoid looking into the sun, to be close to the concession stand). In general, though, by game time, most fans have taken seats on their respective sides of the field.

In much the same way, as neurons are created and begin migrating through the layers of cortex, cellular biochemistry makes some paths more attractive than others. Yet, just as each fan can potentially sit anywhere because there are no reserved seats, an individual neuron can end up in many different locations because genetic instructions do not assign specific brain regions. Thus, the human brain *is* plastic—its organization and function can be affected by experience—but its development follows some general biochemical instructions that ensure most people end up with brains organized along similar lines.

Finally, it's important to emphasize the role of environmental stimulation in normal brain development. To return to the analogy of the brain as a building, the newborn's brain is perhaps best conceived as a partially finished, partially furnished house: A general organizational framework is there, with preliminary neural pathways designed to perform certain functions. The left hemisphere no doubt has some language pathways and the frontal cortex has some emotion-related pathways. However, completing the typical organization of the mature brain requires input from the environment that stimulates other "general purpose" neurons to specialize. When infants hear speech, these experiences may stimulate other neurons in the brain to specialize in language processing. In this manner, experience is the catalyst that converts the partially furnished, partially finished newborn brain into a mature, specialized brain (Johnson, 2000; Webb et al., 2001).

## CHECK YOUR LEARNING

1. The _____ is the part of the neuron that contains the basic machinery that keeps the cell alive.

2. Terminal buttons release _____, chemicals that carry neural transmissions to nearby neurons.

3. The wrinkled surface of the brain is the _____.

4. During prenatal development, the brain forms from a flat group of cells called the _____.

5. During the first year, axons and dendrites grow and many synapses form; however, starting at about the first birthday, _____.

6. To study brain organization, researchers study children with brain damage, _____, and use imaging techniques.

7. Human speech elicits more electrical activity from the _____ of an infant's brain.

8. A good example of brain plasticity is the fact that, although children with brain damage often have impaired cognitive processes, _____.

**CONNECTIONS**
How does the development of the brain, as described in this module, compare to the general pattern of physical growth described in Module 5.1?

**Answers:** (1) cell body, (2) neurotransmitters, (3) cerebral cortex, (4) neural plate, (5) unnecessary synapses disappear, a phenomenon known as synaptic pruning, (6) measure electrical activity in children's brains (EEGs), (7) left hemisphere, (8) over time, they often regain their earlier skills

# Unifying Themes: Connections

This chapter is an excellent opportunity to highlight the theme that *development in different domains is connected.* Consider the impact of the timing of puberty. Whether a child matures early or late affects social development (early-maturing boys date more often), self-esteem (early-maturing boys feel good about themselves but early-maturing girls don't), and academic performance (early-maturing girls often do poorly in school). Or consider the impact of malnutrition. Malnourished youngsters are often listless, which affects how their parents interact with them (they're less likely to provide stimulating experiences). Less stimulation, in turn, slows the children's intellectual development. Physical, cognitive, social, and personality development are linked: Change in one area generally leads to change of some kind in the others.

## See for Yourself

Children love playgrounds. Unfortunately, hundreds of thousands of American children are injured on playgrounds annually. Some of these accidents could have been prevented had parents (or other adults) been present, or, if present, had they been paying closer attention to the children at play.

Go to a local playground and watch children as they play. Notice how many unknowingly put themselves at risk as they play. Also notice how well the children's play is monitored by adults. See for yourself!

## Resources

For more information about...

**ways to help children and adolescents stay physically fit,** try Kenneth Cooper's *Kid Fitness* (Random House, 1992), which describes a program of diet and exercise developed by the originator of the concept of aerobic fitness.

**children's nutrition,** visit the Web site of Children's Nutrition Research Center at Baylor College of Medicine: **http://www.bcm.tmc.edu/cnrc/**

## Key Terms

**anorexia nervosa** 128
**axon** 133
**basal metabolic rate** 129
**body mass index** 129
**bulimia nervosa** 128
**cell body** 133
**cerebral cortex** 133
**corpus callosum** 133
**dendrite** 133
**electroencephalogram (EEG)** 135
**epiphyses** 116
**frontal cortex** 133
**functional magnetic resonance imaging (F-MRI)** 135
**growth hormone** 117
**hemispheres** 133
**malnutrition** 127

**menarche** 123
**myelin** 133
**neural plate** 134
**neuron** 133
**neurotransmitters** 133
**osteoporosis** 121
**plasticity** 138
**positron emission tomography (PET) scan** 136
**primary sex characteristics** 122
**puberty** 120
**secular growth trends** 116
**secondary sex characteristics** 122
**spermarche** 123
**synapse** 133
**synaptic pruning** 134
**terminal buttons** 133

# SUMMARY

## 5.1 Physical Growth

### Features of Human Growth

Physical growth is particularly rapid during infancy, slows during the elementary-school years, and then accelerates again during adolescence. Physical growth refers not only to height and weight but also to development of muscle, fat, and bones.

Children are taller today than in previous generations. Average heights vary around the world and within any culture there is considerable variation in the normal range of height.

### Mechanisms of Physical Growth

Physical growth depends on sleep, in part because most growth hormone is secreted while children sleep. Nutrition is also important, particularly during periods of rapid growth, such as infancy and adolescence. Breast-feeding provides babies with all the nutrients they need and has other advantages. Many children and adolescents do not get adequate nutrients because of poor diets.

### The Adolescent Growth Spurt and Puberty

Puberty includes the adolescent growth spurt as well as sexual maturation. Girls typically begin the growth spurt earlier than boys, who acquire more muscle, less fat, and greater heart and lung capacities. Sexual maturation, which includes primary and secondary sex characteristics, occurs in predictable sequences for boys and girls.

Pubertal changes occur when the pituitary gland signals the adrenal gland, ovaries, and testes to secrete hormones that initiate physical changes. The timing of puberty is influenced strongly by health, nutrition, and social environment.

Pubertal change affects adolescents' psychological functioning. Teens become concerned about their appearance. Early maturation tends to be beneficial for boys but not girls.

## 5.2 Challenges to Healthy Growth

### Malnutrition

Malnutrition is a global problem—including in the United States—that is particularly harmful during infancy, when growth is so rapid. Malnutrition can cause brain damage, affecting children's intelligence and ability to pay attention. Treating malnutrition requires improving children's diet and training their parents to provide stimulating environments.

### Anorexia and Bulimia

Anorexia and bulimia are eating disorders that typically affect adolescent girls. They are characterized by an irrational fear of being overweight. Several factors contribute to these disorders, including cultural standards of thinness, a need for independence within an autocratic family, and heredity.

### Obesity

Many obese children and adolescents are unpopular, have low self-esteem, and are at risk for medical disorders. Obesity reflects both heredity and acquired eating habits. In the most effective programs for treating obesity in youth, both children and their parents set eating and exercise goals and monitor their daily progress.

### Disease

Millions of children around the world die annually from infectious diseases. Integrated Management of Childhood Illness is a new, integrated approach designed to promote children's health.

### Accidents

In the United States, children and adolescents are more likely to die from accidents than any other single cause. Many of these fatalities involve motor vehicles and could be prevented if passengers were restrained properly. Older children and adolescents are sometimes involved in accidents because parents overestimate their abilities.

## 5.3 The Developing Nervous System

### Organization of the Mature Brain

Nerve cells, called *neurons*, are composed of a cell body, a dendrite, and an axon. The mature brain consists of billions of neurons organized into nearly identical left and right hemispheres connected by the corpus callosum. The frontal cortex is associated with personality and goal-directed behavior; the cortex in the left hemisphere, with language; and the cortex in the right hemisphere, with nonverbal processes.

### The Developing Brain

Brain structure begins in prenatal development, when neurons form at an incredible rate. After birth, neurons in the central nervous system become wrapped in myelin, allowing them to transmit information more rapidly. Throughout childhood, unused synapses disappear gradually through a process of pruning.

Methods used to investigate brain functioning in children include (a) studying children with brain damage, (b) recording electrical activity (the electroencephalogram or EEG), and (c) using imaging techniques. Research with these methods reveals that many regions of an infant's brain specialize early in life: the frontal cortex specializes in decision making, the left hemisphere in language, the right hemisphere in processing spatial information. The infant's brain is moderately flexible: It has a preliminary organization that tends to be followed as long as infants receive typical stimulation from the environment.

# 6

When my son, Ben, was a preschooler, he loved to watch *CHiPs* with Erik Estrada zooming around L.A. on his Kawasaki. Ben was totally absorbed by the show and oblivious to everything else around him. His behavior illustrates perception in action: Our senses are assaulted with stimulation, but much of it is ignored. **Sensory and perceptual processes are the means by which people receive, select, modify, and organize stimulation from the world.** Sensory and perceptual processes are the first step in the complex process that eventually results in "knowing." We'll begin studying perceptual development, in Module 6.1, by looking at the origins of sensory processes in infancy. In Module 6.2 we'll see how more complex perceptual and attentional processes develop in childhood.

**Perceptual processes are closely linked to motor skills—coordinated movements of the muscles and limbs.** Perception often guides a child's movement: A child uses vision to avoid obstacles. In turn, a child's movement in the environment provides enormous variety in perceptual stimulation. In Module 6.3, we'll see how improvements in motor skill enhances children's ability to explore, understand, and enjoy the world.

# Perceptual and Motor Development

**6.1**   Basic Sensory and Perceptual Processes

**6.2**   Complex Perceptual and Attentional Processes

**6.3**   Motor Development

# 6.1 | Basic Sensory and Perceptual Processes

## LEARNING OBJECTIVES

- Are newborn babies able to smell and taste? Do they respond to touch and experience pain?

- How well do infants hear? How do they use sounds to understand their world?

- How accurate is infants' vision? Do infants perceive color?

- How do infants integrate information from different senses?

> *Darla adores her 3-day-old daughter, Olivia. She loves holding her, talking to her, and simply watching her. Darla is certain that Olivia is already getting to know her, coming to recognize her face and the sound of her voice. Darla's husband, Steve, thinks she is crazy. He tells her, "Everyone knows that babies are born blind. And they probably can't hear much either." Darla doubts that Steve is right, but she wishes someone would tell her about babies' vision and hearing.*

Darla's questions are really about her newborn daughter's sensory and perceptual skills. To help her understand, we need to remember that humans have different kinds of sense organs, each receptive to a unique kind of physical energy. The retina at the back of the eye, for example, is sensitive to some types of electromagnetic energy, and sight is the result. The eardrum detects changes in air pressure, and hearing is the result. Cells at the top of the nasal passage detect airborne molecules, and smell is the result. In each case, the sense organ translates the physical stimulation into nerve impulses that are sent to the brain.

**Techniques used to study infants' perception typically involve presenting several distinct stimuli, then determining if infants respond the same to all or differently.**

The senses begin to function early in life, which is why this module is devoted entirely to infancy. How can we know what an infant senses? Because infants can't tell us what they smell, hear, or see, researchers have had to devise other ways to find out. In many studies, an investigator presents two stimuli to a baby, such as a high-pitched tone and a low-pitched tone or a sweet-tasting substance and a sour-tasting substance. Then the investigator records the baby's responses, such as heart rate, facial expression, or head movement. If the baby consistently responds differently to the two stimuli (e.g., she looks in the direction of one tone, but not the other), the baby must be distinguishing between them.

Another approach is based on the fact that infants usually prefer novel stimuli over familiar stimuli. **When a novel stimulus is presented, babies pay much attention, but they pay less attention as it becomes more familiar, a phenomenon known as habituation.** Researchers use habituation to study perception by repeatedly presenting a stimulus such as a low-pitched tone until an infant barely responds. Then they present a second stimulus, such as a higher-pitched tone. If the infant responds strongly, then he can distinguish the two stimuli.

In this module, you'll learn what researchers using these techniques have discovered about infants' perception. We begin with smell, taste, and touch because these senses are particularly mature at birth.

## Smell, Taste, and Touch

Newborns have a keen sense of smell; they respond positively to pleasant smells and negatively to unpleasant smells (Mennella & Beauchamp, 1997). They have a relaxed, contented-looking facial expression when they smell honey or chocolate, but they frown, grimace, or turn away when they smell rotten eggs or ammonia. Young babies can also recognize familiar odors. Newborns will look in the direction of a pad that is saturated with their own amniotic fluid (Schaal, Marlier, & Soussignan, 1998). They will also turn toward a pad saturated with the odor of their mother's breast or her perfume (Porter & Winburg, 1999).

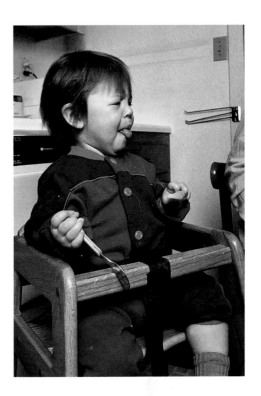

Newborns also have a highly developed sense of taste. They readily differentiate salty, sour, bitter, and sweet tastes (Rostenstein & Oster, 1997). Most infants seem to have a "sweet tooth." They react to sweet substances by smiling, sucking, and licking their lips (e.g., Steiner et al., 2001). In contrast, you can probably guess what the infant in the photo has tasted! This grimace is typical when infants are fed bitter- or sour-tasting substances (Kaijura, Cowart, & Beauchamp, 1992). Infants are also sensitive to changes in the taste of breast milk that reflect a mother's diet. Infants will nurse more after their mother has consumed a sweet-tasting substance such as vanilla (Mennella & Beauchamp, 1996).

Newborns are sensitive to touch. As I described in Module 4.4, many areas of the newborn's body respond reflexively when touched. Touching an infant's cheek, mouth, hand, or foot produces reflexive movements, documenting that infants perceive touch.

If babies react to touch, does this mean they experience pain? This is difficult to answer because pain has such a subjective element to it. The same pain-eliciting stimulus that leads some adults to complain of mild discomfort causes others to report that they are in agony. Because infants cannot express their pain to us directly, we must use indirect evidence.

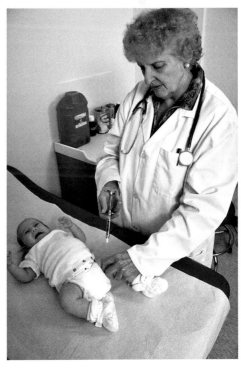

The infant's nervous system definitely is capable of transmitting pain: Receptors for pain in the skin are just as plentiful in infants as they are in adults (Anand & Hickey, 1987). What's more, babies' behavior in response to apparent pain-provoking stimuli also suggests that they experience pain (Buchholz et al., 1998). Look, for example, at the baby in the photo who is receiving an inoculation. She's opened her mouth to cry and, although we can't hear her, the sound of her cry is probably the unique pattern associated with pain. The pain cry begins suddenly, is high-pitched, and is not easily soothed. This baby is also agitated, her heart rate has jumped, and she's moving her hands, arms, and legs (Craig et al., 1993; Goubet et al., 2001). All together, these signs strongly suggest that babies experience pain.

Perceptual skills are extraordinarily useful to newborns and young babies. Smell and touch help them recognize their mothers and make it much easier for them to learn to eat. Early development of smell, taste, and touch prepares newborns and young babies to learn about the world.

## Hearing

Do you remember, from Module 4.1, the study with mothers in late pregnancy who read *The Cat in the Hat* aloud every day? This research showed that the fetus can hear at 7 or 8 months. As you would expect from these results, newborns typically respond to sounds in their surroundings. If a parent is quiet but then coughs, an infant may startle, blink his eyes, and move his arms or legs. These responses may seem natural, but they do indeed indicate that infants are sensitive to sound.

Not surprisingly, infants do not hear as well as adults. **Auditory threshold refers to the quietest sound that a person can hear.** An adult's auditory threshold is fairly easy to measure: A tone is presented, and the adult simply tells when he or she hears it. To test auditory thresholds in infants, who obviously cannot report what they hear, researchers have devised a number of clever techniques (Aslin, Jusczyk, & Pisoni, 1998). For example, in one simple method, the infant is seated on a parent's lap. Both parent and baby wear headphones, as does an observer seated in another room who watches the baby through an observation window. When the observer believes the baby is attentive, he signals the experimenter, who sometimes presents a tone over the baby's headphones and at other times does nothing. Neither the observer nor the parent knows when tones are going to be presented, and they can't hear the tones through their headphones. On each trial, the observer simply judges if the baby responds in any fashion, such as by turning her head or changing her facial expression or activity level. Afterwards, the experimenter determines how well the observer's judgments match the trials: If a baby can hear the tone, the observer should have noted a response only when a tone was presented.

> Infants can distinguish different sounds and they use sound to judge the distance and location of objects.

This type of testing reveals that, overall, adults can hear better than infants; adults can hear some very quiet sounds that infants can't (Aslin et al., 1998). More importantly, this testing shows that infants hear sounds best that have pitches in the range of human speech—neither very high- nor very low-pitched. Infants can differentiate vowels from consonant sounds, and by $4\frac{1}{2}$ months they can recognize their own names (Jusczyk, 1995; Mandel, Jusczyk, & Pisoni, 1995).

Infants also use sound to locate objects, determining whether they are to the left or to the right, and nearby or far away. In one study (Clifton, Perris, & Bullinger, 1991), experimenters showed a rattle to 7-month-old infants. Then the experimenters darkened the room and shook the rattle, either 6 inches away from the infant or about 2 feet away. Infants often reached for the rattle in the dark when it was 6 inches away but seldom did so when it was 2 feet away. These 7-month-olds were quite capable of using sound to estimate distance—in this case, distinguishing a toy they could reach from one they could not.

Thus, by the middle of the first year, most infants respond to much of the information provided by sound. However, not all infants are able to do so, which is the topic of the "Improving Children's Lives" feature.

## IMPROVING CHILDREN'S LIVES

### Hearing Impairment in Infancy

Some infants are born with limited hearing. Others are born deaf. (Exact figures are hard to determine, because infants' hearing is rarely tested precisely.) African, Asian, European, and Hispanic American babies are equally susceptible. Heredity is the leading cause of hearing impairment in newborns. After birth, the leading cause is meningitis, an inflammation of the membranes surrounding the brain and spinal cord.

What are signs of hearing impairment that a parent should watch for? Obviously, parents should be concerned if a young baby never responds to sudden, loud sounds. They should also be concerned if their baby has repeated ear infections, if he does not turn his head in the direction of sounds by 4 or 5 months, does not respond to his own name by 8 or 9 months, and does not begin to imitate speech sounds and simple words by 12 months.

If parents see these problems, their baby should be examined by a physician, who will check for ear problems, and an audiologist, who will measure the infant's hearing. Parents should never delay checking for possible hearing impairment. The earlier the problem is detected, the more the baby can be helped (Smith et al., 1998).

If testing reveals that a baby has impaired hearing, several treatments are possible, depending on the degree of hearing loss. Some children with partial hearing benefit from mechanical devices. Hearing aids help some children, but others—like the child in the photo—benefit from a cochlear implant, in which an electronic device placed in the ear converts speech into electric signals that stimulate nerve cells in the inner ear. Training in lipreading helps others. Children with profound hearing loss can learn to communicate with sign language. By mastering language (either oral language or sign language) and communicating effectively, a child's cognitive and social development will be normal. The key is to recognize impairment promptly. 

## Seeing

If you've watched infants, you've probably noticed that, while awake, they spend a lot of time looking around. Sometimes they seem to be scanning their environment broadly, and sometimes they seem to be focusing on nearby objects. But what do they actually see? Is their visual world a sea of gray blobs? Or do they see the world essentially as adults do? Actually, neither is the case, but, as you'll see, the second is closer to the truth.

From birth, babies respond to light and can track moving objects with their eyes. But what is the clarity of their vision, and how can we measure it? **Visual acuity is defined as the smallest pattern that can be distinguished dependably.** You've undoubtedly had your visual acuity measured by trying to read rows of progressively smaller letters or numbers from a chart. The same basic logic is used in tests of infants' acuity, which are based on two premises. First, most infants will look at patterned stimuli instead of plain, nonpatterned stimuli. For example, if we were to show the two stimuli in the top diagram to infants, most would look longer at the striped pattern than at the gray pattern. Second, as we make the lines narrower (along with the spaces between them), there comes a point at which the black and white stripes become so fine that they simply blend together and appear gray, just like the all-gray pattern.

To estimate an infant's acuity, then, we pair the gray square with squares that differ in the width of their stripes, like those in the bottom diagram: When infants look at the two stimuli equally, it indicates that they are no longer able to distinguish the stripes of the patterned stimulus. By measuring the width of the

FIG.6–1

FIG.6–2

stripes and their distance from an infant's eye, we can estimate acuity (detecting thinner stripes indicates better acuity). Measurements of this sort indicate that newborns and 1-month-olds see at 20 feet what normal adults see at 200 to 400 feet. Infants' acuity improves rapidly and, by the first birthday, is essentially the same as that of a normal adult (Kellman & Banks, 1998).

Infants begin to see the world not only with greater acuity during the first year, but also in color! How do we perceive color? The wavelength of light is the source of color perception. The diagram shows that lights we see as red have a relatively long wavelength, whereas violet, at the other end of the color spectrum, has a much shorter

wavelength. **We detect wavelength—and therefore color—with specialized neurons called cones that are in the retina of the eye.** Some cones are particularly sensitive to short-wavelength light (blues and violets), others are sensitive to medium-wavelength light (greens and yellows), and still others are sensitive to long-wavelength light (reds and oranges). These different kinds of cones are linked in complex circuits of neurons in the eye and in the brain, and this neural circuitry allows us to see the world in color.

These circuits gradually begin to function in the first few months

FIG.6–3

after birth. Newborns and young babies can perceive few colors, but by 3 months the three kinds of cones and their associated circuits are working and infants are able to see the full range of colors (Kellman & Banks, 1998). In fact, by 3 to 4 months, infants' color perception seems similar to that of adults (Adams & Courage, 1995). In particular, infants, like adults, tend to see categories of color. For example, if a yellow light's wavelength is gradually increased, the infant will suddenly perceive it as a shade of red rather than a shade of yellow (Dannemiller, 1998).

The ability to perceive color, along with rapidly improving visual acuity, gives infants great skill in making sense out of their visual experiences. What makes this growing visual skill even more powerful is that, as we'll see in the next section, infants are also starting to connect information obtained from different senses.

## Integrating Sensory Information

So far, we have discussed infants' sensory systems separately. In reality, of course, most infant experiences are better described as "multimedia events." A nursing mother like the one in the photo provides visual and taste cues to her baby. A rattle stimulates vision, hearing, and touch. In fact, much stimulation is not specific to one sense but spans multiple senses. Temporal information, such as duration or tempo, can be conveyed by sight or sound. For example, you can detect the rhythm of a person clapping by seeing the hands meet or by hearing the sound of hands striking. Similarly, the texture of a surface—whether it's rough or smooth, for example—can be detected by sight or by feel.

Infants readily perceive many of these relations. For example, infants can recognize visually an object that they have only touched previously. Similarly, they can detect relations between information presented visually and auditorily. They know, for example, that an object moving into the distance looks smaller and is harder to hear (Bahrick & Lickliter, 2002). And they can link the temporal properties of visual and auditory stimulation, such as duration and rhythm (Lewkowicz, 2000).

Traditionally, coordinating information from different senses (e.g., vision with hearing, vision with touch) was thought to be a challenging task for infants. **More recently, however, some researchers have argued that the infant's sensory systems are particularly attuned to intersensory redundancy, that is, to information that is presented simultaneously to different sensory modes** (Bahrick & Lickliter, 2002). When we see and hear a person talking (auditory + visual), we focus on this information because it is presented to both senses, instead of paying attention to information available to only one sense, such as the color of the person's hair or the sound of an unseen dog barking. The "Focus on Research" feature provides evidence of the importance of intersensory redundancy in infants' perception.

> Infants readily integrate information from different senses, linking seeing to hearing and seeing to touch.

## FOCUS ON RESEARCH

### Infants Attend to Intersensory Redundancy

*Who were the investigators, and what was the aim of the study?* If infants are particularly attentive to information presented redundantly to multiple senses, then they should be better able to notice when that information changes. In other words, if a person claps slowly at first but then quickly, infants should be able to detect this change more readily if they see and hear the clapping than if they see or hear—but not both. Testing this hypothesis was the aim of a study by Lorraine Bahrick and Robert Lickliter (2000).

*How did the investigators measure the topic of interest?* Bahrick and Lickliter wanted to determine the conditions under which 5-month-olds could detect a change in a rhythmic pattern. Consequently, they included three different conditions, shown in the table.

| | Familiarization Trials | | Test Trials | |
| --- | --- | --- | --- | --- |
| Condition | Visual | Auditory | Visual | Auditory |
| Audio + Video | Moving hammer striking a surface | Tapping sounds, synchronized with video | Moving hammer striking a surface, in a new rhythm | Silence |
| Video Only | Moving hammer striking a surface | Silence | Moving hammer striking a surface, in a new rhythm | Silence |
| Audio Only | Still photo of hammer | Tapping sounds | Still photo of hammer | Tapping sounds, in a new rhythm |

**Conditions in the Bahrick and Lickliter (2000) Study**

TABLE 6–1

In the condition of primary interest—audio + video—the infants watched a videotape in which they saw and heard a hammer striking a wooden surface. After several of these familiarization trials, test trials began: The hammer continued to strike the surface, but in a different rhythm and in the absence of sound. The question was whether infants would look longer at the videotape during the test trials, indicating that they had detected the change in rhythm. Performance in this condition was compared to performance in two other conditions: The video-only condition was exactly the same as the audio + video condition, except no audio was presented during the familiarization or test trials. In the audio-only condition, the tapping sounds were exactly as in the audio + video condition, but the videotape depicted a motionless hammer throughout all trials.

*Who were the children in the study?* Each condition included eight 5-month-olds.

*What was the design of the study?* This study was experimental. The independent variable was the manner in which the information was presented: audio + video, video only, and audio only. The dependent variable was the change in infants' looking at the video on the test trials (following the change in rhythm). The study included only 5-month-olds, tested once, so it was not developmental.

*Were there ethical concerns with the study?* No. Most infants seemed to enjoy watching the videos.

*What were the results?* If infants detect the change in the rhythm, they should look more at the video following the change. If they do not detect the change, they should look about the same amount or less (reflecting growing boredom with what seems to be the same stimulus). The graphs show that infants detected the change in rhythm only when auditory and visual information was redundant. Visual or auditory information alone was not enough for infants to detect the change.*

Infants detected a change only when auditory and visual information was synchronized.

FIG.6–4

*What did the investigators conclude?* Bahrick and Lickliter (2000) concluded that "Multimodal stimulation makes overlapping, temporally coordinated information available to the different senses. This 'redundancy' has a powerful impact on the deployment of attention" (p. 198).

*What converging evidence would strengthen these conclusions?* Bahrick and Lickliter could explore other instances of intersensory redundancy. That is, this study focused solely on rhythm, which is just one case of auditory and visual integration. Many other elements need to be explored (e.g., duration) and, of course, this effect needs to be shown for other combinations of senses (e.g., vision and touch, vision and taste). ●

Integrating information from different senses is yet another variation on the theme that has dominated this module: Infants' sensory and perceptual skills are im-

---

*Perhaps you've thought of a problem with this procedure. Infants might look longer not because they notice a change in the pace of hammering but simply because the sound was turned off. To evaluate this possibility, Bahrick and Lickliter also included a condition in which the sound was turned off but the rhythm did not change. In this case, infants did not increase their looking. So, the change in rhythm, not the absence of sound, is the critical variable.

pressive. Darla's newborn daughter, from the opening vignette, can definitely smell, taste, and feel pain. She can distinguish sounds, and at about 7 months she will use sound to locate objects. Her vision is a little blurry now but will improve rapidly, and in a few months she'll see the full range of colors. Within only a month, she'll be making connections between sights and sounds and between other senses. In short, Darla's daughter, like most infants, is well prepared to make sense out of her environment.

## CHECK YOUR LEARNING

1. Babies react to sweet substances by smiling and sucking but grimace when fed substances with a _____ taste.

2. Babies probably experience pain because their nervous system is capable of transmitting pain and because _____.

3. Studies of auditory thresholds reveal that adults can hear better than infants, particularly _____.

4. Infants use sound to judge the distance and _____ of objects.

5. By age _____, infants have approximately the same visual acuity as adults.

6. At 3 months, infants see the full range of colors and, like adults, perceive colors as _____.

7. Infants readily integrate information from different senses and their sensory systems seem to be particularly attuned to _____.

### NATURE AND NURTURE
Are infants' sensory and perceptual skills primarily the effect of nature, nurture, or both?

**Answers:** (1) bitter or sour, (2) they respond to pain-provoking stimulation, (3) softer sounds, (4) location, (5) 1 year, (6) categories, (7) information presented redundantly to multiple senses

# Complex Perceptual and Attentional Processes

# 6.2

## LEARNING OBJECTIVES

- How do infants perceive objects?

- How does attention improve as children grow older?

- What is attention deficit hyperactivity disorder?

Perceiving Objects

Attention

Attention Deficit Hyperactivity Disorder

> *Linda was only 36 hours old when John and Jean brought her home from the hospital. They quickly noticed that loud noises startled Linda, which worried them because their apartment was near an entrance ramp to a freeway. Trucks accelerating to enter the freeway made an incredible amount of noise that caused Linda to "jump" and sometimes cry. John and Jean wondered if Linda would get enough sleep. However, within days, the trucks no longer disturbed Linda; she slept blissfully. Why was a noise that had been so troubling no longer a problem?*

Where we draw the dividing line between "basic" and "complex" perceptual processes is quite arbitrary. As you'll see, Module 6.2 is a logical extension of the information presented in Module 6.1. We'll begin by looking at how we perceive objects. We'll also look at the processes of attention and some children who have attentional problems. By the end of the module, you'll know why Linda is no longer bothered by noises that once disturbed her.

## Perceiving Objects

When you look at this pattern, what do you see? You probably recognize it as part of a human eyeball, even though all that's physically present in the photograph are many different colored dots. In this case, perception actually creates an object from sensory stimulation. That is, our perceptual processes determine that certain features go together to form objects. This is particularly challenging because we often see only parts of objects—nearby objects often obscure parts of more distant objects. Nevertheless, in the photo below we recognize that the orange is one object even though it is partially hidden by the apple.

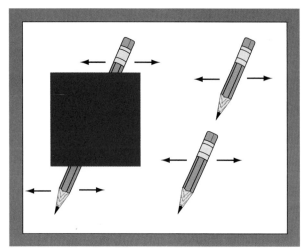

FIG.6–5

Perception of objects is limited in newborns but develops rapidly in the first few months after birth (Johnson, 2001). By 4 months, infants use a number of cues to determine which elements go together to form objects. One important cue is motion: Elements that move together are usually part of the same object (Kellman & Banks, 1998). For example, at the left of the diagram, a pencil appears to be moving back and forth behind a colored square. If the square were removed, you would be surprised to see a pair of pencil stubs, as shown on the right side of the diagram. The common movement of the pencil's eraser and point lead us to believe that they're part of the same pencil.

Young infants, too, are surprised by demonstrations like this. If they see a display like the moving pencils, they will then look very briefly at a whole pencil, apparently because they expected it. In contrast, if after seeing the moving pencil they're shown the two pencil stubs, they look much longer, as if trying to figure out what happened (Eizenman & Bertenthal, 1998; Johnson & Aslin, 1995). Evidently, even very young babies use common motion to create objects from different parts.

Motion is one clue to object unity, but infants use others, too, including, color, texture, and aligned edges. As you can see in the diagram, infants more often group features together (i.e., believe they're part of the same object), when they're the same color, have the same texture, and when their edges are aligned (Johnson, 2001).

Grouping features is an important first step in perceiving objects, but only the first. Perceptual constancies are important, too.

**PERCEPTUAL CONSTANCIES.**  Any time a mother moves away from her baby, the image that she casts on the retinas of her baby's eyes gets smaller. Do babies have a nightmare that their mother's head is shrinking as she moves away? No. **Early on, infants master size constancy, the realization that an object's actual size remains the same despite changes in the size of its retinal image.**

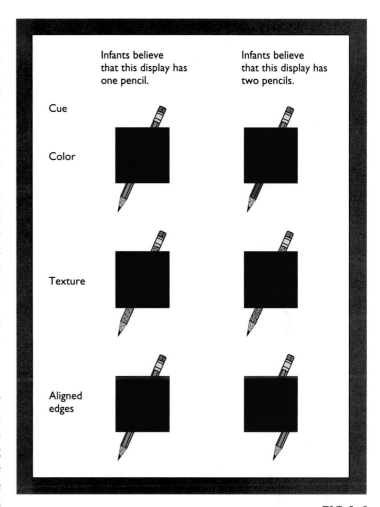

FIG.6–6

How do we know that infants have a rudimentary sense of size constancy? Suppose we let an infant look at an unfamiliar teddy bear. Then we show the infant the same bear, at a different distance, paired with a larger replica of the bear. If infants lack size constancy, the two bears will be equally novel and babies should respond to each similarly. If, instead, babies have size constancy, they will recognize the first bear as familiar, the larger bear as novel, and be more likely to respond to the novel bear. In fact, by 4 or 5 months, babies treat the bear that they've seen twice at different distances—and, therefore, with different retinal images—as familiar (Granrud, 1986). This outcome is possible only if infants have size constancy. Thus, infants do not believe that mothers (and other people or objects) constantly change size as they move closer or farther away.

Size is just one of several perceptual constancies. Others are brightness and color constancy as well as shape constancy, shown in the diagram on page 154. All these constancies are achieved, at least in rudimentary form, by 4 months (Aslin, 1987; Dannemiller, 1998).

The message from the perceptual constancies is that "seeing is not always believing." A good part of perception, therefore, is knowing how to make sense out of what

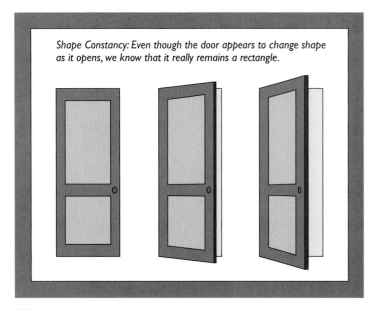

*Shape Constancy: Even though the door appears to change shape as it opens, we know that it really remains a rectangle.*

FIG.6–7

we see. Another important part of "making sense" out of what we see is deciding how near or far an object is.

**DEPTH.**   People see objects as having three dimensions: height, width, and depth. The retina of the eye is flat, so height and width can be represented directly on its two-dimensional surface. But the third dimension, depth, cannot be represented directly on this surface, so how do we perceive depth? How do we decide whether objects are nearby or far away? We use perceptual processing to infer depth.

Can infants perceive depth? Eleanor Gibson and Richard Walk (1960) addressed this question using a special apparatus. **The visual cliff is a glass-covered platform; on one side a pattern appears directly under the glass, but on the other it appears several feet below the glass.** Consequently, one side looks shallow but the other appears to have a steep drop-off, like a cliff. As you can see in the photo, in the experiment the baby is placed on the platform and the mother coaxes her infant to come to her. Most babies willingly crawl to their mothers when she stands on the shallow side. But virtually all babies refuse to cross the deep side, even when the mother calls the infant by name and tries to lure him or her with an attractive toy. Clearly, infants can perceive depth by the time they are old enough to crawl.

What about babies who cannot yet crawl? When babies as young as $1\frac{1}{2}$ months are simply placed on the deep side of the platform, their heartbeat slows down. Heart rate often decelerates when people notice something interesting, so this would suggest that $1\frac{1}{2}$-month–olds notice that the deep side is different. At 7 months, infants' heart rate accelerates, a sign of fear. Thus, although young babies can detect a difference between the shallow and deep sides of the visual cliff, only older, crawling babies are actually afraid of the deep side (Campos et al., 1978).

## Infants use retinal disparity to perceive depth along with several cues provided in the environment.

How do infants infer depth, on the visual cliff or anywhere? They use several kinds of cues. **One, retinal disparity, is based on the fact that the left and right eyes often see slightly different versions of the same scene.** When objects are distant, the images appear in very similar positions on the retina; when objects are near, the images appear in much different positions. Thus, greater disparity in positions of the image on the retina signals that an object is close. By 4 to 6 months, infants use retinal disparity as a depth cue, correctly inferring that objects are nearby when disparity is great (Kellman & Banks, 1998; Yonas & Owsley, 1987).

By 7 months, infants use several cues for depth that depend on the arrangement of objects in the environment. They are illustrated on page 155.

VIDEO 6.1
Gibson's Visual Cliff
CLASSIC MODULE

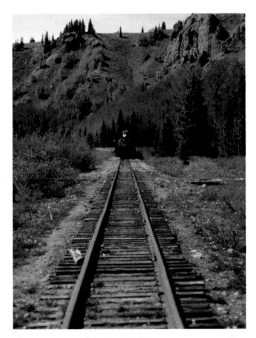

*Linear perspective:* **Parallel lines come together at a single point in the distance.** Thus, we use the space between the lines as a cue to distance and, consequently, decide the train in the photo is far away because the parallel tracks grow close together.

*Texture gradient:* **The texture of objects changes from coarse but distinct for nearby objects to finer and less distinct for distant objects.** In the photo, we judge the distinct flowers to be close and the blurred ones, distant.

*Interposition:* **Nearby objects partially obscure more distant objects.** The glasses obscure the bottle, so we decide the glasses are closer (and use this same cue to decide the grapes are closer than the left glass).

*Relative size:* **Nearby objects look substantially larger than objects in the distance.** Knowing that the runners are really about the same size, we judge the ones that look smaller to be farther away.

So far in this module, we've seen that young babies use simple relations between stimuli to infer an object, recognize that objects are the same despite changes in appearance, and use many cues to infer depth. We can understand infants' perceptual skills from a different perspective by looking at their perception of faces.

**PERCEIVING FACES.**   The human face is a particularly important object to infants. Young babies readily look at faces. From the diagram, which shows a pattern of eye fixations, you can see that 1-month-olds look mostly at the outer edges of the face. Three-month-olds, however, focus almost entirely on the interior of the face, particularly the eyes and lips.

**1-Month-Olds**

**3-Month-Olds**

FIG.6–8

Some theorists argue that babies are innately attracted to stimuli that are face-like. The claim here is that some aspect of the face—perhaps two eyes and a mouth in the correct arrangement—constitutes a distinctive stimulus that is readily recognized, even by newborns. For example, in one study (Morton & Johnson, 1991), newborns turned their eyes to follow a moving face more than they turned their eyes for nonface stimuli. This preference for faces over facelike stimuli supports the view that infants are innately attracted to faces.

Other scientists, however, believe that general principles of perception explain how infants perceive faces (Aslin, 1987). They argue that infants are attracted to faces because faces have stimuli that move (the eyes and mouth) and stimuli with dark and light contrast (the eyes, lips, and teeth). Research by Easterbrooks and her colleagues (1999) supports this view. They found that when face and nonface stimuli are matched for a number of important variables, newborns turn their head and eyes equally for face and nonface stimuli. These results go along with the idea that infants look at faces because of general perceptual principles (for example, babies prefer contrasting stimuli), not because faces are intrinsically attractive to infants.

> **Infants enjoy looking at faces, a preference that may reflect innate attraction to faces or the fact that faces have many properties known to attract infants' attention.**

More research is needed to decide whether face perception follows general perceptual principles or represents a special case. What is clear, though, is that by 3 or 4 months babies have the perceptual skills that allow them to begin to distinguish individual faces (Carey, 1992). And, by 9 months, these skills have become specific to human faces: 6-month-olds recognize human and monkey faces equally well, but 9-month-olds recognize human faces much better than monkey faces (Pascalis, de Haan, & Nelson, 2002). This ability is essential, for it provides the basis for social relationships that infants form during the rest of the first year (which we'll examine in Module 11.3).

## Attention

VIDEO 6.2

Habituation/
Dishabituation

Have you ever been in a class where you knew you should be listening and taking notes, but the lecture was just so boring that you started noticing other things—the construction going on outside or an attractive person seated nearby? After a while, maybe you reminded yourself to "pay attention!" We get distracted because our perceptual systems are marvelously powerful. They provide us with far more information at any time than we could possible interpret. **Attention is the process by which we select information that will be processed further.** In a class, for example, where the task is to direct your attention to the lecture, it is easy to ignore other stimuli if the lecture is interesting. But if the lecture is not interesting, other stimuli intrude and capture your attention.

The roots of attention can be seen in infancy. Remember Linda, the newborn in the vignette who jumped when trucks accelerated past her home? Her response was normal not only for infants but also for children and adults. **When presented with a strong or unfamiliar stimulus, an orienting response usually occurs: A person startles, fixes the eyes on the stimulus, and shows changes in heart rate and brain wave patterns.** Collectively, these responses indicate that the infant is attending to this stimulus. Remember, too, that Linda soon began to ignore the sounds of trucks. After repeated presentations of a stimulus, people become accustomed to it, so their orienting response diminishes and eventually disappears, signs of habituation, which we discussed on page 144. Habituation indicates that attention is selective: A stimulus that once garnered attention no longer does.

The orienting response and habituation can both be demonstrated easily in the laboratory. For example, in one study (Zelazo et al., 1989) speech was played through one of two loudspeakers placed on either side of an infant. At first, most newborns turned their heads toward the source of the speech, but after several trials they no longer responded. Thus, newborns oriented to the novel sound but then gradually habituated to the sound as it became more familiar.

The orienting response and habituation are both useful to infants. On the one hand, orienting makes the infant aware of potentially important or dangerous events in the environment. On the other hand, constantly responding to insignificant stimuli is wasteful, so habituation keeps infants like the one in the photo from wasting too much energy on biologically nonsignificant stimuli (Rovee-Collier, 1987). Given the biological significance of being able to habituate, it's not too surprising that infants who habituate more rapidly tend to grow up to be more intelligent children (Rose et al., 1997).

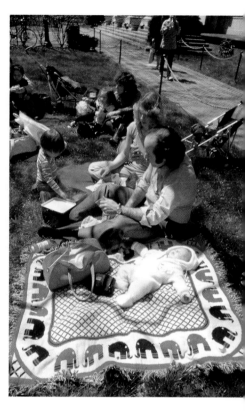

During the preschool years, children gradually become better able to regulate their attention. You can see these changes in the results of a study of $2\frac{1}{2}$- to $4\frac{1}{2}$-year-olds by Ruff, Capozzoli, and Weissberg (1998). These investigators observed preschoolers in several settings. In one, children sat at a table watching hand puppets and dolls enact brief skits. In another, children were told they could play with an assortment of toys on a tabletop. Ruff and her colleagues videotaped children in both settings, then analyzed the tapes for many different behaviors. Children who were actively engaged in the puppet show or free play—as inferred by their posture, facial expressions, spontaneous comments, and the like—exhibited focused attention. Children who left the table exhibited active inattention.

The results, shown in the graph, illustrate two important characteristics of attention during the preschool years. First, attention improved markedly in this period. In both settings, the $4\frac{1}{2}$-year-olds spent much more time than the $2\frac{1}{2}$-year-olds in focused attention and much less time in active inattention. Second, the $4\frac{1}{2}$-year-olds, though much more attentive than the younger children, still spent less than half the time in a state of focused attention. Maintaining focused attention is a demanding skill, one that emerges gradually beyond the preschool and school-age years (Enns, 1990).

Why does attention improve with age? For one thing, older children and adolescents are simply more likely to remind themselves that they need to pay attention. They are also more likely to have mastered some attentional

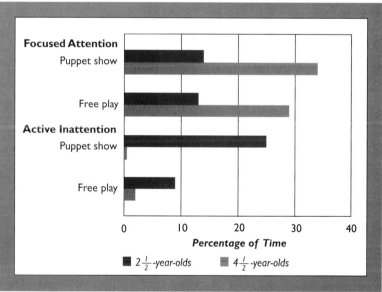

FIG.6–9

"tricks of the trade." For example, if asked to determine whether two objects are the same, older children and adolescents are more likely to compare them feature by feature until they find features that do not match or they run out of features to check (Vurpillot, 1968). By directing their attention in this manner, children are guaranteed that they will do the task accurately and in the least amount of time possible. Asked if the two houses in the diagram at the top of page 158 are the same, older children typically start by comparing the top windows and work down until they have compared all six pairs of windows. In contrast, younger children

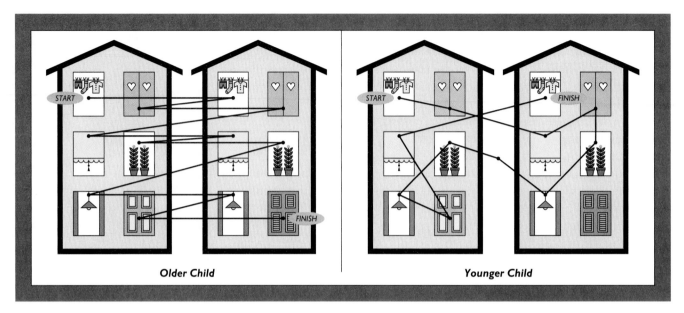

FIG.6–10

direct their attention haphazardly—not systematically checking corresponding windows—so they often don't find the differing windows.

Young children need help to pay attention better. One approach is to make relevant information more salient than irrelevant information. For example, closing a classroom door may not eliminate competing sounds and smells entirely, but it will make them less salient. Or, when preschoolers are working at a table or desk, we can remove all objects that are not necessary for the task. It's also very helpful, particularly for young children, to remind them periodically to pay attention only to relevant information and ignore the rest. These techniques improve some but not all children's attention, as we'll see in the next section.

## Attention Deficit Hyperactivity Disorder

Children with attention deficit hyperactivity disorder—ADHD for short—have special problems when it comes to paying attention. Roughly 3 to 5 percent of all school-age children are diagnosed with ADHD; boys outnumber girls by a 3:1 ratio (Wicks-Nelson & Israel, 1991). The "Real Children" feature describes one boy with ADHD.

### REAL CHILDREN

#### Why Can't Stephen Pay Attention?

Soon after Stephen entered kindergarten, his teacher remarked that he sometimes seemed out of control. Stephen was easily distracted, often moving aimlessly from one activity to another. He also seemed to be impulsive, and compared to other youngsters his age, he had much more difficulty waiting his turn. At first, Stephen's parents just attributed his behavior to boyish energy. But when Stephen progressed to first and second grade, his pattern of behavior continued. He began to fall behind in reading and arithmetic. His classmates were annoyed by his behavior and began to avoid him. This just made Stephen mad, so he often got into fights with his classmates. Finally, Stephen's parents took him to a psychologist, who determined that Stephen had attention deficit hyperactivity disorder.

Stephen exhibits three symptoms at the heart of ADHD (American Psychiatric Association, 1994):

- *Inattention:* Youngsters with ADHD skip from one task to another. They do not pay attention in class and seem unable to concentrate on schoolwork.

- *Hyperactivity:* Children with ADHD are unusually energetic, fidgety, and unable to keep still, especially in situations like school classrooms where they need to limit their activity.

- *Impulsivity:* Children with ADHD often act before thinking; they may run into a street before looking for traffic or interrupt others who are speaking.

**Children with ADHD are overactive, inattentive, and impulsive; they often do poorly in school and are disliked by peers.**

Not all children with ADHD show all these symptoms to the same degree. Some, like the boy in the photograph, may be primarily hyperactive and impulsive. Others may be primarily inattentive and show fewer signs of hyperactivity and impulsivity; their disorder is often described simply as attention-deficit disorder (Barkley, 1990). Children with ADHD often have problems with conduct and academic performance. Like Stephen, many hyperactive children are aggressive and therefore are not liked by their peers (Barkley, 1990; McGee, Williams, & Feehan, 1992). Although youngsters with ADHD usually have normal intelligence, their scores on reading, spelling, and arithmetic achievement tests are often below average (Pennington, Groisser, & Welsh, 1993).

Many myths surround ADHD. Some concern causes. At one time or another, TV, food allergies, sugar, and poor home life have all been proposed as causes of ADHD, but research does not consistently support any of these (e.g., Wolraich et al., 1994). Instead, ADHD has biological roots and a hereditary component (Edelbrock et al., 1995). Another myth is that most children "grow out of" ADHD in adolescence or young adulthood. More than half the children who are diagnosed with ADHD will have problems related to overactivity, inattention, and impulsivity as adolescents and young adults. Few of these young adults complete college, and some will have work- and family-related problems (Fischer et al., 1993; Rapport, 1995). One final myth is that many healthy children are wrongly diagnosed with ADHD. The number of children diagnosed with ADHD *has* increased substantially over the past 10 to 15 years but not because children are being routinely misdiagnosed; the increased numbers reflect growing awareness of ADHD and more frequent diagnoses of ADHD in girls and adolescents (Goldman et al., 1998).

Because ADHD affects academic and social success throughout childhood and adolescence, researchers have worked hard to find effective treatments. The "Child Development and Family Policy" feature describes these efforts.

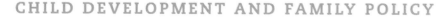

## CHILD DEVELOPMENT AND FAMILY POLICY

### What's the Best Treatment for ADHD?

By the mid 1980s, it was clear that ADHD could be treated. For example, children with ADHD often respond well to stimulant drugs such as Ritalin. It may seem odd that stimulants are given to children who are already overactive, but these drugs stimulate the parts of the brain that normally inhibit hyperactive and impulsive behavior. Thus, stimulants actually have a calming influence for many youngsters with ADHD, allowing them to focus their attention (Aman, Roberts, & Pennington, 1998).

Drug therapy was not the only approach: Psychosocial treatments also worked and were designed to improve children's cognitive and social skills and often included home-based intervention and intensive summer programs (Richters et al., 1995). For example, children can be taught to remind themselves to read instructions before starting assignments. And they can be reinforced by others for inhibiting impulsive and hyperactive behavior (Barkley, 1994).

These treatments were well known by the late 1980s, yet many researchers were troubled by large gaps in our understanding. One gap concerned the long-term success of treatment. Most studies had measured the impact of weeks or months of treatment; virtually nothing was known about the effectiveness of treatment over longer periods. Another gap concerned the most effective combination of treatments and whether this was the same for all children. That is, is medication plus psychosocial treatment the best for all children and for all facets of children's development (i.e., academic and social)?

Prompted by these concerns, scientific advisory groups met in the late 1980s and early 1990s to identify the gaps in understanding and the research needed to fill the gaps. Reports of these groups lead the National Institute of Mental Health to request, in 1992, proposals for research. After intensive review, the top six applications were selected and synthesized to create the Multimodal Treatment Study of Children with ADHD—the MTA for short (Richters et al., 1995). The MTA involves 18 scientists who are experts on ADHD and nearly 600 elementary-school children with ADHD. The children were assigned to different treatment modes and the impact of treatment is measured in several different domains of children's development.

The MTA is ongoing but initial results show that medical treatment alone is the best way to treat hyperactivity per se. However, for a variety of other measures, including academic and social skills as well as parent–child relations, medication plus psychosocial treatment is slightly more effective than medication alone. The MTA also makes it clear that medication treatment is effective only when dosage is monitored carefully with regular follow-up visits to a health care professional, and there is regular communication with schools regarding children's functioning (Jensen et al., 2001).

Thus, the MTA demonstrates one way in which research can influence practices for children, in this case, the treatment of children with ADHD. Scientists identify gaps in understanding of an important childhood disorder, research is proposed and conducted to eliminate the gaps, and evidence indicates the best practices for children, their parents, teachers, and health care professionals.

## CHECK YOUR LEARNING

1. Infants use _____, color, texture, and aligned edges to help distinguish objects.

2. An infant understands _____ if she knows that her father does not really become larger as he moves closer to her.

3. On the visual cliff, infants who can crawl _____, which shows that they can perceive depth.

4. Some theorists explain infants' perception of faces in terms of general principles of perception, but others _____.

5. Older children and adolescents have better attentional skills because they remind themselves to pay attention more often and because _____.

6. The three primary symptoms of ADHD are inattention, hyperactivity, and _____.

**CONTINUITY**

What happens to children with ADHD when they become adolescents and young adults? How does this address the issue of continuity of development?

# Motor Development 6.3

## LEARNING OBJECTIVES

Locomotion
Fine-Motor Skills
Physical Fitness

- What are the component skills involved in learning to walk, and at what age do infants typically master them?

- How do infants learn to coordinate the use of their hands? When and why do most children begin to prefer to use one hand?

- Are children physically fit? Do they benefit from participating in sports?

*Nancy is 14 months old and a world-class crawler. Using hands and knees, she gets nearly anywhere she wants to go. Nancy does not walk and seems to have no interest in learning how. Her dad wonders whether he should be doing something to help Nancy progress beyond crawling. And down deep, he worries that perhaps he should have provided more exercise or training for Nancy when she was younger.*

These photos have a common theme. Each depicts an activity involving motor skills—coordinated movements of the muscles and limbs. In each activity, success demands that each movement be done in a precise way and in a specific sequence. For example, to use a stick shift properly, you need to move the clutch pedal, gas pedal, and the stick shift in specific ways and in exactly the right sequence. If you don't give the car enough gas as you let out the clutch, you'll kill the engine. If you give it too much gas, the engine races and the car lurches forward.

If new activities are demanding for adults, think about the challenges infants face. **Infants must learn locomotion, that is, to move about in the world.** Newborns are relatively immobile, but infants soon learn to crawl, stand, and walk. Learning to move through the environment upright leaves the arms and hands free. Taking full advantage of this arrangement, the human hand has fully independent fingers (instead of a paw), with the thumb opposing the remaining four fingers. An opposable thumb makes it possible for humans to grasp and manipulate objects. **Infants must learn the fine-motor skills associated with grasping, holding, and manipulating objects.** In the case of feeding, for example, infants progress from being fed by others to holding a bottle, to feeding

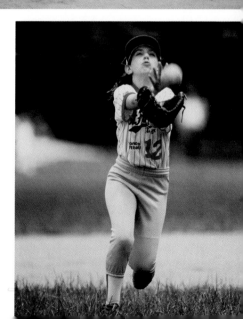

themselves with their fingers, to eating with a spoon. Each new skill requires incredibly complex physical movements.

Although demanding, locomotion and fine-motor skills are well worth mastering because of their benefits. Being able to locomote and to grasp gives children access to an enormous amount of information about their environment. They can explore objects that look interesting, and they can keep themselves close to parents. Improved motor skills promote children's cognitive and social development, not to mention make a child's life more interesting!

In this module, we'll see how children acquire locomotor and fine-motor skills. As we do, we'll find out if Nancy's dad should be worrying about her lack of interest in walking.

## Locomotion

In little more than a year, advances in posture and locomotion change the newborn from an almost motionless being into an upright, standing individual who walks through the environment. The chart shows some of the important milestones in motor development and the age by which most infants achieve them. By about 4 months, most babies can sit upright with support. By 6 or 7 months, they can sit without support, and by 7 or 8 months, can stand if they hold on to an object for support. A typical 11-month-old can stand alone briefly and walk with assistance. **Youngsters at this age are called toddlers, after the toddling manner of early walking.** Of course, not all children walk at exactly the same age. Some walk before their first birthday; others, like Nancy, the world-class crawler in the module-opening vignette, take their first steps as late as 17 or 18 months of age. By 24 months, most children can climb steps, walk backwards, and kick a ball.

FIG.6-11
Source: Based on Shirley, 1931 and Bayley 1993.

Researchers once thought these developmental milestones reflected maturation (e.g., McGraw, 1935). Walking, for example, was thought to emerge naturally when the necessary muscles and neural circuits matured. Today, however, locomotion—and, in fact, all motor development—is viewed from a new perspective. **According to dynamic systems theory, motor development involves many distinct skills that are organized and reorganized over time to meet the demands of specific tasks.** For example, walking includes maintaining balance, moving limbs, perceiving the environment, and having a reason to move. Only by understanding each of these skills and how they are combined to allow movement in a specific situation can we understand walking (Thelen & Smith, 1998).

In the remainder of this section, we'll see how learning to walk reflects the maturity and coalescence of many component skills.

**POSTURE AND BALANCE.** The ability to maintain an upright posture is fundamental to walking. But upright posture is virtually impossible for young infants because the shape of their body makes them top-heavy. Consequently, as soon as a young infant starts to lose her balance, she tumbles over. Only with growth of the legs and muscles can infants maintain an upright posture (Thelen, Ulrich, & Jensen, 1989).

> To walk, infants must acquire distinct skills of standing upright, maintaining balance, stepping alternately, and using perceptual information to evaluate surfaces.

Once infants can stand upright, they must continuously adjust their posture to avoid falling down. By a few months after birth, infants begin to use visual cues and an inner-ear mechanism to adjust their posture. To show the use of visual cues for balance, researchers had babies sit in a room with striped walls that moved. When adults sit in such a room, they perceive themselves as moving (not the walls) and adjust their posture accordingly; so do infants, which shows that they use vision to maintain upright posture (Bertenthal & Clifton, 1998). In addition, when 4-month-olds who are propped in a sitting position lose their balance, they try to keep their head upright. They do this even when blindfolded, which means they are using cues from their inner ear to maintain balance (Woollacott, Shumway-Cook, & Williams, 1989).

Balance is not, however, something that infants master just once. Instead, infants must relearn balancing for sitting, crawling, walking, and other postures. Why? The body rotates around different points in each posture (e.g., the wrists for crawling versus the ankles for walking) and different muscle groups are used to generate compensating motions when infants begin to lose their balance. Consequently, it's hardly surprising that infants who easily maintain their balance while sitting topple over time after time when crawling. Infants must recalibrate the balance system as they take on each new posture, just as basketball players recalibrate their muscle movements when they move from dunking to shooting a three pointer (Adolph, 2000, 2002).

**STEPPING.**   Another essential element of walking is moving the legs alternately, repeatedly transferring the weight of the body from one foot to the other. Children don't step spontaneously until approximately 10 months because they must be able to stand to step.

Can younger children step if they are held upright? Thelen and Ulrich (1991) devised a clever procedure to answer this question. Infants were placed on a treadmill and held upright by an adult. When the belt on the treadmill started to move, infants could respond in one of several ways. They might simply let both legs be dragged rearward by the belt. Or they might let their legs be dragged briefly, then move them forward together in a hopping motion. Many 6- and 7-month-olds demonstrated the mature pattern of alternating steps on each leg that is shown in the photo. Even more amazing is that when the treadmill was equipped with separate belts for each leg that moved at different speeds, babies adjusted, stepping more rapidly on the faster belt. Apparently, the alternate stepping motion that is essential for walking is evident long before infants walk alone. Walking unassisted is not possible, though, until other component skills are mastered.

**PERCEPTUAL FACTORS.**   Many infants learn to walk in the relative security of flat, uncluttered floors at home. But they soon discover that the environment offers a variety of surfaces, some more conducive to walking than others. Infants use perceptual information to judge whether a surface is suitable for walking. When placed on a surface that gives way underfoot (e.g., a waterbed), they quickly judge it unsuitable for walking and resort to crawling (Gibson et al., 1987). And when toddlers encounter a surface that slopes down steeply, few try to walk down (which would result in a fall). Instead, they slide or scoot backwards (Adolph, Eppler, & Gibson, 1993;

Adolph, 1997). Results like these show that infants use perceptual cues to decide whether a surface is safe for walking.

**COORDINATING SKILLS.** Dynamic systems theory emphasizes that learning to walk demands orchestration of many individual skills. Each component skill must first be mastered alone and then integrated with the other skills (Werner, 1948). **That is, mastery of intricate motions requires both differentiation—mastery of component skills—and their integration—combining them in proper sequence into a coherent, working whole.** In the case of walking, not until 9 to 15 months of age has the child mastered the component skills so that they can be coordinated to allow independent, unsupported walking.

Mastering individual skills and coordinating them well does not happen overnight. Instead, they take time and repeated practice. For example, when parents give their infants daily practice in sitting, their infants master sitting at a younger age. However, such practice has no effect on stepping, because different muscles and movements are involved (Zelazo et al., 1993). Similarly, when infants practice crawling on their bellies, this helps them crawl on hands and feet because many of the motions are the same (Adolph, Vereijken, & Denny, 1998). But when infants practice crawling on steep slopes, there is no transfer to walking on steep slopes, because the motions differ (Adolph, 1997). Thus, experience can improve the rate of motor development, but the improvement is limited to the movements that were trained. In other words, just as daily practice kicking a soccer ball won't improve your golf game, infants who receive much practice in one motor skill don't usually improve in others.

These findings from laboratory research are not the only evidence that practice promotes motor development. As you'll see in the "Cultural Influences" feature, cross-cultural research points to the same conclusion.

## CULTURAL INFLUENCES

### Cultural Practices that Promote Motor Development

Compared to infants growing up in Europe and North America, many infants from traditional African cultures reach the motor milestones shown on page 162 at an early age. For example, traditional African infants sit and walk at younger ages. Careful observations of these infants reveal two factors responsible for this early advantage in motor development. First, many common child-care practices in traditional African societies have the unanticipated benefit of improving motor skill. For example, infants are commonly carried by their parents in the "piggyback" style shown in the photo, which helps develop muscles in the infants' trunk and legs. Second, mothers in traditional African cultures believe that practice is essential for motor skills to develop normally and so they (or siblings) provide daily training sessions. For example, they may help children to learn to sit by having them sit while propped up (Super, 1981). The combined effect of this unintentional and deliberate training is to provide additional opportunities for children to learn the elements of different motor skills. Not surprisingly, African infants with these opportunities learn to sit and walk earlier.

**BEYOND WALKING.** If you can recall the feeling of freedom that accompanied your first driver's license, you can imagine how the world expands for infants and toddlers as they learn to move independently. The first tentative steps soon are followed by others that are more skilled. Children's growing skill is evident in their running and hopping. Most 2-year-olds have a hurried walk instead of a true run; they move their legs stiffly (rather than bending them at the knees) and are not airborne as is the case when running. By 5 or 6 years, children run easily, quickly changing directions or speed. Similarly, an average 2- or 3-year-old will hop a few times on one foot, typically keeping the upper body very stiff; by 5 or 6, children can hop long distances on one foot or alternate hopping first on one foot a few times, then on the other.

## Fine-Motor Skills

A major accomplishment in infancy is skilled use of the hands (Bertenthal & Clifton, 1998). Newborns have little apparent control of their hands, but 1-year-olds are extraordinarily talented.

**REACHING AND GRASPING.**   At about 4 months, infants can successfully reach for objects (Bertenthal & Clifton, 1998). These early reaches often look clumsy, and for a good reason. When infants reach, their arms and hands don't move directly and smoothly to the desired object (as is true for older children and adults). Instead, the infant's hand moves like a ship under the direction of an unskilled navigator. It moves a short distance, slows, then moves again in a slightly different direction, a process that's repeated until the hand finally contacts the object (McCarty & Ashmead, 1999). As infants grow, their reaches have fewer movements, though they are still not as continuous and smooth as older children's and adults' reaches (Berthier, 1996).

Reaching requires that an infant move the hand to the location of a desired object. Grasping poses a different challenge: Now the infant must coordinate movements of individual fingers in order to grab an object. Grasping, too, becomes more efficient during infancy. Most 4-month-olds just use their fingers to hold objects. Like the baby in the photo, they wrap an object tightly with their fingers alone. Not until 7 or 8 months do most infants use their thumbs to hold objects (Siddiqui, 1995). At about this age, infants begin to position their hands to make it easier to grasp an object. In trying to grasp a long thin rod, for example, infants place their fingers perpendicular to the rod, which is the best position for grasping (Wentworth et al., 2000). Infants need not see their hand to position it correctly: They position the hand just as accurately in reaching for a lighted object in a darkened room as when reaching in a lighted room (McCarty et al., 2000).

Infants' growing control of each hand is accompanied by greater coordination of the two hands. Although 4-month-olds use both hands, their motions are not coordinated; rather, each hand seems to have a mind of its own. Infants may hold a toy motionless in one hand while shaking a rattle in the other. At roughly 5 to 6 months of age, infants can coordinate the motions of their hands so that each hand performs different actions that serve a common goal. So a child might, for example, hold a toy animal in one hand and pet it with the other (Karniol, 1989).

These many changes in reaching and grasping are well illustrated as infants learn to feed themselves. At about 6 months, they are often given "finger foods" such as sliced bananas and green beans. Infants can easily pick up such foods, but getting them into their mouths is another story. The hand grasping the food may be raised to the cheek, then moved to the edge of the lips, and finally shoved into the mouth. Mission accomplished, but only with many detours along the way! Eye-hand coordination improves rapidly, so before long foods that vary in size, shape, and texture reach the mouth directly.

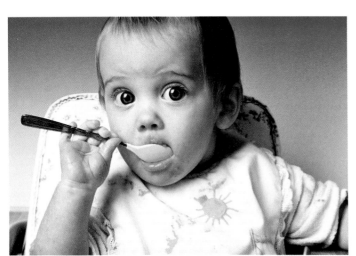

At about the first birthday, youngsters are usually ready to try eating with a spoon. At first, they simply play with the spoon, dipping it in and out of a dish filled with food or sucking on an empty spoon. With a little help, they learn to fill the spoon with food and place it in their mouth, though the motion is awkward because they don't rotate their wrist. Instead, most 1-year-olds fill a spoon by placing it directly over a dish, and lowering it until the bowl of the spoon is full. Then, like the child in the photo, they raise the spoon to the mouth—all the while keeping the wrist rigid. In contrast, 2-year-olds rotate the hand at the wrist while scooping food from a dish and placing the spoon in the mouth—the same motion that adults use.

After infancy, fine-motor skills progress rapidly. Preschool children become much more dexterous, able to make many precise and delicate movements with their hands and fingers. Greater fine-motor skill means that preschool children can begin to care for themselves. No longer must they rely primarily on parents to feed and clothe them; instead, they become increasingly skilled at feeding and dressing themselves. A 2- or 3-year-old, for example, can put on some simple clothing and use zippers but not buttons; by 3 or 4 years, children can fasten buttons and take off their clothes when going to the bathroom; like the child in the photo, most 5-year-olds can dress and undress themselves, except for tying shoes, which children typically master at about age 6.

In each of these actions, the same principles of dynamic systems theory apply as applied to locomotion. Complex acts involve many component movements. Each must be performed correctly and in the proper sequence. Development involves first mastering the separate elements and then assembling them to form a smoothly functioning whole. Eating finger food, for example, requires grasping food, moving the hand to the mouth, then releasing the food.

As the demands of tasks change and as children develop, the same skills are often reassembled to form a different sequence of movements.

**HANDEDNESS.** When young babies reach for objects, they don't seem to prefer one hand over the other; they use their left and right hands interchangeably. They may shake a rattle with their left hand and moments later pick up blocks with their right. In one study, infants and toddlers were videotaped as they played with toys that could be manipulated with two hands, such as a pinwheel (Cornwell, Harris, & Fitzgerald, 1991). The 9-month-olds used their left and right hands equally, but by 13 months most grasped the toy with their right hand.

Then, like the toddler in the photo, they used their left hand to steady the toy while the right hand manipulated the object. This early preference for one hand becomes stronger and more consistent during the preschool years. By the time children are ready to enter kindergarten, handedness is well established and very difficult to reverse (McManus et al., 1988).

What determines whether children become left- or right-handed? Heredity plays a role (Corballis, 1997, 2000). Parents who are both right-handed tend to have right-handed children. Children who are left-handed generally have a parent or grandparent who was also left-handed. But experience also contributes to handedness. Modern industrial cultures favor right-handedness. School desks, scissors, and can openers, for example, are designed for right-handed people and can be used by left-handers only with difficulty.

Sometimes cultural values influence handedness. The Islam religion dictates that the left hand is unclean, and so forbids its use in eating and greeting others. Writing with the left hand is a cultural taboo in China, but when children of Chinese parents grow up elsewhere, about 10 percent of them write with their left hand, the typical figure worldwide (Harris, 1983). In the United States, elementary-school teachers used to urge left-handed children to use their right hands. As this practice has diminished in the last 50 years, the percentage of left-handed children has risen steadily (Levy, 1976). Thus, handedness seems to have both hereditary and environmental influences.

## Physical Fitness

Using one's motor skills—that is, being active physically—has many benefits for children. It promotes growth of muscles and bone, promotes cardiovascular health (National High Blood Pressure Education Program Working Group, 1996), and can help to establish a lifelong pattern of exercise. And, individuals who exercise regularly—30 minutes, at least 3 times a week—reduce their risk for obesity, cancer, heart disease, diabetes, and psychological disorders including depression and anxiety. Running, vigorous walking, swimming, aerobic dancing, biking, and cross-country skiing are all examples of activities that can provide this level of intensity.

> Most youth claim they are active physically, but in reality they are neither active nor physically fit.

How fit are U.S. children and adolescents? According to their own reports, youth are quite active—they report spending more than 2 hours each day in moderate to vigorous activity (Simons-Morton et al., 1997). However, when children are tested against objective criteria, the picture is different. In studies that include a full battery of fitness tests, such as the mile run, pull-ups and sit-ups, fewer than half the children usually meet standards for fitness on all tasks (Corbin & Pangrazi, 1992; Looney & Plowman, 1990). And, you'll remember, from Module 5.2, the U.S. Surgeon General pronounced that obesity has reached epidemic proportions among American children and adolescents (U.S. Department of Health and Human Services, 2001).

Many factors contribute to low levels of fitness. In most schools, physical education classes meet only once or twice a week. And, even when students are in these classes, they spend a surprisingly large proportion of time—nearly half—standing around instead of exercising (Lowry et al., 2001; Parcel et al., 1987). Television and other sedentary leisure-time activities may contribute, too. Children who watch TV often tend to be less fit physically, but the nature of this relation remains poorly understood: Children who watch TV a lot may have fewer opportunities to exercise, but it may be that children who are in poor physical condition would rather watch TV than exercise.

Many experts believe that U.S. schools should offer physical education more frequently each week. And many believe that physical education classes should offer a range of activities in which all children can participate and that can be the foundation for a lifelong program of fitness. Thus, instead of emphasizing team sports such as touch football, physical education classes should emphasize activities like running, walking, racquet sports, and swimming; these can be done throughout adolescence and adulthood and either alone or with another person (American Academy of Pediatrics Committee on Sports Medicine and Committee on School Health, 1989). Families can encourage fitness, too. Instead of spending an afternoon watching TV and eating popcorn, they can, like the family in the photo, go biking together.

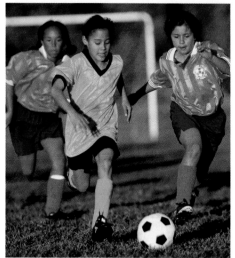

**PARTICIPATING IN SPORTS.** Many children and adolescents get exercise by participating in many team sports, including baseball, softball, basketball, and soccer. Obviously, when children like the girls in the photo play sports, they get exercise and improve their motor skills. But there are other benefits. Sports can enhance participants' self-esteem and can help them to learn initiative (Larson, 2000; Whitehead & Corbin, 1997). And sports can provide children a chance to learn important social skills, such as how to work effectively as part of a group, often in complementary roles. Finally, playing sports allows children to use their emerging cognitive skills as they devise new playing strategies or modify the rules of a game.

In days gone by, children gathered together informally—at a playground, a vacant lot, or someone's backyard—to play these sports. However, today the setting is often an official league, organized and run by adults. This turns out to be a mixed blessing. Adults' involvement in children's sports has several advantages: Children learn how to improve their skills and get knowledgeable feedback, and they can enjoy spending time with a positive role model. But there are disadvantages as well. Adults sometimes overemphasize competition instead of skill development, they can be so controlling that children have little opportunity to learn leadership skills, and they may so emphasize drills, strategy, and performance that the activity becomes more like work instead of play.

When adult coaches encourage their players and emphasize skill development, children usually enjoy playing, often improve their skills, and increase their self-esteem (Smith & Smoll, 1997; Smoll et al., 1993). In contrast, when coaches—like the man in the photo—emphasize winning over skill development and criticize or punish players for bad plays, children lose interest and stop playing (Bailey & Rasmussen, 1996; Smith & Stoll, 1996). Many youth sports organizations provide guidelines for players, coaches, and parents, so that children will enjoy participating. For example, the American Youth Soccer Organization has a code for coaches that includes the following principles:

- Coach positively: Praise children, don't criticize them.
- Be sure that children have fun!
- Have realistic expectations for children and use these to form reasonable demands.
- Develop children's respect for their opponents, opposing coaches, referees, and the game itself.
- Be a good role model for children.

When coaches (and parents) follow these guidelines, it's a good bet that their players will have fun and continue to play the sport. And everyone involved needs to remember that this is the whole point: Children (and adults) play games for recreation, which means to have fun!

## CHECK YOUR LEARNING

**1.** Motor skills are coordinated movements of the muscles and _____.

**2.** According to _____, motor development involves many distinct skills that are organized and reorganized over time, depending on task demands.

**3.** Skills important in learning to walk include maintaining upright posture and balance, stepping, and _____.

**4.** Motor development involves differentiation of individual skills and their _____ into a cohesive whole.

**5.** When infants practice motor skills, the impact of this practice is _____.

**6.** Not until age _____ do children rotate their wrists while using a spoon.

**7.** Handedness is determined by heredity and _____.

**8.** Although children often report that they spend much time in vigorous physical activity, in fact, fewer than _____ percent of children typically meet all standards for fitness.

**9.** Having parents as coaches has many drawbacks; parents sometimes overemphasize competition, they _____, and their emphasis on drills, strategy and performance can turn play into work.

### CONNECTIONS
Describe how participation in sports illustrates connections between motor, cognitive, and social development.

**Answers:** (1) limbs, (2) dynamic systems theory, (3) using perceptual information, (4) integration, (5) limited to the practiced skill; there is no widespread effect, (6) 2 years, (7) environmental influences, (8) 50, (9) are so controlling that children do not have the opportunity to experience leadership

# Unifying Themes: Active Children

Each module in this chapter touched on the theme that *children influence their own development*. That is, repeatedly in this chapter we saw that infants are extremely well equipped to interpret and explore their environments. In Module 6.1, we saw that most sensory systems function quite well in the first year, providing infants with accurate raw data to interpret. In Module 6.2, we learned that attentional skills originate in infancy—through habituation, infants ignore some stimuli and attend to others. Finally, in Module 6.3, we discovered that locomotor and fine-motor skills improve rapidly in infancy; by the first birthday, infants can move independently and handle objects skillfully. Collectively, these accomplishments make the infants extraordinarily well prepared to explore their world and make sense of it.

## See for Yourself

To see the origins of attention, you need a baby and a small bell. A 1- to 5-month-old is probably best because babies at this age can't locomote, so they won't wander away. While the infant is awake, place it on its back. Then move behind the baby's head (out of sight) and ring the bell a few times. You don't need to ring the bell loudly—an "average" volume will do. You should see the orienting response described on page 156: The baby will open its eyes wide and perhaps try to turn in the direction of the sound. Every 2 or 3 minutes, ring the bell again. You should see the baby respond less intensely each time until, finally, it ignores the bell completely. Attention in action! See for yourself!

## Resources

For more information about . . .

**infant development in general, including perceptual development**, try Charles W. Snow and Cindy G. McGaha's *Infant Development* (3rd edition) (Prentice Hall, 2003)

**ADHD**, visit this Web site, maintained by the U.S. National Institute of Mental Health:
**http://www.nimh.nih.gov/publicat/adhdmenu.cfm**

## Key Terms

**attention** 156
**auditory threshold** 146
**cones** 148
**differentiation** 164
**dynamic systems theory** 162
**fine-motor skills** 161
**habituation** 144
**integration** 164
**interposition** 155
**intersensory redundancy** 149
**linear perspective** 155
**locomotion** 161
**motor skills** 142
**orienting response** 156
**relative size** 155
**retinal disparity** 154
**sensory and perceptual processes** 142
**size constancy** 153
**texture gradient** 155
**toddler** 162
**visual acuity** 147
**visual cliff** 154

# SUMMARY

## 6.1 Basic Sensory and Perceptual Processes

### Smell, Taste, and Touch
Newborns are able to smell and can recognize their mother's odor; they also taste, preferring sweet substances and responding negatively to bitter and sour tastes. Infants respond to touch. Judging from their responses to painful stimuli, which are similar to older children's, we can say they experience pain.

### Hearing
Babies can hear, although they are less sensitive to higher- and lower-pitched sounds than adults. Babies can distinguish different sounds and use sound to locate objects in space.

### Seeing
A newborn's visual acuity is relatively poor, but 1-year-olds can see as well as adults with normal vision. Color vision develops as different sets of cones begin to function; by 3 or 4 months, children can see color as well as adults.

### Integrating Sensory Information
Infants begin to integrate information from different senses (e.g., sight and sound, sight and touch). Infants are often particularly attentive to information presented redundantly to multiple senses.

## 6.2 Complex Perceptual and Attentional Processes

### Perceiving Objects
Infants use motion, color, texture, and edges to distinguish objects. By about 4 months, infants have begun to master size, brightness, shape, and color constancy. Infants perceive depth by means of retinal disparity and other cues such as texture gradient, relative size, and interposition. Infants perceive faces early in the first year. However, it is not clear whether perception of faces involves specific perceptual mechanisms or whether it is based on the same processes used to perceive other objects.

### Attention
Attention helps select information for further processing. Infants orient to a novel stimulus, but as it becomes more familiar, they habituate, meaning that they respond less. Compared to older children, preschoolers are less able to pay attention to a task. Older children are better able to pay attention because they have developed strategies for maintaining attention. Younger children's attention can be improved by getting rid of irrelevant stimuli.

### Attention Deficit Hyperactivity Disorder
Children with ADHD are typically inattentive, hyperactive, and impulsive. They sometimes have conduct problems and do poorly in school. According to the Multimodal Treatment Study of Children with ADHD, the most effective approach to ADHD combines medication with psychosocial treatment.

## 6.3 Motor Development

### Locomotion
Infants progress through a sequence of motor milestones during the first year, culminating in walking a few months after the first birthday. Like most motor skills, learning to walk involves differentiation of individual skills, such as maintaining balance and stepping on alternate legs, and then integrating these skills into a coherent whole. This differentiation and integration of skills is central to the dynamic systems theory of motor development. Experience can accelerate specific motor skills.

### Fine-Motor Skills
Infants first use only one hand at a time, then both hands independently, then both hands in common actions, and, finally, both hands in different actions with a common purpose.

Most people are right-handed, a preference that emerges after the first birthday and that becomes well established during the preschool years. Handedness is determined by heredity but can be influenced by experience and cultural values.

### Physical Fitness
Although children report spending much time being physically active, in fact, fewer than half of American school children meet all standards for physical fitness. Part of the explanation for the lack of fitness is inadequate physical education in school. Television may also contribute. Physical education in the schools needs to be more frequent and more oriented toward developing patterns of lifetime exercise. Families can become more active, thereby encouraging children's fitness.

Participating in sports can promote motor, cognitive, and social development. Adult coaches often can help children to improve their skills but they sometimes overemphasize competition, they are so controlling that children have little opportunity to experience leadership, and they overemphasize drills, strategy, and performance, which turns play into work.

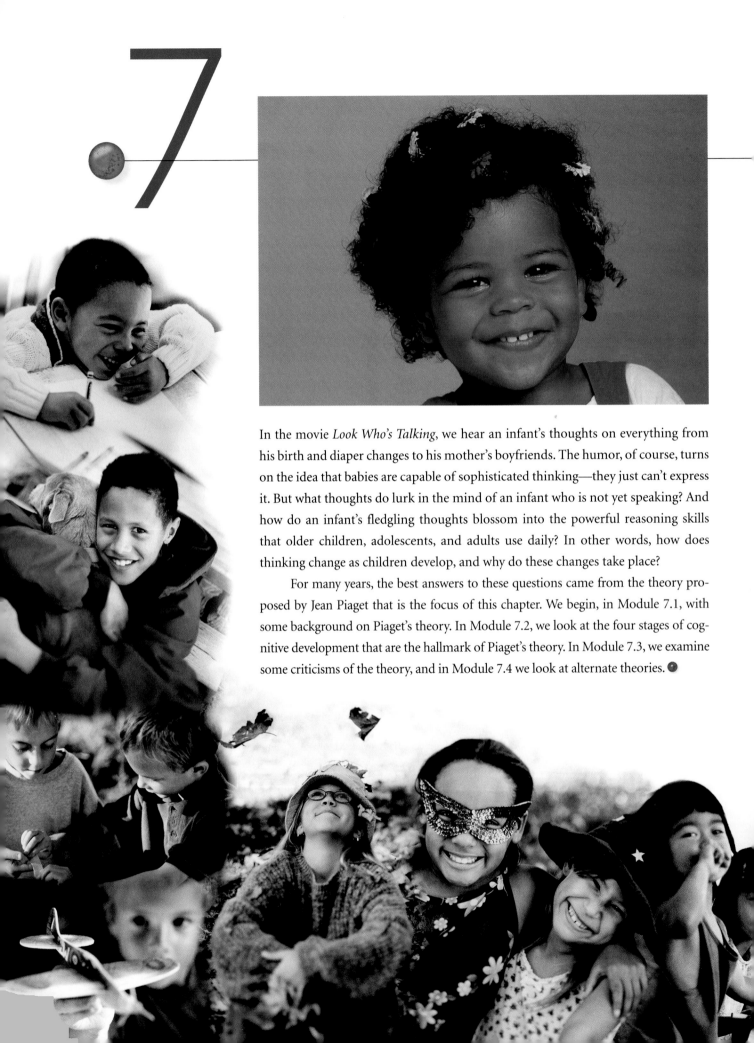

**7**

In the movie *Look Who's Talking*, we hear an infant's thoughts on everything from his birth and diaper changes to his mother's boyfriends. The humor, of course, turns on the idea that babies are capable of sophisticated thinking—they just can't express it. But what thoughts do lurk in the mind of an infant who is not yet speaking? And how do an infant's fledgling thoughts blossom into the powerful reasoning skills that older children, adolescents, and adults use daily? In other words, how does thinking change as children develop, and why do these changes take place?

For many years, the best answers to these questions came from the theory proposed by Jean Piaget that is the focus of this chapter. We begin, in Module 7.1, with some background on Piaget's theory. In Module 7.2, we look at the four stages of cognitive development that are the hallmark of Piaget's theory. In Module 7.3, we examine some criticisms of the theory, and in Module 7.4 we look at alternate theories.

# Piaget's Theory of Cognitive Development

**7.1** General Principles of Piaget's Theory

**7.2** Piaget's Four Stages of Cognitive Development

**7.3** Evaluating Piaget's Theory

**7.4** Beyond Piaget's Theory

# 7.1 General Principles of Piaget's Theory

- Schemes
- Assimilation and Accommodation
- Equilibration and Stages of Cognitive Development

## LEARNING OBJECTIVES

- What are schemes?
- How do assimilation and accommodation help children understand experience?
- What is equilibration, and how does it explain changes in how children think?

> When John, an energetic $2\frac{1}{2}$-year-old, saw a monarch butterfly for the first time, his mother, Patrice, told him, "Butterfly, butterfly; that's a butterfly, John." A few minutes later, a zebra swallowtail landed on a nearby bush and John shouted in excitement, "Butterfly, Mama, butterfly!" A bit later, a moth flew out of another bush; with even greater excitement in his voice, John shouted, "Butterfly, Mama, more butterfly!" As Patrice was telling John, "No, honey, that's a moth, not a butterfly," she marveled at how rapidly John seemed to grasp new concepts with so little direction from her. How was this possible?

For many years, our best answer to Patrice's question came from Jean Piaget, who began work on his theory of mental development in the 1920s. Piaget was trained as a biologist, but he developed a keen interest in the branch of philosophy dealing with the nature and origins of knowledge. He decided to investigate the origins of knowledge not as philosophers had—through discussion and debate—but by doing experiments with children.

We'll begin our study of Piaget's work by looking at some key principles of his theory and, as we do, discover why John understands as quickly as he does.

## Schemes

Piaget believed that children are naturally curious. They constantly want to make sense out of their experience and, in the process, construct their understanding of the world.

For Piaget, children at all ages are like scientists in that they create theories about how the world works. Of course, children's theories are often incomplete. Nevertheless, their theories are valuable because they make the world seem more predictable.

*Schemes are mental categories that organize experience, based on actions in infancy and progressing to abstract properties in adolescence.*

**According to Piaget, children come to understand the world by using schemes, psychological structures that organize experience.** That is, schemes are mental categories of related events, objects, and knowledge. During infancy, most schemes are based on actions. Infants group objects based on the actions they can perform on them. For example, infants suck and grasp, and they use these actions to create categories of objects that can be sucked and objects that can be grasped.

Schemes are just as important after infancy, but then they are based primarily on functional or conceptual relationships, not actions. For example, preschoolers learn that forks, knives, and spoons form a functional category of "things I use to eat." Or they learn that dogs, cats, and goldfish form a conceptual category of "pets."

Like preschoolers, older children and adolescents use schemes based on functional and conceptual schemes, but they also have schemes that are based on increasingly abstract properties. For example, an adolescent might put fascism, racism, and sexism in a category of "ideologies that I despise."

Thus, children use schemes of related objects, events, and ideas throughout development. But as children develop, their basis for creating schemes shifts from physical activity to functional, conceptual, and later abstract properties of objects, events, and ideas.

## Assimilation and Accommodation

Schemes change constantly, adapting to children's experiences. In fact, intellectual adaptation involves two processes working together: assimilation and accommodation. **Assimilation occurs when new experiences are readily incorporated into existing schemes.** Imagine a baby who is familiar with the grasping scheme. Like the baby in the photograph, she will soon discover that the grasping scheme works not only on balls, but also on blocks, rattles, and other small objects. Extending the existing grasping scheme to new objects illustrates assimilation. **Accommodation occurs when schemes are modified based on experience.** Soon the infant learns that some objects can only be lifted with two hands and that some can't be lifted at all. Changing the scheme so that it works for new objects (for example, using two hands to grasp a big stuffed animal) illustrates accommodation.

Assimilation and accommodation are easy to understand if you remember Piaget's belief that infants, children, and adolescents create theories to understand the world around them. The infant whose theory is that objects can be lifted with one hand finds that her theory is confirmed when she tries to pick up small objects, but she's in for a surprise when she tries to pick up a big stuffed animal. The unexpected result forces the infant, like a good scientist, to revise her theory to include this new finding.

Assimilation and accommodation are illustrated in the vignette at the beginning of the module. Piaget would say that when Patrice named the monarch butterfly for John, he formed a scheme something like "butterflies are bugs with big wings." The second butterfly differed in color but was still a bug with big wings, so it was readily assimilated into John's new scheme for butterflies. However, when John referred to the moth as a butterfly, Patrice corrected him. Presumably, John was then forced to accommodate to this new experience. The result was that he changed his scheme for butterflies to make it more precise; the new scheme might be something like "butterflies are bugs with thin bodies and big, colorful wings." He also created a new scheme, something like "a moth is a bug with a bigger body and plain wings."

## Equilibration and Stages of Cognitive Development

Assimilation and accommodation are usually in balance, or equilibrium. That is, children find they can readily assimilate most experiences into their existing schemes, but occasionally they need to accommodate their schemes to adjust to new experiences. This balance between assimilation and accommodation is illustrated both by the baby grasping larger objects and by John's understanding of butterflies.

Periodically, however, the balance is upset and a state of disequilibrium results. Children discover that their current schemes are not adequate because they are spending much more time accommodating than assimilating. **When disequilibrium occurs, children reorganize their schemes to return to a state of equilibrium, a process that**

**Piaget called equilibration.** To restore the balance, current but now-outmoded ways of thinking are replaced by a qualitatively different, more advanced set of schemes.

One way to understand equilibration is to return to the metaphor of the child as a scientist. As discussed in Module 1.2, good scientific theories readily explain some phenomena but usually must be revised to explain others. Children's theories allow them to understand many experiences by predicting, for example, what will happen ("It's morning, so it's time for breakfast") or who will do what ("Mom's gone to work, so Dad will take me to school"), but they too must be modified when predictions go awry ("Dad thinks I'm old enough to walk to school, so he won't take me").

Sometimes scientists find that their theories contain critical flaws, so they can't simply revise; they must create a new theory that draws upon the older theory but is fundamentally different. For example, when the astronomer Copernicus realized that the earth-centered theory of the solar system was wrong, he retained the concept of a central object but proposed that it was the sun, a fundamental change in the theory. In much the same way, children periodically reach a point when their current theories seem to be wrong much of the time, so they abandon these theories in favor of more advanced ways of thinking about their physical and social worlds.

According to Piaget, these revolutionary changes in thought occur three times over the life span, at approximately 2, 7, and 11 years of age. This divides cognitive development into the following four stages:

| Stage of Development | Age Range |
| --- | --- |
| Sensorimotor stage | Infancy (0 to 2 years) |
| Preoperational stage | Preschool and early elementary-school years (2 to 6 years) |
| Concrete operational stage | Middle and late elementary-school years (7 to 11 years) |
| Formal operational stage | Adolescence and adulthood (11 years and older) |

> All children pass through all four of Piaget's stages in the same order, but some do so more rapidly than others.

Each of these stages is marked by a distinctive way of thinking about and understanding the world. The ages listed are only approximate: Some youngsters move through the stages more rapidly than others, depending on their ability and their experience. However, Piaget held that all children go through all four stages and in exactly this sequence. Sensorimotor thinking always gives rise to preoperational thinking; a child cannot "skip" preoperational thinking and move directly from sensorimotor to concrete operational thought.

In the next module, we will look at each of the four stages of cognitive development in detail.

## CHECK YOUR LEARNING

1. In Piaget's theory, a _____ is a mental structure that is used to organize information.

2. Schemes are based primarily on _____ in infancy and progress to abstract properties in adolescence.

**3.** _____ takes place when a scheme is modified based on experience.

**4.** A toddler who has a scheme for flowers sees a tulip for the first time and says, "flower!" This demonstrates _____.

**5.** Piaget believed that when _____ occurs, children reorganize their schemes so that assimilation and accommodation are again in balance.

**CONTINUITY**

Based on what you've learned so far, what would Piaget's position have been on the continuity–discontinuity issue discussed in Module 1.3?

**Answers** (1) scheme, (2) actions, (3) Accommodation, (4) assimilation, (5) disequilibrium

# Piaget's Four Stages of Cognitive Development

# 7.2

## LEARNING OBJECTIVES

- How does thinking become more advanced as infants progress through the sensorimotor stage?

- What are the distinguishing features of the preoperational stage?

- What are the strengths and weaknesses of concrete operational thinking?

- What kinds of reasoning skills define formal operational thinking?

The Sensorimotor Stage

The Preoperational Stage

The Concrete Operational Stage

The Formal Operational Stage

*Three-year-old Jamila loves talking to Aunt Harriett on the telephone, but sometimes these conversations get derailed: When Aunt Harriett asks a question, Jamila often replies by nodding her head. Jamila's dad has explained that Aunt Harriett (and others on the phone) can't see her nodding, that she needs to say "yes" or "no." But, no luck. Jamila invariably returns to head nodding. Her dad can't understand why such a bright and talkative child doesn't realize that nodding is meaningless over the phone.*

If Piaget were here, he would reassure Jamila's dad that her behavior is perfectly normal—children between the ages of 2 and 7 generally believe that others see the world as they do. Piaget would also emphasize the extraordinary amount of cognitive development that has taken place in Jamila's 3 years, development that begins with the sensorimotor period, the first topic in this module.

## The Sensorimotor Stage

We know from Chapter 6 that infants' perceptual and motor skills improve quickly during the first year. Piaget proposed that these rapidly changing perceptual and motor skills in the first 2 years of life form a distinct phase in human development: **The sensorimotor stage spans birth to 2 years, a period during which the infant progresses from simple reflex actions to symbolic processing.** In the 24 months of this stage, infants' thinking progresses remarkably along three important fronts.

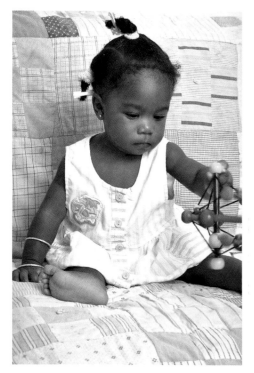

**ADAPTING TO AND EXPLORING THE ENVIRONMENT.** Newborns respond reflexively to many stimuli but between 1 and 4 months, reflexes are first modified by experience. **The chief mechanism for change is the primary circular reaction, which occurs when an infant accidentally produces some pleasing event and then tries to recreate the event.** For example, an infant may inadvertently touch his lips with his thumb, thereby initiating sucking and the pleasing sensations associated with sucking. Later, the infant tries to recreate these sensations by guiding his thumb to his mouth. Sucking no longer occurs only reflexively when a mother places a nipple at the infant's mouth; instead, the infant has found a way to initiate sucking himself.

Between 4 and 8 months, the infant shows greater interest in the world; now objects are more often the focus of circular reactions. For example, the infant shown in the photo accidentally shook a new rattle. Hearing the interesting noise, the infant grasped the rattle again, tried to shake it, and expressed great pleasure at the noise. This sequence was repeated several times.

**Novel actions that are repeated with objects are called secondary circular reactions.** Secondary circular reactions are significant because they represent infants' first efforts to learn about the objects in their environment, to explore their properties and their actions. No longer are infants grasping objects "mindlessly," simply because something is in contact with their hands. Instead, they are learning about the sights and sounds associated with objects.

At about 8 months, infants reach a watershed: The onset of deliberate, intentional behavior. For the first time, the "means" and "end" of activities are distinct. If, for example, a father places his hand in front of a toy, an infant will move his hand to be able to play with the toy. "The moving the hand" scheme is the means to achieve the goal of "grasping the toy." Using one action as a means to achieve another end is the first indication of purposeful, goal-directed behavior during infancy.

Beginning at about 12 months, infants become active experimenters. **An infant will repeat old schemes with novel objects, in what Piaget called a tertiary circular reaction, as if she is trying to understand why different objects yield different outcomes.** An infant may deliberately shake a number of different objects trying to discover which produce sounds and which do not. Or an infant may decide to drop different objects to see what happens. An infant will discover that stuffed animals land quietly whereas bigger toys often make a more satisfying "clunk" when they hit the ground. These actions represent a significant extension of intentional behavior: Now babies repeat actions with different objects solely for the purpose of seeing what will happen.

VIDEO 7.1
Object Permanence

*Sensorimotor thinking involves adapting to the environment, understanding objects, and becoming able to use symbols.*

**UNDERSTANDING OBJECTS.** Objects fill the world. Some, including dogs, spiders, and college students, are animate; others, including cheeseburgers, socks, and this textbook, are inanimate. But they all share a fundamental property—they exist independently of our actions and thoughts toward them. Much as we may dislike spiders, they still exist when we close our eyes or wish they would go away. **Piaget's term for this understanding that objects exist independently was object permanence.** And Piaget made the astonishing claim that infants lacked this understanding for much of the first year. That is, he proposed that an infant's understanding of objects could be summarized as "out of sight, out of mind."

For infants, objects are ephemeral, existing when in sight and no longer existing when out of sight.

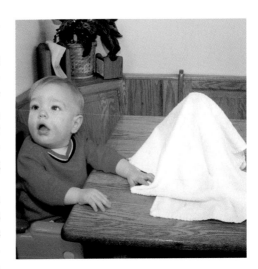

The photo illustrates the sort of research that led Piaget to conclude that infants have little understanding of objects. If a tempting object such as an attractive toy is placed in front of a 4- to 8-month-old, the infant will probably reach and grasp the object. If, however, the object is then hidden by a barrier, or, as in the photo, covered with a cloth, the infant will neither reach nor search. Instead, like the baby in the photo, the infant seems to have lost all interest in the object, as if the now hidden object no longer exists. Paraphrasing the familiar phrase, "out of sight, out of existence!"

Beginning at about 8 months, infants search for an object that an experimenter has covered with a cloth. In fact, many 8- to 12-month-olds love to play this game—an adult covers the object and the infant sweeps away the cover, laughing and smiling all the while! But, despite this accomplishment, their understanding of object permanence remains incomplete according to Piaget. If 8- to 10-month-olds see an object hidden under one container several times, then see it hidden under a second container, they usually look for the toy under the first container. Piaget claimed that this behavior shows only a fragmentary understanding of objects because infants do not distinguish the object from the actions they use to locate it, such as lifting a particular container.

Piaget argued that not until approximately 18 months do infants have full understanding of object permanence. However, in Module 7.4, we'll see research suggesting that infants have greater understanding of objects than Piaget claimed.

**USING SYMBOLS.**   By 18 months, most infants have begun to talk and gesture, evidence of the emerging capacity to use symbols. Words and gestures are symbols that stand for something else. When the baby in the photo waves, it is just as effective and symbolic as saying "goodbye" to bid farewell. Children also begin to engage in pretend play, another use of symbols. A 20-month-old may move her hand back and forth in front of her mouth, pretending to brush her teeth.

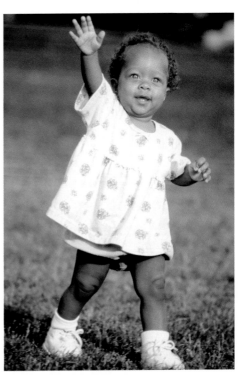

Once infants can use symbols, they can begin to anticipate the consequences of actions mentally instead of having to perform them. Imagine that an infant and parent construct a tower of blocks next to an open door. Leaving the room, a 12- to 18-month-old might close the door, knocking over the tower, because he cannot foresee the outcome of closing the door. But an 18- to 24-month-old can anticipate the consequence of closing the door and move the tower beforehand.

In just 2 years, the infant progresses from reflexive responding to actively exploring the world, understanding objects, and using symbols. These achievements are remarkable and set the stage for preoperational thinking, which we'll examine next.

## The Preoperational Stage

With the magic power of symbols, the child crosses the hurdle into preoperational thinking. **The preoperational stage, which spans ages 2 to 7, is marked by the child's use of symbols to represent objects and events.** Throughout this period, preschool children gradually become proficient at using common symbols, such as words, gestures, graphs, maps, and models.

**VIDEO 7.2**
Egocentrism

FIG.7–1

Although preschool children's ability to use symbols represents a huge advance over sensorimotor thinking, their thinking remains quite limited compared to that of school-age children. Why? To answer this question, we need to look at some important characteristics of thought during the preoperational stage.

EGOCENTRISM.    Preoperational children typically believe that others see the world—both literally and figuratively—exactly as they do. **Egocentrism refers to young children's difficulty in seeing the world from another's viewpoint.** When youngsters stubbornly cling to their own way, they are not simply being contrary. Instead, preoperational children do not comprehend that other people have different ideas and feelings.

Suppose, for example, you ask the preschooler in the drawing to select the photograph that shows how the objects on the table look to you. Most will select photo 1, which shows how the objects look to the child, not photo 2, the correct choice. Preoperational youngsters evidently suppose that the mountains are seen the same way by all; they presume that theirs is the only view, rather than one of many conceivable views (Piaget & Inhelder, 1956).

Egocentrism also explains why Jamila, the 3-year-old in the vignette, nods her head when talking on the phone. Jamila assumes that because she is aware that her head is moving up and down (or side to side!), her aunt must be aware of it, too.

Their egocentrism sometimes leads preoperational youngsters to attribute their own thoughts and feelings to others. **Preoperational children sometimes credit inanimate objects with life and lifelike properties, a phenomenon known as animism** (Piaget, 1929). A $3\frac{1}{2}$-year-old I know, Christine, illustrated preoperational animism in a conversation we had on a rainy day:

RK:    Is the sun happy today?

CHRISTINE:    No. It's sad today.

RK:    Why?

CHRISTINE:    Because it's cloudy. He can't shine. And he can't see me!

RK:    What about your trike? Is it happy?

CHRISTINE:    No, he's very sad, too.

RK:    Why is that?

CHRISTINE:    Because I can't ride him. And because he's all alone in the garage.

Caught up in her egocentrism, Christine believes that objects like the sun and her tricycle think and feel as she does.

## Preoperational children often overlook others' perspectives and focus on one apect of a problem.

**VIDEO 7.3**
Conservation

CENTRATION.    Children in the preoperational stage also have the psychological equivalent of tunnel vision: They often concentrate on one aspect of a problem but totally ignore other equally relevant aspects. **Centration is Piaget's term for this narrowly focused thought that characterizes preoperational youngsters.**

Piaget demonstrated centration in his experiments involving conservation. In the conservation experiments, Piaget wanted to determine when children realize that important characteristics of objects (or sets of objects) stay the same despite changes in their physical appearance. Some tasks that Piaget used to study conservation are shown in the diagram on page 181. Each begins with identical objects (or sets of objects). Then one of the objects (or sets) is transformed and children are asked if the objects are the same in terms of some important feature.

| Type of Conservation | Starting Configuration | Transformation | Final Configuration |
|---|---|---|---|
| Liquid quantity | Is there the same amount of water in each glass? | Pour water from one glass into a shorter, wider glass. | Now is there the same amount of water in each glass, or does one have more? |
| Number | Are there the same number of pennies in each row? | Stretch out the top row of pennies, push together the bottom row. | Now are there the same number of pennies in each row, or does one row have more? |
| Length | Are these sticks the same length? | Move one stick to the left and the other to the right. | Now are the sticks the same length, or is one longer? |
| Mass | Does each ball have the same amount of clay? | Roll one ball so that it looks like a sausage. | Now does each piece have the same amount of clay, or does one have more? |
| Area | Does each cow have the same amount of grass to eat? | Spread out the squares in one field. | Now does each cow have the same amount to eat, or does one cow have more? |

FIG.7–2

A typical conservation problem, involving conservation of liquid quantity, is shown in the photo. Children are shown identical beakers filled with the same amount of juice. After children agree that the two beakers have the same amount, juice is poured from one beaker into a taller, thinner beaker. The juice looks different in the tall, thin beaker—it rises higher—but of course the amount is unchanged. Nevertheless, preoperational children claim that the tall, thin beaker has more juice than the original beaker. (And, if the juice is poured into a wider beaker, they believe it has less.)

What is happening here? According to Piaget, preoperational children center on the level of the juice in the beaker. If the juice is higher after it is poured, preoperational children believe that there must be more juice now than before. Because preoperational thinking is centered, these youngsters ignore the fact that the change in the level of the juice is always accompanied by a change in the diameter of the beaker.

In other conservation problems, preoperational children also tend to focus on only one aspect of the problem. In conservation of number, for example, preoperational children concentrate on the fact that, after the transformation, one row of objects is now longer than the other. In conservation of length, preoperational children concentrate on the fact that, after the transformation, the end of one stick is farther to the right than the end of the other. Preoperational children's centered thinking means that they overlook other parts of the problem that would tell them the quantity is unchanged.

**APPEARANCE AS REALITY.** Preschool children believe an object's appearance tells what the object is really like. For instance, many a 3-year-old has watched with quiet fascination as an older brother or sister put on a ghoulish costume only to erupt in frightened tears when their siblings put on scary makeup. For the youngster in the photo, the scary made-up face is reality, not just something that looks frightening but really isn't.

Confusion between appearance and reality is not limited to costumes and masks. It is a general characteristic of preoperational thinking. Consider the following cases where appearances and reality conflict:

- A boy is angry because a friend is being mean but smiles because he's afraid the friend will leave if he reveals his anger.
- A glass of milk looks brown when seen through sunglasses.
- A piece of hard rubber looks like food (for example, like a piece of pizza).

Older children and adults know that the boy looks happy, the milk looks brown, and the object looks like food but that the boy is really angry, the milk is really white, and the object is really rubber. Preoperational children, however, confuse appearance and reality, thinking the boy is happy, the milk is brown, and the piece of rubber is edible (Siegler, 1998).

> Preoperational children sometimes confuse appearance with reality.

Distinguishing appearance and reality is particularly difficult for children in the early years of preoperational thinking. This difficulty is evident in research on children's use of scale models, which are objects that also symbolize a much larger object. A model of a house, for example, can be an interesting object in its own right as well as a representation of an actual house. The ability to use scale models develops early in the preoperational period. If young children watch an adult hide a toy in a full-size room, then try to find the toy in a scale model of the room that contains all the principal features of the full-scale room (e.g., carpet, window, furniture), 3-year-olds find the hidden toy readily but $2\frac{1}{2}$-year-olds do not (DeLoache, 1995).

Why is this task so easy for 3-year-olds and so difficult for $2\frac{1}{2}$-year-olds? Do the younger children simply forget the location of the toy by the time they look at the scale model of the room? No. If returned to the full-size room, they easily find the hidden toy. Judy DeLoache and her colleagues believe that $2\frac{1}{2}$-year-olds' "attention to a scale model as an interesting and attractive object makes it difficult for them to simultaneously think about its relation to something else" (DeLoache,

Miller, & Rosengren, 1997, p. 308). In other words, young children are drawn to the model as a real object and therefore find it hard to think about the model as a symbol of the full-size room.

If this argument is correct, $2\frac{1}{2}$-year-olds should be more successful using the model if they don't have to think of it as a symbol for the full-size room. DeLoache tested this hypothesis in the study described in the "Focus on Research" feature. (This study is one of my 10 favorite studies of all time, for reasons that will soon be obvious.)

## FOCUS ON RESEARCH

### Finding Toys in a Shrunken Room

*Who were the investigators, and what was the aim of the study?* Judy De-Loache, Kevin Miller, and Karl Rosengren (1997) believed that $2\frac{1}{2}$-year-olds could not find the toy in the model because it was difficult for them to think of the model as an object and as a symbol of the full-size room. To test this argument, they created a condition designed to eliminate the need for children to think of the model as an object and as a symbol. Children were told that a machine could shrink the full-size room. In this case, the model is no longer a symbol of the full-size room; it *is* the room, just shrunken. Consequently, DeLoache and her colleagues expected $2\frac{1}{2}$-year-olds to find the hidden toy because they believed the model was the full-size room shrunken to miniature size.

*How did the investigators measure the topic of interest?* Some children were tested with the usual procedures: hiding the toy in the full-size room and asking children to find it in the scale model. Other children were tested in the new condition designed to help them find the toy. Children saw the oscilloscope shown in the photograph, which was described as a shrinking machine. They saw a toy doll—"Terry the Troll"—placed in front of the oscilloscope; then the experimenter and child left the room briefly while a tape recorder played sounds that were described as sounds "the machine makes when it's shrinking something." When experimenter and child returned, Terry had shrunk from 8 inches to 2 inches. Next, Terry was hidden in the full-size room, the experimenter aimed the "shrinking machine" at the full-size room, then experimenter and child left the room. While the tape recorder played shrinking sounds, research assistants quickly removed everything from the full-size room and substituted the model. Experimenter and child returned and the child was asked to find Terry. This procedure was repeated so that children searched for Terry on four separate trials.

*Who were the children in the study?* DeLoache and her colleagues tested 32 children whose average age was $2\frac{1}{2}$ years.

*What was the design of the study?* The study was experimental. The independent variable was the presence or absence of the shrinking machine. The dependent variable was the percentage of trials on which the children found Terry.

*Were there ethical concerns with the study?* For children tested with the "shrinking machine," the study involved deception. Parents were fully informed about the shrinking machine before they gave consent, and parents were present throughout the experiment. Immediately after the experiment, children were told that the machine could not really shrink objects. They were shown the model, the full-size room, and both small and large versions of Terry. The deception seemed warranted, and no children seemed upset when they were told what really happened.

Children usually found Terry in the "shrinking room" condition, but rarely in the standard condition.

Percentage of Trials When Children Found Terry

Percentage of Children Finding Terry on at Least 3 of 4 Trials

■ Standard condition  ■ "Shrinking room" condition

FIG.7–3

*What were the results?* The top part of the graph shows the percentage of trials in which children found the toy. Children rarely found the toy in the standard condition, but they frequently found it in the "shrinking machine" condition. The bottom part of the graph shows the percentage of children who found Terry on at least three of the four trials. No children in the standard condition were this accurate, but most children in the "shrinking machine" condition were.

*What did the investigators conclude?* When $2\frac{1}{2}$-year-olds must think of the model as an object and as a symbol—so that appearance conflicts with reality—they find this very difficult and, consequently, cannot find the hidden toy, even though the model is an exact replica of the full-size room. In contrast, when children can think of the model as the room, but much smaller—thereby avoiding the conflict between appearance and reality—they readily find the toy.

*What converging evidence would strengthen these conclusions?* Because the changes observed by DeLoache and her colleagues appeared across a fairly narrow age range, this would be an ideal opportunity to conduct a microgenetic study: The goal would be to show, for individual children, the age at which they understand that the model is a symbol of something else. Additional useful research would be to compare the results with other situations in which an object also serves a symbolic function (e.g., children's understanding that a map is a colorful piece of paper as well as a symbol of a much larger physical space). ●

The appearance of a colorful, interesting object that beckons "come play with me" is reality for $2\frac{1}{2}$-year-olds; they cannot "see through" the model to realize that in this task the model really is a symbol for something else (DeLoache, 2000). Difficulty in distinguishing appearance and reality is a deep-seated characteristic of preoperational thinking (especially in the early years of this stage), as are egocentrism and centration.

The defining characteristics of preoperational thought are summarized in the table.

**SUMMARY TABLE**

## CHARACTERISTICS OF PREOPERATIONAL THINKING

| Characteristic | Definition | Example |
|---|---|---|
| Egocentrism | Child believes that all people see the world as he or she does. | A child gestures during a telephone conversation, not realizing that the listener cannot see the gestures. |
| Centration | Child focuses on one aspect of a problem but ignores other relevant aspects. | In conservation of liquid quantity, child pays attention to the height of the liquid in the beaker but ignores the diameter of the beaker. |
| Appearance as reality | Child assumes that an object really is what it appears to be. | Child believes that a person smiling at another person is really happy even though the other person is being mean. |

## The Concrete Operational Stage

During the early elementary-school years, children enter a new stage of cognitive development that is distinctly more adultlike and much less childlike. **In the concrete operational stage, which spans ages 7 to 11, children first use mental operations to solve problems and to reason.** What are the mental operations that are so essential to concrete operational thinking? **Mental operations are strategies and rules that make thinking more systematic and more powerful.** Some mental operations apply to numbers. For example, addition, subtraction, multiplication, and division are familiar arithmetic operations that concrete operational children use. Other mental operations apply to categories of objects. For example, classes can be added (mothers + fathers = parents) and subtracted (parents − mothers = fathers). Still other mental operations apply to spatial relations among objects. For example, if point A is near points B and C, then points B and C must be close to each other.

> Concrete operational thinking is based on mental operations that yield consistent results and that can be reversed.

Mental operations give concrete operational thinking a rule-oriented, logical flavor that is missing in preoperational thought. Applied properly, mental operations yield consistent results. Taking the familiar case of arithmetic operations, 4 + 2 is always 6, not just usually or only on weekends.

Another important property of mental operations is that they can be reversed. Each operation has an inverse that can "undo" or reverse the effect of an operation. If you start with 5 and add 3, you get 8; by subtracting 3 from 8, you reverse your steps and return to 5. For Piaget, reversibility of this sort applied to all mental operations. Concrete operational children are able to reverse their thinking in a way that preoperational youngsters cannot. In fact, reversible mental operations is part of why concrete operational children pass the conservation tasks described on page 181: Concrete operational thinkers understand that if the transformation were reversed (for example, the juice was poured back into the original container), the objects would be identical.

Concrete operational thinking is much more powerful than preoperational thinking. Remember that preoperational children are egocentric (believing that others see the world as they do), are centered in their thinking, and confuse appearances with reality. None of these limitations applies to children in the concrete operational stage.

Egocentrism wanes as youngsters have more experiences with friends and siblings who assert their own perspectives on the world (LeMare & Rubin, 1987). Learning that events can be interpreted in different ways helps children realize that many problems have different facets (thereby avoiding centration) and that appearances can be deceiving.

Concrete operational thinking is a major cognitive advance, but it has its own limits. As the name implies, concrete operational thinking is limited to the tangible and real, to the here and now. The concrete operational youngster takes "an earthbound, concrete, practical-minded sort of problem-solving approach, one that persistently fixates on the perceptible and inferable reality right there in front of him" (Flavell, 1985, p. 98). That is, thinking abstractly and hypothetically is beyond the ability of concrete operational thinkers.

## The Formal Operational Stage

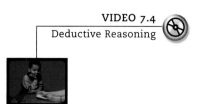

VIDEO 7.4
Deductive Reasoning

**In the formal operational stage, which extends from roughly age 11 into adulthood, children and adolescents apply mental operations to abstract entities; they think hypothetically and reason deductively.** Freed from the concrete and the real, adolescents explore the possible—what might be and what could be.

Unlike reality-oriented concrete operational children, formal operational thinkers understand that reality is not the only possibility. They can envision alternative realities and examine their consequences. For example, ask a concrete operational child, "What would happen if gravity meant that objects floated up?" or "What would happen if men gave birth?" and you're likely to get a confused or even irritated look and comments like "It doesn't—they fall" or "They don't—women have babies." Reality is the foundation of concrete operational thinking. In contrast, formal operational adolescents use hypothetical reasoning to probe the implications of fundamental change in physical or biological laws.

Formal operations also allow adolescents to take a different, more sophisticated approach to problem solving. Formal operational thinkers can solve problems by creating hypotheses (sets of possibilities) and testing them. Piaget (Inhelder & Piaget, 1958) showed this aspect of adolescent thinking by presenting children and adolescents with several flasks, each containing what appeared to be the same clear liquid. They were told that one combination of the clear liquids would produce a blue liquid and were asked to determine the necessary combination.

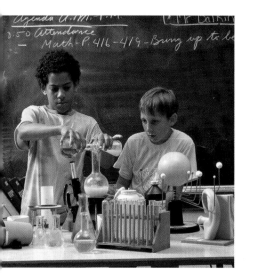

A typical concrete operational youngster, like the ones in the photograph, plunges right in, mixing liquids from different flasks in a haphazard way. In contrast, formal operational adolescents understand that setting up the problem in abstract, hypothetical terms is the key. The problem is not really about pouring liquids but about forming hypotheses about different combinations of liquids and testing them systematically.

A teenager might mix liquid from the first flask with liquids from each of the other flasks. If none of those combinations produces a blue liquid, the adolescent would conclude that the liquid in the first flask is not an essential part of the mixture. Next, he or she would mix the liquid in the second flask with each of the remaining liquids. A formal operational thinker would continue in this manner until he or she found the critical pair that produced the blue liquid. For adolescents, the problem is not one of concrete acts of pouring and mixing; rather, they understand that the problem consists of identifying possible hypotheses (in this case, combinations of liquids) and then evaluating each one. The adolescent's approach to problem solving is also illustrated in the "Real Children" feature.

## REAL CHILDREN

### Hypothetical Reasoning Goes to the Races

As a 15-year-old, I delivered the Indianapolis *Star*. In the spring of 1966, the newspaper announced a contest for all newspaper carriers. The person who created the most words from the letters contained in the words "SAFE RACE" would win two tickets to the Indianapolis 500 auto race.

I realized that this was a problem in hypothetical reasoning. All I needed to do was create all possible combinations of letters, then look them up. Following this procedure I had to win (or, at worst, tie). So, I created endless lists of possible words, beginning with each of the letters individually, then all possible combinations of two letters, and worked my way up to possible combinations of all eight letters (e.g., SCAREEFA, SCAREEAF). This was monotonous enough, but no more than looking up all these possible words in a dictionary. (Remember, this was in the days before computerized spell checkers.) Weeks later, I had generated a list of 126 words. A few months later, I learned that I had won the contest. Hypothetical reasoning has its payoffs!

Because adolescents' thinking is not concerned solely with reality, they are also better able to reason logically from premises and draw appropriate conclusions. **The ability to draw appropriate conclusions from facts is known as deductive reasoning.** Suppose we tell a person the following two facts:

1. If you hit a glass with a hammer, the glass will break.
2. Don hit a glass with a hammer.

The correct conclusion is that "the glass broke," a conclusion that formal operational adolescents will reach. Concrete operational youngsters, too, will sometimes reach this conclusion, but based on their experience and not because the conclusion is logically necessary. To see the difference, imagine that the two facts are now:

1. If you hit a glass with a feather, the glass will break.
2. Don hit a glass with a feather.

The conclusion "the glass broke" follows from these two statements just as logically as it did from the first pair. In this instance, however, the conclusion is counterfactual—it goes against what experience tells us is really true. Concrete operational 10-year-olds resist reaching conclusions that are counter to known facts; they reach conclusions based on their knowledge of the world. In contrast, formal operational 15-year-olds often reach counterfactual conclusions (Markovits & Vachon, 1989). They understand that these problems are about abstract entities that need not correspond to real-world relations.

**Formal operational adolescents can think hypothetically and reason deductively.**

Hypothetical reasoning and deductive reasoning are powerful tools for formal operational thinkers. In fact, we can characterize this power by paraphrasing the quotation about concrete operational thinking that appears on page 185: "Formal operational youth take an abstract, hypothetical approach to problem solving; they are not constrained by the reality that is staring them in the face but are open to different possibilities and alternatives." The ability to ponder different alternatives makes possible the experimentation with lifestyles and values that occurs in adolescence, topics we'll encounter on several occasions later in this book.

With the achievement of formal operations, cognitive development is over in Piaget's theory. Adolescents and adults acquire more knowledge as they grow older, but their fundamental way of thinking remains unchanged, in Piaget's view. The table summarizes Piaget's description of cognitive changes between birth and adulthood.

**SUMMARY TABLE**

## PIAGET'S FOUR STAGES OF COGNITIVE DEVELOPMENT

| Stage | Approximate Age | Characteristics |
|---|---|---|
| Sensorimotor | Birth to 2 years | Infant's knowledge of the world is based on senses and motor skills. By the end of the period, infant explores the world, understands objects, and uses symbols. |
| Preoperational thought | 2 to 6 years | Child learns how to use symbols such as words and numbers to represent aspects of the world, but relates to the world only through his or her perspective. |
| Concrete operational thought | 7 to 11 years | Child understands and applies logical operations to experiences, provided they are focused on the here and now. |
| Formal operational thought | Adolescence and beyond | Adolescent or adult thinks abstractly, speculates on hypothetical situations, and reasons deductively about what may be possible. |

## CHECK YOUR LEARNING

**1.** Sensorimotor thought begins with reflexive responding and ends with _____.

**2.** In a _____, an infant accidentally produces something pleasant, then tries to recreate that pleasing event.

**3.** An important characteristic of preoperational thought is _____, which refers to children's inability to see the world as others do.

**4.** Because of their egocentrism, preoperational children sometimes attribute life-like properties to inanimate objects, a phenomenon known as _____.

**5.** Unlike preoperational children, concrete operational children are capable of _____, which are actions that can be performed on objects or ideas.

**6.** During the concrete operational stage, children cannot reason _____.

**7.** The formal operational period marks the onset of _____ reasoning and deductive reasoning.

**NATURE AND NURTURE**
How might nature and nurture be involved in an infant's progression through the sensorimotor stage?

Answers: (1) symbolic processing, (2) primary circular reaction, (3) egocentrism, (4) animism, (5) mental operations, (6) abstractly and hypothetically, (7) hypothetical

# 7.3 Evaluating Piaget's Theory

— **Piaget's Contributions to Child Development**

— **Criticisms of the Theory**

## LEARNING OBJECTIVES

● How have parents and teachers applied Piaget's theory?

● What are some criticisms of Piaget's theory?

*Chris, a 14-year-old boy, was an enigma to his mother, Terri. On the one hand, Chris's growing reasoning skills impressed and sometimes even surprised her. He not only readily grasped technical discussions of her medical work, but he was becoming adept at finding loopholes in her explanations of why he wasn't allowed to do some things with his friends. On the other hand, sometimes Chris was a real teenage "space cadet." Simple problem solving stumped him, or he made silly mistakes and got the wrong answer. Chris didn't correspond to Terri's image of the formal operational thinker that she remembered from her college child-development class.*

Like Terri, child-development researchers have observed that adolescents' thinking is not always as sophisticated as Piaget's theory predicts. This is one of several criticisms of Piaget's work that we'll examine in the second part of this module. But first, let's look at some of the enduring contributions of Piaget's theory to our understanding of children and their development.

## Piaget's Contributions to Child Development

Ask a child-development researcher who dominated the field for much of the 20th century and most will say Piaget; his impact on every aspect of child-development research was and is profound. As one writer phrased it, "many of Piaget's contributions have become so much a part of the way we view cognitive development nowadays that they are virtually invisible" (Flavell, 1996, p. 202). I want to emphasize three of these enduring, now nearly invisible contributions (Brainerd, 1996; Siegler & Ellis, 1996):

- *The study of cognitive development itself.* Before Piaget, cognition simply was not part of the research agenda for child-development scientists. Piaget showed why cognitive processes are central to development and offered some methods that could be used to study them.
- *A new view of children.* **Piaget emphasized constructivism, the view that children are active participants in their own development who systematically construct ever more sophisticated understandings of their worlds.** This view now pervades thinking about children (so much so that it's one of the themes in this book), but it began with Piaget.
- *Fascinating, often counterintuitive discoveries.* One reason why Piaget's work attracted so much attention is that many of the findings were completely unexpected and became puzzles that child-development researchers couldn't resist trying to solve. In the words of one commentator, "Piaget had the greenest thumb ever for unearthing fascinating and significant developmental progressions" (Flavell, 1996, p. 202).

Piaget's contributions extended beyond child-development research per se. Many teachers and parents also have found Piaget's theory a rich source of ideas for fostering children's development (Siegler, 1998). Some of these ideas are described in the "Improving Children's Lives" feature.

> Piaget's lasting contributions include an emphasis on cognitive development, a view of children as active participants in development, and many unexpected discoveries.

## IMPROVING CHILDREN'S LIVES

### Teaching Practices that Foster Cognitive Growth

Piaget's view of cognitive development has some straightforward implications for teaching practices that promote cognitive growth:

1. Cognitive growth occurs as children construct their own understanding of the world, so the teacher's role is to create environments where children can discover for themselves how the world works. A teacher shouldn't simply try to tell children how addition and subtraction are complementary but instead should provide children with materials that allow them to discover the complementarity themselves.

2. Children profit from experience only when they can interpret this experience with their current cognitive structures. It follows, then, that the best teaching experiences are slightly ahead of the children's current level of thinking. As a youngster begins to master basic addition, don't jump right to subtraction but first go to slightly more difficult addition problems.

3. Cognitive growth can be particularly rapid when children discover inconsistencies and errors in their own thinking. Teachers should therefore encourage children to look at the consistency of their thinking but then let children take the lead in sorting out the inconsistencies. If a child is making mistakes in borrowing on subtraction problems, a teacher shouldn't correct the error directly but should encourage the child to look at a large number of these errors to discover what he or she is doing wrong. ⦿

## Criticisms of the Theory

Although Piaget's contributions to child development are legendary, some elements of his theory have held up better than others. Let's look at some of the problems critics have identified.

**ALTERNATIVE EXPLANATIONS OF PERFORMANCE.** Piaget explained cognitive development with constructs like accommodation, assimilation, and equilibration. Subsequent researchers, however, have found other ways to explain age differences in children's performance on Piaget's tasks.

For example, preoperational children's performance on the conservation task appears to reflect, at least in part, their growing sensitivity to language—not purely their centration. In fact, it is the questions concerning the amount of water that are critical (Winer, Craig, & Weinbaum, 1992). Remember that in this procedure youngsters are twice asked if the amount of juice in the two beakers is the same—once before the juice is poured and once after. In everyday conversation, a question is usually repeated like this because the answer was wrong the first time. Or it may be repeated because the answer was correct at first but something has changed so that it is now wrong. Both of these rules about questions would lead young children who had answered "yes" to the first question to wonder if they were wrong or if a different answer is expected and perhaps say "no" the second time. In fact, when the procedure is changed (for example, by asking the question only once), preschoolers are more likely to conserve. Thus, children's performance on conservation problems is based partly on language development, rather than just the processes that Piaget described.

> A criticism of Piaget's theory is that researchers have discovered better ways to explain children's performance on Piaget's tasks.

Researchers have also reexamined Piaget's account of the development of object permanence. You'll recall, from pages 178–179, Piaget's conclusion that understanding of objects develops fairly slowly from birth to 18 months. Many child-development researchers have since questioned Piaget's conclusions (Smith et al., 1999). Some fairly minor changes in procedures can affect 8- to 10-month-olds' success on the hidden object task. An infant is more likely to look under the correct container if, for example, the interval between hiding and looking is brief and if the containers are easily distinguished from each other. Therefore, infants who are unsuccessful at this task may be showing poor memory rather than inadequate understanding of the nature of objects (Wellman, Cross, & Bartsch, 1986).

In addition, by devising some clever procedures, other investigators have shown that babies understand objects much earlier than Piaget claimed. Renée Baillargeon (1987, 1994), for example, assessed object permanence using a procedure in which infants first saw a silver screen that appeared to be rotating back and forth. When they were familiar with this display, one of two new displays was shown. In the possible event, an orange box appeared in a position behind the screen, making it impossible for the screen to rotate as far back as it had previously. Instead, the screen rotated until it made contact with the box, then rotated forward. In the impossible event, shown in the diagram, the orange box appeared, but the screen continued to rotate as before. The screen rotated back until it was flat, then rotated forward, again revealing the orange box. The illusion was possible because the box was mounted on a movable platform that allowed it to drop out of the way of the moving screen. However, from the infant's perspective, it appeared as if the box vanished behind the screen, only to reappear.

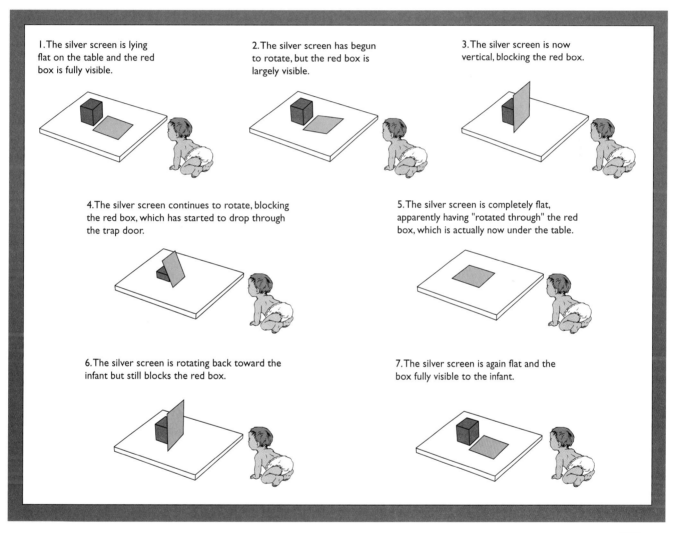

1. The silver screen is lying flat on the table and the red box is fully visible.

2. The silver screen has begun to rotate, but the red box is largely visible.

3. The silver screen is now vertical, blocking the red box.

4. The silver screen continues to rotate, blocking the red box, which has started to drop through the trap door.

5. The silver screen is completely flat, apparently having "rotated through" the red box, which is actually now under the table.

6. The silver screen is rotating back toward the infant but still blocks the red box.

7. The silver screen is again flat and the box fully visible to the infant.

FIG.7–4

The disappearance and reappearance of the box violates the idea that objects exist permanently. Consequently, an infant who understands the permanence of objects should find the impossible event a truly novel stimulus and look at it longer than the possible event. Baillargeon found that $4\frac{1}{2}$-month-olds consistently looked longer at the impossible event than the possible event. Infants apparently thought that the impossible event was novel, just as we are surprised when an object vanishes from a magician's scarf. Evidently, then, infants have some understanding of object permanence early in the first year of life.

**CONSISTENCY IN PERFORMANCE.**  In Piaget's view, each stage of intellectual development has unique characteristics that leave their mark on everything a child does. Just as you can recognize McDonald's by its golden arches, you can recognize preoperational thinking by its egocentrism and formal operational thinking by its abstractness. Consequently, children's performance on different tasks should be very consistent. On the conservation and the three-mountains tasks, for instance, a 4-year-old should always respond in a preoperational way: He should say the water is not the same after pouring, and the other person sees the mountains the same way he does.

> Contrary to Piaget's theory, children performance is often inconsistent across tasks that have the same logical structure.

What does research tell us about the consistency of children's performance on different tasks? There is some consistency, but exceptions are common, too. A good illustration comes from Siegler (1981), who tested children on three different Piagetian tasks. Only one-third of the children performed at the same level on all three tasks. The remainder were inconsistent, sometimes differing considerably from one task to the next. This inconsistent performance on different tasks does not support Piaget's view that children's thinking should always reflect the distinctive imprint of their current stage of cognitive development.

**TRAINING PIAGETIAN CONCEPTS.**  According to Piaget, children master different concepts as they move from one stage to the next. Children master conservation as they move from preoperational to concrete operational thinking, and they master hypothetical reasoning as they move from concrete to formal operational thinking. Consequently, it should not be possible to teach children concepts at an earlier stage: Preoperational children should not be able to learn conservation, for instance. However, many investigators have shown that children can be taught Piagetian concepts ahead of schedule.

In an early study, Gelman (1969) argued that a preschool child's attention is drawn to many cues in the conservation task, such as the size, height, and diameter of the beakers and the level of the liquid. Most of these cues change as the liquid is poured from one beaker to another, which may lead youngsters to believe that the amount of liquid has changed. Gelman wondered if, by teaching children that quantities are the same despite looking different, they could learn to conserve. Consequently, she presented many problems in which two quantities were the same but a third differed; the task was to select the two quantities that were the same. For example, in the problem in the figure, the child chose the two rows that had the same number of dots. To answer correctly, children had to pay attention only to the number of dots and ignore other distracting cues, such as the length of the rows. After training, 5-year-olds were quite successful on a variety of conservation tasks. Thus, when trained to focus strictly on one cue and when given many examples, children ignored misleading cues and recognized that quantity does not change in the conservation task.

FIG.7–5

Training procedures like Gelman's, although successful, may seem artificial because children don't ordinarily experience such a structured set of problems. However, children can learn to conserve another way—through discussion with peers. When, as shown in the photo, conservers and nonconservers solve conservation problems together, their joint answer is likely to be a conservation response. More importantly, when nonconservers are later tested alone, they conserve. These children are not simply parroting the conservers' answers; they explain the conservation response correctly, and the training generalizes to new conservation tasks (Miller & Brownell, 1975). Thus, contrary to what Piaget's theory predicts, with appropriate instruction, preoperational children can master concrete operational concepts.

**A THEORY OF ACTUAL THINKING OR POSSIBLE THINKING?**   Simply because children and adolescents attain a particular level of reasoning in Piaget's theory does not mean that they always reason at that level. Children who are in the concrete operational period often revert to preoperational thinking. Adolescents often fail to reason logically, even when they are capable and when it would be beneficial. For example, adolescents typically show more sophisticated reasoning when the problems are relevant to them personally than when they are not (Ward & Overton, 1990). Also, when the product of reasoning is consistent with adolescents' own beliefs, they are less likely to find flaws in the reasoning (Klaczynski & Narasimham, 1998): Hearing a flawed argument, for example, that Baptists make better parents, Baptist adolescents are more likely to overlook the errors in the argument, in part because they use less rigorous standards of reasoning when the evidence is inconsistent with what they believe (Jacobs & Klaczynski, 2002; Klaczynski, 2000).

Thus, Terri, the mother in the opening vignette, should not be so perplexed by her son's seemingly erratic thinking: Adolescents (and adults, for that matter) simply do not always use the most powerful levels of thinking that they possess. Piaget's account of intellectual development is really a description of how children and adolescents *can* think, not how they always or even usually think.

Because of the criticisms of Piaget's theory, many researchers have taken several different paths in studying cognitive development. In the next module, we'll look at three different approaches that are linked to Piaget's work. In Chapter 8, we'll look at a very different view of cognitive development, the information-processing approach.

## CHECK YOUR LEARNING

1. According to Piaget's theory, the best teaching experiences are _____.

2. Cognitive growth can be very rapid when children discover _____.

3. One criticism of Piaget's theory is that children's performance on tasks like conservation and object permanence is _____.

4. When tested on many different Piagetian tasks, children's level of performance typically _____.

5. Researchers have found that they can teach children Piagetian concepts and, more importantly, that such teaching _____.

6. Compared to what would be expected from Piaget's theory, adolescents' thinking is often _____.

**ACTIVE CHILDREN**
Piaget championed the view that children participate actively in their own development. How do the sensorimotor child's contributions differ from the formal-operational child's contributions?

**Answers:** (1) slightly ahead of the child's level of thinking, (2) inconsistencies and errors in their own thinking, (3) better explained by ideas that are not part of Piaget's theory, (4) varies from one task to the next, (5) generalizes to other, new tasks (6) less sophisticated

# 7.4

# Beyond Piaget's Theory

## LEARNING OBJECTIVES

● How do neo-Piagetian theories differ from Piaget's original theory?

● What naive theories do children hold about physics, psychology, and biology?

● Why did Vygotsky view development as an apprenticeship?

> *Victoria, a 4-year-old, enjoys solving jigsaw puzzles, coloring, and building towers with blocks. While doing these activities, she often talks to herself. For example, once while coloring a picture, she said, "Where's the red crayon? Stay inside the lines. Color the blocks blue." These remarks were not directed at anyone else; after all, Victoria was alone. Why did she say these things? What purpose did they serve?*

Many theories have been proposed to complement Piaget's view of cognitive development. In this last module, we'll look at three. As we do, you'll learn why Victoria often talks to herself.

## Neo-Piagetian Approaches to Cognitive Development

Beginning in the 1970s, several researchers (e.g., Case, 1998; Fischer & Granott, 1995; Halford, 1993; Pascual-Leone, 1970) proposed theories that elaborated on and updated Piaget's theory. **As a group, these are called neo-Piagetian theories because they are modern theories rooted in Piaget's basic assumptions about cognitive development.** The neo-Piagetian theorists generally retain Piaget's belief that important qualitative changes occur in thinking as children develop, but their theories reflect the new research findings we have just been discussing and thus allow for much greater variation in performance from task to task.

Three basic ideas are at the heart of most neo-Piagetian theories:

- Between infancy and adulthood there are three or four qualitatively different levels of cognitive functioning, with each successive level building on elements of the previous level.

- Children develop many distinct conceptual structures (e.g., understanding numbers, understanding spatial relations) that reflect a child's own experiences and culture, and that consequently are quite variable from one child to the next.

- The capacity and efficiency of working memory—a structure that includes ongoing cognitive processes and the information required for those processes—improves with age, making it possible for children's thinking to become more complex.

The first idea comes directly from Piaget's theory and is largely why these theories are called neo-Piagetian. The second idea is quite different from Piaget's idea that the mind is homogeneous at each developmental stage. Neo-Piagetian theories believe that cognitive development in different areas may progress at different rates, which fits with research showing that children are often more advanced in some areas than others. Of course, this same research shows that there is some consistency in children's performance on different tasks (but not the near-perfect consistency expected by Piaget's theory). Working

> Neo-Piagetian theories include qualitatively different stages of thought, but also include the idea that children develop many distinct conceptual structures.

memory helps explain this consistency by showing that, at any age, there is a limit to the cognitive complexity that children can handle.

Thus, in Piaget's view, children's thinking changes quantitatively as they develop, at a fairly common pace in all domains. Developmental change reflects the equilibration process described on page 176. In contrast, in neo-Piagetian views, children's thinking changes quantitatively as they develop, at different rates in different domains, depending on children's experiences. Developmental change reflects greater capacity and efficiency of working memory.

Phrased somewhat differently, neo-Piagetian theories share Piaget's effort to provide a general account of cognitive development, one that has at its core the idea that thinking changes qualitatively with development. However, neo-Piagetian theories also incorporate a mechanism to explain why a child's thinking may mature more rapidly in some areas than others.

In the next section, you'll see that some researchers take the second neo-Piagetian idea that children develop distinct conceptual structures in different areas as their starting point for explaining cognitive development.

## The Child as Theorist

Piaget believed that children, like scientists, formulate theories about how the world works. Children's theories are usually called *naive theories* because, unlike real scientific theories, they are not created by specialists and they are rarely evaluated by formal experimentation. Naive theories are nevertheless valuable because they allow children (and adults) to understand new experiences and predict future events.

In Piaget's view, children formulate a grand, comprehensive theory that attempts to explain an enormous variety of phenomena—including reasoning about objects, people, and morals, for example—within a common framework. More recent views cling to the idea of children as theorists, but propose that children, like real scientists, develop specialized theories about much narrower areas. **For example, according to the core knowledge hypothesis, infants are born with rudimentary knowledge of the world; this knowledge is elaborated based on children's experiences** (Carey & Spelke, 1994). Some of the theories that young children first develop concern physics, biology, and psychology. That is, infants and toddlers rapidly develop theories that organize their knowledge about properties of objects, people, and living things (Wellman & Gelman, 1998).

In the next few pages, we'll look at children's naive theories in each of these areas.

NAIVE PHYSICS.   As a scientific discipline, physics concerns matter (physical objects) and energy. In contrast, naive physics refers to a person's understanding of objects and their properties. Examples would include understanding that an unsupported object falls and that tall objects are partially visible when placed behind shorter objects. For child-development researchers, the goal is to discover when children are first aware of these kinds of object properties. The usual method to assess infants' knowledge is to show events that conform to physical laws as well as events that violate them (e.g., an object seems to "float" in air, with no visible means of support). If infants look longer or shower greater surprise at the "impossible" events, this suggests that they have an expectation about how objects are supposed to act.

Child-development researchers have discovered that infants are aware of many important basic facts about objects. They know, for instance, that objects move along connected, continuous paths and that objects cannot move "through" other objects (Spelke, 1994; von Hofsten et al., 1998). Infants look longer at moving objects that

Infants understand many of the basic properties of objects, such as the idea that objects must be supported.

violate these properties (e.g., a ball that somehow rolls "through" a solid wall) than moving objects that are consistent with them, suggesting that infants are surprised when objects move in ways not predicted by their naive theory of physics. By the middle of the first year, babies also understand that one object striking a second object will cause the latter to move (Kotovsky & Baillargeon, 1998; Spelke, 1994).

Later in the first year, if infants are shown the two situations shown in the figure, they will look at intently at the object that appears unsupported, apparently because it violates their expectations about what happens to unsupported objects (Baillargeon, 1998). And infants are surprised when a tall object is completely hidden when placed behind a shorter object, apparently because it violates their expectations about concealment (Aguiar & Baillargeon, 2002; Hespos & Baillargeon, 2001).

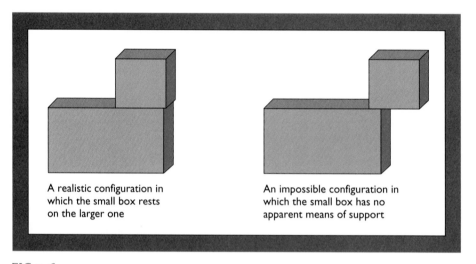

A realistic configuration in which the small box rests on the larger one

An impossible configuration in which the small box has no apparent means of support

FIG.7–6

These amazing demonstrations attest to the fact that the infant is indeed an accomplished naive physicist. Of course, the infant's theories are far from complete; physical properties can be understood at many different levels (Hood, Carey, & Prosada, 2000). Using gravity as an example, infants can expect that unsupported objects will fall, elementary-school children know that such objects fall due to gravity, and physics students know that the force of gravity equals the mass of an object times the acceleration caused by gravity. Obviously, infants do not understand objects at the level of physics students. However, the important point is that infants rapidly create a reasonably accurate theory of some basic properties of objects, a theory that helps them to expect that objects such as toys will act in predictable ways.

**NAIVE BIOLOGY.** Fundamental to adults' naive theories is the distinction between living and nonliving things. Adults know that living things, for example, are made of cells, inherit properties from parents, and move spontaneously. Adults' theories of living things begin in infancy, when youngsters first distinguish animate objects (e.g., people, insects, other animals) from inanimate objects (e.g., rocks, plants, furniture, tools). Motion is critical in early understanding of the difference between animate and inanimate objects: That is, infants and toddlers use motion to identify animate objects and by 12 to 15 months, have determined that animate objects are self-propelled, can move in irregular paths, and act to achieve goals (Rakison & Poulin-Dubois, 2001).

By the preschool years, children's naive theories of biology have come to include many of the specific properties associated with living things (Wellman & Gelman, 1998). Many 4-year-olds' theories of biology include the following elements:

- *Movement:* Children understand that animals can move themselves but inanimate objects can only be moved by other objects or by people. Shown the events in the diagram—an animal and a toy car hopping across a table in exactly the same manner—preschoolers claim that only the animal can really move itself (Gelman & Gottfried, 1996).

FIG.7–7

- *Growth:* Children understand that, from their first appearance, animals get bigger and physically more complex but that inanimate objects do not change in this way. They believe, for example, that sea otters and termites become larger as time goes by but that tea kettles and teddy bears do not (Rosengren et al., 1991).

- *Internal parts:* Children know that the insides of animate objects contain different materials than the insides of inanimate objects. Preschool children judge that blood and bones are more likely to be inside an animate object but that cotton and metal are more likely to be inside an inanimate object (Simons & Keil, 1995).

- *Inheritance:* Children realize that only living things have offspring that resemble their parents. Asked to explain why a dog is pink, preschoolers believe that some biological characteristic of the parents probably made the dog pink; asked to explain why a phone is pink, preschoolers rely on mechanical causes (e.g., a worker used a machine), not biological ones (Springer & Keil, 1991; Weissman & Kalish, 1999).

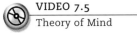
VIDEO 7.5
Theory of Mind

• *Healing:* Children understand that, when injured, animate things heal by re-growth whereas inanimate things must be fixed by humans. Preschoolers know that hair will grow back when cut from a child's head but must be repaired by a person when cut from a doll's head (Backscheider, Shatz, & Gelman, 1993).

Findings like these make it clear that preschoolers' naive theories of biology are complex. Of course, their theories aren't complete; they don't know, for instance, that genes are the biological basis for inheritance (Springer & Keil, 1991). And preschoolers' theories include some misconceptions. They believe that adopted children will physically resemble their adoptive parents (Solomon et al., 1996) and that body parts have intentions—that the heart "wants" to pump blood and bones "want" to grow (Morris, Taplin, & Gelman, 2000). Nevertheless, children's naive theories of biology, when joined with their naive theory of physics, provide powerful tools for making sense of their world and for understanding new experiences.

**NAIVE PSYCHOLOGY.**   The last of the three fundamental theories concerns naive psychology. Think back to the last time you wanted to figure out why someone—a friend, lover, coworker, sibling, or parent—acted as he or she did. Why did your friend go to a movie with someone else instead of going to a concert with you? Why did your brother say nothing about your brand new coat? In common situations like this, adults are often naive psychologists—we try to explain why people act as they do and usually our explanations emphasize that desires or goals cause people's behavior. Your friend went to the movie because she was mad at you for not loaning her your car; your brother didn't comment on your coat because he was preoccupied with something else. Just as naive physics allows us to predict how objects act and naive biology allows us to understand living things, naive psychology allows us to predict how people act (Lillard, 1999).

**Collectively, a person's ideas about connections among thoughts, beliefs, and behavior form a theory of mind, a naive understanding of the relations between mind and behavior.** One of the leading researchers on theory of mind, Henry Wellman (1992; 1993; 2002), believes that children's theory of mind moves through three phases during the preschool years. In the earliest phase, common in 2-year-olds, children are aware of desires, and they often speak of their wants and likes, as in "Lemme see" or "I wanna sit." Also, they often link their desires to their behavior, as in "I happy there's more cookies" (Wellman, 1990). Thus, by age 2, children understand that they and other people have desires and that desires can cause behavior.

By about age 3, an important change takes place. Now children clearly distinguish the mental world from the physical world. For example, if told about one girl who has a cookie and another girl who is thinking about a cookie, 3-year-olds know that only the first girl's cookie can be seen, touched, and eaten (Harris et al., 1991). And, most 3-year-olds use "mental verbs" like *think, believe, remember,* and *forget,* which suggests that they have a beginning understanding of different mental states (Bartsch & Wellman, 1995). Although 3-year-olds talk about thoughts and beliefs, they nevertheless emphasize desires when trying to explain why people act as they do.

Not until age 4 do mental states really take center stage in children's understanding of their own and other people's actions. That is, by 4 years, children understand that their own and other people's behavior is based on their beliefs about events and situations, even when those beliefs are wrong.

This developmental transformation is particularly evident when children are tested on false belief tasks like the one shown in the diagram. In all false-belief tasks, a situation is set up so that the child being tested has accurate information, but someone else does not. For example, in the story in the figure, the child being tested knows that the marble is really in the box, but Sally, the girl in the story, believes that the marble is still in the basket. Remarkably, although 4-year-olds correctly say that Sally will look for the marble in the basket (acting on her false belief), most 3-year-olds say she will look in the box. The 4-year-olds understand that Sally's behavior is based on her beliefs, despite the fact that her beliefs are incorrect (Frye, 1993).

This basic developmental progression is remarkably robust. Wellman, Cross, and Watson (2001) conducted a meta-analysis of approximately 175 studies in which more than 4,000 young children were tested on false-belief tasks. Before $3\frac{1}{2}$ years, children typically make the false-belief error: Attributing their own knowledge of the marble's location to Sally, they say she will search in the correct location. Yet six short months later, children now understand that Sally's false belief will cause her to look for the marble in the basket. This rapid developmental transition from incorrect to correct performance is unaffected by many procedural variables (e.g., whether Sally is a doll, a picture, a person in a videotape, or a real person) and is much the same whether the children are from Europe, North America, Africa, or Asia.

Thus, this pattern signifies a fundamental change in children's understanding of the centrality of beliefs in a person's thinking about the world. By age 4, children "realize that people not only have thoughts and beliefs, but also that thoughts and beliefs are crucial to explaining why people do things; that is, actors' pursuits of their desires are inevitably shaped by their beliefs about the world" (Bartsch & Wellman, 1995, p. 144).

After the preschool years, children's naive psychology moves beyond theory of mind and embraces an ever-expanding range of psychological phenomena. Children begin to connect their naive theories of biology and psychology. For example, at about age 10, children know that such psychological states as being nervous or frustrated can produce physical states such as vomiting or having a headache (Notaro, Gelman, & Zimmerman, 2001). In Module 11.1, we'll trace children's growing understanding of the links among emotions, thoughts, and behavior. For example, although 8-year-olds understand that mental states—thoughts and feelings—can cause a person's mood, most 5-year-olds attribute such mood changes to external, observable causes (Flavell, Flavell, & Green, 2001). Finally, in Module 12.3, we'll discover that, as children develop, their descriptions of other people become more abstract and more psychological.

For now, the important point is that children's naive psychology flourishes in the preschool years. Armed with this theory, children see that other people's behavior is not unpredictable but follows regular patterns.

FIG. 7–8

During the preschool years, children form a theory of mind–a naive understanding of links between thoughts, beliefs, and behavior.

## The Sociocultural Perspective: Vygotsky's Theory

Like many authors, I often refer to child development as a journey that can proceed along many different paths. For Piaget and neo-Piagetian theorists, children make the journey alone. Other people (and culture in general) certainly influence the direction that children take, but the child is seen as a solitary adventurer-explorer boldly forging ahead.

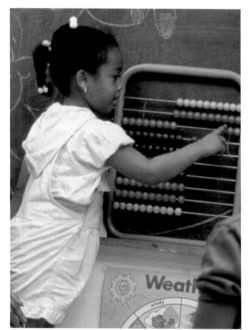

In contrast, within the sociocultural perspective, cognitive development is inseparable from the social and cultural contexts in which children live. To illustrate, Gauvain (1998) argues that cultural contexts organize cognitive development in several ways. First, culture often defines which cognitive activities are valued: American youngsters are expected to learn to read but not to navigate using the stars. Second, culture provides tools that shape the way children think. The cognitive skills that children use to solve arithmetic problems, for example, depend on whether their culture provides an abacus like the one in the photograph, or paper and pencil, or a hand-held calculator. Third, higher-level cultural practices help children to organize their knowledge and communicate it to others. For instance, in most American schools, students are expected to think and work alone rather than collaborate (Matusov, Bell, & Rogoff, 2002). Thus, as Gauvain (1998) emphasizes, "Culture penetrates human intellectual functioning and its development at many levels, and it does so through many organized individual and social practices" (p. 189).

One of the original—and still quite influential—sociocultural theories was proposed by Lev Vygotsky (1896–1934), the Russian psychologist described in Chapter 1. Vygotsky saw development as an apprenticeship in which children advance when they collaborate with others who are more skilled. That is, according to Vygotsky (1978), child development is never a solitary journey. Instead, children always travel with others and usually progress most rapidly when they walk hand in hand with an expert partner.

Vygotsky died of tuberculosis when he was only 37 years old, so he never had the opportunity to formulate a complete theory of cognitive development as Piaget did. Nevertheless, his ideas are influential because they fill some gaps in the Piagetian and neo-Piagetian accounts. Three of Vygotsky's most important contributions are the zone of proximal development, scaffolding, and private speech.

**THE ZONE OF PROXIMAL DEVELOPMENT** Four-year-old Ian and his dad often work on puzzles together. Ian does most of the work; like the father in the photo, his dad sometimes finds a piece that Ian needs or correctly orients a piece. When Ian tries to do the same puzzles himself, he rarely can complete them. **The difference between what Ian can do with assistance and what he can do alone defines the zone of proximal development.** That is, the zone refers to the difference between the level of performance a child can achieve when working independently and the higher level of performance that is possible when working under the guidance of more skilled adults or peers (Wertsch & Tulviste, 1992).

Think, for example, about a preschooler who is asked to clean her bedroom. She doesn't know where to begin. By structuring the task for the child—"start by putting away your books, then your toys, then your dirty clothes"—an adult can help the child accomplish what she cannot do by herself. Just as training wheels help children learn to ride a bike by allowing them to concentrate on other aspects of bicycling, collaborators help children perform effectively by providing structure, hints, and reminders.

The idea of a zone of proximal development follows naturally from Vygotsky's basic premise that cognition develops first in a social setting and only gradually comes under the child's independent control. Understanding how the shift from social to individual learning occurs brings us to the second of Vygotsky's key contributions.

**SCAFFOLDING**   Have you ever had the good fortune to work with a master teacher, one who seemed to know exactly when to say something to help you over an obstacle but otherwise let you work uninterrupted? **Scaffolding refers to a teaching style that matches the amount of assistance to the learner's needs.** Early in learning a new task, when a child knows little, the teacher provides a lot of direct instruction. But, as the child begins to catch on to the task, the teacher provides less instruction and only occasional reminders (McNaughton & Leyland, 1990).

We saw earlier how a parent helping a preschooler clean her room must provide detailed structure. But, as the child does the task more often, the parent needs to provide less structure. Similarly, when high-school students first try to do proofs in geometry, the teacher must lead them through each step; as the students begin to understand how proofs are done and can do more on their own, the teacher gradually provides less help.

Do parents worldwide scaffold their children's learning? If so, do they use similar methods? The "Cultural Influences" feature answers these questions.

VIDEO 7.6
Scaffolding

Vygotsky viewed cognitive development as a collaboration between a novice child and more skilled teachers who scaffold children's learning.

## CULTURAL INFLUENCES

### How Do Parents in Different Cultures Scaffold Their Children's Learning?

Cross-cultural research by Barbara Rogoff and her colleagues (1993) suggests that parents and other adults in many cultures scaffold learning, but they do it in different ways. These researchers studied parents and 1- to 2-year-olds in four different settings: a medium-sized U.S. city, a small tribal village in India, a large city in Turkey, and a town in the highlands of Guatemala. In one part of the study, parents tried to get their toddlers to operate a novel toy (for example, a wooden doll that danced when a string was pulled). No ground rules or guidelines concerning teaching were given; parents were free to be as direct or uninvolved as they cared.

What did parents do? In all four cultural settings, the vast majority attempted to scaffold their children's learning, either by dividing a difficult task into easier subtasks or by doing parts of the task themselves, particularly the more complicated parts. However, as the graphs show, parents in different cultures scaffold in different ways. Turkish parents give the most verbal instruction and use some

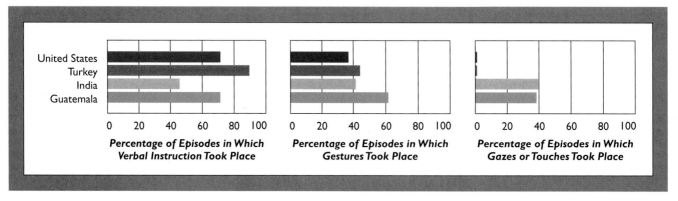

FIG.7–9

gestures (pointing, nodding, shrugging). U.S. parents also use these methods but to slightly lesser degrees. Turkish and U.S. parents almost never touch (such as nudging a child's elbow) or gaze (use eye contact, such as winking or staring). Indian parents seem to use roughly equal amounts of speech, gesture, and touch or gaze to scaffold. Guatemalan parents also use all three techniques, and, overall, Guatemalan parents give the most scaffolding of the four cultures. Evidently, parents worldwide try to simplify learning tasks for their children, but the methods that they use to scaffold learning vary across cultures.

The defining characteristic of scaffolding—giving help but not more than is needed—clearly promotes learning (Plumert & Nichols-Whitehead, 1996). Youngsters do not learn readily when they are constantly told what to do or when they are simply left to struggle through a problem unaided. However, when teachers collaborate with them—allowing children to take on more and more of a task as they master its different elements—they learn more effectively (Murphy & Messer, 2000). Scaffolding is an important technique for transferring skills from others to the child, both in formal settings like schools and in informal settings like the home or playground.

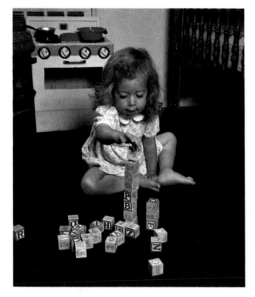

**PRIVATE SPEECH** Like Victoria from the vignette, the little girl in the photo is talking to herself as she is playing. **This behavior demonstrates private speech, comments not directed to others but intended to help children regulate their own behavior.** Vygotsky (1934/1986) viewed private speech as an intermediate step toward self-regulation of cognitive skills. At first, children's behavior is regulated by speech from other people that is directed toward them. When youngsters first try to control their own behavior and thoughts without others present, they instruct themselves by speaking aloud. **Finally, as children gain ever greater skill, private speech becomes inner speech, Vygotsky's term for thought.**

If children use private speech to help control their behavior, then we should see children using it more often on difficult tasks than on easy tasks, and more often after a mistake than after a correct response. These predictions are generally supported in research (Berk, 1992), which documents the power of language in helping children learn to control their own behavior and thinking.

Vygotsky's view of cognitive development as an apprenticeship, a collaboration between expert and novice, complements the other views of cognitive development described in this module. Each perspective—the neo-Piagetian approaches, the child as theorist, and Vygotsky's work—provides a unique lens for viewing cognitive development. The chief characteristics of each perspective are described in the table.

Contributing further to our understanding of cognitive development is information processing, the topic of Chapter 8.

**SUMMARY TABLE**

| CHARACTERISTICS OF SOME ALTERNATIVES TO PIAGET'S THEORY | |
|---|---|
| **Approach** | **Characteristics** |
| Neo-Piagetian theory | The closest of the alternatives to Piaget's original theory; includes qualitatively different stages of thinking, distinct conceptual structures, and increasing capacity of working memory. |
| The child as theorist | Key element is the idea that children form extensive naive theories in specialized areas, including physics, biology, and psychology; though incomplete and sometimes wrong, children's naive theories help them to understand their world. |
| Vygotsky's theory | Views cognitive development as a social enterprise; experts use scaffolding to help a novice acquire knowledge; children use private speech to regulate their own thinking. |

## CHECK YOUR LEARNING

**1.** Neo-Piagetian theories typically retain Piaget's belief that _____.

**2.** By 3 or 4 months, infants know that objects move _____.

**3.** Most 4-year-olds know that living things move, _____, have internal parts, resemble their parents, and heal when injured.

**4.** According to Wellman, the basic element of 2-year-olds' theory of mind is that _____.

**5.** The _____ refers to the difference between what children can do alone and what they can do with skilled help.

**6.** Children use private speech more on difficult tasks than on easy tasks and more often after _____.

**NATURE AND NURTURE**
Compare the role of cultural influences in Piaget's theory, neo-Piagetian theory, and Vygotsky's theory.

**Answers:** (1) cognitive development includes qualitatively different stages of thinking, (2) along connected, continuous paths, (3) grow, (4) people have desires that cause behavior, (5) zone of proximal development, (6) they've made a mistake

# Unifying Themes: Active Children

This chapter emphasizes that *children influence their own development*. This idea is the cornerstone of Piaget's theory. Beginning in infancy and continuing through childhood and adolescence, children are constantly trying to make sense out of what goes on around them. Their understanding of the world and their systematic *misunderstanding* is what propels cognitive development to more sophisticated levels. Experiences provide intellectual food for children to digest. Parents, teachers, and peers are important in cognitive development, not so much for what they teach directly as for the guidance and challenges they provide. Thus, as children take their developmental journeys, Piaget's child is a busy navigator, trying to understand the routes available and trying to decide among them.

## See for Yourself

The best way to see some of the developmental changes that Piaget described is to test some children with the same tasks that Piaget used. The conservation tasks shown on page 181 are good because they're simple to set up and children usually enjoy them. For each task, ask a 3- or 4-year-old and a 7- or 8-year-old to confirm that the two amounts are the same. Then transform one quantity as illustrated in the diagram on page 181 and ask children if the quantities are still the same. Ask them to explain their answers. The differences between 3- and 7-year-olds' answers are truly remarkable. See for yourself!

## Resources

For more information about...

activities for babies that promote cognitive development, read S. H. Jacobs's *Your Baby's Mind* (Bob Adams, 1992), which describes learning games and exercises for babies that are derived from Piaget's view of sensorimotor intelligence.

Piaget's life, his theory, and his research (as well as related research on cognitive development), visit the Web site of the Jean Piaget Society:
**http://www.piaget.org**

## Key Terms

accommodation 175
animism 180
assimilation 175
centration 180
concrete operational stage 185
constructivism 189
core knowledge hypothesis 195
deductive reasoning 187
egocentrism 180
equilibration 176
formal operational stage 185
inner speech 202
mental operations 185

neo-Piagetian theories 194
object permanence 178
preoperational stage 179
primary circular reaction 178
private speech 202
scaffolding 200
schemes 174
secondary circular reaction 178
sensorimotor stage 177
tertiary circular reaction 178
theory of mind 198
zone of proximal development 200

SUMMARY

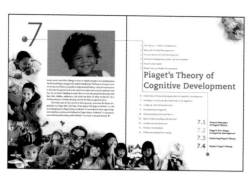

# 7.1 General Principles of Piaget's Theory

### Schemes

In Piaget's view, children construct their understanding of the world by creating schemes—mental categories of related events, objects, and knowledge. Infants' schemes are based on actions, but older children's and adolescents' schemes are based on functional, conceptual, and abstract properties.

### Assimilation and Accommodation

Schemes change constantly. In assimilation, experiences are readily incorporated into existing schemes. In accommodation, experiences cause schemes to be modified.

### Equilibration and Stages of Cognitive Development

When accommodation becomes much more frequent than assimilation, it is a sign that children's schemes are inadequate, so children reorganize them. This reorganization produces four different stages of mental development from infancy through adulthood. All individuals go through all four phases, but not necessarily at the same rate.

# 7.2 Piaget's Four Stages of Cognitive Development

### The Sensorimotor Stage

The first 2 years of life constitute Piaget's sensorimotor stage. Over these 2 years, infants adapt to and explore their environment, understand objects, and begin to use symbols.

### The Preoperational Stage

From ages 2 to 7 years, children are in Piaget's preoperational stage. Although now capable of using symbols, their thinking is limited by egocentrism, the inability to see the world from another's point of view. Preoperational children also are centered in their thinking and sometimes confuse appearance with reality.

### The Concrete Operational Stage

Between ages 7 and 11 children begin to use and can reverse mental operations to solve perspective-taking and conservation problems. The main limit to thinking at this stage is that it is focused on the concrete and real.

### The Formal Operational Stage

With the onset of formal operational thinking, adolescents can think hypothetically and reason abstractly. In deductive reasoning, they understand that conclusions are based on logic, not experience.

# 7.3 Evaluating Piaget's Theory

### Piaget's Contributions to Child Development

Among Piaget's enduring contributions are emphasizing the importance of cognitive processes in development, viewing children as active participants in their own development, and discovering many counterintuitive developmental phenomena. Teachers and parents have used Piaget's theory to foster children's development. The theory emphasizes the roles of discovery in learning, of providing experiences slightly ahead of the child's level, and of learning from inconsistencies and errors.

### Criticisms of the Theory

Piaget's theory has been faulted because children's performance on tasks is sometimes better explained by ideas that are not part of his theory. A second shortcoming is that children's performance from one task to the next is not as consistent as the theory predicts. A third is that, with training, children can readily grasp ideas that should be too advanced for them based on their Piagetian stage. A fourth shortcoming is that children and adolescents often use simpler forms of reasoning than they should for their Piagetian stage.

# 7.4 Beyond Piaget's Theory

### Neo-Piagetian Approaches to Cognitive Development

Neo-Piagetian theorists adhere to the basic premise of Piaget's theory that thought progresses through qualitatively different stages. However, neo-Piagetian theories propose that children develop distinct conceptual structures in different domains. In these theories, development to more advanced cognitive structures is thought to reflect, in part, increases in the capacity of working memory.

### The Child as Theorist

Another approach to cognitive development is rooted in Piaget's metaphor of the child as scientist. However, in contrast to Piaget's idea that children create a comprehensive theory that integrates all their knowledge, the modern view is that children are specialists, generating naive theories in particular domains, including physics, biology, and psychology.

### The Sociocultural Perspective: Vygotsky's Theory

Vygotsky believed that cognition develops first in a social setting and only gradually comes under the child's independent control. The difference between what children can do with assistance and what they can do alone defines the zone of proximal development.

Control of cognitive skills is most readily transferred from others to the child through scaffolding, a teaching style that allows children to take on more and more of a task as they master its different components.

Children often talk to themselves, particularly when the task is difficult or after they have made a mistake. Such private speech is one way that children regulate their behavior, and it represents an intermediate step in the self-regulation of cognitive skills.

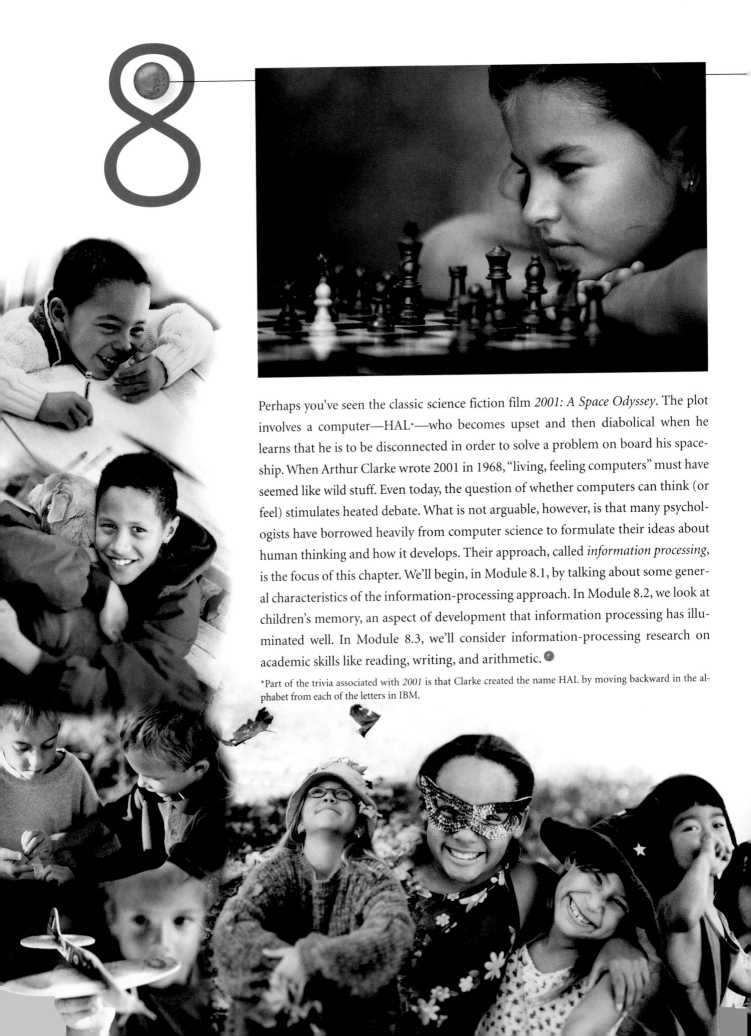

8

Perhaps you've seen the classic science fiction film *2001: A Space Odyssey*. The plot involves a computer—HAL*—who becomes upset and then diabolical when he learns that he is to be disconnected in order to solve a problem on board his spaceship. When Arthur Clarke wrote 2001 in 1968, "living, feeling computers" must have seemed like wild stuff. Even today, the question of whether computers can think (or feel) stimulates heated debate. What is not arguable, however, is that many psychologists have borrowed heavily from computer science to formulate their ideas about human thinking and how it develops. Their approach, called *information processing*, is the focus of this chapter. We'll begin, in Module 8.1, by talking about some general characteristics of the information-processing approach. In Module 8.2, we look at children's memory, an aspect of development that information processing has illuminated well. In Module 8.3, we'll consider information-processing research on academic skills like reading, writing, and arithmetic.

*Part of the trivia associated with *2001* is that Clarke created the name HAL by moving backward in the alphabet from each of the letters in IBM.

# Information-Processing Approaches to Cognitive Development

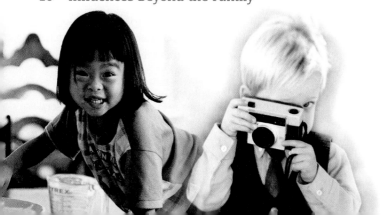

# 8.1 An Introduction to Information Processing

## LEARNING OBJECTIVES

- What are the basic characteristics of the information-processing approach?
- According to information-processing psychologists, how does thinking change as children develop?
- How does information processing differ from Piaget's theory?

*Phung, a 15-year-old girl, has just completed driver's ed and loves getting behind the wheel. Most of the time, her parents are okay when she drives; they don't scream or get hysterical if she goes a little fast or hits the brakes too hard. But every time Phung turns on the radio, they go ballistic. "No, no, no, you need to pay attention to your driving, not listen to music," they say. Phung thinks this is stupid. What does listening to music have to do with how well she drives?*

Phung's question is a good one, and later in this module we'll see that information-processing researchers have an answer for her. But first, let's learn more about information processing as a theoretical approach.

## Basic Features of the Information-Processing Approach

A few weeks ago, a friend of mine, Jim, bought a new computer for his office. Jim was eager to use the new machine to handle his correspondence, prepare graphs for sales meetings, and when his boss wasn't looking, surf the Web. But enthusiasm soon turned to disappointment: Although Jim's computer could do all these things, it was incredibly slow and time consuming. The word-processing software seemed to take forever to load, and it seemed to Jim that he'd spent hours staring at the Windows XP© hourglass while waiting for Web pages to appear. After some oaths not fit to print in a G-rated textbook, Jim gradually realized that saving a few hundred dollars by getting a slower processor and less memory was probably a mistake. His computer simply lacked the hardware necessary to make the software run efficiently.

> In the information-processing approach, mental hardware includes sensory, working, and long-term memories.

**This simple distinction between computer hardware and computer software is the basis of an approach to human thinking known as information processing.** The information-processing approach arose in the 1960s and is now one of the principal approaches to cognitive development (Kail & Bisanz, 1992; Klahr & MacWhinney, 1998). You remember, from Module 1.2, that information-processing theorists believe human thinking is based on both mental hardware and mental software. Mental hardware refers to mental and neural structures that are built in and that allow the mind to operate. If the hardware in a personal computer refers to random-access memory, the central processor, and the like, what does mental hardware refer to? Information-processing theorists generally agree that mental hardware has three components: sensory memory, working memory, and long-term memory. The diagram at the top of page 209 shows how they are related.

**Sensory memory is where information is held in raw, unanalyzed form very briefly (no longer than a few seconds).** For example, look at your hand as you clench your fist, then rapidly open your hand (so that your fingers are extended) and

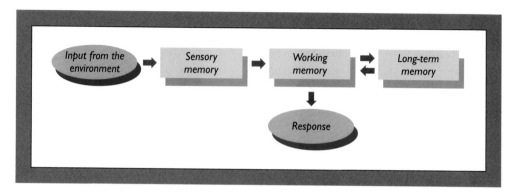

FIG.8–1

then rapidly reclench your fist. If you watch your fingers, you'll see an image of your fingers that lasts momentarily after you reclench your hand. What you're seeing is an image stored in sensory memory.

**Working memory is the site of ongoing cognitive activity.** Some theorists liken working memory to a carpenter's workbench, which includes space for storing the materials for a current project as well as space for the carpenter to do the sawing, nailing, and painting involved in the project (Klatzky, 1980). In much the same way, working memory includes both ongoing cognitive processes and the information that they require (Baddeley, 1996). For example, as you read these sentences, part of working memory is allocated to the cognitive processes responsible for determining the meanings of individual words; working memory also stores the results of these analyses briefly while they are used by other cognitive processes to give meaning to sequences of words.

This description of working memory probably has a familiar ring to it. That's because working memory is a common element in neo-Piagetian approaches to cognitive development, described in Module 7.4. And you may have heard of short-term memory, which refers to the storage aspect of working memory (but not the space set aside for actual construction). Finally, if you're familiar with personal computers, you'll recognize that working memory resembles random-access memory because that's where we load programs we want to run and temporarily store the data those programs are using.

**Long-term memory is a limitless, permanent storehouse of knowledge of the world.** Long-term memory is like a computer's hard drive, a fairly permanent storehouse of programs and data. It includes facts (e.g., Charles Lindbergh flew the Atlantic in the "Spirit of St. Louis"), personal events (e.g., "I moved to Maryland in July 1999"), and skills (e.g., how to play the cello).

Information rarely is forgotten from long-term memory, though it is sometimes hard to access. For example, do you remember the name of the African American agricultural chemist who pioneered crop rotation methods and invented peanut butter? If his name doesn't come to mind, look at this list:

*Marconi     Carver     Fulton     Luther*

Now do you know the answer? (If not, it appears before "Check Your Learning," on page 215.) Just as books are sometimes misplaced in a library, you sometimes cannot find a fact in long-term memory. Given a list of names, though, you can go directly to the location in long-term memory associated with each name and determine which is the famed chemist.

Mental hardware allows us to "run" mental software, so the next question is, what is mental software? To answer this question, think about personal computer software you've used, such as programs for word processing, spreadsheets, or graphing. In each case, the software was designed to accomplish a specific function. In much the same way, mental software refers to mental programs that are the basis for performing particular tasks. According to information-processing psychologists, children have special mental software that allows them to accomplish particular tasks, such as reading, doing arithmetic, or finding their way to and from school.

Let's look at a simple example to see how information-processing psychologists analyze cognitive processes. Suppose a mother asks her son to make his bed, brush his teeth, and take out the trash. A bit later, the mother wonders if she asked her son about the trash, so she says, "Did I ask you to take out the trash?" Almost immediately, he says, "Yes." Despite the speed of the boy's reply, information-processing theorists believe that his mental software has gone through four general steps to answer the question, as shown in the diagram. First, the mental software must understand the mother's question. That is, the software must decode the sounds of the mother's speech and give them meaning. Next, the software searches working memory and long-term memory for the mother's earlier requests. When that information is located and retrieved, the software compares "take out the trash" with each of the mother's requests. Finding a match, the software selects "yes" as the appropriate answer to the question.

Thus, the processes of understanding, searching, comparing, and responding create a mental program that allows the boy to answer his mother. The mental software for solving a calculus problem or writing a poem is more elaborate—involving more processes and more steps—but the basic idea of breaking down a task into many simpler components is the same.

In the next section, we'll see how child development researchers use these ideas to understand how children's thinking changes as they grow older.

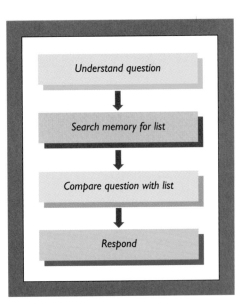

FIG.8–2

## How Information Processing Changes with Development

All theories of cognitive development try to explain how experiences and mental structures interact to produce cognitive growth. You may recall from Module 7.1 that Piaget's explanation of cognitive development emphasized equilibration—the process by which mental structures are massively reorganized so that schemes can assimilate information more readily. Information-processing theorists believe that developmental change comes in several important forms, rather than through a single mechanism like equilibration (Kail & Bisanz, 1992; Siegler, 1989). Let's look at five of them.

**BETTER STRATEGIES.**   Older children usually use better strategies to solve problems (Shrager & Siegler, 1998; Schneider & Bjorklund, 1998). That is, as children develop they use strategies that are faster, more accurate, and easier. Having lost a hat on the way to school, a younger child might search the entire route; an older child might recall taking off the hat midway to school and so only search the last half of the route (Sophian & Wellman, 1987). Both children will probably find the missing hat, but the older child's approach is more efficient.

How do children learn more effective strategies? Of course, parents and teachers often help youngsters learn more effective strategies. In Module 7.4, for example, we saw how parents sometimes scaffold children's learning. By structuring children's actions and providing hints, adults demonstrate new strategies and how best to use them. However, youngsters also learn new strategies by watching and working with more skilled children (Tudge, Winterhoff, & Hogan, 1996). For example, children and adolescents at an arcade watch others play in order to learn good game strategies. Children also discover new strategies on their own (Siegler & Jenkins, 1989). For example, when my daughter was 5, I watched her match words with their antonyms in a language workbook. The pages always had an equal number of words and antonyms, so she quickly learned to connect the last word with the one remaining antonym, without thinking about the meaning of either.

> As children develop, they use more efficient strategies and more working memory.

To explain how children come to use better strategies to solve arithmetic problems, spell, tell time, and reason scientifically, Siegler (1996) proposed the overlapping waves model. According to Siegler, children use multiple approaches to solve most problems and over time they tend to use more efficient strategies (faster, more accurate, less effort) whenever possible (Siegler, 1996). For example, there are many ways that a child might try to spell a word. She might know the correct spelling and simply retrieve it from long-term memory, she could sound out each syllable and figure out the letters corresponding to each sound, or she could find the spelling in a dictionary. She is likely to try to retrieve an answer first (in spelling and other tasks) because memory retrieval is fast and takes little effort. If retrieval does not produce an answer that the child trusts, she will turn to other backup strategies such as sounding out and using a dictionary. Thus, a typical 7-year-old would retrieve the spelling of "cat" from memory but use backup strategies to spell "invention." However, after the child has used backup strategies several times to solve a word, the spelling would be stored in long-term memory and the child could simply retrieve it (Rittle-Johnson & Siegler, 1999).

Thus, with input from parents, teachers, peers, and their own observations, children's mental software becomes more powerful and more efficient. Sometimes these changes occur abruptly—when children immediately see the benefits of a better way of solving a problem—but more often they occur gradually (Alibali, 1999).

**INCREASED CAPACITY OF WORKING MEMORY.** Remember that working memory is the part of mental hardware responsible for ongoing mental activity—the mental workspace. What would happen if this workspace became larger as children grew? To answer this question, think about technological change in personal computers: Modern personal computers run much more impressive software than previously, in part because they have much more random-access memory available than their counterparts from the 1980s and 1990s. If you use this technological change as a metaphor for children's development, the implication is clear. The diagram shows that, compared to younger children, older children have more working memory to allocate to mental software and to information storage (Case, 1992; Kail, 1995). Consequently, older children usually outperform younger children on tasks where working memory is important for performance, such as reading or solving complicated problems.

FIG.8–3

**MORE EFFECTIVE INHIBITORY PROCESSES AND EXECUTIVE FUNCTIONING.**
Yesterday I was listening to the radio and heard that classic oldie "The Lion Sleeps Tonight." Unfortunately, I spent the rest of the afternoon hearing "aweem away, aweem away" over and over in my mind. Undoubtedly, you, too, have had this experience—a thought gets into your head and you can't get rid of it. Returning to the workbench metaphor of working memory, interfering ideas are tools or materials left from previous projects that are not needed for a current project but nevertheless take up precious space on the workbench.

Fortunately, most of the time irrelevant and unwanted ideas do not intrude on our thinking. Why not? **Inhibitory processes prevent task-irrelevant information from entering working memory.** These processes, which rely on the attentional processes described in Module 6.2, improve steadily during childhood (Dempster, 1995). Consequently, thinking in older children and adolescents is more sophisticated because better inhibition means fewer disruptions from irrelevant stimulation and, therefore, more efficient working memory. When an older child is deciding the best way to a new friend's house, the sound of popcorn popping or thoughts of an upcoming swim meet are less likely to intrude on working memory and disrupt his planning (Kail, 2003).

**Inhibitory processes, along with planning and cognitive flexibility, define executive functioning.** In many ways, executive functioning is synonymous with skilled problem solving, which helps to explain the presence of each of the elements in the definition. That is, good problem solving usually involves a plan and often requires flexibility (the ability to respond differently when the old response no longer works) and the ability to inhibit irrelevant responses (Roberts & Pennington, 1996; Zelazo et al., 1997). Each of the elements of executive functioning has been linked to the frontal cortex, a brain region known to develop throughout infancy and childhood (Passler, Isaac, & Hynd, 1985). Thus, with age children are better able to inhibit irrelevant responses, to formulate effective plans, and to adjust those plans as needed.

**INCREASED AUTOMATIC PROCESSING.** Think back to the days when you were learning a brand new skill, like how to type. In the beginning, you had to think about every single step in the process. If, as a novice typist, you were asked to type "child," you probably started like the child in the photograph, by trying to remember the location of "c" on the keyboard and then deciding which finger to use to reach that key. You had to repeat this process for each of the remaining four letters. But as your skill grew, each step became easier until you could type "child" without even thinking about it; your fingers seem to move automatically to the right keys, in the right sequence. **Cognitive activities that require virtually no effort are known as automatic processes.**

To understand how automatic processes affect developmental change, we need to return to working memory. In the early phases of learning a skill, each individual step (such as finding a "c" on the keyboard) must be stored in working memory. Because there are so many steps, an unmastered skill can easily occupy much of the capacity of working memory. In contrast, when a skill has been mastered, individual steps are no longer stored in working memory, which means that more capacity is available for other activities. Thus, beginning drivers like Phung are told to keep the music turned off because listening would consume capacity of working memory that is needed for driving. However, with more experience behind the wheel, many driving skills become automatic, freeing capacity that can be used to listen to the radio. (Patience, Phung, your time will come!)

Compared to adolescents and adults, children have limited experience in most tasks, so they perform few processes automatically. Instead, like Phung, their processing requires substantial working memory capacity. As children gain experience, however, some processes become automatic, freeing working memory capacity for other processes (Kail & Park, 1990). Thus, when faced with complex tasks involving many processes, older children are more likely to succeed because they can perform some of the processes automatically. In contrast, younger children must think about all or most of the processes, taxing or even exceeding the capacity of their working memory.

> Older children have better inhibitory processes, more automatic processes, and more rapid processing.

**INCREASED SPEED OF PROCESSING.** As children develop, they complete most mental processes at an ever-faster rate (Cerella & Hale, 1994). Improved speed is obvious when we measure how fast children of different ages respond on tasks. Across a wide range of cognitive tasks such as deciding which of two numbers is greater, naming a pictured object, and searching memory, 4-and 5-year-olds are generally one-third as fast as adults, whereas 8- and 9-year-olds are one-half as fast as adults (Kail, 2000).

Age differences in processing speed are critical when a specified number of actions must be completed in a fixed period of time. For example, perhaps you've had the unfortunate experience of trying to understand a professor who lectures at warp speed. The instructor's speech was so rapid that your cognitive processes couldn't keep up, which meant that you didn't get much out of the lecture. The problem is even more serious for children, who process information much more slowly than adults.

The five types of developmental change, summarized in the table at the top of page 214, occur throughout infancy, childhood, adolescence, and adulthood. Furthermore, sometimes the different types of change interact with each other. To understand this interaction, think back to the analogy of working memory as a workbench. Carpenters who quickly find the tools they need can complete the project on their workbench promptly and move on to other projects. Carpenters who must search endlessly for tools will complete the project much more slowly. In much the same way, as children process information more rapidly, they use working memory more efficiently. With the five types of change interacting in this fashion (and functioning independently), information processing provides a very detailed account of cognitive development.

## Comparing Information Processing and Piaget's Theory

Piaget's theory is so influential that it has long been the gold standard for theories of cognitive development. By comparing information processing with Piaget's theory, you can see some of the strengths and weaknesses of each (Kail & Bisanz, 1992).

One important difference is that Piaget's work is a single comprehensive theory, whereas information processing represents a general approach encompassing many different theories to describe specific components of cognitive development. Thus, the advantage of Piaget's work is that it is comprehensive—all the links between different facets of cognitive development are included in his theory. But the advantage of the information-processing approach is that specific components of

## TYPES OF DEVELOPMENTAL CHANGE IN INFORMATION PROCESSING

| Type of Developmental Change | Defined | Example |
| --- | --- | --- |
| Better strategies | Older children use faster, more accurate, and easier strategies. | Younger children may "sound out" a word's spelling but older children simply retrieve it. |
| Increased capacity of working memory | Older children have a larger mental workspace for cognitive processes. | An older child could simultaneously watch TV and converse with a friend but a younger child could do one but not both. |
| More effective inhibitory processing and executive functioning | Older children are less prone to interference from irrelevant stimulation and more flexible in their thinking. | Asked by a teacher to format assignments in a new way (e.g., place name in a different location, provide the day but not the date), older children are more successful in adopting to the new format and less likely to incorrectly use the old format. |
| Increased automatic processing | Older children can execute more processes automatically (without using working memory). | Asked to get ready for bed, an older child goes through all the tasks (e.g., brush teeth, put on pajamas) thinking about other things, whereas a younger child focuses on each task as well as what to do next. |
| Increased speed of processing | Older children can execute mental processes more rapidly than younger children. | Shown a picture of a dog, the older child can retrieve the name "dog" from memory more rapidly. |

cognition are described with sharp precision. In essence, Piaget emphasized the "whole" of cognitive development, whereas information processing emphasizes the "parts." Both the whole and the parts are important for complete understanding of cognitive development, so Piaget's theory and information processing complement each other.

A second difference is that Piaget emphasized periodic, qualitative change in cognition: Children's thinking remains at one stage for years, then changes abruptly as equilibration propels thinking into the next, qualitatively different stage. In contrast, when the five types of change in information processing are combined, the result is a steady age-related increase in cognitive skill. Unlike Piaget's account, there are no abrupt or qualitative changes that create distinct cognitive stages. Instead, as you can see in the diagram, cognitive change is constant and gradual. Since both types of change play a role in development, here, too, Piaget's theory and information processing complement each other.

Keep these differences in mind as you read about the development of memory (Module 8.2) and academic skills (Module 8.3). Think about the need to balance the "whole" with the "parts," and think about the role of abrupt change versus gradual change in cognitive development.

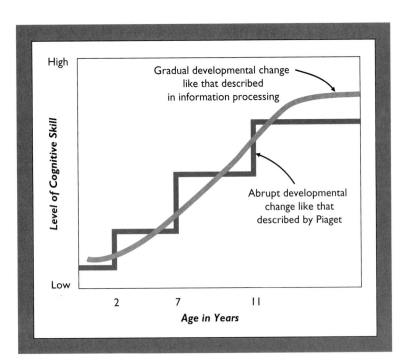

FIG.8–4

*Response to question on page 209:* The agricultural chemist who pioneered crop rotation while on the faculty of Tuskegee Institute of Technology is George Washington Carver.

## CHECK YOUR LEARNING

**1.** Information-processing psychologists believe that mental hardware includes sensory memory, working memory, and _____ .

**2.** Random-access memory in a personal computer is analogous to _____ , according to the information-processing view.

**3.** _____ refers to specialized processes that allow children to complete particular tasks, such as reading or arithmetic.

**4.** According to the information-processing view, the older child's greater cognitive skill can be traced to better strategies, _____ , more effective inhibition and executive functioning, increased automatic processing, and more rapid speed of processing.

**5.** Piaget's theory provides a comprehensive account of cognitive development, whereas information processing provides _____ .

**6.** Piaget emphasizes distinct stages in cognitive development, whereas information processing emphasizes _____ .

**NATURE AND NURTURE**
Do the five types of developmental change emphasized in information processing emphasize nature, nurture, or both? How?

Answers: (1) long-term memory, (2) working memory, (3) Mental software, (4) increased working memory capacity, (5) very detailed explanations of specific aspects of cognitive growth, (6) steady, gradual change

# Memory

# 8.2

## LEARNING OBJECTIVES

- How well do infants remember?

- How do strategies help children to remember?

- How does children's knowledge influence what they remember?

Origins of Memory

Strategies for Remembering

Knowledge and Memory

> *One afternoon 4-year-old Cheryl came home sobbing and reported that Mr. Johnson, a neighbor and longtime family friend, had taken down her pants and touched her "private parts." Her mother was shocked. Mr. Johnson had always seemed an honest, decent man, which made her wonder if Cheryl's imagination had simply run wild. Yet, at times, he did seem a bit peculiar, so her daughter's claim had a ring of truth.*

Regrettably, episodes like this are all too common in America today. When child abuse is suspected, and the child is the sole eyewitness, the child must testify to prosecute the alleged abuser. But can preschool children like Cheryl be trusted to recall events accurately on the witness stand? To answer this question, we need to understand more about how memory develops. We'll start by examining the origins of memory in infancy, then see what factors contribute to the development of memory in childhood and adolescence.

## Origins of Memory

Roots of memory are laid down in the first few months after birth. Young babies remember events for days or even weeks at a time. Some of the studies that opened our eyes to the infant's ability to remember were conducted by Carolyn Rovee-Collier (1997, 1999). The method used in her studies is shown in the photo. A ribbon from a mobile is attached to a 2- or 3-month-old's leg; within a few minutes, the babies learn to kick to make the mobile move. When Rovee-Collier brought the mobile to the infants' homes several days or a few weeks later, babies would still kick to make the mobile move. If Rovee-Collier waited several weeks to return, most babies forgot that kicking moved the mobile. When that happened, she gave them a reminder—she moved the mobile herself without attaching the ribbon to their foot. Then she would return the next day, hook up the apparatus, and the babies would kick to move the mobile.

Rovee-Collier's experiments show that three important features of memory exist as early as 2 and 3 months of age: (1) an event from the past is remembered, (2) over time, the event can no longer be recalled, and (3) a cue can serve to dredge up a memory that seems to have been forgotten.

From these humble origins, memory improves rapidly in older infants and toddlers (Rose, Feldman, & Jankowski, 2001). Youngsters can recall more of what they experience and remember it longer. When shown novel actions with toys and later asked to imitate what they saw, toddlers can remember more than infants and remember the actions for longer periods (Bauer, Burch, & Kleinknecht, 2002). For example, if shown how to make a rattle by first placing a wooden block inside a container, then putting a lid on the container, toddlers are more likely than infants to remember the necessary sequence of steps.

These improvements in memory can be traced, in part, to growth in the brain regions that support memory (Carver & Bauer, 2001; Nelson, 1997). On the one hand, the brain structures primarily responsible for the initial storage of information, including the hippocampus and amygdala, seem to develop very early—by age 6 months. On the other hand, the structure responsible for retrieving these stored memories, the frontal cortex, develops much later—into the second year. Development of memory during the first two years reflects growth in these two different brain regions.

Once youngsters begin to talk, we can study their memory skills using most of the same methods we use with older children and adults. Research using these methods has linked age-related improvement in memory to two factors (Kail, 1990; Schneider & Bjorklund, 1998). First, as children grow, they use more effective strategies for remembering. Second, children's growing factual knowledge of the world allows them to organize information more completely and, therefore, to remember better. We'll look at each of these factors in the next few pages.

## Strategies for Remembering

Last week, I wrote four pages for this book that would have made Tom Clancy green with envy, when the unthinkable happened—a power failure knocked out my computer and all those wonderful words were lost. If I had only saved the text to the hard drive . . . but I hadn't.

This tale of woe sets the stage for understanding how strategies aid memory. Recall that working memory is used for briefly storing a small amount of information, such as the words in these sentences. However, as you read additional sentences, they displace words read earlier from working memory. For you to learn this information, it must be transferred to long-term memory. Anything not transferred from working memory to long-term memory is lost, just as my words vanished from the computer's memory with the power failure.

**Memory strategies are activities that improve remembering.** Some strategies help maintain information in working memory. Others help transfer information to long-term memory. Still others help retrieve information from long-term memory. Obviously, there are many memory strategies.

> As children develop, they begin to use different strategies to improve memory.

Children begin to use memory strategies early. Preschool children look at or touch objects that they've been told to remember (DeLoache, 1984). Looking and touching aren't very effective, but they tell us that preschoolers understand that they should be doing something to try to remember; remembering doesn't happen automatically!

During the elementary-school years, children begin to use more powerful strategies. **For example, 7- and 8-year-olds use rehearsal, a strategy of repetitively naming information that is to be remembered.** A child wanting to call a new friend will rehearse the phone number from the time she finds the number in the phone book until she dials the phone.

As children get older, they learn other memory strategies. **One is organization: information to be remembered should be structured so that related information is placed together.** For example, a seventh grader trying to remember major battles of the American Civil War could organize them geographically (e.g., Shiloh and Fort Donelson in Tennessee, Antietam and Monocacy in Maryland) or chronologically (e.g., Fort Sumter and First Manassas in 1861, Gettysburg and Vicksburg in 1863). **Another strategy is elaboration—embellishing information to be remembered to make it more memorable.** To see elaboration in action, imagine a child who can never remember if the second syllable of *rehearsal* is spelled *her* (as it sounds) or *hear*. The child could remember the correct spelling by reminding herself that *rehearsal* is like *re-hear-ing*. Thus, thinking about the derivation of *rehearsal* makes it easier to remember its spelling. Finally, as children grow they're also more likely to use external aids to memory: they are more likely to make notes and to write down information on calendars so that, like the girl in the photo, they won't forget future events (Eskitt & Lee, 2002).

**METACOGNITION.**    Just as there's not much value to a filled toolbox if you don't know how to use the tools, memory strategies aren't much good unless children know when to use them. For example, rehearsal is a great strategy for remembering phone numbers but lousy for remembering amendments to the U.S. Constitution or the plot of *Hamlet*. During the elementary-school years and adolescence, children gradually learn to identify different kinds of memory problems and the memory strategies most appropriate to each. For example, when reading a textbook or watching a television newscast, outlining or writing a summary are good strategies because they identify the main points and organize them. Children gradually become more skilled at selecting appropriate strategies, but even high-school students do not always use effective learning strategies when they should (Kuhn, 2000; Pierce & Lange, 2000).

After children choose a memory strategy, they need to monitor its effectiveness. That is, they need to decide if the strategy is working. If it's not, they need to begin anew, reanalyzing the memory task to select a better approach. If the strategy is working, they should determine the portion of the material they have not yet mastered and concentrate their efforts there. Monitoring improves gradually with age. For example, elementary-school children can accurately identify which material they have not yet learned, but they do not consistently focus their study efforts on this material (Kail, 1990).

> Metamemory includes the ability to diagnose problems accurately and to monitor effectiveness of a memory strategy.

**Diagnosing memory problems accurately and monitoring the effectiveness of memory strategies are two important elements of metamemory, which refers to a child's informal understanding of memory.** That is, as children develop, they learn more about how memory operates and devise intuitive theories of memory that represent an extension of the theory of mind described in Module 7.4. For example, children learn that memory is fallible (i.e., they sometimes forget!) and that some types of memory tasks are easier than others (e.g., remembering the main idea of the Gettysburg address is simpler than remembering it word-for-word). This growing knowledge of memory helps children to use memory strategies more effectively, just as an experienced carpenter's accumulated knowledge of wood tells her when to use nails, screws, or glue to join two boards.

Of course, children's growing understanding of memory is paralleled by growing understanding of all cognitive processes. **Such knowledge and awareness of cognitive processes is called metacognitive knowledge.** Metacognitive knowledge grows rapidly during the elementary-school years: Children come to know much about perception, attention, intentions, knowledge, and thinking (Flavell, 1999, 2000). For example, school-age children know that sometimes they deliberately direct their attention—as in searching for a parent's face in a crowd—but that sometimes events capture attention—as with an unexpected clap of thunder (Parault & Schwanenflugel, 2000).

One of the most important features of children's metacognitive knowledge is their understanding of the connections among goals, strategies, monitoring, and outcomes. That is, as shown in the diagram, children come to realize that on a broad spectrum of tasks—ranging from learning words in a spelling list to learning to spike a volleyball to learning to get along with an overly talkative classmate seated nearby—they need to regulate their learning by understanding the goal and selecting a means to achieve that goal. Then they determine whether the chosen method is working. **Effective cognitive self-regulation—that is, skill at identifying goals, selecting effective strategies, and monitoring accurately—is a characteristic of successful students** (McCormick & Pressley, 1997; Zimmerman, 2001). A student may decide that writing each spelling word twice before the test is a good way to get all the words right. When the student only gets 70 percent correct on the first test, he switches to a new strategy (e.g., writing each word four times, plus writing its definition), showing the adaptive nature of cognitive processes in self-regulated learners.

Strategies, metamemory, and metacognition are essential for effective remembering, but as you'll see in the next few pages, knowledge is also an aid to memory.

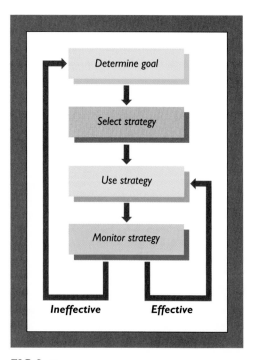

FIG.8–5

## Knowledge and Memory

Let's start our examination of how knowledge influences memory by looking at a study by Michelene Chi (1978). She asked 10-year-olds and adults to remember sequences of numbers. In the graph, you can see that adults remembered more numbers than children. Next she asked participants to remember the positions of objects in a matrix. This time 10-year-olds' recall was much better than that of adults.

What was responsible for this unusual reversal of the expected age difference? Actually, the objects were chess pieces on a chessboard, and the children were skilled chess players but the adults were novices. The positions of the pieces were taken from actual games, so they were familiar configurations for the child chess players. For the adults, who lacked knowledge of chess, the patterns seemed arbitrary. But the children had the knowledge to organize and give meaning to the patterns, so they could recognize and then recall the whole configuration instead of many isolated pieces. It was as if the adults were seeing this meaningless pattern:

n n c c b a s b c c b n

whereas the children were seeing this:

n b c   c b s   a b c   c n n.

The link between knowledge and memory is also illustrated in the "Real Children" feature.

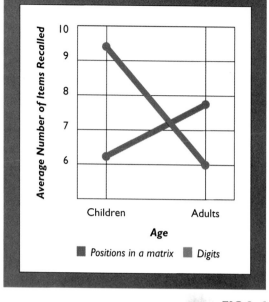

FIG.8–6

## REAL CHILDREN

### Keith Visits the Air Force Museum

A few years ago, I went with a troop of Boy Scouts to visit the U.S. Air Force Museum in Dayton, Ohio. On the drive home, I asked James, a 12-year-old who likes computers and basketball but not airplanes, what he had seen in the museum. "Uh, lotsa planes. Some jets and prop jobs. Oh, and some rockets, too," was his reply. I posed the same question to Keith, another 12-year-old, whose father is a pilot and aeronautical engineer and who lives and breathes airplanes. Keith began, "This was so incredibly cool. I started in the Air Power Gallery and saw a Lightning, a Mustang, a Thunderbolt, a Mitchell, a Liberator, a Flying Fortress, and a Super Fort. Then we went to the Modern Flight hangar. They had a Stratojet, a Stratofort, and a Hustler. There was a Sabre and a Super Sabre there, too." Keith went on like this for another 5 minutes. When he was done, I estimated that Keith had remembered the names of 40 to 50 airplanes.

Amused, I asked Keith to try to remember the following words: *table, green, rain, bus, spoon, dad, coal, doll, salt, doctor, hill, tennis, shirt, piano, nickel, robin.* He paused for a moment, then began to remember words. He finished with 6 words from the list of 16. How could Keith recall so few words from my list when he had remembered 7 or 8 times that many planes? The key is Keith's extensive aeronautical knowledge, which allowed him to organize his recall of planes. He began by recalling World War II fighters (Lightning, Mustang, Thunderbolt), then World War II bombers (Mitchell, Liberator, Flying Fortress, Super Fortress). He continued this way, organizing his recall by category. However, when asked to recall my 16 words,

FIG.8–7
Source: Kail, 1990.

where his knowledge of airplanes was useless, Keith had just an average 12-year-old's memory. For Keith, as for Chi's chess experts, knowledge is memory power.

Usually, of course, the knowledge that allows a child to organize information and give it meaning increases gradually with age (Schneider & Bjorklund, 1998). Researchers often depict knowledge as a network like the one in the diagram, which shows part of a 13-year-old's knowledge of animals. The entries in the network are linked by different types of associations. Some of the links denote membership in categories (dalmatian is a dog), and others denote properties (elephant has a trunk). **Still others denote a script, a memory structure used to describe the sequence in which events occur.** The list of events in walking the dog is a script.

A network diagram like this for a younger child would have fewer entries and fewer and weaker connecting links. Consequently, the youngster cannot organize information as extensively, which makes remembering more difficult than for an older child.

Nevertheless, the knowledge that young children have is organized, and this turns out to be a powerful asset. In the case of events that fit scripts, for example, they needn't try to remember each individual activity; instead, they simply remember the script. When the preschooler in the photo wants to tell his dad about baking cookies, he can simply retrieve the "baking cookies" script and use it to organize his recall of the different events.

Though knowledge can improve memory, it can also distort memory. If a specific experience does not match a child's knowledge (e.g., it differs from a script), the experience is sometimes forgotten or distorted so that it conforms to the existing knowledge (Farrar & Boyer-Pennington, 1999; Levy & Boston, 1994). For example, told a story about a female helicopter pilot, many youngsters will remember the pilot as a man because their knowledge network specifies that pilots are men. And newly acquired knowledge sometimes clouds children's recall of prior knowledge. Suppose a child can't find her new CD, then learns that a classmate often takes things. When asked later about her missing CD, the child's memory will be that the classmate stole the CD (Greenhoot, 2000).

Scripts, too, can distort memory because children cannot distinguish what they experienced from what is specified in the script. For example, the boy baking cookies may remember greasing the cookie sheet simply because this is part of the cookie-baking script, not because he actually did the greasing (Hudson, 1988).

Thus, although children's growing knowledge usually helps them to remember, sometimes it can interfere with accurate memory. In the next section, we'll look at another link between knowledge and memory—children's memory of their own lives.

**AUTOBIOGRAPHICAL MEMORY.**   Start by answering these questions:

Who was your teacher in fourth grade?

Where (and with whom) was your first kiss?

Was your high-school graduation indoors or outdoors?

In answering these questions, you searched memory, just as you would search memory to answer questions such as "What is the capitol of Ohio?" and "Who invented the sewing machine?" However, answers to questions about Ohio and sewing machines are based on general knowledge that you have not experienced personally; answers to questions about your fourth-grade teacher, your first kiss, and your high-school graduation are based on knowledge unique to your own life. **Autobiographical memory refers to people's memory of the significant events and experiences of their own lives.** Autobiographical memory is important because it helps people construct a personal life history. In addition, autobiographical memory allows people to relate their experiences to others, creating socially shared memories (Conway & Pleydell-Pearce, 2000; Nelson, 1993).

> Infantile amnesia, in which people can't recall events from early in life, may be due to limits in toddlers' language and their sense of self.

Autobiographical memory originates in the preschool years, when parents encourage children to think about the past by talking with them about recent events (Hudson, 2001). Picking up a $2\frac{1}{2}$-year-old from day care, a parent may ask, "What did you play?" "What did you have for snack?" In questions like these, parents usually focus on *who, what, where, when,* and *why.* In this way, they teach their children the important features of events and how events are organized. Children's autobiographical memories are richer when parents talk about past events in detail and encourage their children to participate in these conversations. In contrast, when parents' talk is limited to direct questions that can be answered "yes" or "no," children's autobiographical memories are less extensive (Farrant & Reese, 2000).

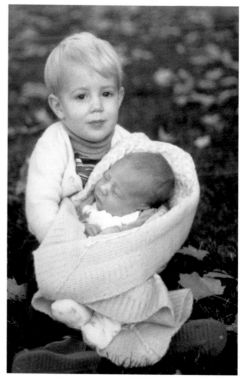

Although autobiographical memory begins in the preschool years, older children, adolescents, and adults remember little from these years (Kail, 1990). **Infantile amnesia refers to the inability to remember events from one's early life.** Adults recall nothing from infancy, but they remember an ever-increasing number of events from about age 3 or 4 years (Eacott, 1999; Schneider & Bjorklund, 1998). For example, when the 2-year-old in the photo is older, he won't remember his brother's birth (Peterson & Rideout, 1998; Quas et al., 1999).* But there's a good chance the older boy will remember his brother's second—or certainly his third—birthday.

Infantile amnesia has several possible explanations. One emphasizes language, the topic of Chapter 10. Once children learn to talk (at about age 2 years), they tend to rely on language to represent their past (Nelson,

---

*Perhaps you're not convinced because you vividly recall significant events that occurred when you were 2, such as the birth of a sibling, a move to a different home, or the death of a close friend or relative. In reality, you are probably not remembering the actual event. Instead, I can almost guarantee that you're remembering others' retelling of these events and your role in them, not the events themselves. Events like these are often socially shared memories and that's the basis for your memory.

1993). Consequently, their earlier, prelingual experiences may be difficult to retrieve from memory, just as after you reorganize your bedroom you may have trouble finding things (Simcock & Hayne, 2002).

Another explanation for infantile amnesia is based on a child's sense of self. I describe this in detail in Module 12.1, but the key idea is that 1- and 2-year-olds rapidly acquire a sense that they exist independently. Some theorists (Howe & Courage, 1997) argue that a child's sense of self provides an organizing framework for autobiographical memory. Infants and toddlers lack a sense of self, so their experiences are not represented in autobiographical memory, which is why they can't be recalled later in life.

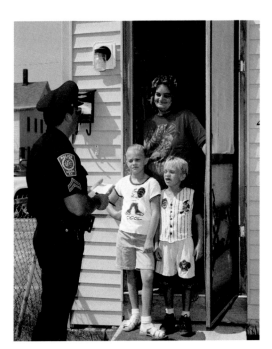

Thus, personal experiences from our earliest years usually can't be recalled because of inadequate language or inadequate sense of self (Harley & Reese, 1999). Beginning in the preschool years, however, autobiographical memory provides a cohesive framework for remembering life's significant events. Unfortunately, some children's autobiographical memories include memories of abuse. Can these memories be trusted? We'll see in the next section.

**EYEWITNESS TESTIMONY.** Remember Cheryl, the 4-year-old in the module-opening vignette who claimed that a neighbor had touched her "private parts"? If Cheryl's comments lead to a police investigation, Cheryl's testimony will be critical. But can her recall of events be trusted? This question is difficult to answer. In legal proceedings, children are often interviewed repeatedly, sometimes as many as 10 to 15 times. Over the course of repeated questioning, they may confuse what actually happened with what others suggest may have happened. When, as in the situation in the photo, the questioner is an adult in a position of authority, children often believe that what is suggested by the adult actually happened (Lampinen & Smith, 1995). As you'll see in the "Focus on Research" feature, preschoolers are particularly prone to confusion of this sort (Ceci & Bruck, 1995, 1998).

## FOCUS ON RESEARCH

### Do Stereotypes and Suggestions Influence Preschoolers' Reports?

*Who were the investigators, and what was the aim of the study?* During legal proceedings, children are often interviewed repeatedly. In the process, interviewers sometimes suggest that certain events took place. Cheryl might be asked, "When Mr. Johnson touched your private parts, was anyone else around?" a question implying that Mr. Johnson definitely touched Cheryl. Furthermore, interviewers may suggest to children that the accused is a "bad person," which may make suggestions of abuse more plausible to children. Michelle D. Leichtman and Stephen J. Ceci (1995) wanted to know if repeated questioning and hints about an adult's "nature" would influence preschool children's recall of events.

*How did the investigators measure the topic of interest?* Leichtman and Ceci had a man named Sam Stone briefly visit classes of 3- and 4-year-olds and 5- and 6-year-olds at a day-care center. During his visit, Sam greeted the teacher, who introduced him to the class. Sam mentioned that the story being read by the teacher was one of his favorites; then he waved goodbye and left the room.

Leichtman and Ceci created four different conditions, shown in the diagram, that differed in what children were told before and after Sam's visit. Children in the control condition were interviewed after the visit, every week for 4 weeks. In these interviews, youngsters were simply asked to describe Sam's visit.

| Condition | Phase 1 | Phase 2 | Phase 3 | Phase 4 |
|---|---|---|---|---|
| Control | | | 4 neutral interviews | |
| Stereotypes | Sam is nice but clumsy | Sam visits the day-care center briefly | 4 neutral interviews | Neutral interview with specific questions about Sam's actions |
| Suggestions | | | 4 suggestive interviews | |
| Stereotypes plus Suggestions | Sam is nice but clumsy | | 4 suggestive interviews | |

FIG.8–8

The stereotype condition differed from the control condition in one way: Three times prior to Sam's visit, teachers described Sam as a nice but clumsy man, thereby implying that children should expect Sam to be clumsy. The suggestions condition also differed from the control condition: During each of the four weekly interviews that followed Sam's visit, the interviewer made misleading suggestions that Sam had ripped a book and soiled a teddy bear, such as "Remember when Sam Stone ripped the book? Did he rip it on purpose or by accident?" (p. 577). Of course, he had done neither. In the fourth condition, stereotypes plus suggestions, teachers told children about Sam's clumsiness before the visit and interviewers made misleading suggestions afterward.

Finally, 10 weeks after Sam had visited the classroom, a different interviewer, one not present during Sam's visit or the previous interviews, asked children several questions about what had happened when Sam visited, including whether Sam had ripped a book or soiled a teddy bear.

*Who were the children in the study?* A total of 176 preschool children participated. Half were 3- and 4-year-olds and half were 5- and 6-year-olds.

*What was the design of the study?* This study was experimental. There were three independent variables: (a) the age of the child, (b) whether the child was told before Sam's visit that he was clumsy, and (c) whether the child received misleading suggestions after Sam's visit. The dependent variable was the child's answer to the interviewers' misleading questions. That is, Leichtman and Ceci counted the percentage of time that children said they had actually seen Sam rip a book or soil the teddy bear, events that never happened. The study was also cross-sectional because it included a group of younger children (3- and 4-year-olds) and a group of older children (5- and 6-year-olds).

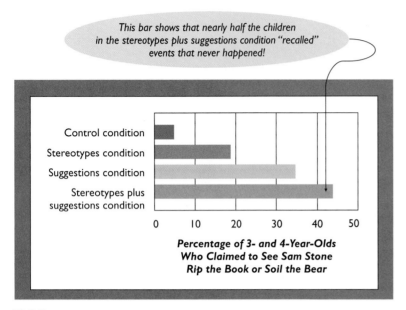

FIG.8–9

This bar shows that nearly half the children in the stereotypes plus suggestions condition "recalled" events that never happened!

*Percentage of 3- and 4-Year-Olds Who Claimed to See Sam Stone Rip the Book or Soil the Bear*

*Were there ethical concerns with the study?* No. Sam's visit, the teachers' comments about Sam beforehand, and the interviews afterward posed no special risks to children.

*What were the results?* Children's answers to the misleading questions are shown in the graph. For simplicity, I've shown only the data for 3- and 4-year-olds. The data for 5- and 6-year-olds were similar but the effects were smaller. (That is, the older children were less suggestible than the younger children.) Almost no children in the control condition claimed to have seen Sam rip a book or soil a bear. However, some children in the stereotyped condition claimed to have seen Sam rip a book or soil a bear, and more than one-third of the children in the suggestions condition claimed he did one or the other. When stereotypes and suggestions were combined, almost half the children said they had seen events that never took place. Although the 5- and 6-year-olds described events much more accurately, even 15 percent of these youngsters claimed to have seen Sam rip a book or soil a bear.

*What did the investigators conclude?* Leichtman and Ceci believe that whether preschoolers are suggestible depends entirely on how their memory for events is probed. The results from their control condition suggest that, without stereotypes and suggestions, preschoolers are unlikely to report events that never happened. However, when adults suggest that a person is likely to behave in a particular way and later imply that some events actually did happen, many preschoolers will go along. From their results, since Cheryl's report was spontaneous, not elicited by repeated questions, it is probably trustworthy.

*What converging evidence would strengthen these conclusions?* Falsely claiming that a visitor ripped a book is a far cry from testifying falsely in a case of child abuse. You can think of many ways in which the target events differ: Abuse involves the child directly, is very embarrassing to the child, and is extraordinarily stressful; observing the torn book is none of these. Consequently, it would be valuable to determine whether young children are equally suggestible when remembering incidents of abuse. Of course, designing an experiment of this sort would be unethical; we can't expose children directly to abuse nor can we suggest to them that others have been abused. A compromise is to study children's memory for the events of a physical exam by a health care professional. These exams involve the child's body and are often mildly embarrassing and mildly stressful. Research such as this can demonstrate whether young children are suggestible in settings that more closely resemble actual child abuse, yet still preserves the right of children as research participants. ◉

Perhaps you're skeptical of findings like these. Surely it must be possible to tell when a young child is describing events that never happened. In fact, although law enforcement officials and child protection workers believe they can usually tell whether children are telling the truth, professionals often cannot distinguish true and false reports (Gordon, Baker-Ward, & Ornstein, 2001). And maybe you doubt that interviewers routinely ask the leading or suggestive questions that are the seeds of false memories. But analyses of videotapes of actual interviews reveal that trained investigators often ask children leading questions and make suggestive comments (Lamb, Steinberg, & Esplin, 2000).

Adults aren't the only ones who taint children's memories; peers can, too! When, for example, some children in a class experience an event (e.g., a class field trip or a special class visitor), they often talk about the event with classmates who weren't there; later, these absent classmates readily describe what happened and often insist they were actually there (Principe & Ceci, 2002).

> Unless misled by others, preschoolers rarely "recall" events that didn't happen.

School-age children are much better able to distinguish actual and false memories (Brainerd & Reyna, 2002), but what can we conclude about preschoolers on the witness stand? If Cheryl's parents press charges against Mr. Johnson, can Cheryl's testimony be trusted? Preschoolers *can* provide reliable testimony, but many commonly used legal procedures can undermine their credibility. Here are guidelines derived from research for improving the reliability of child witnesses (Ceci & Bruck, 1995, 1998; Gordon et al., 2001):

- Warn children that interviewers may sometimes try to trick them or suggest things that didn't happen.
- Ensure that interviewers' questions evaluate alternative explanations of what happened and who was involved.
- Do not question children repeatedly on a single issue.

Following these guidelines will foster the conditions under which preschoolers (and older children, too) are likely to recall the past more accurately and thereby be better witnesses. The "Child Development and Family Policy" feature shows one way in which research findings have changed the methods used to interview children.

## CHILD DEVELOPMENT AND FAMILY POLICY

### Interviewing Children Effectively

Toward the end of the 20<sup>th</sup> century, the number of instances of child abuse had skyrocketed, followed soon by reports that some adults were wrongly convicted based on children's false memories. Consequently, many state and federal agencies created task forces to determine the best way to respond to the challenges of evaluating allegations of child abuse. In Michigan, for example, the Governor's Task Force on Children's Justice was created in 1992 and quickly identified the need for a standard protocol for interviewing children in child-abuse cases. Debra Poole, a psychologist at Central Michigan University and a leading expert on children's eyewitness testimony, was hired to develop the protocol. Poole was an obvious choice because she had recently written a book with Michael E. Lamb (1998), *Investigative Interviews of Children: A Guide for Helping Professionals,* that was published by the American Psychological Association. Working with agencies in nine Michigan counties, Poole devised a preliminary interview protocol that was tested in those counties. The revised protocol was then published by the Governor's Task Force (1998) and the procedures were implemented statewide. The new procedures, derived largely from research like that which I described earlier in this module, is designed to meet the needs of all parties involved: the procedures "will reduce trauma to children, make the information gained more credible in the court process, and protect the rights of the accused" (Governor's Task Force, 1998, p. v). And the new procedures document that research findings can be the stable foundation for public policy.

### CHECK YOUR LEARNING

**1.** Four-month-old Tanya has forgotten that kicking moves a mobile. To remind her of the link between kicking and the mobile's movement, we could _____.

**2.** Children and adolescents often select a memory strategy after they _____.

**3.** The term _____ refers to periodically evaluating a strategy to determine whether it is effective.

**4.** The knowledge that children acquire can distort their recall, either by causing them to forget information that does not conform to their knowledge or by _____.

**5.** A _____ is a memory structure that describes the sequence in which events occur.

**6.** Infantile amnesia, the inability to remember events from early in life, may be due to infants' and toddlers' limited language skills or to their lack of a _____.

**7.** Preschoolers' testimony is more likely to be reliable if interviewers test alternate hypotheses and avoid repeated questioning, and if we warn children that _____.

**CONNECTIONS**
Describe how research on children's eyewitness testimony illustrates connections among emotional, cognitive, and social development.

**Answers:** (1) show her a moving mobile, (2) determine the goal of a memory task, (3) monitoring, (4) causing them to recall events that are part of a script but that did not actually take place, (5) script, (6) sense of self, (7) interviewers may try to trick them

# 8.3  Academic Skills

- Reading
- Writing
- Knowing and Using Numbers

### LEARNING OBJECTIVES

- What are the components of skilled reading?
- As children develop, how does their writing improve?
- When do children understand and use quantitative skills?

*When Susan, a bubbly 3-year-old, is asked how old she'll be on her next birthday, she proudly says, "Four!" while holding up five fingers. Asked to count four objects, whether they're candies, toys, or socks, Susan almost always says, "1, 2, 6, 7 . . . SEVEN!" Susan's older brothers find all this very funny, but her mother thinks that, the obvious mistakes notwithstanding, Susan's behavior shows that she knows a lot about numbers and counting. But what, exactly, does Susan understand? That question has her mother stumped!*

According to information-processing psychologists, cognitive development consists of acquiring mental software for specific domains. Some of the mental software that children must acquire for success in school is in the domains of reading, writing, and quantitative skill. Information-processing psychologists have studied these domains extensively, as you'll see in this module, which examines the traditional 3 Rs: reading, 'riting, and 'rithmetic. We'll start with reading, then examine writing, and end with numbers, where you'll learn why Susan counts as she does.

## Reading

Try reading the following sentence:

Sumisu-san wa nawa o naifu de kirimashita.

Unless you know Japanese, you probably didn't make much headway, did you? Now try this one:

Snore secretary green plastic sleep trucks.

These are English words and you probably read them quite easily, but did you get anything more out of this sentence than the one in Japanese? These examples show two important processes involved in skilled reading. **Word recognition is the process of identifying a unique pattern of letters.** Without knowing Japanese, your word recognition was not successful in the first sentence. You did not know that *nawa* means *rope* or that *kirimashita* is the past tense of the English verb *cut*. Furthermore, because you could not recognize individual words, you had no idea of the meaning of this sentence. **Comprehension is the process of extracting meaning from a sequence of words.** In the second sentence, your word recognition was perfect, but comprehension was still impossible because the words were presented in a random sequence. These examples remind us just how difficult learning to read can be.

In the next few pages, we'll look at how children read. We'll start with the skills that children must have if they are to learn to read, then move to word recognition and comprehension.

FOUNDATIONS OF READING SKILL.   English words are made up of individual letters, so children need to know their letters before they can learn to read. Consequently, it's not surprising that knowledge of letter names is consistently one of the best predictors of success in learning to read: That is, youngsters who know most of their letters learn to read more easily than their peers who don't know their letters (Treiman & Kessler, 2003).

A second essential skill is sensitivity to language sounds. **The ability to hear the distinctive sounds of letters is a skill known as phonological awareness.** One way to measure phonological awareness is to present several words—*fun, pin, bun, gun*—and then ask the child to pick the word that didn't rhyme with the others. Another way is to ask children to say the first, last, or middle sound of a word: "What's the first sound in *cat*?" These measures have been used in dozens of studies and the outcome is always the same: Phonological awareness is strongly related to success in learning to read (Hulme et al., 2000). That is, children who can readily distinguish language sounds learn to read more readily than children who do not.

Prereading skills include knowing the letters of the alphabet and the sounds they make.

As children get older, phonological skill continues to be an excellent predictor of reading ability (Wagner et al., 1999). What's more, phonological skill is important in learning to read not only in alphabet-based languages such as English, but also in non-alphabet-based languages such as Chinese (McBride-Chang & Kail, 2002).

If phonological skill is so essential, how can we help children master them? The "Improving Children's Lives" feature describes one easy way.

## IMPROVING CHILDREN'S LIVES

### Rhyme Is Sublime Because Sounds Abounds

*The Cat in the Hat* and *Green Eggs and Ham* are two books in the famous Dr. Seuss series. You probably know these stories for their zany plots and extensive use of rhyme. When parents frequently read rhymes—not just Dr. Seuss, but also Mother Goose and other nursery rhymes—their children become more aware of word sounds. Passages like the one below draw children's attention to the different sounds that make up words:

*I do not like them in a house. I do not like them with a mouse. I do not like them here or there. I do not like them anywhere. I do not like green eggs and ham. I do not like them, Sam-I-am (Geisel, 1960, p. 20).*

The more parents read rhymes to their children, the greater their children's phonological awareness, which makes learning to read much easier (Baker et al., 1998; Bradley & Bryant, 1983).

So the message is clear. Read to children—the more, the better. As the photo shows, children love it when adults read to them, and learning more about word sounds is icing on the cake!

Storybook reading like that described in this feature is an informal way that parents can foster pre-reading skills. Sometimes, however, parents go beyond simply reading and take on the role of teacher. They may talk about the names of letters and the sounds they make: "This is a *u*. Sometimes it goes *oo-oo-oo* and sometimes it goes *uh*." Both activities—reading for fun and teaching letter names and sounds while reading—promote phonological awareness and early reading skill (Sénéchal & LeFevre, 2002). And the benefits are not limited to the first steps in learning to read but persist into the middle elementary-school years: Third graders read better when they spent much time as preschoolers reading with their parents (de Jong & Leseman, 2001; Sénéchal & LeFevre, 2002).

**RECOGNIZING WORDS.** The first step in actual reading is identifying individual words. One way to do this is to say the sounds associated with each letter and then blend the sounds to produce a recognizable word. Such "sounding out" is a common technique among beginning readers. Older children sometimes sound out words, but only when they are unfamiliar, which points to another common way of recognizing words (Coltheart et al., 1993). Words are recognized through direct retrieval from long-term memory: As the individual letters in a word are identified, long-term memory is searched to see if there is a matching sequence of letters. After the child knows that the letters are, in sequence, *c-a-t*, long-term memory is searched for a match and the child recognizes the word as *cat*.

So far, word recognition may seem like a one-way street where readers first recognize letters and then recognize words. In reality, we know that information flows both ways: Readers constantly use context to help them recognize letters and words. For example, readers typically recognize *t* faster in *cast* than in *asct*. That is, readers recognize letters faster when they appear in words than in nonwords. How do the nearby letters in *cast* help readers to recognize the *t*? As children recognize the first letters in the word as *c*, *a*, and *s*, the possibilities for the last letter become more limited. Because English only includes four four-letter words that start with *cas* (well, five if you include *Cass*), the last letter can only be *e, h, k,* or *t*. In contrast, there are no four-letter words (in English) that begin with *acs*, so all 26 letters must be checked, which takes more time than just checking four letters. In this way, a reader's knowledge of words simplifies the task of recognizing letters, which in turn makes it easier to recognize words (Seidenberg & McClelland, 1989).

**Even beginning readers use context to help recognize letters and words.**

Readers also use the sentence context to speed word recognition. Read these two sentences:

The last word in this sentence is cat.

The little girl's pet dog chased the cat.

Most readers recognize cat more rapidly in the second sentence. The reason is that the first seven words put severe limits on the last word: It must be something "chaseable," and because the "chaser" is a dog, cat is a very likely candidate. In contrast, the first seven words in the first sentence put no limits on the last word; virtually any word could end the sentence. Readers use sentence context like this to help them recognize words, particularly difficult ones (Archer & Bryant, 2001; Kim & Goetz, 1994).

As you can imagine, most beginning readers, like the child in the photo, rely more heavily on "sounding out" because they know fewer words. As they gain more reading experience, they are more likely to be able to retrieve a word directly from long-term memory. You might be tempted to summarize this as "Beginning readers sound out and more advanced readers retrieve directly." Don't! From their very first efforts to read, most children use direct retrieval for a few words. From that point on, the general strategy is to try retrieval first and, if that fails, to sound out the word or ask a more skilled reader for help (Siegler, 1986). For example, when my daughter Laura was just beginning to read, she knew *the, Laura,* and several one-syllable words that ended in *at,* such as *bat, cat,* and *fat*. Shown a sentence like

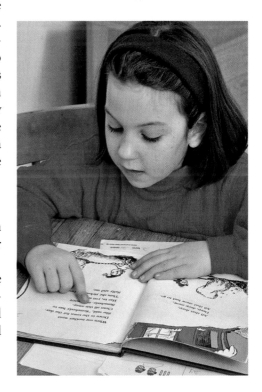

Laura saw the fat cat run,

she would say, "Laura s-s-s . . . ah-h . . . wuh . . . saw the fat cat er-r-r . . . uh-h-h . . . n-n-n . . . run." Familiar words were retrieved rapidly, but the unfamiliar ones were slowly sounded out.

With more experience, children sound out fewer words and retrieve more (Siegler, 1986). That is, by sounding out novel words, children store information about words in long-term memory that is required for direct retrieval (Cunningham et al., 2002; Share, 1999). Of course, all readers sometimes fall back on sounding out when they confront unfamiliar words. Try reading

The rock star rode to the concert in a palanquin.

You may well need to do some sounding out, then consult a dictionary (or look at the answers just before "Check Your Learning") for the correct meaning.

**COMPREHENSION.**    Once individual words are recognized, reading begins to have a lot in common with understanding speech. That is, the means by which people understand a sequence of words is much the same whether the source of words is printed text or speech or, for that matter, Braille or sign language (Crowder & Wagner, 1992). **In all these cases, children derive meaning by combining words to form propositions or ideas and then combining propositions.** For example, as you read

The tall boy rode his bike,

you spontaneously derive a number of propositions, including "There is a boy," "The boy is tall," and "The boy was riding." If this sentence were part of a larger body of text, you would derive propositions for each sentence, then link the propositions together to derive meaning for the passage as a whole (Perfetti & Curtis, 1986).

As children gain more reading experience, they better comprehend what they read. Several factors contribute to this improved comprehension (Siegler, 1998):

> Older children comprehend more because they recognize words easier, have more working memory, know more of the world, monitor their reading, and use appropriate reading strategies.

- *Children become more skilled at recognizing words, allowing more working capacity to be devoted to comprehension* (Zinar, 2000): When children struggle to recognize individual words, they often cannot link them to derive the meaning of a passage. In contrast, when children recognize words effortlessly, they can focus their efforts on deriving meaning from the whole sentence.

- *Working memory capacity increases, which means that older and better readers can store more of a sentence in memory as they try to identify the propositions it contains* (De Beni & Palladino, 2000; Nation et al., 1999): This extra capacity is handy when readers move from sentences like "Kevin hit the ball" to "In the bottom of the ninth, with the bases loaded and the Cardinals down 7-4, Kevin put a line drive into the left-field bleachers, his fourth home run of the series."

- *Children acquire more general knowledge of their physical, social, and psychological worlds, which allows them to understand more of what they read* (Ferreol-Barbey, 2000; Graesser, Singer, & Trabasso, 1994): For example, even if a 6-year-old could recognize all of the words in the longer sentence about Kevin's home run, the child would not fully comprehend the meaning of the passage because he or she lacks the necessary knowledge of baseball.

- *With experience, children better monitor their comprehension*: When readers don't grasp the meaning of a passage because it is difficult or confusing, they read it again (Baker, 1994). Try this sentence (adapted from Carpenter & Daneman, 1981): "The Midwest State Fishing Contest would draw fishermen from all around the region, including some of the best bass guitarists in Michigan." When you first encountered "bass guitarists" you probably interpreted "bass" as a fish. This didn't make much sense, so you reread the phrase to determine that "bass" refers to a type of guitar. Older readers are better able to realize that their understanding is not complete and take corrective action.

- *With experience, children use more appropriate reading strategies*: The goal of reading and the nature of the text dictate how you read. When reading a novel, for example, do you often skip sentences (or perhaps paragraphs or entire pages) to get to "the good parts"? This approach makes sense for pleasure reading but not for reading textbooks, recipes, or how-to manuals. Reading a text-book requires attention to both the overall organization and the relationship of details to that organization. Older, more experienced readers are better able to select a reading strategy that suits the material being read; in contrast, younger, less-skilled readers less often adjust their reading to fit the material (Brown et al., 1996; Cain, 1999).

Greater word recognition skill, greater working memory capacity, greater world knowledge, greater monitoring skill, and use of more appropriate reading strategies are all part of the information-processing explanation of how older and more experienced readers get more meaning from what they read. In the next part of this module, you'll see how information-processing psychologists use similar ideas to explain children's developing ability to write.

## Writing

Though few of us end up being a Maya Angelou, a Sandra Cisneros, or a John Grisham, most adults do write, both at home and at work. The basics of good writing are remarkably straightforward (Williams, 1997), but writing skill develops very gradually during childhood, adolescence, and young adulthood. Research indicates a number of factors that contribute to improved writing as children develop (Adams, Treiman, & Pressley, 1998; Siegler, 1998).

**GREATER KNOWLEDGE AND ACCESS TO KNOWLEDGE ABOUT TOPICS.** Writing is about telling "something" to others. With age, children have more to tell as they gain more knowledge about the world and incorporate this knowledge into their writing (Benton et al., 1995). For example, asked to write about a mayoral election, children are apt to describe it as much like a popularity contest; adolescents more often describe it in terms of political issues that are both subtle and complex. Of course, students are sometimes asked to write about topics quite unfamiliar to them. In this case, older children's and adolescents' writing is usually better because they are more adept at finding useful reference material and incorporating it into their writing.

**GREATER UNDERSTANDING OF HOW TO ORGANIZE WRITING.** One difficult aspect of writing is organization, arranging all the necessary information in a manner that readers find clear and interesting. In fact, children and young adolescents organize their writing differently than older adolescents and adults (Bereiter & Scardamalia, 1987). **Young writers often use a knowledge-telling strategy, writing down information on the topic as they retrieve it from memory.** For example, asked to write about the day's events at school, a second grader wrote:

> *It is a rainy day. We hope the sun will shine. We got new spelling books. We had our pictures taken. We sang Happy Birthday to Barbara. (Waters, 1980, p. 155)*

The story has no obvious structure. The first two sentences are about the weather, but the last three deal with completely independent topics. Apparently, the writer simply described each event as it came to mind.

**During adolescence, writers begin to use a knowledge-transforming strategy, deciding what information to include and how best to organize it for the point they wish to convey to their reader.** This approach involves considering the purpose

> Older children write better because they know how to organize their writing, have mastered the mechanical aspects of writing, and revise more effectively.

of writing (e.g., to inform, to persuade, to entertain) and the information needed to achieve this purpose. It also involves considering the needs, interests, and knowledge of the anticipated audience.

Asked to describe the day's events, older adolescents' writing can take many forms, depending on the purpose and audience. An essay written to entertain peers about humorous events at school would differ from one written to convince parents about problems in schoolwork. And both of these essays would differ from one written to inform an exchange student about a typical day in a U.S. high school. In other words, although children's knowledge-telling strategy gets words on paper, the more mature knowledge-transforming strategy produces a more cohesive text for the reader.

**GREATER EASE IN DEALING WITH THE MECHANICAL REQUIREMENTS OF WRITING.** Soon after I earned my pilot's license, I took my son Matt for a flight. A few days later, he wrote the following story for his second-grade weekly writing assignment:

> *This weekend I got to ride in a one propellered plane. But this time my dad was alone. He has his license now. It was a long ride. But I fell asleep after five minutes. But when we landed I woke up. My dad said, "You missed a good ride." My dad said, "You even missed the jets!" But I had fun.*

Matt spent more than an hour writing this story, and the original (hanging in my office) is filled with erasures where he corrected misspelled words, ill-formed letters, and incorrect punctuation. Had Matt simply described our flight aloud (instead of writing it), his task would have been much easier. In oral language, he could ignore capitalization, punc-

tuation, spelling, and printing of individual letters. These many mechanical aspects of writing can be a burden for all writers, but particularly for young writers.

In fact, research shows that when youngsters like the one in the photo are absorbed by the task of printing letters correctly, the quality of their writing usually suffers; as children master printed and cursive letters, they can pay more attention to other aspects of writing (Graham, Harris, & Fink, 2000; Jones & Christensen, 1999). Similarly, correct spelling and good sentence structure are particularly hard for younger writers; as they learn to spell and to generate clear sentences, they write more easily and more effectively (Graham et al., 1997; McCutchen et al., 1994).

**GREATER SKILL IN REVISING.** Few authors get it down right the first time. Instead, they revise and revise, then revise some more. In the words of one expert, "Experienced writers get something down on paper as fast as they can, just so they can revise it into something clearer" (Williams, 1997, p. 11).

Unfortunately, young writers often don't revise at all—the first draft is usually the final draft. To make matters worse, when young writers revise, the changes do not necessarily improve their writing (Fitzgerald, 1987). Effective revising requires being able to detect problems and knowing how to correct them (Baker & Brown, 1984; Beal, 1996). As children develop, they're better able to find problems and to know how to correct them. Children and adolescents are more likely to find flaws in others' writing than in their own (Cameron et al., 1997). And they are more likely to revise successfully when the topic is familiar to them and when more time passes between initial writing and revising (Chanquoy, 2001; McCutchen, Francis, & Kerr, 1997).

If you look over these past few paragraphs, it's quite clear why good writing is so long in developing. Many different skills are involved and each is complicated in its own right. Mastering them collectively is a huge challenge, one that spans all of childhood, adolescence, and adulthood. Much the same could be said for mastering quantitative skills, as we'll see in the next section.

## Knowing and Using Numbers

Basic number skills originate in infancy, long before babies learn names of numbers. Many babies experience daily variation in quantity. They play with two blocks and see that another baby has three; they watch as a father sorts laundry and finds two black socks but only one blue sock, and they eat one hot dog for lunch while an older brother eats three.

From these experiences, babies apparently come to appreciate that quantity or amount is one of the ways in which objects in the world can differ. This conclusion is based on research in which babies are tested with sequences of pictures like those shown in the diagram. The actual objects in the pictures differ, as do their size, color, and position in the picture. Notice, however, that the first three pictures each show two things: two flowers, two cats, two butterflies.

FIG.8–10

When the first of these pictures is shown, infants look at it for several seconds. But, as more pictures of "two things" are presented, infants habituate (Module 6.2): They glance at the picture briefly, then look away, as if saying, "Enough of these pictures of two things; let's move on to something else." And, in fact, if a picture of a single object or, like the last drawing in the diagram, a picture of three objects is then shown, infants again look for several seconds, their interest apparently renewed. Because the only systematic change is the number of objects depicted in the picture, we know that babies can distinguish stimuli on the basis of number. Typically, 5-month-olds can distinguish two objects from three and, less often, three objects from four (Canfield & Smith, 1996; Wynn, 1996).

How do infants distinguish differences in quantity? Older children might count, but, of course, infants have not yet learned names of numbers. Instead, the process is probably more perceptual in nature. As we saw in Module 6.1, the infant's perceptual system is sensitive to characteristics such as shape and color (Bornstein, 1981). Quantity may well be another characteristic of stimuli to which infants are sensitive. That is, just as colors (reds, blues) and shapes (triangles, squares) are basic perceptual properties, small quantities ("twoness" and "threeness") may be perceptually obvious (Strauss & Curtis, 1984).

Strictly speaking, studies like these tell us that infants can distinguish one object from two objects and two objects from three objects. Of course, for older children and adults, these sets don't simply differ; one set has *more* objects than the other. **Ordinality refers to the fact that numbers can differ in magnitude; some values are greater than others.** Near the first birthday, infants can identify the larger set. If 10-month-olds watch an adult place two crackers in one container but three crackers in a second container, the infants usually reach for the container with more crackers (Feigenson, Carey, & Hauser, 2002), showing early sensitivity to the ordinal properties of sets.

**LEARNING TO COUNT.**   Names of numbers are not among most babies' first words, but by 2 years, youngsters know some number words and have begun to count. Usually, their counting is full of mistakes. In Susan's counting sequence that was described in the vignette—"1, 2, 6, 7"—she skips 3, 4, and 5. But research has shown that if we ignore her mistakes momentarily, the counting sequence reveals that she does understand a great deal. Gelman and Meck (1986) simply placed several objects in front of a child and asked, "How many?" By analyzing children's answers to many of these questions, they discovered that by age 3 most children have mastered three basic principles of counting, at least when it comes to counting up to five objects.

- **One-to-one principle: There must be one and only one number name for each object that is counted.** A child who counts three objects as "1, 2, a" understands this principle because the number of number words matches the number of objects to be counted.
- **Stable-order principle: Number names must be counted in the same order.** A child who counts in the same sequence—for example, consistently counting four objects as "1, 2, 4, 5"—shows understanding of this principle.
- **Cardinality principle: The last number name differs from the previous ones in a counting sequence by denoting the number of objects.** Typically, 3-year-olds reveal their understanding of this principle by repeating the last number name, often with emphasis: "1, 2, 4, 8 . . . EIGHT!"

During the preschool years, children master these basic principles and apply them to ever larger sets of objects. By age 5, most youngsters apply these counting principles to as many as nine objects. Of course, children's understanding of these principles does not mean that they always count accurately. To the contrary, children can apply all these principles consistently while counting incorrectly. They must master the conventional sequence of the number names and the counting principles to learn to count accurately. (To see if you understand the counting principles, go back to Susan's counting in the vignette and decide which principles she has mastered; my answer is given before "Check Your Learning" on page 238.)

Learning the number names beyond 9 is easier because the counting words can be generated based on rules for combining decade number names (20, 30, 40) with unit names (1, 2, 3, 4). Later, similar rules are used for hundreds, thousands, and so on. By age 4, most youngsters know the numbers to 20, and some can count to 99. Usually, they stop counting at a number ending in 9 (29, 59), apparently because they don't know the next decade name (Siegler & Robinson, 1982).

Learning to count beyond 10 is more complicated in English than in other languages. For example, *eleven* and *twelve* are completely irregular names, following no rules. Also, the remaining "teen" number names differ from the 20s, 30s, and the rest in that the decade number name comes after the unit (thir-*teen*, four-*teen*) rather than before (*twenty*-three, *thirty*-four). Also, some decade names only loosely correspond to the unit names on which they are based: *twenty*, *thirty*, and *fifty* resemble *two*, *three*, and *five* but are not the same.

In contrast, the Chinese, Japanese, and Korean number systems are almost perfectly regular. *Eleven* and *twelve* are expressed as *ten-one* and *ten-two*. There are no special names for the decades: *Two-ten* and *two-ten-one* are names for 20 and 21. These simplified number names help explain why youngsters growing up in Asian countries count more accurately than U.S. preschool children of the same age (Miller et al., 1995). What's more, the direct correspondence between the number names and the base-ten system makes it easier for Asian youngsters to learn some mathematical concepts. For example, if a child has 10 blocks, then gets 6 more, an American 5-year-old will carefully count the additional blocks to determine that he now has 16. In contrast, a Chinese 5-year-old will not count but quickly say "16" because she understands that in the base-ten system, 10 + 6 = 16 (Ho & Fuson, 1998).

**ADDING AND SUBTRACTING.**    By 4 or 5 years, most children have encountered arithmetic problems that involve simple addition or subtraction. A 4-year-old might put one green bean on her plate, then watch in dismay as her dad gives her three more. Now she wonders, "How many do I have in all?" Like the child in the photo, many youngsters solve this sort of problem by counting. They first count out four fingers on one hand, then count out two more on the other. Finally, they count all six fingers on both hands. To subtract, they do the same procedure in reverse (Siegler & Jenkins, 1989; Siegler & Shrager, 1984).

Youngsters soon abandon this approach for a slightly more efficient method. Instead of counting the fingers on the first hand, they simultaneously extend the number of fingers on the first hand corresponding to the larger of the two numbers to be added. Next, they count out the smaller number with fingers on the second hand. Finally, they count all of the fingers to determine the sum (Groen & Resnick, 1977).

After children begin to receive formal arithmetic instruction in first grade, addition problems are solved less frequently by counting aloud or by counting fingers. Instead, children add and subtract by counting mentally. That is, children act as if they are counting silently, beginning with the larger number, and adding on. By age 8 or 9, children have learned the addition tables so well that sums of the single-digit integers (from 0 to 9) are facts that are simply retrieved from memory (Ashcraft, 1982).

These counting strategies do *not* occur in a rigid developmental sequence. Instead, as I mentioned in describing Siegler's (1996) overlapping waves model (page 211), individual children use many different strategies for addition, depending on the problem. Children usually begin by trying to retrieve an answer from memory. If they are not reasonably confident that the retrieved answer is correct, then they resort to counting aloud or on fingers (Siegler, 1996). Retrieval is most

Children use many strategies to add, including counting on fingers, counting aloud, and retrieving sums directly from memory.

likely for problems with small addends (e.g., 1 + 2, 2 + 4) because these problems are presented frequently in textbooks and by teachers. Consequently, the sum is highly associated with the problem, which makes the child confident that the retrieved answer is correct. In contrast, problems with larger addends, such as 9 + 8, are presented less often. The result is a weaker link between the addends and the sum and, consequently, a greater chance that children need to determine an answer by resorting to a backup strategy such as counting.

Of course, arithmetic skills continue to improve as children move through elementary school. They become more proficient in addition and subtraction, learn multiplication and division, and move on to the more sophisticated mathematical concepts involved in algebra, geometry, trigonometry, and calculus.

**COMPARING U.S. STUDENTS WITH STUDENTS IN OTHER COUNTRIES.** Let's return to the issue of cultural differences in mathematical competence. When compared to students worldwide in terms of math skills, U.S. students don't fare well. For example, the graph shows the math results from a major international comparison involving students in 38 countries (National Center for Educational Statistics, 2000). U.S. eighth graders have substantially lower scores than eighth graders in the leading nations. Phrased another way, the very best U.S. students only perform at the level of average students in Asian countries like Singapore and Korea. Furthermore, the cultural differences in math achievement hold for both math operations and math problem solving (Stevenson & Lee, 1990).

Why do American students rate so poorly? The "Cultural Influences" feature gives some answers.

FIG. 8–11

## CULTURAL INFLUENCES

### Fifth Grade in Taiwan

Shin-ying is an 11-year-old attending school in Taipei, the largest city in Taiwan. Like most fifth graders, Shin-ying is in school from 8 A.M. until 4 P.M. daily. Most evenings, she spends 2 to 3 hours doing homework. This academic routine is grueling by U.S. standards, where fifth graders typically spend 6 to 7 hours in school each day and less than an hour doing homework. I asked Shin-ying what she thought of school and schoolwork. Her answers surprised me.

RK: Why do you go to school?

SHIN-YING: I like what we study.

RK: Any other reasons?

SHIN-YING The things that I learn in school are useful.

RK: What about homework? Why do you do it?

SHIN-YING: My teacher and my parents think it's important. And I like doing it.

RK: Do you think that you would do nearly as well in school if you didn't work so hard?

SHIN-YING: Oh no. The best students are always the ones who work the hardest.

Schoolwork is the focal point of Shin-ying's life. Although many American schoolchildren are unhappy when schoolwork intrudes on time for play and television, Shin-ying is enthusiastic about school and school-related activities.

Shin-ying is not unusual among Chinese elementary-school students. Many of her comments illustrate findings that emerge from detailed analyses of classrooms, teachers, students, and parents in studies comparing students in Japan, Taiwan, and the United States (Perry, 2000; Stevenson & Lee, 1990; Stigler, Gallimore, & Hiebert, 2000):

> Student in Asia spend more time on school tasks and their parents set higher standards.

- *Time in school and how it is used.* By fifth grade, students in Japan and Taiwan spend 50 percent more time than American students in school, more of this time is devoted to academic activities than in the United States, and instruction in Asian schools is often better organized and more challenging.

- *Time spent in homework and attitudes toward it.* Students in Taiwan and Japan spend more time on homework and value homework more than American students.

- *Parents' attitudes.* American parents are more often satisfied with their children's performance in school; in contrast, Japanese and Taiwanese parents set much higher standards for their children.

- *Parents' beliefs about effort and ability.* Japanese and Taiwanese parents believe more strongly than American parents that effort, not native ability, is the key factor in school success.

Thus, students in Japan and Taiwan excel because they spend more time both in and out of school on academic tasks. Furthermore, their parents (and teachers) set loftier scholastic goals and believe that students can attain these goals with hard work. Japanese classrooms even post a motto describing ideal students—*gambaru kodomo*—those who strive the hardest.

Parents underscore the importance of schoolwork in many ways to their children. For example, even though homes and apartments in Japan and China are very small by U.S. standards, Asian youngsters, like the child in the photo, typically have a desk in a quiet area where they can study undisturbed (Stevenson & Lee, 1990). For Japanese and Taiwanese teachers and parents, academic excellence is paramount, and it shows in their children's success.

What can Americans learn from Japanese and Taiwanese educational systems? From their experiences with Asian students, teachers, and schools, Stevenson and Stigler (1992) suggest several ways American schools could be improved:

- Give teachers more free time to prepare lessons and correct students' work.
- Improve teachers' training by allowing them to work closely with older, more experienced teachers.
- Organize instruction around sound principles of learning such as providing multiple examples of concepts and giving students adequate opportunities to practice newly acquired skills.
- Set higher standards for children, who need to spend more time and effort in school-related activities in order to achieve those standards.

U.S. schools could be improved by giving teachers better training and more time to prepare lessons, basing teaching on principles of learning, and setting higher standards.

Changing teaching practices and attitudes toward achievement would begin to reduce the gap between American students and students in other industrialized countries, particularly Asian countries. Ignoring the problem will mean an increasingly under-educated workforce and citizenry in a more complex world—an alarming prospect.

*Definition on page 229:* A palanquin is a covered couch resting on two horizontal poles that are carried by four people, one at each end of the poles.

*Response to question about Susan's counting on page 234:* Since Susan uses four number names to count four objects ("1, 2, 6, 7 ... SEVEN!"), she understands the one-to-one principle. The four number names are always used in the same order, so she grasps the stable-order principle. And, finally, she repeats the last number name with emphasis, so she understands the cardinality principle.

## CHECK YOUR LEARNING

1. Important prereading skills include knowing letters and _____.
2. Beginning readers typically recognize words by sounding them out; with greater experience, readers are more likely to be able to _____.
3. Older and more experienced readers understand more of what they read because their word recognition skills improve, the capacity of working memory increases, they have more general knowledge of the world, _____, and they are more likely to use appropriate reading strategies.
4. Children typically use a _____ to organize their writing.
5. Children revise best when revising other children's writing and when _____.
6. By age 3 years, most children have mastered the _____, stable-order, and cardinality principles of counting.
7. The simplest way of solving addition problems is to _____; the most advanced way is to retrieve sums from long-term memory.

**8.** Compared to students in U.S. elementary schools, students in Japan and Taiwan spend more time in school, and a greater proportion of that time is _____.

### ACTIVE CHILDREN

Imagine two children just entering first grade. One has mastered prereading skills, can sound out many words, and recognizes a rapidly growing set of words. The second child knows most of the letters of the alphabet, but knows only a handful of letter-sound correspondences. How are these differences in reading skills likely to lead to different experiences in first grade?

**Answers:** (1) sounds associated with each letter, (2) retrieve words from long-term memory, (3) they monitor their comprehension more effectively, (4) knowledge-telling strategy, (5) the topic is familiar to them, (6) one-to-one, (7) count on one's fingers, (8) devoted to academic activities

## Unifying Themes: Active Children

This chapter highlights the theme that *children influence their own development*: Japanese and Chinese elementary-school children typically like studying (an attitude fostered by their parents), and this makes them quite willing to do homework for 2 or 3 hours nightly. This, in turn, contributes to their high levels of scholastic achievement. American schoolchildren usually abhor homework and do as little of it as possible, which contributes to their relatively lower level of scholastic achievement. Thus, children's attitudes help to determine how they behave, which determines how much they will achieve over the course of childhood and adolescence.

### See for Yourself

Create several small sets of objects that vary in number. You might have two pennies, three candies, four buttons, five pencils, six erasers, seven paper clips, and so on. Place each set of objects on a paper plate. Then find some preschool children; 4- and 5-year-olds would be ideal. Put a plate in front of each child and ask, "How many?" Then watch to see what the child does. If possible, tape-record the children's counting so that you can analyze it later. If this is impossible, try to write down exactly what each child says as he or she counts. Later, go back through your notes and determine whether the children follow the counting principles described on page 234. You should see that children, particularly younger ones, more often follow the principles while counting small sets of objects than larger sets. See for yourself!

### Resources

For more information about...

cultural differences in scholastic achievement, try Harold W. Stevenson and James W. Stigler's *The Learning Gap* (Summit Books, 1992), which describes research comparing schooling in the United States and in Asia.

tips and exercises to help develop better study skills for college, visit the Web site of the University Counseling Center of the Virginia Polytechnic Institute and State University, **http://www.ucc.vt.edu/stdysk/stdyhlp.html**

## Key Terms

autobiographical memory  221
automatic processes  212
cardinality principle  234
cognitive self-regulation  218
comprehension  227
elaboration  217
executive functioning  212
infantile amnesia  221
information processing  208
inhibitory processes  212
knowledge-telling strategy  231
knowledge-transforming strategy  231
long-term memory  209
memory strategies  217

metacognitive knowledge  218
metamemory  218
one-to-one principle  234
ordinality  234
organization  217
phonological awareness  227
propositions  230
rehearsal  217
script  220
sensory memory  208
stable-order principle  234
word recognition  227
working memory  209

# 8.1 An Introduction to Information Processing

### Basic Features of the Information-Processing Approach

According to the information-processing approach, cognitive development involves changes in mental hardware and mental software. Mental hardware refers to mental processes that are built-in and allow the mind to function, including sensory, working, and long-term memories. Mental software refers to mental programs that allow people to perform specific tasks.

### How Information Processing Changes with Development

Information-processing psychologists believe that cognitive development reflects more effective strategies, increased capacity of working memory, more effective inhibitory processes, increased automatic processing, and increased speed of processing.

### Comparing Information Processing and Piaget's Theory

Piaget's theory is a single, comprehensive theory, whereas information processing is a general approach encompassing many specific theories. In addition, Piaget's theory emphasizes qualitative change in development, whereas information processing emphasizes quantitative change.

# 8.2 Memory

### Origins of Memory

Rovee-Collier's studies of kicking show that infants can remember, forget, and be reminded of events that occurred in the past.

### Strategies for Remembering

Beginning in the preschool years, children use strategies to help them remember. With age, children use more powerful strategies, such as rehearsal and outlining. Using memory strategies successfully depends, first, on analyzing the goal of a memory task and, second, on monitoring the effectiveness of the chosen strategy. Analyzing goals and monitoring are two important elements of metamemory, which is a child's informal understanding of how memory operates.

### Knowledge and Memory

A child's knowledge of the world can be used to organize information that is to be remembered. When several events occur in a specific order, they are remembered as a single script. Knowledge improves memory for children and adolescents, although older individuals often reap more benefit because they have more knowledge. Knowledge can also distort memory by causing children and adolescents to forget information that does not conform to their knowledge or to remember events that are part of their knowledge but that did not actually take place.

Autobiographical memory refers to a person's memory about his or her own life. Autobiographical memory emerges in the early preschool years, often prompted by parents' asking children about past events. Infantile amnesia, children's and adults' inability to remember events from early in life, may reflect the absence of language or a sense of self.

Young children's memory in court cases is often inaccurate because children are questioned repeatedly, which makes it hard for them to distinguish what actually occurred from what adults suggest may have occurred. Children's testimony would be more reliable if interviewers tested alternate hypotheses during their questioning, avoided repeated questioning, and warned children that they may try to trick them.

# 8.3 Academic Skills

### Reading

Information-processing psychologists divide reading into a number of component skills. Prereading skills include knowing letters and the sounds associated with them. Word recognition is the process of identifying a word. Beginning readers more often accomplish this by sounding out words; advanced readers more often retrieve a word from long-term memory. Comprehension, the act of extracting meaning from text, improves with age because of several factors: working memory capacity increases, readers gain more world knowledge, and readers are better able to monitor what they read and to match their reading strategies to the goals of the reading task.

### Writing

As children develop, their writing improves, reflecting several factors: They know more about the world and so they have more to say; they use more effective ways of organizing their writing; they master the mechanics (e.g., handwriting, spelling) of writing; and they become more skilled at revising their writing.

### Knowing and Using Numbers

Infants can distinguish quantities, probably by means of basic perceptual processes. Children begin to count by about age 2, and by 3 years most children have mastered the one-to-one, stable-order, and cardinality principles, at least when counting small sets of objects. Counting is how children first add, but it is replaced by more effective strategies such as retrieving sums directly from memory.

In mathematics, American students lag behind students in most other industrialized nations, chiefly because of cultural differences in the time spent on schoolwork and homework and in parents' attitudes towards school, effort, and ability.

Have you ever stopped to think how many standardized tests you've taken in your student career? You probably took either the SAT or the ACT to enter college. Before that, you took countless achievement and aptitude tests during elementary school and high school. Psychological testing began in schools early in the 20th century and continues to be an integral part of American education in the 21st century.

Of all standardized tests, none attracts more attention and generates more controversy than tests designed to measure intelligence. Intelligence tests have been hailed by some as one of psychology's greatest contributions to society and cursed by others. Intelligence tests and what they measure are the focus of Chapter 9. We'll start, in Module 9.1, by looking at different definitions of intelligence. In Module 9.2, we'll see how intelligence tests work and examine some factors that influence test scores. Finally, in Module 9.3, we'll look at special children—youngsters whose intelligence sets them apart from their peers.

# Intelligence and Individual Differences in Cognition

9.1   What Is Intelligence?

9.2   Measuring Intelligence

9.3   Special Children, Special Needs

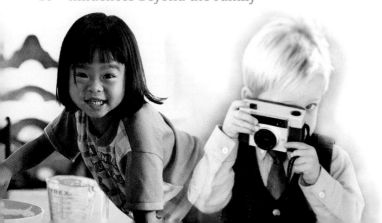

# 9.1                    What Is Intelligence?

## LEARNING OBJECTIVES

● What is the psychometric view of the nature of intelligence?

● How does Gardner's theory of multiple intelligences differ from the psychometric approach?

● What are the three components of Sternberg's triarchic theory of intelligence?

*Max is 22 years old and is moderately mentally retarded. That is, he performs most tasks at the level of a normally developing 5- or 6-year-old. For example, he can't do many of Piaget's conservation tasks and he reads very slowly and with much effort. Nevertheless, if Max hears a song on the radio, he can immediately sit down at the piano and play the melody flawlessly, despite having had no musical training. Everyone who sees Max do this is astonished. How can a person who is otherwise so limited intellectually perform such an amazing feat?*

Before you read further, how would you define intelligence? If you're typical of most Americans, your definition probably includes the ability to reason logically, connect ideas, and solve real problems. You might mention verbal ability, meaning the ability to speak clearly and articulately. You might also mention social competence, referring, for example, to an interest in the world at large and an ability to admit when you make a mistake (Sternberg & Kaufman, 1998).

As you'll see in this module, many of these ideas about intelligence are included in psychological theories of intelligence. We'll begin by considering the oldest theories of intelligence, those associated with the psychometric tradition. Then we'll look at two newer approaches and, along the way, get some insights into Max's uncanny musical skill.

## Psychometric Theories

**Psychometricians are psychologists who specialize in measuring psychological characteristics such as intelligence and personality.** When psychometricians want to research a particular question, they usually begin by administering a large number of tests to many individuals. Then they look for patterns in performance across the different tests. The basic logic underlying this technique is similar to the logic a jungle hunter uses to decide whether some dark blobs in a river are three separate rotting logs or a single alligator (Cattell, 1965). If the blobs move together, the hunter decides they are part of the same structure, an alligator. If they do not move together, they are three different structures—three logs. Similarly, if changes in performance on one psychological test are accompanied by changes in performance on a second test—that is, if they move together—one assumes the tests are measuring the same attribute or factor.

*Using patterns of test scores, psychometricians have found evidence for general intelligence as well as for specific abilities.*

Suppose, for example, that you believe there is such a thing as general intelligence. In other words, you believe that some people are smart regardless of the situation, task, or problem, whereas others are not so smart. According to this view, children's performance should be very consistent across tasks. Smart children should always receive high scores, and the less smart youngsters should always get lower scores. As early as 1904, Charles Spearman reported findings supporting the idea that a general factor for intelligence, or *g*, is responsible for performance on all mental tests.

Other researchers, however, have found that intelligence consists of distinct abilities. For example, Thurstone and Thurstone (1941) analyzed performance on a wide range of tasks and identified seven distinct patterns, each reflecting a unique ability: perceptual speed, word comprehension, word fluency, space, number, memory, and induction. Thurstone and Thurstone also acknowledged a general factor that operated in all tasks, but they emphasized that the specific factors were more useful in assessing and understanding intellectual ability.

These conflicting findings have led many psychometric theorists to propose hierarchical theories of intelligence that include both general and specific components. John Carroll (1993, 1996), for example, proposed the hierarchical theory with three levels that's shown in the diagram. At the top of the hierarchy is *g*, general intelligence. In the middle level are eight broad categories of intellectual skill. **For example, fluid intelligence refers to the ability to perceive relations among stimuli.** Each of the abilities in the second level is further divided into the skills listed in the bottom and most specific level. **Crystallized intelligence, for example, comprises a person's culturally influenced accumulated knowledge and skills, including understanding printed language, comprehending language, and knowing vocabulary.**

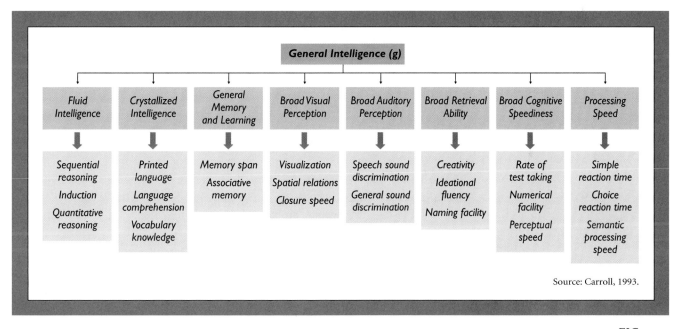

FIG. 9–1

Carroll's hierarchical theory is, in essence, a compromise between the two views of intelligence—general versus distinct abilities. But some critics still find it unsatisfactory because it ignores the research and theory on cognitive development described in Chapters 7 and 8. They believe we need to look beyond the psychometric approach to understand intelligence. In the remainder of this module, then, we'll look at two newer theories that have gained a following.

## Gardner's Theory of Multiple Intelligences

Only recently have developmental psychologists viewed intelligence from the perspective of Piaget's theory and information-processing psychology. These new theories present a much broader theory of intelligence and how it develops. Among the most ambitious is Howard Gardner's (1983, 1999, 2002) theory of multiple intelligences. Rather than using test scores as the basis for his theory, Gardner drew on research in child development, studies of brain-damaged persons, and studies of exceptionally talented people. Using these resources, Gardner identified seven distinct intelligences when he first proposed the theory in 1983. In subsequent work, Gardner (1999, 2002) has identified two additional intelligences; the complete list is shown in the table.

## Nine Intelligences in Gardner's Theory of Multiple Intelligences

| Type of Intelligence | Definition |
| --- | --- |
| Linguistic | Knowing the meanings of words, having the ability to use words to understand new ideas, and using language to convey ideas to others |
| Logical-mathematical | Understanding relations that exist among objects, actions, and ideas, as well as the logical or mathematical operations that can be performed on them |
| Spatial | Perceiving objects accurately and imagining in the "mind's eye" the appearance of an object before and after it has been transformed |
| Musical | Comprehending and producing sounds varying in pitch, rhythm, and emotional tone |
| Bodily-kinesthetic | Using one's body in highly differentiated ways, as dancers, craftspeople, and athletes do |
| Interpersonal | Identifying different feelings, moods, motivations, and intentions in others |
| Intrapersonal | Understanding one's emotions and knowing one's strengths and weaknesses |
| Naturalistic | Recognizing and distinguishing among members of a group (species) and describing relations between such groups |
| Existential | Considering "ultimate" issues, such as the purpose of life and the nature of death |

Source: Gardner, 1983, 1999, 2002.

TABLE 9–1

The first three intelligences in this list—linguistic intelligence, logical-mathematical intelligence, and spatial intelligence—are included in psychometric theories of intelligence. The last six intelligences are not: Musical, bodily-kinesthetic, interpersonal, intrapersonal, naturalistic, and existential intelligences are unique to Gardner's theory. According to Gardner, Yo-Yo Ma's wizardry on the cello, the Williams sisters' remarkable shots on the tennis court, and Oprah Winfrey's grace and charm in dealing with people are all features of intelligence that are totally ignored in traditional theories.

How did Gardner arrive at these nine distinct intelligences? First, each has a unique developmental history. Linguistic intelligence, for example, develops much earlier than the other eight. Second, each intelligence is regulated by distinct regions of the brain, as shown in studies of brain-damaged persons. Spatial intelligence, for example, is regulated by particular regions in the brain's right hemisphere. Third, each has special cases of talented individuals. **Musical intelligence is often shown by savants, individuals with mental retardation who are extremely talented in one domain.** Max, the 22-year-old in the module-opening vignette, is a savant whose special talent is music. Like Max, Eddie B., the 10-year-old savant in the photo, can play a tune correctly after a single hearing and without ever having had formal musical training (Shuter-Dyson, 1982).

Prompted by Gardner's theory, researchers have begun to look at nontraditional aspects of intelligence. **Probably the best known is emotional intelligence, which is the ability to use one's own and others' emotions effectively for solving problems and living happily.** Emotional intelligence made headlines in 1995 due to a best-selling book, *Emotional Intelligence*, in which the author, Daniel Goleman (1995), argued that "emotions [are] at the center of aptitudes for living" (p. xiii). In fact, research shows that emotional intelligence has a number of different components, including perceiving emotions accurately (in others and in oneself) and regulating one's emotions. People who are emotionally intelligent tend to have high scores on traditional IQ tests, have higher self-esteem, and are more sociable (Mayer, Caruso, & Salovey, 1999; Mayer, Salovey, & Caruso, 2000).

> From research in child development, studies of brain-damaged persons, and studies of talented people, Gardner proposed nine distinct intelligences.

Most of the research on emotional intelligence has been done with adults, in large part because Goleman (1998; Goleman, Bayatzis, & McKee, 2002) has argued that emotional intelligence can be the key to a successful career. Child-development researchers have studied emotion, but usually from a developmental angle—they've wanted to know how emotions change with age. We'll look at their research in Module 11.1.

**IMPLICATIONS FOR EDUCATION.**   The theory of multiple intelligence has important implications for education. Gardner (1993, 1995) believes that schools should foster all intelligences, rather than just the traditional linguistic and logical-mathematical intelligences. Teachers should capitalize on the strongest intelligences of individual children. Some students may best understand unfamiliar cultures, for example, by studying their dance, whereas other students may understand these cultures by studying their music.

These guidelines do not mean that teachers should gear instruction solely to a child's strongest intelligence, pigeonholing youngsters as "numerical learners" or "spatial learners." Instead, whether the topic is the signing of the Declaration of Independence or Shakespeare's *Hamlet*, instruction should try to engage as many different intelligences as possible (Gardner, 1999, 2002). The typical result is a much richer understanding of the topic by all students.

Some American schools have enthusiastically embraced Gardner's ideas (Gardner, 1993). Are these schools better than those that have not? Educators in schools using the theory think so; they claim that their students have higher test scores and better discipline and that their parents are more involved (Project Zero, 1999). Although these opinions are encouraging, they need to be supported by research that evaluates children's learning and achievement. In the mean time, there is no doubt that Gardner's work has helped liberate researchers from narrow psychometric-based views of intelligence.

A comparably broad but different view of intelligence comes from another new theory that we'll look at in the next section.

## Sternberg's Triarchic Theory

Robert Sternberg's (1977) early work included a theory of how adults solve problems on intelligence tests. **He elaborated this theory into what he called the triarchic theory because it includes three parts or subtheories** (Sternberg, 1985, 1997). The three subtheories are shown in the diagram on page 248.

**According to the contextual subtheory, intelligent behavior involves skillfully adapting to an environment.** That is, intelligence is always partly defined by

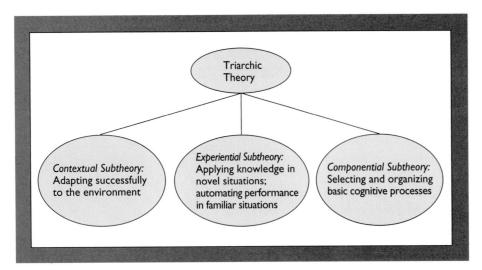

the demands of an environment or cultural context. What is intelligent for children growing up in cities in North America may not be intelligent for children growing up in the Sahara desert, in the Australian outback, or on a remote island in the Pacific Ocean. And, what is intelligent at home may not be intelligent in the neighborhood. The "Cultural Influences" feature illustrates how intelligent behavior is always defined by the context.

FIG. 9–2

## CULTURAL INFLUENCES

### How Culture Defines What Is Intelligent

In Brazil, many elementary-school-age boys like the two in the left photo sell candy and fruit to bus passengers and pedestrians. These children often cannot identify the numbers on paper money, yet they know how to purchase their goods from wholesale stores, make change for customers, and keep track of their sales (Saxe, 1988).

Adolescents who live on Pacific Ocean islands near New Guinea learn to sail boats like the one in the right photo hundreds of miles across open seas to get from one small island to the next. They have no formal training in mathematics, yet they can use a complex navigational system based on the positions of stars and estimates of the boat's speed (Hutchins, 1983).

If either the Brazilian vendors or the island navigators were given the tests that measure intelligence in U.S. students, they would fare poorly. Does this mean they are less intelligent than U.S. children? Of course not. The skills that are important to American conceptions of intelligence and that are assessed on our intelligence tests are less valued in these other cultures and so are not cultivated in the young. And, by the same token, most bright U.S. children would be lost trying to navigate a boat in the open sea. Each culture defines what it means to be intelligent, and the specialized computing skills of vendors and navigators are just as intelligent in their cultural settings as verbal skills are in American culture (Sternberg & Kaufman, 1998).

The triarchic theory includes two other subtheories. **According to the experiential subtheory, intelligence is revealed in both novel and familiar tasks.** For novel tasks, intelligence is associated with the ability to apply existing knowledge to a new situation. At the start of a new school year, for example, readily adjusting to new tasks is a sign of intelligence. Bright children learning multiplication readily draw upon relevant math knowledge to grasp what's involved in multiplication.

For familiar tasks, intelligence is associated with the automatic processing that was described in Module 8.1. Completing a task automatically means using few mental resources. At the end of a school year, performing now-familiar school tasks automatically rather than with effort is a sign of intelligence. Bright children now solve multiplication problems automatically, without thinking about the intermediate steps.

**According to the componential subtheory, intelligence depends on basic cognitive processes called components.** A component is simply Sternberg's term for the different information-processing skills described in Chapter 8, such as monitoring and retrieval. Whether the task is solving an item on an intelligence test, reading a newspaper, or understanding a conversation, components must be selected and organized in the proper sequence to complete the task successfully. In this subtheory, intelligence reflects more efficient organization and use of components.

In contrast to the psychometric approach and to Gardner's theory, the triarchic theory does not identify specific *contents* of intelligence. Instead, Sternberg defines intelligence in terms of *processes*: the relevance of the tasks to personal and cultural goals (contextual subtheory), the familiarity of those tasks (experiential subtheory), and the strategies people use to complete tasks (componential subtheory).

Sternberg's theory also underscores the dangers of comparing test scores of different cultural, ethnic, or racial groups. Comparisons are typically invalid because some test items are usually more relevant and familiar in one culture than in another. A vocabulary test, for example, is useful in assessing intelligence in cultures where formal education is essential to skilled adaptations (because skilled use of language is important for success in schools). In cultures where schooling is not a key to success, a vocabulary test would not provide useful information because it would be irrelevant to cultural goals and much too novel.

As with Gardner's theory, researchers are still evaluating Sternberg's theory. And, as you can see in the table that summarizes the different approaches, theorists are still debating the question of what intelligence is. But, however it is defined, the fact is that individuals differ substantially in intellectual ability, and numerous tests have been devised to measure these differences. The construction, properties, and limitations of these tests are the focus of the next module.

> In the triarchic theory, intelligence reflects strategies children use to complete tasks plus the familiarity and relevance of those tasks.

**SUMMARY TABLE**

## FEATURES OF MAJOR APPROACHES TO INTELLIGENCE

| Approach | Distinguishing Features |
|---|---|
| Psychometric | Intelligence is a hierarchy of general and specific skills |
| Gardner's theory of multiple intelligences | Nine distinct intelligences exist—linguistic, logical-mathematical, spatial, musical, bodily-kinesthetic, interpersonal, intrapersonal, naturalistic, and existential |
| Sternberg's triarchic theory | Intelligence is defined by context, experience, and information-processing components |

## CHECK YOUR LEARNING

1. If some children consistently have high scores on different intelligence tests while other children consistently have lower scores on the same tests, this would support the view that intelligence _____.

2. According to _____ theories, intelligence includes both general intelligence as well as more specific abilities, such as verbal and spatial skill.

3. Gardner's theory of multiple intelligences includes linguistic, logical-mathematical, and spatial intelligences, which are included in psychometric theories, as well as musical, _____, interpersonal, intrapersonal, naturalistic, and existential intelligences, which are ignored in psychometric theories.

4. Based on Gardner's view of intelligence, teachers should _____.

5. According to Sternberg's _____ subtheory, intelligence refers to adapting to an environment to achieve goals.

6. Sternberg's theory emphasizes that comparing test scores of children from cultural groups is dangerous because _____.

**CONNECTIONS**

Compare and contrast the major approaches to intelligence in terms of the extent to which they make connections between different aspects of development. That is, to what extent does each perspective emphasize cognitive processes versus integrating physical, cognitive, social, and emotional processes?

**Answers:** (1) consists of a general factor, *g* (2) hierarchical, (3) bodily-kinesthetic, (4) be sure that their teaching engages many different intelligences, (5) contextual, (6) test items are neither equally relevant nor equally novel for children from different groups

# 9.2    Measuring Intelligence

- Binet and the Development of Intelligence Testing
- Do Tests Work?
- Hereditary and Environmental Factors
- Impact of Ethnicity and Socioeconomic Status

## LEARNING OBJECTIVES

- Why were intelligence tests devised initially? What are modern tests like?
- How well do modern intelligence tests work?
- What are the roles of heredity and environment in determining intelligence?
- How do ethnicity and socioeconomic status influence intelligence test scores?

*Charlene, an African American third grader, received a score of 75 on an intelligence test administered by a school psychologist. Based on the test score, the psychologist believes that Charlene is mildly mentally retarded and should receive special education. Charlene's parents are indignant; they believe that the tests are biased against African Americans and that the score is meaningless.*

American schools faced a crisis at the beginning of the 20th century. Between 1890 and 1915, school enrollment nearly doubled nationally as great numbers of immigrants arrived and as reforms restricted child labor and emphasized education (Chapman, 1988). Increased enrollment meant that teachers now had larger numbers of students who did not learn as readily as the "select few" who had populated their classes previously. How to deal with these less capable children was one of the pressing issues of the day. In this module, you'll see how intelligence tests were devised initially to address a changed school population. Then we'll look at a simple question: "How well do modern tests work?" Finally, we'll examine how race, ethnicity, social class, environment, and heredity influence intelligence, and we'll learn how to interpret Charlene's test score.

## Binet and the Development of Intelligence Testing

The problems facing educators at the beginning of the 20th century were not unique to the United States. In 1904, the minister of public instruction in France asked two noted psychologists, Alfred Binet and Theophile Simon, to formulate a way to identify children who were likely to succeed in school. Binet and Simon's approach was to select simple tasks that French children of different ages ought to be able to do, such as naming colors, counting backwards, and remembering numbers in order. Based on preliminary testing, Binet and Simon determined problems that normal 3-year-olds could solve, that normal 4-year-olds could solve, and so on. **Children's mental age or MA referred to the difficulty of the problems that they could solve correctly.** A child who solved problems that the average 7-year-old could pass would have an MA of 7.

*Binet and Simon created the first intelligence test by using simple tasks to distinguish children who would do well in school from those who wouldn't.*

Binet and Simon used mental age to distinguish "bright" from "dull" children. A "bright" child would have the MA of an older child; for example, a 6-year-old with an MA of 9 was considered bright. A "dull" child would have the MA of a younger child, for example, a 6-year-old with an MA of 4. Binet and Simon confirmed that "bright" children did better in school than "dull" children. Voilá—the first standardized test of intelligence!

**THE STANFORD-BINET.**   Lewis Terman, of Stanford University, revised Binet and Simon's test and published a version known as the Stanford-Binet in 1916. **Terman described performance as an intelligence quotient, or IQ, which was simply the ratio of mental age to chronological age, multiplied by 100:**

$$IQ = MA/CA \times 100$$

At any age, children who are perfectly average will have an IQ of 100 because their mental age equals their chronological age. The figure shows the typical distribution of test scores in the population. Roughly two-thirds of children taking a test will have IQ scores between 85 and 115 and 95 percent will have scores between 70 and 130.

The IQ score can also be used to compare intelligence in children of different ages. A 4-year-old with an MA of 5 has an IQ of 125(5/4 × 100), the same as an 8-year-old with an MA of 10(10/8 × 100).

IQ scores are no longer computed in this manner. Instead, children's IQ scores are determined by comparing their test performance to that of others their age. When children perform at the average for their age, their IQ is 100. Children who perform above the average have IQs greater than 100; children who perform below the average have IQs less than 100. Nevertheless, the concept of IQ as the ratio of MA to CA helped popularize the Stanford-Binet test.

By the 1920s, the Stanford-Binet had been joined by many other intelligence tests. Educators enthusiastically embraced the tests as an efficient and objective way to assess a student's chances of succeeding in school (Chapman, 1988).

FIG. 9-3

**VIDEO 9.1**
Mental Age Testing
CLASSIC MODULE

The Stanford-Binet measures overall IQ; the WISC-III measures verbal and performance IQ

Today, more than 80 years later, the Stanford-Binet remains a popular test; the latest version was revised in 2003. Like the earlier versions, the modern Stanford-Binet consists of various cognitive and motor tasks, ranging from the extremely easy to the extremely difficult. The test may be administered to individuals ranging in age from approximately 2 years to adulthood, but the test items depend on the child's age. For example, preschool children may be asked to name pictures of familiar objects, string beads, answer questions about everyday life, or fold paper into shapes. Older individuals may be asked to define vocabulary words, solve an abstract problem, or decipher an unfamiliar code. The examiner determines, according to specific guidelines, the appropriate starting place on the test and administers progressively more difficult questions until the child fails all the questions at a particular level. An IQ score is assigned on the basis of how many questions the child passed compared with the average number passed by children of the same age.

Another test used frequently with children is the Wechsler Intelligence Scale for Children-III, or WISC-III for short. Unlike the Stanford-Binet, the WISC-III includes subtests for verbal and performance skills, some of which are shown in the figure. Based on their performance, children receive three scores: verbal IQ, performance IQ, and a combination of the two, the full-scale IQ.

The Stanford-Binet and the WISC-III are alike in that they are administered to one person at a time. Other tests can be administered to groups of individuals, which has the advantage of providing information about many individuals quickly and inexpensively, typically without the need of trained psychologists. But individual testing like that shown in the photo on page 253 optimizes the motivation and attention of the child and provides an opportunity for a sensitive examiner to assess factors that may influence test performance. The examiner may notice that the child is relaxed and that test performance is therefore a reason-

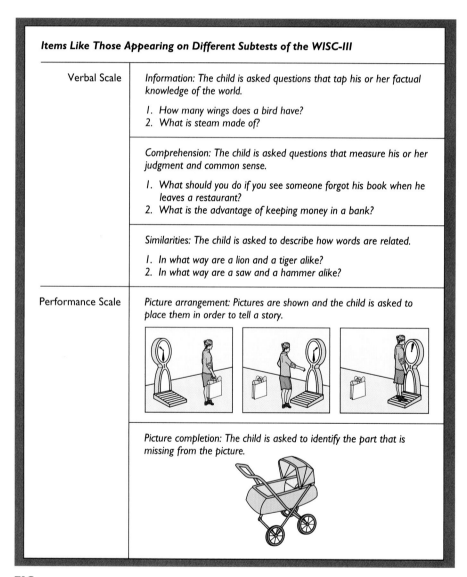

*Items Like Those Appearing on Different Subtests of the WISC-III*

| Verbal Scale | *Information: The child is asked questions that tap his or her factual knowledge of the world.*<br><br>1. How many wings does a bird have?<br>2. What is steam made of? |
| --- | --- |
| | *Comprehension: The child is asked questions that measure his or her judgment and common sense.*<br><br>1. What should you do if you see someone forgot his book when he leaves a restaurant?<br>2. What is the advantage of keeping money in a bank? |
| | *Similarities: The child is asked to describe how words are related.*<br><br>1. In what way are a lion and a tiger alike?<br>2. In what way are a saw and a hammer alike? |
| Performance Scale | *Picture arrangement: Pictures are shown and the child is asked to place them in order to tell a story.* |
| | *Picture completion: The child is asked to identify the part that is missing from the picture.* |

FIG. 9–4

Source: Simulated items similar to those in the Wechsler Intelligence Scales for Adult and Children. Copyright 1949, 1955, 1974, 1981, and 1990 by the Psychological Corporation. Reproduced by permission. All rights reserved.

able sample of the individual's talents. Or the examiner may observe that child is so anxious that she cannot do her best. Such determinations are not possible with group tests. Consequently, most psychologists prefer individualized tests of intelligence over group tests.

**INFANT TESTS.** The Stanford-Binet and the WISC-III cannot be used to test intelligence in infants. For this purpose, many psychologists use the Bayley Scales of Infant Development (Bayley, 1970, 1993). Designed for 2- to 42-month-olds, the Bayley Scales consist of mental and motor scales. The mental scale assesses adaptive behavior, such as attending to visual and auditory stimuli, following directions, looking for a fallen toy, and imitating. The motor scale assesses an infant's control of its body, its coordination, and its ability to manipulate objects. For example, 6-month-olds should turn their head toward an object that the examiner drops on the floor, 12-month-olds should imitate the examiner's actions, and 16-month-olds should build a tower from three blocks. In addition, other items are used to assess abilities such as habituation, memory, and problem solving.

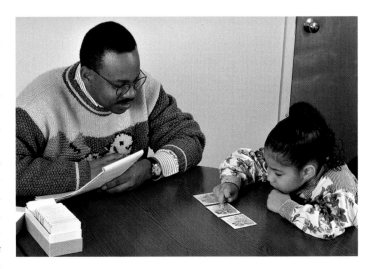

## Do Tests Work?

To determine whether intelligence tests work, we need to consider two separate issues, reliability and validity.

**RELIABILITY.** As I described in Module 2.1, a test is reliable if it yields scores that are consistent. Reliability is often measured by administering similar forms of a test on two occasions. If the test is reliable, a child will have similar scores both times. Today's intelligence tests are very reliable. If a child takes an intelligence test and then retakes it days or a few weeks later, the two scores are usually quite similar (Wechsler, 1991).

Reliability over the long term is more complex. In general, scores from infant intelligence tests are not related to IQ scores obtained later in childhood, adolescence, or adulthood (McCall, 1989). Apparently, children must be at least 18 to 24 months old before their Bayley scores, or scores from similar scales, can predict later IQ scores on the Wechsler or Stanford-Binet scales (Kopp & McCall, 1982).

Why don't scores on infant intelligence tests predict childhood or adult IQ more accurately? One reason is that infant tests measure different abilities than tests administered to children and adolescents: Infant tests place more emphasis on sensorimotor skills and less on tasks involving cognitive processes such as language, thinking, and problem solving.

According to this reasoning, a measure of infant cognitive processing might yield more accurate predictions of later IQ. In fact, habituation, a measure of information processing described in Module 6.1, does predict later IQ more effectively than scores from the Bayley. The average correlation between habituation and later IQ is approximately .5 (Bornstein, 1997). That is, 1- to 6-month-olds who habituate to visual stimuli more rapidly tend to have higher IQs as children. Apparently, infants who rapidly make sense of their world—in this case, thinking "I've seen this picture before, so let's see something new!"—are smarter during the elementary-school years.

If scores on the Bayley Scales do not predict later IQs, why are these tests used at all? The answer is that they are important diagnostic tools: Researchers and health care professionals use scores from the Bayley Scales to determine whether development is progressing normally.

FIG. 9–5

Although infant test scores don't reliably predict IQ later in life, scores obtained in childhood do. The graph shows the results from several longitudinal studies that correlated IQ scores obtained at different points in childhood or adolescence and at maturity. Each line in the graph represents a different study. You can see that the correlation between IQ at 5 years and maturity is approximately .5 and that the correlations get steadily larger as children get older.

These correlations appear to support the idea that intelligence is relatively stable from early childhood on. However, when individual performance over time is examined, stability is not a hard-and-fast rule. McCall, Appelbaum, and Hogarty (1973) conducted a longitudinal study in which 80 individuals had their intelligence tested roughly 14 times between ages 2 and 17. They discovered several different developmental patterns. The most common pattern—found in nearly 50 percent of the participants—was for little change in IQ from 2 to 17 years of age. However, for about 15 percent of the participants, IQ scores first increased, then decreased with age. For another 15 percent, the pattern was just the opposite: IQ scores first decreased, then increased with age.

McCall and his colleagues (1973) also found that children were most likely to have increasing IQ scores when their parents deliberately trained their intellectual and motor skills. When parents did not train their youngsters' intellectual and motor development (or, in some cases, actually discouraged it), IQ scores were likely to decline as children got older. Thus, although IQ is often relatively stable throughout childhood and adolescence, this is definitely not the only pattern. For many children, IQ will change both up and down as they develop.

**VALIDITY.** Reliability of tests, whether short- or long-term, is not the only criterion for evaluating a test. What do test scores mean? Are they really measuring intelligence? These questions raise the issue of *validity*, which refers to the extent that a test really measures what it claims to measure. Validity is usually measured by determining the relation between test scores and other independent measures of what the test is thought to measure. For example, to measure the validity of a test of extroversion, we would have children take the test, then observe them in a social setting, such as a school recess, and record who is outgoing and who is shy. The test would be valid if scores correlated highly with our independent observations of extroverted behavior.

> Most test developers argue that their tests are valid by showing that test scores are related to children's grades in school.

How would we extend this approach to intelligence tests? Ideally, we would administer the intelligence tests and then correlate the scores with other independent estimates of intelligence. But this approach has a fundamental flaw: There are no other independent ways to estimate intelligence; the only way to measure intelligence is with tests. Consequently, many researchers follow Binet's lead and obtain measures of performance in school, such as grades or teachers' ratings of their students. Correlations between these measures and scores on intelligence tests typically fall somewhere between .4 and .6 (Neisser et al., 1996). For example, the correlation between scores on the WISC-III and grade point average is .47 (Wechsler, 1991). This correlation is positive but far from a correlation of 1. Obviously, some youngsters with high test scores do not excel in school, whereas others with low test scores manage to get good grades. In general, however, tests do a reasonable job of predicting school success.

Intelligence tests are reasonable predictors of performance not only in school, but also in the workplace, particularly for more complex jobs (Gottfredson, 1997; Schmidt & Hunter, 1998). Workers with higher IQ scores tend to be more successful in their on-the-job training and, after training, more successful in their actual work performance. If, for example, two teenagers have summer jobs running tests in a biology lab, the smarter of the two will probably learn the procedures more rapidly and, once learned, conduct them more accurately.

**INCREASING VALIDITY WITH DYNAMIC TESTING.** Traditional tests of intelligence such as the Stanford-Binet and the WISC-III measure knowledge and skills that a child has accumulated up to the time of testing. These tests do not directly measure a child's potential for future learning; instead, the usual assumption is that children who have learned more in the past will probably learn more in the future. Critics argue that tests would be more valid if they directly assessed a child's potential for future learning.

**Dynamic testing measures a child's learning potential by having the child learn something new in the presence of the examiner and with the examiner's help.** Thus, dynamic testing is interactive and measures new achievement rather than past achievement. It is based on Vygotsky's ideas of the zone of proximal development and scaffolding (see pages 200–201). Learning potential can be estimated by the amount of material the child learns during interaction with the examiner and from the amount of help the child needs to learn the new material (Grigorenko & Sternberg, 1998; Sternberg & Grigorenko, 2002).

To understand the difference between traditional, static methods of intelligence testing and new, dynamic approaches, imagine a group of children attending a week-long basketball camp. On the first day, all children are tested on a range of basketball skills and receive a score that indicates their overall level of basketball skill. If this score were shown to predict later success in basketball, such as number of points scored in a season, this would be a valid static measure of basketball skill. To make this a dynamic measure of basketball skill, children would spend all week at camp being instructed in new skills. At the end of the week, the test of basketball skills would be readministered. The amount of the child's improvement over the week would measure learning potential, with greater improvement indicating greater learning potential.

Dynamic testing is a recent innovation that is still being evaluated. Preliminary research does indicate, however, that static and dynamic testing both provide useful and independent information. If the aim is to predict future levels of a child's skill, it is valuable to know a child's current level of skill (static testing) as well as the child's potential to acquire greater skill (dynamic testing). By combining both forms of testing, we achieve a more comprehensive view of a child's talents than by relying on either method alone (Day et al., 1997).

## Hereditary and Environmental Factors

Joanna, a 5-year-old girl, took the WISC-III and obtained a score of 112. Ted, a 5-year-old boy, took the same test and received a score of 92. What accounts for the 20-point difference in these youngsters' scores? Heredity and experience both matter.

Some of the evidence for hereditary factors is shown in the graph. If genes influence intelligence, then siblings' test scores should become more alike as siblings become more similar genetically (Plomin & Petrill, 1997). In other words, since

FIG. 9–6

identical twins are identical genetically, they typically have virtually identical test scores, which would be a correlation of 1. Fraternal twins have about 50 percent of their genes in common, just like nontwin siblings of the same biological parents. Consequently, we could predict that their test scores should be (a) less similar than scores for identical twins, (b) similar to scores of other siblings who have the same biological parents, and (c) more similar than scores of children and their adopted siblings. You can see in the graph that each of these predictions is supported.

Heredity also influences developmental profiles for IQ scores (Wilson, 1983). Developmental profiles for IQ are more alike for identical twins than for fraternal twins. If one identical twin gets higher IQ scores with age, the other twin almost certainly will, too. In contrast, if one fraternal twin gets higher scores with age, the other twin may not necessarily show the same pattern. Thus, identical twins are not only more alike in overall IQ, but in developmental change in IQ as well.

**Studies of siblings and adopted children show that heredity contributes to children's intelligence.**

Studies of adopted children also suggest the impact of heredity on IQ: If heredity helps determine IQ, then children's IQs should be more like those of their biological parents than of their adoptive parents. In fact, as I described in the "Focus on Research" feature in Module 3.1, throughout childhood and adolescence, the correlation between children's IQ and their biological parents' IQ is greater than the correlation between children's IQ and their adoptive parents' IQ. What's more, as adopted children get older, their test scores increasingly resemble those of their biological parents. These results are evidence for the greater impact of heredity on IQ as a child grows.

Do these results mean that heredity is the sole determiner of intelligence? No. Three areas of research show the importance of environment on intelligence. The first is research on characteristics of families and homes. If intelligence were solely due to heredity, environment should have little or no impact on children's intelligence. But we know that many characteristics of parents' behavior and home environments are related to children's intelligence. For example, children with high test scores tend to come from homes that are well organized and, like the one in the photo, have plenty of appropriate play materials (Bradley et al., 1989).

The impact of the environment on intelligence is also implicated by research on historical change in IQ scores. During most of the 20th century, IQ test scores rose dramatically (Flynn, 1998). For example, scores on the WISC increased by nearly 10 points over a 25-year-period (Flynn, 1999). Heredity cannot account for such a rapid increase over a few decades (a mere fraction of a second in genetic time). Consequently, the rise must reflect the impact of some aspect of the environment. The change might reflect smaller, better-educated families with more leisure time (Daley et al., 2003; Dickens & Flynn, 2001). Or it might be due to movies, television, and, more recently, the computer and the Internet, providing children with an incredible wealth of virtual experience (Greenfield, 1998). Although the exact cause remains a mystery, the increase per se shows the impact of changing environmental conditions on intelligence.

The importance of a stimulating environment for intelligence is also demonstrated by intervention programs that prepare economically disadvantaged children for school. Without preschool, children from low-income families often enter kindergarten or first grade lacking key readiness skills for academic success, which means they rapidly fall behind their peers who have these skills. Consequently, providing preschool experiences for children from poor families has long been a part of federal policies to eliminate poverty. The "Child Development and Family Policy" feature traces the beginnings of these programs.

## CHILD DEVELOPMENT AND FAMILY POLICY

### Providing Children with a Head Start for School

For more than 35 years, Head Start has been helping to foster the development of preschool children from low-income families. This program's origins can be traced to two forces. First, in the early 1960s, child-development researchers argued that environmental influences on children's development were much, much stronger than had been estimated previously. The year 1961 marked the appearance of *Intelligence and Experience* by psychologist Joseph McVicker Hunt. Hunt reviewed the scientific evidence concerning the impact of experience on intelligence and concluded that children's intellectual development could reach unprecedented heights once child-development scientists identified optimal environmental influences. In addition, a novel program in Tennessee directed by Susan Gray (Gray & Klaus, 1965) gave credibility to the argument by showing that a summer program coupled with weekly home visits throughout the school year could raise intelligence and language in preschool children living in poverty. Gray's findings suggested that Hunt's claims were not simply pipe dreams.

The second force was a political twist of fate. When President Lyndon Johnson launched the War on Poverty in 1964, the Office of Economic Opportunity (OEO) was the command center. Sargent Shriver, OEO's first director, found himself with a huge budget surplus. Most of the War on Poverty programs targeted adults; and because many of these programs were politically unpopular, Shriver was reluctant to spend more money on them. Shriver realized that no programs were aimed at children per se and that such programs would be much less controversial politically. (After all, critics may try to argue that poor adults "deserve their fate" because they're lazy or irresponsible financially, but such arguments are not very convincing when applied to young children.) What's more, he was personally familiar with the potential impact of programs targeted at young children through his experience as the president of the Chicago School Board and his wife's work on the President's Panel on Mental Retardation (Zigler & Muenchow, 1992).

Shriver envisioned a program that would better prepare poor children for first grade. In December 1964, he convened a 14-member planning committee that included professionals from medicine, social work, education, and psychology. Over a 6-week period, the planning committee devised a comprehensive program that would, by involving professionals and parents, meet the health and educational needs of young children. In May 1965, President Johnson announced the opening of Head Start and by that summer, a half-million American youngsters were enrolled. The program continues today and has now served the needs of millions of American children living in poverty.

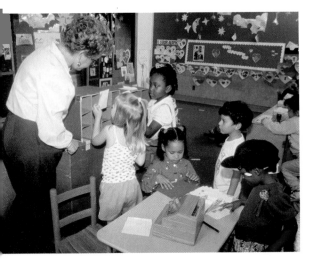

How effectively do these programs meet the needs of preschool youngsters? This turns out to be a question that's hard to answer because of the very nature of Head Start. Since the beginnings in the 1960s, Head Start has been tailored to meet the needs of individual communities; no two Head Start programs are exactly alike. Because Head Start takes on different forms in different communities, this makes it difficult to make blanket statements about the overall effectiveness of the program. However, high-quality Head Start programs *are* effective overall. When children like those in the photo attend good Head Start programs, they are healthier and do better in school (Lazar & Darlington, 1982; Zigler & Styfco, 1994). For example, Head Start graduates are less likely to repeat a grade level or to be placed in special education classes. And they are more likely to graduate from high school.

One of the success stories is the Carolina Abecedarian Project designed by Frances Campbell and Craig Ramey (1994; Campbell et al., 2001; Ramey & Campbell, 1991). This project included 111 children; most were born to African American mothers who had less than a high-school education, an average IQ score of 85, and typically no income. About half the children were assigned to a control group in which they received no special attention. The others attended a special day-care facility daily from age 4 months until 5 years. The curriculum emphasized mental, linguistic, and social development for infants, and prereading skills for preschoolers.

Every few years, the children were assessed on a battery of tests. The results for cognitive scores are shown in the graph. You can see that during the period of the intervention (i.e., the preschool years), the groups differ substantially: Youngsters in the treatment group have above-average IQ scores but those in the control group have below-average scores. For the remaining 15 years, scores for both groups decline slowly, but the children who participated in the special preschool programs always have higher scores, even as young adults. Intervention had a similar benefit on students' reading and math achievement.

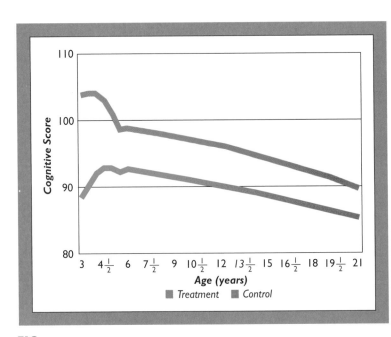

FIG. 9-7

Thus, intervention works. Of course, massive intervention over many years is expensive. But so are the economic consequences of poverty, unemployment, and their byproducts. Programs like the Abecedarian Project show that the repetitive cycle of school failure and education can be broken. In the process, they show that intelligence is fostered by a stimulating and responsive environment.

> Massive long-term intervention increases children's intelligence and achievement.

## Impact of Ethnicity and Socioeconomic Status

On many intelligence tests, ethnic groups differ in their average scores: Asian Americans tend to have the highest scores, followed by European Americans, Hispanic Americans, and African Americans (Loehlin, 2000). To a certain extent, these differences in test scores reflect group differences in socioeconomic status. Children from economically advantaged homes tend to have higher test scores than children from economically disadvantaged homes; and European American and Asian American families are more likely to be economically advantaged, whereas Hispanic American and African American families are more likely to be economically disadvantaged. Nevertheless, when children of comparable socioeconomic status are compared, group differences in IQ test scores are reduced but not eliminated (Brooks-Gunn, Klebanov, & Duncan, 1996). Let's look at four explanations for this difference.

**A ROLE FOR GENETICS?**   On page 256, you learned that heredity helps determine a child's intelligence: Smart parents tend to beget smart children. Does this also mean that group differences in IQ scores reflect genetic differences? No. Most researchers agree that there is no evidence that some ethnic groups have more "smart genes" than others. Instead, they believe that the environment is largely responsible for these differences (Bronfenbrenner & Morris, 1998; Neisser et al., 1996).

A popular analogy (Lewontin, 1976) demonstrates the thinking here. Imagine two kinds of corn: Each kind produces both short and tall plants; and height is known to be due to heredity. If one kind of corn grows in a good soil—with plenty of water and nutrients—the mature plants will reach their genetically determined heights; some short, some tall. If the other kind of corn grows in poor soil, few of the plants will reach their full height and overall the plants of this kind will be much shorter. Thus, even though height is quite heritable for each type of corn, the difference in height between the two groups is due solely to the quality of the environment.

The same conclusion applies to ethnic groups. Differences within ethnic groups are partly due to heredity, but differences among groups apparently reflect environmental influences. Three potential influences have been studied and we'll look at these next.

**EXPERIENCE WITH TEST CONTENTS.**   Some critics contend that differences in test scores reflect bias in the tests themselves. They argue that test items reflect the cultural heritage of the test creators, most of whom are economically advantaged European Americans, and so tests are biased against economically disadvantaged children from other groups. They point to test items like this one:

A conductor is to an orchestra as a teacher is to what?

book     school     class     eraser

Children whose background includes exposure to orchestras are more likely to answer this question correctly than children who lack this exposure.

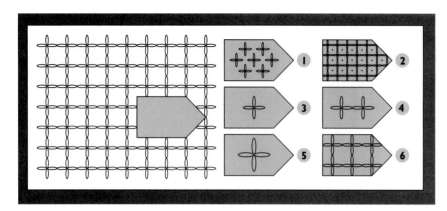

FIG. 9–8

**The problem of bias led to the development of culture-fair intelligence tests, which include test items based on experiences common to many cultures.** An example is Raven's Progressive Matrices, which consist solely of items like the one shown here. Examinees are asked to select the piece that would complete the design correctly (6, in this case). Although items like this are thought to reduce the impact of specific experience, ethnic group differences remain in performance on so-called culture-fair intelligence tests (Anastasi, 1988; Herrnstein & Murray, 1994). Apparently, familiarity with test-related items per se is not the key factor responsible for group differences in performance.

**STEREOTYPE THREAT.** When people know that they belong to a group that is said to lack skill in a domain, this makes them anxious when performing in that domain for fear of confirming the stereotype and they often do poorly as a result. **This self-fulfilling prophecy, in which knowledge of stereotypes leads to anxiety and reduced performance consistent with the original stereotype, is called stereotype threat.** Applied to intelligence, the argument is that African American children experience stereotype threat when they take intelligence tests and this contributes to their lower scores (Steele, 1997; Steele & Aronson, 1995). For example, imagine two 10-year-olds taking an intelligence test for admission to a special program for gifted children. The European American child worries that if he fails the test, he won't be admitted to the program. The African American child has the same fears but also worries that if he does poorly it will confirm the stereotype that African American children don't get good scores on IQ tests.

> Because they worry about stereotypes and are wary in testing situations, children from minority groups often get lower scores on intelligence tests.

**TEST-TAKING SKILLS.** The impact of experience and cultural values can extend beyond particular items to a child's familiarity with the entire testing situation. Tests underestimate a child's intelligence if, for example, the child's culture encourages children to solve problems in collaboration with others and discourages them from excelling as individuals. What's more, because they are wary of questions posed by unfamiliar adults, many economically disadvantaged children often answer test questions by saying, "I don't know." Obviously, this strategy guarantees an artificially low test score. When these children are given extra time to feel at ease with the examiner, they respond less often with "I don't know" and their test scores improve considerably (Zigler & Finn-Stevenson, 1992).

**CONCLUSION: INTERPRETING TEST SCORES.** If all tests reflect cultural influences, at least to some degree, how should we interpret test scores? Remember that tests assess successful adaptation to a particular cultural context. Most intelligence tests predict success in a school environment, which usually espouses middle-class values. Regardless of ethnic group—African American, Hispanic American, or European American—a child with a high test score has the intellectual skills needed for academic work based on middle-class values. A child with a low test score, like Charlene in the module-opening vignette, apparently lacks those skills. Does a low score mean Charlene is destined to fail in school? No. It simply means that, based on her current skills, she's unlikely to do well. Improving Charlene's skills will improve her school performance.

I want to end this module by emphasizing a crucial point: By focusing on groups of people, it's easy to overlook the fact that the average difference in IQ scores between various ethnic groups is relatively small compared to the entire range of scores for these groups. You can easily find youngsters with high IQ scores from all ethnic groups, just as you can find youngsters with low IQ scores from all groups. And, in the next module, we'll look at children at these extremes of ability.

## CHECK YOUR LEARNING

**1.** The Stanford-Binet included the idea of the intelligence quotient, which was _____, multiplied by 100.

**2.** The WISC-III provides a verbal IQ score and a _____.

**3.** Infant intelligence tests, such as the Bayley Scales, do not predict childhood IQ scores but are useful for _____.

**4.** Modern intelligence tests are typically validated by _____.

**5.** As identical twins develop, their IQ scores _____.

**6.** As adopted children get older, their IQ scores increasingly resemble the IQ scores of their _____ parents.

**7.** Evidence for the impact of environment on intelligence comes from studies of children's homes, from historical change in IQ scores, and from _____.

**8.** The problem of cultural bias on intelligence tests led to the development of _____.

**NATURE AND NURTURE**
What findings document the roles of heredity and environment on intelligence?

**Answers:** (1) MA/CA, (2) performance IQ score, (3) determining whether development is progressing normally, (4) showing that test scores correlate with measures of performance in school, (5) follow the same developmental profile, (6) biological, (7) studies on the impact of intervention and enrichment programs, (8) culture-fair intelligence tests, which have test items common to many cultures

# Special Children, Special Needs 9.3

## LEARNING OBJECTIVES

- What are the characteristics of gifted and creative children?
- What are the different forms of mental retardation?
- What are learning disabilities?

Gifted and Creative Children

Children with Mental Retardation

Children with Learning Disabilities

> *Sanjit, a second grader, has taken two separate intelligence tests, and both times he had above-average scores. Nevertheless, Sanjit absolutely cannot read. Letters and words are as mysterious to him as Metallica's music would be to Mozart. His parents took him to an ophthalmologist, who determined that Sanjit's vision was 20-20; nothing is wrong with his eyes. What is wrong?*

Throughout history, societies have recognized children with limited mental abilities as well as those with extraordinary talents. Today, we know much about the extremes of human talents. We'll begin this module with a look at gifted and creative children. Then we'll look at children with mental retardation and learning disabilities and discover why Sanjit can't read.

## Gifted and Creative Children

In many respects the boy in the photo, Bernie, is an ordinary middle-class 12-year-old: He is the goalie on his soccer team, takes piano lessons on Saturday mornings, sings in his church youth choir, and likes to go roller blading. However, when it comes to intelligence and academic prowess, Bernie leaves the ranks of the ordinary. He received a score of 175 on an intelligence test and is taking a college calculus course. **Bernie is gifted, which traditionally has referred to individuals with scores of 130 or greater on intelligence tests** (Horowitz & O'Brien, 1986).

Because giftedness was traditionally defined in terms of IQ scores, exceptional ability is often associated primarily with academic skill. But modern definitions of giftedness are broader and include exceptional talent in an assortment of areas, including art, music, creative writing, and dance (Robinson & Clinkenbeard, 1998; Winner, 2000).

Whether the field is music or math, though, exceptional talent seems to have several prerequisites (Rathunde & Csikszentmihalyi, 1993):

- The child loves the subject and has an almost overwhelming desire to master it.
- Instruction to develop the child's special talent usually begins at an early age with inspiring and talented teachers.
- Parents are committed to promoting their child's talent.

The message here is that exceptional talent must be nurtured. Without encouragement and support from parents and stimulating and challenging mentors, a youngster's talents will wither. Talented children need a curriculum that is challenging and complex; they need teachers who know how to foster talent; and they need like-minded peers who stimulate their interests (Feldhusen, 1996).

The stereotype is that gifted children are often thought to be emotionally troubled and unable to get along with their peers. In reality, gifted youngsters tend to be more mature than their peers and have fewer emotional problems (Luthar, Zigler, & Goldstein, 1992).

CREATIVITY. If you ever saw the movie *Amadeus*, you know the difference between being talented and being creative. Mozart and Salieri were rival composers in Europe during the 18th century. Both were talented, ambitious musicians. Yet, more than 200 years later, Mozart is revered and Salieri is all but forgotten. Why? Then and now, Mozart was considered creative but Salieri was not. What is creativity, and how does it differ from intelligence?

**Intelligence is associated with convergent thinking, using information that is provided to determine a standard, correct answer. In contrast, creativity is associated with divergent thinking, where the aim is not a single correct answer (often there isn't one) but novel and unusual lines of thought** (Callahan, 2000).

Divergent thinking is often measured by asking children to produce many ideas in response to some specific stimulus (Kogan, 1983). For example, children might be asked to name different uses for a common object, such as a coat hanger. Or they might be shown a page filled with circles and asked to draw as many different pictures as they can, as shown in the figure. Both the number of responses and the originality of the responses are used to measure creativity.

FIG. 9–9

Creativity, like giftedness, must be cultivated. The "Improving Children's Lives" feature gives some guidelines for fostering children's creativity.

## IMPROVING CHILDREN'S LIVES

### Fostering Creativity

Here are some guidelines for helping children be more creative.

1. Encourage children to take risks. Not all novel ideas bear fruit; some won't work and some are silly. But only by repeatedly thinking in novel and unusual ways are children likely to produce something truly original.

2. Encourage children to think of alternatives to conventional wisdom. Have them think what would happen if accepted practices were changed. For example, "What would life be like without cars?" or "Why not eat breakfast in the evening and dinner in the morning?"

3. Praise children for working hard. As the saying goes, creativity is one part inspiration and nine parts perspiration. The raw creative insight must be polished to achieve the luster of a finished product.

4. Help children get over the "I'm not creative" hurdle. Too often they believe that only others are creative. Assure children that anyone who follows these guidelines will become more creative.

Gifted and creative children represent one extreme of human ability. At the other extreme are youngsters with mental retardation, the topic of the next section.

## Children with Mental Retardation

"Little David" was the oldest of four children. He learned to sit only days before his first birthday, he began to walk at 2, and he said his first words as a 3-year-old. By age 5, David was far behind his age-mates developmentally. David had Down syndrome, described in Module 3.2. An extra 21st chromosome caused David's retarded mental development.

**Mental retardation refers to substantially below-average intelligence and problems adapting to an environment that emerge before the age of 18.** Below-average intelligence is defined as a score of 70 or less on an intelligence test such as the Stanford-Binet. Adaptive behavior is usually evaluated from interviews with a parent or other caregiver and refers to the daily living skills needed to live, work, and play in the community—skills for caring for oneself and social skills. Only individuals who are under 18, have problems in these areas, and IQ scores of 70 or less are considered mentally retarded (Detterman, Gabriel, & Ruthsatz, 2002).

Mental retardation is defined by below-average scores on intelligence tests and problems adapting to the environment.

TYPES OF MENTAL RETARDATION    Your image of a mentally retarded child may be someone with Down syndrome, like the child shown on page 64. In reality, mentally retarded individuals are just as varied as nonretarded people. How, then, can we describe this variety? One approach is to distinguish the causes of mental retardation. **Some cases of mental retardation—no more than 25 percent—can be traced to a specific biological or physical problem and are known as organic mental retardation.** Down syndrome is the most common organic form of mental retardation. Other types of mental retardation apparently do not involve biological damage. **Familial mental retardation simply represents the lower end of the normal distribution of intelligence.**

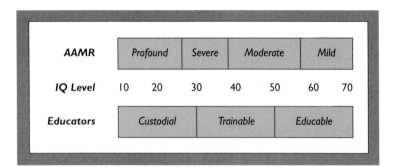

| AAMR | Profound | Severe | Moderate | Mild |
|------|----------|--------|----------|------|
| **IQ Level** | 10    20    30 | 40    50 | 60    70 | |
| **Educators** | Custodial | Trainable | Educable | |

FIG. 9–10

Organic mental retardation is usually substantial, and familial mental retardation is usually less pronounced. The American Association on Mental Retardation (AAMR) identifies four levels of retardation. The levels, along with the range of IQ scores associated with each level, are shown in the chart. Also shown are the three levels of retardation typically used by educators in the United States (Cipani, 1991).

Fortunately, the most severe forms of mental retardation are relatively uncommon. Profound, severe, and moderate retardation together make up only 10 percent of all cases. Individuals who are profoundly and severely retarded usually have so few skills that they must be supervised constantly. Consequently, they usually live in institutions for persons with mental retardation, where they can sometimes be taught self-help skills such as dressing, feeding, and toileting (Reid, Wilson, & Faw, 1991).

Persons who are moderately retarded may develop the intellectual skills of a nonretarded 7- or 8-year-old. With this level of functioning, they can sometimes support themselves, typically at a sheltered workshop, where they perform simple tasks under close supervision.

The remaining 90 percent of individuals with mental retardation are classified as mildly or educable mentally retarded. These individuals go to school and can master many academic skills, but at an older age than a nonretarded child. Individuals with mild mental retardation can lead independent lives. Like the man in the photograph, many people who are mildly retarded work. Some marry. Comprehensive training programs that focus on vocational and social skills help individuals with mild mental retardation be productive citizens and satisfied human beings (Ellis & Rusch, 1991), as you can see by learning more about "little David" in the "Real Children" feature.

## REAL CHILDREN

### Little David, the Rest of the Story

"Little David," so named because his father was also named David, was the oldest of four children; none of his siblings was mentally retarded. As the children grew up, they interacted the way most siblings do—laughing and playing together and sometimes fighting and arguing. Beginning as a teenager and continuing into adulthood, each day David took a city bus from home to his job at a sheltered workshop. He worked 6 hours at such tasks as making bows for packages and stuffing envelopes. He saved his earnings to buy what became his prized possessions—a camera, a color TV, and a VCR. As David's siblings entered adulthood, they began their own families. David relished his new role as "Uncle David" and looked forward to visits from his nieces and nephews. As David entered his 40s, he began to suffer memory loss and was often confused. When he died, at age 47, family and friends grieved over their loss. Yet they all marveled at the richness of David's life. By any standards, David had led a full and satisfying life.

Little David's mental retardation represents one instance of a special need; Bernie's precocity represents another. A third type of special-needs child is one with a learning disability.

## Children with Learning Disabilities

For some children with normal intelligence, learning is a struggle. **These youngsters have a learning disability: they (a) have difficulty mastering an academic subject, (b) have normal intelligence, and (c) are not suffering from other conditions that could explain poor performance, such as sensory impairment or inadequate instruction** (Hammill, 1990).

In the United States, about 5 percent of school-age children are classified as learning disabled, which translates into roughly 2 million youngsters (Moats & Lyon, 1993). The number of distinct disabilities and the degree of overlap among them are still debated (Stanovich, 1993). However, one common classification scheme distinguishes disability in language (including listening, speaking, and writing), in reading, and in arithmetic (Dockrell & McShane, 1993).

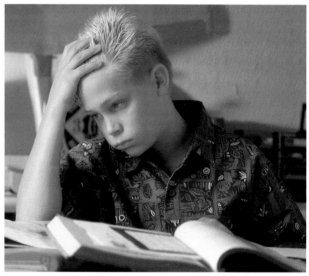

The variety of learning disabilities complicates the task for teachers and researchers because it suggests that each type of learning disability may have its own cause and treatment (Lyon, 1996). Take reading, the most common area of learning disability, as an example. Many children with a reading disability have problems in phonological awareness (described in Module 8.3), which refers to understanding and using the sounds in written and oral language. For a reading-disabled child like Sanjit (in the vignette that opened this module) or the boy in the photograph, all vowels sound alike. Thus *pin* sounds like *pen*, which sounds like *pan*. These youngsters benefit from explicit, extensive instruction on the connections between letters and their sounds (Lyon, 1996).

The "Focus on Research" feature looks at one such successful training program.

## FOCUS ON RESEARCH

### Improving Reading Skill in Children with Reading Disability

*Who were the investigators, and what was the aim of the study?* Most reading experts agree that, compared to children who read normally, children with reading disability have difficulty translating print into sound. Experts also agree that the aim of treatment should be to improve such translation skills. Where experts disagree is in the best way to achieve this aim. Some emphasize exercises in which children manipulate sounds and letters in syllables (e.g., "Which one is 'ook'?" "Which is 'koo'?"). Other experts emphasize articulatory awareness in which children learn the positions of their mouth and tongue as they make different vowel and consonant sounds. Barbara Wise, Jerry Ring, and Richard Olson (1999) wanted to compare the effects of these two approaches in improving reading in children with reading disability.

*How did the investigators measure the topic of interest?* Children in the study were assigned to one of four conditions. Some were in a control group that received no special treatment. Others were in a sound-manipulation condition, an articulatory-awareness condition, or a condition that included both sound-manipulation and articulatory-awareness. The training included exercises like those that I just mentioned

> Children with reading disability have problems understanding and using language sounds.

and lasted 6 months. All children took many reading-related tests before and after training. For simplicity, I'm going to focus on just one outcome measure: children's ability to read individual words accurately.

*Who were the children in the study?* Wise and her colleagues tested 122 children with reading disability from grades 2 through 5. About one-fourth of the children were assigned to each of the four conditions.

*What was the design of the study?* The study was experimental. The independent variable was the condition to which the child was assigned; the dependent variable was the number of words that children read accurately. The study was also longitudinal: Students were tested in October and again in May of the same school year.

*Were there ethical concerns with the study?* No. Parental permission was obtained for all children who participated. You may question the ethics of denying treatment to one-fourth of the children (those in the control group). However, all these children were promised treatment in the following school year and this was deemed an acceptable risk by the review panel at the University of Colorado, where the study was conducted.

*What were the results?* As I mentioned, the children were given a large battery of tasks. On some of the tasks, the training groups differed. For example, children who had sound-manipulation training were more accurate on phoneme deletion tasks (e.g., "Say 'pran' without the 'r'?"). But the most important result is shown in the graph: In actual reading, the various training methods were equally effective. That is, in terms of the increase in reading skill from before training to after training, all three experimental groups improved 12 to 15 percent, compared to 4 percent for the control group.

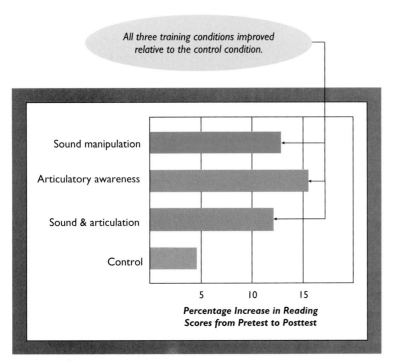

FIG. 9–11

*What did the investigators conclude?* Children with reading disability must learn about language sounds, but apparently there is no single best method. Consequently, teachers can be successful with either method and can alter their approach based on their own background and their students' strengths.

*What converging evidence would strengthen these conclusions?* Two types of findings would complement the results of this study. First, it would be useful to include a group of children who read normally as another way to assess the effectiveness of training. By comparing the performance of this group to the groups of children who received training, we could determine whether training improved children's reading to normal or near-normal levels. Second, it would be important to test these children in subsequent years to determine whether the training has long-lasting benefits. 

The findings in the "Focus on Research" feature are good news for children with learning disabilities, such as reading disability. The key to helping these children is to move beyond the generic label *learning disability* to pinpoint specific cognitive and academic deficits that hamper an individual child's performance in school (e.g., for children with reading disability, processing language sounds). Then instruction can be specifically tailored to improve the child's skills (Moats & Lyon, 1993).

Planning effective instruction for children with learning disabilities is much easier said than done, however, because diagnosing learning disability is very difficult. Some children have both reading and language disabilities; other children have reading and arithmetic disabilities. Despite these difficulties, with ingenuity, hard work, and care, children with learning disabilities—and all exceptional children, for that matter—can develop their full intellectual potential.

## CHECK YOUR LEARNING

**1.** Traditionally, giftedness was defined solely in terms of _____.

**2.** Creativity is associated with _____ thinking, in which the goal is to think in novel and unusual directions.

**3.** Cases of _____ mental retardation are due to specific biological or physical problems.

**4.** Most individuals with mental retardation are classified as _____.

**5.** Children with a learning disability are unable to master an academic subject, have _____, and have no other condition, such as sensory impairment, that could explain their poor performance.

**6.** Children with reading disability often benefit from instruction on _____.

**CONNECTIONS**
How does mental retardation show connections between motor, cognitive, and social development?

**Answers:** (1) IQ scores, (2) divergent, (3) organic, (4) mildly or educably retarded, (5) normal intelligence, (6) connections between letters and their sounds

# Unifying Themes: Nature and Nurture

In this chapter, I want to underscore the theme that *development is always jointly influenced by heredity and environment.* In no other area of child development is this theme as important, because the implications for social policy are so profound. If intelligence were completely determined by heredity, for example, intervention programs would be a waste of time and tax dollars because no amount of experience would change nature's prescription for intelligence. But we've seen several times in this chapter that neither heredity nor environment is all-powerful when it comes to intelligence. Studies of twins, for example, remind us that heredity clearly has substantial impact on IQ scores. Identical twins' IQs are consistently more alike than fraternal twins', a result that documents heredity's influence on intelligence. Yet, at the same time, intervention studies such as Head Start and the Carolina Abecedarian Project show that intelligence is malleable. Children's intelligence can be enhanced by intensely stimulating environments.

Thus, heredity imposes some limits on how a child's intelligence will develop, but the limits are fairly modest. We can nurture all children's intelligence considerably if we are willing to invest the time and effort.

## See for Yourself

We've seen that the definition of intelligence differs across cultural settings. See how parents define intelligence by asking them to rate the importance of four common aspects of intelligence:

- Problem-solving skill (thinking before acting, seeing different sides to a problem)
- Verbal skill (speaking clearly, having a large vocabulary)
- Creative skill (asking many questions, trying new things)

- Social skill (playing and working well with other people, respecting and caring for others)

Ask parents to rate the importance of each element on a 6-point scale, where 1 means extremely unimportant to intelligence and 6 means extremely important. Try to ask parents from different ethnic groups; then compare your results with other students' results to see if parents' views of intelligence are similar or different and if cultural background affects parents' definitions. See for yourself!

## Resources

For more information about...

**the lives of brilliant and creative people**, read Howard Gardner's *Creating Minds* (Basic Books, 1993), which illustrates each different intelligence in Gardner's theory by tracing its development in the life of an extraordinary person, including Albert Einstein, Martha Graham, and Pablo Picasso.

**learning disabilities**, visit the Web site of the National Center for Learning Disabilities **www.ncld.org**

## Key Terms

componential subtheory 249
components 249
contextual subtheory 247
convergent thinking 262
crystallized intelligence 245
culture-fair intelligence tests 260
divergent thinking 262
dynamic testing 255
emotional intelligence 247
experiential subtheory 249
familial mental retardation 263

fluid intelligence 245
gifted 262
intelligence quotient (IQ) 251
learning disability 265
mental age (MA) 251
mental retardation 263
organic mental retardation 263
psychometricians 244
savants 246
stereotype threat 260
triarchic theory 247

## 9.1 What Is Intelligence?

### Psychometric Theories
Psychometric approaches to intelligence include theories that describe intelligence as a general factor as well as theories that include specific factors. Hierarchical theories include both general intelligence as well as various specific skills, such as verbal and spatial ability.

### Gardner's Theory of Multiple Intelligences
Gardner's theory of multiple intelligences proposes nine distinct intelligences. Three are found in psychometric theories (linguistic, logical-mathematical, and spatial intelligence), but six are new (musical, bodily-kinesthetic, interpersonal, intrapersonal, naturalistic, and existential intelligence). Gardner's theory has stimulated research on nontraditional forms of intelligence, such as emotional intelligence. The theory also has implications for education, suggesting, for example, that schools should adjust teaching to each child's unique intellectual strengths.

### Sternberg's Triarchic Theory
Robert Sternberg's triarchic theory includes (a) the contextual subtheory, which specifies that intelligent behavior must always be considered in relation to the individual's culture, (b) the experiential subtheory, which specifies that intelligence is associated with the familiarity of the task, and (c) the componential subtheory, which specifies that intelligent behavior involves organizing basic cognitive processes into an efficient strategy for completing a task.

## 9.2 Measuring Intelligence

### Binet and the Development of Intelligence Testing
Binet created the first intelligence test to identify students who would have difficulty in school. Using this work, Terman created the Stanford-Binet, which introduced the concept of the intelligence quotient (IQ). Another widely used test, the WISC-III, provides IQs based on verbal and performance subtests. Infant tests, such as the Bayley Scales, typically assess mental and motor development.

### Do Tests Work?
In the short term, intelligence tests are reliable, which means that people usually get consistent scores on the tests. In the longer term, scores on infant intelligence tests do not predict adult IQ scores, but infant habituation predicts childhood IQs, and preschool IQ scores predict adult IQs. Intelligence tests are reasonably valid measures of achievement in school. They also predict people's performance in the workplace. Dynamic tests are designed to improve validity by measuring children's potential for future learning.

### Hereditary and Environmental Factors
Evidence for the impact of heredity on IQ comes from the findings that (a) siblings' IQ scores become more alike as siblings become more similar genetically, and (b) adopted children's IQ scores are more like their biological parents' test scores than their adoptive parents' scores. Evidence for the impact of the environment comes from the finding that children who live in responsive, well-organized home environments tend to have higher IQ scores, as do children who participate in intervention programs.

### Impact of Ethnicity and Socioeconomic Status
Ethnic groups differ in their average scores on IQ tests. This difference is not due to genetics or to familiarity with specific test items but is due to children's familiarity and comfort with the testing situation. Nevertheless, IQ scores remain valid predictors of school success because middle-class experience is often a prerequisite for school success.

## 9.3 Special Children, Special Needs

### Gifted and Creative Children
Traditionally, gifted children have been those with high scores on IQ tests. Modern definitions of giftedness are broader and include exceptional talent in, for example, the arts. Gifted children are socially mature and emotionally stable.

Creativity is associated with divergent thinking, thinking in novel and unusual directions. Tests of divergent thinking can predict which children are most likely to be creative when they are older. Creativity can be fostered by experiences that encourage children to think flexibly and explore alternatives.

### Children with Mental Retardation
Individuals with mental retardation have IQ scores of 70 or lower and problems in adaptive behavior. Organic mental retardation is due to specific biological or physical causes; familial mental retardation reflects the lower end of the normal distribution of intelligence. Most retarded persons are classified as mildly or educably retarded; they attend school, work, and have families.

### Children with Learning Disabilities
Children with a learning disability have normal intelligence but have difficulty mastering specific academic subjects. The most common is reading disability, which often can be traced to inadequate understanding and use of language sounds. When such language-related skills are taught, children's reading improves.

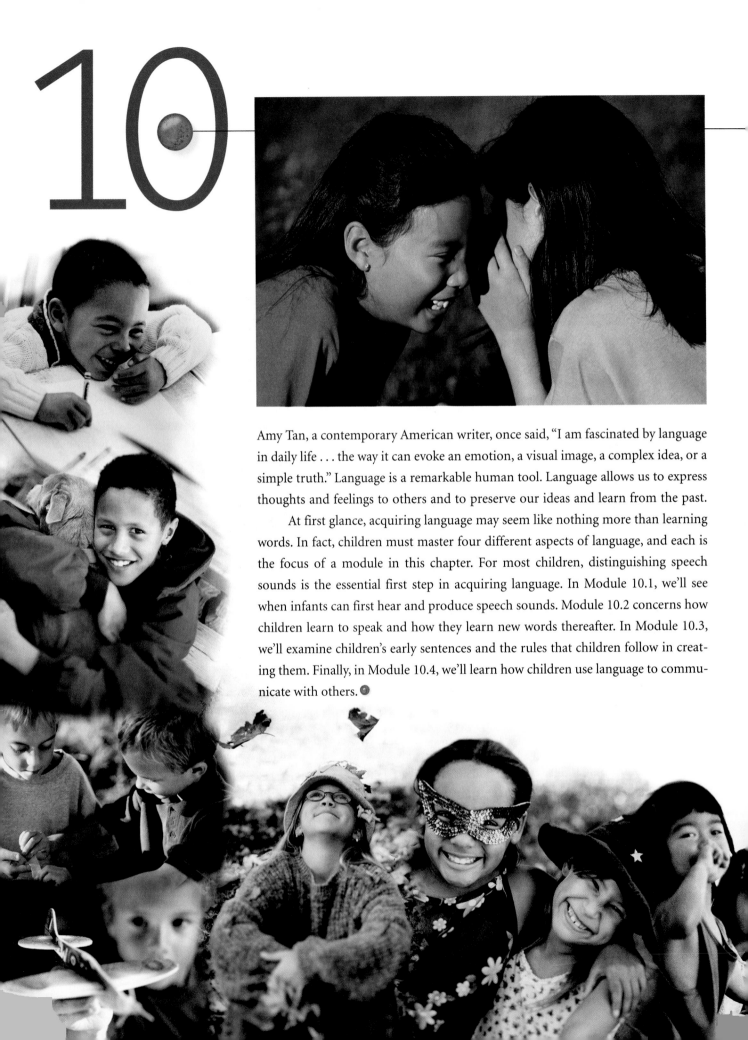

# 10

Amy Tan, a contemporary American writer, once said, "I am fascinated by language in daily life . . . the way it can evoke an emotion, a visual image, a complex idea, or a simple truth." Language is a remarkable human tool. Language allows us to express thoughts and feelings to others and to preserve our ideas and learn from the past.

At first glance, acquiring language may seem like nothing more than learning words. In fact, children must master four different aspects of language, and each is the focus of a module in this chapter. For most children, distinguishing speech sounds is the essential first step in acquiring language. In Module 10.1, we'll see when infants can first hear and produce speech sounds. Module 10.2 concerns how children learn to speak and how they learn new words thereafter. In Module 10.3, we'll examine children's early sentences and the rules that children follow in creating them. Finally, in Module 10.4, we'll learn how children use language to communicate with others.

# Language and Communication

**10.1**  The Road to Speech

**10.2**  Learning the Meanings of Words

**10.3**  Speaking in Sentences

**10.4**  Using Language to Communicate

# 10.1

## The Road to Speech

**LEARNING OBJECTIVES**

- What are phonemes, and how well can infants distinguish them?
- How does infant-directed speech help children learn about language?
- What is babbling, and how does it become more complex in older infants?

> As a 7-month-old, Chelsea began to make her first wordlike sounds, saying "dah" and "nuh." Several weeks later, she began to repeat these syllables, saying "dah-dah" and "nuh-nuh." By 11 months her speech resembled sentences with stressed words: "dah-NUH-bah-BAH!" Chelsea's parents were astonished that her sentences could sound so much like real speech yet still be absolutely meaningless!

From birth, infants make sounds—they laugh, cry, and, like Chelsea, produce sounds that resemble speech. Yet, for most of their first year, infants do not talk. This contrast raises two important questions about infants as nonspeaking creatures. First, can babies who are unable to speak understand any of the speech that is directed to them? Second, how do infants like Chelsea progress from crying to more effective methods of oral communication, such as speech? We'll answer both questions in this module, but let's begin by considering exactly what we mean by *language*.

## Elements of Language

When you think of language, what comes to mind? English, perhaps? Or maybe German, Spanish, Korean, or Zulu? What about American Sign Language? **Defined broadly, language is a system that relates sounds (or gestures) to meaning.** Languages are expressed in many forms—through speech, writing, and gesture. Furthermore, languages consist of different subsystems. Spoken languages usually involve four distinct but interrelated elements:

*The elements of language include phonology, semantics, grammar, and pragmatics.*

- **Phonology refers to the sounds of a language.** For example, all the different words in English are constructed from about 45 different sounds.
- **Semantics is the study of words and their meaning.** *Webster's Third New International Dictionary* has roughly a half million entries, and a typical college-educated English speaker has a vocabulary of about 150,000 words.
- **Grammar refers to the rules used to describe the structure of a language. The most important element of grammar is** syntax, **rules that specify how words are combined to form sentences.**
- **Pragmatics is the study of how people use language to communicate effectively.** Our communication must be appropriate, suited to the audience and occasion. We wouldn't, for example, use fancy vocabulary and long sentences with a 5-year-old.

Learning language involves mastering each of these elements. Children must learn to hear the differences in speech sounds and how to produce them; they must learn the meaning of words and rules for combining them in sentences; and they must learn appropriate and effective ways to talk with others. In the remainder of this module (and the three others in this chapter), we'll see how children come to understand language and speak it themselves.

## Perceiving Speech

We learned in Module 6.1 that even newborn infants hear remarkably well. But can babies distinguish speech sounds? To answer this question, we first need to know more about the elements of speech. **The basic building blocks of language are phonemes, unique sounds that can be joined to create words.** Phonemes include consonant sounds such as the sound of *t* in *toe* and *tap* along with vowel sounds such as the sound of *e* in *get* and *bed*. Infants can distinguish most of these sounds, many of them by as early as 1 month after birth (Aslin, Jusczyk, & Pisoni, 1998).

FIG. 10–1

How do we know that infants can distinguish different vowels and consonants? Researchers have devised a number of clever techniques to determine if babies respond differently to distinct sounds. One approach is illustrated in the diagram. A rubber nipple is connected to a tape recorder so that sucking turns on the tape and sound comes out of a loudspeaker. In just a few minutes, 1-month-olds learn the relation between their sucking and the sound: They suck rapidly to hear a tape that consists of nothing more than the sound of *p* as in *pin, pet,* and *pat* (pronounced "puh").

After a few more minutes, infants seemingly tire of this repetitive sound and suck less often, which represents the habituation phenomenon described in Module 6.1. But, if the tape is changed to a different sound such as the sound of *b* in *bed, bat,* or *bird* (pronounced "buh") babies begin sucking rapidly again. Evidently, they recognize that the sound of *b* is different from *p* because they suck more often to hear the new sound (Jusczyk, 1995).

Of course, the language environment for young infants is not solely auditory; much exposure to language comes in face-to-face interaction with adults. These interactions provide many visual cues about sounds and infants use these cues: Shown a video of an adult saying "ba," infants notice when the adult looks to be saying "sha" even though the audio still presents "ba" (Lewkowicz, 2000a).

THE IMPACT OF LANGUAGE EXPOSURE.  Not all languages use the same set of phonemes; a distinction that is important in one language may be ignored in another. For example, unlike English, French and Polish differentiate between nasal and nonnasal vowels. To hear the difference, say the word *rod*. Now repeat it, but holding your nose. The subtle difference between the two sounds illustrates a nonnasal vowel (the first version of *rod*) and a nasal one (the second).

Because an infant might be exposed to any of the world's languages, it would be adaptive for young infants to be able to perceive a wide range of phonemes. In fact, research shows that infants can distinguish phonemes that are not used in their native language. For example, Japanese does not distinguish the consonant sound of *r* in *rip* from the sound of *l* in *lip* and Japanese adults trying to learn English have great difficulty distinguishing these sounds. At about 6 months, infants in both Japanese- and English-speaking environments can distinguish them, but by 11 or 12 months, only infants in English-speaking environments can (Werker & Tees, 1999).

Newborns apparently are biologically capable of hearing the entire range of phonemes in all languages worldwide. But as babies grow and are more exposed to a particular language, they only notice the linguistic distinctions that are meaningful in their own language. Specialization in one language apparently comes at a cost; the potential to hear other language sounds easily is lost (Best, 1995).

**IDENTIFYING WORDS.** Of course, hearing individual phonemes is only the first step in perceiving speech. One of the biggest challenges for infants is identifying recurring patterns of sounds—words. Imagine, for example, an infant overhearing this conversation between a parent and an older sibling:

> SIBLING: Jerry got a new *bike*.
>
> PARENT: Was his old *bike* broken?
>
> SIBLING: No. He'd saved his allowance to buy a new mountain *bike*.

An infant listening to this conversation hears *bike* three times. Can the infant learn from this experience? Yes. When 7- to 8-month-olds hear a word repeatedly in different sentences, they later pay more attention to this word than to words they haven't heard previously. Evidently, 7- and 8-month-olds can listen to sentences and recognize the sound patterns that they hear repeatedly (Juscyzk & Aslin, 1995; Saffran, Aslin, & Newport, 1996). And, by 6 months, infants pay more attention to content words (e.g., nouns, verbs) than to function words (e.g., articles, prepositions) and they look at the correct parent when they hear "mommy" or "daddy" (Shi & Werker, 2001; Tincoff & Jusczyk, 1999).

*Infants use stress and the co-occurrence of sounds to identify words in speech.*

In normal conversation, there are no silent gaps between words, so how do infants pick out words? Stress is one important clue. English contains many one-syllable words that are stressed and many two-syllable words that have a stressed syllable followed by an unstressed syllable (e.g., *dough'-nut, tooth'-paste, bas'-ket*). Infants pay more attention to stressed syllables than unstressed syllables, which is a good strategy for identifying the beginnings of words (Aslin et al., 1998; Mattys et al., 1999).

Of course, stress is not a foolproof sign. Many two-syllable words have stress on the second syllable (e.g., *gui-tar', sur-prise'*), so infants need other methods to identify words in speech. One method is statistical. Infants notice syllables that go together frequently (Jusczyk, 2002). For example, in a study by Aslin, Saffran, and Newport (1998), 8-month-olds heard the following sounds, which consisted of 4 three-syllable artificial words, said over and over in a random order.

<u>pa bi ku</u>  <u>go la tu</u>  <u>da ro pi</u>  <u>ti bu do</u>  <u>da ro pi</u>  <u>go la tu</u>  <u>pa bi ku</u>  <u>da ro pi</u>...

I've underlined the words and inserted gaps between them so that you can see them more easily, but in the study there were no breaks at all—just a steady flow of syllables for 3 minutes. Later, infants listened to these words less than to new words that were novel combinations of the same syllables. They had detected *pa bi ku, go la tu, da ro pi,* and *ti bu do* as familiar patterns and listened to them less than to words like *tu da ro,* a new word made up from syllables they'd already heard.

Yet another way that infants identify words is through their emerging knowledge of how sounds are used in their native language. For example, think about these two pairs of sounds: *s* followed by *t* and *s* followed by *d*. Both pairs of sounds are quite common at the end of one word and the beginning of the next: bu*s t*akes, ki*ss t*ook; thi*s d*og, pa*ss d*irectly. However, *s* and *t* occur frequently within a word (*st*op, li*st*, pe*st*, *st*ink) but *s* and *d* do not. Consequently, when *d* follows an *s*, it probably starts a new word. In fact, 9-month-olds follow rules like this one because when they hear novel words embedded in continuous speech, they're more likely to identify the novel word when the final sound in the preceding word occurs infrequently with the first sound of the novel word (Mattys & Jusczyk, 2001).

Thus, infants use many powerful tools to identify words in speech. Of course, they don't yet understand the meanings of these words; they just recognize a word as a distinct configuration of sounds.

Parents (and other adults) often help infants master language sounds by talking in a distinctive style. **In infant-directed speech, adults speak slowly and with exaggerated changes in pitch and loudness.** If you could hear the mother in the photo talking to her baby, you would notice that she alternates between speaking softly and loudly and between high and low pitches and that her speech seems very expressive emotionally (Trainor, Austin, & Desjardins, 2000). (Infant-directed speech is also known as *motherese*, because this form of speaking was first noted in mothers, although it's now known that most caregivers talk this way to infants.)

Infant-directed speech may attract infants' attention more than adult-directed speech (Kaplan et al., 1995; Lewkowicz, 2000a) because its slower pace and accentuated changes provide infants with increasingly more salient language clues. In addition, infant-directed speech includes especially good examples of vowels (Kuhl et al., 1997), which may help infants learn to distinguish these sounds.

Infant-directed speech, then, helps infants perceive the sounds that are fundamental to their language. Unfortunately, some babies cannot hear speech sounds because they are deaf. How can these infants best learn language? The "Child Development and Family Policy" feature addresses this question.

## CHILD DEVELOPMENT AND FAMILY POLICY

### Are Cochlear Implants Effective for Young Children?

About 2 infants and toddlers out of 1,000 are born deaf or have profound hearing loss before they master language. Of these youngsters, about 10 percent are born to deaf parents. In these cases, the child's deafness is usually detected early and parents communicate with their children using sign language. Deaf infants and toddlers seem to master sign language in much the same way and at about the same pace that hearing children master spoken language. For example, deaf 10-month-olds often babble in signs: They produce sequences of signs that are meaningless but resemble the tempo and duration of real signs.

The remaining 90 percent of deaf infants and toddlers have parents with normal hearing. For these children, communicating with signs is not really an option because their parents don't know sign language. Consequently, the usual recommendation for deaf children of hearing parents is to master spoken language, sometimes through methods that emphasize lip reading and speech therapy and sometimes with these methods along with signs and gestures. Unfortunately, with any of these methods, deaf children and parents rarely master spoken language. Their ability to produce and comprehend spoken language falls years behind their peers with normal language (Hoff, 2001).

Since the mid 1990s, however, deaf children have had a new option. As I described on page 147, the cochlear implant is a device that picks up speech sounds and converts them to electrical impulses that stimulate nerve cells in the ear. Cochlear implants are a tremendous benefit for people who lose their hearing after they master language. Adults with cochlear implants can converse readily with hearing speakers and some can converse on the phone (which is difficult otherwise because they can't lip read and because telephone lines sometimes distort speech sounds).

The potential benefit of cochlear implants for young children is a more controversial issue. Some critics (e.g., Lane, 1992; Lane & Bahan, 1998) argue that although cochlear implants benefit adults who have already learned language, there is no evidence that they can help young children to learn language. That is, the critics doubt that the quality of sensory information provided by cochlear implants is sufficient to guide language acquisition.

To determine whether cochlear implants should be recommended for deaf infants and toddlers, researchers would need to compare language development in deaf children who have cochlear implants with that in deaf children who do not. Mario Svirsky and his colleagues (2000) provided such data in a study of 70 children who had become profoundly deaf before age 3 and had received cochlear implants at an average age of $4\frac{1}{2}$ years. Their results were clear: Language development was enhanced in children with cochlear implants. That is, language skills improved more rapidly in children who had cochlear implants than in children who did not. In fact, after children had received cochlear implants, their language acquisition progressed at the same rate as language in children with normal hearing.

But this good news comes with several cautions. First, because most children did not receive their cochlear implants until 4 or 5 years of age, their language skills are still substantially behind that of hearing children. Second, a cochlear implant does not replace other forms of therapy for deaf children; a cochlear implant is used with these other forms to make them more effective. Third, the benefits of a cochlear implant are not the same for all children: Improvements in language are astonishing for some children but modest for others.

These findings, along with similar outcomes from other studies (e.g., Blamey et al., 2001; Szagun, 2001) have clear implications for policies that concern young deaf children. A cochlear implant is an effective tool that can enhance children's language; it should be made available to deaf children. At the same time, research is needed to determine, first, the value of cochlear implants for younger infants and, second, why cochlear implants are so beneficial for some children but not others.

## First Steps to Speech

As any new parent can testify, newborns and young babies make many sounds—they cry, burp, and sneeze. However, language-based sounds don't appear immediately. **At 2 months, infants begin to produce vowel-like sounds, such as "ooooooo" or "ahhhhhh," a phenomenon known as cooing.** Sometimes infants become quite excited as they coo, perhaps reflecting the joy of simply playing with sounds.

*Babbling appears at 5 or 6 months with a single consonant and vowel, then combines different speech sounds and, later, adds intonation.*

**After cooing comes babbling, speechlike sound that has no meaning.** A typical 6-month-old might say "dah" or "bah," utterances that sound like a single syllable consisting of a consonant and a vowel. Over the next few months, babbling becomes more elaborate as babies apparently experiment with more complex speech sounds. Older infants sometimes repeat a sound as in "bahbahbah" and begin to combine different sounds, "dahmahbah" (Hoff, 2001).

At roughly 8 to 11 months, infants' babbling sounds more like real speech because infants like Chelsea (in the vignette) stress some syllables and they vary the pitch of their speech (Davis et al., 2000). In English declarative sentences, for example, pitch first rises, then falls toward the end of the sentence. In questions, however, the pitch is level, then rises toward the end of the question. **This pattern of rising or falling pitch is known as intonation.** Older babies' babbling reflects these patterns: Babies who are brought up by English-speaking parents have both the declarative and question patterns of intonation in their babbling. Babies exposed to a language with different patterns of intonation, such as Japanese or French, reflect their language's intonation in their babbling (Levitt & Utman, 1992).

The appearance of intonation in babbling indicates a strong link between perception and production of speech: Infants' babbling is influenced by the characteristics of the speech that they hear. Beginning in the middle of the first year, infants try to reproduce the sounds of language that others use in trying to communicate with them (or, in the case of deaf infants with deaf parents, the signs that others use). Hearing *dog*, an infant may first say "dod," then "gog" before finally saying "dog" correctly. In the same way that beginning typists gradually link movements of their fingers with particular keys, through babbling infants learn to use their lips, tongue, and teeth to produce specific sounds, gradually making sounds that approximate real words (Poulson et al., 1991). Fortunately, learning to produce language sounds is easier for most babies than the cartoon suggests!

The ability to produce sound, coupled with the 1-year-old's advanced ability to perceive speech sounds, sets the stage for the infant's first true words. In Module 10.2, we'll see how this happens.

## CHECK YOUR LEARNING

**1.** Phonology, semantics, _____, and pragmatics are the four principal elements of language.

**2.** _____ is the study of how people use language to communicate appropriately and effectively.

**3.** Young infants can distinguish many language sounds, but older infants are more likely to notice only _____.

**4.** Infants identify words in speech by detecting stressed syllables and _____.

**5.** Adults using infant-directed speech speak slowly and exaggerate the loudness and _____ of their speech.

**6.** At about 2 months, infants begin to coo, making sounds that resemble _____.

**7.** At about 7 months, most infants' babbling begins to sound like real speech because infants start to stress some syllables and because they _____.

**ACTIVE CHILDREN**

How does the research in this module support the view that children actively try to interpret and understand the world?

# 10.2     Learning the Meanings of Words

**LEARNING OBJECTIVES**

● How do children make the transition from babbling to talking?

● What different styles of language learning do young children use?

● What rules do children follow to learn new words?

● What conditions foster children's learning of new words?

*Efrat is 20 months old and loves to talk. What amazes her parents is how quickly she adds words to her vocabulary. For example, the day her parents brought home a computer, Efrat watched as they set it up. The next day, she spontaneously pointed to the computer and said, "puter." This happens all the time— Efrat hears a word once or twice, then uses it correctly herself. Efrat's parents wonder how she does this, particularly because learning vocabulary in a foreign language is so difficult for them!*

At about their first birthday, most youngsters say their first words. Typically, these words are an extension of advanced babbling, consisting of a consonant-vowel pair that may be repeated. *Mama* and *dada* are probably the most common first words that stem from advanced babbling. Other early vocabulary words include animals, food, body parts, and clothing (Nelson, 1973). Also common are words that denote actions (for example, *go*). By age 2, most youngsters have a vocabulary of a few hundred words, and by age 6, a typical child's vocabulary includes over 10,000 words (Anglin, 1993).

Like Efrat, most children learn new words with extraordinary ease and speed. How do they do it? We'll answer that question in this module.

## Understanding Words as Symbols

When my daughter, Laura, was 9 months old, she sometimes babbled "bay-bay." A few months later, she still said "bay-bay" but with an important difference. As a 9-month-old, "bay-bay" was simply an interesting set of sounds that she made for no reason (at least, none that was obvious to us). As a 13-month-old, "bay-bay" was her way of saying "baby." What had happened between 9 and 13 months? Laura had begun to understand that speech is more than just entertaining sound. She realized that sounds form words that refer to objects, actions, and properties. Put another way, Laura recognized that words are symbols, entities that stand for other entities. She already had formed concepts such as "round, bouncy things" and "furry things that bark" and "little humans that adults carry" based on her own experiences. With the insight that speech sounds can denote these concepts, she began to match sound patterns (words) and concepts (Reich, 1986).

If this argument is correct, we should find that children use symbols in other areas, not just in language. They do. Gestures are symbols, and like the baby in the photo, infants begin to gesture shortly before their first birthday (Goodwyn & Acredolo, 1993). Young children may smack their lips to indicate hunger or wave "bye-bye" when leaving. In these cases, gestures and words convey a message equally well. Both reflect the child's developing ability to use symbols to represent actions and objects, which is one of the grand achievements of human development.

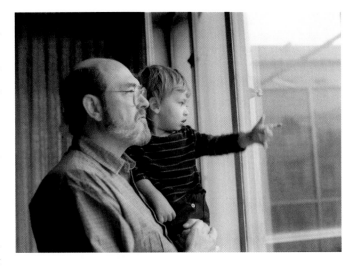

## Styles of Learning Language

As youngsters expand their vocabulary, they often adopt a distinctive style of learning language (Bates, Bretherton, & Snyder, 1988). **Some children have a referential style; their vocabularies mainly consist of words that name objects, persons, or actions. Other children have an expressive style; their vocabularies include some names but also many social phrases that are used like a single word, such as "go away," "what'd you want?" and "I want it."**

Katherine Nelson (1973) was the investigator who discovered these two basic styles of learning language. She studied 18 children for about a year, starting at approximately their first birthdays, a period during which the children's vocabularies increased from fewer than 10 words to nearly 200. She visited each child monthly for about an hour to tape-record samples of spontaneous speech and to test language development.

By the time children had 50-word vocabularies—typically at about $1\frac{1}{2}$ years—two distinct groups had emerged. Children in the referential group had vocabularies dominated by names of objects, persons, or actions, such as *milk, Jo-Jo,* and *up.* Other children, the expressive group, learned some names but knew a much higher percentage of words that were used in social interactions (*go away, I want it, lemme see*) and question words (*what, where*). For example, Rachel, a referential child, had 41 name words in her 50-word vocabulary but only 2 words for social interaction or questions. Elizabeth, an expressive child, had a more balanced vocabulary: 24 name words and 14 for social interactions and questions.

We know now that referential and expressive styles represent end points on a continuum; most children are somewhere in between. For children with referential emphasis, language is primarily an intellectual tool—a means of learning and talking about objects (Masur, 1995). In contrast, for children with expressive emphasis, language is more of a social tool—a way of enhancing interactions with others. Of course, both of these functions—intellectual and social—are important functions of language, which explains why most children blend the referential and expressive styles of learning language.

> Language is primarily an intellectual tool for referential children and primarily a social tool for expressive children.

## Fast Mapping Meanings to Words

Once children have the insight that a word can symbolize an object or action, their vocabularies grow slowly at first. A typical 15-month-old, for example, may learn 2 to 3 new words each week. **However, at about 18 months, many children experience a naming explosion during which they learn new words—particularly names of**

**objects—much more rapidly than before.** Children now learn 10 or more new words each week (Fenson et al., 1994).

This rapid rate of word learning is astonishing when we realize that most words have many plausible but incorrect referents. To illustrate, imagine what's going through the mind of the child in the photo. The mother has just pointed to the flowers, saying, "Flowers. These are flowers. See the flowers." To the mother (and you), this all seems crystal clear and incredibly straightforward. But what might a child learn from this episode? Perhaps the correct referent for "flowers." But a youngster could, just as reasonably, conclude that "flowers" refers to the petals, to the color of the flowers, or to the mother's actions in pointing to the flowers.

Surprisingly, though, most youngsters learn the proper meanings of simple words in just a few presentations. **Children's ability to connect new words to their meanings so rapidly that they cannot be considering all possible meanings for the new word is termed fast mapping.** How can young children learn new words so rapidly? Researchers believe that many distinct factors contribute to young children's rapid word learning (Hollich et al., 2000).

**JOINT ATTENTION.** Parents encourage word learning by carefully watching what interests their children. When toddlers touch or look at an object, parents often label it for them. When a youngster points to a banana, a parent may say, "Banana, that's a banana." Of course, to take advantage of this help, infants must be able to tell when parents are labeling instead of just conversing. In fact, when adults label an unfamiliar object, 18- to 20-month-olds assume that the label is the object's name *only* when adults show signs that they are referring to the object. For example, toddlers are more likely to learn the name of an object or action when adults look at the object or action while saying its name than when adults look elsewhere while labeling (Baldwin et al., 1996; Poulin-Dubois & Forbes, 2002). Thus, beginning in the toddler years, parents and children work together to create conditions that foster word learning: Parents label objects and youngsters rely on adults' behavior to interpret the words they hear.

Although joint attention helps children to learn words, it is not required: Children learn new words when they are used in ongoing conversation and when they overhear others use novel words (Akhtar, Jipson, & Callanan, 2001). And when speakers appear unfamiliar with a novel person or object, 4- and 5-year-olds are less likely to learn new words, as if they doubt that speakers know what they're talking about (Birch & Bloom, 2002; Sabbagh & Baldwin, 2001).

**CONSTRAINTS ON WORD NAMES.** Joint attention simplifies word learning for children, but the problem still remains: How does a toddler know that *banana* refers to the object that she's touching, as opposed to her activity (touching) or to the object's color? Many researchers believe that young children follow several simple rules that limit their conclusions about what labels mean.

A study by Au and Glusman (1990) identified one of the rules that young children use. These researchers presented preschoolers with a stuffed animal with pink horns that otherwise resembled a monkey and called it a *mido*. *Mido* was then repeated several times, always referring to the monkeylike stuffed animal with pink horns. Later, these youngsters were asked to find a *theri* in a set of stuffed animals that included several *mido*. Never having heard of a *theri*, what did the children do? They never picked a *mido*; instead, they selected other stuffed animals. Knowing that *mido* referred to monkeylike animals with pink horns, evidently they decided that *theri* had to refer to one of the other stuffed animals.

Apparently children were following this simple but effective rule for learning new words:

- If an unfamiliar word is heard in the presence of objects that already have names and objects that don't, the word refers to one of the objects that doesn't have a name.

Researchers have discovered several other simple rules that help children match words with the correct referent (Hoff, 2001; Woodward & Markman, 1998):

- A name refers to a whole object, not its parts or its relation to other objects, and refers not just to this particular object but to all objects of the same type. For example, when a grandparent points to a stuffed animal on a shelf and says "dinosaur," children conclude that *dinosaur* refers to the entire dinosaur, not just its ears or nose, not to the fact that the dinosaur is on a shelf, and not to this specific dinosaur but to all dinosaurlike objects.

> Young children use several simple rules to learn word names, such as the rule that a name applies to an entire object.

- If an object already has a name and another name is presented, the new name denotes a subcategory of the original name. If the child who knows the meaning of *dinosaur* sees a brother point to another dinosaur and hears the brother say "T-rex," the child will conclude that *T-rex* is a special type of dinosaur.

- Given many similar category members, a word applied consistently to only one of them is a proper noun. If a child who knows *dinosaur* sees that one of a group of dinosaurs is always called "Dino," the child will conclude that *Dino* is the name of that dinosaur.

Rules like these make it possible for children like Efrat, the child in the vignette, to learn words rapidly because they reduce the number of possible referents. The child in the photo on page 280 follows these rules to decide that *flower* refers to the entire object, not its parts or the action of pointing to it.

**SENTENCE CUES.** Children hear many unfamiliar words embedded in sentences containing words they already know. The other words and the overall sentence structure can be helpful clues to a word's meaning.

For example, when a parent describes an event using familiar words but an unfamiliar verb, children often infer that the verb refers to the action performed by the subject of the sentence (Fisher, 1996; Woodward & Markman, 1998). When the youngsters in the photo hear, "The man is juggling," they will infer that *juggling* refers to the man's actions with the bowling pins, because they already know *man* and because *-ing* refers to ongoing actions.

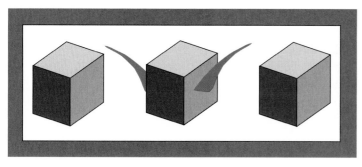

FIG. 10–2

As another example of how sentence context aids word learning, look at the blocks in the diagram and point to "the boz block." I imagine you pointed to the middle block. Why? In English, adjectives usually precede the nouns they modify, so you inferred that *boz* is an adjective describing *block*. Since *the* before *boz* implies that only one block is *boz*, you picked the middle one, having decided that *boz* means "winged." Toddlers, too, use sentence cues like these to judge word meanings. Hearing "This is a Zav," 2-year-olds will interpret *zav* as a category name but hearing "This is Zav" (without the *a*), they interpret *zav* as a proper name (Hall, Lee, & Belanger, 2001).

**COGNITIVE FACTORS.** The naming explosion coincides with a time of rapid cognitive growth, and children's increased cognitive skill helps them to learn new words. As children's thinking becomes more sophisticated and, in particular, as they start to have goals and intentions, language becomes a means to express those goals and to achieve them. Thus, intention provides children with an important motive to learn language—to help achieve their goals (Bloom & Tinker, 2001). In addition, young children's improving attentional and perceptual skills also promote word learning. Many objects with the same name have a common shape (e.g., balls are round, pencils are slender rods), and children's growing ability to detect perceptual similarities allows them to extend new words to novel instances of objects (Smith et al., 2002).

**NAMING ERRORS.** Of course, these rules for learning new words are not perfect; initial mappings of words onto meanings are often only partially correct (Hoff & Naigles, 2002). **A common mistake is underextension, defining a word too narrowly.** Using *car* to refer only to the family car and *ball* to a favorite toy ball are examples of underextension. **Between 1 and 3 years, children sometimes make the opposite error, overextension, defining a word too broadly.** Children may use *car* to also refer to buses and trucks or use *doggie* to refer to all four-legged animals.

The overextension error occurs more frequently when children are producing words than when they are comprehending words. Two-year-old Jason may say "doggie" to refer to a goat but nevertheless correctly point to a picture of a goat when asked. Because overextension is more common in word production, it may actually reflect another fast-mapping rule that children follow: "If you can't remember the name for an object, say the name of a related object" (Naigles & Gelman, 1995).

Both underextension and overextension disappear gradually as youngsters refine meanings for words with more exposure to language.

## Encouraging Word Learning

How can parents and other adults help children learn words? For children to expand their vocabularies, they need to hear others speak. Not surprisingly, then, children learn words more rapidly if their parents speak to them frequently (Huttenlocher et al., 1991; Roberts, Burchinal, & Durham, 1999). Of course, sheer quantity of parental speech is not all that matters. Parents can foster word learning by naming objects that are the focus of a child's attention (Dunham, Dunham, & Curwin, 1993). Parents can name different products on store shelves as they point to them. During a walk, parents can label the objects—birds, plants, vehicles—that the child sees. In addition, children

**Children learn new words when they participate in activities that force them to understand the meanings of new words.**

learn more words when their parents' speech is rich in different words and is grammatically sophisticated (Hoff & Naigles, 2002), and when parents respond promptly and appropriately to their children's talk (Tamis-Lemonda & Bornstein, 2002).

Parents can also help children learn words by reading books with them. Reading together is fun for parents and children alike, and it provides opportunities for children to learn new words. However, the way that parents read makes a difference. When parents carefully describe pictures as they read, preschoolers' vocabularies increase (Reese & Cox, 1999). Asking children questions also helps. In a study of 4-year-olds (Sénéchal, Thomas, & Monker, 1995), some parents simply read the story and children listened. Other parents read the story but stopped periodically to ask a "what" or "where" question that the child could answer with the target word. Later, the researchers tested children's abilities to recognize the target words and produce them. The graph shows that children who answered questions comprehended more target words than children who only listened. Children who answered questions were also much more likely to produce the target words.

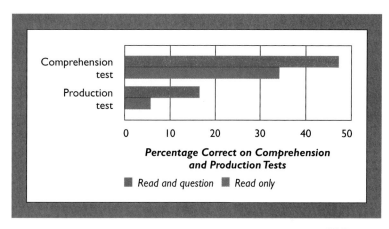

FIG. 10–3

Why is questioning effective? When an adult reads a sentence (e.g., "Arthur is *angling*"), then asks a question (e.g., "What is Arthur doing?"), a child must match the new word (*angling*) with the pictured activity (fishing) and say the word aloud. When parents read without questioning, children can ignore words they don't understand. Questioning forces children to identify meanings of new words and practice saying them.

Viewing television can also help word learning under some circumstances. For example, preschool children who regularly watch *Sesame Street* usually have larger vocabularies by the time they enter kindergarten than preschoolers who watch *Sesame Street* only occasionally (Rice et al., 1990). Other television programs, notably cartoons, do not have this positive influence. What accounts for the difference? *Sesame Street* involves children in language activities that help them learn words (in the photo, words with E). Cartoons, however, require no interaction at all.

For school-age children, parents remain an important influence on vocabulary development: Children learn words when exposed to a parent's advanced vocabulary, particularly in the context of instructive and helpful interactions (Weizman & Snow, 2001). Reading is another great way to learn new words. Written material—books, magazines, newspapers, textbooks—almost always contains more unfamiliar words than conversational language, so reading is rich in opportunities to expand vocabulary (Hayes, 1988). Not surprisingly, children who read frequently tend to have larger vocabularies than children who read less often (Allen, Cipielewski, & Stanovich, 1992).

Research on reading, along with research on television and parents' influence, points to a simple but powerful conclusion: Children are most likely to learn new words when they participate in activities that force them to understand the meanings of new words and use those new words. Is learning new words (and other aspects of language) more difficult for children learning two languages? The "Cultural Influences" feature has the answer.

## CULTURAL INFLUENCES

### Growing Up Bilingual

About 6 million American schoolchildren come from homes where English is not the primary language. In some states, 25 percent or more of the children are bilingual, and the percentages are even higher in some urban areas (U.S. Bureau of the Census, 1995). These youngsters usually speak English and another language, such as Spanish or, like the children in the photo, Chinese.

Is learning two languages easier or harder than learning just one language? For much of the 20th century, the general view was that bilingualism harmed children's development. One child psychology text published in 1952 surveyed the research and concluded, "There can be no doubt that the child reared in a bilingual environment is handicapped in his language growth" (Thompson, 1952, p. 367). Today, we know that this conclusion is wrong because it was based on studies of poor, immigrant children's scores on intelligence tests. In retrospect, immigrant children's test scores had more to do with their poverty and unfamiliarity with a new culture than with their bilingualism.

In fact, modern studies lead to a different picture. When 1- and 2-year-olds learn two languages simultaneously, they often progress somewhat slowly at first because they mix words from the two languages. By age 3 or 4, however, children separate the languages; and by the time they begin elementary school, they are proficient in both languages (Baker, 1993; Lanza, 1992). When each language is considered separately, bilingual children often have somewhat smaller vocabularies than monolingual children (Umbel et al., 1992). However, since bilingual youngsters often know words in one language but not the other, their total vocabulary (i.e., words known in both language + words known in either language but not both) is greater than that of monolingual children.

What's more, bilingual children surpass monolingual children in other language skills. Bilingual preschoolers are more likely to understand that the printed form of a word is unrelated to the meaning of the word (Bialystok, 1997; Bialystok, Shenfield, & Codd, 2000). For example, bilingual preschoolers are less likely to believe that words denoting large objects (e.g., *bus*) are longer than words denoting small objects (e.g., *bug*). Bilingual children also better understand that words are simply arbitrary symbols. Bilingual youngsters, for instance, are more likely than monolingual children to understand that, as long as all English speakers agreed, *dog* could refer to cats and *cat* could refer to dogs (Bialystok, 1988; Campbell & Sais, 1995).

> Bilingual children learn language as rapidly as monolingual children and they better understand the symbolic nature of words.

Of course, many children in America can't speak English at the time when they should begin school. How to teach these children has prompted much national debate. One view is that all Americans should speak English and so all teaching should be in English. Another view is that children learn more effectively in their native tongue and so all teaching should be done in that language.

Much of the debate over the proper language of instruction is political, reflecting people's desire for a society with a universal cultural heritage and language rather than a society with pluralistic heritages and languages. Ignoring the political aspects, research shows that the best method uses the child's native language *and* English (Padilla et al., 1991; Wong-Fillmore et al., 1985). Initially, children receive basic English-language teaching while they are taught other subjects in their native language. Gradually, more instruction is in English, in step with children's growing proficiency in the second language. When instruction is in children's native language and English, they are most likely to master academic content and English, outcomes that are less likely when instruction is solely in the native language or in English.

## CHECK YOUR LEARNING

1. Children begin to _____ at about the same age that they begin to talk, and both apparently reflect children's growing understanding of symbols.

2. Children with a(n) _____ style of language learning typically have many social phrases (e.g., *go away*) in their vocabularies.

3. When children have a referential style of language learning, they tend to use language primarily as a(n) _____ tool.

4. Many strategies help children learn words, including joint attention, constraints on word learning, and _____.

5. When young children hear an unfamiliar word in the presence of a novel object, they _____.

6. Sometimes children define a word too broadly, an error known as _____.

7. Young children are most likely to learn new words when parents _____, when they regularly watch TV programs like *Sesame Street*, and when parents ask questions while reading to them.

**CONNECTIONS**
How do the factors responsible for the naming explosion show connections among language, cognitive, and social development?

**Answers:** (1) gesture, (2) expressive, (3) intellectual, (4) sentence cues, (5) infer that the word denotes the novel object, (6) overextension, (7) label objects

# Speaking in Sentences                               10.3

## LEARNING OBJECTIVES

● How do children progress from speaking single words to complicated sentences?

● How do children acquire the grammar of their native language?

From Two-Word Speech to Complex Sentences

How Do Children Acquire Grammar?

> *Jaime's daughter, Luisa, is a curious $2\frac{1}{2}$-year-old who bombards her father with questions. Jaime enjoys Luisa's questioning, but he is bothered by the way she phrases her questions. Luisa will say, "What you are doing?" and "Why not she sleep?" Obviously, Jaime doesn't talk this way, so he wonders where Luisa learned to ask questions like this. Is it normal, or is it a symptom of some type of language disorder?*

Not long after children begin to talk, they start combining words to form simple sentences. These simple sentences are the first step in a new area of language learning, mastering *syntax*—a language's rules for combining words to create sentences. We'll begin this module by tracing the stages in children's acquisition of syntax and, along the way, see that Luisa's way of asking questions is quite normal for youngsters learning English. Then we'll examine different factors that influence children's mastery of syntax.

## From Two-Word Speech to Complex Sentences

At about $1\frac{1}{2}$ years, children begin to combine individual words to create two-word sentences, like *more juice, gimme cookie, truck go, my truck, Daddy go, Daddy bike.* **Researchers call this kind of talk telegraphic speech because, like telegrams of days gone by, it consists of only words directly relevant to meaning.** Before phones and e-mail, people sent urgent messages by telegraph, and the cost was based on the number of words. Consequently, telegrams were brief and to the point, containing only the important nouns, verbs, adjectives, and adverbs, much like children's two-word speech.

In their two-word speech, children follow rules to express different meanings. For example, the sentences *truck go* and *Daddy eat* are both about agents—people or objects that do something and the actions they perform. Here the rule is "agent + action." In contrast, *my truck* is about a possessor and a possession; the rule for creating these sentences is "possessor + possession."

When children are in the two-word stage, they use several basic rules to express meaning (Brown, 1973). These are listed in the table.

| Rules Used to Express Meaning During the Two-Word Stage | |
|---|---|
| **Rule** | **Example** |
| agent + action | "Daddy eat" |
| possessor + possession | "my truck" |
| action + object | "gimme cookie" |
| agent + object | "boy car" (meaning the boy is pushing the car) |
| action + location | "put chair" (meaning put the object on the chair) |
| entity + location | "truck chair" (meaning the truck is on the chair) |
| attribute + entity | "big car" |
| demonstrative + entity | "that cup" |
| Source: Based on Brown, 1973. | |

TABLE 10-1

Of course, not all children use all eight rules, but most do. And this is true of children around the world (Tager-Flusberg, 1993). Regardless of the language they learn, children's two-word sentences follow a common set of rules that are very useful in describing ideas concerning people and objects, their actions, and their properties.

When children move beyond two-word sentences, they quickly begin to use much longer sentences. For example, at $1\frac{1}{2}$ years, my daughter Laura would say, "gimme juice" or "bye-bye Mom." As a $2\frac{1}{2}$-year-old, she had progressed to "When I finish my ice cream, I'll take a shower, okay?" and "Don't turn the light out—I can't see better!" Her improvement was characteristic of most children.

> Children use a common set of rules to create two-word sentences that describe people, objects, actions, and properties.

Beginning at about the second birthday, children move to three-word and even longer sentences. **Their longer sentences are filled with grammatical morphemes, words or endings of words (such as *-ing, -ed,* or *-s*) that make a sentence grammatical.** To illustrate, a $1\frac{1}{2}$-year-old might say, "kick ball," but a 3-year-old would be more likely to say, "I am kicking the ball." Compared to the $1\frac{1}{2}$-year-old's telegraphic speech, the 3-year-old has added several elements, including a pronoun, *I,* to serve as the subject of the sentence, the auxiliary verb *am,* *-ing* to the verb *kick,* and an article, *the,* before *ball.* Each of these grammatical morphemes makes the older child's sentence slightly more meaningful and much more grammatical.

How do children learn all of these subtle nuances of grammar? Conceivably, a child might learn that *kicking* describes kicking that is ongoing and that *kicked* describes kicking that occurred in the past. Later, the child might learn that *raining* describes current weather and *rained* describes past weather. But learning different tenses for individual verbs—one by one—would be remarkably slow going. More effective would be to learn the general rules that "verb + *-ing*" denotes an ongoing activity and "verb + *-ed*" denotes a past activity. In fact, this is what children do: They learn general rules about grammatical morphemes.

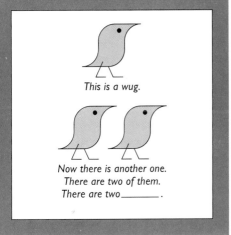

*This is a wug.*

*Now there is another one.*
*There are two of them.*
*There are two_____.*

FIG. 10-4

Jean Berko (1958) conducted one of the first studies showing that children's use of grammatical morphemes is based on their growing knowledge of grammatical rules, rather than merely their memory for individual words. She showed preschoolers pictures of nonsense objects like the one in the diagram. The experimenter labeled it, saying, "This is a wug." Then youngsters were shown pictures of two of the objects while the experimenter said, "Now there is another one. There are two of them. There are two . . ." Most children spontaneously said, "Wugs." Because *wug* is a novel word, children could answer correctly only by applying the rule of adding *-s* to indicate plural.

Sometimes, of course, applying the general rule can lead to very creative communication. As a 3-year-old, my daughter would say, "unvelcro it," meaning detach the Velcro. She had never heard *unvelcro,* but she created this word from the rule that "*un-* + verb" means to reverse or stop the action of a verb. Creating such novel words is, in fact, evidence that children learn grammar by applying rules, not learning individual words.

**Additional evidence that children master grammar by learning rules comes from preschoolers' overregularization, applying rules to words that are exceptions to the rule.** Youngsters learning English may incorrectly add an *-s* instead of using an irregular plural—*two mans* instead of *two men* or *two foots* instead of *two feet.* With the past tense, children may add *-ed* instead of using an irregular past tense—*I goed* instead of *I went* or *she runned* instead of *she ran* (Marcus et al., 1992). Children apparently know the general rule but not all the words that are exceptions.

The rules governing grammatical morphemes range from fairly simple to very complex. The rule for plurals—add *-s*—is simple to apply, and, as you might expect, it's one of the first grammatical morphemes that children master. Adding *-ing* to denote ongoing action is also simple, and it too is mastered early. More complex forms, such as the various forms of the verb *to be,* are mastered later; but, remarkably, by the end of the preschool years, children typically have mastered most of the rules that govern grammatical morphemes.

At the same time that preschoolers are mastering grammatical morphemes, they extend their speech beyond the subject-verb-object construction that is basic in English. You can see these changes in the way children ask questions. Children's questions during two-word speech are marked by intonation alone. Soon after a child can declare, "My ball," he can also ask "My ball?" Children quickly discover *wh* words (*who, what, when, where, why*), but they don't use them correctly. Like Luisa, the $2\frac{1}{2}$-year-old in the module-opening vignette, many youngsters merely attach the *wh* word to the beginning of a sentence without changing the rest of the sentence: *What he eating? What we see?* But by 3 or $3\frac{1}{2}$ years, youngsters insert the required auxiliary verb before the subject, creating *What is he eating?* or *What will we see?* (deVilliers & deVilliers, 1985).

> As children move beyond two-word speech, they begin to master questions, negation, and other more complex sentences.

Between ages 3 and 6, children also learn to use negation ("That isn't a butterfly") and embedded sentences ("Jennifer thinks that Bill took the book"). They begin to comprehend passive voice ("The ball was kicked by the girl") as opposed to the active voice ("The girl kicked the ball"), although full understanding of this form continues into the elementary-school years (Tager-Flusberg, 1993). In short, by the time most children enter kindergarten, they use most of the grammatical forms of their native language with great skill.

## How Do Children Acquire Grammar?

Ponder young children's grammatical accomplishments for a moment, particularly in light of their other cognitive skills. Most youngsters can neither read nor do arithmetic, and some don't know the letters of the alphabet, but virtually all have mastered the fundamentals of grammar of their native tongue. How do they do it? Theorists have proposed several different answers to this question.

**THE BEHAVIORIST ANSWER.** If you were asked to explain how children master grammar, where would you begin? You might propose that children learn to speak grammatically by listening to and then copying adult sentences. Children might simply copy the grammatical forms they hear. In fact, B. F. Skinner (1957) and other learning theorists once claimed that all aspects of language—sounds, words, grammar, and communication—are learned through imitation and reinforcement (Whitehurst & Vasta, 1975).

Critics were quick to point to some flaws in the learning explanation of grammar, however. One problem is that children produce many sentences they've never ever heard. In fact, most of children's sentences are novel, which is difficult to explain in terms of simple imitation of adults' speech. For example, when young children create questions by inserting a *wh* word at the beginning of a sentence ("What she doing?"), who are they imitating?

Also troublesome for the learning view is that, even when children imitate adult sentences, they do not imitate adult grammar. In simply trying to repeat "I am drawing a picture," young children will say "I draw picture." Furthermore, linguists, particularly Noam Chomsky (1957, 1995), have argued that grammatical rules are far too complex for toddlers and preschoolers to infer them solely on the basis of speech that they hear.

**THE LINGUISTIC ANSWER.** Beginning with Chomsky (1957), linguists proposed children are born with mechanisms that simplify the task of learning grammar (Slobin, 1985). According to this view, children are born with neural circuits in the brain that allow them to infer the grammar of the language that they hear. That is, grammar itself is not built into the child's nervous system, but processes that guide the learning of grammar are.

This proposal that inborn mechanisms help children learn grammar might not be as intuitively appealing as imitation, but many findings indirectly support this view:

1. *Specific regions of the brain are known to be involved in language processing.* If children are born with a "grammar-learning processor," it should be possible to locate a specific region or regions of the brain that are involved in learning grammar. In fact, you may remember from Module 5.3 that for most people the left hemisphere of the brain plays a critical role in understanding language. Some functions of language have been located even more precisely. For example, the area in blue in the diagram is Broca's area—a region in the left frontal cortex that is necessary for combining words into meaningful sentences. The fact that specific areas in the brain, such as Broca's area, have well-defined functions for language makes it plausible that children have specialized neural circuits that help them learn grammar.

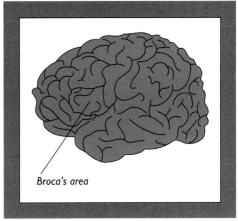

*Broca's area*

FIG. 10–5

2. *Only humans learn grammar readily.* If grammar is learned solely through imitation and reinforcement, then it should be possible to teach rudimentary grammar to nonhumans. If, instead, learning grammar depends on specialized neural mechanisms that are unique to humans, then efforts to teach grammar to nonhumans should fail. This prediction has been tested many times by trying to teach grammar to chimpanzees, the species closest to humans on the evolutionary ladder. For example, the chimpanzee in the photo, Nim Chimpsky, was taught to communicate using gestures taken from sign language. Other chimps have been taught using plastic chips to stand for words. The result? Chimps master a handful of grammatical rules governing two-word speech, but only with massive effort that is completely unlike the preschool child's learning of grammar (Savage-Rumbaugh et al., 1993; Seyfarth & Cheney, 1996). And the resulting language is unlike children's grammar in many ways (Kako, 1999). For example, Nim gradually used longer sentences but because he repeated himself (e.g., "eat Nim eat Nim"), not because he expressed more complicated ideas. Because numerous efforts to teach grammar to chimps have failed, this suggests that children rely on some type of mechanism specific to humans to master grammar.

3. *There is a critical period for learning language.* The period from birth to about 12 years is a critical period for acquiring language generally and mastering grammar particularly. If children do not acquire language in this period, they will never truly master language later. Evidence of a critical period for language comes from studies of isolated children. In one tragic instance, a baby girl named Genie was restrained by a harness during the day and a straightjacket-like device at night. No one was permitted to talk to Genie, and she was beaten when she made any noise. When Genie was discovered, at age 13, she did not speak at all. After several years of language training, her mastery of grammar remains limited, resembling the telegraphic speech of a 2-year-old (Curtiss, 1989; Rymer, 1993).

Further evidence for a critical period for language comes from studies of

**VIDEO 10.1**
Teaching Sign Language to the Chimpanzee Washoe
CLASSIC MODULE

individuals learning second languages. Individuals master the grammar of a foreign language at the level of a native speaker only if they are exposed to the language prior to adolescence (Newport, 1991). Why is it that one period of time can be so much more influential for language than others? Why can't missed language experiences be made up after age 12? A critical period for language answers these questions. That is, just as females ovulate for only a limited portion of the life span, the neural mechanisms involved in learning grammar may function only during infancy and childhood.

Although these findings are consistent with the idea that children have innate grammar-learning mechanisms, they do *not* prove the existence of such mechanisms. Consequently, scientists have continued to look for other explanations.

**Children learn grammar by relying on some language-specific mechanisms, by noting regularities in the speech they hear, and by participating in linguistically rich interactions**

**THE COGNITIVE ANSWER.** Not all researchers believe that children must have specialized mechanisms to learn grammar. Some theorists (e.g., Braine, 1992) believe that children learn grammar through powerful cognitive skills that help them rapidly detect regularities in their environments, including patterns in the speech they hear. According to this approach, it's as if children establish a huge Excel spread sheet that has the speech they've heard in one column and the context in which they heard it in a second column; periodically infants scan the columns looking for recurring patterns (Maratsos, 1998). For example, children might be confused the first time they hear -*s* added to the end of a familiar noun. However, as the database expands to include many instances of familiar nouns with an added -*s*, children discover that -*s* is always added to a noun when there are multiple instances of the object. Thus, they create the rule: noun + -*s* = plural. With this view, children learn language by searching for regularities across many examples that are stored in memory, not through an inborn grammar-learning device.

**THE SOCIAL-INTERACTION ANSWER.** This approach is eclectic, drawing on each of the views we've considered so far. From the behaviorist approach, it takes an emphasis on the environment; from the linguistic approach, that language learning is unique; and, from the cognitive view, that children have powerful cognitive skills they can use to master language. The unique contribution of this perspective is emphasizing that children master language generally and grammar specifically in the context of social interactions (Bloom & Tinker, 2001). That is, much language learning takes place in the context of interactions between children and adults, with both parties eager for better communication. Children have an ever-expanding repertoire of ideas and intentions that they wish to convey to others and caring adults want to understand their children, so both parties work to improve language skills as a means toward better communication. Thus, improved communication provides an incentive for children to master language and for adults to help them.

You can see the nature of these interactions in the following example, in which a child wants a cookie (after Hulit & Howard, 2002, pp. 37–38). Like the child in the photo, a 9-month-old who wants a cookie might point to it while looking at the mother. In turn, the mother gives the cookie, saying, "Here's the cookie." By age 2, a child might say,

"Gimme cookie, please?" with the mother responding, "Yes, I'll give you the cookie." At 9 months and 2 years, the child's desire to have the cookie motivates communication (pointing at 9 months, spoken language at 2 years) and gives the mother opportunities to demonstrate more advanced forms of language.

None of these accounts, summarized in the table, provides a comprehensive account of how grammar is mastered. But many scientists believe the final explanation will include contributions from the linguistic, cognitive, and social-interaction accounts. That is, children's learning of grammar will be explained in terms of some mechanisms specific to learning grammar, children actively seeking to identify regularities in their environment, and linguistically rich interactions between children and adults (MacWhinney, 1998).

SUMMARY TABLE

| DIFFERENT APPROACHES TO EXPLAINING CHILDREN'S ACQUISITION OF GRAMMAR | |
| --- | --- |
| Approach | Children are thought to master grammar . . . |
| Behaviorist | by imitating speech they hear |
| Linguistic | with inborn mechanisms that allow children to infer the grammatical rules of their native language |
| Cognitive | using powerful cognitive mechanisms that allow children to find recurring patterns in the speech they hear |
| Social Interaction | in the context of social interactions with adults in which both parties want improved communication |

Of course, many parents don't care much about theories of language, but they do want to know how they can help their children master grammar and other aspects of language. The "Improving Children's Lives" feature provides some guidelines.

## IMPROVING CHILDREN'S LIVES

### Promoting Language Development

Adults eager to promote children's language development can follow a few guidelines:

1. Talk with children frequently and treat them as partners in conversation. That is, try talking with children interactively, not directively.

2. Use a child's speech to show new language forms. Expand a child's remark to introduce new vocabulary or new grammatical forms. Rephrase a child's ungrammatical remark to show the correct grammar.

3. Encourage children to go beyond minimal use of language. Have them answer questions in phrases and sentences, not single words. Have them replace vague words such as *stuff* or *somebody* with more descriptive ones.

4. Listen. This guideline has two parts. First, because children often talk slowly, it's tempting for adults to complete their sentences for them. Don't. Let children express themselves. Second, pay attention to what children are saying and respond appropriately. Let children learn that language works.

5. Make language fun. Use books, rhymes, songs, jokes, and foreign words to increase a child's interest in learning language.

Of course, as children's language improves during the preschool years, others can understand it more readily, which means that children become better at communicating. The emergence and growth of communication skills is the topic of the next module.

### CHECK YOUR LEARNING

**1.** Children's first sentences are referred to as telegraphic speech because _____.

**2.** Children's two-word sentences are based on a common set of rules that are useful in describing _____.

**3.** As children move beyond two-word sentences, _____ appear in their speech, beginning with those that follow simple rules.

**4.** Evidence that children learn grammatical rules comes from overregularization, in which children _____.

**5.** One flaw in the learning explanation of grammar is that children say many novel sentences; another is that _____.

**6.** Evidence that children are born with specialized neural circuits for learning grammar includes the facts that specific brain regions are associated with language processing, _____, and there is a critical period for learning language.

**7.** According to the cognitive approach, children _____ to discover grammatical rules.

**ACTIVE CHILDREN**
How do the various explanations of grammatical development differ in their view of the child's role in mastering grammar?

**Answers:** (1) they include only words that are essential to meaning, (2) ideas about people and objects, their actions, and their properties, (3) grammatical morphemes, (4) apply grammatical rules to words that are exceptions to the rule, (5) young children who imitate adults' speech do not imitate adults' grammar, (6) only humans learn grammar, (7) detect regular patterns in speech

# 10.4 Using Language to Communicate

— Taking Turns

— Speaking Effectively

— Listening Well

### LEARNING OBJECTIVES

● When and how do children learn to take turns in conversation?

● What are the skills required to be an effective speaker?

● What is involved in becoming a good listener?

*Marla and Kitty, both 7-year-olds, usually are good friends, but right now they're boiling mad at each other. Marla was going to the mall with her dad to buy some new markers. Kitty found out and gave Marla money to buy some markers for her, too. Marla returned with the markers, but they weren't the kind that Kitty liked, so she was angry. Marla was angry because she didn't think Kitty should be mad; after all, it was Kitty's fault for not telling her what kind to buy. Meanwhile, Marla's dad hopes they come to some understanding soon and cut out all the shouting.*

Imagining these girls arguing is an excellent way to learn what is needed for effective communication. Both talk at the same time, their remarks are rambling and incoherent, and neither bothers to listen to the other. In other words, for effective oral communication, don't do what they do. These girls need to follow a few simple guidelines for effective communication:

- People should take turns, alternating as speaker and listener.
- A speaker's remarks should relate to the topic and be understandable to the listener.
- A listener should pay attention and let the speaker know if his or her remarks don't make sense.

Complete mastery of these guidelines is a lifelong pursuit; after all, even adults often miscommunicate with one another because they don't observe one or more of these rules. However, in this module, we'll trace the development of effective communication skills and, along the way, discover why young children like Marla and Kitty sometimes fail to communicate.

## Taking Turns

Many parents begin to encourage turn taking long before infants say their first words (Field & Widmayer, 1982):

|  |  |
|---|---|
| PARENT: | Can you see the bird? |
| INFANT (COOING): | ooooh |
| PARENT: | It is a pretty bird. |
| INFANT: | ooooh |
| PARENT: | You're right, it's a cardinal. |

Soon after 1-year-olds begin to speak, parents like the father in the photo encourage their youngsters to participate in conversational turn taking. To help children along, parents often carry both sides of a conversation to demonstrate how the roles of speaker and listener alternate (Shatz, 1983):

|  |  |
|---|---|
| PARENT (TO INFANT): | What's Amy eating? |
| PARENT (ILLUSTRATING REPLY): | She's eating a cookie. |

Parents and other caregivers seem to do whatever is necessary to allow infants and toddlers to "fit in" to a conversation. That is, caregivers scaffold youngsters' attempts to converse, making it more likely that children will succeed.

Such early "conversations" between caregivers and infants are not universal. In some non-Western cultures, preverbal infants are not considered appropriate conversational partners, so adults don't talk to them. Only after infants are older do others begin to converse with them (Ochs, 1988).

By age 2, spontaneous turn taking is common in conversations between youngsters and adults (Barton & Tomasello, 1991). And by age 3, children have progressed to the point that if a listener fails to reply promptly, the child repeats his or her remark in order to elicit a response (Garvey & Berninger, 1981). A 3-year-old might say, "Hi, Paul" to an older sibling who's busy reading. If Paul doesn't answer in a few seconds, the 3-year-old might say, "Hi, Paul" again. When Paul remains unresponsive, the 3-year-old is likely to shout, "PAUL!"—showing that by this age children understand the rule that a comment deserves a response. Preschool children seem to interpret the lack of a response as, "I guess you didn't hear me, so I'll say it again, louder!"

## Speaking Effectively

When do children first try to initiate communications with others? Wanting to tell something to someone else is a deliberate act, and, based on Piaget's description of sensorimotor thinking (pages 177–179), we wouldn't expect much communication until near the first birthday. In fact, what appear to be the first deliberate attempts to communicate typically emerge at 10 months (Bates et al., 1979; Golinkoff, 1993). Infants at this age may touch or point to an object while simultaneously looking at another person. They continue this behavior until the person acknowledges them. It's as if the child is saying, "This is a neat toy! I want you to see it, too."

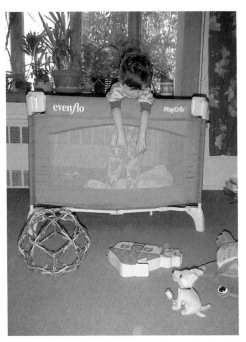

Beginning at 10 months, an infant may point, touch, or make noises to get an adult to do something. An infant in a playpen like the one in the photo who wants a toy that is out of reach may make noises while pointing to the toy. The noises capture an adult's attention, and the pointing indicates what the baby wants (Blake, O'Rourke, & Borzellino, 1994). The communication may be a bit primitive by adult standards, but it works for babies!

After the first birthday, children begin to use speech to communicate and often initiate conversations with adults (Bloom et al., 1996). Toddlers' first conversations are about themselves, but their conversational scope expands rapidly to include objects in the environment (e.g., toys, food). Later, conversations begin to include more abstract notions, such as hypothetical objects and past or future events (Foster, 1986).

Of course, young children are not always skilled conversational partners. At times their communications are confusing, leaving a listener to wonder, "What was that all about?" Every message—whether an informal conversation or a formal lecture—should have a clear meaning. But saying something clearly is often difficult because clarity can only be judged by considering the listener's age, experience, and knowledge of the topic, along with the context of the conversation. For example, think about the simple request, "Please hand me the Phillips-head screwdriver." This message may be clear to older listeners familiar with different types of screwdrivers, but it won't mean much to younger listeners who think all screwdrivers are alike. And, if the toolbox is filled with Phillips-head screwdrivers of assorted sizes, the message won't be clear even to a knowledgeable listener.

Constructing clear messages is a fine art, but, amazingly, by the preschool years, youngsters begin to adjust their messages to match the listener and the context. In a classic study, Marilyn Shatz and Rochel Gelman (1973) asked 4-year-olds to explain how a toy worked, once to a 2-year-old and once to an adult. Shatz and Gelman found that 4-year-olds talked more overall to adults than to 2-year-olds and used longer sentences with adult listeners than with 2-year-old listeners. Also, children used simpler grammar and more attention-getting words, such as *see, look, watch,* and *hey,* when speaking with 2-year-olds. Here, for example, is how one 4-year-old child explained the toy to her two different listeners (the toy is a garage with drivers and trucks that carry marbles to a dumping station):

*Adult listener: You're supposed to put one of these persons in, see? Then one goes with the other little girl. And then the little boy. He's the little boy and he drives. And then they back up. . . . And then the little girl falls out and then it goes backwards.*

> *2-year-old listener: Watch, Perry. Watch this. He's back in here. Now he drives up. Look, Perry. Look here, Perry. Those are marbles, Perry. Put the men in here. Now I'll do it. (Shatz & Gelman, 1973, p. 13)*

Shatz and Gelman's findings show that preschoolers are already sensitive to characteristics of the listener in formulating a clear message. More recent findings also show that children consider the listener and setting in devising clear messages:

## Young children adjust their messages based on a listener's age and knowledge.

- Preschool children give more elaborate messages to listeners who lack critical information than to listeners who have the information (Nadig & Sedivy, 2002; O'Neill, 1996). For example, a child describing where to find a toy will give more detailed directions to a listener whose eyes were covered when the toy was hidden.

- School-age children speak differently to adults and peers. They are more likely to speak politely with adults and be more demanding with peers (Warren-Leubecker & Bohannon, 1989). A child might ask a parent, "May I have one of your cookies?" but say to a peer, "Give me one of your cookies."

- **Some African Americans speak African American English, a variant of standard English that has slightly different grammatical rules.** For example, "He be tired" in African American English is synonymous with "He usually is tired" in standard English. Many African American children learn both African American English and standard English, and they switch back and forth, depending on the situation (Warren & McCloskey, 1993). They use standard English more often in school and when talking with European Americans but use African American English more often at home and when talking with African American peers.

All these findings show that school-age children (and sometimes preschoolers) are well on their way to understanding the factors that must be considered in creating clear messages. Even so, sometimes messages are not clear to listeners. Speakers need to pay attention to listeners; if they don't seem to understand the message, they need to try again. The "Focus on Research" feature shows that even young children have mastered this basic step toward effective communication.

## FOCUS ON RESEARCH

### When Listeners Don't Understand, Preschoolers Try Again

*Who were the investigators, and what was the aim of the study?* A good general rule for effective communication is that speakers should monitor their listeners' comprehension. When listeners get puzzled expressions on their faces, this is usually a sign that the message was not crystal clear and the speaker should clarify. Do preschool children know this important communicative rule? Do they pay attention to a listener's comprehension? These were the questions that Helen Shwe and Ellen Markman (1997) wanted to answer.

*How did the investigators measure the topic of interest?* Shwe and Markman showed two objects (e.g., a toy car and a sock) to $2\frac{1}{2}$-year-olds and asked which one they'd like to see. After the child had chosen, the experimenter said, "You asked for the _____. I think you want the _____. I'm going to give you the _____. Here's the _____." In one condition, the experimenter mentioned the chosen toy and actually gave the child the chosen toy. In three other conditions, the experimenter sometimes mentioned the wrong toy or gave the wrong toy or both. Then the experimenter recorded what the child did.

*Who were the children in the study?* Shwe and Markman tested 22 preschoolers with an average age of 31 months.

*What was the design of the study?* This study was experimental: There were two independent variables. One was whether the experimenter mentioned the correct toy in replying to the child's choice; the other was whether the experimenter gave the child the chosen toy. The dependent variable was the frequency with which children repeated their preference for the original toy, either by vocalizing, pointing, or gazing. The study was not developmental (only $2\frac{1}{2}$-year-olds participated and they were tested just once), so it was neither cross-sectional nor longitudinal.

*Were there ethical concerns with the study?* No. The task asking children to choose a toy posed no danger to the children. Mothers were present during testing.

*What were the results?* The top of the graph shows what children did when they received the wrong toy. Not surprisingly, they were much more likely to repeat their preference spontaneously when they received the wrong toy than when they received

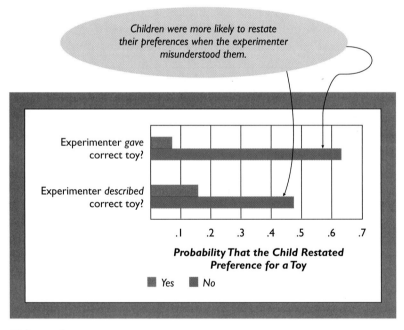

FIG. 10–6

the right one. (After all, when the child received the expected object, there was no reason to repeat the request.) More interesting are the results in the bottom of the graph, which show what children did when the experimenter described the wrong toy. Children were much more likely to restate their preference when the experimenter described it incorrectly than when the experimenter described it correctly.

*What did the investigators conclude?* Even very young children seem to understand that, when listeners misunderstand, speakers need to do something. In the grander scheme of things, repeating what you've just said is not a very good strategy. But in this simple experimental setting, it was adequate to convey to the adult, "You think I wanted the sock but, no, I wanted the car." As Shwe and Markman (1997) phrased it, "Young children monitor their communicative partner's knowledge state and care about their listener's comprehension . . ." (p. 636).

*What converging evidence would strengthen these conclusions?* One interesting extension of this study would involve naturalistic observation of young children's communications. Observing young children communicating with peers might be particularly fruitful because young listeners often do not understand what speakers mean. Doing this research as part of a longitudinal study would be useful in revealing developmental change in effective communication during the preschool years. 🔘

Thus, from a surprisingly young age, children express themselves to others and adjust their conversations to fit listeners. Are young children equally adept at listening? We'll find out in the next section.

## Listening Well

Listening well may seem easy, but it's not. A skilled listener must continuously decide whether a speaker's remarks make sense. If they do, then a listener needs to make an appropriate reply, typically by extending the conversation with another remark that's on the topic.

Few toddlers master this fundamental conversation skill. Their replies are more likely to be unrelated to the topic than related to it (Bloom, Rocissano, & Hood, 1976). Asked "Where's the sock?" a $1\frac{1}{2}$-year-old may say something like "I'm hungry!" By 3 years, children are more adept at continuing conversations by making remarks that relate to the topic being discussed.

If a message is vague or confusing, the listener should ask the speaker to clarify the message. This seems obvious enough, but young children do not always realize when a message is ambiguous. Told to find "the red toy," they may promptly select the red ball from a pile that includes a red toy car, a red block, and a red toy hammer. Instead of asking the speaker which *specific* red toy, young listeners often assume that they know which toy the speaker had in mind (Beal & Belgrad, 1990). Only when messages almost defy comprehension—when they are too quiet to be heard or when they impart obviously ambiguous or even conflicting information—do youngsters detect a problem.

> Young children often ignore ambiguities in messages.

Because young children's remarks often contain ambiguities and because, as listeners, they often do not detect ambiguities, young children often miscommunicate, just like Marla and Kitty in the opening vignette. Kitty probably didn't communicate exactly what kind of markers she wanted, and Marla didn't understand that the directions were unclear. Throughout the elementary-school years, youngsters gradually master the many skills involved in determining whether a message is consistent and clear (Ackerman, 1993).

Sometimes messages are confusing because they conflict with what a listener thinks is true. For example, suppose a child is told that the family cat, which always stays indoors, has run away. Even preschoolers are more likely to believe such a message when told by a parent than by a classmate because they know the parent is better informed about this particular topic (Robinson, Champion, & Mitchell, 1999).

Sometimes listeners must go beyond the words to understand the real meaning of a message. Metaphor is one example. When parents tell their teenagers, "Your bedroom is a junk yard," you (and they) know that this remark is not to be taken literally. Instead, the metaphor highlights the fact that the bedroom is a mess and filled with things that could be thrown away.

As you might expect, understanding nonliteral meanings of messages develops slowly (e.g., Dews et al., 1996). In the case of metaphor, young children easily understand simple metaphors in which the nonliteral meaning is based on references to concrete objects and their properties. For example, a parent might say to a 5-year-old, "You're a fish," referring to how well the child swims and enjoys the water, and the child will likely understand.

More complex metaphors require that children make connections based on abstract relations. For example, in Shakespeare's *Romeo and Juliet*, Romeo proclaims that "Juliet is the sun." You might interpret this line to mean that Juliet is the center of Romeo's universe or that without Juliet Romeo will die. The first interpretation depends on your knowledge of astronomy; the second, on your knowledge of biology. Younger children lack this sort of knowledge to comprehend metaphors, so they try to interpret them literally. Only when children gain the necessary content knowledge do they understand metaphors based on abstract relations (Franquart-Declercq & Gineste, 2001).

> Understanding of nonliteral messages, including metaphor and sarcasm, develops slowly.

Sarcasm is another form of communication that is not to be interpreted literally. When a soccer player misses the ball entirely and a teammate says, "Nice kick," the literal meaning of the remark is the opposite of the intended meaning. Like understanding of metaphor, understanding of sarcasm develops gradually (Creusere, 1999). When people emphasize their sarcasm by speaking in mocking or overly enthusiastic tones, school-age children can detect their meaning. However, if sarcasm must be detected solely from the context—by realizing that the comment is the opposite of what would be expected—only adolescents and adults are likely to understand the real meaning of the remark (Capelli, Nakagawa, & Madden, 1990).

This discussion of listening skills completes our catalog of the important accomplishments that take place in communication during childhood. As children enter kindergarten, they have mastered many of the fundamental rules of communication, and as they grow older, they acquire even greater proficiency.

## CHECK YOUR LEARNING

1. In some non-Western cultures, preverbal infants are not seen as _____.

2. If a listener doesn't respond promptly, a 3-year-old speaker will _____.

3. Before they can talk, infants often try to communicate by making noises or by _____.

4. One example of the way that children adjust their speech to consider listeners is that many African American children _____.

5. When listeners do not understand them, toddlers will sometimes _____.

**6.** When toddlers respond to a remark, their comment is often _____.

**7.** Young children often ignore ambiguities in messages because _____.

 **CONNECTIONS**

According to Piaget's theory, preschool children are egocentric. How do you think this egocentrism influences their communication skill? Are the findings described in this module consistent with Piaget's view?

**Answers:** (1) appropriate conversational partners, (2) repeat the remark in an effort to elicit a reply, (3) touching or pointing at an object, (4) use African American English more often at home than in school, (5) repeat their remark, (6) not relevant to the speaker's topic, (7) they assume that they know what the speaker means

# Unifying Themes: Connections

This chapter is an appropriate occasion to stress the theme that *development in different domains is connected*: Language has important connections to biological, cognitive, and social development. A link to biological development would be children's mastery of grammar: In ways that we don't yet fully understand, children seem to be endowed with a mechanism that smooths the path to mastering grammar. A link to cognitive development would be children's first words: Speaking words reflects the cognitive insight that speech sounds are symbols. A link to social development would be the communication skills that enable children to interact with peers and adults.

## See for Yourself

Berko's (1958) "wugs" task is fun to try with preschool children. Photocopy the drawing on page 287 and show it to a preschooler, repeating the instructions that appear on that page. You should find that the child quite predictably says, "two wugs." Create some pictures of your own to examine other grammatical morphemes, such as adding *-ing* to denote ongoing activity or adding *-ed* to indicate past tense. See for yourself!

## Resources

For more information about . . .

**Genie,** the girl whose tragic childhood provided some fascinating insights into the impact of experience on language development, read Russ Rymer's *Genie* (Harper-Collins, 1993), which describes Genie's childhood and the debates about how best to rehabilitate her.

**American Sign Language (ASL),** visit the Animated American Sign Language Dictionary Web site, **http://www.bconnex.net/~randys/index_nf.html**

## Key Terms

## 10.1 The Road to Speech

### Elements of Language

Language includes four distinct elements: phonology (sounds), semantics (word meaning), grammar (rules for language structure), and pragmatics (rules for communication). Syntax, which is part of grammar, describes how words are ordered in sentences.

### Perceiving Speech

Phonemes are the basic units of sound that make up words. Infants can hear phonemes soon after birth. They can even hear phonemes that are not used in their native language, but this ability is lost by the first birthday. Before they speak, infants can recognize words, apparently by noticing stress and syllables that go together. Infants prefer infant-directed speech—adults' speech to infants that is slower and has greater variation in pitch—because it provides them additional language clues.

### First Steps to Speech

Newborns are limited to crying, but at about 3 months, babies coo. Babbling soon follows, consisting of a single syllable; over several months, infants' babbling includes longer syllables and intonation.

## 10.2 Learning the Meanings of Words

### Understanding Words as Symbols

Children's first words represent a cognitive accomplishment that is not specific to language. Instead, the onset of language is due to a child's ability to interpret and use symbols. Consistent with this view, there are parallel developments in the use of gestures.

### Styles of Learning Language

Some youngsters use a referential style in learning words that emphasizes words as names and views language as an intellectual tool. Other children use an expressive style that emphasizes phrases and views language as a social tool.

### Fast Mapping Meanings to Words

Most children learn the meanings of words too rapidly for them to consider all plausible meanings systematically. Instead, children use a number of fast-mapping rules to determine probable meanings of new words. Joint attention, constraints, sentence cues, and cognitive

skills all help children learn words. The rules do not always lead to the correct meaning. An underextension denotes a child's meaning that is narrower than an adult's meaning; an overextension denotes a child's meaning that is broader.

### Encouraging Word Learning

Children's word learning is fostered by experience, including being read to, watching television, and, for school-age children, reading to themselves. The key ingredient is making children think about the meanings of new words.

## 10.3 Speaking in Sentences

### From Two-Word Speech to Complex Sentences

Not long after their first birthday, children produce two-word sentences that are based on simple rules for expressing ideas or needs. These sentences are sometimes called telegraphic because they use the fewest possible words to convey meaning. Moving from two-word to more complex sentences involves adding grammatical morphemes. Children first master grammatical morphemes that express simple relations, then those that denote complex relations.

As children acquire grammatical morphemes, they also extend their speech to other sentence forms, such as questions, and later to more complex constructions, such as passive sentences.

### How Do Children Acquire Grammar?

Behaviorists proposed that children acquire grammar through imitation, but that explanation is incorrect. Today's explanations come from three perspectives: the linguistic emphasizes inborn mechanisms that allow children to infer the grammatical rules of their native language, the cognitive perspective emphasizes cognitive processes that allow children to find recurring patterns in the speech they hear, and the social-interaction perspective emphasizes social interactions with adults in which both parties want improved communication.

## 10.4 Using Language to Communicate

### Taking Turns

Parents encourage turn taking even before infants talk and later demonstrate both the speaker and listener roles for their children. By age 3, children spontaneously take turns and prompt one another to speak.

### Speaking Effectively

Before they can speak, infants use gestures and noises to communicate. During the preschool years, children gradually become more skilled at constructing clear messages, in part by adjusting their speech to fit their listeners' needs. They also begin to monitor their listeners' comprehension, repeating messages if necessary.

### Listening Well

Toddlers are not good conversationalists because their remarks don't relate to the topic. Preschoolers are unlikely to identify ambiguities in another's speech. Also, they sometimes have difficulty understanding messages that are not to be taken literally, such as metaphor and sarcasm.

If you're a fan of *Star Trek*, you know that Mr. Spock feels little emotion because he's half Vulcan and people from the planet Vulcan don't have emotions. Would you like to live an emotionless life like Mr. Spock? Probably not. For most of us, feelings enrich our lives. As partial testimony to their importance, the English language has more than 500 words that refer to emotions (Averill, 1980). Joy, happiness, satisfaction, and yes, anger, guilt, and humiliation are just a few of the feelings that give life meaning.

In this chapter, we'll see how emotions emerge and how they affect development. In Module 11.1, we'll discuss when children first express different emotions and recognize emotions in others. Next, in Module 11.2, we'll see that children have different behavioral styles and that these styles are rooted, in part, in emotions. Finally, in Module 11.3, we'll examine the infant's first emotional relationship, the one that develops with the primary caregiver.

# Emotional Development

11.1   Emerging Emotions

11.2   Temperament

11.3   Attachment

# 11.1

## Emerging Emotions

**LEARNING OBJECTIVES**

- Why do people "feel"? Why do they have emotions?

- At what ages do children begin to experience and express different emotions?

- When do children begin to understand other people's emotions? How do they use this information to guide their own behavior?

- When do children show evidence of regulating emotion, and why is this an important skill?

> *Nicole was ecstatic that she was finally going to see her 7-month-old nephew, Claude. She rushed into the house and, seeing Claude playing on the floor with blocks, swept him up in a big hug. After a brief, puzzled look, Claude burst into angry tears and began thrashing around, as if saying to Nicole, "Who are you? What do you want? Put me down! Now!" Nicole quickly handed Claude to his mother, who was surprised by her baby's outburst and even more surprised that he continued to sob while she rocked him.*

This vignette illustrates three common emotions. Nicole's initial joy, Claude's anger, and his mother's surprise are familiar to all of us. In this module, we begin by discussing *why* people have feelings at all. Then we look at when children first express emotions, how children come to understand emotions in others, and, finally, how children regulate their emotions. As we do, we'll learn why Claude reacted to Nicole as he did and how Nicole could have prevented Claude's outburst.

## The Function of Emotions

Why do people feel emotions? Wouldn't life be simpler if people were emotionless like computers or residents of Mr. Spock's Vulcan? Probably not. Think, for example, about activities that most adults find pleasurable: a good meal, sex, holding one's children, and accomplishing a difficult but important task. These activities were and remain essential to the continuity of humans as a species, so it's not surprising that we find them pleasant (Gaoulin & McBurney, 2001).

**Basic emotions such as happiness and fear include a subjective feeling, a physiological response, and an overt behavior.**

Modern theories emphasize the functional value of emotion. That is, according to the functional approach, emotions are useful because they help people adapt to their environment (Izard & Ackerman, 2000). Take fear as an example. Most of us would rather not be afraid but there are instances in which feeling fearful is very adaptive. Imagine you are walking alone, late at night, in a poorly lighted section of campus. You become frightened and, as a consequence, are particularly attentive to sounds that might signal the presence of threat, and you probably walk quickly to a safer location. Thus, fear is adaptive because it organizes your behavior around an important goal—avoiding danger (Cosmides & Tooby, 2000).

Similarly, other emotions are adaptive. Happiness, for example, is adaptive in contributing to stronger interpersonal relationships: When people are happy with another person, they smile, and this often causes the other person to feel happy too, strengthening their relationship (Izard & Ackerman, 2000). Disgust is adaptive in keeping people away from substances that might make them ill: As we discover that the milk in a glass is sour, we experience disgust and push the glass away. Thus, in the functional approach, most emotions developed over the course of human history to meet unique life challenges and help humans to survive.

## Experiencing and Expressing Emotions

The three emotions from the vignette—joy, anger, and surprise—are considered "basic emotions," as are interest, disgust, distress, sadness, and fear (Dragh-Lorenz, Reddy, & Costall, 2001). **Basic emotions are experienced by people worldwide, and each consists of three elements: a subjective feeling, a physiological change, and an overt behavior** (Izard, 1991). For example, suppose you wake to the sound of a thunderstorm and then discover your roommate has left for class with your umbrella. Subjectively, you might feel ready to explode with anger; physiologically, your heart would beat faster; and behaviorally, you would probably be scowling.

**MEASURING EMOTIONS.**   How can we determine when infants first experience basic emotions? Overt behaviors such as facial expressions provide important clues. To see for yourself, look at the photos of young babies. Which one is angry? Which are the sad and happy babies? The facial expressions are so revealing that I'm sure you guessed that the babies are, in order, sad, happy, and angry. But do these distinctive facial expressions mean that the infants are actually experiencing these emotions? Not necessarily. Facial expressions are only one component of emotion—the behavioral manifestation. Emotion also involves physiological responses and subjective feelings. Of course, infants can't express their feelings to us verbally, so we don't know much about their subjective experiences. But at least some of the physiological responses that accompany facial expressions are the same in infants and adults. For example, when infants and adults smile—which suggests they're happy—the left frontal cortex of the brain tends to have more electrical activity than the right frontal cortex (Fox, Kimmerly, & Schafer, 1991).

Research has revealed several other reasons to believe that facial expressions are an accurate barometer of an infant's emotional state:

- Infants (and adults) worldwide express basic emotions in much the same way (Izard, 1991). For example, the boy in the photo on page 306 shows the universal signs of fear. His eyes are open wide, his eyebrows are raised, and his mouth is relaxed but slightly open. The universality of emotional expression

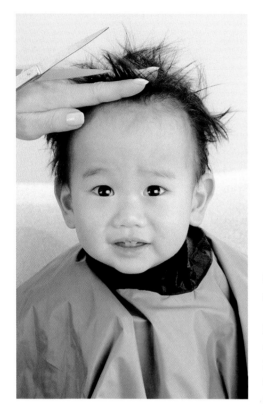

suggests that humans are biologically programmed to express basic emotions in a specific way.

- By 5 to 6 months, infants' facial expressions change predictably and meaningfully in response to events. When a happy mother greets her baby, the baby usually smiles in return; when a tired, distracted mother picks up her baby roughly, the baby usually frowns at her (Izard et al., 1995; Weinberg & Tronick, 1994).

- When adults are really happy or amused, they smile differently than when they smile to greet an acquaintance or to hide hurt feelings. In "joyful" smiles, the muscles around the eyes contract, which lifts the cheeks. Similarly, infants smile at both moms and interesting objects, but are more likely to raise their cheeks during smiling when looking at mom (Messinger, 2002). The close parallel between the details of infants' and adults' smiles suggests that smiling has the same meaning, emotionally, for infants and adults.

Collectively, these findings make it reasonable to assume that facial expressions reflect an infant's underlying emotional state.

**DEVELOPMENT OF BASIC EMOTIONS.**   Using facial expressions and other overt behaviors, scientists have traced the growth of basic emotions in infants. According to one influential theory (Lewis, 2000), newborns experience only two general emotions: pleasure and distress. Rapidly, though, more discrete emotions emerge, and by 8 or 9 months of age, infants are thought to experience all basic emotions. For example, joy emerges at about 2 or 3 months. **At this age, social smiles first appear: Infants smile when they see another human face.** Sometimes social smiling is accompanied by cooing, the early form of vocalization described in Module 10.1 (Sroufe & Waters, 1976). Smiling and cooing seem to be the infant's way of expressing pleasure at seeing another person. Sadness is also observed at about this age: Infants look sad, for example, when their mothers stop playing with them (Lewis, 2000).

VIDEO 11.1
Stranger Anxiety

Anger typically emerges between 4 and 6 months. Infants will become angry, for example, if a favorite food or toy is taken away (Sternberg & Campos, 1990). Reflecting their growing understanding of goal-directed behavior (see Module 7.2), infants also become angry when their attempts to achieve a goal are frustrated. For example, if a parent restrains an infant trying to pick up a toy, the guaranteed result is a very angry baby.

Like anger, fear emerges later in the first year. **At about 6 months, infants become wary in the presence of an unfamiliar adult, a reaction known as stranger wariness.** When a stranger approaches, a 6-month-old typically looks away and begins to fuss (Mangelsdorf, Shapiro, & Marzolf, 1995). The baby in the photo is showing the signs of stranger wariness. The grandmother has picked him up without giving him a chance to warm up to her, and the outcome is as predictable as it was with Claude, the baby in the vignette who was frightened by his aunt: He cries, looks frightened, and reaches with arms outstretched in the direction of someone familiar.

How wary an infant feels around strangers depends on a number of factors (Thompson & Limber, 1991). First, infants tend to be less fearful of strangers when the environment is familiar and more fearful when it is not. Many parents know this firsthand from traveling with their infants: Enter a friend's house for the first time and the baby clings tightly to its mother. Second, the amount of anxiety depends on the stranger's behavior. Instead of rushing to greet or pick up the baby, as Nicole did in the vignette, a stranger should talk with other adults and, in a while, perhaps offer the baby a toy (Mangelsdorf, 1992). Handled this way, many infants will soon be curious about the stranger instead of afraid.

Wariness of strangers is adaptive because it emerges at the same time that children begin to master creeping and crawling (described in Module 6.3). Like Curious George, the monkey in a famous series of children's books, babies are inquisitive and want to use their new locomotor skills to explore their worlds. Being wary of strangers provides a natural restraint against the tendency to wander away from familiar caregivers. However, as youngsters learn to interpret facial expressions and recognize when a person is friendly, their wariness of strangers declines.

**EMERGENCE OF COMPLEX EMOTIONS.** In addition to basic emotions such as joy and anger, people feel complex emotions such as pride, guilt, and embarrassment. **Sometimes known as the self-conscious emotions, they involve feelings of success when one's standards or expectations are met and feelings of failure when they aren't.** Most scientists (e.g., Lewis, 2000) believe that complex emotions don't surface until 18 to 24 months of age, because they depend on the child having some understanding of the self, which typically occurs between 15 and 18 months. Children feel guilty or embarrassed, for example, when they've done something they know they shouldn't have done (Kochanska et al., 2002). For example, a child who breaks a toy is thinking, "You told me to be careful. But I wasn't!" Similarly, children feel pride when they accomplish a challenging task for the first time. The toddler in the photo is probably thinking something like, "I've never done this before, but this time I did it—all by myself!" Thus, children's growing understanding of themselves (which I discuss in detail in Module 12.1), allows them to experience complex emotions like pride and guilt (Lewis, 2000).

The features of basic and complex emotions are summarized in the table.

**SUMMARY TABLE**

| INFANTS' EXPRESSION OF EMOTIONS | | | |
|---|---|---|---|
| Type | Defined | Emerge | Examples |
| Basic | Experienced by people worldwide and include a subjective feeling, a physiological response, and an overt behavior | Birth to 9 months | Joy, anger, fear |
| Complex (self-conscious) | Responses to meeting or failing to meet expectations or standards | 18 to 24 months | Pride, guilt, embarrassment |

**LATER DEVELOPMENTS.** As children grow, they continue to experience basic and complex emotions but different situations or events elicit these emotions. In the case of complex emotions, cognitive growth means that elementary-school children experience shame and guilt in situations where they would not have when they were younger (Reimer, 1996). For example, unlike preschool children, many school-age children would be ashamed if they neglected to defend a classmate who had been wrongly accused of a theft.

Fear is another emotion that can be elicited in different ways, depending on a child's age. Many preschool children are afraid of the dark and of imaginary creatures. These fears typically diminish during the elementary-school years as children grow cognitively and better understand the difference between appearance and reality (see Module 7.2). Replacing these fears are concerns about school, health, and personal harm (Silverman, La Greca, & Wasserstein, 1995). Such worries are common and not cause for concern in most children. In some youngsters, however, they become so extreme they overwhelm the child (Chorpita & Barlow, 1998). For example, a 7-year-old's worries about school would not be unusual unless her concern grew to the point that she refused to go to school. In the "Improving Children's Lives" feature, we'll look at this form of excessive fear and how it can be treated.

## IMPROVING CHILDREN'S LIVES

### "But I Don't Want to Go to School!"

Many youngsters plead, argue, and fight with their parents daily over going to school. **An overwhelming fear of going to school and active resistance to attending school constitutes school phobia.** For example, every school day, 9-year-old Keegan would cling to his mother and start to sob as soon as he finished his breakfast. When it was time to leave the house to catch the bus, he would drop to the floor and start kicking.

Children may develop school phobia because they are overanxious generally and school is full of situations that can cause anxiety, such as reading aloud, taking tests, or learning new activities with competitive classmates. **School-phobic children can be helped with systematic desensitization, a technique that associates deep relaxation with progressively more anxiety-provoking situations.** First the therapist asks the child to generate a list of school-related situations, from pleasant ("I got the highest grade on my math test") to neutral ("We say the pledge of allegiance every morning") to very anxiety provoking ("I got home and realized that I'd left my assignments in my locker"). Setting the list aside, the therapist then teaches the child how to reduce tension by relaxing different muscle groups. When the child masters the relaxation techniques, the therapist asks the child to relax and imagine the pleasant school-related situations. Over several sessions, the child imagines progressively more anxiety-provoking situations while relaxed, so that the anxiety the child used to feel is replaced by feelings of calm relaxation. Children taught this technique report feeling much less anxious, and their school attendance improves (Kearney & Silverman, 1995).

**CULTURAL DIFFERENCES IN EMOTIONAL EXPRESSION.** Children worldwide express many of the same basic and complex emotions. However, cultures differ in the extent to which emotional expression is encouraged (Hess & Kirouac, 2000). In many Asian countries, for example, outward displays of emotion are discouraged in favor of emotional restraint. Consistent with these differences, in one study (Camras et al., 1998), European American 11-month-olds cried and smiled more often than Chinese 11-month-olds. In another study (Zahn-Waxler et al., 1996), U.S. preschoolers were more likely than Japanese preschoolers to express anger in interpersonal conflicts.

Cultures also differ in the events that trigger emotions, particularly complex emotions. Situations that evoke pride in one culture may evoke embarrassment or shame in another. For example, American elementary-school children often show pride at personal achievement, such as getting the highest grade on a test or, as shown in the photo, coming in first place in a county fair. In contrast, Asian elementary-school children are embarrassed by a public display of individual achievement but show great pride when their entire class is honored for an achievement (Stevenson & Stigler, 1992).

Thus, culture can influence when and how much children express emotion. Of course, expressing emotion is only part of the developmental story. Children must also learn to recognize others' emotions, which is our next topic.

## Recognizing and Using Others' Emotions

Imagine you are broke and plan to borrow $20 from your roommate when she returns from class. Shortly, she storms into your apartment, slams the door, and throws her backpack on the floor. Immediately, you change your plans, realizing that now is hardly a good time to ask for a loan. This example reminds us that, just as it is adaptive to be able to express emotions, it is adaptive to be able to recognize others' emotions and sometimes change our behavior as a consequence.

By the first birthday, infants can recognize others' emotions and use these emotions to direct their own behavior.

When can infants first identify emotions in others? Perhaps as early as 4 months and definitely by 6 months, infants begin to distinguish facial expressions associated with different emotions. They can, for example, distinguish a happy, smiling face from a sad, frowning face (Ludemann, 1991; Montague & Walker-Andrews, 2001). Of course, infants might be able to distinguish an angry face from a happy one but not know the emotional significance of the two faces. How can we tell whether infants understand the emotions expressed in a face? The best evidence is that infants often match their own emotions to other people's emotions. When happy mothers smile and talk in a pleasant voice, infants express happiness themselves. If mothers are angry or sad, infants become distressed, too (Haviland & Lelwica, 1987; Montague & Walker-Andrews, 2001).

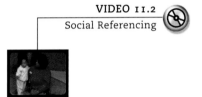

VIDEO 11.2
Social Referencing

Also like adults, infants use others' emotions to direct their behavior. **Infants in an unfamiliar or ambiguous environment often look at their mother or father, as if searching for cues to help them interpret the situation, a phenomenon known as social referencing.** If a parent looks afraid when shown a novel object, 12-month-olds are less likely to play with the toy than if a parent looks happy (Repacholi, 1998). Furthermore, an infant can use parents' facial expressions or their vocal expressions alone to decide whether they want to explore an unfamiliar object (Mumme, Fernald, & Herrera, 1996). And infants' use of parents' cues is precise. If two unfamiliar toys are shown to a parent, who expresses disgust at one toy but not the other, 12-month-olds will avoid the toy that elicited the disgust but not the other toy (Moses et al., 2001). Thus, social referencing shows that infants are remarkably skilled in using their parents' emotions to help them direct their own behavior.

As their cognitive skills grow, children begin to understand why people feel as they do. By kindergarten, for example, children know that undesirable or unpleasant events often make a person feel angry or sad (Levine, 1995). Children even know that they more often feel sad when they think about the undesirable event itself (e.g., a broken toy or a friend who moves away) but feel angry when they think about the person who caused the undesirable event (e.g., the person who broke the toy or the friend's parents who wanted to live in another city). Kindergarten children also understand that remembering past sad events can make a person unhappy again (Lagattuta, Wellman, & Flavell, 1997).

During the elementary-school years, children begin to comprehend that people sometimes experience "mixed feelings." Wintre and Vallance (1994) read sentences describing emotionally evocative situations to 4- through 8-year-olds and asked them how happy, angry, sad, scared, or loving they would feel in each situation. A sentence describing a fear-provoking situation was "You are home all alone," and one describing a sad situation was "Your best friend moves away." You can see in the results, shown in the figure, that by about 8 years of age children realize how people can feel good and bad at the same time. The increased ability to see multiple, differing emotions coincides with the freedom from centered thinking that characterizes the concrete operational stage (Module 7.2).

| Stage | Age | Understanding | Example |
|---|---|---|---|
| 1 | 5 years | A situation can cause a person to experience two different emotions. | A child could be sad and angry that a best friend is moving away. |
| 2 | 6 1/2 years | A situation can cause a person to experience two different emotions that differ in intensity. | A child could be very sad and a little angry that a best friend is moving away. |
| 3 | 8 years | A situation can cause a person to feel positively and negatively at the same time. | A child could be happy and scared about staying home alone. |

**Stages in the Development of Children's Understanding That People Can Experience Multiple Emotions Simultaneously**

FIG. 11-1

As children develop, they also begin to learn **display rules,** culturally specific standards for appropriate expressions of emotion in a particular setting or with a particular person or persons. Adults know, for example, that expressing sadness is appropriate at funerals but expressing joy is not. Similarly, expressing sadness is appropriate with relatives and close friends but less so with strangers. Preschool children's understanding of display rules is shown by the fact that they control their anger more when provoked by peers they like than when provoked by peers they don't like (Fabes et al., 1996). Also, school-age children and adolescents are more willing to express anger than sadness and, like the child in the photo, more willing to express both anger and sadness to parents than to peers (Zeman & Garber, 1996; Zeman & Shipman, 1997).

What experiences contribute to children's understanding of emotions? Not surprisingly, children learn about emotions when parents talk about feelings, explaining how they differ and the situations that elicit them (Brown & Dunn, 1996; Cervantes & Callanan, 1998). Also, a positive, rewarding relationship with parents and siblings is related to children's understanding of emotions (Brown & Dunn, 1996; Thompson, Laible, & Ontai, 2003). The nature of this connection is still a mystery. One possibility is that within positive parent–child and sibling relationships, people express a fuller range of emotions (and do so more often) and are more willing to talk about why they feel as they do, providing children more opportunities to learn about emotions.

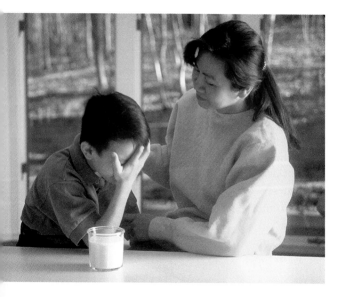

Children's growing understanding of emotions in others contributes in turn to a growing ability to help others. They are more likely to recognize the emotions that signal a person's need. Better understanding of emotions in others also contributes to children's growing ability to play easily with peers because they can see the impact of their behavior on others. We'll cover empathy and social interaction in detail later in the book; for now, the important point is that recognizing emotions in others is an important prerequisite for successful, satisfying interactions. Another element of successful interactions is regulating emotions, our next topic.

## Regulating Emotions

Think back to a time when you were *really* angry at a good friend. Did you shout at the friend? Did you try to discuss matters calmly? Or did you simply ignore the situation altogether? Shouting is a direct expression of anger, but calm conversation and overlooking a situation are deliberate attempts to regulate emotion. People often regulate emotions; for example, we routinely try to suppress fear (because we know there's no real need to be afraid of the dark), anger (because we don't want to let a friend know just how upset we are), and joy (because we don't want to seem like we're gloating over our good fortune).

Child-development researchers have studied two aspects of emotion regulation: its origins and its links to social competence. Emotion regulation clearly begins in infancy. By 4 to 6 months, infants use simple strategies to regulate their emotions (Buss & Goldsmith, 1998; Mangelsdorf, Shapiro, & Marzolf, 1995). When something frightens or confuses an infant—for example, a stranger or a mother who suddenly stops responding—he or she often looks away (just as older children and even adults often turn away or close their eyes to block out disturbing stimuli). Frightened infants also move closer to a parent, another effective way of helping to control their fear (Parritz, 1996).

> Even infants can regulate their emotions and school-age children have mastered several techniques for regulating their emotions.

Older children and adolescents encounter a wider range of emotional situations, so it's fortunate they develop a number of related new ways to regulate emotion (Eisenberg & Morris, 2002):

- Children begin to regulate their own emotions and rely less on others to do this for them. A fearful child no longer runs to a parent but instead devises her own methods for dealing with fear. For example, she might reassure herself by saying, "I know the thunderstorm won't last long and I'm safe inside the house."
- Children more often rely on mental strategies to regulate emotions. For example, a child might reduce his disappointment at not receiving a much-expected gift by telling himself that he didn't really want the gift in the first place.
- Children more accurately match the strategies for regulating emotion with the particular setting. For example, when faced with emotional situations that are unavoidable, such as going to the dentist to have a cavity filled, children adjust to the situation (for instance, by thinking of the positive consequences of treating the tooth) instead of trying to avoid the situation.

Collectively, these age-related trends give older children and adolescents plenty of tools for regulating emotions. Nevertheless, not all children regulate their emotions well and those who don't tend to have problems interacting with peers and have adjustment problems (Eisenberg & Morris, 2002; Lengua, 2002). When children can't control their anger, worry, or sadness, they often have difficulty resolving the conflicts that inevitably surface in peer relationships (Fabes et al., 1999). For example, when children argue over which game to play or which movie to watch, their unregulated anger can interfere with finding a mutually satisfying solution. Thus, ineffective regulation of emotions leads to more frequent conflicts with peers, and, consequently, less satisfying peer relationships and less adaptive adjustment to school (Eisenberg et al., 2001).

In this module, we've seen how children express, recognize, and regulate emotions; in the next module, we'll discover that emotion is an important feature of children's temperament.

**CHECK YOUR LEARNING**

**1.** According to the functional approach, emotions are important because
_____.

**2.** Basic emotions include a subjective feeling, a physiological change, and
_____.

**3.** According to one theory, newborns experience only pleasure and _____.

**4.** The first detectable form of fear is _____, which emerges at about 6 months.

**5.** Wariness of strangers is adaptive because it emerges at about the same time that
_____.

**6.** Complex emotions, such as guilt and shame, emerge later than basic emotions because _____.

**7.** In social referencing, infants use a parent's facial expression _____.

**8.** School-age children and adolescents express anger and sadness more often with
_____ than with peers.

**9.** When children cannot regulate their emotions well, they tend to have problems in _____.

🔀 **CONNECTIONS**
Most theories of cognitive development, such as Piaget's and the information-processing approach, don't explicitly consider emotion. How might emotions affect thinking? How could these approaches include emotion?

**Answers:** (1) they are useful—they help people adapt to their environment, (2) an overt behavior, (3) distress, (4) wariness of strangers, (5) infants master creeping and crawling, (6) complex emotions require more advanced cognitive skills, (7) to direct their own behavior (for example, deciding if an unfamiliar situation is safe or frightening), (8) parents, (9) interacting with peers, especially when conflicts arise

# 11.2

# Temperament

What Is Temperament?

Hereditary and Environmental
Contributions to Temperament

Stability of Temperament

Temperament and Other Aspects
of Development

**LEARNING OBJECTIVES**

● What are the different features of temperament?

● How do heredity and environment influence temperament?

● How stable is a child's temperament across childhood?

● What are the consequences of different temperaments?

*Soon after Yoshimi arrived in the United States from Japan to begin graduate studies, she enrolled her 5-month-old son in day care. She was struck by the fact that, compared to her son, the European American babies in the day-care center were "wimps" (slang she had learned from American television). The other babies cried often and with minimal provocation. Yoshimi wondered whether her son was unusually "tough" or whether he was just a typical Japanese baby.*

When you've observed young babies—perhaps as part of "See for Yourself" in Chapter 4—were some babies like Yoshimi's, quiet most of the time, while others cried often and impatiently? Maybe you saw some infants who responded warmly to strangers and others who seemed very shy. **Such behavioral styles, which are fairly stable across** situations and are biologically based, make up an infant's temperament. For example, all babies become upset occasionally and cry. However, some, like Yoshimi's son, recover quickly and others are very hard to console. These differences in emotion and style of behavior are evident in the first few weeks after birth and are important throughout life.

We'll begin this module by looking at different ways that scientists define temperament.

## What Is Temperament?

Alexander Thomas and Stella Chess (Thomas, Chess, & Birch, 1968) pioneered the study of temperament with the New York Longitudinal Study, in which they traced the lives of 141 individuals from infancy through adulthood. Thomas and Chess gathered their initial data by interviewing the babies' parents and asking individuals unfamiliar with the children to observe them at home. Based on these interviews and observations, Thomas and Chess suggested that infants' behavior varied along nine temperamental dimensions. One dimension was activity, which referred to an infant's typical level of motor activity. A second was persistence, which referred to the amount of time that an infant devoted to an activity, particularly when obstacles are present.

Using these and other dimensions, Thomas and Chess identified three patterns of temperament. Most common were "easy" babies, who were usually happy and cheerful, tended to adjust well to new situations, and had regular routines for eating, sleeping, and toileting. A second, less common group were "difficult" babies, who tended to be unhappy, were irregular in their eating and sleeping, and often responded intensely to unfamiliar situations. Another less common group were "slow to warm up" babies. Like difficult babies, slow-to-warm-up babies were often unhappy; but unlike difficult babies, slow-to-warm-up were not upset by unfamiliar situations.

*In the New York Longitudinal Study, most infants could be placed in one of three temperamental groups: easy, difficult, and slow to warm up.*

The New York Longitudinal Study launched research on infant temperament, but today's researchers no longer emphasize creating different categories of infants, such as "easy" or "slow to warm up." Instead, researchers want to determine the different dimensions that underlie temperament. Instead of the nine dimensions proposed by Thomas and Chess, most scientists now agree that temperament consists of somewhere between two and six dimensions (Rothbart & Bates, 1998). For example, the table lists five dimensions of temperament included in most current accounts of temperament (Caspi, 1998).

| **Five Dimensions of Temperament** | |
|---|---|
| **Dimension** | **Description** |
| Activity level | The amount of physical and motor activity in daily situations |
| Positive affect | The extent to which the child expresses pleasure, enthusiasm, and contentment |
| Persistence | The amount of time a child devotes to an activity, particularly when obstacles or distractions are present, and the child's ability to resist distraction from competing stimuli |
| Inhibition | The extent to which a child is shy and withdrawn, particularly in unfamiliar settings |
| Negative affect | The extent to which a child is irritable, easily distresses, and is prone to anger |

TABLE 11–1

Some theories have fewer dimensions because they combine dimensions listed in the table. For example, one view is that activity level and positive affect are really a common dimension that refers to a child's enthusiasm for approaching and engaging novel situations. Other theories have more dimensions because dimensions listed in the table are subdivided. An example would be negative affect: Sometimes this is divided into *fearful distress*, a response to a novel social situation or a novel object, and *irritated distress*, a response to frustrating situations (Wachs & Bates, 2001). These fine points of temperament are still being studied.

## Hereditary and Environmental Contributions to Temperament

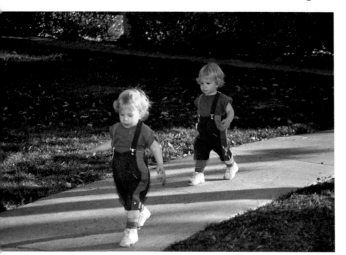

Most theories agree that temperament reflects both heredity and experience. The influence of heredity is shown in twin studies: Identical twins are more alike in most aspects of temperament than fraternal twins. For example, Goldsmith, Buss, and Lemery (1997) found that the correlation for identical twins' activity level was .72, but the correlation for fraternal twins was only .38. In other words, like the youngsters in the photo, if one identical twin is temperamentally active, the other usually is, too. However, the impact of heredity also depends on the temperamental dimension and the child's age. For example, negative affect is more influenced by heredity than the other dimensions; and temperament in childhood is more influenced by heredity than is temperament in infancy (Wachs & Bates, 2001).

The environment also contributes to children's temperament. Positive emotionality—laughing often, being generally happy, and often expressing pleasure—seems to reflect environmental influences (Goldsmith et al., 1997). Conversely, infants more often develop intense, difficult temperaments when mothers are abrupt in dealing with them and lack confidence (Belsky, Fish, & Isabella, 1991).

Heredity and experience may also explain why Yoshimi, the Japanese mother in the vignette, has such a hardy son. The "Cultural Influences" feature tells the story.

## CULTURAL INFLUENCES

### Why Is Yoshimi's Son So Tough?

If you've ever watched an infant getting an injection, you know the inevitable response. After the syringe is removed, the infant's eyes open wide and then the baby begins to cry, as if saying, "Wow, that hurt!" Infants differ in how intensely they cry and in how readily they are soothed, reflecting differences in the emotionality dimension of temperament, but virtually all European American babies cry. It's easy to suppose that crying is a universal response to the pain from the inoculation, but it's not.

In such stressful situations, Japanese and Chinese infants are less likely to become upset (Kagan et al., 1994). Lewis, Ramsay, and Kawakami (1993) found that most European American 4-month-olds cried loudly within 5 seconds of an injection, but only half the Japanese babies in their study cried. What's more, when Japanese and Chinese babies become upset, they are soothed more readily than European American babies.

Lewis and his colleagues found that about three-fourths of the Japanese babies were no longer crying 90 seconds after the injection, compared to fewer than half the European American babies. The conclusion seems clear: Yoshimi's son appears to be a typical Japanese baby in crying less often and less intensely than the European American babies at his day-care center.

Why are Asian infants less emotional than their European American counterparts? Heredity may be involved. Perhaps the genes that contribute to emotionality are less common among Asians than among European Americans. But we can't overlook experience. Compared to European American mothers, Japanese mothers spend more time in close physical contact with their babies, constantly and gently soothing them; this may reduce the tendency to respond emotionally. 🔊

There's no question that heredity and experience cause babies' temperaments to differ, but how stable is temperament across childhood and adolescence? We'll find out in the next section.

## Stability of Temperament

Do calm, easygoing babies grow up to be calm, easygoing children, adolescents, and adults? Are difficult, irritable infants destined to grow up to be cranky, whiny children? The first answers to these questions came from the Fels longitudinal project, a study of many aspects of physical and psychological development from infancy. Although not a study of temperament per se, Jerome Kagan and his collaborators (Kagan, 1989; Kagan & Moss, 1962) found that fearful preschoolers in the Fels project tended to be inhibited as older children and adolescents.

> Temperament is moderately stable through infancy, childhood, and adolescence.

Spurred by findings like this one, later investigators attempted to learn more about the stability of temperament. This research shows that temperament is moderately stable throughout infancy, childhood, and adolescence (Wachs & Bates, 2001). For example, newborns who cry under moderate stress tend, as 5-month-olds, to cry when they are placed in stressful situations like the one in the photo, in which the mother is not allowing her baby to move its body (Stifter & Fox, 1990). In addition, inhibited 2-year-olds tend to be shy as 4-year-olds, especially when their mothers are intrusive (e.g., provide help when it's not needed) or frequently make derisive remarks about their shyness, such as "Don't be such a baby!" (Rubin, Burgess, & Hastings, 2002).

In many respects, temperament resembles personality, so it's not surprising that many child-development researchers have speculated about potential connections between the two. In fact, personality in adulthood includes many of the same dimensions observed for temperament in infancy and childhood (Caspi, 1998; Costa & McCrae, 2001). For example, extroversion is a dimension of personality that refers to a person's warmth, gregariousness, and activity level. Extroverted individuals tend to be affectionate, prefer the company of others, and like being active; introverted people tend to be more reserved, enjoy solitude, and prefer a more sedate pace (Costa & McCrae, 2001).

Extroversion looks like a blend of the temperamental dimensions of positive affect and activity level; and longitudinal studies find that inhibited children are more likely as adults to be introverted than extroverted (Caspi & Silva, 1995). However, research of this sort also reveals many instances in which temperament is poorly related to personality in adulthood (Wachs &

Bates, 2001). This may seem surprising, but remember that temperament changes as children develop, depending on their experiences. An inhibited child who finds herself in a school group with children with similar interests may "open up" and become much more outgoing over time; her early inhibited temperament is not related to her later outgoing personality. Thus, we should not expect children's temperament to be consistently related to their personality as adults.

In the next section, we'll see some of the connections between temperament and other aspects of development.

## Temperament and Other Aspects of Development

One of the goals of Thomas and Chess's New York Longitudinal Study was to discover temperamental features of infants that would predict later psychological adjustment. In fact, Thomas and Chess discovered that about two-thirds of the preschoolers with difficult temperaments had developed behavioral problems by the time they entered school. In contrast, fewer than one-fifth of the children with easy temperaments had behavioral problems (Thomas et al., 1968).

> Temperament is linked to school success, good peer relations, compliance to parents' requests, and to depression.

Other scientists have followed the lead of the New York Longitudinal Study in looking for links between temperament and outcomes of development, and they've found that temperament is an important influence on development. Consider these examples:

- Persistent children are likely to succeed in school, whereas active and distractible children are less likely to succeed (Martin, Olejnik, & Gaddis, 1994).

- Shy, inhibited children often have difficulty interacting with their peers and often do not cope effectively with problems (Eisenberg et al., 1998; Kochanska & Radke-Yarrow, 1992).

- Anxious, fearful children are more likely to comply with a parent's rules and requests, even when the parent is not present (Kochanska, 1995).

- Children who are frequently angry or fearful are more prone to depression (Lengua, West, & Sandler, 1998).

The "Focus on Research" feature shows that temperament is also related to children's tendency to help people in distress.

## FOCUS ON RESEARCH

### Temperament Influences Helping Others

*Who were the investigators, and what was the aim of the study?* When people are in obvious distress, some children readily step forward to help but others seem reluctant to help. Why are some children so helpful whereas others aren't? Shari Young, Nathan Fox, and Carolyn Zahn-Waxler (1999) argued that temperament may be part of the answer. Specifically, inhibited, shy youngsters may find it difficult to overcome their reticence to help another, particularly when they do not know the person and when the other person does not specifically request help. Young and her colleagues examined this hypothesis by studying inhibition and helping in 2-year-olds.

*How did the investigators measure the topic of interest?* The researchers videotaped children as they interacted with their mother and a stranger during free play. At some point during the session, the experimenter feigned injury (e.g., she pretended that she had caught her fingers in the clipboard). Later in the session, the mother also feigned injury (e.g., she pretended to bump into a chair). While feigning injury, the experimenter and the mother did not solicit the child's help in any way, either directly (e.g., by saying, "Help me, help me") or indirectly (e.g., by calling the child's name). Later, observers scored children's behaviors on several dimensions, including:

- *Inhibition:* The extent to which children avoided the experimenter, even when he began playing with a novel, attractive toy.
- *Concerned expression:* The extent to which children displayed obvious concern for the injured experimenter or mother, as shown by, for example, expressions of sadness.
- *Helpful behavior:* The extent to which children acted in ways apparently aimed at reducing distress, such as sharing a toy or stroking the injured body part.

*Who were the children in the study?* The study involved fifty 2-year-olds. Children were tested within 2 weeks of their second birthday.

*What was the design of the study?* This study was correlational because Young and her colleagues were interested in the relation that existed naturally between inhibition and helping. The study was actually longitudinal (children were also tested at 4 months), but I'm only describing the results from the second testing session, which took place at age 2 years.

*Were there ethical concerns with the study?* No. The children enjoyed most of the free play session. The experimenters and mothers "recovered" quickly from their feigned injuries—in approximately 1 minute—and no children were visibly upset by the injury.

*What were the results?* The graph shows some correlations between inhibition and (a) expressing concern, and (b) helping behavior, separately for helping the mother and helping the experimenter. Let's begin with the correlations for mothers. Neither correlation is significant, which indicates that when interacting with their moms, shy and outgoing children were equally likely to express concern and to provide help. The results differ for helping the experimenter. The correlation between inhibition and expressing concern is again small, indicating that shy and outgoing youngsters were equally likely to express concern when the experimenter feigned injury. However, the correlation between inhibition and helping is negative: shy, inhibited 2-year-olds were less likely than outgoing 2-year-olds to help an experimenter who appeared to be hurt.

*What did the investigators conclude?* A young child's temperament helps determine whether that child will help. When mothers and experimenters feigned injury, both shy and outgoing children noticed and were disturbed by their distress. Outgoing children typically translated this concern into action, helping both mothers and experimenters. In contrast, shy youngsters helped mothers but could not overcome their reticence to help an unfamiliar adult who did not specifically ask for help. Even though shy children see that a person is suffering, their apprehensiveness in unfamiliar social settings often prevents them from helping.

*What converging evidence would strengthen these conclusions?* One way to test the generality of these results would be to repeat the experiment, replacing the mother and adult experimenter with an older sibling and unfamiliar child who is the same age as the older sibling. The prediction is that shy and outgoing

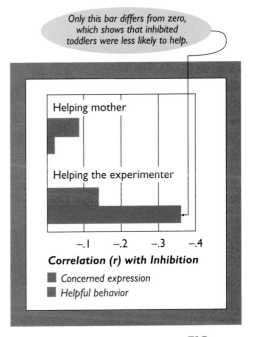

FIG. 11–2

children would help the familiar older sibling, but only outgoing children would help the unfamiliar older child. ⬤

Although these findings underscore that temperament is an important force in children's development, temperament rarely is the sole determining factor. Instead, the influence of temperament often depends on the environment in which children develop. To illustrate, let's consider the link between temperament and behavior problems. Infants and toddlers who temperamentally resist control—those who are difficult to manage, who are often unresponsive, and who are sometimes impulsive—tend to be prone to behavior problems, particularly aggression, when they are older. However, more careful analysis shows that resistant temperament leads to behavior problems primarily when mothers do not exert much control over their children. Among mothers who do exert control—those who prohibit, warn, and scold their children when necessary—resistant temperament is not linked to behavior problems (Bates et al., 1998).

Similarly, young adolescents are more likely to drink, smoke, and use drugs when they experience many life stressors (e.g., when someone in the family has a serious accident or illness, when a parent loses a job, or when parents and the child are frequently in conflict) and their parents themselves smoke and drink. But this is less true for young adolescents with temperaments marked by positive affect (Wills et al., 2001). That is, young adolescents who are temperamentally cheerful apparently are less affected by life stressors and consequently are less likely to drink, smoke, or use drugs.

This research reminds us that emotion is a fundamental element of temperament. In the next module, we'll look at emotion from yet another perspective, that of the emotional relationship formed between an infant and its primary caregiver.

## CHECK YOUR LEARNING

1. In their New York Longitudinal Study, Thomas and Chess identified nine dimensions of temperament, but today most scientists believe that _____.

2. Compared to European American infants, Asian infants are calmer and _____.

3. Research on the stability of temperament in infancy, childhood, and adolescence typically finds that _____.

4. Thomas and Chess found that by the time difficult preschool children had entered school, many had _____.

5. Although temperament is an important developmental force, the influence of temperament often depends on _____.

Ⓘ **NATURE AND NURTURE**
What are the biological bases of temperament? How does the environment influence temperament? How do nature and nurture interact to influence temperament?

**Answers:** (1) Thomas and Chess overestimated the number of temperamental dimensions; instead of nine, there are two to six dimensions; (2) are soothed more readily when upset, (3) temperament is moderately stable, (4) developed behavioral problems, (5) the environment in which children develop

# Attachment

**LEARNING OBJECTIVES**

● How does an attachment relationship develop between an infant and primary caregiver?

● What different types of attachment relationships are there? What are the consequences of different types of relationships?

*Ever since Samantha was a newborn, Karen and Dick looked forward to going to their favorite restaurant on Friday night. Karen enjoyed the break from childcare responsibilities and Dick liked being able to talk to Karen without interruptions. But recently they've had a problem. When they leave her with a sitter, 8-month-old "Sam" gets a frightened look on her face and usually begins to cry hysterically. Karen and Dick wonder if Sam's behavior is normal and if their Friday night dinners are coming to an end.*

The social-emotional relationship that develops between an infant and a parent (usually, but not necessarily, the mother) is special. This is a baby's first social-emotional relationship, so scientists and parents alike believe it should be satisfying and trouble-free to set the stage for later relationships. In this module, we'll look at the steps involved in creating the baby's first emotional relationship. Along the way, we'll see why 8-month-old Sam has begun to cry when Karen and Dick leave her with a sitter.

## The Growth of Attachment

Sigmund Freud was the first modern theorist to emphasize the importance of emotional ties to the mother for psychological development. Today, the dominant view of early human relationships comes from John Bowlby (1969, 1991). **According to Bowlby, children who form an attachment to an adult—that is, an enduring social-emotional relationship—are more likely to survive.** This person is usually the mother but need not be; the key is a strong emotional relationship with a responsive, caring person. Attachments can form with fathers, grandparents, or someone else.

Bowlby (1969) argued that evolutionary pressure favored behaviors likely to elicit caregiving from an adult, such as clinging, sucking, crying, and smiling. That is, over the course of human evolution, these behaviors have become a standard part of the human infant's biological heritage, and the responses they evoke in adults create an interactive system that leads to the formation of attachment relationships.

The attachment relationship develops gradually over the first several months after birth, reflecting the baby's growing perceptual and cognitive skills described in Chapters 6 and 7. The first step is for the infant to learn the difference between people and other objects. Typically, in the first few months, babies begin to respond differently to people and to objects—for example, smiling more at people and vocalizing more to people—suggesting that they have begun to identify members of the social world.

During these months, mother and infant begin to synchronize their interactions. Remember from Module 4.4 that young babies' behaviors go through cycles. Infants move between states of alertness and attentiveness to states of distress and

**Many infant behaviors such as crying and smiling are designed to elicit caregiving from adults and thus promote the development of an emotional bond between parent and child.**

VIDEO 11.3
Nature and Development of Affection: Harlow's Monkeys
CLASSIC MODULE

inattentiveness. Caregivers begin to recognize these states of behavior and adjust their own behavior accordingly. A mother who notices that her baby is awake and alert will begin to smile at and talk to her baby. These interactions often continue until the baby's state changes, which prompts the mother to stop. In fact, by 3 months of age, if a mother does not interact with her alert baby (but instead stares silently), babies become at least moderately distressed, looking away from her and sometimes crying (Toda & Fogel, 1993).

Thus, interactions between mothers and infants gradually become well coordinated. When vocalizing, mothers and infants alternate smoothly between speaking and listening (Jaffe et al., 2001). And they begin to calibrate their behaviors so that they are both "on" at the same time (Gable & Isabella, 1992). These interactions provide the foundation for more sophisticated communication and foster the infant's trust that the mother will respond predictably and reassuringly.

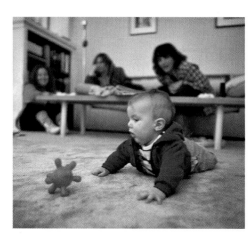

By approximately 7 or 8 months, most infants have singled out the attachment figure—usually the mother—as a special individual. An infant will smile at the mother and cling to her more than to other people. The attachment figure is now the infant's stable social-emotional base. For example, a 7-month-old like the one in the photo will explore a novel environment but periodically look toward his mother, as if seeking reassurance that all is well. The behavior suggests the infant trusts his mother and indicates the attachment relationship has been established. In addition, this behavior reflects important cognitive growth: It means that the infant has a mental representation of the mother, an understanding that she will be there to meet the infant's needs (Lewis et al., 1997).

The formation of the attachment bond also explains why 8-month-old Sam cries whenever Karen and Dick try to leave her with a sitter. Sam is attached to Karen, expects her to be nearby, and is upset when separated from her.

**THE ROLE OF FATHERS.** Attachment typically first develops between infants and their mothers because mothers are usually the primary caregivers of American infants. Babies soon become attached to fathers, too, despite some consistent differences in the ways that American mothers and fathers interact with infants. In a

typical two-parent family, fathers spend far less time than mothers with infants and are far less likely than mothers to be responsible for child-care tasks. For example, in a nationally representative sample of mothers and fathers of infants and toddlers, fathers spent an average of 32 minutes each day in caregiving tasks (e.g., feeding, bathing) compared to 70 minutes for mothers (Yeung et al., 2001). Over the past 40 years, child care has shifted some from being "women's work" to a responsibility that can be shared equally by mothers and fathers. But women are still far more likely to be involved in direct care of infants and toddlers, despite no evidence that they provide better care than fathers do (Parke, 2002).

Another difference between mothers and fathers is *how* they interact with young children. Fathers typically spend much more time playing with their babies than taking care of them. And even their style of play differs. Physical play like that shown in the photo is the norm for fathers, whereas mothers spend more time reading and talking to babies, showing them toys, and playing games like patty-cake (Parke, 2002). Given the opportunity to play with mothers or fathers, infants more often choose their fathers. However, when infants are distressed, mothers are preferred (Field, 1990). Thus, although most infants become attached to both parents, mothers and fathers typically have distinctive roles in their children's early social development.

VIDEO 11.4
Separation Anxiety

## The Quality of Attachment

Attachment between infant and mother usually occurs by 8 or 9 months of age, but the attachment can take on different forms. Mary Ainsworth (1978, 1993) pioneered the study of attachment relationships using a procedure that has come to be known as the Strange Situation. You can see in the diagram that the Strange Situation involves a series of episodes, each about 3 minutes long. The mother and infant enter an unfamiliar room filled with interesting toys. The mother leaves briefly, then mother and baby are reunited. Meanwhile, the experimenter observes the baby, recording its response to both events.

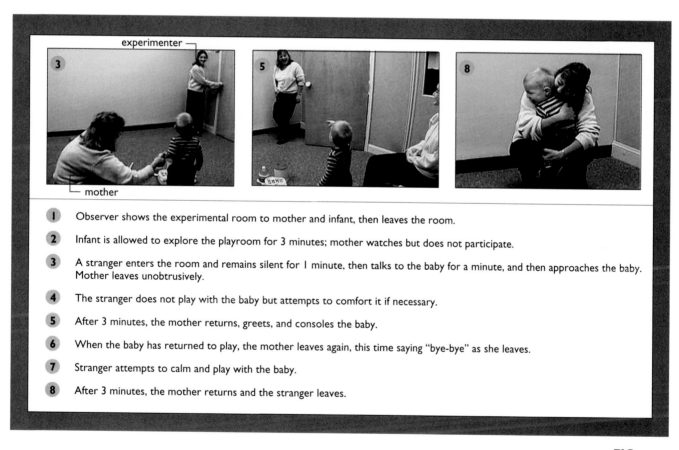

experimenter

mother

1  Observer shows the experimental room to mother and infant, then leaves the room.

2  Infant is allowed to explore the playroom for 3 minutes; mother watches but does not participate.

3  A stranger enters the room and remains silent for 1 minute, then talks to the baby for a minute, and then approaches the baby. Mother leaves unobtrusively.

4  The stranger does not play with the baby but attempts to comfort it if necessary.

5  After 3 minutes, the mother returns, greets, and consoles the baby.

6  When the baby has returned to play, the mother leaves again, this time saying "bye-bye" as she leaves.

7  Stranger attempts to calm and play with the baby.

8  After 3 minutes, the mother returns and the stranger leaves.

FIG. 11-3

Based on how the infant reacts to separation from the mother and then reunion, Ainsworth (1993) and other researchers (Main & Cassidy, 1988) have identified four primary types of attachment relationships. One is a secure attachment and three are insecure attachments (avoidant, resistant, disorganized):

• **Secure attachment: The baby may or may not cry when the mother leaves, but when she returns, the baby wants to be with her and if the baby is crying,**

**it stops.** Babies in this group seem to be saying, "I missed you terribly, but now that you're back, I'm okay." Approximately 60 to 65 percent of American babies have secure attachment relationships.

- **Avoidant attachment: The baby is not visibly upset when the mother leaves and, when she returns, may ignore her by looking or turning away.** Infants with an avoidant attachment look as if they're saying, "You left me again. I always have to take care of myself!" About 20 percent of American infants have avoidant attachment relationships, which is one of the three forms of insecure attachment.

- **Resistant attachment: The baby is upset when the mother leaves and remains upset or even angry when she returns, and is difficult to console.** Like the baby in the photo, these babies seem to be telling the mother, "Why do you do this? I need you desperately and yet you just leave me without warning. I get so angry when you're like this." About 10 to 15 percent of American babies have this resistant attachment relationship, which is another form of insecure attachment.

- **Disorganized (disoriented) attachment: The baby seems confused when the mother leaves and, when she returns, seems as if it doesn't really understand what's happening.** The baby often has a dazed look on its face as if wondering, "What's going on here? I want you to be here, but you left and now you're back. I don't know whether to laugh or cry!" About 5 to 10 percent of American babies have this disorganized attachment relationship, the last of the three kinds of insecure attachment.

More than 30 years later, the Strange Situation remains an important tool for studying attachment. But some scientists have criticized its emphasis on separation and reunion as the primary means for assessing quality of attachment; they suggest that what is considered an appropriate response to separation may not be the same in all cultures (Rothbaum et al., 2000). Consequently, investigators now use other methods to complement the Strange Situation. One of them, the Attachment Q-Set, can be used with young children as well as infants and toddlers. In this method, trained observers watch mothers and children interact at home; then the observer rates the interaction on many attachment-related behaviors (e.g., "Child greets mother with a big smile when she enters the room"). The ratings are totaled to provide a measure of the security of the child's attachment.

Whether measured with the Strange Situation or the Attachment Q-Set, secure attachments are the most common throughout the world (van IJzendoorn & Kroonenberg, 1988; van IJzendoorn & Sagi, 1999). As you can see in the graph, in many countries roughly two out of three infants are securely attached. This is fortunate because, as we'll see, a secure attachment provides a solid base for later social development.

Infants typically form the same type of attachment relationships with both parents (Fox, Kimmerly, & Schafer, 1991). An infant who is securely attached to his mother is usually securely attached to

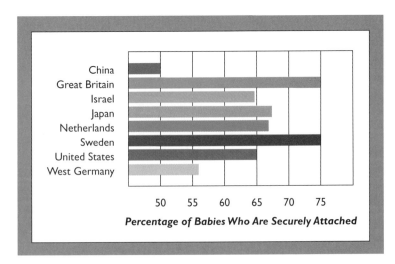

*Percentage of Babies Who Are Securely Attached*

FIG. 11-4

his father, too. In addition, when an infant is securely attached, the infant's siblings are likely to be securely attached, too, especially when they're the same sex (van IJzendoorn et al., 2000). However, you shouldn't conclude that security of attachment is etched in stone in infancy: Attachment security can and does change, particularly when changes in family circumstances (e.g., birth of a sibling, divorce) produce a change in the quality of care that a child receives (Sagi et al., 2002; Thompson, 2000).

**CONSEQUENCES OF QUALITY OF ATTACHMENT.** Erikson, Bowlby, and other theorists (Waters & Cummings, 2000) believe that attachment, as the first social relationship, provides the basis for all of an infant's later social relationships. In this view, infants who experience the trust and compassion of a secure attachment should develop into preschool children who interact confidently and successfully with their peers. In contrast, infants who do not experience a successful, satisfying first relationship should be more prone to problems in their social interactions as preschoolers.

> Infants with a secure attachment relationship tend to interact successfully with peers.

Many findings are consistent with these predictions. For example, children with secure attachment relationships have higher-quality friendships and fewer conflicts in their friendships than children with insecure attachment relationships (Lieberman, Doyle, & Markiewicz, 1999). And, school-age children are less likely to have behavior problems if they have secure attachment relationships and more likely if they have insecure attachment relationships (Carlson, 1998; Moss et al., 1998).

However, the most compelling evidence comes from a meta-analysis of 63 studies that examined possible links between parent–child attachment and children's peer relations (Schneider, Atkinson, & Tardif, 2001). As predicted, children with secure attachments tended to have better relations with their peers and, in particular, had higher-quality friendships. And, although some theorists (Thompson, 1998) have argued that an insecure attachment is particularly detrimental to peer relations in children who are exposed to other risk factors (e.g., if they have a history of maltreatment or if one of their parents has a psychiatric disorder), the positive relation between attachment and peer relations was evident in children from high- and low-risk groups.

The conclusion seems inescapable: As infants who have secure attachment relationships develop, their social interactions tend to be more satisfying. Why? Secure attachment evidently promotes trust and confidence in other humans, which leads to more skilled social interactions later in childhood. Of course, attachment is only one step along the long road of social development. Infants with insecure attachments are not doomed, but this initial misstep can interfere with their social development.

**FACTORS DETERMINING QUALITY OF ATTACHMENT.** Because secure attachment is so important to a child's later development, researchers have tried to identify the factors involved. Undoubtedly the most important is the interaction between parents and their babies (De Wolff & van IJzendoorn, 1997). A secure attachment is most likely when parents respond to infants predictably and appropriately. For example, the mother in the photo has promptly responded to her baby's crying and is trying to reassure the baby. The mother's behavior evidently conveys that social interactions are predictable and satisfying, and apparently this behavior instills in infants the trust and confidence that are the hallmark of secure attachment.

A secure attachment relationship is most likely to develop when parents respond to the infant's needs reliably and sensitively.

Why does predictable and responsive parenting promote secure attachment relationships? To answer this question, think about your own friendships and romantic relationships. These relationships are usually most satisfying when we believe we can trust the other people and depend on them in times of need. The same formula seems to hold for infants. **Infants develop an internal working model, a set of expectations about parents' availability and responsiveness, generally and in times of stress.** When parents are dependable and caring, babies come to trust them, knowing they can be relied upon for comfort. That is, babies develop an internal working model in which they believe their parents are concerned about their needs and will try to meet them (Bretherton, 1992; Thompson, 2000).

Many research findings attest to the importance of a caregiver's sensitivity for developing secure attachment:

- In a longitudinal study, infants were more likely to have a secure attachment relationship at 12 months when their parents were sensitive and responded quickly and appropriately to their infant at 3 months (Cox et al., 1992).

- In a study conducted in Israel, infants were less likely to develop secure attachment when they slept in dormitories with other children under 12, where they received inconsistent (if any) attention when they became upset overnight (Sagi et al., 1994).

- In a study conducted in the Netherlands, infants were more likely to form a secure attachment when their mother had 3 months of training that emphasized monitoring an infant's signals and responding appropriately and promptly (van den Boom, 1994, 1995).

Thus, secure attachment is most likely when parents are sensitive and responsive. Of course, not all caregivers react to babies in a reliable and reassuring manner. Some respond intermittently or only after the infant has cried long and hard. And when these caregivers finally respond, they are sometimes annoyed by the infant's demands and may misinterpret the infant's intent. Over time, these babies tend to see social relationships as inconsistent and often frustrating, conditions that do little to foster trust and confidence.

Why are some parents more responsive (and thus are more likely to foster secure attachment) than others? According to modern attachment theory (e.g., Cassidy, 1994), parents have internal working models of the attachment relationship with their own parents, and these working models guide interactions with their own infants. When questioned about attachment relationships with the Adult Attachment Interview (George, Kaplan, & Main, 1985), adults can be classified into one of three groups, one corresponding to the secure attachment of childhood and the other two corresponding to insecure attachments:

- **Secure adults describe childhood experiences objectively and value the impact of their parent–child relationship on their development.**

- **Dismissive adults sometimes deny the value of childhood experiences and sometimes are unable to recall those experiences precisely, yet they often idealize their parents.**

- **Preoccupied adults describe childhood experiences emotionally and often express anger or confusion regarding relationships with their parents.**

According to attachment theory, only parents with autonomous attachment representations are likely to provide the sensitive caregiving that promotes secure attachment relationships. In fact, many studies show that parents' secure attachment representations are associated with sensitive caregiving, and, in turn, with secure attachment in their infants (van IJzendoorn, 1995; Pederson et al., 1998). Furthermore, some studies (Hamilton, 2000; Waters et al., 2000) show that infants with secure attachment relations tend to become adults with secure attachment representations, completing the circle. However, as I mentioned earlier, a secure attachment is not determined forever in infancy; when children with secure attachments experience many stressful life events, their attachment representations often become insecure (Waters et al., 2000).

The sensitive and responsive caregiving that is essential for secure attachments is often taxing, particularly for babies with difficult temperaments. That is, babies who fuss often and are difficult to console are more prone to insecure attachment (Goldsmith & Harman, 1994; Seifer et al., 1996). Insecure attachment may also be more likely when a difficult, emotional infant has a mother whose personality is rigid and traditional than when the mother is accepting and flexible (Mangelsdorf et al., 1990). Rigid mothers do not adjust well to the often erratic demands of their difficult babies; instead, they want the baby to adjust to them. This means that rigid mothers less often provide the responsive, sensitive care that leads to secure attachment.

Fortunately, even brief training for mothers of newborns can help them respond to their babies more effectively (Wendland-Carro, Piccinini, & Millar, 1999). Mothers can be taught how to interact more sensitively, affectionately, and responsively, paving the way for secure attachment and the lifelong benefits associated with a positive internal working model of interpersonal relationships.

**WORK, ATTACHMENT, AND CHILD CARE.**   Since the 1970s, more women in the workforce and more single-parent households have made child care a fact of life for many American families. I describe child care in detail in Module 16.3, but here I want to focus on one specific aspect: What happens to mother–infant attachment when other people care for the infant much of the time? Parents and policymakers alike have been concerned about the impact of such care. Is there, for example, a maximum amount of time per week that infants should spend in care outside the home? Is there a minimum age below which infants should not be placed in care outside the home? The "Child Development and Family Policy" feature describes work that has attempted to answer these and other questions about the impact of early child care on children's development.

## CHILD DEVELOPMENT AND FAMILY POLICY

### Determining Guidelines for Child Care for Infants and Toddlers

Because so many American families need child care for their infants and toddlers, a comprehensive study of early child care was required to provide parents and policymakers with appropriate guidelines. The task fell to the U.S. National Institute of Child

Health and Human Development, which began the Early Child Care study in 1991. Researchers recruited 1,364 mothers and their newborns from 12 U.S. cities. Both mothers and children have been tested repeatedly (and the testing continues, since the study is ongoing).

From the outset, one of the concerns was the impact of early child care on mother–infant attachment. In fact, the results so far show no overall effects of child-care experience on mother–infant attachment, for either 15- or 36-month-olds (NICHD Early Child Care Research Network, 1997, 2001). In other words, a secure mother–infant attachment was just as likely, regardless of the quality of child care, the amount of time the child spent in care, the age when the child began care, how frequently the parents changed child-care arrangements, and the type of child care (e.g., at a child-care center or in the home with a non-relative).

However, when the effects of child care were considered along with characteristics of mothers, an important pattern was detected: At 15 and 36 months, insecure attachments were more common when less sensitive mothering was combined with low quality or large amounts of child care (NICHD Early Child Care Research Network, 1997, 2001). As the investigators put it "poor quality, unstable, or more than minimal amounts of child care apparently added to the risks already inherent in poor mothering, so that the combined effects were worse than those of low maternal sensitivity and responsiveness alone" (1997, p. 877). These conclusions are particularly convincing because the same pattern of results was found in Israel in a large-scale study of child care and attachment that was modeled after the NICHD Early Child Care study (Sagi et al., 2002).

These results provide clear guidelines for parents. The essential ingredient for secure attachment is high-quality parenting. With such parenting, a secure attachment is likely regardless of a child's experience in child care. Of course, parents should still look for high-quality child care; and we'll explore this topic in detail in Module 16.3. ⦿

## CHECK YOUR LEARNING

1. By approximately _____ months of age, most infants have identified a special individual—typically, but not always, the mother—as the attachment figure.

2. Around the world, _____ is the customary role for fathers.

3. Joan, a 12-month-old, was separated from her mother for about 15 minutes. When they were reunited, Joan would not let her mother pick her up. When her mother approached, Joan looked the other way and toddled to another part of the room. This behavior suggests that Joan has a(n) _____ attachment relationship.

4. _____ is the most common form of attachment worldwide.

5. The single, most important factor in fostering a secure attachment relationship is _____.

**6.** Adults with _____ representations of the attachment relationships with their own parents are most likely to have secure attachments with their own children.

**ACTIVE CHILDREN**

How do an infant's behaviors contribute to the formation of attachment? How do the caregiver's behaviors contribute?

**Answers:** (1) 7 or 8, (2) playmate, (3) avoidant, (4) Secure attachment, (5) responsive parenting that fosters an infant's trust and confidence, (6) secure

# Unifying Themes: Active Children

Temperament is one of the best examples in the entire book of the theme that *children influence their own development.* Temperament helps determine how parents, peers, and other adults respond to children. Parents and peers, for example, usually respond positively to temperamentally easy children. Parents find it more straightforward to establish a secure attachment with an easy child than with a difficult child. Peers get along better with easy children than with shy, inhibited children. Children's temperament does not alone dictate the direction of their development, but it makes some directions much easier to follow than others.

## See for Yourself

Arrange to visit a local day-care center where you can unobtrusively observe preschoolers for several days. As you watch the children, see if you can detect the temperamental differences that are described in Module 11.2. Can you identify an emotional child, an active child, and a social child? Also, notice how adults respond to the children. See if the same behaviors lead to different responses from adults, depending on the child's temperament. See for yourself!

## Resources

For more information about...

the **development of emotion**, read Carolyn Saarni's *The Development of Emotional Competence* (Guilford, 1999) which focuses on the growth of eight key emotional skills.

**attachment**, visit the Web site of a group of prominent attachment researchers:
**http://www.johnbowlby.com**

## Key Terms

SUMMARY

# 11.1 Emerging Emotions

### The Function of Emotions
Modern theories emphasize the functional value of emotion. Emotions such as fear, happiness, and disgust are valuable because they help people adapt: keeping them away from danger and strengthening social relationships.

### Experiencing and Expressing Emotions
Scientists often use infants' facial expressions to judge when different emotional states emerge in development. Basic emotions, which include joy, anger, and fear, emerge in the first year. Fear first appears in infancy as stranger wariness. Complex emotions have an evaluative component and include guilt, embarrassment, and pride. They appear between 18 and 24 months and require more sophisticated cognitive skills than basic emotions like happiness and fear. Cultures differ in the rules for expressing emotions and the situations that elicit particular emotions.

### Recognizing and Using Others' Emotions
By 6 months, infants have begun to recognize the emotions associated with different facial expressions. They use this information to help them evaluate unfamiliar situations. Beyond infancy, children understand the causes and consequences of different emotions, that people can feel multiple emotions simultaneously, and the rules for displaying emotions appropriately.

### Regulating Emotions
Infants use simple strategies to regulate emotions such as fear. As children grow, they become better skilled at regulating their emotions. Children who do not regulate emotions well tend to have problems interacting with others.

# 11.2 Temperament

### What is Temperament?
Temperament refers to biologically based, stable patterns of behavior that are evident soon after birth. The New York Longitudinal Study suggested nine distinct dimensions of temperament, but most modern theories include two to six dimensions. According to one view, temperament includes the five dimensions of activity level, positive affect, persistence, inhibition, and negative affect.

### Hereditary and Environmental Contributions to Temperament
The major theories agree that both heredity and environment contribute to temperament. For many dimensions of temperament, identical twins are more alike than fraternal twins. Positive emotionality reflects environmental influences, and difficult temperament is linked to abrupt parenting.

### Stability of Temperament
Temperament is moderately stable in infancy, childhood, and adolescence. Temperament in childhood is somewhat related to personality in adulthood. The relations are not very strong because temperament itself is changing as children develop.

### Temperament and Other Aspects of Development
Many investigators have shown that temperament is related to other aspects of development. Difficult babies are more likely to have behavioral problems by the time they are old enough to attend school. Persistent children are more successful in school, shy children sometimes have problems with peers, anxious children are more compliant with parents, and angry or fearful children are prone to depression. However, the impact of temperament always depends on the environment in which children develop.

# 11.3 Attachment

### The Growth of Attachment
Attachment is an enduring social-emotional relationship between infant and parent. Many of the behaviors that contribute to the formation of attachment are biologically programmed. Attachment develops gradually over the first year of life; by about 7 or 8 months, infants have identified an attachment figure, typically the mother. In the ensuing months, infants often become attached to other family members, including fathers, whose usual role is playmate.

### The Quality of Attachment
Research with the Strange Situation, in which infant and mother are separated briefly, reveals four primary forms of attachment. Most common is a secure attachment, in which infants have complete trust in the mother. Less common are three types of insecure attachment relationships that lack this trust. In avoidant relationships, infants deal with the lack of trust by ignoring the mother; in resistant relationships, infants often seem angry with her; in disorganized (disoriented) relationships, infants seem to not understand the mother's absence.

Children who have had secure attachment relationships during infancy often interact with their peers more readily and more skillfully. Secure attachment is most likely to occur when mothers respond sensitively and consistently to their infants' needs. Adults who value their relationship with their own parents are most likely to use the sensitive caregiving that promotes secure attachments with their own infants.

A century ago, G. Stanley Hall, an influential American developmental psychologist, wrote that adolescence was "strewn with wreckage of mind, body, and morals" (1904, p. xiv). Judging by today's movies and media, Hall's analysis seems to have stood the test of time: When teens aren't presented as runaways, drug addicts, and shoplifters, they're moody and withdrawn or manic. But how accurate is this picture? What does current research show about adolescence and the process of developing independence and identity?

In Module 12.1, we'll look at the mechanisms that give rise to a person's identity, and we'll see if "storm and stress" is a necessary step in achieving an identity. Of course, people are often happier with some aspects of themselves than with others. These evaluative aspects of identity are the focus of Module 12.2. Finally, in Module 12.3, we'll look at how we develop an understanding of others, because as we learn more about ourselves, we learn more about other people, too.

# Understanding Self and Others

# 12.1

## Who Am I? Self-Concept

### LEARNING OBJECTIVES

● When do infants first acquire a sense of self?

● How does self-concept become more elaborate as children grow?

● How do adolescents achieve an identity?

> *Dea was born in Seoul of Korean parents but was adopted by a Dutch couple in Michigan when she was 3 months old. Growing up, she considered herself a red-blooded American. In high school, however, Dea realized that others saw her as an Asian American, an identity about which she had never given much thought. She began to wonder, who am I really? American? Dutch American? Asian American?*

Like Dea, do you sometimes wonder who you are? **Answers to "Who am I?" reflect a person's self-concept, which refers to the attitudes, behaviors, and values that a person believes make him or her a unique individual.** One answer to "Who am I?"—from a teenage girl—shows just how complex a person's self-concept can be.

> *I'm sensitive, friendly, outgoing, popular, and tolerant, though I can also be shy, self-conscious, and even obnoxious! I'd like to be friendly and tolerant all of the time. That's the kind of person I want to be, and I'm disappointed when I'm not. I'm responsible, even studious now and then, but on the other hand, I'm a goof-off, too, because if you're too studious, you won't be popular (Harter, 1990, p. 352).*

VIDEO 12.1
Self Awareness

As an adult, your answer is probably even more complex because, after all, most people are complex creatures. But how did you acquire this complex self-concept? We'll answer that question in this module, beginning with the origins of an infant's sense of self. Later, we'll see how identity becomes elaborated after infancy and see how individuals like Dea develop an ethnic identity.

### Origins of Self-Recognition

What is the starting point for self-concept? Following the lead of the 19th-century philosopher and psychologist William James, modern researchers believe that the foundation of self-concept is the child's awareness that he or she exists. At some point early in life, children must realize that they exist independently of other people and objects in the environment and that their existence continues over time.

Measuring the onset of this awareness is not easy. Obviously, we can't simply ask a 3-year-old, "So, tell me, when did you first realize that you existed and weren't simply part of the furniture?" A less direct approach is needed, and the photo shows one route that many investigators have taken. Like many babies his age, the 9-month-old in the photo is smiling at the face he sees in the mirror. Babies at this age sometimes touch the face in the mirror or wave at it, but none of their behaviors indicates that they recognize themselves in the mirror. Instead, babies act as if the face in the mirror is simply a very interesting stimulus.

How would we know that infants recognize themselves in a mirror? One clever approach is to have the mother place a red mark on her infant's nose; she does this surreptitiously, while wiping the baby's face. Then the infant is returned to the mirror. Many 1-year-olds touch the red mark on the mirror, showing that they notice the mark on the face in the mirror. At about 15 months, however, an important change occurs: Many babies see the red mark in the mirror, then reach up and touch *their own* noses. By age 2, most children do this (Bullock & Lütkenhaus, 1990; Lewis, 1997). When these older toddlers notice the red mark in the mirror, they understand that the funny-looking nose in the mirror is their own.

Do you doubt that the mirror task shows an infant's emerging sense of self? Perhaps you think it tells more about an infant's growing understanding of mirrors than the baby's self-awareness. One way to examine this possibility would be to test infants who have never seen mirrors previously. Priel and deSchonen (1986) took this approach, testing infants from Israeli desert communities. These babies had never seen mirrors or, for that matter, virtually any reflective surfaces. Nevertheless, the same developmental trend appeared in the desert infants as in a comparison group of infants living in a near-by city. No 6- to 12-month-olds in either group touched their noses after they saw the mark, a few 13- to 19-month-olds did, and nearly all the 20- to 26-month-olds did.

> By 2 most children recognize themselves and refer to themselves by name or with *I* and *me.*

We don't need to rely solely on the mirror task to know that self-awareness emerges between 18 and 24 months. During this same period, toddlers look more at photographs of themselves than at photos of other children. They also refer to themselves by name or with a personal pronoun, such as *I* or *me*, and sometimes they know their age and their gender. These changes suggest that self-awareness is well established in most children by age 2 (Lewis, 1987).

The self-awareness that's evident in toddlers clearly has its roots in infancy (Rochat, 2001). Some of the roots are social. From regular, predictable interactions with caregivers, infants learn that those interactions involve different roles—one for the infant and one for the caregiver. Such differentiation of roles into the "my" and "other" roles is an important early step toward self-awareness. Other roots of self-awareness involve infants' understanding of their own bodies. As adults, we know that when we raise our hand to scratch our nose, the hand we see "doing the scratching" is our hand; it's part of our physical self. From experience watching their bodies move, infants learn this aspect of self-awareness—"that's not any old hand, that's my hand"—by 3 to 5 months of age.

Soon after children are self aware, autobiographical memory (described in Module 8.2) begins to emerge (Harley & Reese, 1999). That is, children begin to recognize continuity in the self over time; the "I" in the present is linked to the "I" in the past (Nelson, 2001). Awareness of a self that is extended in time is fostered by conversations with parents about the past and the future. Through such conversations, a 3-year-old celebrating a birthday understands that she's an older version of the same person who had a birthday a year previously.

Children's growing awareness of a self extended in time is also revealed by children's understanding of ownership (Fasig, 2000). When a toddler sees his favorite toy and says "mine," this implies awareness of continuity of the self over time: "In the past, I played with that." And when toddlers like the girl in the photo say "Mine!" they are often not being aggressive or selfish; instead "mine" is a way of indicating ownership and in the process defining themselves. Thus, the girl in the photo is not trying to deny the doll to the other girl; she is simply saying that playing with dolls is part of who she is (Levine, 1983).

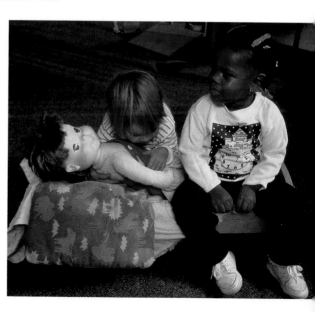

Finally, once self-awareness is established, children begin to acquire a self-concept. That is, once children fully understand that they exist and that they have a unique mental life, they begin to wonder who they are. They want to define themselves. In the next section, we'll see how this self-concept becomes more complex as children develop.

## The Evolving Self-Concept

Before you go any further, return to the quotation on page 332 from the teenager. In describing herself, this girl relies heavily on psychological traits. The first sentence alone includes eight adjectives referring to these traits: *sensitive, friendly, outgoing, popular, tolerant, shy, self-conscious,* and *obnoxious.* How do children develop such a complex view of themselves? For toddlers and preschoolers, self-concept is *much* simpler. Asked to describe themselves, preschoolers are likely to mention physical characteristics ("I have blue eyes"), their preferences ("I like cookies"), their possessions ("I have trucks"), and their competencies ("I can count to 50"). What these features have in common is a focus on a child's characteristics that are observable and concrete (Damon & Hart, 1988).

> A preschooler's self-concept is linked to the concrete and real but an adolescent's self-concept is more abstract and psychological.

At about 6 to 8 years of age, children's self-descriptions begin to change (Harter, 1994, 1999). Children are more likely to mention emotions ("Sometimes I get angry"). They are also more likely to mention the social groups to which they belong ("I'm on the lacrosse team"). Finally, in contrast to preschool children, who simply mention their competencies, elementary-school children describe their level of skill in relation to their peers ("I'm the best speller in my whole class").

Self-concepts change again as children enter adolescence (Harter & Monsour, 1992). They now include attitudes ("I love algebra") and personality traits ("I'm usually a very happy person"). Adolescents also begin to make religious and political beliefs part of their self-concept ("I'm a Catholic" or "I'm a conservative Republican"). Another change is that adolescents' self-concepts often vary with the setting. A teenager might say, "I'm really shy around people that I don't know, but I let loose when I'm with my friends and family."

Yet another change is that adolescents' self-concepts are often future oriented: Adolescents often describe themselves in terms of what they will be when they reach adulthood (Harter, 1990, 1999). These descriptions may include occupational goals ("I'm going to be an English teacher"), educational plans ("I plan to go to a community college to learn about computers"), or social roles ("I want to get married as soon as I finish high school").

The gradual elaboration of self-concept from the preschool years to adolescence is summarized in the table. Two general changes are evident: First, self-concept

**SUMMARY TABLE**

**DEVELOPMENTAL CHANGE IN SELF-CONCEPT**

| Preschoolers | School-Age Children | Adolescents |
|---|---|---|
| Possessions | Emotions | Attitudes |
| Physical characteristics | Social groups | Personality traits |
| Preferences | Comparisons with peers | Beliefs vary with the setting |
| Competencies | | Future oriented |

becomes richer as children grow; adolescents simply know much more about themselves than preschoolers. Second, the type of knowledge that children have of themselves changes. Preschoolers' understanding is linked to the concrete, the real, and the here and now. Adolescents' understanding, in contrast, is more abstract and more psychological, and sees the self as evolving over time. The change in children's knowledge of themselves should not surprise you because it's exactly the type of change that Piaget described. Concrete operational children's focus on the real and tangible extends to their thoughts about themselves, just as formal operational adolescents' focus on the abstract and hypothetical applies to their thoughts about themselves.

Adolescence is also a time of increasing self-reflection. Adolescents look for an identity to integrate the many different and sometimes conflicting elements of the self (Marcia, 1991). We'll look at this search for identity in detail in the next section.

VIDEO 12.2
Imaginary Audience

## The Search for Identity

Erik Erikson (1968) believed that adolescents struggle to achieve an identity that will allow them to participate in the adult world. How exactly do they accomplish this? To learn more about possible identities, adolescents use the hypothetical reasoning skills of the formal operational stage to experiment with different selves (Nurmi, Poole, & Kalakoski, 1996). Adolescents' advanced cognitive skills allow them to imagine themselves in different roles.

Much of the testing and experimentation is career oriented. Some adolescents, like the ones shown in the photo, may envision themselves as rock stars; others may imagine being a professional athlete, a Peace Corps worker, or a best-selling novelist. Other testing is romantically oriented. Teens may fall in love and imagine living with the loved one. Still other exploration involves religious and political beliefs (King, Elder, & Whitbeck, 1997; Yates & Youniss, 1996). Teens give different identities a trial run just as you might test drive different cars before selecting one. By fantasizing about their future, adolescents begin to discover who they will be.

**The self-absorption that marks the teenage search for identity is referred to as adolescent egocentrism** (Elkind, 1978). Unlike preschoolers, adolescents know that others have different perspectives on the world. At the same time, many adolescents believe, wrongly, that they are the focus of others' thinking. A teen like the one in the photo who spills food on herself may imagine that all her friends are thinking only about the stain on her blouse and how sloppy she is. **Many adolescents feel that they are, in effect, actors whose performance is being watched constantly by their peers, a phenomenon known as the imaginary audience.**

**Adolescent self-absorption is also demonstrated by the personal fable, teenagers' tendency to believe that their experiences and feelings are unique, that no one has ever felt or thought as they do.** Whether the excitement of first love, the despair of a broken relationship, or the confusion of planning for the future, adolescents often believe they are the first to experience these feelings and that no one else could possibly understand the power of their emotions (Elkind & Bowen, 1979). **Adolescents' belief in their uniqueness also contributes to an illusion of invulnerability—the belief that misfortune only happens to others.** They think they can have sex without becoming pregnant or drive recklessly without being in an auto accident. Those misfortunes, according to them, only happen to others.

Adolescent egocentrism, imaginary audiences, personal fables, and the illusion of invulnerability become less common as adolescents make progress toward achieving an identity. What exactly is involved in achieving an identity? Most adolescents progress through different phases or statuses, though not necessarily in this order (Marcia, 1980, 1991):

> *In achieving an identity, adolescents often begin in the diffusion status and end in the achievement status.*

VIDEO 12.3
Invincibility Fable

- **Diffusion: Individuals in this status are confused or overwhelmed by the task of achieving an identity and are doing little to achieve one.**
- **Foreclosure: Individuals in this status have an identity determined largely by adults, rather than from personal exploration of alternatives.**
- **Moratorium: Individuals in this status are still examining different alternatives and have yet to find a satisfactory identity.**
- **Achievement: Individuals in this status have explored alternatives and have deliberately chosen a specific identity.**

Unlike Piaget's stages, these four phases do not necessarily occur in sequence. Most young adolescents are in a state of diffusion or foreclosure. The common element in these phases is that teens are not exploring alternative identities. They are avoiding the crisis altogether or have resolved it by taking on an identity suggested by parents or other adults. However, as individuals move beyond adolescence and into young adulthood and have more opportunity to explore alternative identities, diffusion and foreclosure become less common, and, achievement and moratorium become more common (Kroger, 2000).

Typically, young people do not reach the achievement status for all aspects of identity at the same time (Dellas & Jernigan, 1990; Kroger & Green, 1996). Some adolescents may reach the achievement status for occupations before achieving it for religion and politics. Others reach the achievement status for religion before other domains. Evidently, few youth achieve a sense of identity all at once; instead, the crisis of identity is first resolved in some areas and then in others.

CHOOSING A CAREER.   One element of identity that has been examined in some detail is career development. According to a theory proposed by Donald Super (1976, 1980), identity is a primary force in an adolescent's choice of a career. **At about age 13 or 14, adolescents use their emerging identities as a source of ideas about careers, a process called crystallization.** Teenagers use their ideas about their own talents and interests to limit potential career prospects. A teenager who is extroverted and sociable may decide that working with people would be the career for him. Another who excels in math and science may decide she'd like to teach math. Decisions are provisional, and adolescents experiment with hypothetical careers, trying to envision what each might be like. Rarely, however, are careers as hypothetical as the one imagined by the teenager in the cartoon!

At about age 18, adolescents extend the activities associated with crystallization and enter a new phase. **During specification, individuals further limit their career possibilities by learning more about specific lines of work and starting to obtain the training required for a specific job.** Our extroverted teenager who wants to work with people may decide that a career in sales would be a good match for his abilities and interests. The teen who likes math may have learned more about careers and decided she'd like to be an accountant. Some teens, like the young man in the photo, may begin an apprenticeship as a way to learn a trade.

"Your son has made a career choice, Mildred. He's going to win the lottery and travel a lot."

By permission of Bunny Hoest, Wm. Hoest Enterprises, Inc.

The end of the teenage years or the early 20s marks the beginning of the third phase. **During implementation, individuals enter the workforce and learn firsthand about jobs.** This is a time of learning about responsibility and productivity, of learning to get along with coworkers, and of altering one's lifestyle to accommodate work. This period is often unstable; individuals may change jobs frequently as they adjust to the reality of life in the workplace.

In each of Super's three phases of career development, there is continuous give and take between an individual's identity and career choice. A person's self-concept makes some careers more attractive than others; occupational experiences, in turn, refine and shape a person's identity.

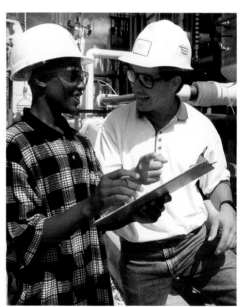

What circumstances help adolescents decide on a career and achieve identity? Parents are influential (Marcia, 1980). When parents encourage discussion and recognize their children's autonomy, their children are more likely to reach the achievement status. Apparently these youth feel encouraged to undertake the personal experimentation that leads to identity. In contrast, when parents set rules with little justification and enforce them without explanation, children are more likely to remain in the foreclosure status. These teens are discouraged from experimenting personally; instead, their parents simply tell them what identity to adopt. Overall, adolescents are most likely to establish a well-defined identity in a family atmosphere where parents encourage children to explore alternatives on their own but do not pressure or provide explicit direction (Harter, 1990, 1999).

**ETHNIC IDENTITY.** For many adolescents growing up in North America today, achieving an identity is even more challenging because they are members of ethnic minority groups. The "Cultural Influences" feature describes one example.

## CULTURAL INFLUENCES

### Dea's Ethnic Identity

Dea, the adolescent in the opening vignette, belongs to the one-third of adolescents and young adults living in the United States who are members of ethnic minority groups. They include African Americans, Asian Americans, Hispanic Americans, and Native Americans. **These individuals typically develop an ethnic identity:**

**They feel a part of their ethnic group and learn the special customs and traditions of their group's culture and heritage** (Phinney, 1996).

An ethnic identity seems to be achieved in three phases. Initially, adolescents have not examined their ethnic roots. A teenage African American girl in this phase remarked, "Why do I need to learn about who was the first Black woman to do this or that? I'm just not too interested" (Phinney, 1989, p. 44). For this girl, ethnic identity is not yet an important personal issue.

In the second phase, adolescents begin to explore the personal impact of their ethnic heritage. The curiosity and questioning that are characteristic of this stage are captured in the comments of a teenage Mexican American girl who said, "I want to know what we do and how our culture is different from others. Going to festivals and cultural events helps me to learn more about my own culture and about myself" (Phinney, 1989, p. 44). Part of this phase involves learning cultural traditions; for example, like the girl in the photo, many adolescents learn to prepare ethnic food.

In the third phase, individuals achieve a distinct ethnic self-concept. One Asian American adolescent explained his ethnic identification like this: "I have been born Filipino and am born to be Filipino. . . . I'm here in America, and people of many different cultures are here, too. So I don't consider myself only Filipino, but also American" (Phinney, 1989, p. 44).

To see if you understand the differences between these stages of ethnic identity, reread the vignette on page 332 about Dea and decide which stage applies to her. The answer appears on page 340, just before "Check Your Learning." ⊙

Older adolescents are more likely than younger ones to have achieved an ethnic identity because they are more likely to have had opportunities to explore their cultural heritage (Phinney & Chavira, 1992). Also, as with overall identity, adolescents are most likely to achieve an ethnic self-concept when their parents encourage them to explore alternatives instead of pressuring them to adopt a particular ethnic identity (Rosenthal & Feldman, 1992).

> Adolescents with an ethnic identity have higher self-esteem, find interactions with others more satisfying, and do better in school.

Ethnic identity poses a special challenge for immigrant adolescents. Unlike native-born ethnic children, who have exposure to mainstream and ethnic culture from a young age, from the time immigrant adolescents enter a new country, they face the task of negotiating a culture largely unfamiliar to them. And many immigrant adolescents have already established a strong identity with their native land. Consequently, it's not surprising that immigrant adolescents do not immediately identify with their new culture. For example, in one study (Birman & Trickett, 2001), Jewish adolescents who had fled the former Soviet Union reported that, although they acted like most American teenagers (e.g., they ate American food, spent time with native-born American teens), they still "felt Russian" despite having lived in the United States for nearly 10 years.

Do adolescents benefit from a strong ethnic identity? Yes. Adolescents who have achieved an ethnic identity tend to have higher self-esteem and find their interactions with family and friends more satisfying (R. E. Roberts et al., 1999). In addition, many investigators have found that adolescents with a strong ethnic identity do better in school than adolescents whose ethnic identities are weaker (Stalikas & Gavaki, 1995; Taylor et al., 1994).

Some individuals achieve a well-defined ethnic self-concept and, at the same time, identify strongly with the mainstream culture. In the United States, for example, many Chinese Americans embrace both Chinese and American culture; in England, many Indians identify with both Indian and British cultures. For other individuals, the cost of strong ethnic identification is a weakened tie to mainstream culture. Some investigators report that, for Hispanic Americans, strong identification with American culture is associated with a weaker ethnic self-concept (Phinney, 1990).

We shouldn't be too surprised that identifying with mainstream culture weakens ethnic identity in some groups but not others (Berry, 1993). Racial and ethnic groups living in the United States are diverse. African American, Asian American, Hispanic American, and Native American cultures and heritages differ, and so we should expect that the nature and consequences of a strong ethnic self-concept will differ across these and other ethnic groups.

Even within any particular group, the nature and consequences of ethnic identity may change over successive generations (Cuellar et al., 1997). As successive generations become more assimilated into mainstream culture, they may identify less strongly with ethnic culture. Thus, parents may maintain strong feelings of ethnic identity that their children don't share (Phinney, Ong, & Madden, 2000).

**STORM AND STRESS.**   According to American novelists and filmmakers, the search for identity that I've described in the past few pages is inherently a struggle, a time of storm and stress for adolescents. Although this view may make for best-selling novels and hit movies, in reality the rebellious teen is largely a myth. Think about the following conclusions derived from research findings (Steinberg, 1990). Most adolescents

- admire and love their parents,
- rely upon their parents for advice,
- embrace many of their parents' values, and
- feel loved by their parents.

Not exactly the image of the rebel, is it? Cross-cultural research provides further evidence that for most teens adolescence is not a time of turmoil and conflict. Offer and his colleagues (1988) interviewed adolescents from 10 different countries: the United States, Australia, Germany, Italy, Israel, Hungary, Turkey, Japan, Taiwan, and Bangladesh. These investigators found most adolescents moving confidently and happily toward adulthood. As the graphs show, most adolescents around the world reported that they were usually happy, and few avoided their homes.

Of course, parent–child relations do change during adolescence. As teens become more independent, their relationships with their parents become more egalitarian. Parents must adjust to their children's growing

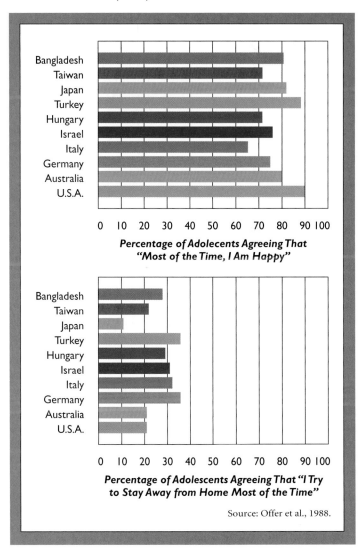

*Percentage of Adolescents Agreeing That "Most of the Time, I Am Happy"*

*Percentage of Adolescents Agreeing That "I Try to Stay Away from Home Most of the Time"*

Source: Offer et al., 1988.

FIG. 12–1

sense of autonomy by treating them more like equals (Laursen & Collins, 1994). This growing independence means that teens spend less time with their parents, are less affectionate toward them, and argue more often with them about matters of style, taste, and freedom. Teenagers are also more moody and more likely to enjoy spending some time alone (Larson, 1997; Wolfson & Carskadon, 1998). But these changes are natural byproducts of an evolving parent–child relationship in which the "child" is nearly a fully independent young adult (Steinberg, 1990).

> Depression is often triggered when adolescents blame themselves for a negative event.

The challenges of adolescence can lead some youth to become depressed. As we saw in Chapter 3, depressed individuals have pervasive feelings of sadness, are irritable, have low self-esteem, sleep poorly, and are unable to concentrate. About 3 to 8 percent of adolescents are depressed; adolescent girls are more often affected than boys, probably because social challenges in adolescence are often greater for girls than boys (Avenevoli & Steinberg, 2001; Nolen-Hoeksema & Girgus, 1994).

Depression is often triggered when adolescents experience a serious loss (e.g., the death of a loved one), disappointment (e.g., a much anticipated date is a fiasco), or failures (e.g., a defender falls down, allowing the opponent to score a game-winning goal). Of course, many adolescents and adults experience negative events like these, but most don't become depressed. Why? **One view emphasizes adolescents' attributions, their personal explanations of success and failure** (Nevid, Rathus, & Greene, 2003). Depression-prone adolescents are, for example, more likely to blame themselves for failure. Thus, after the disappointing date, a depression-prone teen is like to think, "I acted like a fool" instead of placing blame elsewhere by thinking "Gee. What a jerk!" And depression-prone teens more often believe that such personal "flaws" are stable and wide ranging (e.g., "I just don't get along well with other people!") instead of thinking of them as temporary (e.g., "I was just getting over the flu, so it's not surprising that the date went poorly") or specific (e.g., "I think softball is boring, so going to a game on a first date was really stupid").

Although attributions can lead to depression, biology also contributes, apparently through neurotransmitters. **Some depressed adolescents have reduced levels of norepinephrine and serotonin, neurotransmitters that help regulate brain centers that allow people to experience pleasure.** Some adolescents may feel depressed because lower levels of neurotransmitters make it difficult for them to experience happiness, joy, and other pleasurable emotions (Peterson, 1996).

To treat depression, some adolescents take antidepressant drugs designed to correct the imbalance in neurotransmitters. The well-known drug, Prozac, for example, is designed to reduce depression by increasing levels of serotonin (Peterson, 1996). However, drug treatment has no lasting effects—it only works while people are taking the drugs. More long-lasting effects are observed with psychotherapy. The most effective forms emphasize cognitive and social skills—adolescents learn how to have rewarding social interactions and to interpret them appropriately (Hollon, Haman, & Brown, 2002). These treatments *are* effective and depressed adolescents do need help; left untreated, depression can interfere with performance in school and social relationships, and may also lead to recurring depression in adulthood (Nevid et al., 2003).

*Response to question on page 338 about Dea's ethnic identity:* Dea, the Dutch Asian American high-school student, doesn't know how to integrate the Korean heritage of her biological parents with the Dutch American culture in which she was reared. This would put her in the second phase of acquiring an ethnic identity. On the one hand, she is examining her ethnic roots, which means she's progressed beyond the initial stage. On the other hand, she has not yet integrated her Asian and European roots, and so has not reached the third and final phase.

## CHECK YOUR LEARNING

**1.** Apparently children become self-aware by age 2 because at this age they recognize themselves in a mirror and in photographs, and they _____.

**2.** During _____, children's self-concepts begin to include emotions, membership in social groups, and comparisons with peers.

**3.** A focus on attitudes, personality traits, and the future characterizes self-concept during _____.

**4.** _____ refers to the fact that adolescents sometimes believe that their lives are a performance, with their peers watching them constantly.

**5.** The _____ status would describe an adolescent who has attained an identity based almost entirely on her parents' advice and urging.

**6.** A person who has simply put off searching for an identity because it seems too confusing and too overwhelming is in the _____ status.

**7.** In Super's theory of career development, at about 18 years individuals enter the _____ phase; at this time they limit career possibilities by learning more about specific lines of work or start training.

**8.** When individuals have a strong ethnic identity, their identification with mainstream culture _____.

**9.** Children's relations with their parents change in adolescence, reflecting adolescents' growing independence and a _____ parent–child relationship.

### ➤◄ CONNECTIONS

Although Piaget's theory was not concerned with identity formation, how might his theory explain why identity is a central issue in adolescence?

**Answers:** (1) refer to themselves by name or with the pronouns *I* and *me*, (2) the elementary-school years, (3) adolescence, (4) Imaginary audience, (5) foreclosure, (6) diffusion, (7) specification, (8) is sometimes strong and sometimes weak, depending on specific circumstances, (9) more egalitarian

---

# Self-Esteem

# 12.2

## LEARNING OBJECTIVES

● What is self-esteem? How is it measured?

● How does self-esteem change as children develop?

● What factors influence the development of self-esteem?

● How is children's development affected by low self-esteem?

> *Darnel, age 10, loves school and for good reason: Every year, he is always one of the best students in his class. Darnel's mother, Karen, wants to enroll him in a program for gifted children, where she believes the pace will be more appropriate for her talented son. Darnel's dad, Jon, doesn't think this is such a great idea. He's afraid that if Darnel doesn't do well against all those other bright kids, his son will begin to doubt his academic ability.*

Measuring Self-Esteem —

Change and Stability — in Self-Esteem

Sources of Self-Esteem —

Consequences of Low — Self-Esteem

**Jon is concerned about Darnel's self-esteem, which refers to a person's judgment and feelings about his or her own worth.** Children with high self-esteem judge themselves favorably and feel positive about themselves. In contrast, children with low self-esteem judge themselves negatively, are unhappy with themselves, and often would rather be someone else. In this module, we'll see how self-esteem is measured, how it changes as children develop, and what forces shape it.

## Measuring Self-Esteem

Think about your own self-esteem. Do you think you have high self-esteem or low self-esteem? To help you answer this question, read each of these sentences and decide how well each applies to you:

I'm very good at schoolwork.

I find it very easy to make friends.

I do very well at all kinds of different sports.

I'm happy with the way I look.

If you agreed strongly with each of these statements, you definitely have high self-esteem. Usually, however, people agree with some of these statements more strongly than others. This tells us that, in addition to an overall sense of self-worth, people evaluate themselves in different areas. That is, people have multiple self-esteems, each linked to a specific content area. This phenomenon should seem familiar because it's like intelligence: In Module 9.1, we saw that hierarchical theories of intelligence begin with a general intelligence that is divided into more specific abilities, such as verbal ability and spatial ability.

How can we measure different aspects of self-esteem? The method depends on the age of the child. With 4- to 7-year-olds, one popular approach devised by Harter and Pike (1984) uses pairs of pictures. The sample pictures show a girl either solving a puzzle easily or having difficulty. During testing, children are first asked to point to the pictured child who is most like them. Then they point to the larger circle if they believe that they are "a lot" like the child in that picture or the smaller one if they believe they are "a little" like the child in that picture. Harter and Pike used 24 pairs of

FIG. 12–2

pictures like these to measure children's self-worth in four areas: cognitive competence, physical competence, acceptance by peers, and acceptance by mother.

Another productive approach with young children uses puppets (Ablow & Measelle, 1993; Measelle et al., 1998). One puppet describes itself to the child: "I like pizza." A second puppet then describes itself in opposite terms—"I don't like pizza"—and then motions to the child, "How about you?" Children can respond verbally ("I like pizza, too!"), by nodding their heads in agreement or disagreement, or by pointing to one of the puppets. Children are presented pairs of statements measuring academic competence ("I learn/don't learn things well"), achievement motivation ("I try/don't try my best at school"), social competence ("It's hard/not hard for me to make new friends"), and peer acceptance ("Kids are/are not nice to me").

> The *Self-Perception Profile for Children* measures children's self-worth overall and in five specific areas.

Self-esteem in older children and adolescents can be measured with a questionnaire. The child reads statements like the ones at the beginning of this section. The most widely used self-esteem questionnaire of this sort is the *Self-Perception Profile for Children* (SPPC) devised by Susan Harter (1985, 1988). The SPPC is designed to evaluate self-worth in children age 8 and older in five domains (Harter, 1988, p. 62):

- *Scholastic competence:* How competent or smart the child feels in doing schoolwork
- *Athletic competence:* How competent the child feels at sports and games requiring physical skill or athletic ability
- *Social acceptance:* How popular or accepted the child feels in social interactions with peers
- *Behavioral conduct:* How adequate the child feels about behaving the way one is supposed to
- *Physical appearance:* How good-looking the child feels and how much the child likes his or her physical characteristics, such as height, weight, face, and hair

The SPPC includes six statements for each domain. For example, the figure on page 344 lists two of the statements used to evaluate scholastic competence, shown as they actually appear on the SPPC. In both statements, the child has checked the response that indicates the highest level of self-esteem. A child's answers to all six statements are used to create an average level of self-esteem in that domain. The averages for each of the five domains are then used to generate a self-perception profile for each child. Two profiles are illustrated in the figure. Allison's self-esteem is high across all five domains; Colleen's self-esteem is much more varied. She feels positive about her social acceptance and physical appearance and, to a lesser extent, about her conduct. However, she feels negative about her scholastic and athletic competence.

Notice that each profile ends with a bar graph depicting the child's overall self-worth. Overall self-worth is measured on the SPPC with six more items, such as "Some kids like the way they are leading their life" and "Some kids like the kind of person they are." Children's responses to these statements are then averaged to create a measure of overall self-worth.

Are you surprised that overall self-worth is measured separately? Why not simply average children's ratings on the five dimensions? The reason is that children's overall self-worth is usually not simply the average of their self-worth in specific domains. You can see that this is true in the profiles for Allison and Colleen. Both girls feel very

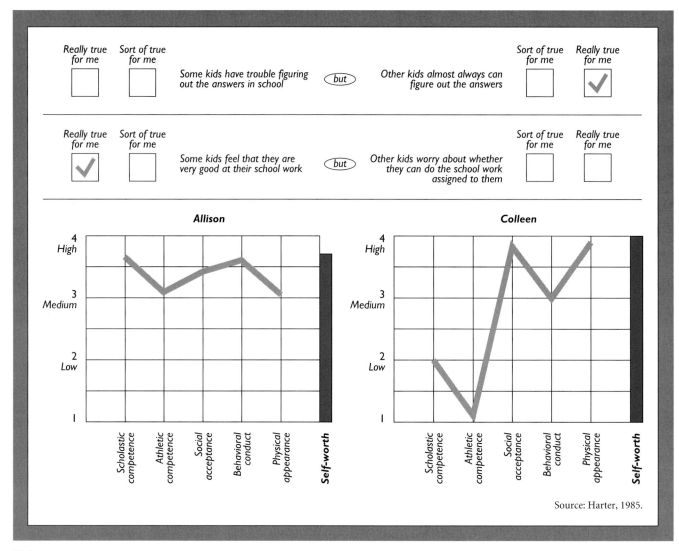

Really true
for me

Sort of true
for me

☐

☐

Some kids have trouble figuring
out the answers in school

( but )

Other kids almost always can
figure out the answers

Sort of true
for me

☐

Really true
for me

☑

Really true
for me

Sort of true
for me

☑

☐

Some kids feel that they are
very good at their school work

( but )

Other kids worry about whether
they can do the school work
assigned to them

Sort of true
for me

☐

Really true
for me

☐

Source: Harter, 1985.

FIG. 12–3

positive about themselves overall. This isn't surprising for Allison based on her ratings in the individual domains. But it is hardly what we would expect for Colleen if overall self-worth were simply the sum of self-worth in specific domains. Evidently, overall feelings of self-worth somehow transcend feelings of self-worth in specific domains.

The SPPC is intended for use with children and young adolescents. For assessing self-esteem in older adolescents and young adults, Harter (1990) created a more extensive scale. This scale includes the five domains in the SPPC, along with job competence, close friendships, and romantic appeal. These additional domains were included because self-esteem becomes more differentiated during adolescence.

In the next section, we'll see that greater differentiation is only one of several important developmental changes in self-esteem.

## Change and Stability in Self-Esteem

At what age is self-esteem greatest? The answer may surprise you—it's during the preschool years. Most preschool children have very positive views of themselves across many different domains. For example, when Harter and Pike (1984) used the pictures shown on page 342 to estimate kindergarten children's cognitive competence, the average score was 3.6 out of a possible 4. In other words, virtually all the children said they were either a little or a lot like the competent child.

As children progress through the elementary-school years, self-esteem usually drops somewhat. Why? In reality, of course, all children are *not* above average. During the elementary-school years, children begin to compare themselves with peers (Ruble et al., 1980). When they do, they discover that they are not necessarily the best readers or the fastest runners. They may realize, instead, that they are only average readers. Or, like the girl in the background of the photo, they come to understand that they are among the slowest runners in the class. This realization means that children's self-esteem usually drops somewhat at the beginning of elementary school.

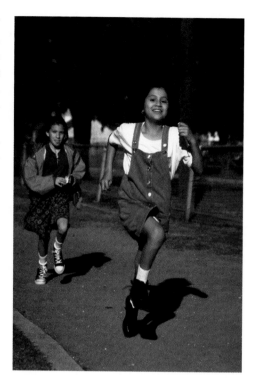

By the end of the elementary-school years, children's self-esteem has usually stabilized (Harter, Whitesell, & Kowalski, 1992) as children learn their place in the "pecking order" of different domains and adjust their self-esteem accordingly. However, self-esteem sometimes drops when children move from elementary school to middle school or junior high (Twenge & Campbell, 2001). Apparently, when students from different elementary schools enter the same middle school or junior high, they know where they stand compared to their old elementary-school classmates but not compared to students from other elementary schools. Thus, peer comparisons begin anew, and self-esteem often suffers temporarily. But, as a new school becomes familiar and students gradually adjust to the new pecking order, self-esteem again increases.

There is more to developmental change in self-esteem, however. The pattern of change also depends on the specific domain and the child's sex, as we'll see in the "Focus on Research" feature.

## FOCUS ON RESEARCH

### Developmental Change in Self-Esteem in Different Domains

*Who were the investigators, and what was the aim of the study?* The developmental change that we see in global self-esteem need not hold for all domains. Specific domains (e.g., academic, behavior) might change in different ways as children develop. In addition, developmental change in self-esteem in specific domains might differ for boys and girls. To study these issues, David Cole and his colleagues (2001) examined developmental change in five domains of self-esteem between grades 3 and 11.

*How did the investigators measure the topic of interest?* The investigators assessed self-perception in five domains—academic, sports, social, appearance, and behavior—using Harter's SPPC. Examples of items included: "very good at schoolwork" (academic), "popular with others" (social), "better than others at sports" (sports), "happy with the way they look" (appearance), and "act as supposed to" (behavior). Each domain was assessed with five different items.

*Who were the children in the study?* The study began in the fall of 1993 with 435 third graders and 420 sixth graders attending public schools in a medium-sized city in the midwestern United States. The sample included approximately equal numbers of boys and girls; roughly half of the participants were European American and one-third were African American. The children completed the SPPC every fall and spring for a 5-year-period. Thus, the younger participants were eighth graders when the study ended and the older participants were eleventh graders.

*What was the design of the study?* This study was correlational because Cole and his colleagues were interested in the relations that existed naturally between children's self-perception and their age and sex. The study was longitudinal-sequential because children in the two groups (those in grades 3 and 6 at the start of the study) were tested repeatedly over a 5-year-period.

*Were there ethical concerns with the study?* No. The investigators obtained permission from the parents for the children to participate.

*What were the results?* Average levels of self-esteem are shown in the graphs. For simplicity, I've only shown the results for three domains: academic, behavioral, and social. Let's look at three aspects of these findings. First, compare the outcomes for boys and girls. Their self-perceptions were similar for the academic and social domains, but in the behavioral domain, girls have greater self-esteem than boys in the elementary-school years but not during middle school and high school. Next, let's examine developmental change in different domains: Academic self-perception changes little with age,

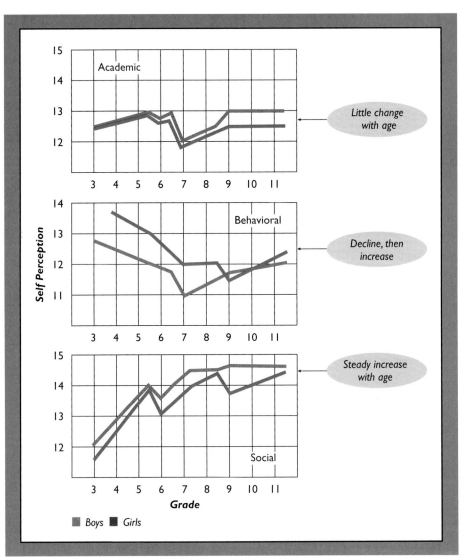

FIG. 12–4

social self-perception increases substantially, and behavioral self-perception declines during the elementary-school years but increases somewhat in middle school and high school. Finally, let's consider the impact of school transitions on children's self-perceptions: These students entered middle school in grade 7 and high school in grade 9. You can see that the middle-school transition affects children's self-perceptions in the academic domain more than in the social and behavioral domains.

*What did the investigators conclude?* Each of the three results leads to a straightforward conclusion. Let's review them in order. First, boys' and girls' self-perceptions are similar in some domains but not others. Second, the nature of developmental change in self-perception depends on the domain. Third, school transitions do affect self-perceptions—more so in some domains than in others.

*What converging evidence would strengthen these conclusions?* One limitation of the study concerns the sample. The results may be specific to children and adolescents growing up in the midwestern United States. Testing samples from other populations would strengthen the authors' conclusions. Another limit concerns the assessment of self-perception. Although the SPPC is the gold standard for measuring children's self-esteem, it is always a good idea to confirm that the same results are obtained when self-esteem is assessed with other measures.

These changes in overall level of self-esteem are accompanied by the change that I mentioned earlier: Self-esteem becomes more differentiated as children become older (Boivin, Vitaro, & Gagnon, 1992). Children are able to evaluate themselves in more domains as they develop, and their evaluations in each domain are increasingly independent. That is, younger children's ratings of self-esteem are often like Allison's (on page 344): The ratings are consistent across the different dimensions. In contrast, older children's and adolescents' ratings more often resemble Colleen's, with self-esteem varying from one domain to another.

During the school years, children's academic self-concepts become particularly well defined (Byrne & Gavin, 1996; Marsh & Yeung, 1997). As children accumulate successes and failures in school, they form beliefs about their ability in different content areas (e.g., English, math, science), and these beliefs contribute to their overall academic self-concept. A child who believes that she is skilled at English and math but not so skilled in science will probably have a positive academic self-concept overall. But a child who believes he is untalented in most academic areas will have a negative academic self-concept.

> As children develop, self-esteem becomes more differentiated.

Self-esteem and self-concept vary not only with age, but also across settings. To show this variation, Harter and her colleagues (1998) modified SPPC items dealing with overall self-worth so they could assess self-worth in the context of specific relationships. For example, the item "some kids like the kind of person they are" was changed to "some kids like the kind of person they are when they are around _____" and the blank was filled with *parents, teachers, male classmates*, or *female classmates*. In this manner, adolescents were asked to describe their self-worth in the context of different relationships. The important finding was that most adolescents clearly distinguish self-worth across these interpersonal settings. Adolescents who judge themselves positively in the context of adults, for example, might value themselves less positively in the context of classmates. Or adolescents who feel negative about themselves at home may feel positive about themselves in relationships outside the home.

Sadly, at all ages and in all settings, many individuals do not view themselves very positively. Some children are ambivalent about who they are; others actually feel

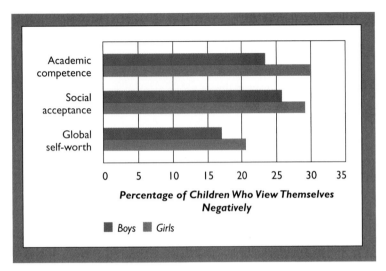

FIG. 12–5

negative about themselves. The graph shows that roughly 25 percent of 9- and 10-year-olds in one study (Cole, 1991) had negative self-esteem on three scales of the SPPC. Why do these children have so little self-worth compared to their peers? We'll answer this question in the next section.

## Sources of Self-Esteem

Think back to Allison and Colleen, the two girls whose self-perceptions are graphed on page 344. Both girls evaluated their overall self-worth very positively. In general, they were happy with themselves and with their lives. Why do these girls feel so positive while some children feel so negative about themselves? You won't be surprised to learn that parenting plays a key role.

Children are more likely to view themselves positively when their parents are affectionate toward them and involved with them (Lord, Eccles, & McCarthy, 1994). Around the world, children have higher self-esteem when families live in harmony and parents nurture their children (Scott, Scott, & McCabe, 1991). A father who routinely hugs his daughter and gladly takes her to piano lessons is saying to her, "You are important to me." When children hear this regularly from parents, they evidently internalize the message and come to see themselves positively.

Parents' discipline also is related to self-esteem. Children with high self-esteem generally have parents who aren't afraid to set rules but are also willing to discuss rules and discipline with their children (Coopersmith, 1967). Parents who fail to set rules are, in effect, telling their children that they don't care—they don't value them enough to go to the trouble of creating rules and enforcing them. In much the same way, parents who refuse to discuss discipline with their children are saying, "Your opinions don't matter to me." Not surprisingly, when children internalize these messages, the result is lower overall self-worth.

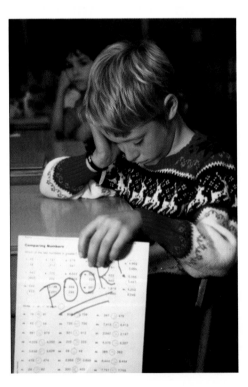

Allison's and Colleen's positive self-worth can therefore be credited, at least in part, to their parents for being warm and involved, for establishing rules, and for discussing these rules with them. But how can we account for the fact that Allison views herself positively in all domains whereas Colleen's self-perceptions are more varied? As I've suggested before, social comparisons are important (Butler, 1992). Both girls have many opportunities during each day to compare themselves with peers. Allison is almost always the first to finish assignments, usually gets one of the highest grades in the class on exams, and is often asked by her teacher to help classmates on math and science problems. Meanwhile, Colleen is usually among the last to finish assignments, typically gets low grades on tests, and is one of the students Allison helps with math and science. Daily classroom routines give every student ample opportunities to discover everyone's academic standing within the room. Soon, everyone knows that Allison is one of the most capable students and Colleen is one of the least capable. Allison understands that her classmates see her as talented academically, so her academic self-esteem is quite high. Like the boy in the photo, Colleen knows that her classmates see her as not very talented academically, so her academic self-esteem is low.

Thus, although parents contribute to children's self-esteem through their affection and discipline, comparisons to peers also matter. Children's self-esteem is high when they compare themselves favorably to others (Hoge, Smit, & Hanson, 1990). This explanation has implications for academically talented youngsters, like Darnel in the opening vignette, who might be placed in classes for gifted children. We'll look at these implications in the "Improving Children's Lives" feature.

## IMPROVING CHILDREN'S LIVES

### Self-Esteem in Gifted Classes

In a traditional classroom of students with a wide range of ability, talented youngsters compare themselves with other students and develop positive academic self-esteem. But in classes for gifted students, many talented youngsters are only average and some are below average. The resulting social comparisons cause these children's academic self-esteem to drop (Marsh et al., 1995).

There is a clear lesson here for parents and teachers: When parents like Karen and Jon (from the module-opening vignette) think about enrolling their child in classes for gifted children, they should understand that accelerated academic progress often comes at a price: Children's academic self-esteem often declines somewhat, even though their actual skills are improving.

What can parents do? First, they should look honestly at their child and decide whether he or she values learning per se versus being at the top of the class. Students who value being at the top of the class will be more affected by social comparisons in a gifted class than students who are more intent on mastering challenging academic material. Second, parents should find out whether common assignments and comparative evaluations are made, as in typical classrooms, or whether the gifted class emphasizes individualized work. The latter is more conducive to self-esteem. Carefully considering these factors can help parents decide if a gifted program is likely to lower their child's self-esteem, a very unwelcome side effect.

In examining sources of self-esteem—not just for children in gifted classes, but for all children—several characteristics of teachers and schools should also be taken into account (Hoge et al., 1990). In general, self-esteem is greater when students work hard in school, get along with their peers, and avoid disciplinary problems. In addition, self-esteem is greater when students participate in extracurricular activities, such as music, student council, sports, and clubs. Finally, students' self-esteem is enhanced when the overall climate of the school is nurturing—when students believe that teachers care about them and listen to them. Grades matter, too, but good grades affect students' self-esteem in specific disciplines—in math or English—not their overall self-esteem (Hoge et al., 1990; Marsh & Yeung, 1997).

> Children have greater self-esteem when they work hard in school and when they feel that teachers care about them.

By encouraging students to work to the best of their ability and by being genuinely interested in their progress, teachers can enhance the self-esteem of all students, regardless of their talent. Parents can do the same and, by encouraging their children to participate in extracurricular activities that match their talents, further promote self-esteem.

## Consequences of Low Self-Esteem

It is important that parents and teachers make an effort to enhance children's self-esteem because children with low self-esteem are at risk for many developmental problems. Children with low self-esteem are

- more likely to have problems with peers (Verschueren, Buyck, & Marcoen, 2001),
- more prone to psychological disorders such as depression (Button et al., 1996; Garber, Robinson, & Valentiner, 1997),
- more likely to be involved in bullying, as bullies, victims, or both (O'Moore & Kirkham, 2001), and
- more likely to do poorly in school (Marsh & Yeung, 1997).

In looking at these outcomes, we need to be cautious about stating that each is "caused" by low self-esteem. In fact, in many cases, low self-esteem contributes to the outcome but is itself also caused by the outcome. Poor school performance is a case in point: Over time, children who are unskilled academically do not keep up in school, which causes a drop in their academic self-esteem, making them less confident and probably less successful in future school learning (Marsh & Yeung, 1997). Much the same vicious circle probably applies to the poor peer relationships seen in children with low self-esteem. Poor social skills lead to peer rejection, reducing self-esteem in the peer context and disrupting future peer interactions.

> Children with low self-esteem typically have poor peer relations, are at risk for psychological disorders, have poor peer relations, are involved in antisocial activities, and poorly in school.

Understanding this complex cause-effect-cause pattern is important in deciding how to help children with low self-esteem. Some children benefit directly from therapy that increases their low self-esteem. Others, however, who need to change their own behavior, also benefit from learning how to improve their social skills (a topic that I discuss again in Modules 13.4 and 16.1). And, we need to remember that all children have some talents that can be nurtured. Taking the time to recognize each child creates the feelings of "being special" that promote self-esteem.

Thus far in this chapter, we've focused on children's growing understanding of themselves. In the next module, we'll look at parallel changes that occur in children's understanding of other people.

## CHECK YOUR LEARNING

1. One way to measure self-esteem in young children is to show pictures of children succeeding or failing in different domains; another is to _____.

2. Harter's *Self-Perception Profile for Children* (SPPC) is used to assess a child's self-esteem in five domains (scholastic competence, athletic competence, social acceptance, behavioral conduct, physical appearance) and the child's _____.

3. Self-esteem is usually at its peak during the _____ years.

4. Self-esteem often drops when children leave elementary school for middle school because _____.

5. As children develop, levels of self-esteem change and self-esteem becomes _____.

6. Children are more likely to have positive self-worth when parents are affectionate and involved with them and when parents _____.

7. A gifted child's self-esteem will not be harmed by a gifted class if the child values learning for its own sake or if the gifted class emphasizes _____.

8. Children with low self-esteem are more likely to have poor peer relations, _____, be involved in bullying, and do poorly in school.

**CONNECTIONS**

How do the long-term consequences of low self-esteem show connections among cognitive, social, and emotional development?

**Answers:** (1) have puppets describe themselves, then ask children which puppet is more like them, (2) overall self-worth, (3) preschool, (4) peer comparisons begin anew when children enter middle school, (5) more differentiated, (6) set rules and discuss discipline with their children, (7) individualized work, (8) be prone to psychological disorders such as depression

# Understanding Others

# 12.3

## LEARNING OBJECTIVES

- As children develop, how do they describe others differently?
- How does understanding of others' thinking change as children develop?
- When do children develop prejudice toward others?

Describing Others —

Understanding What Others Think —

Prejudice —

> *When 12-year-old Ian agreed to baby-sit for his 5-year-old brother, Kyle, his mother reminded him to keep Kyle out of the basement because Kyle's birthday presents were there, unwrapped. But as soon as their mother left, Kyle wanted to go to the basement to ride his tricycle. When Ian told him no, Kyle burst into angry tears and shouted, "I'm gonna tell Mom you were mean to me!" Ian wished he could explain to Kyle, but he knew that would just cause more trouble!*

We know from Modules 12.1 and 12.2 that Ian, as a young adolescent, has a growing understanding of himself. This vignette suggests that his understanding of other people is also growing. He understands why Kyle is angry, and he also knows that if he gives in to Kyle, his mother will be angry when she returns. Children's growing understanding of others is the focus of this module. We'll begin by looking at how children describe others, then examine their understanding of how others think. We'll also see how children's recognition of different social groups can lead to prejudices.

## Describing Others

As children develop, their self-descriptions become richer, more abstract, and more psychological. These same changes occur in children's descriptions of others. Children begin by describing other people in terms of concrete features, such as behavior and appearance, and progress to describing them in terms of abstract traits (Barenboim, 1981; Livesley & Bromley, 1973). The "Real Children" feature shows this progression in one child.

## REAL CHILDREN

### Tell Me About a Girl You Like

Every few years, Tamsen was asked to describe a girl that she liked a lot. Each time, she described a different girl. More importantly, the contents of her descriptions changed, focusing less on behavior and emphasizing psychological properties. Let's start with the description she gave as a 7-year-old:

*Vanessa is short. She has black hair and brown eyes. She uses a wheelchair because she can't walk. She's in my class. She has dolls just like mine. She likes to sing and read.*

Tamsen's description of Vanessa is probably not too different from the way she would have described herself: The emphasis is on concrete characteristics, such as Vanessa's appearance, possessions, and preferences. Contrast this with the following description, which Tamsen gave as a 10-year-old:

> ## Children's descriptions of others first focus on concrete features, then focus on psychological traits, then on integrating different characteristics.

*Kate lives in my apartment building. She is a very good reader and is also good at math and science. She's nice to everyone in our class. And she's very funny. Sometimes her jokes make me laugh so-o-o hard! She takes piano lessons and likes to play soccer.*

Tamsen's account still includes concrete features, such as where Kate lives and what she likes to do. However, psychological traits are also evident: Tamsen describes Kate as nice and funny. By age 10, children move beyond the purely concrete and observable in describing others. During adolescence, descriptions become even more complex, as you can see in the following, from Tamsen as a 16-year-old:

*Jeannie is very understanding. Whenever someone is upset, she's there to give a helping hand. Yet, in private, Jeannie can be so sarcastic. She can say some really nasty things about people. But I know she'd never say that stuff if she thought people would hear it because she wouldn't want to hurt their feelings.*

This description is more abstract: Tamsen now focuses on psychological traits like understanding and concern for others' feelings. It's also more integrated: Tamsen tries to explain how Jeannie can be both understanding and sarcastic. ◉

FIG. 12–6

Each of Tamsen's three descriptions is very typical. As a 7-year-old, she emphasized concrete characteristics; as a 10-year-old, she began to include psychological traits; and as a 16-year-old, she tried to integrate traits to form a cohesive picture.

The progression in how children perceive others was illustrated vividly in a classic study by Livesley and Bromley (1973). They interviewed 320 7- to 15-year-olds attending school in Merseyside, England (near Liverpool, home of the Beatles). All participants were asked to describe eight people that they knew: two boys, two girls, two men, and two women. The examiner told the participants, "I want you to describe what sort of person they are. I want you to tell me what you think about them and what they are like" (p. 97).

The participants at different ages typically produced descriptions much like Tamsen's at different ages. Livesley and Bromley then categorized the contents of the descriptions. Some of their results appear in the graph. Descriptions referring to appearances or possessions become less common as children grow older, as do descriptions giving general information, such as the person's age, sex, religion, or school. In contrast, descriptions of personality traits (for example, "friendly" or "conceited") increase between ages 8 and 14 years. This pattern of changes in children's descriptions of others resembles children's changing understanding of the self, which I explained on pages 334-335.

By age 5, children use the information in their descriptions to predict others' future behavior (Heyman & Gelman, 1999; Yuill & Pearson, 1998). To illustrate, suppose kindergarten children are told that Alissa did something nice (e.g., helped another child finish a difficult puzzle), but Celeste did something mean (e.g., scribbled in another child's favorite book). Kindergarten children will judge that, in the future, Alissa is more likely than Celeste to help a child who is hurt, to give money to a needy child, and to hope that an elaborate art project turns out well for the child who created it. Thus, descriptions of others are useful, even for young children, because they allow children to predict how others will behave in the future.

## Understanding What Others Think

One trademark of the preschool child's thinking is difficulty in seeing the world from another's point of view. Piaget's term for this was *egocentrism*, and it was a defining characteristic of his preoperational stage of development (see Module 7.2). In much the same way, preschool children's communication is often ineffective because they don't consider the listener's perspective when they talk (see Module 10.4). As children move beyond the preschool years, though, they realize that others see the world differently, both literally and figuratively. For example, in the module-opening vignette, 12-year-old Ian knows why his little brother, Kyle, is angry: Kyle thinks that Ian is being bossy and mean. Ian understands that Kyle doesn't know there is a good reason why he can't go to the basement.

Sophisticated understanding of how others think is achieved gradually throughout childhood and adolescence. Robert Selman (1980, 1981) has proposed a theory of how understanding others' thinking—or *perspective taking*—occurs. Selman's theory is based on two of Piaget's key assumptions, namely, that understanding of others occurs in stages and that movement from one stage to the next is based on cognitive development. The table shows Selman's five stages of perspective taking.

| Selman's Stages of Perspective Taking | | |
|---|---|---|
| **Stage** | **Approximate Ages** | **Description** |
| Undifferentiated | 3–6 years | Children know that self and others can have different thoughts and feelings, but often confuse the two. |
| Social-informational | 4–9 years | Children know that perspectives differ because people have access to different information. |
| Self-reflective | 7–12 years | Children can step into another's shoes and view themselves as others do; they know that others can do the same. |
| Third-person | 10–15 years | Children and adolescents can step outside the immediate situation to see how they and another person are viewed by a third person. |
| Societal | 14 years to adult | Adolescents realize that a third person's perspective is influenced by broader personal, social, and cultural contexts. |

TABLE 12-1

A good way to appreciate the progression from stage to stage is to look at one of the social dilemmas that Selman used to explore children's perspective taking.

*Holly is an 8-year-old girl who likes to climb trees. She is the best tree climber in the neighborhood. One day while climbing down from a tall tree she falls off the bottom branch but does not hurt herself. Her father sees her fall. He is upset and asks her to promise not to climb trees anymore. Holly promises.*

*Later that day, Holly and her friends meet Sean. Sean's kitten is caught up in a tree and cannot get down. Something has to be done right away or the kitten may fall. Holly is the only one who climbs well enough to reach the kitten and get it down, but she remembers her promise to her father (Selman & Byrne, 1974, p. 805).*

> In Selman's theory, young children confuse their own and others' views, but adolescents can see their own and another's views from a third person's perspective.

This dilemma is typical in that it includes people who don't share the same knowledge about the events taking place. After hearing the story, children are asked questions to investigate their ability to take on each character's view and predict what Holly does.

As children grow, their answers reflect ever more sophisticated understanding of who is thinking what and why in these dilemmas (Selman, 1980, 1981; Selman & Byrne, 1974). The youngest children, those in the undifferentiated stage, might reply, "Holly's father will be happy if she gets the kitten because he likes kittens." This answer confuses the child's own feelings with the father's and ignores Holly's promise. Children in the social-informational stage might say, "If Holly's father knew why she climbed the tree, he probably wouldn't be angry." This answer indicates that the child thinks the father's response depends on whether he knows the reason for Holly's behavior.

In the self-reflective stage, a child might say, "Holly's father would understand that she thought saving the kitten's life was really important, so he wouldn't be mad. He'd probably be proud." This comment shows Holly's father stepping into Holly's shoes, the defining characteristic of the self-reflective stage.

At the next level, the third-person stage, a child might respond, "Holly remembers the promise, but she doesn't think her father will be angry when she explains that she wouldn't have climbed the tree except to save the kitten's life. Her father might wish that Holly had asked an adult for help, but he'd also understand why it was important to Holly to save the kitten." This child simultaneously considers both Holly's and her father's perspectives on the dilemma. In answering, the child has stepped outside the immediate situation to take the perspective of a neutral third party who can look at both Holly's and her father's views.

At the most advanced level, the societal stage, an adolescent might reply, "Holly and her father both know that she almost always obeys him. So, they'd both know that if she disobeyed him to climb the tree, there would have to be an awfully good reason. So, they'd talk about it." This child's answer, like the previous one, considers Holly's and her father's perspectives simultaneously. The difference is that this comment puts the issue in the broader context of the history of their father–daughter relationship.

As predicted by Selman's theory, research shows that, as children develop, their reasoning moves through each stage, in sequence. In addition, regardless of age, children at more advanced cognitive levels tend to be at more advanced stages in perspective taking (Gurucharri & Selman, 1982; Krebs & Gillmore, 1982).

Additional support for Selman's theory comes from studies on perspective taking and social behavior. In the photo on page 355, the children with the soccer ball apparently recognize that the girl on the sideline wants to play, so they're inviting her to join the game. Children who can anticipate what others are thinking should get along better with their peers, and research indicates that they do. For example, children with good perspective-taking skills are typically well liked by their peers (LeMare & Rubin, 1987). Of course, mere understanding does not guarantee good social behavior; sometimes children who understand what another child is thinking take advantage of that child. But, in general, greater understanding of others seems to promote positive interactions, a topic that we'll discuss further in Chapter 13 on moral understanding and behavior.

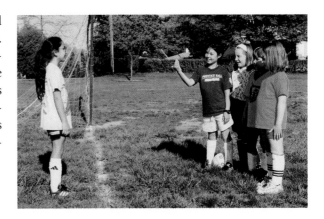

## Prejudice

As children learn more about others, they discover that people belong to different social groups, based on variables such as sex, ethnicity, and social class. By the preschool years, most children can distinguish males from females and can identify people from different ethnic groups (Aboud, 1993). **Once children learn their membership in a specific group, they typically show prejudice, a negative view of others based on their membership in a specific group.** Actually, in young children prejudice is not so much a negative view of others as it is an enhanced view of one's own group. That is, preschool and kindergarten children attribute many positive traits such as being friendly and smart to their own group and few negative traits such as being mean (Bigler, Jones, & Lobliner, 1997; Black-Gutman & Hickson, 1996).

As children move into the elementary-school years, prejudice usually declines somewhat (Powlishta et al., 1994). Cognitive development explains the decline. Preschool and kindergarten children usually view people in social groups as much more homogeneous than they really are. People from other groups are seen as all alike and, typically, not as good as people from the child's own group. As children grow, they begin to understand that people in social groups are heterogeneous—they know that individual European Americans, girls, and obese children, for example, are not all alike. And they have learned that people from different groups may be more alike than people from the same group. Gary, an African American whose passion is computers, finds that he enjoys being with Vic, an Italian American who shares his love of computers, but not Curtis, another African American whose passion is music. As children realize that social groups consist of all kinds of different people, prejudice lessens.

During early adolescence, prejudice often increases again. This resurgence apparently reflects two different processes (Black-Gutman & Hickson, 1996; Teichman, 2001). One is experiential: Exposed to prejudices of those around them, children and adolescents internalize some of these views. A second process concerns adolescents' identity. In the search for identity (described on pages 335-340), adolescents' preferences for their own groups often intensifies. Thus, greater prejudice in older children and adolescents reflects both a more positive view of their own group as well as a more negative view of other groups. Bob, a 14-year-old European American growing up in Arizona, becomes more prejudiced because he views his own European American heritage more positively and acquires prejudicial attitudes toward Native Americans from his parents and peers.

Identifying *how* children form actual prejudices is challenging because ethical concerns limit us to correlational studies. (Obviously, we could not do an experiment in which some children are deliberately exposed to biased information about actual groups of children.) Consequently, to study the processes underlying prejudice, researchers sometimes conduct experiments in which children are temporarily assigned to different groups.

To illustrate this approach, many theorists believe that social status contributes to prejudice: Children are more likely to develop strong preferences for their group when it has high status. In experimentation designed to test this prediction (Bigler, Brown, & Markell, 2001; Brown & Bigler, 2002), children attending a summer-school program were assigned to wear either a blue or yellow T-shirt. To increase the status of children wearing yellow shirts, children were told that in the previous summer, students wearing yellow shirts were smarter, better leaders, and better athletes. Throughout the 4-week program, teachers mentioned T-shirt color frequently (e.g., had children sit with others wearing the same color of shirt), but did *not* favor one group over the other. Nevertheless, at the end of the program, children wearing yellow shirts viewed themselves much more positively than they viewed children wearing blue shirts; in contrast, children wearing blue shirts (low status) had no biases. Thus, high status breeds a preference for one's own group (Nesdale & Flesser, 2001).

What can parents, teachers, and other adults do to rid children of prejudice? One way is to encourage friendly and constructive contacts between children from different groups (Ramsey, 1995). Adults can create situations in which children from different groups work together toward common goals. In class, this might be a class project, as shown in the photo. In sports, it might be mastering a new skill. By working together, Gary starts to realize that Vic acts, thinks, and feels as he does simply because he's Vic, not because he's an Italian American.

Another useful approach is to ask children to play different roles (Davidson & Davidson, 1994). They can be asked to imagine that, because of their race, ethnic background, or sex, they have been insulted verbally or not allowed to participate in special activities. A child might be asked to imagine that she can't go to a private swimming club because she's African American or that she wasn't invited to a party because she's Hispanic. Afterwards, children reflect on how they felt when prejudice and discrimination were directed at them. And they're asked to think about what would be fair—what should be done in situations like these?

**Prejudice is reduced with friendly and constructive contacts between children from different groups.**

From such experiences, children and adolescents discover for themselves that a person's membership in a social group tells us very little about that person. They learn, instead, that all children are different, each a unique mix of experiences, skills, and values.

Increasing interaction between children of different racial groups was one of the consequences of the U.S. Supreme Court's decision in *Brown v. Board of Education*, a case that shows how child-development research influenced social policy.

## CHILD DEVELOPMENT AND FAMILY POLICY

### Ending Segregated Schools

In 1950, African American children in most states attended separate schools. Segregated schooling had been the law of the land for more than 100 years, bolstered by several famous Supreme Court decisions. In the fall of 1950, the chapter of the National Association for the Advancement of Colored People (NAACP) in Topeka, Kansas, decided to test the constitutionality of the law. Thirteen African American parents, including Oliver Brown, attempted to enroll their children in white-only schools; when they were turned away, the NAACP sued the Topeka Board of Education.

A key element in the NAACP's case was that separate schools were inherently harmful to African American children because such schools apparently legitimized their second-class status. To support this claim, the NAACP legal team relied on testimony from Dr. Kenneth B. Clark. In previous work, Clark (1945; Clark & Clark, 1940) had shown that African American children typically thought that white dolls were "nice" but that brown dolls were "bad." He found the same results in African American children attending segregated Topeka schools, leading him to testify that,

> these children . . . , like other human beings who are subjected to an obviously inferior status in the society in which they live, have been definitely harmed in the development of their personalities . . .

In May 1954, the Supreme Court rendered the landmark decision that segregated schools were unconstitutional. The impact of Clark's research and testimony was evident in the decision in *Brown v. Board of Education*, delivered by Chief Justice Earl Warren:

> Segregation of white and colored children in public schools has a detrimental effect upon the colored children. The impact is greater when it has the sanction of the law, for the policy of separating the races is usually interpreted as denoting the inferiority of the negro group. A sense of inferiority affects the motivation of a child to learn. Segregation with the sanction of law, therefore, has a tendency to [retard] the educational and mental development of negro children and to deprive them of . . . benefits they would receive in a racial[ly] integrated school system.

After the *Brown* decision, Clark continued his work on civil rights and worked on behalf of African American youth. For his lifelong effort to inform public policy on African American children and their families, in 1987 he received the Gold Medal for Life Achievement in Psychology in the Public Interest from the American Psychological Foundation. 🌐

Clark's work is a compelling demonstration of the manner in which child-development research can have far-reaching implications for policy—in this case, helping to eliminate racially segregated schools in America. And the integrated schools that resulted have helped to reduce prejudice by providing children with opportunities to learn about peers from other ethnic and racial groups.

## CHECK YOUR LEARNING

1. Children's descriptions of others begin with concrete characteristics (e.g., appearance, possessions) and next begin to include _____.

2. When adolescents describe others, they usually _____.

3. Selman's theory of perspective taking is based on Piaget's assumption that understanding of others consists of stages and that _____.

4. In Selman's theory, at the most advanced stage of perspective taking, adolescents _____.

5. Prejudice declines somewhat as children get older because _____.

6. One way to reduce prejudice is to encourage friendly and constructive contacts between people from different groups; another is to _____.

**ACTIVE CHILDREN**
How might children's growing understanding of other people affect their interactions with peers?

discrimination and prejudice

alize that social groups are not homogeneous, (6) have children play roles that let them experience
recognize the influence of context on this perspective, (5) with cognitive development, children re-
from one stage to the next reflects cognitive development, (4) take a third person's perspective and
**Answers:** (1) psychological traits, (2) try to provide a cohesive, integrated picture, (3) movement

# Unifying Themes: Nature and Nurture

This chapter is a good occasion to feature the theme that *development is always jointly influenced by heredity and environment*. The emergence of self-awareness between 15 and 24 months is primarily due to biological forces. Regardless of circumstances, children become self-aware between ages 1 and 2. However, elaborating self-awareness into a specific self-concept depends largely on a child's experiences at home and in school. The specific direction that children take in establishing an identity is strongly influenced by those around them, particularly their parents and teachers.

## See for Yourself

The mirror recognition task, described on pages 332-333, is great fun to do, and you'll be astonished by the rapid change in children's responses between 1 and 2 years. For this task, you simply need a mirror, some tissue, blush, and a few cooperative parents of 12- to 18-month-olds. Have the parents play with their toddler near the mirror and, in the process, wipe the toddler's nose with a tissue that has blush on it. Then see how the toddler responds to the now red nose. Some 12-month-olds will do nothing; others will touch the red nose in the mirror. When the 15- or 18-month-olds see themselves, though, they should stop, get a curious expression on their faces, and then reach up to touch their nose. See for yourself!

## Resources

For more information about...

**adolescent search for identity**, read Erik Erikson's *Gandhi* (Norton, 1969), a Pulitzer Prize–winning book in which Erikson shows how the adolescent search for identity influenced the development of this great leader of India.

**deciding on a career or finding a job that's right for you**, visit a Web site maintained by the *Wall Street Journal*: **http://www.collegejournal.com/careersqa/findcareerpath/**

## Key Terms

achievement status 336
adolescent egocentrism 335
attributions 340
crystallization 336
diffusion status 336
ethnic identity 337
foreclosure status 336
illusion of invulnerability 336
imaginary audience 335

implementation 337
moratorium status 336
norepinephrine 340
personal fable 336
prejudice 355
self-concept 332
self-esteem 342
serotonin 340
specification 337

Understanding Self
and Others

12.1  What Am I? Self-Concept
12.2  Self-Esteem
12.3  Understanding Others

# SUMMARY

## 12.1 Who Am I? Self-Concept

### Origins of Self-Recognition

At about 15 months, infants begin to recognize themselves in the mirror, one of the first signs of self-recognition. They also begin to prefer to look at pictures of themselves, to refer to themselves by name and with personal pronouns, and sometimes to know their age and gender. Evidently, by 2 years, most children have the rudiments of self-awareness.

### The Evolving Self-Concept

Preschoolers often define themselves in terms of observable characteristics, such as possessions, physical characteristics, preferences, and competencies. During the elementary-school years, self-concept begins to include emotions, a child's membership in social groups, and comparisons with peers. During adolescence, self-concept includes attitudes, personality traits, beliefs, and future plans. In general, adolescents' self-concepts are more abstract, more psychological, and more future oriented than self-concepts in younger children.

### The Search for Identity

The search for identity typically involves four statuses. Diffusion and foreclosure are more common in early adolescence; moratorium and achievement are more common in late adolescence and young adulthood. Adolescents are most likely to achieve an identity when parents encourage discussion and recognize their autonomy; they are least likely to achieve an identity when parents set rules and enforce them without explanation.

According to Super's theory, an adolescent's developing identity is a primary influence on his or her career aspirations. Super proposes three phases of vocational development during adolescence and young adulthood: crystallization, when basic ideas about careers are identified, based on the person's identity; specification, when lines of work associated with interests are identified; and implementation, which marks entry into the workforce.

Adolescents from ethnic groups often progress through three phases in acquiring an ethnic identity: initial disinterest, exploration, and identity achievement. Achieving an ethnic identity usually results in higher self-esteem but is not consistently related to the strength of one's identification with mainstream culture.

Contrary to myth, adolescence is not usually a period of storm and stress. Most adolescents love their parents, feel loved by them, rely on them for advice, and adopt their values. The parent–child relationship becomes more egalitarian during the adolescent years, reflecting adolescents' growing independence. A small number of adolescents become depressed, often because their explanations of their own behavior is flawed.

## 12.2 Self-Esteem

### Measuring Self-Esteem

Most tasks assess self-esteem in different areas. One of the most common measures is Harter's *Self-Perception Profile for Children* (SPPC), which is designed for children as young as 8 years. It assesses self-esteem in five areas: scholastic competence, athletic competence, social acceptance, behavioral conduct, and physical appearance. It also measures overall self-worth. For measuring self-esteem in older adolescents, job competence, close friendships, and romantic appeal are added.

### Change and Stability in Self-Esteem

Global self-esteem is very high during the preschool years but declines in the elementary-school years as children compare themselves to peers. Self-esteem also declines, temporarily, when children make school transitions. Some specific domains of self-esteem increase steadily with age but others decline. Self-esteem becomes more differentiated in older children and adolescents as they evaluate themselves on more aspects of self-esteem, including different types of academic skills.

### Sources of Self-Esteem

Children's self-esteem is greater when parents are affectionate and involved with them and when parents set rules and discuss disciplinary action. Self-esteem also depends on peer comparisons. Self-esteem is usually greater when children know that others view them positively.

### Consequences of Low Self-Esteem

When children have low self-esteem, they are more likely to have poor peer relations, suffer psychological disorders such as depression, be involved in antisocial activities, and do poorly in school. Therapy and improved social skills can enhance children's self-esteem.

## 12.3 Understanding Others

### Describing Others

Children's descriptions of others change in much the same way that their descriptions of themselves change. During the early elementary-school years, descriptions emphasize concrete characteristics. In the late elementary-school years, they emphasize personality traits. In adolescence, they emphasize an integrated picture of a person. Children use their descriptions to predict others' behaviors.

### Understanding What Others Think

According to Selman's perspective-taking theory, children's understanding of how others think progresses through five stages. In the first, the undifferentiated stage, children often confuse their own and another's view. In the last, the societal stage, adolescents take a third person's perspective and understand that this perspective is influenced by context.

### Prejudice

Prejudice emerges in the preschool years, soon after children recognize different social groups. Prejudice declines during childhood, as children's cognitive growth helps them understand that social groups are heterogeneous, not homogeneous, but often increases in older children and adolescents. The best way to reduce prejudice is with additional exposure to individuals from other social groups and through role play that allows children to experience prejudice and discrimination.

# 13

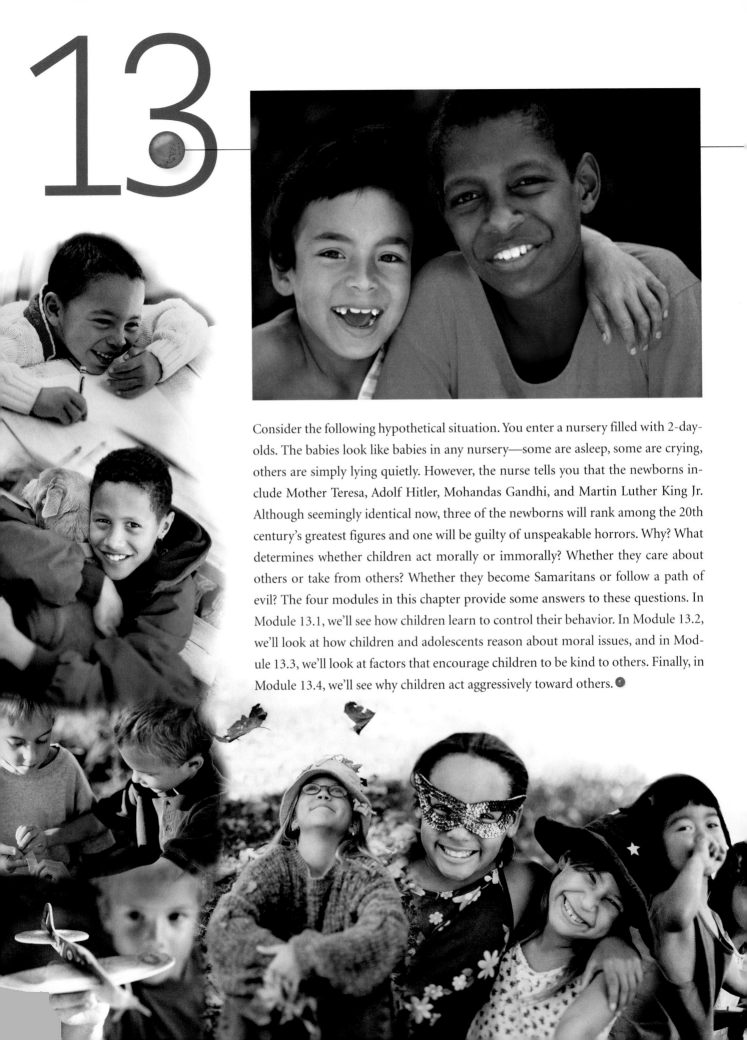

Consider the following hypothetical situation. You enter a nursery filled with 2-day-olds. The babies look like babies in any nursery—some are asleep, some are crying, others are simply lying quietly. However, the nurse tells you that the newborns include Mother Teresa, Adolf Hitler, Mohandas Gandhi, and Martin Luther King Jr. Although seemingly identical now, three of the newborns will rank among the 20th century's greatest figures and one will be guilty of unspeakable horrors. Why? What determines whether children act morally or immorally? Whether they care about others or take from others? Whether they become Samaritans or follow a path of evil? The four modules in this chapter provide some answers to these questions. In Module 13.1, we'll see how children learn to control their behavior. In Module 13.2, we'll look at how children and adolescents reason about moral issues, and in Module 13.3, we'll look at factors that encourage children to be kind to others. Finally, in Module 13.4, we'll see why children act aggressively toward others.

# Moral Understanding and Behavior

# 13.1 Self-Control

## LEARNING OBJECTIVES

● When does self-control begin, and how does it change as children develop?

● What factors influence children's ability to maintain self-control?

● What strategies can children use to improve their self-control?

*Shirley returned from a long day at work tired but eager to celebrate her son Ryan's fourth birthday. Her excitement quickly turned to dismay when she discovered that Ryan had taken a huge bite of icing from the birthday cake while the baby sitter fixed lunch. Before she had left for work that morning, Shirley had explicitly told Ryan not to touch the cake. Why couldn't Ryan wait? Why did he give in to temptation? What could she do to help Ryan control himself better in the future?*

In this vignette, Shirley wishes that Ryan had **greater self-control, the ability to rise above immediate pressures and not give in to impulse.** A child who saves her allowance to buy a much-desired object instead of spending it immediately on candy is showing self-control, as is an adolescent who studies for an exam instead of going to the mall with his friends, knowing that tomorrow he can enjoy the mall and a good grade on his exam.

Self-control is one of the first steps toward moral behavior because children must learn that they cannot constantly do whatever tempts them at the moment. Instead, society has rules for behavior in certain situations, and children must learn to restrain themselves.

In this module, we'll first see how self-control emerges during the preschool years. Then we'll learn some of the factors that determine how well children control themselves. Finally, we'll look at strategies that children use to improve their self-control.

## Beginnings of Self-Control

In this cartoon, Calvin shows little self-control. Is he typical for his age? Thankfully, no. Self-control emerges in infancy and gradually improves during the preschool years (Kopp, 1987, 1997). A rough chronology looks like this:

# Calvin and Hobbes                    by Bill Watterson

- At approximately the first birthday, infants become aware that people impose demands on them and they must react accordingly. Infants learn that they are not entirely free to behave as they wish; instead, others set limits on what they can do. These limits reflect both concern for their safety ("Don't touch! It's hot") as well as early socialization efforts ("Don't grab Ravisha's toy").

- At about 2 years, toddlers have internalized some of the controls imposed by others and are capable of some self-control in parents' absence. For example, although the boy on the left in the photo certainly looks as if he wants to play with the toy that the other toddler has, so far he has inhibited his desire to grab the toy, perhaps because he remembers that his parents have told him not to take things from others.

- At about 3 years, children become capable of self-regulation, which "involves flexible and adaptive control processes that can meet quickly changing situational demands" (Kopp, 1987, p. 38). Children can devise ways to regulate their own behavior. To return to the example of a playmate's interesting toy, children might tell themselves that they really don't want to play with it, or they might turn to another activity that removes the temptation to grab it.

By age 3, children are capable of self-regulation, because they can make simple plans to deal with the demands of different situations.

These gradual improvements in self-control are revealed in the study profiled in the "Focus on Research" feature.

## FOCUS ON RESEARCH

### Growth of Effortful Control in Toddlers and Preschoolers

*Who were the investigators, and what was the aim of the study?* Grazyna Kochanska and her colleagues Kathleen Murray and Elena Harlan (2000) wanted to examine improvements in self-control between 2 and 3 years of age. In addition, they wanted to determine if self-control in situations where children must comply with prohibitions ("Don't look!") was related to their ability to regulate their own emotions.

*How did the investigators measure the topic of interest?* Kochanska and her colleagues tested children on many measures of control; for simplicity, I'm only going to describe four. In one measure of self-control, children were asked to sit with their backs turned away from an adult as she wrapped a gift; the experimenter recorded how quickly children peeked at the gift. In a second measure of self-control, an adult placed a nicely wrapped gift on a table and told children not to touch the gift while she went to get a bow; the experimenter recorded how quickly children touched the gift. To measure regulation of anger, mothers strapped the child tightly in a car seat; the experimenter recorded how quickly and intensely the child became angry. To measure regulation of joy, an adult presented a funny puppet show to children that ended with the puppets tickling the child; the experimenter recorded how much children smiled and laughed during this episode.

*Who were the children in the study?* Kochanska and her colleagues tested 106 2-year-olds and retested 103 of them approximately one year later. Most of the children were European American.

FIG. 13–1

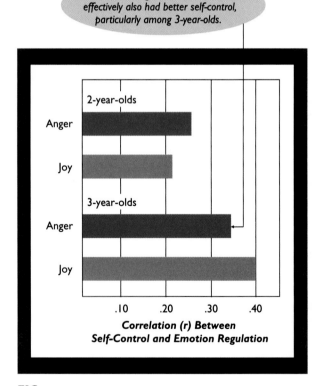

FIG. 13–2

*What was the design of the study?* This study was correlational because Kochanska was interested in relations that existed naturally between age and children's self-control and between children's self-control and their regulation of emotion (anger, joy). The study was longitudinal because children were tested twice, at approximately 2 and 3 years of age.

*Were there ethical concerns with the study?* No. The tasks involved minimal risk and weren't much different from experiences that children would encounter in daily life.

*What were the results?* Let's begin by looking at age differences in self-control. The top graph shows that 3-year-olds waited longer than 2-year-olds to peek at the gift being wrapped and to touch the gift after the adult left. Of course, these improvements should not obscure the fact almost no children in either group are truly showing self-control. All children eventually turn to look at the gift being wrapped or touch the wrapped gift on the table.

The bottom graph shows correlations between children's performance on the self-control and emotional self-regulation tasks. You can see that the correlations were positive: Children who showed good self-control (by waiting longer to peek or touch) tended to regulate their emotions better (e.g., they were less angry when strapped in the car seat).

*What did the investigators conclude?* Self-control improves considerably between 2 and 3 years (but is still far from perfect). And the ability to control one's behavior in the face of temptation is related to the ability to control one's emotions.

*What converging evidence would strengthen these conclusions?* Kochanska and her colleagues measured children's self-control with specially designed tasks. Consequently, a useful next step would be to complement the results from those tasks with observations of self-control as it occurs naturally in children's homes. Also, since the 3-year-olds have hardly mastered self-control, another logical extension would be to continue the longitudinal study, testing children annually as they get older. ◉

As we've seen, preschoolers have much to learn about regulating impulsive behavior, and control is achieved only gradually throughout the elementary-school years. For example, in a study by Rotenberg and Mayer (1990), after children had completed a task, they were offered the choice of a relatively small reward immediately or a much larger reward if they waited one day. About one-third of the 6- to 8-year-olds opted to wait for the larger reward. In contrast, half of the 9- to 11-year-olds and nearly all of the 12- to 15-year-olds waited a day to obtain the larger reward. Thus, although self-control may be evident in toddlers, mastery occurs gradually throughout childhood.

Perhaps you wonder about the validity of these tasks. That is, are these tasks measuring important aspects of self-control in children's natural environments? Mothers' reports of their youngsters' self-control represent one source of evidence for the validity of these tasks. Children who are less likely to touch prohibited toys are, according to their mothers' reports, more likely to spontaneously confess to misdeeds at home and more likely to do as asked at home, without parental supervision (Kochanska et al., 1994).

Even more remarkable are the results from longitudinal studies on the long-term consistency of self-control. Shoda, Mischel, and Peake (1990) tracked down nearly 200 15- to 18-year-olds who had participated in self-control experiments as 4-year-olds. In the original experiments, 4-year-olds were told that if they waited alone in a room until the experimenter returned, they would receive a big prize. If they rang a bell to signal the experimenter to return, they would receive a much smaller prize. Then the researchers simply recorded the length of time children waited until the experimenter returned. Amazingly, how long 4-year-olds waited was related to a host of characteristics some 11 to 14 years later. The table shows some of the significant correlations between the 4-year-olds' ability to delay gratification and their coping skills, personality characteristics, and SAT scores as adolescents. In general, 4-year-olds who waited the longest before calling the experimenter were still, as 15- to 18-year-olds, better able to exert self-control and more attentive and able to plan, and they had higher SAT scores.

Preschoolers who are better able to resist temptation often grow up to be adolescents who have better self-control, are more planful, and have higher SAT scores.

### Correlations Between Children's Delay of Gratification as Preschoolers and Their Coping, Personality, and Academic Achievement as Adolescents

| Measure | r |
| --- | --- |
| *Coping* | |
| Is likely to yield to temptation | −.50 |
| Distractibility when trying to concentrate | −.41 |
| *Personality* | |
| Is planful, thinks ahead | .36 |
| Tends to go to pieces under stress, becomes rattled and disorganized | −.34 |
| *SAT scores* | |
| Verbal scale | .42 |
| Quantitative scale | .57 |

Source: Shoda, Mischel, and Peake, 1990.

TABLE 13-1

These individuals were tested one more time, when they were in their late 20s (Ayduk et al., 2000). The 4-year-olds who waited the longest were, as 27-year-olds, better educated and had higher self-esteem.

Obviously, individuals differ in their ability to resist temptation, and this characteristic is remarkably stable over time. But why are some children and adults better able than others to exert self-control? As you'll see in the next section of this module, parents play an important role in determining children's self-control.

## Parental Influences

In the neighborhood where I grew up, there were next-door neighbors where both husbands had similar jobs with an engineering company, and both wives were full-time homemakers. Nevertheless, their lifestyles had little in common. One family always seemed to be the first on the block to own new "toys": the first stereo record player, the first color TV, the first Ford Mustang in 1964, and so on. The other family was as frugal as the first family was free spending: Occasional trips to the repair shop kept the black-and-white TV working, children wore hand-me-down clothes, and the dad rode a bus to work.

Obviously, the children growing up in these two families were exposed to very different models of self-control. Adults in the first family preferred immediate gratification, but those in the second family preferred to save their money for deferred goals. Is children's self-control influenced by their exposure to such models? Can self-control be changed by exposure to a model with less (or more) self-control?

Some of the first answers to these questions came from a classic study by Albert Bandura and Walter Mischel (1965). In the first phase of the study, fourth and fifth graders made several choices between a small immediate reward and a larger delayed outcome (for example, a small candy bar immediately or a larger one in a week). Children who most preferred immediate reward and the ones who most preferred delayed reward then went on to a second phase. Now they watched an adult choose between a less valuable item that could be obtained immediately and a more valuable item that required delay. For children who preferred waiting for a larger reward, the adult always chose the immediate reward. For children who had preferred immediate but small rewards, the adult always chose the delayed reward item. In both cases, the adult also briefly explained his behavior. For example, when the choice was between getting a plastic chess set immediately and a more expensive wooden set in two weeks, the adult commented, "Chess figures are chess figures. I can get much use out of the plastic ones right away" (p. 701).

Immediately after watching the model, children had the opportunity to choose between immediate but small rewards or delayed but larger rewards. What happened? Most children imitated the adult's behavior. Children exposed to a model who delayed gratification also delayed their choices. Similarly, most children exposed to models who showed little self-control were easily swayed and abandoned their own self-control. Apparently, children can show self-restraint or be incredibly impulsive, simply depending on how they observe others behave in similar situations.

Are you skeptical of Bandura and Mischel's (1965) results, maybe because the setting seems artificial? Perhaps children's self-control can't be so easily influenced outside of the laboratory, in a normal home setting? In fact, correlational studies show that parents' behavior is related to their children's self-control, but not in a way that you may expect. Self-control is usually *lower* in children whose parents are very strict with them (Donovan, Leavitt, & Walsh, 2000; Feldman & Wentzel, 1990).

One interpretation of this finding is that strict parents "overcontrol" their children: By constantly directing them to do one thing but not another, parents do not give their children either the opportunity or the incentive to internalize control (Kochanska, Coy, & Murray, 2001). Consistent with this argument is the finding that children have greater self-control when parents encourage them to be independent and make their own decisions (Silverman & Ragusa, 1990).

So far, the story seems reasonably straightforward: For children to gain self-control, parents must relinquish control. By gradually giving children more opportunities to regulate their own behavior and see the consequences of their choices, parents foster self-control. For example, instead of insisting that elementary-school children follow a set after-dinner routine, parents can allow children to decide how to balance entertainment, homework, and household chores.

But more recent research shows that the story is not so simple after all. Remember from Module 11.2 that temperament affects children's responses to parents' efforts to promote self-control. We'll look at this research in the next section.

## Temperamental Influences on Self-Control

Children's temperament helps determine their level of self-control. Emotional toddlers and preschoolers are less able to control themselves (Stifter, Spinrad, & Braungart-Rieker, 1999). That is, youngsters who have difficulty regulating their emotions usually have difficulty regulating their behavior.

Temperament also influences how children respond to parents' efforts to teach self-control. In children, the aspect of temperament that's most important for self-control is anxiety and fearfulness (Kochanska, 1991, 1993). Some anxious and fearful children become nervous at the prospect of potential wrongdoing. When told not to eat a cookie until after dinner, fearful children may leave the room because they're afraid that otherwise they might give in to temptation. With these children, a simple parental reminder usually guarantees compliance because they are so anxious about not following instructions, getting caught, or having to confess to a misdeed.

> Parents foster self-control by using gentle discipline with fearful children and by using appeals to cooperate with fearless children.

For children who are not naturally fearful at the thought of misdeeds, other approaches are necessary. More effective with these children are positive appeals to the child to cooperate, appeals that build on the strong attachment relationship between parent and child. Fearless children comply with parental requests out of positive feelings for a loved one, not out of distress caused by fear of misdeeds (Kochanska, 1997a).

Of course, regardless of their temperament, children are not perfectly consistent in their self-control. Children who are able to resist temptation on one occasion may give in the next time. Why do children show self-control on some tasks but not on others? As we'll see in the next section, the answer lies in children's plans for resisting temptation.

## Improving Self-Control

Imagine it's one of the first nice days of spring. You have two major exams that you should study for, but it's so-o-o-o tempting to spend the entire day with your friends, sitting in the sun. What do you do to resist this temptation and stick to studying? You might remind yourself that these exams are very important. You might also move to a windowless room to keep your mind off the tempting weather. Stated more generally, effective ways to resist temptation include (a) reminding yourself of the importance of long-term goals over short-term temptations and (b) reducing the attraction of the tempting event.

During the preschool years, some youngsters begin to use both of these methods spontaneously. In an experiment by Mischel and Ebbesen (1970), 3- to 5-year-olds were asked to sit alone in a room for 15 minutes. If they waited the entire time, they would receive a desirable reward. Children could call the experimenter back to the room at any time by a prearranged signal; in this case, they would receive a much less desirable reward.

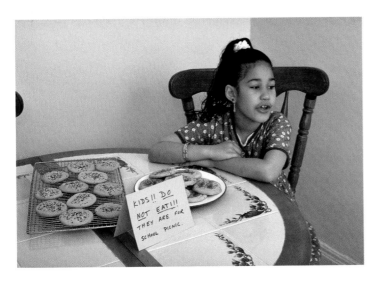

Some children, of course, were better able than others to wait the full 15 minutes. How did they do it? Some children talked to themselves: "I've gotta wait to get the best prize!" As Vygotsky described (Module 7.4), these youngsters were using private speech to control their own behavior. Others, like the child in the photograph, sang. Still others invented games. All were effective techniques for enduring 15 boring minutes to receive a desired prize.

Later studies show that children who have a concrete way of handling such a situation are far better able to resist temptation (Mischel, Cantor, & Feldman, 1996). Effective plans include (a) reminders to avoid looking at the tempting object, (b) reminders of rules against touching a tempting object, and (c) activities designed to divert attention from the tempting object, such as playing with other objects. For example, in the vignette, Shirley could have helped Ryan make a plan to resist temptation. She might have told him, "When you feel like you want to eat some cake, tell yourself, 'No cake until Mom gets home' and go play in your bedroom."

Overall, then, how children think about tempting objects or outcomes makes all the difference. Even preschoolers can achieve self-control by making plans that include appropriate self-instruction. As children learn to regulate their own behavior, they also begin to learn about moral rules—cultural rights and wrongs—which are described in the next module.

## CHECK YOUR LEARNING

1. At approximately age _____, children first learn that other people make demands of them.

2. Fifteen- to 18-year-olds who were better able to resist temptation as preschoolers still have better self-control, are more attentive and planful, and have _____.

3. Bandura and Mischel's classic study of adults' influence on children's self-control revealed that, after viewing adults who showed little self-control, children _____.

4. When parents are very controlling, their children tend to _____.

5. With fearful children, parents can foster self-control by using gentle discipline; with fearless children, parents can foster self-control by _____.

6. Children can maintain self-control more effectively when they remind themselves to resist temptation and _____.

**≈ CONTINUITY**
Review the findings from the longitudinal study of delay of gratification, shown in Table 13–1 on page 365. What do these results tell us about the continuity of development? How strongly is early development related to later development?

**Answers:** (1) 1, (2) higher SAT scores, (3) imitated the adults' poor self-control, (4) have poor self-control, (5) asking them to cooperate, which appeals to their strong attachment relationship, (6) they divert their attention from the tempting object or event

# Reasoning About Moral Issues

# 13.2

## LEARNING OBJECTIVES

● How does reasoning about moral issues change during childhood and adolescence?

● How do concern for justice and caring for other people contribute to moral reasoning?

● What factors help promote more sophisticated reasoning about moral issues?

*Howard, the least popular boy in the eighth grade, had been wrongly accused of stealing a sixth-grader's portable CD player. Min-shen, another eighth grader, knew that Howard was innocent but said nothing to the school principal for fear of what his friends would say about siding with Howard. A few days later, when Min-shen's father heard about the incident, he was upset that his son apparently had so little "moral fiber." Why hadn't Min-shen acted in the face of an injustice?*

On one of the days when I was writing this module, my local paper had two articles about youth from the area. One article was about a 14-year-girl who was badly burned while saving her younger brothers from a fire in their apartment. Her mother said she wasn't surprised by her daughter's actions because she had always been an extraordinarily caring person. The other article was about two 17-year-old boys who had beaten an elderly man to death. They had only planned to steal his wallet, but when he insulted them and tried to punch them, they became enraged.

Reading articles like these, you can't help but question why some people act in ways that earn our deepest respect and admiration, whereas others earn our utter contempt as well as our pity. And, at a more mundane level, we wonder why Min-shen didn't tell the truth about the theft to the lunchroom supervisor. In this module, we'll begin our exploration of moral understanding and behavior by looking at children's thinking about moral issues: How do children judge what is "good" and what is "bad"? Let's start by looking at Jean Piaget's ideas about the development of moral reasoning.

## Piaget's Views

Once, when my son Matt was about 6, we were playing Chutes and Ladders®. This is a board game in which you can advance rapidly when you land on a space that has a ladder but must go backward if you land on a chute. To speed up the game, I suggested to Matt that we be allowed to advance if we landed on a chute as well as a ladder. I reminded him that he liked to climb up slides at playgrounds, so my suggestion had some logic to it. Matt would have none of this. He told me, "It's a rule that you have to go backward when you land on a chute. You can't go forward. The people who made Chutes and Ladders® say so. Just read the instructions, Daddy." I tried again to persuade him (because, in my humble opinion, Chutes and Ladders® gives new meaning to "bored" games), but he was adamant.

Matt's inflexibility, which is typical of 6-year-olds, can be explained by Piaget's stage theory of moral development. Based on children's play and their responses to stories about children who misbehave, Piaget proposed one of the first theories of moral development. In the first stage of moral development, which lasts from age 2 years to about 4, children have no well-defined ideas about morality. **But, beginning at about 5 years and continuing through age 7, children are in a stage of moral** realism; they believe that rules are created by wise adults and therefore must be followed and cannot be changed. Another characteristic of the stage of moral realism is that children believe in **immanent justice,** the idea that breaking a rule always leads to punishment. Suppose I had forced Matt to use my new rules for Chutes and Ladders® and that, the next day, he had tripped on his way to school, scraping his knee. Believing in immanent justice, he would have seen the scraped knee as the inevitable consequence of breaking the rule the previous day.

**At about age 8, children progress to the stage of moral relativism, the understanding that rules are created by people to help them get along.** Children progress to this more advanced level of moral reasoning in part because advances in cognitive development allow them to understand the reasons for rules. Furthermore, from interactions with their peers, children come to understand the need for rules and how they are created. For example, as the boys in the photograph decide where to ride their skateboards, they might follow a rule that everybody can suggest some place and then they'll vote. The boys understand that this rule isn't absolute; they follow it because it's reasonably fair and, by using this rule, they spend more time skating and less time arguing.

Children in the stage of moral relativism also understand that because people agree to set rules in the first place, they can also change them if they see the need. If the skateboarding boys decided another rule would be fairer and would help them get along better, they could adopt the new rule.

Some of Piaget's ideas about moral reasoning have stood the test of time better than others. For example, later research has showed that children's early moral reasoning does not consider adult authority final and absolute. Instead, preschool children believe adults' authority is limited. Preschoolers believe that pushing a child or damaging another child's possession is wrong even when an adult says that it's okay (Tisak, 1993). A lasting contribution of Piaget's work, however, is the idea that moral reasoning progresses through a sequence of stages, driven by cognitive development and interactions with peers. One important theory that builds on Piaget's stage approach comes from Lawrence Kohlberg; it's the focus of the next section.

*In Piaget's view, 5- to 7-year-olds believe that rules are absolute; by age 8, children understand that rules are created by people to help them get along.*

## Kohlberg's Theory

To begin, I'd like to tell you a story about Heidi, a star player on a soccer team that I coached. Heidi was terribly upset because our team was undefeated and scheduled to play in a weekend tournament to determine the league champion. But on Sunday of this same weekend, a Habitat-for-Humanity house was to be dedicated to her grandfather, who had died a few months previously. If Heidi skipped the tournament game, her friends on the team would be upset; if she skipped the dedication, her family would be disappointed. Heidi couldn't do both and didn't know what to do.

Kohlberg created stories like this one to study how people reason about moral dilemmas. He made it very difficult to reach a decision in his stories because every alternative involved some undesirable consequences. In fact, there is no "correct" answer—that's why the stories are referred to as moral "dilemmas." For Heidi, pleasing her friends means disappointing her family; pleasing her family means letting down her teammates. Kohlberg was more interested in the reasoning used to justify a decision—Why should Heidi go to the tournament? Why should she go to the dedication?—not the decision itself.[*]

Kohlberg's best-known moral dilemma is about Heinz, whose wife is dying:

*In Europe, a woman was near death from cancer. One drug might save her, a form of radium that a druggist in the same town had recently discovered. The druggist was charging $2,000, ten times what the drug cost him to make. The sick woman's husband, Heinz, went to everyone he knew to borrow the money, but he could only get together about half of what it cost. He told the druggist that his wife was dying and asked him to sell it cheaper or let him pay later. But the druggist said, "No." The husband got desperate and broke into the man's store to steal the drug for his wife (Kohlberg, 1969, p. 379).*

Although more hangs in the balance for Heinz than for Heidi, both are moral dilemmas in that the alternative courses of action have desirable and undesirable features.

Kohlberg analyzed children's, adolescents', and adults' responses to a large number of dilemmas and identified three levels of moral reasoning, each divided into two stages. Across the six stages, the basis for moral reasoning shifts. In the earliest stages, moral reasoning is based on external forces, such as the promise of reward or the threat of punishment. At the most advanced levels, moral reasoning is based on a personal, internal moral code and is unaffected by others' views or society's expectations. You can clearly see this gradual shift in the three levels:

- **Preconventional level: For most children, many adolescents, and some adults, moral reasoning is controlled almost solely by obedience to authority and by rewards and punishments.**

  *Stage 1: Obedience orientation.* People believe that adults know what is right and wrong. Consequently, a person should do what adults say is right to avoid being punished. A person at this stage might argue that Heinz should not steal the drug because it is against the law (which was set by adults).

  *Stage 2: Instrumental orientation.* People look out for their own needs. They often are nice to others because they expect the favor to be returned in the future. A person at this stage might say it was all right for Heinz to steal the drug because his wife might do something nice for him in return (that is, she might reward him).

- **Conventional level: For most adolescents and most adults, moral decision making is based on social norms—what is expected by others.**

  *Stage 3: Interpersonal norms.* Adolescents and adults believe that they should act according to others' expectations. The aim is to win the approval of others by behaving like "good boys" and "good girls." An adolescent or adult at this stage might argue that Heinz should not steal the drug because then others would see him as an honest citizen who obeys the law.

  *Stage 4: Social system morality.* Adolescents and adults believe that social roles, expectations, and laws exist to maintain order within society and to promote the good of all people. An adolescent or adult in this stage might reason that Heinz should steal the drug because a husband is obligated to do all that he possibly can

---

[*]As it turned out, Heidi didn't have to resolve the dilemma. We lost our tournament game on Saturday, so she went to the dedication on Sunday.

to save his wife's life. Or a person in this stage might reason that Heinz should not steal the drug because stealing is against the law and society must prohibit theft.

- **Postconventional level: For some adults, typically those older than 25, moral decisions are based on personal, moral principles.**

> In Kohlberg's theory, moral reasoning is first based on reward and punishment, but ultimately is based on a personal moral code.

*Stage 5: Social contract orientation.* Adults agree that members of cultural groups adhere to a "social contract" because a common set of expectations and laws benefits all group members. However, if these expectations and laws no longer promote the welfare of individuals, they become invalid. Consequently, an adult in this stage might reason that Heinz should steal the drug because social rules about property rights are no longer benefiting individuals' welfare.

*Stage 6: Universal ethical principles.* Abstract principles like justice, compassion, and equality form the basis of a personal moral code that may sometimes conflict with society's expectations and laws. An adult at this stage might argue that Heinz should steal the drug because life is paramount and preserving life takes precedence over all other rights.

The table puts all the stages together, providing a quick summary of Kohlberg's theory.

**SUMMARY TABLE**

**STAGES IN KOHLBERG'S THEORY OF MORAL DEVELOPMENT**

*Preconventional Level: Punishment and Reward*

Stage 1: Obedience to authority

Stage 2: Nice behavior in exchange for future favors

*Conventional Level: Social Norms*

Stage 3: Live up to others' expectations

Stage 4: Follow rules to maintain social order

*Postconventional Level: Moral Codes*

Stage 5: Adhere to a social contract when it is valid

Stage 6: Personal morality based on abstract principles

**SUPPORT FOR KOHLBERG'S THEORY.** Kohlberg proposed that his stages form an invariant sequence. That is, individuals move through the six stages in the order listed and in only that order. If his stage theory is right, then level of moral reasoning should be strongly associated with age and level of cognitive development: Older and more advanced thinkers, on the average, should be more advanced in their moral development, and indeed they usually are (Stewart & Pascual-Leone, 1992).

For example, the graph on page 373 shows developmental change in the percentage of individuals who reason at Kohlberg's different stages. Stages 1 and 2 are common among children and young adolescents but not older adolescents and adults. Stages 3 and 4 are common among older adolescents and adults. The graph also shows that most individuals do not progress to the final stages. Most adults' moral reasoning is at Stages 3 and 4.

Support for Kohlberg's invariant sequence of stages also comes from longitudinal studies measuring individuals' level of reasoning over several years. Individuals do progress through each stage in sequence, and virtually no individuals skip any stages (Colby et al., 1983). Longitudinal studies also show that, over time, individuals become more advanced in their level of moral reasoning or remain at the same level. They do not regress to a lower level (Walker & Taylor, 1991).

Additional support for Kohlberg's theory comes from research on the link between moral reasoning and moral behavior. In general, level of moral reasoning should be linked to moral behavior. Remember that less advanced moral reasoning reflects the influence of external forces such as rewards and social norms, whereas more advanced reasoning is based on a personal moral code. Therefore, individuals at the preconventional and conventional levels would act morally when external forces demand, but otherwise they might not. In contrast, individuals at the postconventional level, where reasoning is based on personal principles, should be compelled to moral action even when external forces may not favor it.

FIG. 13-3

Let's return to the example in the vignette. Suppose you knew that one of the least popular students has been wrongly accused of stealing a CD player; you know that some friends in your group are actually responsible. What would you do? Speaking out on behalf of the unpopular student is unlikely to lead to reward. Furthermore, there are strong social norms against "squealing" on friends. So if you are in the preconventional or conventional level of moral reasoning like Min-shen, the boy in the vignette, you would probably let the unpopular student be punished unfairly. But if you are at the postconventional level and see the situation in terms of principles of justice and fairness, you would be more likely to identify the real perpetrators, despite the price to be paid in rejection by the group.

Many researchers report findings that support the hypothesized link between moral reasoning and moral action. In one study (Gibbs et al., 1986), high-school teachers were asked to judge whether their students would defend their principles in difficult situations or if they would act morally only when it was fashionable or handy. High-school students who were judged by their teachers to have greater moral courage tended to be more advanced in Kohlberg's stages than students who were judged less courageous. That is, students like those in the photograph who protest social conditions tend to have higher moral reasoning scores. The converse is also true: Delinquent adolescents, whose actions are more likely to be morally offensive, tend to have lower moral reasoning scores than nondelinquent adolescents (Chandler & Moran, 1990). That is, delinquent adolescents are more likely to emphasize punishment and reward in their moral reasoning, rather than social norms and personal moral codes.

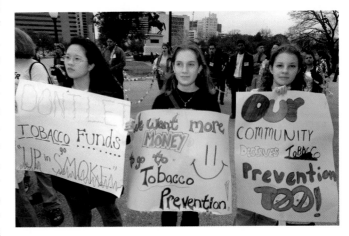

On another point of Kohlberg's theory, support is mixed. Kohlberg claimed that his sequence of stages is universal: All people in all cultures should progress through the six-stage sequence. Some research shows that children and adolescents in cultures worldwide reason about moral dilemmas at Stages 2 or 3, just like North American children and adolescents. But, as we'll see in the "Cultural Influences" feature, beyond the earliest stages, moral reasoning in other cultures is often not described well by Kohlberg's theory (Turiel & Neff, 2000).

## CULTURAL INFLUENCES

### Moral Reasoning in India

Many critics note that Kohlberg's emphasis on individual rights and justice reflects traditional American culture and Judeo-Christian theology. Not all cultures and religions share this emphasis; consequently, moral reasoning might be based on different values in other cultures (Carlo et al., 1996; Keller et al., 1998).

The Hindu religion, for example, emphasizes duty and responsibility to others, not individual rights and justice (Simpson, 1974). Accordingly, children and adults reared with traditional Hindu beliefs might emphasize caring for others in their moral reasoning more than individuals brought up in the Judeo-Christian tradition.

Miller and Bersoff (1992) tested the hypothesis that cultural differences affect moral reasoning by constructing dilemmas with both justice- and care-based solutions. For example:

> Ben planned to travel to San Francisco in order to attend the wedding of his best friend. He needed to catch the very next train if he was to be on time for the ceremony, as he had to deliver the wedding rings. However, Ben's wallet was stolen in the train station. He lost all of his money as well as his ticket to San Francisco.
>
> Ben approached several officials as well as passengers . . . and asked them to loan him money to buy a new ticket. But, because he was a stranger, no one was willing to lend him the money he needed.
>
> While Ben . . . was trying to decide what to do next, a well-dressed man sitting next to him walked away. . . . Ben noticed that the man had left his coat unattended. Sticking out of the man's coat pocket was a train ticket to San Francisco. . . . He also saw that the man had more than enough money in his coat pocket to buy another train ticket (p. 545).

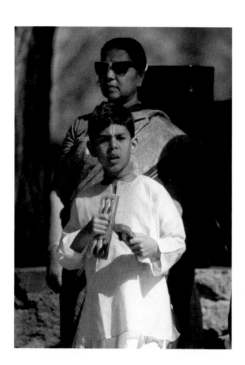

One solution emphasized individual rights and justice:

> Ben should not take the ticket from the man's coat pocket even though it means not getting to San Francisco in time to deliver the wedding rings to his best friend (p. 545).

The other solution placed a priority on caring for others:

> Ben should go to San Francisco to deliver the wedding rings to his best friend even if it means taking the train ticket from the other man's coat pocket (p. 545).

When children and adults living in the United States responded to dilemmas like this one about Ben, a slight majority selected the justice-based alternative. In contrast, when Hindu children and adults living in India, like the mother and son in the photo, responded to the same dilemmas, the overwhelming majority selected the care-based alternative.

Clearly, moral reasoning reflects the culture in which a person is reared. Consistent with Kohlberg's theory, judgments by American children and adults reflect their culture's emphasis on individual rights and justice. But judgments by Indian children and adults reflect their culture's emphasis on caring for other people. The bases of moral reasoning are not universal as Kohlberg claimed; instead, they reflect cultural values.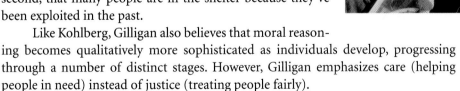

## Beyond Kohlberg's Theory

Kohlberg's theory obviously is not the final word on moral development. Much about his theory seems valid, but investigators have addressed its shortcomings. The next few pages describe some work that helps complete our picture of the development of moral thinking.

**GILLIGAN'S ETHIC OF CARING.** Findings like those described in the "Cultural Influences" feature indicate that Kohlberg's theory is not universal but applies primarily to cultures with Western philosophical and religious traditions. But researcher Carol Gilligan (1982; Gilligan & Attanucci, 1988) questions how applicable Kohlberg's theory is even within the Western tradition. Gilligan argues that Kohlberg's emphasis on justice applies more to men than to women, whose reasoning about moral issues is often rooted in concern for others. Gilligan writes, "The moral imperative that emerges repeatedly in interviews with women is an injunction to care, a responsibility to discern and alleviate the real and recognizable trouble of this world" (1982, p. 100).

Gilligan proposes a developmental progression in which individuals gain greater understanding of caring and responsibility. In the first stage, children are preoccupied with their own needs. In the second stage, people care for others, particularly those who are less able to care for themselves, like infants and the aged. The third stage unites caring for others and for oneself by emphasizing caring in all human relationships and by denouncing exploitation and violence between people. For example, consider the teen in the photo, who is helping at a homeless shelter. She does so not because she believes the homeless are needy but because she believes, first, that all humans should care for each other, and second, that many people are in the shelter because they've been exploited in the past.

Like Kohlberg, Gilligan also believes that moral reasoning becomes qualitatively more sophisticated as individuals develop, progressing through a number of distinct stages. However, Gilligan emphasizes care (helping people in need) instead of justice (treating people fairly).

What does research tell us about the importance of justice and care in moral reasoning? Do females and males differ in the bases of their moral reasoning? The best answer to these questions comes from a comprehensive meta-analysis conducted by Jaffee and Hyde (2000) that included 113 studies with more than 12,000 participants. Overall, boys and men tended to get slightly higher scores on problems that emphasized justice, whereas girls and women tended to get slightly higher scores on problems that emphasized caring. But the differences are small and do not indicate that moral reasoning by females is predominated by a concern with care and

Gilligan proposed that moral reasoning is sometimes based on concern for others, not solely on justice and individual rights.

moral reasoning by males is predominated by a concern with justice. Instead, girls and boys as well as men and women reason about moral issues similarly (Walker, 1995); both often think about moral issues in terms of care and interpersonal relationships.

**EISENBERG'S LEVELS OF PROSOCIAL REASONING.**    Nancy Eisenberg (1982; Eisenberg et al., 1995) argues that Kohlberg's theory is flawed because the dilemmas are unrealistic. They involve breaking a law or disobeying a person in authority. In real life, says Eisenberg, most children's moral dilemmas involve choosing between self-interest and helping others. For example, in one of Eisenberg's moral dilemmas, a child walking to a party comes upon a child injured from a fall. The first child must decide whether to continue to the party or help the second child and miss the party.

Like Kohlberg, Eisenberg focuses on how children explain their choices. **Most preschool and many elementary-school children have a hedonistic orientation: They pursue their own pleasure.** These children do not help the injured child because they would miss the party. Or they might help because they expect that the injured child would return the favor in the future. In either case, self-interest is the basis of their decision.

**Some preschool and many elementary-school children have a needs-oriented orientation: They are concerned about others' needs and want to help.** Children at this stage have learned a simple rule, to help others. They often explain their desire to help as a straightforward, "He needs my help." Their desire to help is not based on imagining how the injured child feels or on a personal moral code.

**Many elementary-school children and adolescents have a stereotyped, approval-focused orientation, behaving as they think society expects "good people" to behave.** The helpful teen in the photo would explain her behavior by saying that the person she's helping will like her more because she's helping.

**Finally, some children and many adolescents develop an empathic orientation; they consider the injured child's perspective and how their own actions will make them feel.** An adolescent with this orientation might say, "He'd be in pain, so I'd feel bad if I didn't help."

The same kinds of evidence that support Kohlberg's theory support Eisenberg's. For example, longitudinal studies indicate that children in many countries move through Eisenberg's different orientations in sequence (Eisenberg, 1986; Eisenberg et al., 1995). Moreover, children who reason at more advanced levels are more likely to actually help others than children who reason at less advanced levels (Miller et al., 1996).

Eisenberg's theory is like Kohlberg's in emphasizing that moral development involves a developmental shift away from self-centered thinking to social norms and moral principles. Her theory is like Gilligan's in emphasizing that caring for others is an important element in everyday moral reasoning.

**DEVELOPMENT OF DOMAINS OF SOCIAL JUDGMENT.**    The research I've described so far tells us that there is more to moral reasoning than justice; concern for others is important, too. Elliot Turiel (1997, 1998) has taken these ideas a step further and argued that moral judgments (whether based on justice or care) represent one of several important domains that make up social judgments. To illustrate the domains, think about the following preschool children:

- Brian, who often kicks or pushes his younger brother when their mom isn't looking.

- Kathryn, who never puts her toys away when she's done playing with them.
- Brad, who likes to wear his underpants inside out.

Although each child's behavior is in some sense "wrong," only the first child's behavior—kicking and pushing—represents a moral transgression because Brian's actions can harm another person. **In contrast, social conventions are arbitrary standards of behavior agreed to by a cultural group to facilitate interactions within the group.** Thus social convention says that we can eat French fries but not green beans with our fingers and that, in the case of Kathryn, children should clean up after themselves. **Finally, the personal domain pertains to choices concerning one's body (e.g., what to eat and wear) and choices of friends or activities.** Decisions here are not right or wrong but instead are seen as personal preferences left up to the individual (Smetana, 2002). Thus, Brad's decision to wear his underpants inside out is unusual but not wrong.

> Preschool children distinguish moral decisions and social conventions from the personal domain.

During the preschool years, children begin to differentiate these domains (Turiel, 1998). For example, they believe that breaking a moral rule is more serious and should be punished more severely than breaking a social convention. Furthermore, preschool children believe that adults have authority over social conventions but not moral rules (which stem from higher authority) or the personal domain (which is up to the individual). For example, preschool children believe that teachers could decide it is okay for students to talk during storytime, but could not decide it is okay for students to hit each other; and teachers should not tell students what clothes to wear to school (Nucci & Weber, 1995; Smetana, Schlagman, & Adams, 1993).

Children's early understanding of these different domains of social judgment is rooted in their experiences and parents' responses to different kinds of transgressions (Turiel, 1998). When a child breaks a moral rule, adults talk about the impact of the act on the victim and how that person could be hurt. In contrast, when a child violates a social convention, adults more often talk about the need to follow rules and to obey parents, teachers, and other people in authority. Finally, conversations in the personal domain are different: Here adults typically do not specify a "right" or "wrong" choice but instead encourage children to make their own choices (Nucci & Weber, 1995). Thus, in Turiel's (1998, Turiel & Neff, 2000) view, moral reasoning is part of a much larger developmental accomplishment: children understand that there are different domains of social decision making, each with unique rules of authority and sanctions for misbehavior. And, by the preschool years, children have made remarkable progress in understanding the distinction between the moral, social-conventional, and personal domains.

The net result of Gilligan's work, Eisenberg's research, and Turiel's study of domains of social judgment is much a broader view of moral reasoning. As Kohlberg claimed, moral reasoning becomes progressively more sophisticated as children develop. However, contrary to Kohlberg's original claims, moral reasoning is not always based on justice and rights. Concern for others is sometimes the basis. And moral reasoning is simply one important part of children's understanding of domains of social judgment.

## Promoting Moral Reasoning

Whether it is based on justice or care, most cultures and most parents want to encourage adolescents to think carefully about moral issues. What can be done to help adolescents develop more mature forms of moral reasoning? Sometimes simply being exposed to more advanced moral reasoning is sufficient to promote developmental change (Walker, 1980). Adolescents may notice, for example, that older friends do not wait to be rewarded to help others. Or a teenager may notice that respected peers take courageous positions regardless of the social consequences. Such experiences apparently cause adolescents to re-evaluate their reasoning on moral issues and propel them toward more sophisticated thinking.

Discussion can be particularly effective in revealing shortcomings in moral reasoning. When people, like the adolescents in the photo, reason about moral issues with others whose reasoning is at a higher level, the usual result is that individuals reasoning at lower levels improve (Berkowitz & Gibbs, 1985). This is particularly true when the conversational partner with the more sophisticated reasoning makes an effort to understand the other's view, by requesting clarification or paraphrasing what the other child is saying (Walker, Hennig, & Krettenauer, 2000).

The "Child Development and Family Policy" feature shows how Kohlberg used research results like these to foster moral thinking.

## CHILD DEVELOPMENT AND FAMILY POLICY

### Promoting More Advanced Moral Reasoning

Kohlberg wasn't content to simply chart how moral reasoning changed with age. He also wanted to devise ways to foster sophisticated moral reasoning.

**To foster discussion and expose students to more advanced moral thinking, Kohlberg and his colleagues set up "Just Communities," special groups of students and teachers within public high schools** (Higgins, 1991; Power, Higgins, & Kohlberg, 1989). Teachers and students met weekly to plan school activities and discuss school policies. Decisions were reached democratically, with teachers and students alike each having one vote. However, during discussions, teachers acted as facilitators, encouraging students to consider the moral consequences of different courses of action. Students who participated in Just Communities tended to be more advanced in their moral thinking (Higgins, 1991; Power, Higgins, & Kohlberg, 1989).

Research findings such as these send an important message to parents: Discussion is probably the best way for parents to help their children think about moral issues in more mature terms (Walker & Taylor, 1991). Research consistently shows that mature moral reasoning comes about when adolescents are free to express their opinions on moral issues to their parents, who are, in turn, expressing their own opinions and, consequently, exposing their adolescent children to more mature moral reasoning (Hoffman, 1988, 1994).

**Discussion is the best way to foster more mature moral reasoning.**

In this module, we've seen how moral reasoning changes as children develop. To see how these changes lead to changes in moral action, we'll look at children's prosocial behavior in the next module.

### CHECK YOUR LEARNING

1. Children in Piaget's stage of moral realism believe that rules are created by _____.

2. Kohlberg's theory includes the preconventional, conventional, and _____ stages of moral reasoning.

3. For children in the preconventional level, moral reasoning is strongly influenced by _____.

4. Gilligan's views of morality emphasize _____ instead of justice.

5. When boys' and girls' moral reasoning is compared, the typical result is that _____.

6. Preschoolers distinguish moral, _____, and personal domains of social judgment.

7. In Just Communities, teachers encouraged students to _____.

8. If parents wish to foster their children's moral development, they should _____ with them.

**CONNECTIONS**

How similar is Piaget's concrete operational thinking (see Module 7.2) to Kohlberg's preconventional level of moral reasoning? How similar are formal operational thinking and conventional moral reasoning?

**Answers:** (1) wise adults and therefore cannot be changed, (2) postconventional, (3) reward or punishment, (4) caring for others, (5) they differ slightly, but not to the extent that would indicate predominantly male and female styles of moral reasoning, (6) social-conventional, (7) consider the moral consequences of their decisions, (8) discuss moral issues

# Helping Others

# 13.3

## LEARNING OBJECTIVES

- At what age do children begin to act prosocially? How does prosocial behavior change with age?

- What skills do children need to behave prosocially?

- What situations influence children's prosocial behavior?

- How can parents foster prosocial behavior in their children?

Development of Prosocial Behavior

Skills Underlying Prosocial Behavior

Situational Influences

Socializing Prosocial Behavior

> Six-year-old Juan got his finger trapped in the VCR when he tried to remove a tape. While he cried and cried, his 3-year-old brother, Antonio, and his 2-year-old sister, Carla, watched but did not help. Later, when their mother had soothed Juan and saw that his finger was not injured, she worried about her younger children's reactions. In the face of their brother's obvious distress, why had Antonio and Carla done nothing?

Most parents, most teachers, and most religions try to teach children to act in cooperative, helping, giving ways—at least most of the time and in most situations. **Actions that benefit others are known as prosocial behavior.** Of course, cooperation often "works" because individuals gain more than they would by not cooperating. **Altruism is prosocial behavior that helps another with no direct benefit to the individual.** Altruism is driven by feelings of responsibility for other people. Two youngsters pooling their funds to buy a candy bar to share demonstrates cooperative behavior. One youngster giving half her lunch to a friend who forgot his demonstrates altruism.

But, as the story of Juan and his siblings shows, children (and adults, for that matter) are not always helpful or cooperative. In this module, you'll learn how prosocial behavior changes with age and some factors that promote prosocial behavior.

## Development of Prosocial Behavior

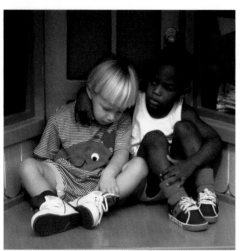

Simple acts of altruism can be seen by 18 months. When toddlers and preschoolers see other people who are obviously hurt or upset, they appear concerned, like the child in the photo. They try to comfort the person by hugging him or patting him, and they try to determine why the person is upset (Zahn-Waxler et al., 1992). Apparently, at this early age, children recognize signs of distress.

During the preschool years, children gradually begin to understand others' needs and learn appropriate altruistic responses (Farver & Branstetter, 1994). Their early attempts at altruistic behavior are limited because their knowledge of what they can do to help is modest. As youngsters acquire more strategies to help others, their preferred strategies become more adult-like (Strayer & Schroeder, 1989).

Thus, as a general rule, intentions to act prosocially increase with age, as do children's strategies for helping. Of course, not all children respond to the needs of others, either in toddlerhood or at later ages. Some children attach greater priority to looking out for their own interests. What makes some children more likely than others to help? We'll answer this question in the next section.

## Skills Underlying Prosocial Behavior

Think back to an occasion when you helped someone. How did you know that the person needed help? Why did you decide to help? Although you didn't realize it at the time, your decision to help was probably based on several skills:

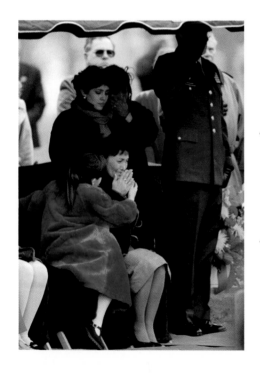

- *Perspective taking.* In Module 7.2, you learned about Piaget's concept of egocentrism, the preoperational youngster's inability to see things from another's point of view. Egocentrism limits children's ability to share or help because they simply do not realize the need for prosocial behavior. They have only one perspective—their own. For example, young children might not help someone carrying many packages because they cannot envision that carrying lots of bulky things is a burden. Older children, however, can take the perspective of others, so they recognize the burden and are more inclined to help. In general, the better children understand the thoughts and feelings of other people, the more willing they are to share and help others (Eisenberg, 1988).

- *Empathy.* **The ability to experience another person's emotions is empathy.** Children who deeply feel another person's fear, disappointment, sorrow, or loneliness are more inclined to help that person than children who do not feel these emotions (Kochanska, Padavich, & Koenig, 1996; Roberts & Strayer, 1996). In other words, youngsters like the one in the photo, who is obviously distressed by what she is seeing, are most likely to help others.

- *Moral reasoning.* In Module 13.2, you learned that reward and punishment influence young children's moral reasoning, whereas a concern for moral principles characterizes adolescents' and adults' moral decision making. Therefore, as you would expect, prosocial behavior in young children is usually determined by the chance of reward or punishment. It also follows that, as children mature and begin to make moral decisions on the basis of fairness and justice, they become more prosocial. Consistent with this idea, Eisenberg, Zhou, and

Koller (2001) found that Brazilian 13- to 16-year-olds were more likely to act prosocially when their moral reasoning was more advanced (e.g., based on internalized moral standards).

In sum, children and adolescents who help others tend to be better able to take another's view, to feel another's emotions, and to act on the basis of principles, rather than rewards, punishments, or social norms. For example, a 15-year-old who spontaneously loans his favorite video game to a friend does so because he sees that the friend would like to play the game, he feels the friend's disappointment at not owning the game, and he believes that friends should share with others.

Of course, perspective taking, empathy, and moral reasoning skills do not guarantee that children always act altruistically. Even though children have the skills needed to act altruistically, they may not because of the particular situation, as we'll see in the next section.

## Situational Influences

Kind children occasionally disappoint us by being cruel, and children who are usually stingy sometimes surprise us by their generosity. Why? The setting helps determine whether children act altruistically or not.

- *Feelings of responsibility.* Children act altruistically when they feel responsible to the person in need. They are more likely to help siblings and friends than strangers, simply because they feel a direct responsibility to people that they know well (Costin & Jones, 1992).

- *Feelings of competence.* Children act altruistically when they feel that they have the skills necessary to help the person in need. Suppose, for example, that a preschooler is growing more and more upset because she can't figure out how to work a computer game. A classmate who knows little about computer games is not likely to help because he doesn't know what to do to help. By helping, he could end up looking foolish (Peterson, 1983).

> Children are most likely to help when they feel responsible, have the needed skills, are happy, and believe they will lose little by helping.

- *Mood.* Children act altruistically when they are happy or feeling successful but not when they are sad or feeling as if they have failed. In other words, a preschooler who has just spent an exciting morning as the "leader" in nursery school is more inclined to share treats with siblings than a preschooler who was punished by the teacher (Moore, Underwood, & Rosenhan, 1973).

- *Cost of altruism.* Children act altruistically when it entails few or modest sacrifices. A preschooler who has received a snack that she doesn't particularly like is more inclined to share it than a child who has received her very favorite snack (Eisenberg & Shell, 1986).

When, then, are children most likely to help? When they feel responsible to the person in need, have the skills that are needed, are happy, and do not think they have to give up a lot by helping. When are children least likely to help? When they feel neither responsible nor capable of helping, are in a bad mood, and believe that helping will entail a large personal sacrifice.

Using these guidelines, how do you explain why Antonio and Carla, the children in the vignette, watched idly as their older brother cried? Hint: The last two factors—mood and cost—are not likely to be involved. However, the first two factors may explain Antonio and Carla's failure to help their older brother. My explanation appears on page 384, just before "Check Your Learning."

So far, we've seen that altruistic behavior is determined by children's skills (such as perspective taking) and by characteristics of situations (such as whether children feel competent to help in a particular situation). Whether children are altruistic is also determined by socialization, the topic of the next section.

## Socializing Prosocial Behavior

Dr. Martin Luther King Jr. said that his pursuit of civil rights for African Americans was particularly influenced by three people: Henry David Thoreau (a 19th-century American philosopher), Mohandas Gandhi (the leader of the Indian movement for independence from England), and his father, Dr. Martin Luther King Sr. As is true of many humanitarians, Dr. King's prosocial behavior started in childhood, at home. But how do parents foster altruism in their children? The key factors are reasoning, modeling, and praise.

Parents whose favored disciplinary strategy is reasoning tend to have children who behave prosocially (Hoffman, 1988, 1994). The "Real Children" feature shows this approach in action.

### REAL CHILDREN

**Using Reasoning to Promote Prosocial Behavior**

 Jim's 4-year-old daughter, Annie, was playing with a friend, Maurice. Annie asked Maurice if she could borrow his crayons. When Maurice refused, Annie pushed him aside and grabbed the crayons, which caused Maurice to cry. At this point, Jim returned the crayons to Maurice and had the following conversation with Annie:

JIM: Why did you take the crayons away from Maurice?

ANNIE: Because I wanted them.

JIM: How do you think he felt? Happy or sad?

ANNIE: I dunno.

JIM: I think you know.

ANNIE: Okay. He was sad.

JIM: Would you like it if I took the crayons away from you? How would you feel?

ANNIE: I'd be mad. And sad, too.

JIM: Well, that's how Maurice felt, and that's why you shouldn't just grab things away from people. It makes them angry and unhappy. Ask first, and if they say "no," then you mustn't take them.

Jim's approach to discipline is to reason with Annie to help her see how her actions affect others. He emphasizes the rights and needs of others as well as the impact of one child's misbehavior on others. Repeated exposure to reasoning during discipline seems to promote children's ability to take the perspective of others (Hoffman, 1988).

Reasoning is one way that parents can influence prosocial behavior; modeling is another. Children imitate others' behavior, including prosocial behavior. In laboratory studies, children imitate their peers' altruism (Wilson, Piazza, & Nagle, 1990). For example, children are more likely to donate toys to hospitalized children or to help older adults with household chores when they see other children doing so.

Of course, parents are the models to whom children are most continuously exposed, so they exert a powerful influence. For example, parents who report frequent feelings of warmth and concern for others tend to have children who experience stronger feelings of empathy (Eisenberg et al., 1991). When a mother is helpful and responsive, her children often imitate her by being cooperative, helpful, sharing, and less critical of others (Bryant & Crockenberg, 1980).

Perhaps the most obvious way to foster sharing and other altruistic behavior in children is to reward them directly for acts of generosity. Many parents reward prosocial acts with praise. **Particularly effective is dispositional praise, which links the child's altruistic behavior to an underlying altruistic disposition.** In other words, a parent might say, "Thanks for helping me make breakfast; I knew I could count on you because you are such a helpful person." When children like the one in the photo repeatedly hear remarks like this, their self-concept apparently changes to include these characteristics. Children begin to believe they really are helpful (or nice or friendly). Consequently, when they encounter a situation in which prosocial behavior is appropriate, their self-concept prompts them to act prosocially (Mills & Grusec, 1989).

One last, surprising way that parents can promote prosocial behavior is by having adolescents routinely help with household tasks, such as setting and clearing the table, helping to prepare meals, and helping with laundry. Adolescents (but not children) who perform these chores regularly are more helpful spontaneously. One interpretation of this finding is that helping with household tasks that benefit the entire family sensitizes adolescents to the welfare of others (Grusec, Goodnow, & Cohen, 1996).

Thus, a host of factors, summarized in the table, contribute to children's prosocial behavior.

Parents can foster altruism by using reasoning to discipline their children, by behaving altruistically themselves, by having children help with chores, and by praising children's altruism.

**SUMMARY TABLE**

| FACTORS CONTRIBUTING TO CHILDREN'S PROSOCIAL BEHAVIOR | | |
| --- | --- | --- |
| **General Category** | **Types of Influence** | **Children are more likely to help when . . .** |
| Skills | Perspective taking | they can take another person's point of view |
| | Empathy | they feel another person's emotions |
| | Moral reasoning | they base moral decisions on fairness |
| Situational influences | Feelings of responsibility | they feel responsible to the person in need |
| | Feelings of competence | they feel competent to help |
| | Mood | they're in a good mood |
| | Cost of altruism | the cost of prosocial behavior is small |
| Parents' influence | Disciplinary strategy | parents use reasoning as their primary form of discipline |
| | Modeling | parents behave prosocially themselves |
| | Reward | parents reward prosocial behavior |

Combining all these ingredients, we can describe the development of children's altruistic behavior this way: As children get older, their perspective taking and empathic skills develop, which enables them to see and feel another's needs. Nonetheless, children are never invariably altruistic (or, fortunately, invariably nonaltruistic) because properties of situations dictate altruistic behavior, too.

As parents and other adults try to encourage children's prosocial behavior, one of the biggest obstacles is aggressive behavior, which is common throughout childhood and adolescence. In the next module, we'll look at some of the forces that contribute to children's aggression.

*Answer to question on page 381 about why Antonio and Carla didn't help:* Here are two explanations: First, neither Antonio nor Carla may have felt sufficiently responsible to help because (a) with two children who could help, each child's feeling of individual responsibility is reduced, and (b) younger children are less likely to feel responsible for an older brother. Second, it's my guess that neither child has had many opportunities to use the VCR. In fact, it's likely they both have been strongly discouraged from even touching it! Consequently, they don't feel competent to help because they don't know how it works or what they should do to help Juan remove his finger.

## CHECK YOUR LEARNING

1. Simple acts of altruism, such as hugging an unhappy peer, emerge at age _____.

2. Preschool children who want to act prosocially may not because _____.

3. The factors that contribute to prosocial behavior are prosocial skills, _____, and socialization.

4. The skills that help children behave prosocially include _____, empathy, and moral reasoning.

5. Children are more likely to behave prosocially when they feel responsible, competent, and happy and when _____.

6. Parents can encourage prosocial behavior by using reasoning when they discipline their children, _____, having children do household chores that benefit the entire family, and praising children for behaving prosocially.

7. In _____, parents link a child's altruistic behavior to an underlying altruistic disposition.

**ACTIVE CHILDREN**
Most parents want their children to be helpful to others, and parents can influence the extent to which their children are helpful. But altruism also depends on characteristics of children themselves. Describe some of these characteristics and how they influence whether children will be helpful.

**Answers:** (1) 18 months, (2) their knowledge of appropriate prosocial behaviors is limited, (3) situational influences, (4) perspective taking, (5) the costs of prosocial behavior are minimal, (6) modeling prosocial behavior, (7) dispositional praise

# Aggression

# 13.4

## LEARNING OBJECTIVES

● When does aggressive behavior first emerge? How stable is aggression across childhood, adolescence, and adulthood?

● How do families, television, and the child's own thoughts contribute to aggression?

● Why are some children victims of aggression?

> *Every day, 7-year-old Reza follows the same routine when he gets home from school: He watches one action-adventure cartoon on TV after another until it's time for dinner. Reza's mother is disturbed by her son's constant TV viewing, particularly because of the amount of violence in the shows that he likes. Her husband tells her to stop worrying: "Let him watch what he wants to. It won't hurt him and, besides, it keeps him out of your hair."*

If you think back to your years in elementary school, you can probably remember a class "bully"—a child who was always teasing classmates and picking fights. **Such acts typify aggression, behavior meant to harm others.** Aggressiveness is not the same as assertiveness, even though laypeople often use these words interchangeably. You've probably heard praise for an "aggressive businessperson" or a ballplayer who was "aggressive at running the bases." Psychologists and other behavioral scientists, however, would call these behaviors assertive. Assertive behaviors are goal-directed actions to further the legitimate interests of individuals or the groups they represent, while respecting the rights of other persons. In contrast, aggressive behavior, which may be physical or verbal, is intended to harm, damage, or injure and is carried out without regard for the rights of others.

In this module, we will examine aggressive behavior in children and see how it changes with age. Then we'll examine some causes of children's aggression and, in the process, learn more about the impact of Reza's TV watching on his behavior.

VIDEO 13.1
Bullying

## Change and Stability

By the time youngsters are old enough to play with one another, they show aggression. When 1- and 2-year-olds play, conflicts frequently arise over contested playthings, and youngsters often use aggression to resolve their conflicts (Cummings, Iannotti, & Zahn-Waxler, 1989). Among toddlers and preschoolers, common aggressive behaviors include hitting, kicking, pushing, or biting the other child or, as shown in the photo, trying to grab a toy from another child.

By the end of the preschool years, different forms of aggression are evident (Coie et al., 1991). **The most common form of aggression is bullying, in which the aggression is unprovoked and seems to have as its sole goal to intimidate, harass, or humiliate another child.**

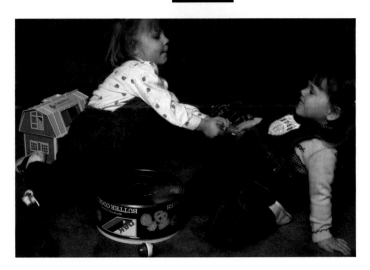

**Bullying and instrumental and reactive aggression are common in the preschool years.**

VIDEO 13.2
Reactive Aggression

VIDEO 13.3
Relational Aggression

Bullying is illustrated by a child who spontaneously says, "You're stupid!" and then kicks the child.

Two other forms of aggression are less common than bullying but still occur fairly often. **In instrumental aggression, a child uses aggression to achieve an explicit goal.** Instrumental aggression would include shoving a child to get at the head of a lunch line or grabbing a toy away from another child. **In reactive aggression, one child's behavior leads to another child's aggression.** Reactive aggression would include a child who loses a game and then punches the child who won or a child not chosen for the starring role in a play kicking the child who was.

Bullying and instrumental and reactive aggression are most likely to be expressed physically in younger children. As children get older, they more often use language to express their aggression. **A particularly common form of verbal aggression is relational aggression, in which children try to hurt others by undermining their social relationships.** In relational aggression, which is more typical of girls than boys, children try to hurt others by telling friends to avoid a particular classmate, by spreading malicious gossip, or by making remarks meant to hurt others (Crick & Werner, 1998; French, Jansen, & Pidada, 2002). Two true stories from my child-development students portray relational aggression. After a heated argument in second grade, one student's former friend had written "Erin is a big jerk" in block letters on the sidewalk where everyone walking to school would see the message. Another student, Beth, told me that after she'd beaten a classmate in the fifth-grade spelling bee, the classmate's friends formed the "I hate Beth" club.

Although verbal aggression occurs more often as children grow, physical aggression still occurs during childhood and early adolescence, particularly among boys. In one study, fourth- and seventh-grade boys reported that nearly 50 percent of their conflicts with other boys involved physical aggression (Cairns et al., 1989).

Although forms of aggression change with development, individual children's tendencies to behave aggressively are moderately stable over time, especially among boys. In a study conducted in Sweden by Stattin and Magnusson (1989), teachers rated the aggressive behavior of more than one thousand 10-year-olds. Their results, shown in the graph, indicate that teachers' ratings accurately predicted subsequent criminal activity. Boys in the least aggressive group committed relatively few criminal offenses of any sort, whereas two-thirds of the most aggressive boys had committed offenses, and nearly half had committed major offenses such as assault, theft, or robbery. Overall, girls committed far fewer offenses, but teachers' ratings of aggressive behavior still predicted which girls were more likely to have criminal records.

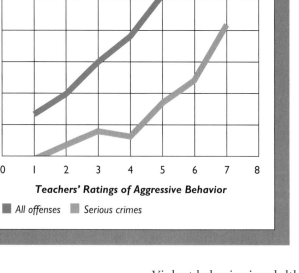

FIG. 13–4

Violent behavior in adulthood is not the only long-term outcome of childhood aggression; poor adjustment to high school (e.g., dropping out, failing a grade) and unemployment are others (Ladd, 2003). In one study, aggressive 8-year-olds tended to do poorly in high school, leaving them few options for work as young adults and putting them at risk for problem drinking. By their early 30s, many highly aggressive 8-year-olds had been unemployed for more than 2 years (Kokko & Pulkkinen, 2000).

Findings from these and similar studies show that aggression is *not* simply a case of playful pushing and shoving that most children outgrow. To the contrary, a small minority of children who are highly aggressive develop into young adults who create havoc in society. What causes children to behave aggressively? Let's look at some of the roots of aggressive behavior.

## Roots of Aggressive Behavior

For many years, psychologists believed that aggression was caused by frustration. The idea was that when children or adults were blocked from achieving a goal, they became frustrated and they aggressed, often against the interfering person or object. Although frustration can lead to aggression (Berkowitz, 1989), researchers no longer believe that it's the sole cause of aggression, and therefore they have considered other causes, including the family, television, and the child's own thoughts.

IMPACT OF THE FAMILY.   Early family experiences are a prime training ground for learning patterns of aggression. The pioneering work in this area was conducted by Gerald Patterson (1984), whose findings were based almost entirely on careful, systematic observation of aggressive children in their home environments. Patterson showed that parents and siblings play an enormous role in cultivating aggressive behavior in children. Many parents and older siblings, for example, use physical punishment or threats to stop aggressive behavior. Although the immediate effect may be to suppress aggression, physical punishment also serves as a model, vividly demonstrating that physical force "works" as a means of controlling others. A parent like the one in the photo is saying, in effect, "You were right. The best way to get people to do what you want, or to stop them from doing what you don't want, is to hit them hard enough."

Not surprisingly, parents' use of harsh physical punishment is associated with aggressive behavior in children. Dodge, Bates, and Pettit (1990) studied children who were so harshly punished physically that they were bruised or needed medical treatment. These children were rated twice as aggressive by both teachers and peers as children who had not experienced such harsh punishment. But strong or aggressive parental responses are not essential in making a child aggressive. When parents are coercive, unresponsive, and emotionally uninvested, their children are more likely to be aggressive (Hart et al., 1998; Rubin, Bukowski, & Parker, 1998).

In many families with aggressive children, a vicious circle seems to develop. Compared to families with nonaggressive children, both aggressive children and their parents are more likely to respond to neutral behavior with aggression. What's more, once an aggressive exchange has begun, both parents and children are likely to escalate the exchange, rather than break it off. And once a child has been labeled aggressive by parents and others, that child is more likely to be accused of aggression and to be singled out for punishment, even when the child has been behaving entirely appropriately on the occasion in question (Patterson, 1984). The "aggressive child" will be accused of all things that go wrong—from missing cookies to broken appliances—and other children's misbehaviors will be ignored.

Patterson's work emphasizes the point that hitting a child for aggression does not usually inhibit aggression for very long. What is the best response to a child's aggression? Discourage it—either by ignoring it or punishing it—while encouraging and rewarding other forms of nonaggressive social behavior. An older brother who simply grabs the remote control from a younger sister should be punished ("No TV for 3 days!"), and then shown a better way to resolve the conflict ("Wait until your sister finishes her program, then ask if you can change the channel. If she says 'no', come see me."). Later, the child should be praised for cooperating rather than aggressing ("Thanks for asking your sister instead of just grabbing the remote control.").

Parents are not the only family members who influence children's aggression—siblings matter, too. Among aggressive children, those who have good relationships with their siblings tend to be less aggressive and better adjusted than aggressive children who have conflicted relationships with their siblings (Stormshak et al., 1996). Good sibling relationships may provide aggressive children with opportunities to improve their social skills, or they may provide emotional support for aggressive youngsters.

> In families with aggressive children, a vicious circle often develops in which parents and children respond to neutral behavior aggressively and escalate aggressive exchanges.

Finally, it's important to remember that children may elicit some of the very parental behaviors that foster their aggression. Recall our description in Module 3.3 of evocative gene-environment interactions, in which children inherit characteristics that make some experiences more likely than others. In the case of aggression, adoption and twin studies point to hereditary components in aggression (Deater-Deckard & Plomin, 1999; Rowe, Almeida, & Jacobson, 1999). Some children inherit a tendency to be impulsive, to have an angry temperament, or to regulate their own behavior poorly. These characteristics often lead parents to discipline these children more harshly, which then makes them more aggressive (Ge et al., 1996). Thus, parents and child can both contribute to a vicious circle of escalating aggression.

**IMPACT OF TELEVISION.**   Most children today watch television regularly by the time they're 3 years old, and by the time they turn 15, they have spent more time watching television than going to school. In fact, throughout childhood they will have spent more time watching television than in any other activity except going to school and sleeping (Liebert & Sprafkin, 1988).

What do children see when they watch all this television? The answer varies somewhat from child to child, but most American children spend considerable time watching action-adventure programs that contain a heavy dose of modeled aggression. Heroes and "good guys" on these shows almost invariably end up in a fight with the "bad guys." The good guys always win, of course, and are typically rewarded with praise, admiration, and sometimes more tangible rewards (such as a vacation in the sun).

What are the effects of watching all these rewarded aggressive models for so long? This question first attracted attention in the mid-1950s. At that time, only about half the households in the United States had television sets, yet the public was already aware of the frequent portrayal of violence in TV programs and worried about its effects on viewers, especially young ones. Anecdotal evidence suggested a link. One 6-year-old fan of Hopalong Cassidy (a TV cowboy of the 1950s) asked his father for real bullets for his toy gun because his toy bullets didn't kill people the way Hopalong's did (Schramm, Lyle, & Parker, 1961).

More than 50 years later, we are still concerned about violence on TV, with good reason. One recent analysis (Wilson et al., 2002) showed that, like the TV program in the photo, nearly 70 percent of TV programs targeted for children contain acts of physical aggression. And the average American youngster will see several thousand murders on TV before reaching adolescence (Waters, 1993). (If you find these numbers hard to believe, try the activities described in "See for Yourself" at the end of the chapter.)

What does research tell us about this steady diet of televised mayhem and violence? According to Bandura's (1986) social cognitive theory, children learn by observing others; so if they watch violent behavior (either real or televised), they will act violently. In fact, laboratory studies conducted in the 1960s by Bandura, Ross, and Ross (1963) made just this point. Children watched specially created TV programs showing an adult kicking

and hitting a plastic "Bobo" doll. When children were given the opportunity to play with the doll, those who had seen the TV program were much more likely to behave aggressively toward the doll than children who had not seen the program.

VIDEO 13.4
Human Aggression:
Bandura's Bobo Doll
CLASSIC MODULE

Critics thought the laboratory setting of this and other early studies affected the results, and they doubted that viewing TV violence in more realistic settings would have such pronounced effects on children (Klapper, 1968). Today, however, we know that viewing TV violence "hardens" children, making them more accepting of interpersonal violence. Suppose, for example, a teen is baby-sitting two youngsters who begin to argue and then fight. Baby sitters who are frequent viewers of TV violence are more inclined to let them "slug it out" because they see this as a normal, acceptable way of resolving conflicts (Drabman & Thomas, 1976).

Is this increased tolerance for aggression reflected in children's behavior? Will Reza, the avid cartoon watcher in the vignette at the beginning of the module, become more aggressive? Or, as his father believes, is his TV watching simply "fun"? The answer from research is clear: Reza's father is wrong. Frequent exposure to TV violence makes children more aggressive.

One of the most compelling studies examined the impact of children's TV viewing at age 8 on criminal activity at age 30 (Huesmann, 1986). The graph shows that 8-year-old boys who watched large doses of TV violence had the most extensive criminal records as 30-year-olds. This was true for both males and females, even though females' overall level of criminal activity was much lower.

More recent studies (e.g., Johnson et al., 2002) confirm the long-term impact of TV on aggression and violence, particularly for boys, even when confounding variables such as parents' education and family income are controlled. What's more, playing violent video games seems to lead to violence in much the same way that watching violent TV does (Anderson & Bushman, 2001). Children and adolescents who play violent video games frequently tend to be more aggressive and less altruistic.

These findings are correlational and thus complicate conclusions about cause and effect. But experimental studies demonstrate that view-

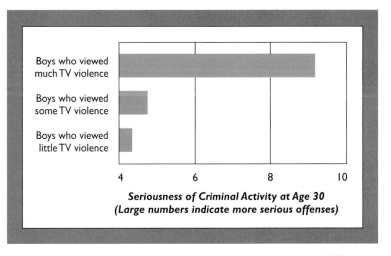

Boys who viewed
much TV violence

Boys who viewed
some TV violence

Boys who viewed
little TV violence

4        6        8        10

*Seriousness of Criminal Activity at Age 30*
*(Large numbers indicate more serious offenses)*

FIG. 13–5

ing televised violence breeds aggression, so it is reasonable to conclude that children who regularly view TV violence resort to aggression in interacting with others. For some, their aggression eventually puts them behind bars. Of course, TV violence is not the sole cause of aggression in children. But it is an important factor in a highly complex process to which parents and peers also contribute.

**COGNITIVE PROCESSES.** The perceptual and cognitive skills described in Chapters 6 through 8 also play a role in aggression. Dodge, Bates, and Pettit (1990) were the first to explore the cognitive aspects of aggression. They discovered that aggressive boys often respond aggressively because they are not skilled at interpreting other people's intentions and, without a clear interpretation in mind, they respond aggressively by default. That is, aggressive boys far too often think, "I don't know what you're up to, and, when in doubt, attack."

From findings like these, Crick and Dodge (1994; Dodge & Crick, 1990) formulated the information-processing model of children's thinking shown in the diagram. According to the model, responding to a social stimulus involves several steps. First, children selectively attend to certain features of the social stimulus but not others, in the manner described on pages 156-158 of Mod-

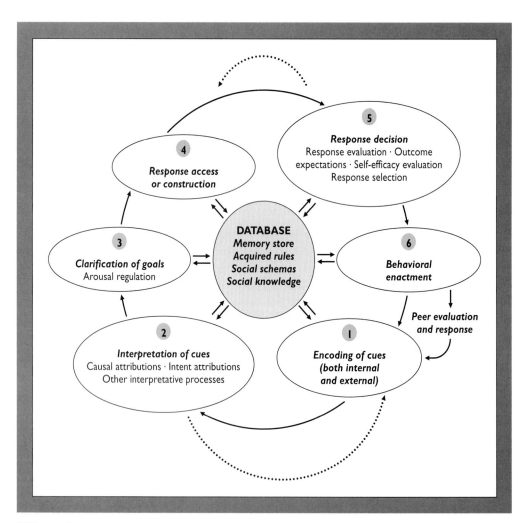

FIG. 13–6

ule 6.2. Second, children try to interpret the features that they have processed; that is, they try to give meaning to the social stimulus. Third, children evaluate their goals for the situation. Fourth, children retrieve from memory a behavioral response that is associated with the interpretation and goals of the situation. Fifth, children evaluate this response to determine if it is appropriate. Finally, the child proceeds with the behavior.

Several investigators have shown that aggressive children's processing is biased and restricted in many of these steps, and that this flawed information processing is associated with increased aggression (Crick & Werner, 1998; Egan, Monson, & Perry, 1998). For example, aggressive children often attribute hostile intentions to others that are not justified (de Castro et al., 2002). When another child has broken a toy and has a surprised, chagrined look on her face, an aggressive child will, nevertheless, believe that the child broke the toy on purpose. Or, seeing two classmates whispering together in the corner of a classroom, an aggressive child often assumes the classmates are planning to do something mean, even when there's no reason to suspect this (Crick, Grotpeter, & Bigbee, 2002). And, based on a personal history of being rejected and ridiculed by peers, many aggressive children believe that unfamiliar peers are unfriendly and uncaring (Burks et al., 1999; MacKinnon-Lewis, Rabiner, & Starnes, 1999).

> Aggressive children often interpret neutral behavior in hostile terms.

If aggressive children are unskilled at interpreting and responding to others' actions, would training in these skills improve their social behavior? The answer seems to be "yes" (Dodge & Crick, 1990). One approach is to teach aggressive children that aggression is painful and does not solve problems, that intentions can be understood by attending to relevant cues, and that there are more effective, prosocial ways to solve interpersonal disputes. In a study by Guerra and Slaby (1990), adolescents incarcerated for committing violent acts received training designed to increase their understanding of social situations. For example, they were taught to pay attention to nonhostile cues in a social situation, to think of alternative ways of responding to social problems, and to evaluate responses in terms of their consequences. Supervisors at the correctional facility judged that the adolescents were better adjusted following training than before. They were less aggressive, less impulsive, and more flexible in their solutions.

Improving social skills in aggressive adolescents is beneficial, but in the long run a more productive approach is to teach young children constructive ways to resolve conflicts without relying on aggression. An example of this approach (Stevahn et al., 2000) involved a program designed to teach kindergarten children to negotiate their conflicts. As shown in the card that was given to children, the elements of the program included recognizing a conflict, both parties communicating their understanding of the situation and their intentions, generating solutions that would benefit both, and agreeing on a solution. Following this training, children were better able to negotiate solutions to hypothetical and actual conflicts. Thus, training in social skills can reduce aggressive behavior and promote more positive ways to resolve conflicts with peers.

FIG. 13–7

To sum up, the vicious cycle of aggression usually begins early. Once youngsters are labeled aggressive, environmental factors may lead them quite unwittingly along an aggressive path. The punishments that parents and teachers dole out may increase the child's hostility and serve as evidence that aggression "works." The child may then choose aggressive companions who further encourage aggressive behavior.

Of course, families are not the sole causes of aggression and violence. Poverty, unemployment, racism, and terrorism create a culture of aggression and violence (Coie & Dodge, 1998). But individual parents can be careful to not set the cycle of aggression in motion. Parents can respond to misbehavior with reasoning instead of physical punishment. And children prone to aggression can be taught equally effective but more prosocial ways to deal with conflict.

## Victims of Aggression

Every aggressive act is directed at someone. Most schoolchildren are the targets of an occasional aggressive act—a shove or kick to gain a desired toy, or a stinging insult by someone trying to save face. However, a small percentage of children are chronic targets of bullying. In both Europe and the United States, about 10 percent of elementary-school children and adolescents are chronic victims of aggression (Kochenderfer & Ladd, 1996; Olweus, 1994). Dorothy Allison provides a frightening glimpse of this victimization in her novel *Bastard Out of Carolina*. As Shannon got on the school bus, she walked

> past a dozen hooting boys and another dozen flushed and whispering girls. As she made her way up the aisle, I watched each boy slide to the end of his seat to block her sitting with him and every girl flinch away as if whatever Shannon had might be catching. In the seat ahead of us Danny Yarboro leaned far over into the aisle and began making retching noises. "Cootie train! Cootie train" somebody yelled as the bus lurched into motion and Shannon still hadn't found a seat (pp. 153–154).

In this episode, Shannon is the victim of verbal bullying. But victimization by physical force also occurs frequently: Think of a child who is beat up daily on the playground. And other children are chronic targets of relational aggression: Think of children who are constantly the subject of rumors spread by their classmates (Crick, Casas, & Nelson, 2002).

As you can imagine, being tormented daily by their peers is hard on children. Research consistently shows that children who are chronic victims of aggression are often lonely, anxious, and depressed; they dislike school; and they have low self-esteem (Graham & Juvonen, 1998; Ladd & Ladd, 1998). And, although most children are happier when no longer victimized, the harmful effects linger for some children: They are still lonely and sad despite not having been victims for 1 or 2 years (Kochenderfer-Ladd & Wardrop, 2001).

**Some children who are chronic victims of aggression overreact when provoked; others withdraw and submit to aggression.**

Why do some children suffer the sad fate of being victims? Some victims are actually aggressive themselves (Olweus, 1978; Schwartz et al., 1997). These youngsters often overreact, are restless, and are easily irritated. Their aggressive peers soon learn that these children are easily baited. A group of children will, for example, insult or ridicule them, knowing that they will probably start a fight even though they are outnumbered. Other victims tend to be withdrawn and submissive. They are unwilling or unable to defend themselves from their peers' aggression, and so they are usually referred to as passive victims (Ladd & Ladd, 1998; Olweus, 1978). When attacked, like the child in the photo, they show obvious signs of distress and usually give in to their attackers, thereby rewarding the aggressive behavior. Thus, both aggressive and withdrawn-submissive children end up as victims; and this pattern holds for children in China as well as for children in North America (Schwartz, Chang, & Farver, 2001).

How do children end up as victims? Family history and parenting help decide. To understand these forces, we need to distinguish victims who overreact from those who respond passively, and within the latter group, distinguish boys from girls. Victims who overreact often come from hostile, punitive, or even abusive family environments (Schwartz et al., 1997). Among passive victims, boys tend to have mothers who are overprotective or emotionally overinvolved with them; in contrast, girls who are passive victims tend to have mothers who are controlling and unresponsive (Ladd & Ladd, 1998).

Some victims try to cope with the problem themselves, but this is complicated because different strategies seem to work best for boys and girls (Kochendefer-Ladd & Skinner, 2002). One strategy for victimized children is to turn to peers for support, by telling them how it feels to be victimized or by asking them for help directly. This strategy works for girls but backfires for boys: Boys' classmates like them even less, perhaps because boys are expected to cope with problems alone and peers shun boys who seek help. A strategy that has costs and benefits for boys is ignoring the victimization—pretending that it's not happening or saying that it doesn't matter. When victimized boys do this, they tend to be more anxious (the cost) but their peers like them more (the benefit).

Rather than letting children cope alone with victimization (using strategies that may or may not work), a better approach is to teach victimized children ways of dealing with aggression that are more effective than either overreacting or withdrawing passively (e.g., don't lash out when you're insulted; don't show that you're afraid when you're threatened). In addition, increasing self-esteem can help. When attacked, children with low self-esteem may think, "I'm a loser and have to put up with this because I have no choice." Increasing children's self-esteem makes them less tolerant of personal attacks (Egan & Perry, 1998). Finally, one of the easiest ways to help victims is to foster their friendships with peers. When children have friends, they're not as likely to be victimized (Hodges, Malone, & Perry, 1997).

Throughout this module, we've seen the harm caused by aggression: victims are hurt and children who are chronically aggressive often lead problem-filled lives. Yet, the research described in this module has also identified many of the roots of aggressive behavior and suggested how children can learn other, more constructive ways to interact with peers.

## CHECK YOUR LEARNING

1. During the elementary-school years, physical aggression becomes less common but _____ becomes more common, especially among girls.

2. After the preschool years, bullying is the most common form of aggression, but instrumental and _____ aggression also occur often.

3. As adults, highly aggressive children are more likely to _____.

4. Aggressive behavior in children is linked to parents' use of _____ punishment.

5. Family influences on children's aggression include parental behavior (including punishment), _____, and inherited tendencies that may evoke harsh parenting.

6. Children who regularly watch televised violence are more likely to behave aggressively, and they also _____.

7. Aggressive children often interpret neutral stimuli in _____ terms.

8. Some chronic victims of aggression tend to overreact when provoked, whereas other chronic victims tend to _____.

**CONNECTIONS**
Crick and Dodge's model of decision making draws on the information-processing approach to cognitive development presented in Chapter 8. Use that approach to suggest other possible causes of and remedies for children's aggressive behavior.

**Answers:** (1) verbal aggression, (2) reactive, (3) engage in criminal activity, (4) harsh physical, (5) the quality of children's relationships with siblings, (6) become hardened to violence, (7) hostile or aggressive, (8) withdraw or submit

# Unifying Themes: Continuity

This chapter has some nice illustrations of the theme that *early development is related to later development but not perfectly*. For example, look at the table on page 365, which shows correlations between preschoolers' delayed gratification and several measures in adolescence. Preschoolers who were best able to delay gratification were, as adolescents, less likely to yield to temptation and to be distractible. Yet the correlations were far from 1, which shows that many preschoolers who quickly gave into temptation became adolescents who were not distractible.

The same conclusion is evident in the results in the graph on page 386. Among children who were rated by their teachers as the most aggressive, about 40 percent had committed serious crimes by age 30, yet 60 percent had not. Among the children who were rated least aggressive, more than 90 percent were crime-free as adults, but 5 percent had committed serious crimes. Behaving aggressively in childhood definitely increases the odds of adult criminal activity, but it does not guarantee it.

## See for Yourself

This assignment may seem like a dream come true—you are being required to watch TV. Pick an evening when you can watch network television programming from 8 until 10 P.M. (prime time). Your job is to count each instance of (a) physical force by one person against another and (b) threats of harm to compel another to act against his or her will. Select one network randomly and watch the program for 10 minutes. Then turn to another network and watch that program for 10 minutes. Continue changing the channels every 10 minutes until the 2 hours are over. Of course, it won't be easy to follow the plots of all these programs, but you will end up with a wider sample of programming this way. Repeat this procedure on a Saturday morning when you can watch 2 hours of children's cartoons (not *South Park*!).

Now simply divide the total number of aggressive acts by 4 to estimate the amount of aggression per hour. Then multiply this figure by 11,688 to estimate the number of aggressive acts seen by an average adolescent by age 19. (Why 11,688? Two hours of daily TV viewing—a very conservative number—multiplied by $365\frac{1}{4}$ days and 16 years.) Then ponder the possible results of that very large number. If your parents told you, nearly 12,000 times, that stealing was okay, would you be more likely to steal? Probably. Then what are the consequences of massive exposure to the televised message, "Solve conflicts with aggression"? See for yourself!

## Resources

For more information about...

 **people who have devoted their lives to helping others**, read Anne Colby and William Damon's *Some Who Do Care: Contemporary Lives of Moral Commitment* (The Free Press, 1992). The authors, developmental psychologists interested in moral development, use biographies of humanitarians to identify the forces that make some people commit their lives to helping others.

**the impact of media violence on children**, visit the Web site of the University of Oregon's Media Literacy On-Line Project,
**http://interact.uoregon.edu/MediaLit/HomePage**

## Key Terms

aggression 385
altruism 379
bullying 385
conventional level 371
dispositional praise 383
empathic orientation 376
empathy 380
hedonistic orientation 376
immanent justice 370
instrumental aggression 386
Just Communities 378
moral realism 370

moral relativism 370
needs-oriented orientation 376
personal domain 377
postconventional level 372
preconventional level 371
prosocial behavior 379
reactive aggression 386
relational aggression 386
self-control 362
social conventions 377
stereotyped, approval-focused orientation 376

# SUMMARY

## 13.1 Self-Control

### Beginnings of Self-Control
At 1 year, infants are first aware that others impose demands on them; by 3 years, youngsters can devise plans to regulate their behavior. During the school-age years, children become better able to control their behavior.

Children differ in their self-control, but individuals are fairly consistent over time: Preschoolers who have good self-control tend to become adolescents with good self-control.

### Parental Influences
When children observe adults who delay gratification, they are more likely to delay gratification themselves. Similarly, when children observe adults who show little self-control, they are likely to show little self-control themselves. Children who have the best self-control tend to have parents who do not use harsh punishment and who encourage their children to be independent and make their own decisions.

### Temperamental Influences on Self-Control
Temperament helps determine how parents influence their children's self-control. With temperamentally fearful children, gentle reminders are effective; with fearless children, parents should appeal to the attachment relationship.

### Improving Self-Control
Children are better able to regulate their own behavior when they have plans to help them remember the importance of the goal and something to distract them from tempting objects.

## 13.2 Reasoning About Moral Issues

### Piaget's Views
Piaget theorized that 5- to 7-year-olds are in a stage of moral realism. They believe that rules are created by wise adults; therefore, rules must be followed and cannot be changed. At about 8 years, children enter a stage of moral relativism, believing that rules are created by people to help them get along.

### Kohlberg's Theory
Kohlberg proposed that moral reasoning includes preconventional, conventional, and postconventional levels. Moral reasoning is first based on rewards and punishments, and, later, on personal moral codes. As predicted by Kohlberg's theory, people progress through the stages in sequence and do not regress, and morally advanced reasoning is associated with more frequent moral behavior. However, few people attain the most advanced levels, and cultures differ in the bases for moral reasoning.

### Beyond Kohlberg's Theory
Gilligan proposed that females' moral reasoning is based on caring and responsibility for others, not justice. Research does not support consistent sex differences, but has found that males and females both consider caring as well as justice in their moral judgments, depending on the situation.

According to Eisenberg, children's reasoning about prosocial dilemmas shifts from a self-interested, hedonistic orientation to concern for others based on empathy.

During the preschool years, children differentiate moral rules, social conventions, and personal choices. They believe, for example, that social conventions can be changed but moral rules cannot. And they understand that breaking a moral rule produces a harsher punishment than breaking a social convention.

### Promoting Moral Reasoning
Many factors can promote more sophisticated moral reasoning, including (a) observing others reason at more advanced levels, and (b) discussing moral issues with peers, teachers, and parents.

## 13.3 Helping Others

### Development of Prosocial Behavior
Even toddlers know when others are upset, and they try to offer comfort. As children grow older, they more often see the need to act prosocially and are more likely to have the skills to do so.

### Skills Underlying Prosocial Behavior
Children are more likely to behave prosocially when they are able to take others' perspectives, are empathic, and have more advanced moral reasoning.

### Situational Influences
Children's prosocial behavior is often influenced by situational characteristics. Children more often behave prosocially when they feel that they should and can help, when they are in a good mood, and when they believe that they have little to lose by helping.

### Socializing Prosocial Behavior
Parenting approaches that promote prosocial behavior include using reasoning in discipline, modeling prosocial behavior, praising children for prosocial behavior, and having adolescents do family-oriented chores.

## 13.4 Aggression

### Change and Stability
As children grow older, physical aggression decreases and verbal aggression becomes more common. Typical forms of aggression include bullying as well as instrumental and reactive aggression. Overall levels of aggression are fairly stable, which means that very aggressive young children often become involved in criminal activities as adolescents and adults.

### Roots of Aggressive Behavior
Children's aggressive behavior has been linked to their parents' use of harsh physical punishment. Other factors that contribute to children's aggression are excessive viewing of televised violence and lack of skill at interpreting others' actions and intentions.

### Victims of Aggression
Children who are chronic targets of aggression are often lonely and anxious. Some victims of aggression tend to overreact when provoked; others tend to withdraw and submit. Victimization can be overcome by increasing children's social skills, their self-esteem, and their number of friends.

# 14

You barely have the phone to your ear before your brother-in-law shouts, "Jeannie had the baby!" "That's great," you say. "A boy or a girl?" Why is this always the first question people ask new parents? Why are people so interested in a baby's sex? The answer is that being a *boy* or *girl* is not simply a biological distinction. Instead, these terms are associated with distinct social roles. **Like a role in a play, a social role is a set of cultural guidelines for how a person should behave.** The social roles associated with gender are among the first that children learn. **Starting in infancy, children learn about gender roles—the culturally prescribed behaviors that are considered appropriate for males and females.** As youngsters learn the behaviors assigned to males and females, they begin to identify with one of these groups. **Children forge a gender identity, the perception of oneself as either male or female.**

In this chapter, we will see how children acquire a gender role and a gender identity. We'll begin, in Module 14.1, by considering cultural stereotypes of males and females. In Module 14.2, we will examine actual psychological differences between boys and girls. In Module 14.3, we'll focus on how children come to identify with one sex. Finally, in Module 14.4, we'll discuss recent changes in gender roles. Throughout this chapter, I'll use *sex* to refer to aspects of males and females that are clearly biological (such as differences in anatomy) and *gender* to refer all other characteristics that relate to maleness and femaleness.

# Gender and Development

14.1    Gender Stereotypes

14.2    Differences Related to Gender

14.3    Gender Identity

14.4    Gender Roles in Transition

# 14.1 Gender Stereotypes

LEARNING OBJECTIVES

● What are gender stereotypes, and how do they differ for males and females?

● How do gender stereotypes influence behavior?

● When do children learn their culture's stereotypes for males and females?

> *When Nancy was 7 months pregnant, her 11-year-old son, Clark, announced that he really wanted a brother, not a sister. Clark explained, "A sister would drive me crazy. Girls never make up their minds about stuff, and they get all worked up over nothin'." "Where did Clark get these ideas?" Nancy wondered. "Is this typical for 11-year-olds?"*

**All cultures have gender stereotypes—beliefs about how males and females differ in personality traits, interests, and behaviors.** Of course, because stereotypes are beliefs, they may or may not be true. In this module, we'll look at the features associated with gender stereotypes and discover when children like Clark learn about gender stereotypes.

## How Do We View Men and Women?

"Terry is active, independent, competitive, and aggressive." As you were reading this sentence, you probably assumed that Terry was a male. Why? Although Terry is a common name for both males and females, the adjectives used to describe Terry are more commonly associated with men than with women. In fact, more than 30 years of research shows that most adults associate different traits with men and women (Best, 2001; Lueptow, Garovich-Szabo, & Lueptow, 2001; Lutz & Ruble, 1995). Men are said to be independent, competitive, aggressive, outgoing, ambitious, self-confident, and dominant. **These male-associated traits are called instrumental because they describe individuals who act on the world and influence it.** In contrast, women are said to be emotional, kind, creative, considerate, gentle, excitable, and aware of others' feelings. **Female-associated traits are called expressive, because they describe emotional functioning and individuals who value interpersonal relationships.**

In the "Cultural Influences" feature, we'll see whether these views are shared by adults worldwide.

### CULTURAL INFLUENCES

#### Around the World with Four Gender Stereotypes

Are men seen as aggressive and independent worldwide? And are women seen as emotional and gentle worldwide? Or are these stereotypes of men and women unique to the United States? John Williams and Deborah Best (1990) addressed these questions in an ambitious project involving 300 different traits and participants in 30 countries. The graphs on page 401 present the results for just 4 traits and 7 countries. You can see that each trait shows considerable cultural variation. For example, virtually all American

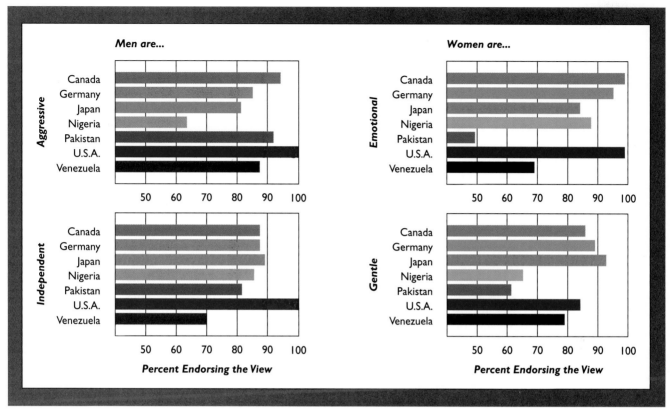

FIG. 14–1

participants consider men aggressive, but only a slight majority of Nigerian participants do. Thus, American views of men and women are not shared worldwide. In fact, what's notable about the research results is that Americans' gender stereotypes are more extreme than are those in any other country listed. Keep this in mind as you think about what men and women can and cannot do and what they should and should not do. Your ideas about gender are shaped by your culture's beliefs, which are not held universally.

Understanding our tendency to stereotype gender behavior is important because stereotypes are very limiting (Smith & Mackie, 2000). If we have stereotyped views, we expect males to act in particular ways and females to act in other ways, and we respond to males and females solely on the basis of gender, not as individuals. For example, do you assume the youngster in the photo is a girl based on her taste in toys? Assuming the child is a girl would, in turn, probably lead you to think she plays more quietly and is more easily frightened than if you assume the child is a boy (Stern & Karraker, 1989). Making stereotyped assumptions about gender leads to a whole host of inferences about behavior and personality that may not be true.

When do children begin to learn their culture's stereotypes for males and females? We'll answer this question in the next section. 🌐

## Learning Gender Stereotypes

By the time children enter elementary school, they are well on their way to forming gender stereotypes; and by the time they complete elementary school, their ideas of gender stereotypes are virtually as well formed as adults'. Children's growing understanding of gender stereotypes was demonstrated in a study by Deborah Best and her colleagues (1977).

Children were asked if 16 stereotypically masculine and 16 stereotypically feminine traits were more typical of boys or girls. At age 5, boys and girls judged one-third of the traits the way adults would; by age 11, they judged about 90 percent of the traits according to adult stereotypes. The table shows the traits that children judged stereotypically at ages 5 and 11. A check means that boys and girls agreed with the listed stereotype.

## Children's Stereotypes of Boys and Girls

| Boys are . . . | | | Girls are . . . | | |
|---|---|---|---|---|---|
| | 5-year-olds | 11-year-olds | | 5-year-olds | 11-year-olds |
| strong | ✓ | ✓ | emotional | ✓ | ✓ |
| aggressive | ✓ | ✓ | gentle | ✓ | ✓ |
| disorderly | ✓ | ✓ | soft-hearted | ✓ | ✓ |
| cruel | ✓ | ✓ | affectionate | ✓ | ✓ |
| coarse | ✓ | ✓ | weak | ✓ | ✓ |
| ambitious | ✓ | ✓ | appreciative | | ✓ |
| dominant | ✓ | ✓ | excitable | | ✓ |
| adventurous | | ✓ | sophisticated | | ✓ |
| independent | | ✓ | fickle | | ✓ |
| loud | | ✓ | meek | | ✓ |
| boastful | | ✓ | submissive | | ✓ |
| jolly | | ✓ | whiny | | ✓ |
| steady | | ✓ | talkative | | ✓ |
| confident | | ✓ | frivolous | | ✓ |

Source: Based on Best et al., 1977.

TABLE 14-1

Obviously, by 11 years, children have adultlike knowledge of gender stereotypes; in this regard, Clark's view of girls in the opening vignette is quite typical for his age. Children understand gender stereotypes by the time they enter kindergarten, and their understanding grows throughout the elementary-school years (Etaugh & Liss, 1992).

During the elementary-school years, children also learn that the traits and occupations associated with males tend to have higher social status than those associated with females. They learn, for example, that lawyers and engineers have more social status than social workers and flight attendants. Children apparently learn a simple rule—something like "Jobs for men are more prestigious than jobs for women"—because children learning unfamiliar jobs (e.g., a chandler makes candles) rate these occupations as more prestigious if they're illustrated with men than with women (Liben, Bigler, & Krogh, 2001).

As children develop, they also begin to understand that gender stereotypes do not always apply; older children are more willing than younger children to ignore stereotypes when judging other children. For example, told about a boy who likes to play with girls and pretend to iron, preschoolers think he would still want to play with masculine toys.

By the middle elementary-school years, however, children realize that this boy's interests are not stereotypic and he would rather play with feminine toys (Martin, 1989).

Thus, although older children are more familiar with gender stereotypes, they see these stereotypes as general guidelines for behavior that are not necessarily binding for all boys and girls (Signorella, Bigler, & Liben, 1993; Taylor, 1996). In fact, older children consider gender stereotypes less binding than many social conventions and moral rules (Levy, Taylor, & Gelman, 1995; Serbin, Powlishta, & Gulko, 1993). This change is due to cognitive growth: As we saw in Chapter 12, in the context of views of different racial and ethnic groups, older children's cognitive development allows them to understand that stereotypes are generalizations that do not necessarily apply to all people (Bigler & Liben, 1992).

Increased age is not the only factor leading to more flexible views of stereotypes. Girls tend to be more flexible about stereotypes (Ruble & Martin, 1998), perhaps because they see that male-stereotyped traits are more attractive and have more status than female-stereotyped traits. Social class also contributes. Adolescents and young adults (but not children) from middle-class homes tend to have more flexible ideas about gender than individuals from lower-class homes (e.g., Serbin et al., 1993). This difference may be due to education: Better-educated middle-class parents may impart less rigid views of gender to their children.

> By the end of elementary school, children know adults' stereotypes of males and females and understand that these stereotypes are not binding on individuals.

Ethnicity is another factor associated with flexible views of gender. Some studies find that African American youngsters have more flexible ideas about gender than their European American peers (e.g., Bardwell, Cochran, & Walker, 1986). Compared to European American mothers, African American mothers are more frequently employed outside the home, and this may contribute to their children's more open attitudes.

At this point, perhaps you're wondering whether there's any truth to gender stereotypes. For example, are boys really more dominant than girls? Are girls really more excitable than boys? For answers to these questions, let's go to Module 14.2.

## CHECK YOUR LEARNING

1. Male gender stereotypes include instrumental traits, whereas female gender stereotypes emphasize _____ traits.

2. Compared to adults from many other countries, Americans' views on gender are _____.

3. Gender stereotypes are harmful because they lead people to make inferences about a child's behavior or personality based solely on the child's _____, not on individual characteristics.

4. Compared to younger children, older children know more of the contents of gender stereotypes, know that male traits and occupations often have more status, and know that _____.

5. _____-class adolescents and adults tend to have more flexible views of gender roles, as do African American children.

## CONNECTIONS

Examine the traits listed in the table on page 402. How might Piaget have explained the differences between 5- and 11-year-olds' responses?

**Answers:** (1) expressive, (2) more stereotyped, (3) sex, (4) gender stereotypes are not binding on all boys and girls, (5) Middle

# 14.2

# Differences Related to Gender

## LEARNING OBJECTIVES

● How do boys and girls differ in physical development, intellectual abilities, and social behavior?

● What factors are responsible for these gender differences?

● What are the implications of these gender differences for boys' and girls' development?

*All through elementary and middle school, Darlene was one of the best students. When she moved into high school, she was particularly proud that she always got the highest grades in her math classes. But she noticed that, as each year went by, even though she got the best grades in math, the boys got higher scores on the standardized tests given every spring.*

Is Darlene's experience typical? Do girls usually get higher grades than boys in math class but lower scores on standardized tests? Some of the first answers to these questions came in *The Psychology of Sex Differences*, a book by Eleanor Maccoby and Carol Jacklin published in 1974. Maccoby and Jacklin did no new research; rather, they summarized results from approximately 1,500 research studies that had been done over the years on gender differences. According to Maccoby and Jacklin,

> *physical differences between the sexes are obvious and universal. The psychological differences are not. The folklore that has grown up about them is often vague and inconsistent. We believe there is a great deal of myth in the popular view about sex differences. There is also some substance. . . . we hope to be able to identify the generalizations that may be relied upon with some confidence (p. 3).*

Maccoby and Jacklin concluded that girls have greater verbal ability, but that boys have greater mathematical and spatial abilities and are more aggressive.

Maccoby and Jacklin's methodology was quite simple: First they searched psychological journals for studies on gender differences. Then they categorized the studies according to the behaviors that were studied and the ages of the children. Finally, they examined the results for gender differences. For example, girls are thought to be more sensitive to touch, but Maccoby and Jacklin found that, in 6 studies of touch sensitivity, infant boys and girls were equally sensitive. In 3 other studies, girls were more sensitive. In 11 studies of older children and adults, 9 found no differences and 2 found that females were more sensitive. Maccoby and Jacklin concluded that "if a sex difference exists in touch sensitivity . . . our survey has revealed only hints of it" (1974, p. 23).

Maccoby and Jacklin examined many studies of cognition and social behavior, and concluded that gender differences had been established in only four areas: Girls have greater verbal ability whereas boys have greater mathematical and visual-spatial ability, and boys are more aggressive than girls. Just as important, Maccoby and Jacklin did not find evidence to support popular ideas that girls are more social and suggestible than boys, have lower self-esteem, are less analytic in thinking, and lack achievement motivation.

Some critics challenged Maccoby and Jacklin on the grounds that they had included some weak studies and defined behaviors in ways that other researchers might not (Block, 1976). Others questioned outright findings about some specific behaviors. The debate stimulated more research; some of this research applied new statistical techniques that allowed for finer analysis (Eagly, 1995). Many develop-mentalists now believe that gender differences are more extensive than Maccoby and Jacklin suggested, but their book remains a classic because its comprehensiveness provided an excellent starting point for further research.

In the remainder of this module, we'll see what we've discovered about gender differences since Maccoby and Jacklin's classic analysis. We'll focus on differences in physical development, cognitive processes, and social behavior.

## Differences in Physical Development and Behavior

Of course, differences in the reproductive system are what differentiate boys and girls, along with differences in secondary sex characteristics such as lower voices and facial hair in boys and breast development and wider hips in girls. Boys are usually larger and stronger than girls, which means that they often physically outperform girls. You can see the difference at high-school track meets: Boys usually run faster, jump higher, and throw objects farther and more accurately. And, as the diagram shows, long before high-school, boys throw and jump farther than girls. Outside of sports, on tasks that involve fine-motor coordination, such as tracing and drawing, girls do better than boys (Thomas & French, 1985).

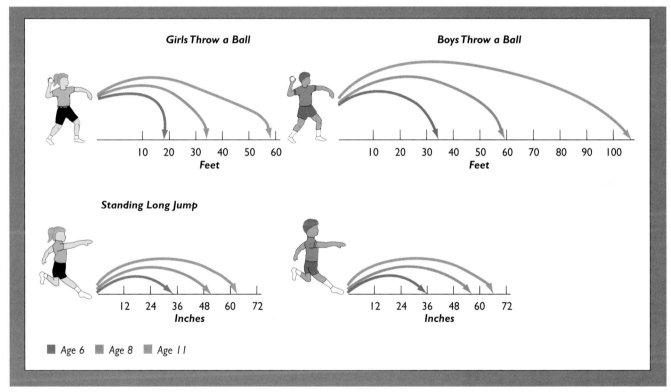

FIG. 14-2

Some of the gender differences in gross-motor skills that require strength re-flect the fact that as children approach and enter puberty, girls' bodies have propor-tionately more fat and less muscle than boys' bodies. This difference explains why, for example, boys can hang from a bar using their arms and hands much longer than girls can. However, for other gross-motor skills, such as running, throwing, and catching, body composition is much less important (Smoll & Schutz, 1990). In these cases, children's experience is crucial. During recess, elementary-school girls are more often found swinging, jumping rope, or perhaps talking quietly in a group; in contrast, boys are playing football or shooting baskets. Many girls and their parents believe that sports and physical fitness are less valuable for girls than boys (Eccles, Jacobs, & Harold, 1990). Consequently, girls spend less time in these sports and fitness-related activities than boys, depriving them of opportunities to practice, which is essential for developing motor skills (Eccles & Harold, 1991).

As infants, boys are more active than girls, and this difference increases during childhood (Eaton & Enns, 1986). For example, in a classroom, boys are more likely than girls to have a hard time sitting still. On playgrounds like those in the photos, boys more often play vigorously and girls, quietly. And, recall from Module 6.2 that boys are three times more likely than girls to be diagnosed with attention deficit hyperactivity disorder.

Girls tend to be healthier than boys. Female embryos are more likely than male embryos to survive prenatal development. This trend continues after birth. Infant boys are more prone to birth complications, and throughout life boys are more prone to many diseases and dysfunctions (Jacklin, 1989). Finally, adolescent boys and young men are more likely to engage in unhealthy, risk-taking behaviors, including drinking, reckless driving, and sexual activity (Byrnes, Miller, & Schafer, 1999).

To summarize, boys tend to be bigger, stronger, and more active; girls tend to have better fine-motor coordination and to be healthier. In the next section, which concerns intellectual skills, you'll again see that gender differences vary from one skill to the next.

## Differences in Intellectual Abilities and Achievement

Of the four gender-based differences discovered by Maccoby and Jacklin (1974), three concern intellectual skills: Girls tend to have greater verbal skill but boys tend to have greater mathematical and visual-spatial skill. Since Maccoby and Jacklin's work, we've learned much about the nature of gender differences in these areas.

VERBAL ABILITY.    During the toddler years, girls have larger vocabularies than boys (Feldman et al., 2000). During elementary school and high school, girls read, write, and spell better than boys, and more boys have reading and other language-related problems such as stuttering (Halpern, 2000).

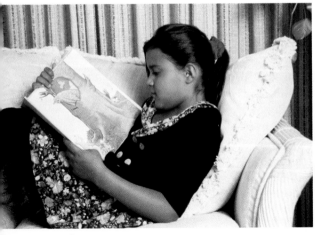

Why are girls more talented verbally than boys? Part of the explanation may lie in biological forces. The left hemisphere of the brain, which is central to language (see Module 5.3), may mature more rapidly in girls than in boys (Diamond et al., 1983). But experience also contributes. During the toddler years, mothers talk more to daughters than to sons (Leaper, Anderson, & Sanders, 1998). And, by the elementary-school years reading is often stereotyped as an activity for girls (Huston, 1983), which may make girls like the one in the photo more willing than boys to invest time and effort in mastering verbal skills like reading.

SPATIAL ABILITY.    In Module 9.1, you saw that spatial ability is a component of most models of intelligence. **One aspect of spatial ability is mental rotation, the ability to imagine how an object will look**

**after it has been moved in space.** The items in the figure below test mental rotation: The task is to determine which of the figures labeled A through E are rotated versions of the figure in the box on the left. From childhood on, boys tend to have better mental-rotation skill than girls (Govier & Salisbury, 2000; Voyer, Voyer, & Bryden, 1995). (The correct answers are C and D.)

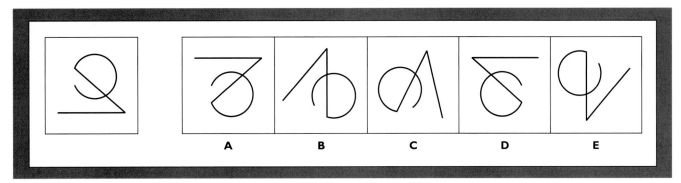

FIG. 14–3

Spatial ability also involves determining relations between objects in space while ignoring distracting information. For example, which of the tilted bottles of water in the figure has the waterline drawn correctly? In an upright bottle, the water-line is at right angles to the sides of the bottle, but selecting the correct answer for the tilted bottle (A, in this case) requires that you ignore the conflicting perceptual in-formation provided by the sides of the bottle. From adolescence on, boys are more accurate than girls on these kinds of spatial tasks (Voyer, Voyer, & Bryden, 1995).

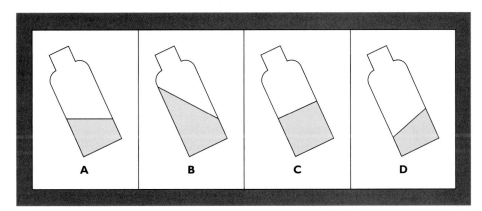

FIG. 14–4

Explanations for gender differences in spatial ability abound:

- A recessive gene on the X chromosome may promote spatial ability (Thomas & Kail, 1991). In this type of inheritance, males only have to inherit a recessive gene from their mother to score high in spatial ability, but females must inher-it the recessive gene from both parents.

- The right hemisphere of the brain may be more specialized for spatial process-ing in males than in females, perhaps because boys mature more slowly than girls (Waber, 1977).

- Boys are more likely than girls to participate in activities that foster spatial skill, such as estimating the trajectory of an object moving through space (e.g., a baseball), using two-dimensional plans to assemble an object such as a scale model (Baenninger & Newcombe, 1995), or, like the boys in the photo, playing video games that involve visual-perceptual skills (Okagaki & Frensch, 1994).

Each of these possible explanations of gender differences in spatial ability is supported by some studies but not by others. And, of course, the explanations are not necessarily mutually exclusive. Biological and experiential forces may both contribute to gender differences in spatial ability, just as both contribute to gender differences in verbal ability. Thus, parents and others can foster verbal and spatial abilities in boys and girls because each is influenced considerably by experience.

MATHEMATICS. Gender differences in math skill are complex. Let's start with performance on standardized math achievement tests. Standardized tests emphasize computational skills during the elementary- and middle-school years, and girls usually score higher than boys. Solving problems and applying math concepts are emphasized in high school and college; here boys often score higher than girls. Thus, initially girls excel in math computation, but later boys excel in math problem solving (Hyde, Fennema, & Lamon, 1990). The gender difference remains even when boys and girls take an equal number of math courses (Kimball, 1989).

The gender difference in performance on math achievement tests is not restricted to the United States. Beller and Gafni (1996) analyzed math scores from the International Assessment of Educational Progress. For 9-year-olds, gender differences were inconsistent; for 13-year-olds, boys' scores exceeded girls' scores in 17 of the 20 countries studied, including Brazil, China, Ireland, and Israel.

Paradoxically, the results are different for grades in math courses. Often no differences are detected in boys' and girls' grades, but when a difference occurs, it invariably favors girls. This is even true for courses in high school and college—when males are getting higher scores on achievement tests (Kimball, 1989). Darlene's experience, described in the module-opening vignette, is common: Girls get better grades in math courses but lower scores on standardized tests of math achievement.

Why should females get lower scores on tests of math achievement but higher grades in math courses? One explanation is based on the concept of stereotype threat, which was introduced in Module 9.2. According to this view, when girls like the ones in the photo take standardized achievement tests, they are anxious for fear of confirming the stereotype and they do poorly as a result (Nosek, Banaji, & Greenwald, 2002; Shih, Pittinsky, & Ambady, 1999).

Because of findings like these, educators have worked hard to reduce gender stereotypes associated with math (Secada, Fennema, & Adajian, 1995). Unfortunately, gender differences in math continue. Hedges and Nowell (1995) evaluated data from the National Assessment of Educational Progress (NAEP), which administers standardized tests in several areas to approximately 70,000 to 100,000 American students in grades 3, 7, and 11. The researchers found that the gender difference in math achievement has been remarkably constant since the NAEP test was first administered in 1978.

Why are gender differences in math so persistent? One possibility is that biological factors contribute. In particular, spatial ability, which we just discussed, may play a role. Some aspects of math are easier to understand if they can be visualized mentally. For example, being able to imagine a three-dimensional space where lines and planes intersect simplifies learning geometry. Boys may be more successful in some areas of math because they more often have the spatial skills that promote understanding (Casey et al., 1997).

Most likely, the gender difference in math is due to multiple factors. Some have roots in biology (e.g., spatial skill) but others have roots in experience (e.g., stereotypes concerning math). As you'll see in the next section, nature and nurture also contribute to gender differences in personality and social behavior.

> Girls often have higher grades than boys in math courses, but boys typically get higher scores on standardized tests of math achievement.

## Differences in Personality and Social Behavior

Are there differences in personality and social behavior between boys and girls? In the 1970s, Maccoby and Jacklin (1974) found convincing evidence of only one gender difference in this realm: Boys were more aggressive than girls. In this section, we'll see what researchers have discovered in the ensuing 30 years.

**AGGRESSIVE BEHAVIOR.** No one doubts Maccoby and Jacklin's conclusion that boys are more aggressive physically than girls. As mentioned in Module 13.4 and as you can see in the photos, the gender difference in physical aggression is readily observed. No matter how you slice it, boys are more aggressive than girls (Collaer & Hines, 1995; Knight, Fabes, & Higgins, 1996). Of course, some qualifications apply. Boys are not always aggressive. They are, for example, more likely to be physically aggressive toward other boys than toward girls (Maccoby & Jacklin, 1980): Boys may try to beat up other boys, but, as a general rule, they don't try to beat up girls. And, when they're provoked, girls can be physically aggressive, too (Bettencourt & Miller, 1996).

Because boys and men are more aggressive in virtually all cultures and because males in nonhuman species are also more aggressive, scientists are convinced that biology contributes heavily to this gender difference. **Aggressive behavior has been linked to androgens, hormones secreted by the testes.** Androgens do not lead to aggression directly. Instead, androgens make it more likely that boys will be aggressive by making boys more excitable or easily angered and by making boys stronger (e.g., Marcus et al., 1985).

Just because hormones are involved, though, we can't ignore experience. The media are filled with aggressive male models—from John Wayne to Jedi Knights—who are rewarded for their behavior. What's more, parents are more likely to use physical punishment with sons than with daughters and are more tolerant of aggressive behavior in sons than in daughters (Block, 1978; Condry & Ross, 1985). As we saw in Module 13.4, these are just the sort of experiences that precipitate a vicious cycle of increasing aggression; and this cycle is much more common for boys than girls. Although androgens may make boys more prone to aggression, experience encourages boys rather than girls to express their aggression physically.

Although boys' aggression may be more obvious because of its physical nature, girls can be aggressive, too, resorting to nonphysical forms such as spreading rumors or malicious gossip (Cairns et al., 1989). The "Focus on Research" feature describes a study that shows how boys and girls differ in their aggressive behavior.

## FOCUS ON RESEARCH

### Aggression Appears in Boys and Girls Differently

*Who were the investigators, and what was the aim of the study?* Throughout the early 1990s, most research on children's aggression focused on physical aggression. Yet children do not have to hit, kick, or push others to harm them. In relational aggression, children try to hurt others by damaging their relationships with peers. They may call children names, make fun of them, spread rumors about them, or—just as bad—pointedly ignore them. Nicki Crick and Jennifer Grotpeter (1995) conducted a study to test the hypothesis that, although physical aggression may be more common among boys, relational aggression is more common among girls.

*How did the investigators measure the topic of interest?* Crick and Grotpeter asked children to complete questionnaires nominating peers who fit different descriptions. To measure physical aggression, children nominated peers who fit descriptions such as "hits, pushes" and "starts fights." For relational aggression, they nominated peers who fit descriptions such as "when mad at a person, ignores them or stops talking to them" and "when mad, gets even by keeping the person from being in their group of friends." Children also completed other questionnaires that measured anxiety, depression, and peer relationships.

> Boys are physically more aggressive than girls, who typically aggress by trying to damage other children's peer relationships.

*Who were the children in the study?* The researchers tested 491 children in grades 3 to 6 in public schools in the Midwest United States. The sample included 60 percent European American children and 37 percent African American children.

*What was the design of the study?* This study was correlational because Crick and Grotpeter were interested in the relation that existed naturally between two variables—children's sex and form of aggression. Although the study included children of different ages, Crick and Grotpeter did not examine age differences in aggression. Thus, the study was neither cross-sectional nor longitudinal.

*Were there ethical concerns with the study?* No. The questionnaires were completed anonymously, so children did not know if peers had nominated them for undesirable characteristics. Crick and Grotpeter obtained permission from the parents for the children to participate.

*What were the results?* Based on how often boys and girls were nominated for different descriptions, Crick and Grotpeter placed each child in one of four categories: not aggressive, physically aggressive, relationally aggressive, or physically *and* relationally aggressive. The graph shows the percentage of children in each category. Thankfully, most children were not aggressive. The top pair of bars shows that nearly three-fourths of the boys and girls in the study were in this category. Unfortunately, the bottom bars show that a small percentage of children mastered both physical and relational aggression.

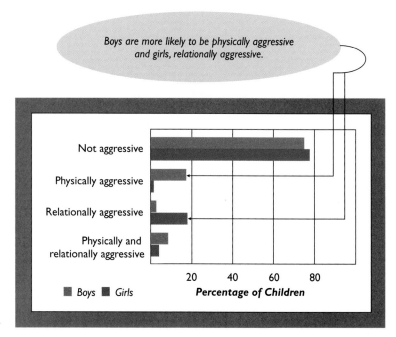

The remaining two categories, however, are the ones that are critical to Crick and Grotpeter's hypothesis. They expected to find a greater percentage of boys who were physically aggressive and a greater percentage of girls who were relationally aggressive, and the two middle pairs of bars show exactly this pattern: Many boys but few girls relied solely upon physical aggression; in contrast, many girls but few boys relied solely upon relational aggression.

FIG. 14–5

*What did the investigators conclude?* Boys and girls are both aggressive; the sexes simply differ in their preferred methods of aggression. When they want to harm peers, boys try to hurt them physically but girls try to damage their relationships with peers. Crick and Grotpeter suggest that previous research underestimated girls' aggressiveness because relational aggression is not as obvious to observers as physical aggression.

*What converging evidence would strengthen these conclusions?* This work could be extended in several different directions. One concerns methods for measuring aggression. Crick and Grotpeter assessed both physical and relational aggression through questionnaires. Observational measures of physical and relational aggression would complement the questionnaire data (although observing relational aggression could be very challenging). A second extension concerns age. Crick and Grotpeter focused on children in the upper elementary grades. Data on physical and relational aggression before and after this period would provide a more complete picture of the development of these forms of aggression.

**EMOTIONAL SENSITIVITY.** According to the stereotypes listed on page 402, girls are better able to express their emotions and interpret others' emotions. In fact, this is a gender difference supported by research (Hall & Halberstadt, 1981; Weinberg et al., 1999). For example, throughout infancy, childhood, and adolescence, girls identify facial expressions (e.g., happy face vs. a sad face) more accurately than boys do (McClure, 2000).

Most developmentalists believe that the gender difference in emotional sensitivity reflects both nature and nurture. On the nature side, regions of the brain's temporal lobe that play a leading role in processing emotional expression develop more rapidly in girls than in boys (McClure, 2000). On the nurture side, parents are more "feeling-oriented" with daughters than with sons. They are more likely to talk about emotions with daughters than with sons and to emphasize the importance of considering others' feelings (Kuebli, Butler, & Fivush, 1995; Zahn-Waxler, Cole, & Barrett, 1991).

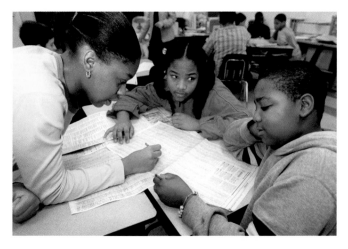

**SOCIAL INFLUENCE.**   Another gender stereotype is that females are more easily influenced by others—that is, they are, more persuadable. In fact, young girls are more likely than young boys to comply with an adult's request, and they are more likely to seek an adult's help (Jacklin & Maccoby, 1978). Girls and women are also influenced more than boys and men by persuasive messages and others' behavior, especially when they are under group pressure (Becker, 1986; Eagly, Karau, & Makhijani, 1995). However, these gender differences may stem from the fact that females value group harmony more than boys and thus seem to give in to others (Miller, Danaher, & Forbes, 1986; Strough & Berg, 2000). For instance, at a meeting like the one in the photo, girls are just as likely as boys to recognize the flaws in a bad idea, but girls are more willing to go along simply because they don't want the group to start arguing.

Depression is more common among adolescent girls than adolescent boys.

**DEPRESSION.**   Depression, a disorder in which individuals are chronically sad and irritable and have low self-esteem, is rare in childhood but becomes much more common in adolescence, particularly among teenage girls like the one in the photo (Avenevoli & Steinberg, 2001). According to current theories (Hankin & Abramson, 2001), depression is often triggered when adolescents experience a negative life event (e.g., flunk a major exam) and interpret this event negatively (e.g., "I'm so stupid; my friends won't want to be with me if they know I'm this dumb").

Applied to the sex difference in depression during adolescence, this approach emphasizes that girls experience more frequent negative life events such as dissatisfaction with their appearance after pubertal change or conflict with close friends. Also, girls are more apt to interpret these negative life events in harmful terms, emphasizing social-emotional consequences, for example, to a far greater extent than boys. For example, I knew a 15-year-old boy who, after 9 years of playing soccer, was the only player cut from the high-school team. Although upset briefly, within days he had decided to go out for cross-country and ended up having a successful and rewarding career running. In the same circumstances, a girl might well have spent more time focusing on the harmful consequences—"I won't be able to hang with my soccer friends," "I stink at sports"—the kind of thinking that would put her at risk for a bout of depression.

At this point, perhaps you're wondering about the role of hormones in depression. After all, adolescence is often portrayed as a time when hormones are running wild and causing huge mood swings. In fact, researchers have found few consistent connections between depression (and other mood disorders) and levels of hormones (Buchanan, Eccles, & Becker, 1992). That is, although levels of female hormones such as progesterone and estrogen definitely rise with the onset of puberty, these changes play no more than a small role in the onset of depression in teenage girls.

## Frank Talk About Gender Differences

The gender differences we've discussed in this module are summarized in the table.

### SEX DIFFERENCES IN PHYSICAL AND BEHAVIORAL DEVELOPMENT

| General Area | Specific Domain | Nature of Difference |
| --- | --- | --- |
| *Physical Development* | | |
| | Motor skills | Boys excel at tasks that require strength but girls do better on tasks that require fine-motor coordination. |
| | Activity | Beginning in infancy, boys are more active than girls. |
| | Health | From conception through adulthood, girls are healthier. |
| *Intellectual Abilities* | | |
| | Verbal ability | Girls have larger vocabularies; they also read, write, and spell better. |
| | Spatial ability | Boys are better on mental-rotation tasks and in determining relations between objects in space. |
| | Mathematics | Girls get better grades in math but boys get higher scores on standardized tests. |
| *Personality and Social Behavior* | | |
| | Aggression | Boys are more aggressive physically; girls rely more on relational aggression. |
| | Emotional sensitivity | Girls are better able to identify and express emotions. |
| | Social influence | Because girls value group harmony more than boys do, girls are more susceptible to others' influence. |
| | Depression | Beginning in adolescence, girls are more prone to depression than boys. |

What should we make of these differences? What do they tell us about the experience of growing up male versus growing up female?

First, remember that the gender differences described in this module represent differences in the *average scores* for boys and girls, differences that are relatively small. For example, the diagram shows the distribution of scores on a hypothetical reading test. As we would expect, overall girls do better than boys. However, the distributions of girls' and boys' scores overlap substantially. The area shaded in green shows the large percentage of boys who have higher reading scores than the average girl and the area

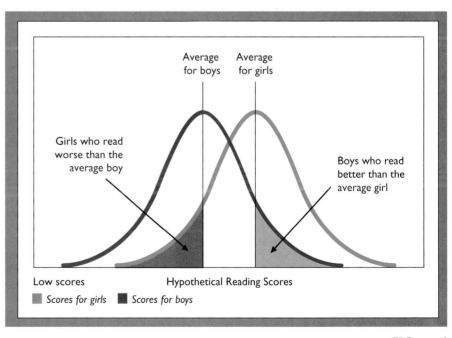

FIG. 14–6

shaded in red shows the large percentage of girls who have lower reading scores than the average boy. The diagram makes it obvious that a difference in average scores does *not* mean that girls read well and boys read poorly. Consequently, a boy who wants to become a writer should not be deterred because of small differences in average scores for boys and girls. Of course, we could draw similar diagrams in the other domains in which boys and girls differ, with the same conclusion. Gender differences are small, which means that boys' and girls' scores overlap considerably.

Second, think about the huge number of abilities, behaviors, and traits that have not been considered in this module. Boys and girls do not differ in many, many aspects of cognition, personality, and social behavior, a point that is easily lost when focusing on gender differences. In reality, a list of ways that boys and girls are similar is much longer than a list of differences. In cognitive processing, memory, and understanding people—to name just a few areas—boys and girls are much more alike than different. If development is a journey, both boys and girls have many choices as they travel; few, if any, routes have signs that say "for girls only" or "for boys only."

In this module, we've focused on the behaviors and skills in which boys and girls differ; in the next, we'll see how children acquire a gender identity, a sense of "being a boy" or "being a girl."

## CHECK YOUR LEARNING

1. Maccoby and Jacklin found that girls had greater verbal skill, that boys excelled in math and visual-spatial ability, and that boys _____.

2. In physical development and behavior, boys are bigger, stronger, and _____.

3. Girls may excel in verbal ability because of gender differences in brain development and because _____.

4. Explanations for the gender difference in spatial ability include a recessive gene, brain specialization, and _____.

5. In math, girls get better grades but boys _____.

6. Boys specialize in physical aggression; girls specialize in _____.

7. When working in groups, girls may be more influenced by other group members than boys because _____.

**NATURE AND NURTURE**
Summarize gender differences in intellectual abilities. How does nature contribute to these differences? How does nurture contribute?

**Answers:** (1) were more aggressive, (2) more active, (3) verbal activities such as reading are stereotyped as "for girls," (4) differences in experiences that promote spatial skill, (5) get higher scores on standardized tests, (6) relational aggression, (7) girls put greater emphasis on maintaining group harmony

# Gender Identity

The Socializing Influences
of People and the Media

Cognitive Theories
of Gender Identity

Biological Influences

LEARNING OBJECTIVES

● How do parents, peers, and the media influence children's learning of gender roles?

● How do cognitive theories explain children's learning of gender roles?

● How does biology influence children's learning of gender roles?

> *Taryn, who has just turned 4, knows that she's a girl but is convinced that she'll grow up to be a man. Taryn plays almost exclusively with boys and her favorite toys are trucks and cars. Taryn tells her parents that when she's bigger, she'll grow a beard and be a daddy. Taryn's father is confident that his daughter's ideas are a natural part of a preschooler's limited understanding of gender, but her mother wonders if they've neglected some important aspect of Taryn's upbringing.*

According to the old saying, "Boys will be boys and girls will be girls," but how, in fact, do boys become boys and girls become girls when it comes to gender roles? That is, how do children acquire their culture's roles for males and females? And how do children develop a sense of identity as a male or female? We'll answer these questions in this module and, as we do, learn whether Taryn's wish to grow up to be a man is typical for youngsters her age.

## The Socializing Influences of People and the Media

Folklore holds that parents and other adults—teachers and television characters, for example—directly shape children's behavior toward the roles associated with their sex. Boys are rewarded for boyish behavior and punished for girlish behavior.

The folklore even has a theoretical basis: According to social learning theorists like Albert Bandura (1977, 1986) and Walter Mischel (1970), children learn gender roles in much the same way they learn other social behaviors—through reinforcement and observational learning. Parents and others thus shape appropriate gender roles in children, and children learn what their culture considers appropriate behavior for males and females by simply watching how adults and peers act. How well does research support social learning theory? Let's look first at research done with parents.

PARENTS.    An extensive meta-analysis of 172 studies involving 27,836 children (Lytton & Romney, 1991) found that parents tend to treat sons and daughters similarly except when it comes to gender-related behavior. That is, parents interact equally with sons and daughters, are equally warm to both, and encourage both sons and daughters to achieve and be independent. But there are some important exceptions to the general rule of comparable treatment:

*Parents treat sons and daughters similarly, except for gender-related behavior.*

- In behavior related to gender roles, parents respond differently to sons and daughters (Lytton & Romney, 1991). Activities such as playing with dolls, dressing up, or helping an adult are encouraged more often in daughters than in sons; rough-and-tumble play and playing with blocks are encouraged more in sons than in daughters.

- Mothers often talk differently to sons and daughters: They tend to use more supportive statements with their daughters and are often more directive with sons (Leaper, Anderson, & Sanders, 1998).

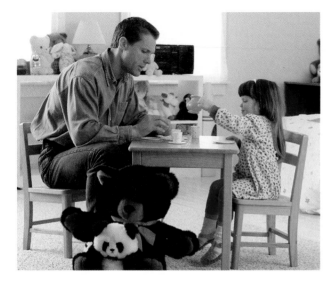

- Parents assign sons and daughters different household chores. Daughters tend to be assigned stereotypically female chores such as washing dishes or housecleaning, whereas sons are assigned stereotypically male chores such as taking out the garbage or mowing the lawn (McHale et al., 1990).

Fathers are more likely than mothers to treat sons and daughters differently. More than mothers, fathers like the one in the photo often encourage gender-related play. Fathers also push their sons more but accept dependence in their daughters (Snow, Jacklin, & Maccoby, 1983). A father, for example, may urge his frightened young son to jump off the diving board ("Be a man!") but not be so insistent with his daughter ("That's okay, honey"). Apparently mothers are more likely to respond based on their knowledge of the individual child's needs, but fathers respond based on gender stereotypes. A mother responds to her son knowing that he's smart but unsure of himself; a father may respond because of what he thinks boys should be like.

**TEACHERS.**    After parents, teachers may be the most influential adults in children's lives. Many teachers help to differentiate gender roles by making gender salient in the classroom. In elementary schools, students may be told to form separate lines for boys and girls like the ones shown in the photo. Or teachers may praise the girls as a group for being quiet during a video while criticizing the boys for laughing (Thorne, 1993). In addition, teachers spend more time interacting with boys than girls. Teachers call on boys more frequently, praise them more for their schoolwork, and spend more time scolding them for disruptive classroom behavior (Good & Brophy, 1996). By using sex as a basis for differentiating children and by giving boys more attention, teachers foster gender role learning.

**PEERS.**    By 3 years, most children's play shows the impact of gender stereotypes—boys prefer blocks and trucks, whereas girls prefer tea sets and dolls—and youngsters are critical of peers who engage in cross-gender play (Langlois & Downs, 1980). This is particularly true of boys who like feminine toys or who play at feminine activities. Boys who play with dolls and girls (like the one in the photo) who play with trucks will both be ignored, teased, or ridiculed by their peers, but a boy will receive harsher treatment than a girl (Levy, Taylor, & Gelman, 1995). Once children learn rules about gender-typical play, they often harshly punish peers who violate those rules.

Peers influence gender roles in another way, too. Between 2 and 3 years of age, children begin to prefer playing with same-sex peers (Martin & Fabes, 2001). Little boys play together with cars, and little girls play together with dolls. This preference increases during childhood, reaching a peak in preadolescence. Then the tide begins to turn, but even in adulthood time spent at work and at leisure is quite commonly segregated by gender (Hartup, 1983). This tendency for boys to play with boys and girls with girls has several distinctive features (Maccoby, 1990, 1998):

- In some cultures, adults select playmates for children. However, in cultures where children choose playmates, boys select boys as playmates and girls select girls.
- Children spontaneously select same-sex playmates. Adult pressure ("James, why don't you play with John, not Amy") is not necessary.
- Children resist parents' efforts to get them to play with members of the opposite sex. Girls are often unhappy when parents encourage them to play with boys, and boys are unhappy when parents urge them to play with girls.
- Children's reluctance to play with members of the opposite sex is not restricted to gender-typed games, such as playing house or playing with cars. Boys and girls prefer same-sex playmates even in gender-neutral activities such as playing tag or doing puzzles.

Boys and girls don't play together because girls don't like boys' style of play and because girls find that their enabling interaction style is ineffective with boys.

Why do boys and girls seem so attracted to same-sex play partners? Eleanor Maccoby (1988, 1990) believes that two factors are critical. First, boys specifically prefer rough-and-tumble play and generally are more competitive and dominating in their interactions. Girls' play is not as rough and is less competitive, so Maccoby argues that boys' style of play may be aversive to girls.

Second, when girls and boys play together, girls do not readily influence boys. **Girls' interactions with one another are typically enabling—their actions and remarks tend to support others and sustain the interaction.** When drawing together, one girl might say to another, "Cool picture" or "What do you want to do now?" **In contrast, boy's interactions are often constricting—one partner tries to emerge as the victor by threatening or contradicting the other, by exaggerating, and so on.** In the same drawing task, one boy might say to another, "My picture's better" or "Drawing is stupid—let's watch TV." When these styles are brought together, girls find that their enabling style is ineffective with boys. The same subtle overtures that work with other girls have no impact on boys. Boys ignore girls' polite suggestions about what to do and ignore girls' efforts to resolve conflicts with discussion.

Regardless of the exact cause, early segregation of playmates by style of play means that boys learn primarily from boys and girls from girls. Over time, such social segregation by sex reinforces sex differences in play. Martin and Fabes (2001), for example, conducted a longitudinal study of same-sex play in preschool and kindergarten children. When young boys spent most of their time playing with other boys at the beginning of the school year, by the end of the year their play was more active and more aggressive. In contrast, when young girls spent most of their time playing with other girls at the beginning of the school year, by the end of the year their play was less active and less aggressive. Boys and girls who spent more time playing with other-sex children didn't show these changes. Thus, young boys and girls teach each other sex-appropriate play. As they do, this helps solidify a youngster's emerging sense of membership in a particular gender group and sharpens the contrast between genders.

**TELEVISION.**   Another source of influence on gender-role learning is television, which often portrays males and females in stereotyped ways. Women on television tend to be cast in romantic, marital, or family roles; they are depicted as emotional, passive, and weak. Men are more often cast in leadership or professional roles and are depicted as rational, active, and strong (Huston et al., 1992).

What is the impact of these stereotyped portrayals? As you can imagine, children who watch a lot of TV end up with more stereotyped views of males and females. For example, Kimball (1986) studied gender-role stereotypes in a small Canadian town that could not receive TV programs until a transmitter was installed in 1974. Children's views of personality traits, behaviors, occupations, and peer relations were measured before and after TV was introduced.

Boys' views became more stereotyped on all four dimensions. For example, in their more stereotyped views of occupations, boys now believed that girls could be teachers and cooks whereas boys could be physicians and judges. Girls' views became more stereotyped only for traits and peer relations. After TV was introduced, girls believed that boasting and swearing were characteristic of boys and that sharing and helping were characteristic of girls. Findings like these indicate that TV viewing causes children to adopt many of the stereotypes that dominate television programming (Signorielli & Lears, 1992).

Let's now return to our original question: How well does research support the social learning explanation of gender roles? Studies of parents, teachers, and peers show that children learn much about gender roles simply by observing males and females. But simple observation of real-life models or television characters cannot be the entire explanation. After all, young boys traditionally have far more opportunities to observe their mother's behavior than their father's, but are more likely to imitate their father (for example, by using hammer and saw) than their mother (for example, by cooking). Thus, an important element in learning about gender is identifying with one gender and then actively seeking out activities that are typical for that gender. This aspect of gender role learning is the focus of cognitive theories, which we'll examine in the next section.

## Cognitive Theories of Gender Identity

According to Lawrence Kohlberg (1966; Kohlberg & Ullian, 1974), full understanding of gender develops gradually and involves three elements:

- **Gender labeling: By age 2 or 3, children understand that they are either boys or girls and label themselves accordingly.**

- **Gender stability: During the preschool years, children begin to understand that gender is stable: Boys become men and girls become women.** However, children in this stage believe that a girl who wears her hair like a boy will become a boy and that a boy who plays with dolls will become a girl (Fagot, 1985).

- **Gender consistency: Between 4 and 7 years, most children understand that maleness and femaleness do not change over situations or according to personal wishes.** They understand that a child's sex is unaffected by the clothing that a child wears or the toys that a child likes.

*According to cognitive theories, after children understand that gender is constant, they learn about activities and behaviors typically associated with their sex.*

VIDEO 14.1
Gender Consistency

Taryn, the 4-year-old in the opening vignette, is in the first stage—she knows that she's a girl. However, she has yet to develop a sense of gender stability or gender consistency. **When children understand labels, stability, and consistency, they have mastered gender constancy.**

According to Kohlberg's theory, only children who understand gender constancy should have extensive knowledge of sex-stereotyped activities (Newman, Cooper, & Ruble, 1995). That is, not until children understand that gender is constant do they begin to learn what is appropriate and possible for their gender and what is not, as you'll see in the "Real Children" feature.

## REAL CHILDREN

### Laura Trades Wrestling for Cheerleading

When my daughter Laura was $2\frac{1}{2}$, she knew that she was a girl, but she also insisted that she would grow up to be a daddy. At about the same time, my son Ben was on a school wrestling team. Laura often went with me to watch Ben wrestle. Afterwards, she thought it was great fun to wrestle on the living room floor, slapping her hand down on the carpet when she pinned me. Never did she comment on the fact that all the wrestlers were boys; evidently this was irrelevant.

By the time she turned 4, Laura knew that she would become a woman. At this age, I remember vividly taking her to watch Ben play football. I wondered if she would become so bored and restless that we'd need to leave. Wrong. Laura immediately discovered the cheerleaders (all girls) and insisted we sit right in front of them. Throughout the game (and the rest of the season), Laura's eyes were riveted to the cheerleaders' every move, and when we'd get home, she'd imitate their routines. According to Kohlberg's theory, 4-year-old Laura knew that cheerleading was for girls and that because she was a girl, cheerleading was for her.*

Laura's interest in gender-typical behavior emerged only after she understood gender constancy. You can see this same pattern in findings from research (Szkrybalo & Ruble, 1999). For example, Martin and Little (1990) measured preschool children's understanding of gender and their knowledge of gender-stereotyped activities (for example, that girls play with dolls and that boys play with airplanes). The youngest children in their study—$3\frac{1}{2}$- to 4-year-olds—did not understand gender constancy and knew little of gender-stereotyped activities. By age 4, children understood gender constancy but still knew little of gender-stereotyped activities. By $4\frac{1}{2}$ years, many children understood gender constancy and knew gender-typical and gender-atypical activities. Importantly, there were no children who lacked gender constancy but knew about gender-stereotyped activities, a combination that is impossible according to Kohlberg's theory.

Kohlberg's theory specifies *when* children begin learning about gender-appropriate behavior and activities (once they understand gender constancy) but not *how* such learning takes place. A theory proposed by Carol Martin (Martin & Halverson, 1987; Martin et al., 1999), illustrated in the diagram, addresses how children learn about gender. **In gender-schema theory, children first decide if an object, activity, or behavior is female or male, then use this information to decide whether or not they should learn more about the object, activity, or behavior.** That is, once children know their gender,

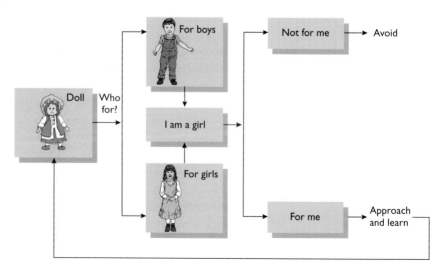

---

*But, as an elementary-school student, she abandoned cheerleading for soccer and basketball.

FIG. 14–7

they pay attention primarily to experiences and events that are gender appropriate (Martin & Halverson, 1987). According to gender-schema theory, the preschool boy in the photo who is watching a group of girls playing in sand will decide that playing in sand is for girls and that, because he is a boy, playing in sand is not for him. Seeing a group of older boys playing football, he will decide that football is for boys, and because he is a boy, football is acceptable and he should learn more about it.

According to gender-schema theory, after children understand gender, it's as if they see the world through special glasses that allow only gender-typical activities to be in focus (Liben & Bigler, 2002). After children understand gender, their tastes in TV programs begin to shift along gender-specific lines (Luecke-Aleksa et al., 1995). In addition, they begin to use gender labels to evaluate toys and activities. Shown an unfamiliar toy and told that children of a specific sex *really* like this toy, children like the toy much more if others of their sex do, too (Martin, Eisenbud, & Rose, 1995).

This selective viewing of the world explains a great deal about children's learning of gender roles, but as we'll see in the next section, there is one final important element that needs to be considered.

## Biological Influences

Most child-development researchers agree that biology contributes to gender roles and gender identity. Evolutionary developmental psychology, for example, reminds us that men and women performed vastly different roles for much of human history: Women were more invested in child rearing and men were more invested in providing important resources (e.g., food, protection) for their offspring (Geary, 2002). In adapting to these roles, different traits and behaviors evolved for men and women. For example, men became more aggressive because that was adaptive in helping them ward off predators.

> According to evolutionary developmental psychology, different traits and behaviors have evolved in men and women.

Another way to consider biological influences on gender is in terms of sex hormones such as androgen and estrogen. In Module 14.2, we saw that hormones are a factor in gender differences in aggression but that research has produced inconsistent findings concerning the impact of hormones on spatial ability and depression. What about the impact of hormones on gender-stereotyped play? **Some fascinating insights come from studies of children with congenital adrenal hyperplasia (CAH), a genetic disorder in which, beginning in prenatal development, the adrenal glands secrete large amounts of androgen.** The extra androgen doesn't affect a baby boy's physical development; but in baby girls it can enlarge the clitoris so that it resembles a penis. Girls affected by CAH have surgery during infancy to correct their physical appearance and they receive hormone therapy to correct the imbalance of androgen. Nevertheless, during childhood and adolescence, girls with CAH prefer masculine activities (such as playing with cars instead of dolls) and male playmates to a much greater extent than girls not exposed to these amounts of androgen (Berenbaum & Snyder, 1995; Collaer & Hines, 1995). And these effects are largest for girls who have the greatest exposure to androgen during prenatal development (Berenbaum, Duck, & Bryk, 2000). Apparently the androgen not only masculinizes the genitals in baby girls, but also affects the prenatal development of brain regions critical for masculine and feminine gender-role behavior.

Perhaps the most accurate conclusion to draw is that biology, the socializing influence of people and media, and the child's own efforts to understand gender-typical behavior all contribute to gender roles and differences. Recognizing the interactive nature of these influences on gender learning also enables us to better understand how gender roles are changing today, which is the focus of the next module.

## CHECK YOUR LEARNING

**1.** Parents treat sons and daughters similarly except when it comes to _____.

**2.** When children engage in cross-gender play, their peers _____.

**3.** Same-sex play is common because most girls don't enjoy boys' rough-and-tumble play and because _____.

**4.** When it comes to gender stereotypes, children who watch TV more often _____.

**5.** In Kohlberg's theory, during the preschool years, children master _____; that is, they understand that boys become men and girls become women.

**6.** According to cognitive theories, children want to learn about gender-typical activities only after _____.

**7.** Some girls exposed to large amounts of male hormones during prenatal development _____.

**ACTIVE CHILDREN:**
The popular view is that children learn gender roles from adults (and society at large). But children are active participants in gender-role learning. Describe how children influence learning of gender roles.

**Answers:** (1) gender-related behavior, (2) criticize, tease, or punish them, (3) girls find that their enabling style of interaction is ineffective with boys, (4) have more stereotyped views of gender than children who watch TV less often, (5) gender stability, (6) they have learned that gender is constant, (7) prefer masculine activities and male playmates

# Gender Roles in Transition

# 14.4

## LEARNING OBJECTIVES

Emerging Gender Roles —

Beyond Traditional Gender Roles —

● What is androgyny, and how is it related to traditional conceptions of masculinity and femininity?

● Can parents rear gender-neutral children?

*Meda and Perry want their 6-year-old daughter, Hope, to pick activities, friends, and ultimately a career based on her interests and abilities, rather than on her gender. They have done their best to encourage gender-neutral values and behavior. Both are therefore astonished that Hope seems to be totally indistinguishable from other 6-year-olds reared by conventional parents. Hope's close friends are all girls. When Hope is with her friends, they play house or play with dolls. What seems to be going wrong with Meda and Perry's plans for a gender-neutral girl?*

Gender roles are not etched in stone; they change with the times. In the United States, the range of acceptable roles for girls and boys and women and men has never been greater than today. For example, fathers like the man in the photo stay home to be the primary caregivers for children, and some women work full time as sole support for the family. What is the impact of these changes on children? In this module, we'll answer this question by looking at new gender roles and at efforts by parents like Meda and Perry to rear gender-neutral children.

## Emerging Gender Roles

Traditionally, masculinity and femininity were seen as ends of a continuum: Children possessing many traits associated with males were considered highly masculine, and youngsters possessing many traits associated with females were considered highly feminine. A newer view of gender roles is based on the independent dimensions of instrumentality and expressiveness that were described in Module 14.1 (Bem, 1984). In this view, traditional males are rated high on instrumentality but low on expressiveness, whereas traditional females are low on instrumentality but high on expressiveness. In other words, this approach recognizes that other combinations of traits are possible. **Androgynous persons are rated high on both the instrumental and expressive dimensions.** (The term *androgyny* originated from the Greek words for male, *andro*, and female, *gyn*.) That is, androgynous individuals combine many of the traits listed in the table on page 402:

They can be both independent and emotional, self-confident and considerate, ambitious and creative.

Many theorists (e.g., Bem, 1984) argue that the ability to react with both instrumental and expressive behaviors is psychologically healthier than reacting primarily with one or the other. In fact, androgynous children often have higher self-esteem than children whose gender roles are highly stereotyped (Markstrom-Adams, 1989). But the benefits of androgyny are greater for girls than for boys. Androgynous girls have higher self-esteem than expressive girls and are more likely to express their thoughts and feelings publicly (Harter et al., 1998). For example, a girl like the one in the photo, who is independent and ambitious as well as considerate and creative, is more likely to feel positive about herself than a girl who embodies only the expressive traits traditionally associated with females. However, highly instrumental boys have nearly as high self-esteem as androgynous boys (Lau, 1989).

Evidently, a balance of expressiveness and instrumentality may be especially adaptive across life's many tasks. Being independent and confident has benefits at home and work, but so does being kind and considerate. Teaching children to adopt nontraditional views of gender is no simple task, however, as we'll see in the next section.

## Beyond Traditional Gender Roles

Many researchers (e.g., Bem, 1989; Eagly, 1995) believe gender is overemphasized to children. They argue that adults often group children by gender unnecessarily. Examples include a minister who rewards perfect church attendance with blue pencils for boys and pink pencils for girls or an elementary-school teacher who has boys and girls form separate lines for lunch. In both cases, children's gender is irrelevant, yet distinguishing boys and girls makes gender seem important and increases children's gender stereotypes (Bigler, 1995).

Many developmentalists believe that gender should be linked strictly to reproductive function instead of, as now, to traits, behaviors, and abilities. Is this possible? Children can certainly learn less stereotyped views of gender, at least in the short run. In one study (Bigler & Liben, 1990), some 6- to 11-year-olds were taught how to decide if a person can perform a particular job or occupation. They were told that the person's sex was not relevant; instead, they should decide if the person would like to do at least some of the activities that are part of the job and if the person has some of the skills necessary for the job. For example, to be a construction worker, a person should like to build things and should know how to drive heavy machinery.

When tested later on their attitudes toward household activities and occupations, these children had significantly fewer stereotyped responses than children who had not been taught to think of occupations in terms of interests and skills. That is, children who have this type of training are more likely to think it perfectly natural for women to be construction workers or men to be nurses.

Short-term interventions like the one just described show that more balanced attitudes and behaviors are possible (Gash & Morgan, 1993). But accomplishing change over the long term in a natural setting may be more complicated, based on some results of the Family Lifestyles Project (Weisner & Wilson-Mitchell, 1990). This research examined families in which the parents were members of the 1960s and 1970s counterculture and deeply committed to rearing their children without traditional gender stereotypes. In these families, men and women shared the household, financial, and child-care tasks.

> Children can be taught to have fewer gender stereotypes, but changing children's style of play and their playmates is difficult.

The Family Lifestyle Project indicates that parents like Meda and Perry in the opening vignette can influence some aspects of gender stereotyping more readily than others. The children studied in the Family Lifestyles Project had few stereotypes about occupations: They agreed that girls could be president of the United States and drive trucks and that boys could be nurses and secretaries. They also had fewer stereotyped attitudes about the use of objects: Boys and girls were equally likely to use an iron, a shovel, hammer and nails, and needle and thread. Nevertheless, children in these families tended to have same-sex friends, and they liked gender-stereotyped activities: The boys enjoyed physical play and the girls enjoyed drawing and reading.

It should not surprise you that some features of gender roles and identities are influenced more readily by experience than others. For 250,000 years, Homo sapiens have existed in small groups of families, hunting animals and gathering vegetation. Because women have borne the children and cared for them, it has been adaptive for women to be caring and nurturing. As we saw in Module 11.3, a nurturing caregiver increases the odds of a secure attachment and, ultimately, the survival of the infant. Men's responsibilities included hunting and protecting the family unit from predators, roles for which physical strength and aggressiveness were crucial.

Circumstances of life at the beginning of the 21st century are, of course, substantially different: Often, both men and women are employed outside the home and both men and women care for children. Nevertheless, the cultural changes of the past few decades cannot erase hundreds of thousands of years of evolutionary history (Geary, 2002). We should not be surprised that boys and girls play differently, that girls tend to be more supportive in their interactions with others, and that boys are usually more aggressive physically.

The "Improving Children's Lives" feature suggests ways children can be helped to go beyond traditional gender roles and learn the best from both roles.

## IMPROVING CHILDREN'S LIVES

### Encouraging Valuable Traits, Not Gender Traits

Parents and other adults can encourage children to learn the best from both of the traditional gender roles. Being independent, confident, caring, and considerate are valuable traits for all people, not just for boys or girls. Here are some guidelines to help achieve these aims:

- Since children learn gender roles from those around them, parents should be sure that they themselves are not gender-bound. Mothers and fathers can mow lawns, make repairs, and work outside the home. Mothers and fathers can prepare meals, do laundry, and care for the young. This *does* make a difference: I've always done most of the laundry in our house, and my daughter, at 5, was astonished when I told her that in most homes mothers do the wash.

- Parents should not base decisions about children's toys, activities, and chores on the child's sex. They should decide if a toy, activity, or chore is appropriate for the child as an individual (based on age, abilities, and interests), rather than because the child is a boy or girl.

- Forces outside the home, such as media and teachers, often work against parents who want their children to go beyond traditional gender roles. It's neither feasible nor wise to shelter children from these influences, but parents can encourage them to think critically about others' gender-based decisions. When band teachers insist that boys play trumpets and trombones while girls play clarinets and flutes, parents should ask children whether this makes sense. When a TV program shows a man coming to aid the stereotypic damsel in distress, parents should ask the child why the woman simply didn't get herself out of her predicament.

By following these guidelines, adults can help children to develop all their talents, not just those that fit traditional views associated with males and females.

### CHECK YOUR LEARNING

1. Androgynous children tend to have higher self-esteem than children with highly stereotyped gender roles, but this difference is found primarily among _____.

2. When children learn that skills and interests are the most important factors in determining whether a person can perform a job, their gender stereotypes of occupations _____.

3. In the Family Lifestyles Project, parents' efforts to rear gender-neutral children have been most successful when it comes to _____.

**NATURE AND NURTURE**
What do the findings from the Family Lifestyles Project suggest about the role of nature and nurture in gender differences and gender roles?

**Answers:** (1) girls, (2) become smaller, (3) children's views of occupations and objects

# Unifying Themes: Connections

Research on gender illustrates the theme that *development in different domains is connected*. Think about how children learn gender roles. According to conventional wisdom, children acquire masculine or feminine traits and behaviors through socialization by parents and other knowledgeable persons in the child's culture. This process is important, but we saw that learning gender roles is not simply a social phenomenon: Cognitive processes are essential. Kohlberg's theory shows that children don't really begin to learn about gender until they understand that they will remain a boy or girl for life. Once they understand gender constancy, gender-schema theory shows how children use this information to decide which experiences are relevant to them. Biology apparently contributes, too, although we still don't really understand how. Biology, cognition, and social forces all shape the unique gender role that individual boys or girls play.

## See for Yourself

To see that older children know more about gender stereotypes and understand that stereotypes are not binding, you'll need to create some simple stories that illustrate stereotyped traits. You could create stories for any of the traits listed in the table on page 402, but I suggest that you use "independent," "confident," "appreciative," and "gentle." Each story should include two to three sentences that describe a child. Be sure that your stories contain no other clues that would hint that the child in the story is a boy or a girl. For example, this story illustrates "independent":

*I know a child who likes to do things without help from adults. This child likes to do homework without help and enjoys traveling alone to visit cousins who live in another city.*

Read your stories to some 11- and 12-year-olds. After you've read each story, ask, "Is this child a boy, a girl, or could it be either?" Record the reply, and then ask, "Would most people think that the child is a boy or would most think that the child is a girl?"

In the first question, you're measuring children's understanding that gender stereotypes are flexible. You should find that children answer with "either one" about half of the time, indicating that they believe in some, but not total, flexibility in gender stereotypes. In the second question, you're measuring children's awareness of gender stereotypes. You should find that most children always answer the second question stereotypically: that people would identify the independent and confident children as boys and the appreciative and gentle children as girls. See for yourself!

## Resources

For more information about...

gender stereotypes and gender differences, try Carol Tavris's *The Mismeasure of Women* (Simon and Schuster, 1992), in which the author argues that women are constantly being measured according to standards developed for men.

ways to encourage girls and young women to pursue interests in science, math, and technology, visit the Web site of the Advocates for Women in Science, Engineering, and Mathematics:
**http://www.awsem.com**

## Key Terms

androgens 409

androgynous 422

congenital adrenal hyperplasia (CAH) 420

constricting 417

enabling 417

expressive traits 400

gender consistency 418

gender constancy 418

gender identity 398

gender labeling 418

gender role 398

gender-schema theory 419

gender stability 418

gender stereotypes 400

instrumental traits 400

mental rotation 406

social role 398

# SUMMARY

# 14.1 Gender Stereotypes

### How Do We View Men and Women?
Instrumental traits describe individuals who are acting on the world and are usually associated with males. Expressive traits describe individuals who value interpersonal relationships and are usually associated with females.

### Learning Gender Stereotypes
By age 5, children have begun to learn some of the traits typically associated with males and females; by 11 years, children's knowledge of these traits is very similar to adults' knowledge. Older children also understand that stereotypes are not necessarily binding.

# 14.2 Differences Related to Gender
In *The Psychology of Sex Differences*, published in 1974, Eleanor Maccoby and Carol Jacklin concluded that males and females differed in only four areas—verbal ability, spatial ability, math achievement, and aggression. Subsequent investigators have used their work as the starting point for analyzing gender differences.

### Differences in Physical Development and Behavior
Boys tend to be bigger, stronger, and more active than girls, who tend to have better fine-motor coordination and to be healthier.

### Differences in Intellectual Abilities and Achievement
Girls excel in verbal skills whereas boys excel in spatial ability. Girls get better grades in math; boys get better scores on math achievement tests. This difference in math skill has remained the same over the past few decades. Differences in intellectual abilities reflect both hereditary and environmental factors.

### Differences in Personality and Social Behavior
Boys are more aggressive physically than girls, and biology probably contributes heavily to this difference. Girls usually express their aggression by trying to damage other children's relations with peers.

Girls are more sensitive to others' feelings and are more influenced by others; both differences are probably due to experience. Adolescent girls are more prone to depression.

### Frank Talk About Gender Differences
Most gender differences are fairly small, which means that abilities for boys and girls overlap considerably. Also, despite the emphasis on gender differences, boys and girls are quite similar in many aspects of cognition, personality, and social behavior.

# 14.3 Gender Identity

### The Socializing Influences of People and the Media
Parents treat sons and daughters similarly, except in gender-related behavior. Fathers may be particularly important in teaching about gender because they are more likely to treat sons and daughters differently. Teachers foster gender-role learning by making gender salient.

By the preschool years, peers discourage cross-gender play by ridiculing peers who do it. Peers also influence gender roles because children play almost exclusively with same-sex peers.

Television depicts men and women in stereotyped fashion, and children who watch a lot of television are likely to have very stereotyped views of men and women.

### Cognitive Theories of Gender Identity
According to Kohlberg's theory, children gradually learn that gender is constant over time and cannot be changed according to personal wishes. After children understand gender constancy, they begin to learn gender-typical behavior. According to gender-schema theory, children learn about gender by paying attention to behaviors of members of their own sex and ignoring behaviors of members of the other sex.

### Biological Influences
The idea that biology influences some aspects of gender roles is supported by research on females exposed to male hormones during prenatal development.

# 14.4 Gender Roles in Transition

### Emerging Gender Roles
Androgynous persons embody both instrumental and expressive traits. Androgynous girls have higher self-esteem than traditional girls and are more likely to express themselves publicly; androgynous boys have about the same level of self-esteem as traditional boys.

### Beyond Traditional Gender Roles
Training studies show that children can learn less-stereotyped views of gender, but studies of parents trying to rear gender-neutral children suggest that many stereotyped behaviors are resistant to change.

# 15

*Family.* The term is as sacred to most Americans as baseball, apple pie, and Chevrolet. But what comes to mind when you think of family? Television gives us one answer—from *Leave It to Beaver* to *Family Ties* to *Everybody Loves Raymond*, the American family is portrayed as a mother, father, and their children. In reality, of course, American families are as diverse as the people in them. Some families consist of a single parent and an only child. Others include two parents, many children, and grandparents or other relatives.

All these family configurations, however, have a common goal: nurturing children and helping them become full-fledged adult members of their culture. To learn how families achieve these goals, we'll begin, in Module 15.1, by looking at relationships between parents and children. Next, in Module 15.2, we'll look at relationships between siblings. Then, in Module 15.3, we'll consider how children are influenced by divorce and remarriage. Finally, in Module 15.4, we'll examine the forces that can cause parents to abuse their children.

# Family Relationships

# 15.1

# Parenting

## LEARNING OBJECTIVES

● What is a systems view of family dynamics?

● What are the primary dimensions of parenting?

● What parental behaviors affect children's development?

● How do children help determine how parents rear them?

● What role do culture and family configuration play in children's development?

*Tanya and Sheila, both sixth graders, wanted to go to an Avril Lavigne concert with two boys from their school. When Tanya asked if she could go, her mom said, "No way!" Tanya responded defiantly, "Why not?" In return, her mother exploded, "Because I say so. That's why. Stop pestering me." Sheila wasn't allowed to go either. When she asked why, her mom said, "I just think you're still too young to be dating. I don't mind your going to the concert. If you want to go just with Tanya, that would be fine. What do you think of that?"*

The vignette illustrates what we all know well from personal experience—parents go about child rearing in many different ways. In this module, you'll learn about different approaches that parents take to raising children. But let's begin by thinking about parents as an important element in the family system.

## The Family as a System

Families are rare in the animal kingdom. Only human beings and a handful of other species form family-like units. Why? Compared to the young in other species, children develop slowly. And because children are immature—unable to care for themselves—for many years, the family structure evolved as a way to protect and nurture young children during their development (Bjorklund, Yunger, & Pellegrini, 2002).

As we think about original and modern families, it's tempting to believe that parents' actions are all that really matter. That is, through their behavior, parents directly and indirectly determine their children's development. This view of parents as "all powerful" was part of early psychological theories (e.g., Watson, 1925) and is held even today by some first-time parents. But most theorists now view families from an ecological perspective (described in Module 1.2). That is, families form a system of interacting elements—parents and children influence one another (Parke & Buriel, 1998).

When viewed as part of an interactive system, parents still influence their children, both directly—for example, by encouraging them to study hard—and indirectly—for example, by being generous and kind to others. However, the influence is no longer exclusively from parent to children but is mutual: Children influence their parents, too. By their behaviors, attitudes, and interests, children affect how their parents behave toward them. When, for example, children resist discipline, parents may become less willing to reason and more inclined to use force.

Even more subtle influences become apparent when families are viewed as systems of interacting elements. For example, fathers' behaviors can affect mother–child relationships. A demanding husband may leave his wife with little time, energy, or interest in helping her daughter with her homework. Or, when siblings argue constantly, parents may become preoccupied with avoiding problems rather than encouraging their children's development.

These many examples show that narrowly focusing on parents' impact on children misses the complexities of family life. But there is even more to the systems view. The family itself is embedded in other social systems, such as neighborhoods and religious institutions (Parke & Buriel, 1998). These other institutions can affect family dynamics. Sometimes they simplify child rearing, as when neighbors are trusted friends and can help care for each other's children. Sometimes, however, they complicate child rearing. Grandparents who live nearby can create friction within the family. At times, the impact of the larger systems is indirect, as when work schedules cause a parent to be away from home or when schools must eliminate programs that benefit children.

The diagram summarizes the numerous interactive influences that exist in a systems view of families. In the remainder of this module, we'll describe parents' influences on children and then how children affect their parents' behavior. Finally, we'll consider how parent–child influences vary with culture and family configuration.

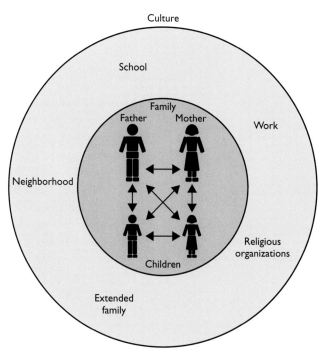

FIG. 15–1

## Dimensions and Styles

Parenting can be described in terms of general dimensions that are like personality traits in that they represent stable aspects of parental behavior—aspects that hold across different situations (Holden & Miller, 1999). Research consistently reveals two general dimensions of parental behavior. One is the degree of warmth and responsiveness that parents show their children. Another is the amount of control parents exert over their children.

WARMTH AND RESPONSIVENESS.    At one end of the spectrum are parents who are openly warm and affectionate with their children. They are involved with them, respond to their emotional needs, and spend considerable time with them. At the other end of the spectrum are parents who are relatively uninvolved with their children and sometimes even hostile toward them. These parents often seem more focused on their own needs and interests than those of their children's. Warm parents enjoy hearing their children describe the day's activities; uninvolved or hostile parents aren't interested, considering it a waste of their time. Warm parents see when their children are upset and try to comfort them; uninvolved or hostile parents pay little attention to their children's emotional states and invest little effort comforting them when they're upset.

> Children benefit from warm, responsive parenting.

As you might expect, children benefit from warm and responsive parenting (Pettit, Bates, & Dodge, 1997; Zhou et al., 2002). When parents are warm toward them, children typically feel secure and happy, and they're better behaved. In contrast, when parents are uninvolved or hostile, their children are often anxious and less controlled. And, as we saw in Module 12.2, children often have low self-esteem when their parents are uninvolved (Rothbaum & Weisz, 1994).

PARENTAL CONTROL. A second general dimension of parental behavior involves control, which refers to parents' efforts to supervise and monitor their children's behavior. Parents who are behaviorally controlling set reasonable standards for their children; they also usually know where their children are, what they're doing, and with whom. Such control is usually good for children. When parents have reasonable expectations for their children and keep tabs on their activity—for example, a mother knows that her 12-year-old is staying after school for choir practice, then going to the library—their children tend to be better adjusted (Kilgore, Snyder, & Lentz, 2000).

Part of the key to effective control is setting standards that are appropriate for the child's age, then showing the child how to meet them, and, finally, rewarding the child for complying (Powers & Roberts, 1995; Rotto & Kratochwill, 1994). Suppose a mother wants her preschooler to fold and put away her socks. This is a reasonable request because the child is physically capable of this simple task and she knows where the socks should be stored. Like the mother in the photo, she should show her daughter how to complete the task, and then praise her when she does.

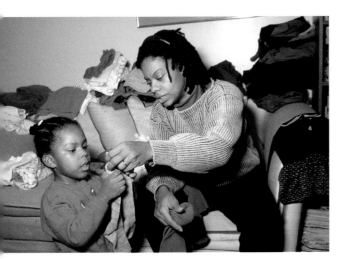

Once standards are set, they should be enforced consistently. Time and time again, research has shown that children and adolescents are more compliant when parents enforce rules regularly. For example, the mother should insist that her daughter always fold and put away her socks, not just occasionally. When parents enforce rules erratically, children come to see rules as optional instead of obligatory, and they try to avoid complying with them (Conger, Patterson, & Ge, 1995). And, in the long run, inconsistent discipline is associated with the onset of psychological problems in children (Hill, Bush, & Roosa, 2003).

Effective control is also based on good communication. Parents should explain why they've set standards and why they reward or punish as they do. If a mother wants her son to clean his room, she should explain that a messy room is unsafe, makes it difficult to find toys that he wants, and makes it difficult for her to clean. Parents can also encourage children to ask questions if they don't understand or disagree with standards. If the son feels that his mother's standards for orderliness are so high that it's impossible to play in his room, he should feel free to raise the issue with his mother without fear of making her angry.

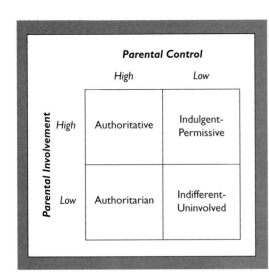

| | Parental Control | |
|---|---|---|
| | **High** | **Low** |
| **Parental Involvement** **High** | Authoritative | Indulgent-Permissive |
| **Low** | Authoritarian | Indifferent-Uninvolved |

FIG. 15–2

PARENTING STYLES. Combining the dimensions of warmth and control produces four prototypic styles of parenting, as shown in the diagram (Baumrind, 1975, 1991).

- **Authoritarian parenting combines high control with little warmth.** These parents lay down the rules and expect them to be followed without discussion. Hard work, respect, and obedience are what authoritarian parents wish to cultivate in their children. There is little give-and-take between parent and child because authoritarian parents do not consider children's needs or wishes. This style is illustrated by Tanya's mother in the opening vignette, who feels no obligation whatsoever to explain her decisions.

- **Authoritative parenting combines a fair degree of parental control with being warm and responsive to children.** Authoritative parents explain rules and encourage discussion. This style is exemplified by Sheila's mother in the opening vignette. She explained why she did not want Sheila going to the concert and encouraged her daughter to discuss the issue with her.

- **Indulgent-permissive parenting offers warmth and caring but little parental control.** These parents generally accept their children's behavior and punish them infrequently. An indulgent-permissive parent would readily agree to Tanya or Sheila's request to go to the concert, simply because it is something the child wants to do.

- **Indifferent-uninvolved parenting provides neither warmth nor control.** Indifferent-uninvolved parents provide for their children's basic physical and emotional needs but little else. These parents try to minimize the amount of time spent with their children and avoid becoming emotionally involved with them. If Tanya or Sheila had parents with this style, she might have simply gone to the concert without asking, knowing that her parents wouldn't care and would rather not be bothered.

> Authoritative parenting fosters achievement in school, self-reliance, and good conduct.

Parenting style is fairly stable over time. Parents who are authoritative with their school-age children tend to be authoritative when their children are adolescents (McNally, Eisenberg, & Harris, 1991). Given this stability, you shouldn't be surprised to learn that parenting style influences children's development (Baumrind, 1991; Maccoby & Martin, 1983):

- Children with authoritarian parents typically have lower grades in school, lower self-esteem, and are less skilled socially.
- Children with authoritative parents tend to have higher grades and be responsible, self-reliant, and friendly.
- Children with indulgent-permissive parents have lower grades and are often impulsive and easily frustrated.
- Children with indifferent-uninvolved parents have low self-esteem and are impulsive, aggressive, and moody.

Thus, most children seem to benefit from authoritative parenting. These benefits are not restricted to European American children. They apply as well to children and parents from several different ethnic groups in the United States, including people of African, Asian, and Hispanic descent (Brody & Flor, 1998; Steinberg et al., 1992). However, some researchers find that authoritarian parenting can benefit children growing up in poverty (Furstenberg, 1993). Why? When youngsters grow up in neighborhoods with a lot of violence and crime, strict obedience to parents can protect children (Kelley, Power, & Wimbush, 1992).

To sum up, a parental style that combines control, warmth, and affection is usually best for children. However, other factors, such as a dangerous neighborhood, may make an authoritarian parenting style more appropriate for some children.

As important as these different dimensions and styles are for understanding parenting, there is more to effective child rearing, as we'll see in the next section.

## Parental Behavior

Dimensions and styles are general characterizations of how parents typically behave. If, for example, I describe a parent as warm or controlling, you immediately have a sense of that parent's usual style in dealing with his or her children. Nevertheless, the price for such a broad description is that it tells us little about how parents behave in specific situations and how these parental behaviors influence children's development. Put another way, what specific behaviors can parents use to influence their children? Researchers who study parents name three: direct instruction, modeling, and feedback.

DIRECT INSTRUCTION.   Parents often tell their children what to do. But simply playing the role of drill sergeant in ordering children around—"Clean your room!" "Turn off the TV!"—is not very effective. **A better approach is direct instruction, telling a child what to do, when, and why.** Instead of just shouting "Share your candy with your brother!" a parent should explain when and why it's important to share with a sibling.

In addition, just as coaches help athletes master sports skills, parents can help their youngsters master social and emotional skills. Parents can explain links between emotions and behavior—"Catlin is sad because you broke her crayon" (Gottman, Katz, & Hooven, 1996). They can also teach how to deal with difficult social situations—"When you ask Lindsey if she can sleep over, do it privately so you won't hurt Kaycee's or Hannah's feelings" (Mize & Pettit, 1997). In general, children who get this sort of parental "coaching" tend to be more socially skilled and, not surprisingly, get along better with their peers. (I'll have more to say about this in Module 16.1.)

Direct instruction and coaching are particularly powerful when paired with modeling. Urging children to act in a particular way, such as sharing with others, is more compelling when children also see others sharing. In the next section, we'll see how children learn by observing others.

LEARNING BY OBSERVING.   Children learn a great deal from parents simply by watching them. For example, in Module 13.4 we saw that youngsters often learn how to interact with others by watching how their parents interact. The parents' modeling and the youngsters' observational learning thus lead to imitation, so children's behavior resembles the behavior they observe. **Observational learning can also produce counterimitation, learning what should not be done.** If an older brother like the one in the photo has been mean to a classmate and the father punishes him, the younger sister may learn to be friendly instead of mean.

FEEDBACK.   By giving feedback to their children, parents indicate whether a behavior is appropriate and should continue or is inappropriate and should stop. Feedback comes in two general forms. **Reinforcement is any action that increases the likelihood of the response that it follows.** Parents may use praise to reinforce a child's studying or give a reward for completing household chores. **Punishment is any action that discourages the reoccurrence of the response that it follows.** Parents may forbid children to watch television when they get poor grades in school or make children go to bed early for neglecting household chores.

Of course, parents have been rewarding and punishing their children for centuries, so what do psychologists know that parents don't know already? In fact, researchers have made some surprising discoveries concerning the nature of reward and punishment. **Parents often unwittingly reinforce the very behaviors they want to discourage, a situation called the negative reinforcement**

**trap** (Patterson, 1980). The negative reinforcement trap occurs in three steps, most often between a mother and her son. In the first step, the mother tells her son to do something he doesn't want to do. She might tell him to clean up his room, to come inside while he's outdoors playing with friends, or to study instead of watching television. In the next step, the son responds with some behavior that most parents find intolerable: He argues, complains, or whines—not just briefly, but for an extended period. In the last step, the mother gives in—saying that the son needn't do as she told him initially—simply to get the son to stop the behavior that is so intolerable.

Parents can influence children through direct instruction, by acting as models, and by providing feedback.

The feedback to the son is that arguing (or complaining or whining) works; the mother rewards that behavior by withdrawing the request that the son did not like. That is, although we usually think a behavior is strengthened when it is followed by the presentation of something that is valued, behavior is also strengthened when it is followed by removing something that is disliked.

As for punishment, research (Parke, 1977) shows that punishment works best when

- administered directly after the undesired behavior occurs, rather than hours later,
- an undesired behavior always leads to punishment, rather than usually or occasionally,
- accompanied by an explanation of why the child was punished and how punishment can be avoided in the future, and
- the child has a warm, affectionate relationship with the person administering the punishment.

At the same time, research reveals some serious drawbacks to punishment. One is that punishment is primarily suppressive: Punished responses are stopped, but only temporarily if children do not learn new behaviors to replace those that were punished. For example, denying TV to brothers who are fighting stops the undesirable behavior, but fighting is likely to recur unless the boys learn new ways of solving their disputes.

A second drawback is that punishment can have undesirable side effects. Children become upset as they are being punished, which makes it unlikely that they will understand the feedback that punishment is meant to convey. A child denied TV for misbehaving may become angry over the punishment itself and ignore why he's being punished. What's more, as we saw in Module 13.4, when children are punished physically, they often imitate this behavior with peers and younger siblings (Whitehurst & Vasta, 1977). Children who are spanked often use aggression to resolve their disputes with others, and are more likely to have behavioral problems (Bradley et al., 2001).

One method combines the best features of punishment while avoiding its shortcomings. **In time-out, a child who misbehaves must briefly sit alone in a quiet, unstimulating location.** Some parents have children sit alone in a bathroom; others have children sit alone in a room, as shown in the photo. Time-out is punishing because it interrupts the child's ongoing activity and isolates the child from other family members, toys, books, and, generally, all forms of rewarding stimulation.

The period is sufficiently brief—usually just a few minutes—for a parent to use the method consistently. During time-out, both parent and child typically calm down. Then, when time-out is over, a parent can talk with the child and explain why the punished behavior is objectionable and what the child should do instead. "Reasoning" like this—even with preschool children—is effective because it emphasizes why a parent punished initially and how punishment can be avoided in the future.

Thus, parents can influence children by direct instruction, by modeling behavior that they value and not modeling what they don't want their children to learn, by giving feedback, and through the parenting styles that we examined in the first section of this module. In the next section, we'll switch perspectives and see how children affect their parents' behavior.

## Children's Contributions

I emphasized earlier that the family is a dynamic, interactive system with parents and children influencing each other. In fact, children begin at birth to influence the way their parents treat them.

One way to see the influence of children on parents is by looking at how parenting changes as children grow. The same parenting that is marvelously effective with infants and toddlers is inappropriate for adolescents. Let's look again at the two basic dimensions of parental behavior—warmth and control. Warmth is beneficial throughout development—toddlers and teens alike enjoy knowing that others care about them. But the manifestation of parental affection changes, becoming more reserved as children develop. The enthusiastic hugging and kissing that delights toddlers embarrasses adolescents.

Parental control also changes gradually as children develop (Maccoby, 1984). As children develop cognitively and are better able to make their own decisions, parents gradually relinquish control and expect children to be responsible for themselves. For instance, parents of elementary-school children often keep track of their children's progress on school assignments, but parents of adolescents don't, expecting their children to do this themselves.

Parents not only change their expressions of warmth and control as children develop, they also behave differently depending on a child's specific behavior (Kochanska, 1993). To illustrate the reciprocal influence of parents and children, imagine two children with different temperaments as they respond to a parent's authoritative style. The first child has an "easy" temperament and readily complies with parental requests and responds well to family discussions about parental expectations. These parent–child relations are a textbook example of successful authoritative parenting. But suppose, like the child in the photo, the second child has a "difficult temperament" and complies reluctantly and sometimes not at all. Over time, the parent becomes more controlling and less affectionate. The child in turn complies even less in the future, leading the parent to adopt an authoritarian parenting style (Bates et al., 1998).

As this example illustrates, parenting behaviors and styles often evolve as a consequence of the child's behavior. With a moderately active young child who is eager to please adults, a parent may discover that a modest amount of control is adequate. But for a very active child who is not as eager to please, a parent may need to be more controlling and directive (Dumas, LaFreniere, & Serketich, 1995; Hastings & Rubin, 1999). Influence is reciprocal: Children's behavior helps determine how parents treat them and the resulting parental behavior influences children's behavior, which in turn causes parents to again change their behavior (Stoolmiller, 2001).

A study by Kim and colleagues (2001) shows reciprocal influence in action in adolescence. Once a year these investigators videotaped parents and their adolescents as they discussed current family conflicts dealing with issues such as household chores, homework, and transportation. When parents were angry and hostile during the discussions, their adolescent children became angry and hostile, too; in turn, their parents became more angry and more hostile. Thus a vicious circle was established in which parents and children each prompted the other to escalate the level of anger and hostility.

As time goes by, these reciprocal influences lead many families to adopt routine ways of interacting with each other. Some families end up functioning smoothly: Parents and children cooperate, anticipate each other's needs, and are generally happy. Unfortunately, other families end up troubled: Disagreements are common, parents spend much time trying unsuccessfully to control their defiant children, and everyone is often angry and upset (Belsky, Woodworth, & Crnic, 1996; Kochanska, 1997).

Over the long term, such troubled families do not fare well, so it's important that these negative reciprocal influences are nipped in the bud (Carrere & Gottman, 1999; Christensen & Heavey, 1999).

> Parents' behavior and styles often evolve over time as a consequence of their children's behavior.

## Cultural Influences and Family Configuration

The general aim of child rearing—helping children become contributing members of their cultures—is much the same worldwide (Whiting & Child, 1953). However, cultures have different ideas of the best ways to achieve this goal. And, within cultures, families do not always consist of a mother, father, and their children; different family configurations can affect family dynamics. We'll look at some of these variations in values and practices in this section.

**CULTURAL DIFFERENCES IN WARMTH AND CONTROL.**   Warmth and control are universal aspects of parents' behavior, but views about the "proper" amount of warmth and the "proper" amount of control vary with particular cultures. European Americans want their children to be happy and self-reliant individuals, and they believe these goals are best achieved when parents are warm and exert moderate control (Goodnow, 1992; Spence, 1985). In many Asian and Latin American countries, however, individualism is less important than cooperation and collaboration (Okagaki & Sternberg, 1993). In China, for example, Confucian principles dictate that parents are always right and that emotional restraint is the key to family harmony (Chao, 1994). In fact, consistent with their cultural values, mothers and fathers in China are more likely to emphasize parental control and less likely to express affection than are mothers and fathers in the United States (Lin & Fu, 1990). Thus, cultural values help specify appropriate ways for parents to interact with their offspring.

**THE ROLE OF GRANDPARENTS.**   With people living longer, three-generation families—with child, parents, and grandparents—are becoming the norm in many industrialized nations. Most American children see their grandparents at least once a month, more often if they live nearby. Grandmothers are usually more involved with grandchildren than grandfathers, and some scientists believe this is an evolutionary adaptation. In humans, the onset of menopause coincides, approximately, with the birth of grandchildren. Genetically speaking, middle-aged women may be more valuable caring for their grandchildren—making sure that they survive to bear further children—than in bearing additional children of their own (Smith & Drew, 2002).

What roles do grandparents play in children's lives? One classic analysis suggested five specific styles of grandparenting (Neugarten & Weinstein, 1964):

- **Formal grandparents express strong interest in the grandchild but maintain a hands-off attitude toward child rearing.**
- **Fun-seeking grandparents see themselves as a primary source of fun for their grandchildren but avoid interactions that are more serious.**
- **Distant grandparents have little contact with children, except as part of holidays or other family celebrations.**
- **Dispensing-family-wisdom grandparents provide information and advice to parents and child alike.**
- **Surrogate-parent grandparents assume many of the normal roles and responsibilities of a parent.**

Of these different styles, we know the most about the surrogate-parent style because it is particularly common in African American families. The "Cultural Influences" feature describes the important role of grandmothers in African American family life.

## CULTURAL INFLUENCES

### Grandmothers in African American Families

Approximately 1 in 8 African American children lives with a grandmother, compared to only 1 in 25 European American children (U.S. Bureau of the Census, 1994). Why is this? A quarter of all African American children grow up in chronic poverty, and living with relatives is one way of sharing—and thereby reducing— the costs associated with housing and child care.

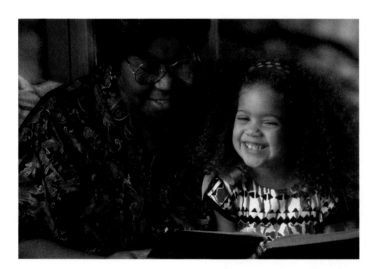

African American grandmothers who live with their daughters and their children frequently become involved in rearing their grandchildren, adopting the surrogate-parent style (Pearson et al., 1990). When the daughter is a teenage mother, the grandmother may be the child's primary caregiver, an arrangement that benefits both the adolescent mother and the child. Freed from the obligations of child rearing, the adolescent mother is able to improve her situation by, for example, finishing school. The child benefits because grandmothers are often more effective mothers than teenage mothers: Grandmothers are less punitive and, like the grandmother in the photo, are very responsive to their grandchildren (Chase-Lansdale, Brooks-Gunn, & Zamsky, 1994; Smith & Drew, 2002).

This family arrangement works well for children. In terms of achievement and adjustment, children living with their mothers and grandmothers resemble children living in two-parent families, and they tend to be better off than children in single-parent families (Wilson, 1989). Even when grandmothers are not living in the house, children benefit when their mothers receive social and emotional support from grandmothers and other relatives: Children are more self-reliant and less likely to become involved in delinquent activities such as drug use and vandalism (Taylor & Roberts, 1995).

Thus, grandmothers and other relatives can ease the burden of child rearing in African American families living in poverty, and, not surprisingly, children benefit from the added warmth, support, and guidance of an extended family.

By acting as surrogate parents, grandparents can affect their grandchildren's lives directly. However, grandparents also affect their grandchildren indirectly, through intergenerational transmission of parental attitudes and practices. For example, if parents are affectionate with their children, when these children become parents themselves, they will tend to be affectionate with their own children. In other words, the grandparents' affectionate behavior results in their grandchildren experiencing affectionate care. Thus, it is important to think about the indirect as well as the direct influences that grandparents have on their grandchildren (Smith & Drew, 2002).

**CHILDREN OF GAY AND LESBIAN PARENTS.**   More than a million youngsters in the United States have a gay or lesbian parent (Patterson, 2002). In most of these situations, children were born in a heterosexual marriage that ended in divorce when one parent revealed his or her homosexuality. Less frequent, but becoming more common, are children born to single lesbians or to lesbian couples.

Research on gay and lesbian parents and their children is scarce, and most has involved children who were born to a heterosexual marriage that ended in divorce when the mother came out as a lesbian. Most of these lesbian mothers are European American and well educated (Patterson, 2002).

As parents, gay and lesbian couples are more similar to heterosexual couples than different. There is no indication that gay and lesbian parents are less effective than heterosexual parents. In fact, some evidence suggests that gay men may be especially responsive to children's needs, perhaps because their self-concepts include emotional sensitivity that is traditionally associated with the female gender role (Bigner & Jacobsen, 1989).

> In most respects—include gender roles, self-concept and social skill—children of gay and lesbian parents resemble children of heterosexual parents.

Children reared by gay and lesbian parents seem to develop much like children reared by heterosexual couples (Patterson, 2002). Preschool boys and girls apparently identify with their own sex and acquire the usual accompaniment of gender-based preferences, interests, activities, and friends. As adolescents and young adults, the vast majority are heterosexual (Bailey et al., 1995). In other respects—such as self-concept, social skill, moral reasoning, and intelligence—children of lesbian mothers resemble children of heterosexual parents. For example, in one study of 80 families—55 headed by a lesbian and 25 headed by a heterosexual—the children were comparable in social competence and behavioral adjustment (Chan, Raboy, & Patterson, 1998).

Research on children reared by gay and lesbian couples, along with findings concerning African American grandmothers and warmth and control in Asian parents, remind us that "good parenting" takes on somewhat different meanings in different cultures. These research results also challenge the conventional wisdom that a two-parent family with mother and father both present necessarily provides the best circumstances for development. Multiple adults *are* important (a fact that will become even clearer in Module 15.3 on divorce), but *who* the adults are seems to matter less than what they do. Children benefit from good parenting skills, whether it's a mother and father or grandparents—or two women or two men—doing the parenting.

## CHECK YOUR LEARNING

**1.** According to the systems approach, the family consists of interacting elements who influence each other and the family itself is _____.

**2.** Children who have low self-esteem and are impulsive, aggressive, and moody often have parents with an _____ style of parenting.

**3.** In a _____, parents unwittingly reinforce undesirable behaviors.

**4.** Parental behaviors that influence children include direct instruction, modeling (learning through observation), and _____.

**5.** The effectiveness of punishment depends on timing, consistency, the presence of an accompanying explanation, and _____.

**6.** Compared to American parents, Chinese parents tend to be more controlling and less _____.

**7.** _____ grandparents are very interested in their grandchildren but avoid becoming involved in child rearing.

### ACTIVE CHILDREN

Most descriptions of parenting focus on the impact of parents on their children's development. Think about the alternative: How do children's actions and characteristics affect a parent's behavior?

**Answers:** (1) embedded in other social systems, such as neighborhoods, (2) indifferent-uninvolved, (3) negative reinforcement trap, (4) feedback (reward and punishment), (5) the child's relationship with the person who is punishing, (6) affectionate, (7) Formal

# 15.2    Brothers and Sisters

**Firstborn, Laterborn, and Only Children**

**Qualities of Sibling Relationships**

## LEARNING OBJECTIVES

● How do firstborn, laterborn, and only children differ?

● How do sibling relationships change as children grow? What determines how well siblings get along?

*Bob and Alice adored their 2-year-old son, Robbie, who was friendly, playful, and always eager to learn new things. In fact, Bob thought Robbie was nearly perfect and saw no reason to tempt fate by having another child. However, Alice had heard stories that only children were conceited, spoiled, and unfriendly. Alice was sure that Robbie would grow up like this unless she and Bob had another child. What to do?*

For most of a year, all firstborn children are only children like Robbie. Some children remain "onlies" forever, but most get brothers and sisters. Some firstborns are joined by many siblings in rapid succession; others are simply joined by a single brother or sister. As the family acquires these new members, parent–child relationships become more complex. Parents can no longer focus on a single child but must adjust to the needs of multiple children. Just as important, siblings influence each other's development, not just during childhood but, as the cartoon on page 441 reminds us, throughout life. To understand sibling influence, let's look at differences between firstborns, laterborns, and only children.

## Firstborn, Laterborn, and Only Children

Firstborn children are often "guinea pigs" for most parents, who have lots of enthusiasm but little practical experience rearing children. Parents typically have high expectations for their firstborns and are both more affectionate and more punitive with them. As more children arrive, parents become more adept at their roles, having learned "the tricks of the parent trade" with earlier children. With laterborn children, parents have more realistic expectations and are more relaxed in their discipline (e.g., Baskett, 1985).

The different approaches that parents take with their firstborns and laterborns help explain differences that are commonly observed between these children. Firstborn children generally have higher scores on intelligence tests and are more likely to go to college. They are also more willing to conform to parents' and adults' requests. Laterborn children, perhaps because they are less concerned about pleasing parents and adults but need to get along with older siblings, are more popular with their peers and more innovative (Eaton, Chipperfield, & Singbeil, 1989).

And what about only children? Alice, the mother in the opening vignette, was well acquainted with the conventional wisdom, which says that parents like the ones in the photo dote on "onlies," with the result that they are selfish and egotistical. Is the folklore correct? From a comprehensive analysis of more than 100 studies, the answer is "no." In fact, only children were found more likely to succeed in school than other children and to have higher levels of intelligence, leadership, autonomy, and maturity (Falbo & Polit, 1986).

This research has important implications for China, where only children are the norm due to government efforts to limit family size. The "Child Development and Family Policy" feature tells the story.

## CHILD DEVELOPMENT AND FAMILY POLICY

### Assessing the Consequences of China's One-Child Policy

With more than a billion citizens, the People's Republic of China has the largest population in the world. The Chinese make up roughly 20 percent of the world's population. For much of the 20th century, Chinese leaders recognized that a large, rapidly growing population was a serious obstacle to economic growth and an improved standard of living. Consequently, the Chinese government implemented several programs to limit family size and since 1979 has had a policy of one child per family. The policy was promoted with billboards like the one in the photo that advertised the benefits of having only one child. Parents were encouraged to use contraceptives and, more importantly, one-child families received many economic benefits: cash bonuses, better health and child care, and more-desirable housing.

The policy has been effective in reducing the birth rate in China; and now social scientists are evaluating the impact of the one-child policy on children and their families. For example, traditionally the Chinese have valued well-behaved children who get along well with others. Would the only children in today's China be less cooperative and more self-centered than previous generations of Chinese youngsters? The answer seems to be "no." Many studies have compared only and non-only children in China; most comparisons find no differences; when differences are found, the advantage often goes to the only child (Jiao, Ji, & Jing, 1996; Yang et al., 1995).

As Chinese only children enter adulthood, a new concern will be care of the elderly. Traditionally, children have been responsible for their aging parents. This task becomes more demanding—financially and psychologically—when it cannot be shared with other siblings. Research will be needed to determine whether older people receive adequate care and to determine the impact on only children of providing such care. Through this sort of research, psychologists and other social scientists will play an important role in helping to determine the long-term consequences of China's decision to limit family size.

**ADOPTED CHILDREN.**   The U.S. government doesn't keep official statistics on the number of adopted children, but the best estimate is that about 2 to 4 percent of U.S. children are adopted. The majority of adoptive parents are middle-class European Americans and, until the 1960s, so were adopted children. However, improved birth control and legalized abortion in the late 1960s meant that hardly any European American infants were relinquished for adoption. Consequently, beginning in the 1960s, parents began to adopt children of other races, as shown in the photo, and children from other countries. At the same time, parents began to adopt children with special needs, such as chronic medical problems or exposure to maltreatment (Brodzinsky & Pinderhughes, 2002; Gunnar, Bruce, & Grotevant, 2000).

As adoption became more common, the myth of the "adopted child syndrome" blossomed. According to this myth, adopted children are more prone to behavioral problems, substance use, and criminal activity, presumably because of the special challenges they face in establishing a unique identity, which we explored in Module 12.1 (Finley, 1999). Is there any truth to the myth? In fact, when compared to children living with biological parents, adopted children are quite similar in terms of temperament, mother–infant attachment, and cognitive development (Brodzinsky & Pinderhughes, 2002).

But some findings *are* consistent with the myth. Adopted children are more prone to problems adjusting to school and to conduct disorders, such as being overly aggressive (Miller et al., 2000). To a certain extent, this finding reflects the fact that adoptive parents are more likely to seek help for their adoptive children because they are more affluent and can afford it, and because they are used to dealing with agencies that provide mental health services. Also, the extent of these problems hinges on the age when the child was adopted and the quality of their care prior to adoption (Brodzinsky & Pinderhughes, 2002; Gunnar et al., 2000). Problems are much more common when children are adopted at an older age (and thus probably are separated from an attachment figure) and when their care before adoption was poor (e.g., they were institutionalized or lived in a series of foster homes).

> Adopted children are more prone to problems, typically due to poor quality of life before being adopted.

Perhaps the best way to summarize this research is that adoption *per se* is not a fundamental developmental challenge for most children. But quality of life before adoption certainly places some adopted children at risk. And it's important to remember that most adopted children fare quite well.

In discussing firstborn, laterborn, only, and adopted children, we have not yet considered relationships that exist between siblings. These can be powerful forces on development, as we'll see in the next section.

## Qualities of Sibling Relationships

From the very beginning, sibling relationships are complicated. On the one hand, most expectant parents are excited by the prospect of another child, and their enthusiasm is contagious: Their children, too, eagerly await the arrival of the newest family member. On the other hand, the birth of a sibling is often distressing for older children, who may become withdrawn or return to more childish behavior because of the changes that occur in their lives, particularly the need to share parental attention and affection (Gottlieb & Mendelson, 1990). However, distress can be avoided if parents remain responsive to their older children's needs (Howe & Ross, 1990). In fact, one of the benefits of a sibling's birth is that fathers become more involved with their older children (Stewart et al., 1987).

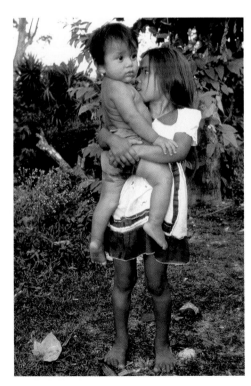

Many older siblings enjoy helping their parents take care of newborns. Older children play with the baby, console it, feed it, or change its diapers. In middle-class Western families, such caregiving often occurs in the context of play, with parents nearby. But in some cultures, children—particularly girls like the one in the photo—play an important role in providing care for their younger siblings (Zukow-Goldring, 2002).

As the infant grows, interactions between siblings become more frequent and more complicated. For example, toddlers tend to talk more to parents than to older siblings. But, by the time the younger sibling is 4 years old, the situation is reversed: Now young siblings talk more to older siblings than to their mother (Brown & Dunn, 1992). Older siblings become a source of care and comfort for younger siblings when they are distressed or upset (Garner, Jones, & Palmer, 1994). And older siblings serve as teachers for their younger siblings, teaching them to play games or how to cook simple foods (Maynard, 2002).

As time goes by, some siblings grow close, becoming best friends in ways that nonsiblings can never be. Other siblings constantly argue, compete, and simply do not get along with each other. The basic pattern of sibling interaction seems to be established early in development and remains fairly stable. Dunn, Slomkowski, and Beardsall (1994), for example, interviewed mothers twice about their children's interaction, first when the children were 3- and 5-year-olds and again 7 years later, when the children were 10- and 12-year-olds. Dunn and her colleagues found that siblings who got along as preschoolers often continued to get along as young adolescents, whereas siblings who quarreled as preschoolers often quarreled as young adolescents.

The "Real Children" feature presents two sibling relationships that, although very different in quality, reveal the stability that Dunn and her colleagues (1994) discovered.

## REAL CHILDREN

### A Tale of Two Sibling Relationships

 When Calvin, age 4, learned that his mother was going to have a baby, he cried uncontrollably and refused to talk to his mother for the rest of the day. After Hope was born, Calvin tried to ignore her, which was impossible because he wanted to be near his mother, and Hope, of course, was there, too. He couldn't see why his mother liked this new baby so much and seemed to have so little time for him. As Hope grew older, Calvin argued with her over just about everything and continued to compete with her for their parents' attention. When Hope entered adolescence and boyfriends entered the scene, Calvin teased her and hassled them. Over the years, Hope was too nice to give Calvin the treatment he deserved, but she was glad when he left for college and only came home for vacations.

In contrast, Hillary and Elizabeth were always close. Beginning in the preschool years, the two sisters played together constantly. When Elizabeth was upset, Hillary was quick to console her. When Hillary had special activities—a piano recital or a soccer match—Elizabeth always wanted to be there, and she was very proud of her sister's accomplishments. When Hillary and Elizabeth were both in high school, they remained as close as ever, sharing clothes and secrets about their teen romances. Hillary still played soccer and Elizabeth remained her biggest fan. Elizabeth had become the family's pianist and was quite talented; she won several state competitions, and Hillary never missed a performance.

Calvin and Hope's relationship is remarkable for Calvin's jealousy and hostility; Hillary and Elizabeth's relationship is remarkable for its enduring intimacy, love, and mutual respect. What the relationships have in common is stability: The quality of relationship that was established early in childhood was maintained.

Why was Hillary and Elizabeth's relationship so filled with love and respect, whereas Calvin and Hope's was dominated by jealousy and resentment? Put more simply, what factors contribute to the quality of sibling relationships? First, children's sex and temperament matter. Sibling relations are more likely to be warm and harmonious between siblings of the same sex than between siblings of the opposite sex (Dunn & Kendrick, 1981) and when neither sibling is temperamentally emotional (Brody, Stoneman, & McCoy, 1994). Age is also important: Sibling relationships generally improve as the younger child approaches adolescence because siblings begin to perceive one another as equals (Buhrmester & Furman, 1990).

Parents contribute to the quality of sibling relationships, both directly and indirectly (Brody, 1998). The direct influence stems from parents' treatment. Siblings more often get along when they believe that parents have no "favorites" but treat all siblings fairly (Kowal & Kramer, 1997). When parents lavishly praise one child's accomplishments while ignoring another's, children notice the difference and their sibling relationship suffers.

> Parents can foster good sibling relationships by treating children fairly and by getting along with each other.

This doesn't mean that parents must treat all their children the same. Children understand that parents should treat their kids differently—based on their age or personal needs. Only when differential treatment is not justified do sibling relationships deteriorate (Kowal & Kramer, 1997).

The indirect influence of parents on sibling relationships stems from the quality of the parents' relationship with each other: A warm, harmonious relationship between parents fosters positive sibling relationships; conflict between parents is associated with conflict between siblings (Erel, Margolin, & John, 1998; Volling & Belsky, 1992). When parents don't get along, they no longer treat their children the same, leading to conflict among siblings (Brody et al., 1994).

One practical implication of these findings is that in their pursuit of family harmony (otherwise known as peace and quiet), parents can influence some of the factors affecting sibling relationships but not others. Parents can help reduce friction between siblings by being equally affectionate, responsive, and caring with all of their children and by caring for one another. At the same time, some dissension is natural in families, especially those with young boys and girls: Children's different interests lead to arguments, like the one in the photo. Faced with common simple conflicts—Who decides which TV show to watch? Who gets to eat the last cookie? Who gets to hold the new puppy?—a 3-year-old brother and a 5-year-old sister *will* argue because they lack the social and cognitive skills that allow them to find mutually satisfying compromises.

When siblings do fight—particularly young children—parents should intervene. When parents explain one sibling's behavior to another (e.g., "He covered his eyes 'cause he was scared"), siblings have more positive interactions (Kojima, 2000). And, by helping their children settle differences, parents show children more sophisticated ways to negotiate; later, children often try to use these techniques themselves instead of fighting (Pearlman & Ross, 1997). Parents especially need to intervene when conflicts escalate to the point that siblings are acting aggressively, yelling or swearing, or making denigrating comments. Obviously, parents need to protect their children from each other. But, more importantly, if left unchecked, over time such conflicts can lead to behavior problems in school (Garcia et al., 2000).

Regardless of the quality of their sibling relationships, American children are more likely than children in other countries to have their family relationships disrupted by divorce. What is the impact of divorce on children and adolescents? Module 15.3 has some answers.

## CHECK YOUR LEARNING

1. Compared to firstborn children, laterborn children are more innovative and more _____.

2. When compared to children who have siblings, only children are, for the most part, _____.

**3.** Adopted children are more likely to have adjustment and conduct problems when they are adopted at an older age and when _____.

**4.** Siblings are more likely to get along when they are of the same sex, not temperamentally emotional, and when the younger child _____.

**5.** Sibling relationships are harmed when parents treat their children differently if _____.

**6.** Parents can influence sibling relationships directly by treating children fairly and indirectly by _____.

 **CONTINUITY**
What research findings suggest continuity in the quality of sibling relationships? What findings suggest discontinuity?

**Answers:** (1) popular, (2) similar, not different, (3) their care before adoption was poor quality, (4) enters adolescence, (5) the differential treatment is not justified, (6) getting along with each other

# 15.3 Divorce and Remarriage

— **Family Life After Divorce**

— **Impact of Divorce on Children**

— **Blended Families**

**LEARNING OBJECTIVES**

● How does family life change for children following divorce?

● What are some of the effects of divorce on children?

● How do children adjust to a parent's remarriage?

> *Jack has lived with his dad for the 4 years since his parents' divorce; he visits his mother every other weekend. Although Jack was confused and depressed when his parents divorced, he has come to terms with the new situation. He's excelling in school, where he is well liked by peers and teachers. One of Jack's friends is Troy. Troy's parents are married but bicker constantly since his dad lost his job. His parents are unable to agree on anything; the pettiest event or remark triggers an argument. Troy's grades have fallen, and whereas he was once a leader among the boys in his class, now he prefers to be alone.*

Like Jack, many American youngsters' parents divorce. Nearly half of all first marriages end in divorce and every year approximately one million American children have parents who divorce (Amato, 2001). According to all theories of child development, divorce is distressing for children because it involves conflict between parents and usually separation from one of them. But what aspects of children's development are most affected by divorce? Are these effects long lasting, or are at least some of them temporary (as seems to be true for Jack)? To begin to answer these questions, let's start with a profile of life after divorce.

## Family Life After Divorce

After divorce, children usually live with their mothers, though fathers are more likely to get custody today than in previous generations. About 15 percent of children live with their fathers after divorce (Meyer & Garasky, 1993). Not much is known about family life in homes headed by single fathers, so the description on the next few pages is based entirely on research done on children living with their mothers.

The best portrait of family life after divorce comes from the Virginia Longitudinal Study of Divorce and Remarriage conducted by Mavis Hetherington (1988, 1999; Hetherington & Kelly, 2002). The Virginia Study traced the lives of families for several years after divorce along with a comparison sample of families with parents who did not divorce.

During the first few months after divorce, many mothers were less affectionate toward their children. They also accepted less mature behavior from their children than they would have before the divorce and had a harder time controlling their children. The overall picture shows both mothers and children suffering the distress of a major change in life circumstances: Children regressed to less mature forms of behavior, and mothers were less able to parent effectively. Fathers, too, were less able to control their children, but this was probably because most were extremely indulgent.

Two years after the divorce, mother–child relationships had improved, particularly for daughters. Mothers were more affectionate. They were more likely to expect age-appropriate behavior from their children and discipline their children effectively. Fathers also demanded more mature behavior of their children, but many had become relatively uninvolved with their children.

> When children living with their divorced mothers enter adolescence, mothers and daughters are often quite close but mothers and sons often fight.

Six years after divorce, the children in the study were adolescents. Family life continued to improve for mothers with daughters; like the mother and daughter in the photo, many grew extremely close over the years following divorce. Unfortunately, family life was problematic for mothers with sons. These mothers often complained about their sons, who resisted discipline. Many mothers fell into the negative reinforcement trap described in Module 15.1. Mothers and sons were frequently in conflict, and neither was very happy with the other or with the general quality of family life. Of course, conflict between mothers and adolescent sons is common when parents are married, but it was more intense with single moms, perhaps because adolescent sons are more willing to confront their single mothers concerning standards for their behavior.

Results like these from the Virginia Study underscore that divorce changes family life for parents and children alike. In the next section, we'll look at the effects of these changes on children's development.

## Impact of Divorce on Children

Do the disruptions, conflict, and stress associated with divorce affect children? Of course they do. Having answered this easy question, however, many more difficult questions remain: Are all aspects of children's lives affected equally by divorce? *How* does divorce influence development? Why is divorce more stressful for some children than others?

**WHAT ASPECTS OF CHILDREN'S LIVES ARE AFFECTED BY DIVORCE?**   By 2000, nearly 200 studies on divorce had been conducted, involving tens of thousands of preschool- through college-age children. Amato (2001; Amato & Keith, 1991) conducted comprehensive meta-analyses of this research. The outcome? In school achievement, conduct, adjustment, self-concept, and parent–child relations, children whose parents had divorced fared poorly compared to children from intact families.

However, the effects of divorce dropped from the 1970s to 1980s, perhaps because as divorce became more frequent in the 1980s, it became more familiar and less frightening. The effects of divorce increased again in the 1990s, perhaps reflecting a widening gap in income between single- and two-parent families (Amato, 2001).

When children of divorced parents become adults, the effects of divorce persist. As adults, children of divorce are more likely to become teenage parents and to become divorced themselves. Also, they report less satisfaction with life and are more likely to become depressed (Furstenberg & Teitler, 1994; Hetherington & Kelly, 2002). For example, in one study (Chase-Lansdale, Cherlin, & Kiernan, 1995), 11 percent of children of divorce had serious emotional problems as adults compared to 8 percent of children from intact families. The difference is small—11 percent versus 8 percent—but divorce does increase the risk of emotional disorders in adulthood.

Life for children after divorce is *not* all gloom and doom. Children adjust to their new circumstances (Chase-Lansdale & Hetherington, 1990). However, certain factors can ease the transition. Children adjust to divorce more readily if their divorced parents cooperate with each other, especially on disciplinary matters (Hetherington, 1989). **In joint custody, both parents retain legal custody of the children.** Children benefit from joint custody if their parents get along (Bauserman, 2002).

Of course, many parents do not get along after a divorce, which eliminates joint custody as an option. Traditionally, mothers have been awarded custody; but in recent years fathers more often have been given custody, especially of sons. This practice coincides with findings that children like Jack, the other boy in the opening vignette, often adjust better when they live with same-sex parents: Boys often fare better with fathers and girls fare better with mothers (Goodman, Emery, & Haugaard, 1998). One reason boys are often better off with their fathers is that boys are likely to become involved in negative reinforcement traps (described in Module 15.1) with their mothers. Another explanation is that both boys and girls may forge stronger emotional relationships with same-sex parents than with other-sex parents (Zimiles & Lee, 1991).

**HOW DOES DIVORCE INFLUENCE DEVELOPMENT?** Divorce usually results in several changes to family life that affect children (Amato & Keith, 1991). First, the absence of one parent means that children lose a role model, a source of parental help and emotional support, and a supervisor. For instance, a single parent may have to choose between helping one child complete an important paper or watching another child perform in a school play. She can't do both, and one child will miss out.

Divorce affects children through the less of a role model, economic hardship, and exposure to conflict.

Second, single-parent families experience economic hardship, which creates stress and often means that activities once taken for granted are no longer available (Goodman et al., 1998). A family may no longer be able to afford books for pleasure reading, music lessons, or other activities that promote child development. Moreover, when a single parent worries about having enough money for food and rent, she has less energy and effort to devote to parenting.

Third, conflict between parents is extremely distressing to children and adolescents (Fincham, 1998), particularly for children who are emotionally insecure (Davies & Cummings, 1998). In fact, many of the problems ascribed to divorce are really caused by marital conflict occurring before the divorce (Erel & Burman, 1995; Shaw, Winslow, & Flanagan, 1999). Children like Troy, the boy in the opening vignette whose parents are married but fight constantly, often show many of the same effects associated with divorce (Katz & Woodin, 2002).

**WHICH CHILDREN ARE MOST AFFECTED BY DIVORCE? WHY?**   Some children are more affected by divorce than others. Amato and Keith's (1991) analysis, for example, showed that although the overall impact of divorce is the same for boys and girls, divorce is more harmful when it occurs during childhood and adolescence than during the preschool or college years. Also, children who are temperamentally more emotional tend to be more affected by divorce (Lengua et al., 1999).

Some children suffer more from divorce because of their tendency to interpret events negatively. We know, from Module 12.4, that two children often have differing interpretations of exactly the same social event. Suppose, for example, that a father forgets to take a child on a promised outing. One child might believe that an emergency prevented the father from taking the child. A second child might believe that the father hadn't really wanted to spend time with the child in the first place and will never make similar plans again. Children who—like the second child—tend to interpret life events negatively are more likely to have behavioral problems following divorce (Mazur et al., 1999).

And, in the "Focus on Research" feature, we'll see that children's efforts to cope with stress can influence how they're affected by divorce.

## FOCUS ON RESEARCH

### Children Who Cope with Divorce

*Who were the investigators, and what was the aim of the study?* For all children, divorce is a major obstacle on the road to healthy development. Some children get around the obstacle fairly easily, but others do so only with great difficulty. Why? One answer to this question comes from studies of how people react to other life stresses (e.g., the death of a loved one). People who deal effectively with such stresses often believe that they can actively shape their own destinies (Bandura, 1997; Lazarus, 1991). For them, a stressor represents a problem to be solved, rather than an insurmountable force that must ruin their lives. Irwin Sandler and his colleagues (2000) conducted a study designed to determine whether the impact of divorce was less when children used active coping strategies. In particular, they hypothesized that when children use such strategies, they begin to believe they can influence the future and thus are less susceptible to psychological disorders.

*How did the investigators measure the topic of interest?* Sandler and his research team were interested in connections among three variables:

- children's use of active strategies to solve problems or to make themselves feel better,
- children's belief in their ability to influence the outcome of future events, and
- children's symptoms of anxiety or depression.

Each construct was measured with a questionnaire. For active strategies, children responded to items like "You did something to make it better" and "You tried to figure out why things like this happen" on a scale ranging from "never" to "most of the time." For belief in their ability to influence future events, children responded to items like "Overall, how good do you think you will be at making things better when problems come up in the future" on a scale ranging from "not at all good" to "very good." Finally, children and their mothers completed multiple questionnaires that probed symptoms of anxiety and depression.

The questionnaires were completed twice—3 months apart.

*Who were the children in the study?* Sandler and his colleagues studied 356 9- to 12-year-olds whose parents had divorced within the previous 2 years.

*What was the design of the study?* This study was correlational because the researchers were interested in the relation that existed naturally among the three primary constructs. The study was longitudinal because children were tested twice, 3 months apart.

*Were there ethical concerns with the study?* No. Parents provided informed consent.

*What were the results?* The primary results of the study are two correlations. First, the correlation between children's active use of strategies at the first testing and belief in the ability to influence future outcomes at the second testing was .39. In other words, those children who reported actively solving problems were more likely, 3 months later, to believe that they could influence problems in the future. Second, at the second testing, the correlation between belief in the ability to influence future outcomes and symptoms of anxiety and depression was −.45. That is, when children believed in their ability to cope with future events, they were less likely to have symptoms of anxiety or depression.

*What did the investigators conclude?* When children actively cope—either by trying to solve a problem or by trying to make it feel less threatening—they gain confidence in their ability to control future events in their lives. This confidence acts as a buffer against anxiety or depression, which are often brought on by the feeling that life's problems are insurmountable.

*What converging evidence would strengthen these conclusions?* The researchers' conclusions would be strengthened if the study were continued and it was shown that beliefs about control had benefits over years (instead of just 3 months). In addition, the conclusions would be more compelling if children's self-reports were complemented with other measures. Teachers, for example, could be asked to judge how actively children worked to solve problems. Finally, future research could ask why some children are active problem solvers in the first place.

Just as children can reduce the harm of divorce by being active problem solvers, parents can make divorce easier on their children. The "Improving Children's Lives" feature has some tips on ways parents can make divorce less stressful for their children.

## IMPROVING CHILDREN'S LIVES

### Helping Children Adjust After Divorce

 Divorce causes major changes in children's lives that are very stressful. Here are some ways parents can reduce stress and help children adjust to their new life circumstances. Parents should

- explain together to children why they are divorcing and what their children can expect to happen to them.

- reassure children that they will always love them and always be their parents; parents must back up these words with actions by remaining involved in their children's lives, despite the increased difficulty of doing so.

- expect that their children will sometimes be angry or sad about the divorce, and they should encourage children to discuss these feelings with them.

Parents should not

- compete with each other for their children's love and attention; children adjust to divorce best when they maintain good relationships with both parents.

- take out their anger with each other on their children.

- criticize their ex-spouse in front of the children.

- ask children to mediate disputes; parents should work out problems without putting the children in the middle.

Following all these rules all the time is not easy. After all, divorce is stressful and painful for adults, too. But parents owe it to their children to try to follow most of these rules most of the time to minimize the disruptive effects of their divorce on their children's development. ●

## Blended Families

Following divorce, most children live in a single-parent household for about 5 years. However, like the adults in the photo, more than two-thirds of men and women eventually remarry (Glick, 1989; Glick & Lin, 1986). **The resulting unit, consisting of a biological parent, stepparent, and children, is known as a blended family.** Because mothers are more often granted custody of children, the most common form of blended family is a mother, her children, and a stepfather (Hetherington & Stanley-Hagan, 2002). Preadolescent boys typically benefit from the presence of a stepfather, particularly when he is warm and involved. Preadolescent girls, however, do not adjust readily to their mother's remarriage, apparently because it disrupts the intimate relationship they have established with her. Nevertheless, as boys and girls enter adolescence, both benefit from the presence of a caring stepfather (Hetherington, 1993).

The best strategy for stepfathers is to be interested in their new stepchildren but avoid encroaching on established relationships. Newly remarried mothers must be careful that their enthusiasm for their new spouse does not come at the expense of time and affection for their children. And both parents and children need to have realistic expectations. The blended family can be successful, but it takes effort because of the complicated relationships, conflicting loyalties, and jealousies that usually exist (Anderson et al., 1999).

Much less is known about blended families consisting of a father, his children, and a stepmother, though several factors make a father's remarriage difficult for his children (Brand, Clingempeel, & Bowen-Woodward, 1988). First, fathers are often awarded custody when judges believe that children are unruly and will profit from a father's "firm hand." Consequently, many children living with their fathers do not adjust well to many of life's challenges, which certainly includes a father's remarriage. Second, fathers are sometimes granted custody because they have a particularly close relationship with their children, especially their sons. When this is the case, children sometimes fear that their father's remarriage will disturb this relationship. Finally, noncustodial mothers are more likely than noncustodial fathers to maintain close and frequent contact with their children (Maccoby et al., 1993). The constant presence of the noncustodial mother may interfere with a stepmother's efforts to establish close relationships with her stepchildren, particularly with her stepdaughters.

> Children in blended families often fear that remarriage will disrupt the close relationship they have with their biological parent.

Over time, children adjust to the blended family. If the marriage is happy, most children profit from the presence of two caring adults. Unfortunately, second marriages are slightly more likely than first marriages to end in divorce, so many children relive the trauma. As you can imagine, another divorce—and possibly another remarriage—severely disrupts children's development, accentuating the problems that followed the initial divorce (Capaldi & Patterson, 1991).

Regrettably, divorce is not the only way that parents can disturb their children's development. As we'll see in the next module, some parents harm their children more directly, by abusing them.

## CHECK YOUR LEARNING

1. In the first few months after divorce, mothers do not parent effectively and children often _____.

2. As children approach adolescence, mother_____ relationships after a divorce remain positive.

3. The impact of divorce on children became _____ in the 1980s.

4. Divorce affects children's development by depriving them of a role model and source of help, _____, and because the conflict associated with divorce is very distressing for children.

5. Children are most likely to be affected by divorce during the _____ years.

6. Fathers are often awarded custody when _____ or when they have a particularly close relationship with their children.

7. One difficulty for custodial fathers and stepmothers is that the children's biological mother _____.

**CONNECTIONS**
How do the consequences of divorce show the connections among cognitive, social, and emotional development?

**Answers:** (1) resort to immature forms of behavior, (2) daughter, (3) smaller, (4) by exposing them to economic hardship, (5) school-age and adolescent, (6) their children are unruly and need a father's "firm hand," (7) may remain very close to the children, making it hard for stepmothers to establish relationships with her stepchildren

# 15.4

# Parent–Child Relationships Gone Awry

— **Consequences of Maltreatment**

— **Causes of Maltreatment**

— **Preventing Maltreatment**

## LEARNING OBJECTIVES

● What are the consequences of child maltreatment?

● What factors cause parents to mistreat their children?

● How can maltreatment be prevented?

*The first time 7-year-old Max came to school with bruises on his face, he said he'd fallen down the basement steps. When Max had similar bruises a few weeks later, his teacher spoke with the school principal, who contacted local authorities. They discovered that Max's mother hit him with a paddle for even minor misconduct; for serious transgressions, she beat Max and made him sleep alone in an unheated, unlighted basement.*

Unfortunately, cases like Max's occur far too often in modern America. Maltreatment comes in many forms (Cicchetti, Toth, & Maughan, 2000). The two that often first come to mind are physical abuse involving assault that leads to injuries and sexual abuse involving fondling, intercourse, or other sexual behaviors. Another form of maltreatment is neglect, not giving children adequate food, clothing, or medical care. And, as the poster reminds us, children can also be harmed by psychological abuse—ridicule, rejection, and humiliation.

The frequency of these various forms of child maltreatment is difficult to estimate because so many cases go unreported. According to the Administration on Children, Youth, and Families (2002), approximately 1 million children annually suffer maltreatment or neglect. About 60 percent are neglected, about 20 percent are abused physically, about 10 percent are abused sexually, and 10 percent are maltreated psychologically (Administration on Children, Youth, and Families, 2002).

We'll begin this module by looking at the consequences of maltreatment, then look at some causes, and, finally, examine ways to prevent maltreatment. As we do, we'll discover what led Max to suffer as he did.

## Consequences of Maltreatment

You probably aren't surprised to learn that the prognosis for youngsters like Max is not very good. Some, of course, suffer permanent physical damage. Even when there is no lasting physical damage, children's social and emotional development is often disrupted. They tend to have poor relationships with peers, often because they are too aggressive (Bolger & Patterson, 2001; Shields, Ryan, & Cicchetti, 2001). Their cognitive development and academic performance are also disturbed. Abused youngsters tend to get lower grades in school, score lower on standardized achievement tests, and be retained in a grade rather than promoted. Also, school-related behavior problems, such as being disruptive in class, are common, in part because maltreated children don't regulate their emotions well (Maughan & Cicchetti, 2002; Shonk & Cicchetti, 2001).

Adults who were abused as children often experience emotional problems such as depression or anxiety, are more prone to think about or attempt suicide, and are more likely to abuse spouses and their own children (Malinosky-Rummell & Hansen, 1993). In short, when children are maltreated, virtually all aspects of their development are affected and these effects do not vanish with time.

## Causes of Maltreatment

Why would a parent abuse a child? Maybe you think parents would have to be severely disturbed or deranged to harm their own flesh and blood. Not really. The vast majority of abusing parents cannot be distinguished from nonabusing parents in terms of standard psychiatric criteria (Wolfe, 1985). That is, adults who mistreat their children are not suffering from any specific mental or psychological disorder, and they have no distinctive personality profile.

Modern accounts of child abuse no longer look to a single or even a small number of causes. Instead, a host of factors put some children at risk for abuse and protect others; the number and combination of factors determine if the child is a likely target for abuse (Cicchetti et al., 2000). Let's look at three of the most important factors: cultural context and community, the parents, and the children themselves.

**CULTURE AND COMMUNITY.**    The most general category of contributing factors has to do with cultural values and the social conditions of the community in which parents rear their children. For example, a culture's view of physical punishment may contribute to child maltreatment. Many countries in Europe and Asia have strong cultural prohibitions against physical punishment. It simply isn't done and would be viewed in much the same way we would view an American parent who punished by not feeding the child for a few days. In Sweden, for example, spanking is against the law and children can report their parents to the police. But the scene in the photo, a father spanking his child, is common in the United States. Countries that do not condone physical punishment tend to have lower rates of child maltreatment than the United States (U.S. Department of State, 2002).

In addition to cultural values, the communities in which children live can put them at risk for maltreatment and abuse. Living in poverty is one important risk factor: Maltreatment is more common in families living in poverty, in part because lack of money increases the stress of daily life (Goodman et al., 1998). When parents are worrying about whether they can buy groceries or pay the rent, they are more likely to punish their children physically instead of making the extra effort to reason with them. A second risk factor is social isolation: Abuse is more likely when families are socially isolated from other relatives or neighbors, because isolation deprives children of adults who could protect them and deprives parents of social support that would help them cope with life stresses (Garbarino & Kostelny, 1992; Korbin, 1987).

Cultural values and community factors clearly contribute to child abuse, but they are only part of the puzzle. After all, although maltreatment is more common among families living in poverty, it does not occur in a majority of these families and it does occur in middle-class families, too. Consequently, we need to look for additional factors to explain why abuse occurs in some families but not others.

**PARENTS.**    Faced with the same cultural values and living conditions, why do only a handful of parents abuse or mistreat their children? That is, which characteristics increase the odds that a parent will abuse his or her children? Child-development researchers have identified several important factors (Cicchetti et al., 2000). First, parents who maltreat their children often were maltreated themselves, which may lead them to believe that abuse is simply a normal part of childhood. Second, parents who mistreat their children often use ineffective parenting techniques (e.g., inconsistent discipline) and have such unrealistic expectations that their children can never meet them. Third, in families where abuse occurs, the couple's interactions are often unpredictable, unsupportive, and unsatisfying for both husbands and wives. Thus, mistreatment of children is simply one symptom of family dysfunction.

**CHILDREN'S CONTRIBUTIONS.**    To place the last few pieces in the puzzle, we must look at the abused children themselves. The discussion in Module 15.1 of reciprocal influence between parents and children should remind you that children may inadvertently, through their behavior, bring on their own abuse. In fact, infants and preschoolers are abused more often than older children. Why? They are easier targets of abuse and they are less able to regulate aversive behaviors that elicit abuse (Belsky, 1993). You've probably heard stories about a parent who shakes a baby to death because the baby won't stop crying. Because younger children are more likely to cry or whine excessively—behaviors that irritate all parents sooner or later—they are more likely to be the targets of abuse.

For much the same reason, children who are frequently ill are more often abused. When children are sick, they're more likely to cry and whine, annoying their parents. Also, when children are sick, they need medical care, which means additional expense. In addition, they can't go to school, which means that parents must arrange alternate child care. By increasing the level of stress in a family, sick children can inadvertently become the targets of abuse (Sherrod et al., 1984).

Stepchildren form another group at risk for abuse (Daly & Wilson, 1996). Just as Cinderella's stepmother doted on her biological children but abused Cinderella, so stepchildren are more prone to abuse and neglect than biological children. Adults are less invested emotionally in their stepchildren, and this lack of emotional investment leaves stepchildren more vulnerable.

Obviously the children are not at fault and do not deserve the abuse. Nevertheless, normal infant or child behavior can provoke anger and maltreatment from some parents.

Thus, many factors, summarized in the table, all contribute to child maltreatment. Any single factor will usually not result in abuse; maltreatment is more likely when risk factors start to add up. For example, several factors placed Max, the boy in the vignette, at risk for abuse: His family had moved to the community recently because his stepfather thought he could find work in the local plant; but the plant wasn't hiring, so his stepfather was unemployed and the family had little money saved. And Max had asthma, which meant there was regular expense for medication and occasional visits to the emergency room when he had a severe attack. All these factors combined to put Max at risk for maltreatment. (How many risk factors? My answer appears just before Check Your Learning on page 456.)

> Children are most likely to be abused when their culture condones physical punishment, their parents lack effective child-rearing skills, and their own behavior is aversive.

**SUMMARY TABLE**

## FACTORS THAT CONTRIBUTE TO CHILD ABUSE

| General Category | Specific Factor |
| --- | --- |
| Cultural and community contributions | Abuse is more common in cultures that tolerate physical punishment. |
| | Abuse is more common when families live in poverty because of the stress associated with inadequate income. |
| | Abuse is more common when families are socially isolated because parents lack social supports. |
| Parents' contributions | Parents who abuse their children were often maltreated themselves as children. |
| | Parents who abuse their children often have poor parenting skills (e.g., unrealistic expectations, inappropriate punishment). |
| Children's contributions | Young children are more likely to be abused because they cannot regulate their behavior. |
| | Ill children are more likely to be abused because their behavior while ill is often aversive. |
| | Stepchildren are more likely to be abused because stepparents are less invested in their stepchildren. |

## Preventing Maltreatment

The complexity of child abuse dashes any hopes for a simple solution. Because maltreatment is more apt to occur when several contributing factors are present, eradicating child maltreatment would entail a massive effort. American attitudes toward "acceptable" levels of punishment and poverty would have to change. American children will be abused as long as physical punishment is considered acceptable and as long as poverty-stricken families live in chronic stress from simply trying to provide food and shelter. Parents also need counseling and training in parenting skills. Abuse will continue as long as parents remain ignorant of effective methods of parenting and discipline.

> Child abuse can be reduced by providing social supports and teaching effective parenting.

It would be naive to expect all of these changes to occur overnight. However, by focusing on some of the more manageable factors, the risk of maltreatment can be reduced. Social supports help. When parents know they can turn to other helpful adults for advice and reassurance, they better manage the stresses of child rearing that might otherwise lead to abuse. And families can be taught more effective ways of coping with situations that might otherwise trigger abuse (Wicks-Nelson & Israel, 1991). Through role-playing sessions, parents can learn the benefits of authoritative parenting and effective ways of using feedback and modeling (described in Module 15.1) to regulate children's behavior.

Providing social supports and teaching effective parenting are typically done when maltreatment and abuse have already occurred. Of course, preventing maltreatment in the first place is more desirable and more cost-effective. For prevention, one useful tool is familiar—early childhood intervention programs. That is, maltreatment and abuse can be cut in half when families participate for two or more years in intervention programs that include preschool education along with family support activities aimed at encouraging parents to become more involved in their children's education (Reynolds & Robertson, 2003). When parents participate in these programs, they become more committed to their children's education. This leads their children to be more successful in school, reducing a source of stress and enhancing parents' confidence in their child-rearing skills, reducing the risks of maltreatment in the process.

Finally, we need to remember that most parents who have mistreated their children deserve compassion, rather than censure. In most cases, parents and children are attached to each other; maltreatment is a consequence of ignorance and burden, not malice.

*Answer to question on page 455 about the number of risk factors:* Four factors put Max at risk: social isolation (just moved to the community), poverty (unemployed, no savings), he is a stepchild, and he has a chronic illness.

### CHECK YOUR LEARNING

1. Maltreatment includes physical abuse, sexual abuse, psychological abuse, and
_____ .

2. Adults who were abused as children are more likely to have emotional problems, to be suicide-prone, and to _____ .

3. Children who are maltreated frequently have poor peer relationships, sometimes because they are _____ .

4. Social factors that contribute to child maltreatment include cultural views toward physical punishment, poverty, and _____.

5. Children who are at special risk for maltreatment include infants and toddlers, children who are ill frequently, and _____.

6. Programs for preventing maltreatment often try to help families learn _____.

**ACTIVE CHILDREN**

How does child abuse demonstrate, in an unfortunate way, that children are sometimes active contributors to their own development?

**Answers:** (1) neglect, (2) abuse spouses and children, (3) too aggressive, (4) social isolation, (5) stepchildren, (6) new ways of coping with situations that might trigger maltreatment

# Unifying Themes: Active Children

In this chapter, I want to emphasize the theme that *children influence their own development*. This may seem to be an unusual chapter to emphasize this theme because, after all, we usually think of how parents influence their children. But several times in this chapter we've seen that parenting is determined, in part, by children themselves. We saw that parents change their behavior as their children grow older. Parents also adjust their behavior depending on how their children respond to previous efforts to discipline. And, in discussing causes of child maltreatment, we discovered that younger and sick children often unwittingly place themselves at risk for abuse because of their behavior. Constant whining and crying is trying for all parents and prompts a small few to harm their children.

Of course, parents do influence their children's development in many important ways. But effective parenting recognizes that there is no all-purpose formula that works for all children or, for that matter, for all children in one family. Instead, parents must tailor their child-rearing behavior to each child, recognizing his or her unique needs, strengths, and weaknesses.

## See for Yourself

Many students find it hard to believe that parents actually use the different styles described in Module 15.1. To observe how parents differ in their warmth and control, visit a place where parents and children interact together. Shopping malls and fast-food restaurants are two good examples. Observe parents and children, then judge their warmth (responsive to the child's needs versus uninterested) and degree of control (relatively controlling versus uncontrolling). As you observe, decide whether parents are using feedback and modeling effectively. You should observe an astonishing variety of parental behavior, some effective and some not. See for yourself!

## Resources

For more information about...

☞ **ways to help deal with divorce**, try Neil Kalter's *Growing Up with Divorce* (Free Press, 1990), which describes practical ways for parents to help their children deal with the stresses of divorce.

↗ **how to deal with all of the different problems large and small that come up in rearing children**, visit the Today's Parent Web site,
**http://www.todaysparent.com**

## Key Terms

authoritarian parenting 432
authoritative parenting 432
blended family 451
counterimitation 434
direct instruction 434
dispensing-family-wisdom grandparents 438
distant grandparents 438
formal grandparents 438
fun-seeking grandparents 438

indifferent-uninvolved parenting 433
indulgent-permissive parenting 433
joint custody 448
negative reinforcement trap 434
punishment 434
reinforcement 434
surrogate-parent grandparents 438
time-out 435

# SUMMARY

**Family Relationships**

15.1 Parenting
15.2 Brothers and Sisters
15.3 Divorce and Remarriage
15.4 Parent–Child Relationships Gone Awry

## 15.1 Parenting

### The Family as a System
According to the systems approach, the family consists of interacting elements—parents and children influence each other. The family itself is influenced by other social systems, such as neighborhoods and religious organizations.

### Dimensions and Styles
One dimension of parenting is the degree of parental warmth: Children clearly benefit from warm, caring parents. Another dimension is control. Effective parental control involves setting appropriate standards and enforcing them consistently.

Combining warmth and control yields four parental styles: (a) authoritarian parents are controlling but uninvolved, (b) authoritative parents are controlling but responsive to their children, (c) indulgent-permissive parents are loving but exert little control, and (d) indifferent-uninvolved parents are neither warm nor controlling. Authoritative parenting is usually best for children.

### Parental Behavior
Parents influence development by direct instruction and coaching. In addition, parents serve as models for their children, who sometimes imitate parents' behavior directly and sometimes in ways that are the opposite of what they've seen (counterimitation).

Parents also use feedback to influence children's behavior. Sometimes parents fall into the negative reinforcement trap, inadvertently reinforcing behaviors that they want to discourage. Punishment is effective when it is prompt, consistent, accompanied by an explanation, and delivered by a person with whom the child has a warm relationship. Punishment has limited value because it suppresses behaviors but does not eliminate them, and it often has side effects. Time-out is one useful form of punishment.

### Children's Contributions
Parenting is influenced by characteristics of children themselves. As children grow, parents display affection more discretely and are less controlling. Over time, families develop routine ways of interacting, which can be harmful if based largely on negative mutual influences.

### Cultural Influences and Family Configuration
Child rearing is influenced by culture and family configuration. Compared to American parents, Chinese parents are more controlling and less affectionate. In African American families, grandmothers often live with their daughters, an arrangement that eases the cost burden of housing and child care and benefits children because grandmothers can play an active role in child rearing.

Research on gay and lesbian parents suggests that they are more similar to heterosexual parents than different and that their children develop much like children reared by heterosexual couples.

## 15.2 Brothers and Sisters

### Firstborn, Laterborn, and Only Children
Firstborn children often are more intelligent and more likely to go to college, but laterborn children are more popular and more innovative. Only children are comparable to children with siblings on most dimensions and better off on some, such as achievement and autonomy. In many respects, adopted children are similar to children living with their biological parents. Some adopted children have problems adjusting to school, primarily when they are adopted at an older age and when their quality of care before being adopted was poor.

### Qualities of Sibling Relationships
The birth of a sibling can be stressful for older children, particularly when parents ignore their older child's needs. Siblings get along better when they are of the same sex, believe that parents treat them fairly, enter adolescence, and have parents who get along well.

## 15.3 Divorce and Remarriage

### Family Life After Divorce
In the months after a divorce, a mother's parenting is often less effective and her children behave immaturely. By 2 years after the divorce, family life is much improved. At 6 years after the divorce, mother–daughter relationships are often very positive but mother–son relationships are often conflict-filled.

### Impact of Divorce on Children
A divorce can harm children in many ways, ranging from school achievement to adjustment. The impact of divorce stems from less supervision of children, economic hardship, and conflict between parents. Children often benefit when parents have joint custody following divorce or when they live with the same-sex parent.

### Blended Families
When a mother remarries, daughters sometimes have difficulty adjusting because the new stepfather encroaches on an intimate mother–daughter relationship. A father's remarriage can cause problems because children fear that the stepmother will disturb intimate father–child relationships and because of tension between the stepmother and the noncustodial mother.

## 15.4 Parent–Child Relationships Gone Awry

### Consequences of Maltreatment
Children who are maltreated sometimes suffer permanent physical damage. Their peer relationships are often poor, and they tend to lag in cognitive development and academic performance.

### Causes of Maltreatment
A culture's views on violence, poverty, and social isolation can foster child maltreatment. Parents who abuse their children are often unhappy, socially unskilled individuals. Younger, unhealthy children are more likely to be targets of maltreatment, as are stepchildren.

### Preventing Maltreatment
Prevention should target each of the factors that contribute to child maltreatment. In reality, prevention programs often focus on providing families with new ways of coping with problems and providing parents with resources to help them cope with stress.

# 16

If you stand outside a kindergarten classroom on the first day of school, you'll probably see some children crying, fearful of facing a novel environment on their own. What may surprise you is that many parents, too, are struggling to hold back their tears. Why? Parents realize that when their children begin school, they are taking an important step toward independence. Other forces now become influential in children's lives, sometimes challenging parents' influence. Among these forces are children's agemates (their peers), the media, and school itself. In this chapter, we'll examine these forces and see how they affect children. We'll look at peer influence in Module 16.1. Next, in Module 16.2, we'll see how electronic media—particularly television and computers—affect children's development. Finally, in Module 16.3, we'll examine the influences on children's development of other cultural institutions, including day care, the workplace, neighborhoods, and schools.

# Influences Beyond the Family

**16.1** Peers

**16.2** Electronic Media

**16.3** Institutional Influences

# 16.1 Peers

**LEARNING OBJECTIVES**

- When do youngsters first begin to interact with each other, and how do these interactions change during infancy, childhood, and adolescence?

- Why do children become friends, and what are the benefits of friendship?

- When do romantic relationships emerge in adolescence?

- What are the important features of groups in childhood and adolescence? How do groups influence individuals?

- Why are some children more popular than others? What are the causes and consequences of being rejected?

> *For 6 months, 17-year-old Gretchen has been dating Jeff, an 18-year-old. They have had sex several times, each time without contraception. Gretchen suggested to Jeff that he buy some condoms but he didn't want to because someone might see him at the drug store and that would be too embarrassing. And, although she never mentions it to Jeff, Gretchen sometimes thinks that getting pregnant would be cool: Then she and Jeff could move into their own apartment and begin a family.*

Many of the major developmental theorists—including Freud, Erikson, Piaget, and Vygotsky—believed that children's development is strongly shaped by their interactions and relationships with peers. Whether occurring with classmates, a small circle of friends, or in a romantic relationship like Gretchen's, children's and adolescents' interactions with peers are important developmental events.

In this module, we'll trace the development of peer interactions. Then we'll look at friendship and romantic relationships, where we'll better understand why Gretchen and Jeff are having unprotected sex. Finally, we'll consider children's membership in groups, including their social status within those groups.

**VIDEO 16.1**
Parten's Play
Categories

## Development of Peer Interactions

Peer interactions begin surprisingly early in infancy. Two 6-month-olds together will look, smile, and point at one another. Over the next few months, infants laugh and babble when with other infants (Hartup, 1983; Rubin, Bukowski, & Parker, 1998).

Beginning at about the first birthday and continuing through the preschool years, peer relations rapidly become more complex. **In a classic early study, Parten (1932) identified a developmental sequence that began with nonsocial play— children playing alone or watching others play but not playing themselves.** Later, children progressed to more elaborate forms of play with each child having a well-defined role. Today, researchers no longer share Parten's view that children move through each stage of play in a rigid sequence, but the different forms of play that she distinguished are useful nonetheless.

**The first type of social play to appear—soon after the first birthday—is parallel play: youngsters play alone but maintain a keen interest in what other children are doing.** For example, each

*Parallel play is the first social play and it is first seen soon after the first birthday.*

boy in the photo has his own toy but is watching the other play, too. During parallel play, exchanges between youngsters begin to occur. When one talks or smiles, the other usually responds (Howes, Unger, & Seidner, 1990).

Beginning at roughly 15 to 18 months, toddlers no longer just watch one another at play. **In simple social play, youngsters engage in similar activities, talk or smile at one another, and offer each other toys.** Play is now truly interactive (Howes & Matheson, 1992). An example of simple social play would be two 20-month-olds pushing toy cars along the floor, making "car sounds," and periodically trading cars.

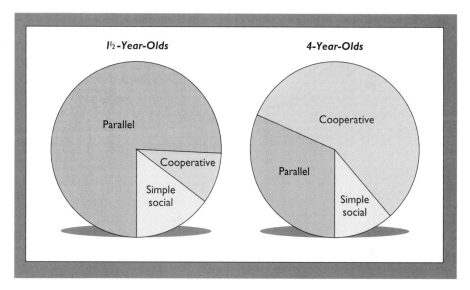

**Toward the second birthday, cooperative play begins: Now children organize their play around a distinct theme and take on special roles based on the theme.** For example, children may play "hide-and-seek" and alternate roles of hider and finder, or they may have a tea party and alternate being the host and guest.

The pie charts show how the nature of young children's play changes dramatically in a few years. These charts are based on observing 1- to 5-year-olds interacting with their peers at a day-care center (Howes & Matheson, 1992). The $1\frac{1}{2}$-year-olds spend the vast majority of their time in parallel play; other forms of play are relatively rare. By the time children are $3\frac{1}{2}$ to 4 years old, parallel play is much less common and cooperative play is the norm. Cooperative play typically involves peers of the same sex, a preference that increases until, by age 6, youngsters choose same-sex playmates about two-thirds of the time (LaFreniere, Strayer, & Gauthier, 1984).

FIG. 16-1

**MAKE-BELIEVE.** During the preschool years, cooperative play often takes the form of make-believe. Preschoolers have telephone conversations with imaginary partners or pretend to drink imaginary juice. In early phases of make-believe, children rely on realistic props to support their play. While pretending to drink, younger preschoolers use a real cup; while pretending to drive a car, they use a toy steering wheel. In later phases of make-believe, children no longer need realistic props; instead, they can imagine that a block is the cup, or, like the boys in the photo, that a paper plate is the steering wheel. Of course, this gradual movement toward more abstract make-believe is possible because of cognitive growth that occurs during the preschool years (Harris & Kavanaugh, 1993).

VIDEO 16.2

Sociodramatic Play
(social pretend play)

When children pretend, are they confused? After all, people take on new roles (the child becomes a teacher) and objects take on new identities (the banana becomes a phone), changes that would seem ripe for children to mistake the real world from the pretend one. In fact, young children rarely mix up pretense with reality. Why? When playing, children usually tell play partners that they want to pretend ("Let's pretend"), then describe those aspects of reality that are being changed ("I'll be the pilot and this is my plane," referring to the couch). It's as if children mutually agree to enter a parallel universe where just a few properties are changed (Lillard, 2001).

As you might suspect, make-believe reflects the values important in a child's culture (Bornstein et al., 1999). For example, Farver and Shin (1997) studied make-believe play of European American preschoolers and Korean American preschoolers. The Korean American children came from recently immigrated families, so they still held traditional Korean values, such as an emphasis on the family and on harmony over conflict. The two groups of children differed in the themes of their make-believe play. Adventure and fantasy were favorite themes for European American youngsters, but family roles and everyday activities were favorites of the Korean American children.

In addition, the groups differed in their style of play during make-believe. European American children were more assertive in their make-believe and more likely to disagree with their play partner's ideas about pretending ("*I* want to be the king; *you* be the mom!"). Korean American children were more polite and more likely to strive for harmony ("Could I *please* be king?"). Thus, cultural values influence both the content and the form of make-believe.

Make-believe play is not only entertaining for children, but also promotes cognitive development (Berk, 1994). Children who spend much time in make-believe play tend to be more advanced in language, memory, and reasoning. They also tend to have a more sophisticated understanding of other people's thoughts, beliefs, and feelings (Howe, Petrakos, & Rinaldi, 1998; Youngblade & Dunn, 1995).

Yet another benefit of make-believe is that it allows children to explore topics that frighten them. Children who are afraid of the dark may reassure a doll who is also afraid of the dark. By explaining to the doll why she shouldn't be afraid, children come to understand and regulate their own fear of darkness. Or children may pretend that a doll has misbehaved and must be punished, which allows them to experience the parent's anger and the doll's guilt. Make-believe allows children to explore other emotions, too, including joy and affection (Gottman, 1986).

> **Make-believe play promotes cognitive development and lets children explore emotional topics that frighten them.**

For many preschool children, make-believe play involves imaginary companions. Children can usually describe their imaginary playmates in some detail, mentioning sex and age as well as hair and eye color. Imaginary companions were once thought to be fairly rare and a sign of possible developmental problems. But recent research shows that many preschoolers, particularly firstborn and only children, report imaginary companions (Gleason, Sebanc, & Hartup, 2000; Taylor, Cartwright, & Carlson, 1993).

What's more, an imaginary companion is associated with many *positive* social characteristics: Preschoolers with imaginary friends tend to be more sociable and have more real friends than other preschoolers. Furthermore, vivid fantasy play with imaginary companions does not mean that the distinction between fantasy and reality is blurred: Children with imaginary companions can distinguish fantasy from reality just as accurately as youngsters without imaginary companions (Taylor et al., 1993).

**SOLITARY PLAY.** At times throughout the preschool years, many children prefer to play alone. Should parents be worried? Usually, no. Solitary play comes in many forms and most are normal—even healthy. Spending free playtime alone coloring, solving puzzles, or assembling Legos® is not a sign of maladjustment. Many youngsters enjoy solitary activities and, at other times, choose very social play.

However, some forms of solitary play *are* signs that children are uneasy interacting with others (Coplan et al., 2001; Harrist et al., 1997). One type of unhealthy solitary play is wandering aimlessly. Sometimes children go from one preschool activity center to the next, as if trying to decide what to do. But really they just keep wandering, never settling into play with others or into constructive solitary play. Another unhealthy type of solitary play is hovering: A child stands nearby peers who are playing, watching them play but not participating. Over time, these behaviors do not bode well for youngsters (as we'll see on pages 475–476), so it's best for these youngsters to see a professional who can help them overcome their reticence in social situations (Ladd, 1998).

**PARENTAL INFLUENCE.** Parents get involved in their preschool children's play in several ways. Sometimes they take the role of playmate (and many parents deserve an Oscar for their performances). They use the opportunity to scaffold their children's play (see Module 7.4), often raising it to more sophisticated levels (Tamis-LeMonda & Bornstein, 1996). For example, if a toddler is stacking toy plates, a parent might help the child stack the plates (play at the same level) or might pretend to wash each plate (play at a more advanced level). When parents demonstrate more advanced forms of play, their children often play at the more advanced levels later (Bornstein et al., 1996).

Another parental role during preschoolers' play is mediator. Preschoolers often disagree, argue, and sometimes fight. As shown in the photo, children play more cooperatively and longer when parents are present to help iron out conflicts (Mize, Pettit, & Brown, 1995; Parke & Bhavnagri, 1989). When young children can't agree on what to play, a parent can negotiate a mutually acceptable activity. When both youngsters want to play with the same toy, a parent can arrange for them to share. Here, too, parents scaffold their preschoolers' play, smoothing the interaction by providing some of the social skills that preschoolers lack.

Yet another parental role is coach. Preschool children often encounter social problems that, although minor from an adult's perspective, seem overwhelming to the child. For example, a child might be coloring when another child approaches and demands the crayon the child is using. Parents can help their preschoolers understand and handle such problems. When parents coach—and when their advice is constructive—their children tend to be skilled socially and less aggressive (Mize & Pettit, 1997).

Parents also influence the success of their children's peer interactions in a much less direct manner. Recall from Module 11.3 that children's relationships with peers are most successful when, as infants, they had a secure attachment relationship with their mother (Ladd & LeSieur, 1995; Lieberman, Doyle, & Markiewicz, 1999).

Why does quality of attachment predict the success of children's peer relationships? One view is that a child's relationship with his or her parents is the internal working model for all future social relationships. When the parent–child relationship is high quality and emotionally satisfying, children are encouraged to form relationships with other people. Another possibility is that a secure attachment relationship with the mother makes an infant feel more confident about exploring the environment, which, in turn, provides more opportunities to interact with peers. These two views are not mutually exclusive; both may contribute to the relative ease with which securely attached children interact with their peers (Hartup, 1992b).

**PEER RELATIONS AFTER PRESCHOOL.** When children attend elementary school, the context of peer relations changes dramatically. Not only does the sheer number of peers increase dramatically, but children are often exposed to a far more diverse set of peers than before. In addition, children find themselves interacting with peers in situations that range from reasonably structured with much adult supervision (e.g., a classroom) to largely unstructured with minimal adult supervision (e.g., a playground during recess).

An obvious change in children's peer relations during the elementary-school years is that children get along better than when they were younger. Children typically resolve conflicts through coercion: One child does whatever necessary (including verbal and physical aggression) to get the other to give in. Adolescents most often "resolve" conflicts by disengaging from them; they simply drop the topic. For example, if one teenager wants to spend more time studying while another thinks they should go to the mall, they will probably just go home and do nothing together. Finally, young adults most often negotiate disagreements—they compromise, seeking a middle ground that appeals to both parties. Of course, sometimes children negotiate and sometimes young adults are coercive, but the general trend is toward more effective, more sophisticated solutions to conflicts, reflecting developmental change in cognitive and social skills (Laursen, Finkelstein, & Betts, 2001).

What do school-age children do when they're together? In one study (Zarbatany, Hartmann, & Rankin, 1990), investigators asked Canadian students in grades 5 and 6 how they spent their time with peers. The students in the study indicated how often they participated with peers in each of 29 different activities. The results, shown in the graph, are not too surprising, eh? The most common activities with peers are simple—just being together and talking (Larson, 2001).

The graph also highlights another important feature of peer relations during the elementary-school years. Children reported that they played physical games a few times each week, which reflects, in part, the emergence of a special type of play in school-age children. **In rough-and-tumble play, children playfully chase, punch, kick, shove, fight, and wrestle with peers.** Notice the word *play* in this definition: Unlike aggression, where the intention is to do harm, rough-and-tumble play is for fun. When chil-

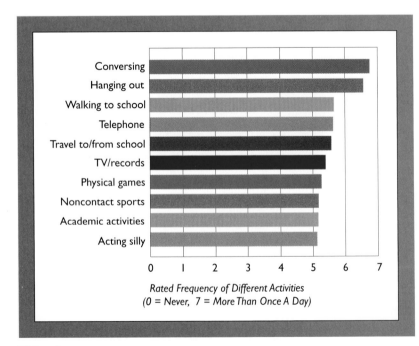

*Rated Frequency of Different Activities*
*(0 = Never, 7 = More Than Once A Day)*

FIG. 16-2

dren are involved in rough-and-tumble play, they are usually smiling and sometimes laughing (Pellegrini & Smith, 1998). When parents or teachers intervene, the youngsters usually explain that there's no problem, they're just playing. Rough-and-tumble play is more common among boys than girls, and girls' rough-and-tumble play tends to emphasize running and chasing over wrestling and fighting.

As children move into adolescence, three features of their peer relationships loom large: Friendships become more intimate, youth have their first romantic relationships, and groups take on greater significance. These changes are so important that we'll consider each one separately. First we'll look at friendship.

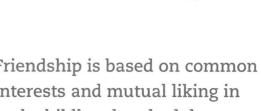

VIDEO 16.3
Rough and Tumble
Play

## Friendship

Over time, even young children develop special relationships with certain peers. **Friendship is a voluntary relationship between two people involving mutual liking.** By age 4 or 5 years, most children claim to have a "best friend." If you ask them how they can tell a child is their best friend, their response will probably resemble 5-year-old Katelyn's:

> INTERVIEWER:  Why is Heidi your best friend?
>
> KATELYN:  Because she plays with me. And she's nice to me.
>
> INTERVIEWER:  Are there any other reasons?
>
> KATELYN:  Yeah, Heidi lets me play with her dolls.

**DEVELOPMENTAL CHANGE IN THE FEATURES OF FRIENDSHIP.**  Of course, older children and adolescents also have best friends, but they describe them differently. Older children and adolescents believe that loyalty, trust, and intimacy are important ingredients of friendship. Also, adolescents, much more so than children, believe that friends should defend one another. They also strongly believe that friends should not deceive or abandon one another (Newcomb & Bagwell, 1995).

You can see these key features of adolescent friendships in the "Real Children" feature.

Friendship is based on common interests and mutual liking in both childhood and adolescence but only in adolescence is intimacy important, particularly for girls.

## REAL CHILDREN

### Heather's Best Friend

I interviewed Heather, a 13-year-old, about Anna, her best friend since third grade.

> RK:  Why is Anna your best friend?
>
> HEATHER:  We have fun together. We both play basketball and we like the same music.
>
> RK:  What else tells you that Anna's your best friend?
>
> HEATHER:  She helps me. And we think alike. My mom says we're like twins!
>
> RK:  I know that Katie is one of your friends, too. But she's not your best friend. How is being friends with Anna different than being friends with Katie?
>
> HEATHER:  Because I can tell Anna stuff—special stuff, like secrets—and I know that she won't tell anybody else.

RK: What else?

HEATHER: Well, once some girls at school were picking on me because my mom said I couldn't go to a movie with them. Anna helped me. She told the girls that she thought the movie was stupid and nobody who had any brains would want to go see it.

RK: Do you and Anna ever fight?

HEATHER: Sure. But later we always make up. And we tell each other that we're sorry.

For Heather, best friends have common interests and like each other. But her friendship with Anna goes further: She and Anna share secrets and defend each other. And, although they do argue, they both agree that their friendship is too important to be spoiled by petty disagreements, so they always make up. ⬤

Loyalty is more important in adolescents' friendships than in children's friendships. The emphasis on loyalty apparently goes hand in hand with the emphasis on intimacy: If a friend is disloyal, adolescents are afraid that they may be humiliated because their intimate thoughts and feelings will become known to a much broader circle of people (Berndt & Perry, 1990).

Intimacy is more common in friendships among girls, who are more likely than boys to have one exclusive "best friend." Because intimacy is at the core of their friendships, girls are also more likely to be concerned about the faithfulness of their friends and worry about being rejected (Buhrmester & Furman, 1987). And when one friend makes another mad, girls' anger tends to be more intense and last longer (Whitesell & Harter, 1996).

The emergence of intimacy in adolescent friendships means that friends also come to be seen as sources of social and emotional support. Levitt, Guacci-Franco, and Levitt (1993) asked African American, European American, and Hispanic American 7-, 10-, and 14-year-olds to whom they would turn if they needed help or were bothered by something. For all ethnic groups, 7- and 10-year-olds relied on close family members—parents, siblings, and grandparents—as primary sources of support, but not friends. However, 14-year-olds relied on close family members less often and said they would turn to friends instead. Because adolescent friends share intimate thoughts and feelings, they can provide support during emotional or stressful periods.

**WHO BECOME FRIENDS?** In childhood and adolescence, most friends are like those shown in the photo—alike in age, sex, and race (Hamm, 2000; Hartup, 1992a). Because friends are supposed to treat each other as equals, friendships are rare between an older, more experienced child and a younger, less experienced child. Because children typically play with same-sex peers (see Module 14.3), boys and girls rarely become friends.

Friendships are more common between children and adolescents from the same race or ethnic group than between those from different groups, reflecting racial segregation in American society. Friendships among children of different groups are more common in schools where classes are smaller (Hallinan & Teixeira, 1987). Evidently, when classes are large, children select friends from the large number of available same-race peers. When fewer same-race peers are available in smaller classes, children more often become friends with other-race children. Interracial friendships are usually confined to school, unless children come from integrated neighborhoods. That is, when children live in different, segregated neighborhoods, their friendship does not extend to out-of-school settings (DuBois & Hirsch, 1990).

Of course, friends are usually alike not only in age, sex, and race, but also in attitudes toward school, recreation, using drugs, and the future (Hamm, 2000; Newcomb & Bagwell, 1995). Tom, who enjoys school, likes to read, and plans to go to Harvard, will probably not befriend Barry, who thinks that school is stupid, listens to MP3s constantly, and plans to quit high school to become a rock star (Haselager et al., 1998). As time passes, friends become more similar in their attitudes and values (Berndt & Murphy, 2002).

Although children's friendships are overwhelmingly with members of their own sex, a few children have friendships with opposite-sex children. Who are these children, and why do they have opposite-sex friendships? Boys and girls are equally likely to have opposite-sex friendships. The important factor in understanding these children is whether they have same- and opposite-sex friends or *only* opposite-sex friends. Children with same- and opposite-sex friendships tend to be very well adjusted, whereas children with only opposite-sex friendships tend to be unpopular and less competent academically and socially, and to have lower self-esteem. Apparently, children with both same- *and* opposite-sex friends are so socially skilled and popular that both boys and girls are eager to be their friends. In contrast, children with only opposite-sex friendships are socially unskilled, unpopular youngsters who are rejected by their same-sex peers and form friendships with opposite-sex children as a last resort (Kovacs, Parker, & Hoffman, 1996).

**QUALITY AND CONSEQUENCES OF FRIENDSHIP.** If you think back to your childhood friendships, you probably remember some that were long lasting and satisfying as well as others that rapidly wore thin and soon dissolved. What accounts for these differences in the quality and longevity of friendships? Sometimes friendships are brief because children have the skills to create friendships—they know funny stories, they kid around, they know good gossip—but lack the skills to sustain them—they can't keep secrets, or they're too bossy (Jiao, 1999; Parker & Seal, 1996). Sometimes friendships end because, when conflicts arise, children are more concerned about their own interests and are unwilling to compromise or negotiate (Fonzi et al., 1997; Rose & Asher, 1999). And sometimes friendships dissolve when children discover that their needs and interests aren't as similar as they thought initially (Gavin & Furman, 1996; Poulin & Boivin, 2000).

When children have good friends, they are more likely to behave prosocially and are better adjusted.

Considering that friendships disintegrate for many reasons, you're probably reminded that truly good friends are to be treasured. In fact, researchers consistently find that children benefit from having good friends. Compared to children who lack friends, children with good friends have higher self-esteem, are less likely to be lonely and depressed, and more often act prosocially—sharing and cooperating with others (Hartup & Stevens, 1999; Ladd, 1998). Children with good friends cope better with life stresses, such as the transition from elementary school to middle school or junior high (Berndt & Keefe, 1995), and they're less likely to be victimized by peers (Schwartz et al., 2000). The benefits of friendship are also long lasting: Children who have friends have greater self-worth as young adults (Bagwell, Newcomb, & Bukowski, 1998).

Thus, friends are not simply special playmates and companions; they are important resources. Children learn from their friends and turn to them for support in times of stress. Friendships are one important way peers influence development. Peers also influence development through romantic relationships, the topic of the next section.

## Romantic Relationships

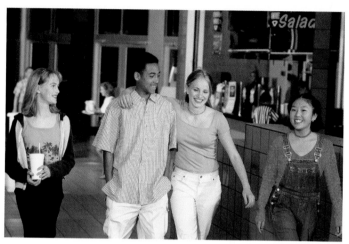

The social landscape adds a distinctive landmark in adolescence—romantic relationships. Children's social interactions are almost exclusively with their own sex; in contrast, adolescents spend 5 to 10 hours each week interacting with members of the other sex and an equal amount of time thinking about them. The first step toward romantic relationships usually consists of activities involving mixed groups of boys and girls; typical would be the group of boys and girls in the photo spending time at a mall. The next step would involve several pairs of boys and several girls going out together as a group; ultimately, relationships involve well-defined couples (Furman, 2002). For younger adolescents, romantic relationships offer companionship like that provided by a best friend and an outlet for sexual exploration. For older adolescents, trust and support become important features of romantic relationships (Shulman & Kipnis, 2001).

Cultural factors influence romantic relationships. European American parents tend to encourage independence in their teenagers more than traditional Hispanic American and Asian American parents, who emphasize family ties and loyalty to parents. Romantic relationships are a sign of independence and usually result in less time spent with family, which explains why Hispanic American and Asian American adolescents often begin to date at an older age and date less frequently (Xiaohe & Whyte, 1990).

**SEXUAL BEHAVIOR.**   We've already seen that sexual exploration is an important feature of romantic relationships for younger adolescents. In fact, by the end of high school, roughly two-thirds of American adolescents will have had intercourse at least once (Kirby, 2001). Why are some adolescents sexually active? Parents are influential: Adolescents are less likely to have sex when they feel close to their parents, when parents monitor their teenagers' activities, and when parents' values discourage sex (Miller, Benson, & Galbraith, 2001). Peers matter, too. Adolescents are more likely to have sex when their peers approve and when they believe their peers are also having sex (Brown & Theobald, 1999).

Adolescents' sexual behavior is a cause for concern because approximately 1 in 11 American adolescent girls becomes pregnant; about half of them give birth. The result is that nearly a half million babies are born to American teenagers annually. African American, Native American, and Hispanic American adolescents are the most likely to become teenage moms; Asian American adolescents are the least likely (Martin et al., 2002).

**Adolescents rarely use contraceptives during sex, which is why so many teens become pregnant.**

As we saw in Module 4.2, teenage mothers and their children usually face bleak futures. If this is the case, why do so many teens become pregnant? The answer is simple: Few sexually active teenagers use birth control. Those who do often use ineffective methods, such as withdrawal, or practice contraception inconsistently (Besharov &

Gardiner, 1997; Kirby, 2001). Adolescents' infrequent use of contraceptives can be traced to several factors (Adler, 1994; Gordon, 1996):

- *Ignorance:* Many adolescents are seriously misinformed about the facts of conception. For example, many do not know when conception is most likely to occur during the menstrual cycle.
- *Illusion of invulnerability:* Too many adolescents deny reality. They believe they are invincible—"It couldn't happen to me"—and that only others become pregnant.
- *Lack of motivation:* For some adolescent girls, like Gretchen from the module-opening vignette, becoming pregnant is appealing. They think having a child is a way to break away from parents, gain status as an independent-living adult, and have "someone to love them."
- *Lack of access:* Some teenagers do not know where to obtain contraceptives, and others, like Jeff in the vignette, are embarrassed to buy them. Still others don't know how to use contraceptives.

What's the best way to reduce adolescent sexual behavior and teen pregnancy? Programs that focus primarily on abstinence receive lots of headlines, but they are not consistently effective; some versions may work, but many do not (Kirby, 2002). In contrast, comprehensive sex education programs *are* effective (Kirby, 2001). These programs teach the biological aspects of sex and emphasize responsible sexual behavior or abstaining from premarital sex altogether. They also include discussions of the pressures to become involved sexually and ways to respond to this pressure. A key element is that in role-playing sessions students practice strategies for refusing to have sex. Youth who participate in programs like these are less likely to have intercourse; when they do have intercourse, they are more likely to use contraceptives (Kirby, 2001).

**SEXUAL ORIENTATION.**   For most adolescents, sexual behavior involves members of the opposite sex. However, roughly 15 percent of adolescent boys and girls report emotional and sexual attractions to members of their own sex. For most adolescents, these experiences are simply a part of the larger process of role experimentation common to adolescence. However, like the teens in the photo, about 5 percent of teenage boys and girls identify their sexual orientation as gay (D'Augelli, 1996).

The roots of sexual orientation are poorly understood. Scientists have, however, discredited several theories of sexual orientation. Research (Bell, Weinberg, & Hammersmith, 1981; Golombok & Tasker, 1996; Patterson, 1992) shows that each of the following is *false:*

- Sons become gay when raised by a domineering mother and a weak father.
- Girls become lesbians when their father is their primary role model.
- Children raised by gay or lesbian parents usually adopt their parents' sexual orientation.
- Gay and lesbian adults were, as children, seduced by an older person of their sex.

If all these ideas are false, what determines a person's sexual orientation? The exact factors probably differ from one person to the next, but many scientists today believe that biology plays an important role (Lalumière, Blanchard, & Zucker, 2000). Some evidence suggests that heredity and hormones influence sexual orientation (Bailey, Dunne, & Martin, 2000). Another idea is based on the finding that men are more often gay when they have older brothers and this effect gets stronger with each additional older brother; the explanation for this effect is that a pregnant woman's immune system responds to some biochemical feature of a male fetus. The response is weak at first but increases with each successive male, ultimately affecting brain development in laterborn sons (Blanchard, 1997; Blanchard et al., 1998).

Yet another intriguing idea—one that applies to males and females—is that genes and hormones don't produce sexual orientation per se but lead to temperaments that affect children's preference for same- and opposite-sex activities (Bem, 1996). Children who do not enjoy gender-typical activities come to see themselves as different and thus ultimately acquire a different gender identity.

Although the origins of sexual orientation are not yet well understood, it is clear that gay and lesbian individuals face many challenges. Their family and peer relationships are often disrupted, and they endure verbal and physical attacks. Given these problems, it's not surprising that gay and lesbian youth often experience mental health problems (D'Augelli, 1996). In recent years, social changes have helped gay and lesbian youth respond more effectively to these challenges. The "official" stigma associated with being gay or lesbian was removed in 1973 when the American Psychological Association and the American Psychiatric Association declared that homosexuality was not a psychological disorder. Other helpful changes include more (and more visible) role models and more centers for gay and lesbian youth. These resources are making it easier for gay and lesbian youth to understand their sexual orientation and to cope with the many other demands of adolescence.

In concluding this section, we need to recognize that sexual behavior and sexuality are enormously complicated and emotionally charged issues, even for adults. Adults who deal with adolescents need to recognize this complexity and help provide teenagers with skills for dealing with the issues involved in their emerging sexuality.

## Groups

During adolescence, groups become an important feature of social life. Two types of groups are particularly common during adolescence. **A clique consists of four to six individuals who are good friends and, consequently, tend to be similar in age, sex, race, and interests.** Members of a clique spend time together and often dress, talk, and act alike. Cliques are often part of a larger group, too. **A crowd is a larger mixed-sex group of older children or adolescents who have similar values and attitudes and are known by a common label.** Maybe you remember some of the different crowds from your own youth? *Jocks, preppies, burnouts, nerds,* and *brains*—adolescents use these or similar terms to refer to crowds of older children or adolescents (Brown et al., 1993; Cairns et al., 1995).

Some crowds have more status than others. For example, students in many junior and senior high schools claim that the "jocks" are the most prestigious crowd, whereas the "burnouts" are among the least prestigious. Self-esteem in older children and adolescents often reflects the status of their crowd. During the school years, youth from high-status crowds tend to have greater self-esteem than those from low-status crowds (Brown & Lohr, 1987).

Why do some students become nerds while others join the burnouts? Parenting style (discussed in Module 15.1) is part of the answer. A study by Brown and his colleagues (1993) examined the impact of three parental practices on students' membership in particular crowds. The investigators measured the extent to which parents emphasized academic achievement, monitored their children's out-of-school activities, and involved their children in joint decision making. When parents emphasized achievement, their children were more likely to be in the popular, jock, and normal crowds and less likely to be in the druggie crowd. When parents monitored out-of-school behavior, their children were more likely to be in the brain crowd and less likely to be in the druggie crowd. Finally, when parents included their children in joint decision making, their children were more likely to be in the brain and normal crowds and less likely to be in the druggie crowd. These findings were true for African American, Asian American, European American, and Hispanic American children and their parents.

What seems to happen is that when parents practice authoritative parenting—they are warm but controlling—their children become involved with crowds that endorse adult standards of behavior (for example, normals, jocks, brains). But, when parents' style is neglectful or permissive, their children are less likely to identify with adult standards of behavior and, instead, join crowds like druggies that disavow adult standards.

**GROUP STRUCTURE.**   Groups—whether in school, at a summer camp, or anyplace else—typically have a well-defined structure. **Most groups have a dominance hierarchy consisting of a leader to whom all other members of the group defer.** Other members know their position in the hierarchy. They yield to members who are above them in the hierarchy and assert themselves over members who are below them. A dominance hierarchy is useful in reducing conflict within groups because every member knows his or her place.

What determines where members stand in the hierarchy? With children, especially boys, physical power is often the basis for the dominance hierarchy. The leader is usually the most physically intimidating child (Pettit et al., 1990). Among girls and older boys, hierarchies are often based on individual traits that relate to the group's main function. At a summer camp, for example, the leaders most often are the children with the greatest camping experience. Among Girl Scouts, girls chosen to be patrol leaders tend to be bright and goal oriented and to have new ideas (Edwards, 1994). These characteristics are appropriate because the primary function of patrols is to help plan activities for the entire troop of Girl Scouts. Thus, leadership based on key skills is effective because it gives the greatest influence to those with the skills most important to group functioning (Hartup, 1983).

> Groups have a dominance hierarchy in which group members defer to a leader, who usually has skills important to the group's function.

**PEER PRESSURE.**   Groups establish *norms*—standards of behavior that apply to all group members—and groups may pressure members to conform to these norms. Such "peer pressure" is often characterized as an irresistible, harmful force. The stereotype is that teenagers exert enormous pressure on each other to behave antisocially. In reality, peer pressure is neither all-powerful nor always evil. For example, most junior and senior high students resist peer pressure to behave in ways that are clearly antisocial, such as stealing (Brown, Lohr, & McClenahan, 1986). Peer pressure can be positive, too; peers often urge one another to participate in school activities, such as trying out for a play or working on the yearbook, or to become involved in community action projects, such as Habitat for Humanity.

Peer pressure is most powerful when the standards for appropriate behavior are not clear-cut. Taste in music and clothing, for example, is completely

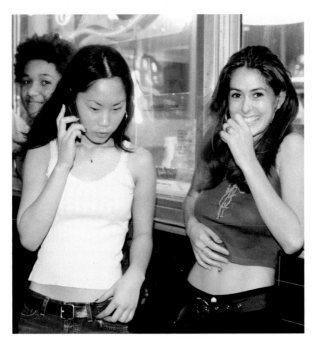

subjective, so youths conform to peer group guidelines, as you can see in the all-too-familiar sight shown in the photo—teen-age girls all wearing "cool" clothing.

Similarly, standards on smoking, drinking, and using drugs are often fuzzy. Drinking is a good case in point. Parents and groups like SADD (Students Against Driving Drunk) may discourage teens from drinking, yet American culture is filled with youthful models who drink, seem to enjoy it, and suffer no apparent ill effects. To the contrary, they seem to enjoy life even more. With such contradictory messages, it is not surprising that youth look to their peers for answers (Urberg, Değirmencioğlu, & Pilgrim, 1997). Consequently, some youth drink (or smoke, use drugs, or have sex) to conform to their group's norms, whereas others abstain, again reflecting their group's norms.

## Popularity and Rejection

Eileen is definitely the most popular child in her class. Other youngsters always want to play with her and sit near her at lunch or on the school bus. In contrast, Jay is the least popular child in the class. When he tries to join a game of foursquare, the others quit. Students in the class dislike Jay as much as they like Eileen.

Popular and rejected children like Eileen and Jay can be found in every classroom and neighborhood. In fact, studies of popularity (Newcomb, Bukowski, & Pattee, 1993) reveal that most children can be placed in one of five categories:

- *Popular children* are liked by many classmates.
- *Rejected children* are disliked by many classmates.
- *Controversial children* are both liked and disliked by classmates.
- *Average children* are liked and disliked by some classmates but without the intensity found for popular, rejected, or controversial children.
- *Neglected children* are ignored by classmates.

Children's classification in a particular category is reasonably stable over time: Children popular in first grade tend to be popular in sixth grade (Brengen et al., 2001).

What determines who's hot and who's not? Why is a child popular, rejected, controversial, average, or neglected? Smarter and physically attractive children are more often popular (Johnstone, Frame, & Bouman, 1992). However, the most important ingredient in popularity is social skill. Popular children are usually friendly, cooperative, and helpful. They are more skillful at communicating and better at integrating themselves into an ongoing conversation or play session—they "fit in" instead of "barging in" (Rubin et al., 1998). However, an exception to this general rule is found among elementary-school boys: Although most boys who are popular are friendly and cooperative, a subgroup of popular boys are aggressive, athletic, and do poorly in school (Rodkin et al., 2000).

**Popular children are socially skilled–they're friendly, cooperative, and helpful.**

VIDEO 16.4
Neglected Child

Why do some children fail in their efforts to be popular and end up in one of the other categories—rejected, controversial, average, or neglected? We know the most about rejected children. Rejected children tend to be socially unskilled (Stormshak et al., 1999). Many rejected children are aggressive, attacking their peers without provocation

(Brendgen et al., 2001; Dodge, Bates, & Pettit, 1990). Other rejected youngsters have poor self-control and are often disruptive in school (French, 1988, 1990). When conflicts arise, rejected children often become angry and retaliate (Bryant, 1992).

Being well liked seems straightforward: Be pleasant and friendly, not obnoxious; share, cooperate, and help instead of being disruptive. Are these rules specific to American children, or do they apply more generally? The "Cultural Influences" feature has the answer.

## CULTURAL INFLUENCES

### Keys to Popularity

In America, popular children seem to know how to get along with others. These results don't apply just to American children; they hold for children in many cultures around the world, including Canada, European countries, Israel, and China (e.g., Casiglia, Coco, & Zappulla, 1998). Sometimes, however, popular children have other characteristics that are unique to their cultural setting. In Israel, for example, popular children are more likely to be direct and assertive than in other countries (Krispin, Sternberg, & Lamb, 1992). In China, popular children are more likely to be shy than in other countries (Chen, Rubin, & Li, 1995). Evidently, good social skills are at the core of popularity in most countries, but other features may also be important, reflecting culturally specific values.

**CONSEQUENCES OF REJECTION.**  No one enjoys being rejected. Not surprisingly, peer rejection poses a major obstacle in children's development. Over the course of kindergarten, for example, rejected youngsters become less involved in classroom activities; they end the year feeling lonely and disliking school (Buhs & Ladd, 2001). Repeated peer rejection in childhood can also have serious long-term consequences (DeRosier, Kupersmidt, & Patterson, 1995; Downey et al., 1998; Ladd, 1998). Rejected youngsters are more likely than youngsters in the other categories to drop out of school, commit juvenile offenses, and suffer from psychopathology. The "Focus on Research" feature describes one study that showed some of the long-term effects of popularity and rejection.

## FOCUS ON RESEARCH

### Long-Term Consequences of Popularity and Rejection

*Who were the investigators, and what was the aim of the study?* Patricia Morison and Ann Masten (1991) set out to determine if the outcome of development is similar for popular and unpopular children. That is, they wanted to know if popular and rejected children take the same or different developmental paths.

*How did the investigators measure the topic of interest?* Morison and Masten identified popular and rejected children by asking children in grades 3 to 6 to nominate classmates for roles in an imaginary class play. Popular children were defined as those who were frequently nominated for roles like "a good leader," "everyone likes to be with," and "has many friends." Rejected children were those frequently nominated for roles like "picks on other kids," "too bossy," and "teases other children too much." Seven years later, the children and their parents completed questionnaires measuring academic achievement, social skill, and self-worth.

*Who were the children in the study?* Initially, 207 children in grades 3 to 6 were tested, and 183 of them completed the questionnaires 7 years later.

*What was the design of the study?* This study was correlational because Morison and Masten were interested in the relation that existed naturally between two sets of variables: popularity and rejection at the first testing and academic achievement, social skill, and self-worth at the second. The study was longitudinal because children were tested twice, once in grades 3 to 6 and again 7 years later.

> When children are rejected, they do less well in school, have lower self-esteem, and more often have behavioral problems.

*Were there ethical concerns with the study?* No. The general purpose of the study was explained and then parents and children consented to participate.

*What were the results?* The table shows the correlations between popularity and rejection in grades 3 to 6 and academic achievement, social skill, and self-worth measured 7 years later. Children who were popular in grades 3 to 6 were doing well in school, were socially skilled, and had high self-esteem. In contrast, children who were rejected in grades 3 to 6 were not doing well in school and had low self-esteem.

### Correlations Between Children's Popularity and Rejection in Grades 3 to 6 and Academic Achievement, Social Skill, and Self-Worth

| Outcome | Popularity in Grades 3–6 | Rejection in Grades 3–6 |
| --- | --- | --- |
| Academic achievement | .27 | −.25 |
| Social skill | .24 | .03 |
| Self-worth | .24 | −.22 |

TABLE 16–1

*What did the investigators conclude?* Popular children fit in with groups instead of trying to make groups adjust to them. When conflicts arise with peers, popular children try to understand the problem and provide useful solutions. Over time, popular children's prosocial skill pays long-term dividends; unfortunately, rejected children's lack of prosocial skill has a price as well.

*What converging evidence would strengthen these conclusions?* One useful step would be to continue the longitudinal study to examine the consequences of rejection later in adolescence. Another important addition would be to replace the questionnaires used to measure social skill with observations of actual social skills in natural settings.

**CAUSES OF REJECTION.**    Peer rejection can be traced, at least in part, to parental influence (Ladd, 1998). Children see how their parents respond to different social situations and often imitate these responses later. Parents who are friendly and cooperative with others demonstrate effective social skills. Parents who are belligerent and combative demonstrate much less effective social skills. In particular, when parents typically respond to interpersonal conflict like the couple in the photo—with intimidation or aggression—their children may imitate them; this hampers their development of social skills and makes them less popular in the long run (Keane, Brown, & Crenshaw, 1990).

Parents' disciplinary practices also affect their children's social skill and popularity. Inconsistent discipline—punishing a child for misbehaving one day and ignoring the same behavior the next—is associated with antisocial and aggressive behavior, paving the way to rejection (Dishion, 1990). Consistent punishment that is tied to parental love and affection is more likely to promote social skill and, in the process, popularity (Dekovic & Janssens, 1992).

In sum, parenting can lead to an aggressive interpersonal style in a child, which in turn leads to peer rejection. The implication, then, is that by teaching youngsters (and their parents) more effective ways of interacting with others, we can make rejection less likely. With improved social skills, rejected children would not need to resort to antisocial behaviors. Rejected children (and other types of unpopular children) can be taught how to initiate interaction, communicate clearly, and be friendly. They can also be discouraged from behaviors that peers dislike, such as whining and fighting. This training is very similar to the training given aggressive adolescents, who are typically unpopular (see Module 13.4). Training of this sort does work. Rejected children can learn skills that lead to peer acceptance and thereby avoid the long-term harm associated with being rejected (LaGreca, 1993; Mize & Ladd, 1990).

Throughout this module, we've seen that peers affect children's development in many ways—for example, through different forms of play, through friendships, and through participation in social groups. Beginning in the next module, we'll look at important *nonsocial* influences on children's development, starting with media such as television and computers.

## CHECK YOUR LEARNING

1. Toddlers often engage in _____ play, which consists of playing separately but looking at one another and sometimes communicating verbally.

2. _____ play promotes cognitive development and helps children explore topics that frighten them.

3. Parents influence play in their roles as playmate, _____, and coach.

4. Beginning in adolescence, friendships include an emphasis on loyalty, trust, and _____.

5. Friends are usually alike in age, sex, race, and _____.

6. In early adolescence, romantic relationships offer companionship and _____.

7. Adolescents usually have unprotected sex because of ignorance, _____, lack of motivation, and they don't know how to get contraceptives.

8. As groups form, a _____ typically emerges, with the leader at the top.

9. Peer pressure is most powerful when _____.

10. Compared to unpopular children, popular children are usually _____.

**CONNECTIONS**
How might developmental change in the nature of friendship be explained by Piaget's stages of cognitive development, described in Module 7.2?

**Answers:** (1) parallel, (2) Make-believe, (3) negotiator, (4) intimacy, (5) interests, (6) the opportunity for sexual exploration, (7) the belief that they are invincible—only others get pregnant, (8) dominance hierarchy, (9) standards for appropriate behavior are vague, (10) more skilled socially

# 16.2    Electronic Media

## LEARNING OBJECTIVES

● How does watching television affect children's attitudes and behavior?

● How does TV viewing influence children's cognitive development?

● How do children use computers at home and in school?

> *Whenever Bill visits his granddaughter, Harmony, he is struck by the amount of time Harmony spends watching television. Many of the programs she watches are worthwhile. Nevertheless, Bill wonders if such a steady diet of TV watching might somehow be harmful. Images pop on and off the screen so rapidly that Bill wonders how Harmony will ever learn to pay attention. And he worries that she won't be as attentive in other settings that aren't as rich in video stimulation.*

Think about some of the technological developments that contemporary children take for granted that were completely foreign to youngsters growing up just a few decades ago. Your list would probably include VCRs, cable TV, CD and DVD players, video game players, personal computers, cell phones, pagers, and the World Wide Web. More forces than ever before can potentially influence children's development. In generations past, children learned their culture's values from parents, teachers, religious leaders, and print media. These sources of cultural knowledge are still with us, but they coexist with new technologies that do not always portray parents' values. Two of these technologies—television and computers—are the focus of this module. As we look at their influence, we'll see if Bill's concern for his granddaughter is well founded.

## Television

MRS. HORTON, COULD YOU STOP BY SCHOOL TODAY?"

The cartoon exaggerates TV's impact on American children, but only somewhat. After all, think about how much time you spent in front of a TV while you were growing up. If you were a typical U.S. child and adolescent, you spent much more time watching TV than interacting with your parents or in school. The numbers tell an incredible story. School-age children spend about 15 to 25 hours each week watching TV (Nielson, 1990; Wright et al., 2001). Extrapolated through adolescence, the typical American high-school graduate has watched 15,000 hours of TV—nearly 2 full years of watching TV 24 hours daily! No wonder social scientists and laypeople alike think TV plays an important role in socializing American children.

For most youngsters, viewing time increases gradually during the preschool and elementary-school years, reaching a peak just before adolescence. Boys watch more TV than girls. Also, children with lower IQs watch more than those with higher IQs; children from lower-income families watch more TV than children from higher-income families (Huston & Wright, 1998).

It is hard to imagine that all this TV viewing would not affect children's behavior. For this reason, scientists have been studying the impact of TV since the 1950s. Much of the research has addressed the impact of the medium per se; other research has examined the impact of the contents of TV programs (Huston & Wright, 1998). In this section, we'll look at the results of both types of research.

**THE MEDIUM IS THE MESSAGE...OR IS IT?**   When TV first became popular, critics argued that the medium itself—independent of the contents of programs—has several harmful effects on viewers, particularly children (Huston & Wright, 1998). Among the criticisms were these:

- Because TV programs consist of many brief segments presented in rapid succession, children who watch a lot of TV develop short attention spans and have difficulty concentrating in school.
- Because TV provides ready-made, simple-to-interpret images, children who watch a lot of TV become passive, lazy thinkers and become less creative.
- Children who spend a lot of time watching TV spend less time in more productive and valuable activities, such as reading, participating in sports, and playing with friends.

In fact, as stated, none of these criticisms is consistently supported by research. The first criticism—TV watching reduces attention—is the easiest to dismiss. Research repeatedly shows that increased TV viewing does not lead to reduced attention, greater impulsivity, reduced task persistence, or increased activity levels (Huston & Wright, 1998). The contents of TV programs can influence these dimensions of children's behavior—children who watch impulsive models behave more impulsively themselves (see Module 13.1)—but TV per se does not harm children's ability to pay attention. Bill, the grandfather in the opening vignette, need not worry that his granddaughter's TV viewing will limit her ability to pay attention later in life.

As for the criticism that TV viewing fosters lazy thinking and stifles creativity, the evidence is mixed. Many studies find no link between the amount of TV viewing and creativity. For example, D. R. Anderson and colleagues (2001) found that the amount of time spent watching TV during the preschool years was unrelated to creativity during adolescence. Other studies, however, find a negative relation: As children watch more TV, they tend to be less creative on tests of divergent thinking like those described in Module 9.3 (Valkenburg & van der Voort, 1994; 1995). Child-development researchers don't know why the negative effects aren't found more consistently, although one idea is that the effects depend on which programs children watch, rather than simply the amount of TV watched.

Finally, according to the last criticism, TV viewing replaces other socially more desirable activities: The simple-minded view is that every hour of TV viewing replaces an hour of some more valuable activity, such as reading or doing homework. To illustrate the problems with this view, let's look at reading. The correlation between time spent watching TV and time spent reading *is* negative—heavy TV viewers read less (Huston & Wright, 1998). But we need to be cautious in interpreting this correlation (see Figure 2-2 on page 33). The easy interpretation is that watching much TV causes children to read less. However, other evidence suggests an alternate interpretation is more plausible: Children who are poor readers (and thus are unlikely to spend much time reading) end up watching a lot of TV. For youngsters who read poorly, an hour spent watching TV replaces some activity, but not an hour that would have been spent reading (Huston & Wright, 1998).

The research on each of these criticisms points to one conclusion: To understand the impact of TV on children, we need to move past the medium per se and consider other variables, including the contents of TV programs. Scientists who have done this have discovered that TV does, indeed, substantially affect children's development, as you'll see in the next three sections.

TV influences children through the contents of programs, not as a medium per se.

**INFLUENCE ON ATTITUDES AND SOCIAL BEHAVIOR.**   Children are definitely influenced by what they see on TV (Anderson et al., 2001). In Module 13.4, for example, we saw how some children become more aggressive after viewing violence on television; and in Module 14.3 we saw how children adopt gender stereotypes from TV.

Television can definitely have negative effects, but can TV be put to prosocial goals? Can TV viewing help children learn to be more generous and cooperative and have greater self-control? Yes, according to early laboratory studies. In these experiments, children were more likely to act prosocially after they watched brief films showing a peer acting prosocially (Liebert & Sprafkin, 1988). For example, children were more likely to share or more likely to resist the temptation to take from others after they watched other children sharing or resisting temptation.

Children are more likely to be cooperative and generous after having seen TV characters who are cooperative and generous.

Research with actual TV programs leads to the same conclusion: Youngsters who watch TV shows that emphasize prosocial behavior, such as *Mister Rogers' Neighborhood*, are more likely to behave prosocially (Huston & Wright, 1998; Sanders, Montgomery, & Brechman-Toussaint, 2000). Nevertheless, two factors restrict the actual prosocial impact of TV viewing. First, prosocial behaviors are portrayed far less frequently than aggressive behaviors, so opportunities to learn the former from television are limited. Second, the relatively small number of prosocial programs compete with other kinds of television programs and other non-TV activities for children's time, so children simply may not watch the few prosocial programs that are televised. Consequently, we are far from harnessing the power of television for prosocial uses.

**INFLUENCE ON CONSUMER BEHAVIOR.**   Sugary cereals, hamburgers and French fries, snack foods, toys, jeans, and athletic shoes.... A phenomenal number of TV advertisements for these products are directed toward children and adolescents. A typical youth may see more than 50 commercials a day! Children as young as 3 years can distinguish commercials from programs, though preschoolers believe commercials are simply a different form of entertainment—one designed to inform viewers. Not until age 8 or 9 do children begin to understand the persuasive intent of commercials. At the same time, children also begin to realize that commercials are not always truthful (Liebert & Sprafkin, 1988; Oates, Blades, & Gunter, 2002). They understand that a toy rocket will not really fly or that a doll will not really talk, contrary to how they're shown in commercials.

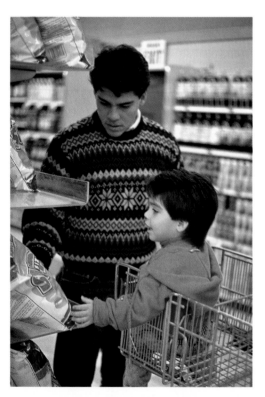

Even though children gradually understand the real intent of commercials, commercials are still effective sales tools (Donkin, Neale, & Tilston, 1993). Children grow to like many of the products advertised on TV and, like the youngster in the photograph, urge parents to buy products they've seen on television. In one study (Greenberg, Fazel, & Weber, 1986), for example, more than 75 percent of the children reported that they had asked their parents to buy a product they had seen advertised on TV. And more often than not, parents had purchased the product for them!

This selling power of TV has long concerned advocates for children because so many commercials are for foods that have little nutritional value and can lead to obesity and tooth decay. The U.S. government once regulated the amount and type of advertising on children's TV programs (Huston, Watkins, & Kunkel, 1989), but today the responsibility falls largely to parents.

**INFLUENCE ON COGNITION.**   The year 1969 was a watershed in the history of children's television. That year marked the appearance of a program designed to use the power of video and animation to foster preschool skills, including recognizing letters and numbers, counting, and building vocabulary. The program achieved its goals. Preschoolers who watched the show regularly were more proficient at the targeted academic skills than preschoolers who watched infrequently. Regular viewers also adjusted to school more readily, according to teachers' ratings (Bogatz & Ball, 1972).

By now, of course, you know that I'm talking about Big Bird, Bert, Ernie, and other members of the cast of *Sesame Street*, shown in the photo. For more than 30 years, *Sesame Street*, produced originally by Children's Television Workshop, has helped educate generations of preschoolers (Fisch, Truglio, & Cole, 1999). Today, mothers and fathers who watched *Sesame Street* as preschoolers are watching with their own youngsters.

More recent studies confirm that *Sesame Street* remains effective. Rice and her colleagues (1990), for example, found that children who had watched *Sesame Street* frequently at age 3 had larger vocabularies as 5-year-olds than children who had watched infrequently. And, remarkably, the time preschool children spend watching *Sesame Street* predicts their grades in high school and the amount of time they spend reading as adolescents (Anderson et al., 2001).

Building on the success of *Sesame Street*, Children's Television Workshop developed a number of other successful programs. *Electric Company* teaches reading skills, *3-2-1 Contact* focuses on science and technology, and *Square One TV* teaches mathematics (Fisch & McCann, 1993). Other public television programs include *Reading Rainbow*, which introduces children's books; *Where in Time Is Carmen Sandiego?*, which teaches history; and *Ghostwriter*, which focuses on writing. Although these programs are no longer in production (except for *Sesame Street*), they are still shown on cable networks and demonstrate that children can learn academic skills and useful social skills from TV. Thus, TV can be beneficial if parents monitor their youngsters' viewing and if they insist that the television industry improves the quality and variety of programs available for children and adolescents.

The "Improving Children's Lives" feature includes some guidelines for ensuring that TV's influence on children is positive.

## IMPROVING CHILDREN'S LIVES

### Get the Kids Off the Couch!

If you know a child who sits glued to the TV screen from after school until bedtime, it's time to take action. Here are some suggestions:

- Children need absolute rules concerning the amount of TV and the types of programs that they can watch. These rules must be enforced consistently.

- Children shouldn't fall into the trap of "I'm bored, so I'll watch TV." Children should be encouraged to know what they want to watch before they turn on the TV.

- Adults should watch TV with children and discuss the programs. For example, parents can express their disapproval of a character's use of aggression and suggest other means of resolving conflicts. Parents can also point to the stereotypes that are depicted. The aim is for children to learn that TV's account of the world is often inaccurate and that TV should be watched critically.

- Parents need to be good TV viewers themselves. The first two tips listed here apply to viewers of all ages. When a child is present, parents shouldn't watch violent programs or others that are inappropriate for the young. And parents should watch TV deliberately and selectively, instead of mindlessly channel surfing.

## Computers

Some observers believe that computers are creating a "digital childhood"—an era in which new media are transforming the lives of American children (Cocking, 2001). In this section, we'll look at children's use of computers at home and in school.

**COMPUTERS IN THE HOME.**  Nearly two-thirds of American families own a computer and, on a given day, about half of American children use a computer outside of school (Roberts et al., 1999). How do children and adolescents use computers? One frequent use is playing games. And, just as children and adolescents are influenced by the TV programs they watch, they are influenced by the contents of the computer games they play. On the one hand, many popular games including *Tetris* and *Star Fox* involve basic perceptual-spatial skills, such as estimating the trajectory of a moving object. When children play such games frequently, their spatial skills often improve (Subrahmanyam et al., 2001). On the other hand, many popular games, such *Counter-Strike* and *Grand Theft Auto 3* are violent, with players killing game characters in extraordinarily gruesome ways. Just as exposure to televised violence can make children behave more aggressively, playing violent video games can make children more aggressive (Sherry, 2001).

In addition to playing games, children use computers to access the Internet. When children are on-line, what are they doing? First, they do their schoolwork—children use the Internet to help them find information for school assignments. Second, they communicate—they use e-mail and instant messaging to "talk" with nearby and distant friends and relatives. Third, they provide their own entertainment—they play games on-line or search for information related to interests and hobbies (Subrahmanyam et al., 2001).

In many respects, home computers have changed the *how* of childhood and adolescence but not the *what*. As with previous generations, children and adolescents still play games, connect with peers, and do homework. The home computer simply provides a different means for accomplishing these tasks. As we'll see in the next section, much the same is true of computers in schools.

**COMPUTERS IN THE CLASSROOM.**  New technologies—whether TV, videotape, or pocket calculator—soon find themselves in the classroom. Personal computers are no exception; virtually all American public schools now use personal computers to aid instruction. Computers serve many functions in the classroom (Lepper & Gurtner, 1989; Roschelle et al., 2000). One is that of tutor: Children use computers to learn reading, spelling, arithmetic, science, and social studies. Computers allow instruction to be individualized and interactive. Students proceed at their own pace, receiving feedback and help when necessary. Computers are also a valuable medium for experiential learning.

Simulation programs allow students to explore the world in ways that would be impossible or dangerous otherwise. Students can change the law of gravity or see what happens to a city when no taxes are imposed. Finally, computers can help students achieve traditional academic goals (Steelman, 1994). A graphics program can allow artistically untalented students to produce beautiful illustrations. A word-processing program can relieve much of the drudgery associated with revising, thereby encouraging better writing.

> Computers are used in schools as tutors, for experiential learning, and to help children accomplish traditional academic goals more simply.

Not all researchers, educators, and policymakers are enthusiastic about computers taking on a pivotal role in education. Some critics fear that computers eliminate an important human element in learning. However, all experts agree on the need for research-based policies concerning children and computer technology. The "Child Development and Family Policy" feature describes progress toward this goal.

## CHILD DEVELOPMENT AND FAMILY POLICY

### How Can Computers Promote Child Development?

Most U.S. children have access to computers at home and at school, and most adults agree that computer literacy is an important skill for children to acquire. Yet some adults worry that the benefits of computers for children are accompanied by some serious costs. Hearing these concerns, the Board on Children, Youth, and Families (BCYF) has worked to create constructive policies for children and computer technology. The BCYF is part of the National Academy of Sciences, a private organization that was chartered by the U.S. Congress in 1863. The BCYF provides nonpartisan critical analysis of policy-related issues concerning children, youth, and their families. Beginning in 2001, the BCYF summarized the existing research on children and computers to determine the additional research needed to help formulate public policy. The work has focused on three key issues, each of which has an associated question for public policy. These are summarized in the table.

| Policy Issues Concerning Children and Computers | |
| --- | --- |
| **Issue** | **Policy Question** |
| *Access to Computer Technology:* Children from low-income families are less likely to have a computer at home; their schools usually have computers, but they tend to be older machines and there are fewer of them. | How can all children have ready access to modern computing equipment? |
| *Use of Computers in Education:* Simply putting computers in classrooms has little impact on quality of instruction. Instead, teachers need additional training, computerized instruction needs to be integrated into curriculums, computers need to have software that is instructionally effective, and software needs to be adjustable to the needs of individual students. | What are effective ways of using computers to impove students' learning? |
| *Computers and Children's Well-Being:* Outside the classroom, computers may have positive and negative effects on children. On the positive side, the Internet allows children to maintain friendship over distances, an asset in today's mobile society. On the negative side, the time that children devote to computers may come at the expense of other activities that promote children's well-being (e.g., physical play, interacting with peers, reading). | What can be done to increase the benefits of computers for children's lives while minimizing the potential harm? |

TABLE 16–2

The BCYF does not have an in-house research team to conduct the necessary studies. Instead, the BCYF works to make these issues well known in the scientific community. In this spirit, in January 2001, BCYF conducted a workshop in which researchers and policymakers met to discuss these issues and the type of research that is needed. The result of this workshop—along with other efforts by the BCYF and other interested organizations—will be to encourage child-development researchers in universities to conduct the studies necessary to provide policy-related information. ●

Overall, then, computers are like television in that the technology per se doesn't necessarily influence children's development. However, the way the technology is used—for example, watching violent TV programs or using word-processing software to revise a short story—can affect children, positively or negatively depending on the use. In the next module, we'll see whether institutions such as neighborhoods and schools also influence children in this manner.

### CHECK YOUR LEARNING

1. Preschool children believe that commercials _____.

2. Youngsters who are frequent viewers of *Sesame Street* typically improve their academic skills and, as adolescents, they have better grades and _____.

3. When children play violent video games, they _____.

4. Children and adolescents use home computers to play games and to _____.

5. Computers are used in schools as tutors, _____, and to help students accomplish traditional academic tasks more simply.

> **ACTIVE CHILDREN**
> How does children's use of computers show that children influence their own development?

**Answers:** (1) represent a different, informative type of program but do not understand their intent to persuade, (2) read more, (3) become more aggressive, (4) access the Internet, (5) as a medium for experiential learning

# 16.3    Institutional Influences

— **Day Care**

— **Part-Time Employment**

— **Neighborhoods**

— **School**

### LEARNING OBJECTIVES

● How are children affected by nonparental child care?

● What is the impact of part-time employment on children's development?

● How are children influenced by their neighborhoods?

● What are the hallmarks of effective schools and effective teachers?

> *When 15-year-old Aaron announced that he wanted an after-school job at the local supermarket, his mother was delighted, believing that he would learn much from the experience. Five months later, she had her doubts. Aaron had lost interest in school, and they argued constantly about how he spent his money.*

So far in this chapter, we've seen the potent influences of peers and media on children's development. Yet there are other noteworthy influences on children and their development—cultural institutions where children spend much of their lives. In this module, we'll look at four such institutions: day care, the workplace, neighborhoods, and school. As we do, we'll see whether part-time jobs like Aaron's help or harm youth.

## Day Care

Each day, approximately 10 million U.S. children age 5 and under are cared for by someone other than their mother, a phenomenon linked to more dual-earner couples and to more single-parent households in the United States in the 21st century. Who is caring for America's children? About one-third of America's infants and preschoolers are cared for in their home, typically by the father or a grandparent (U.S. Bureau of the Census, 1995). Another third receive care in the provider's home. The provider is often—but not always—a relative. Finally, another third attend day-care or nursery-school programs. The patterns are very similar for European American, African American, and Hispanic American youngsters (Singer et al., 1998).

Many parents, particularly mothers, have misgivings about their children spending so much time in the care of others. Should parents worry? Does nonmaternal care harm children? Before turning to research for answers to these questions, let's put them in historical and cross-cultural perspective. Although nonmaternal care of children is often portrayed as unnatural—and therefore potentially harmful—the truth is that for most of history and in most cultures, a majority of children have been cared for by someone other than the mother, at least some of the time (Lamb, 1999). When viewed from the larger perspective of history, there is nothing "natural" or "traditional" about mothers having nearly exclusive responsibility for child care.

Nevertheless, in the United States (and many other industrialized countries) since World War II, the cultural ideal has been that children are better off when cared for at home by their mothers. Does research support the cultural ideal? In answering this question, most researchers worried about the impact of child care on mother–infant attachment. But, as we saw in Module 11.3, the Early Child-Care study conducted by the National Institute of Child Health and Human Development showed that attachment security was affected by child care only when less sensitive mothers had their infants in low-quality child care.

Of course, the effects of day care need not be limited to attachment; other aspects of children's development might be affected, and these have been investigated in other reports from the Early Child-Care study. Here, too, the general finding is that children who have high quality child care do not differ from children who are raised at home by their mothers. However, children who have poor-quality child care are slightly more likely to have behavior problems, to lag in their linguistic and cognitive development, and to be less ready for school (NICHD Early Child Care Research Network, 1998, 2000).

> Parents can roll their children in high-quality day care without fearing harmful consequences.

In general, working parents can enroll their infants and preschoolers in high-quality day-care programs with no fear of harmful consequences. What should parents look for in a day-care center? A first-rate program should have (a) a low ratio of children to caregivers, (b) a well-trained, experienced staff, (c) low staff turnover, (d) ample opportunities for educational and social stimulation, and (e) effective communication between parents and day-care workers concerning the general aims and routine functioning of the day-care program (Lamb, 1999; Rosenthal & Vandell, 1996).

Collectively, these variables do *not* guarantee that a child will receive high-quality care. Sensitive, responsive caregiving—the same behavior that promotes secure attachment relationships—is the real key to high-quality child care. Centers that have well-trained, experienced staff caring for a relatively small number of children are more likely to provide good care, but the only way to know the quality of care with certainty is to see for yourself (Lamb, 1999; NICHD Early Child Care Research Network, 2002).

When children enter elementary school, child care becomes easier for working parents. However, many children still need care before or after school. Formal programs for before- and after-school care have been studied much less than day care for infants and toddlers (Lamb, 1999). Nevertheless, the limited research that has been done suggests that many of the same variables associated with high-quality day care are associated with high-quality before- and after-school care. Children benefit from well-trained, encouraging teachers; from low child-to-teacher ratios; and from a flexible, age-appropriate curriculum (Vandell & Shumow, 1999).

Many school-age children—approximately 10 percent of all 5- to 13-year-olds in the United States—receive no formal care after school; they are left alone to care for themselves (Galambos & Maggs, 1991). **Children who care for themselves are sometimes called latchkey children, a term that originated more than 200 years ago to describe children who raised a door latch to enter their own homes.** Some latchkey children, like the child in photo, stay at home alone (sometimes with parental supervision in absentia via the telephone). Others may stay at friends' homes where adults are sometimes present, or they may be unsupervised in public places such as shopping malls.

The popular perception is that latchkey children are a frightened, endangered lot. But research provides little support for this view. To the contrary, most older children and adolescents who care for themselves at home after school fare as well as children in the care of parents or other adults (Lamb, 1999). In one study, third, fourth, and fifth graders who cared for themselves at home were no more anxious, headstrong, or dependent than children cared for by their mothers (Vandell & Ramanan, 1991).

Research does reveal one group that is at risk—children and adolescents who spend their after-school hours away from home, unsupervised. These individuals are more prone to antisocial influences of peers and more prone to engage in problem behavior (Galamabos & Maggs, 1991; Pettit et al., 1999).

This generally rosy picture does not mean that parents should begin self-care without careful planning. Robinson, Rowland, and Coleman (1986) suggest that parents contemplating self-care for their children should ask themselves several basic questions:

• Is the child old enough and emotionally mature enough, regardless of age, to assume the responsibility of self-care? For example, does the child stay home for short time periods?

**Children can care for themselves after school if they are mature, their neighborhood is safe, and they are supervised by an adult.**

• Does the child live in a safe neighborhood where crime is low and community cohesion is high and where neighbors and community facilities can be depended on as support systems?

• Does the child's self-care arrangement provide for some type of adult supervision, such as a telephone or pager?

If each of these questions can be answered "yes," then self-care will probably work. The next step is to prepare the child for self-care. Children need to know after-school routines (for example, acceptable ways of getting home from school and how to check in with a parent), rules for their own behavior after school (for example, acceptable and unacceptable activities), and guidelines on how to handle emergencies (Peterson, 1989). Posting procedures and emergency phone numbers in a conspicuous location is often enough reassurance for children.

Fortunately, employers have begun to realize that convenient, high-quality child care makes for a better employee. Businesses are realizing that the availability of excellent child care helps attract and retain a skilled labor force. And cities help by modifying their zoning codes so that new shopping complexes and office buildings must include child-care facilities, like those in the top photo. With effort, organization, and help from the community and business, high-quality child care can be available to all families.

## Part-Time Employment

The teen in the middle photo is engaged in an American adolescent ritual—the part-time job. Today, a substantial majority of high-school seniors work part-time. Out of every five adolescent part-time workers, one works at a fast-food restaurant like McDonald's or Burger King, and another works in a retail store as a cashier or salesperson. Boys are more likely to be manual laborers, busboys, or newspaper carriers. Girls are more often baby sitters, housekeepers, or restaurant workers, and they are usually paid less than boys (Call, 1996; Mortimer, 1991).

Most adults praise teens for working, believing that early exposure to the workplace teaches self-discipline, self-confidence, and important job skills (Snedeker, 1982). For most adolescents, however, the reality is very different. Part-time work can actually be harmful, for several reasons:

1. *School performance suffers.* When students work more than approximately 15 hours per week, they devote less time to homework and are more apt to cut classes. Not surprisingly, their grades are lower than those of their peers who work less or not at all (Steinberg, Fegley, & Dornbusch, 1993). Why should 15 hours of work be so detrimental to school performance? A 15-hour work schedule usually means four 3-hour shifts after school and another 3-hour shift on the weekend. This would seem to leave ample opportunity to study, but only if students use their time effectively. In fact, many high-school students apparently do not have the foresight and discipline necessary to consistently meet the combined demands of work and school. Like the boy in the bottom photo, many teens have great difficulty balancing work, study, and sleep.

2. *There are mental health and behavioral problems.* Adolescents who work long hours—more than 15 or 20 hours a week—are more likely to experience anxiety and depression, and their self-esteem often suffers. Many adolescents find themselves in jobs that are repetitive and boring but stressful, and such conditions undermine self-esteem and breed anxiety. Extensive part-time work frequently leads to substance abuse, including cigarettes, alcohol, marijuana, and cocaine (Bachman & Schulenberg, 1993; Mortimer et al., 1996). Extensive work is also associated with more

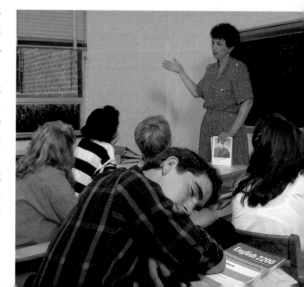

frequent problem behavior, including violence toward others, trouble with police, and arguments with parents (Bachman & Schulenberg, 1993).

Why employment is associated with all of these problems is not clear. Perhaps employed adolescents turn to drugs to help them cope with the anxiety and depression brought on by work. Arguments with parents may become more common because anxious, depressed adolescents are more prone to argue or because wage-earning adolescents may believe that their freedom should match their income. Whatever the exact mechanism, extensive part-time work is clearly detrimental to the mental health of most adolescents.

3. *Affluence is misleading.* Adults sometimes argue that work is good for teenagers because it teaches them "the value of a dollar." Here, too, reality is at odds with the adage. The typical teenage pattern is to "earn and spend." Working adolescents spend most of their earnings on themselves—to buy clothing, snack food, or cosmetics and to pay for entertainment. Few working teens set aside much of their income for future goals, such as a college education, or use it to contribute to their family's expenses (Shanahan et al., 1996a; 1996b). Because parents customarily pay for many of the essential expenses associated with truly independent living—rent, utilities, and groceries, for example—working adolescents often have a vastly higher percentage of their income available for discretionary spending than working adults. Thus, for many teens, the part-time work experience provides unrealistic expectations about how income can be allocated (Bachman, 1983).

The message that emerges repeatedly from research on part-time employment is hardly encouraging. Like Aaron, the teenage boy in the vignette, adolescents who work long hours at part-time jobs do not benefit from the experience. To the contrary, they do worse in school, are more likely to have behavioral problems, and learn how to spend money rather than how to manage it. These effects are similar for adolescents from different ethnic groups (Steinberg & Dornbusch, 1991) and are comparable for boys and girls (Bachman & Schulenberg, 1993).

**When adolescents work many hours in part-time jobs, they do worse in school, often have behavioral problems, and experience misleading affluence.**

Does this mean that teenagers who are still in school should never work part-time? Not necessarily. Part-time employment can be a good experience, depending on the circumstances. One key is the number of hours of work. Although the exact number of hours varies, of course, from one student to the next, most students could easily work 5 hours weekly without harm, and many could work 10 hours weekly. Another key is the type of job. When adolescents have jobs that allow them to use their skills (for example, bookkeeping, computing, or typing) and acquire new ones, self-esteem is enhanced, and they learn from their work experience (Mortimer, Harley, & Staff, 2002). Yet another factor is how teens spend their earnings. When they save their money or use it to pay for clothes and school expenses, relations with their parents often improve (Shanahan et al., 1996a, 1996b).

By these criteria, who is likely to show the harmful effects of part-time work? A teen who spends 30 hours a week bagging groceries and spends most of it on CDs or videos. And who is likely to benefit from part-time work? A teen who likes to tinker with cars, who spends Saturdays working in a repair shop, and who sets aside some of his earnings for college.

Finally, summer jobs typically do not involve conflict between work and school. Consequently, many of the harmful effects associated with part-time employment during the school year do not hold for summer employment. In fact, such employment sometimes enhances adolescents' self-esteem, especially when they save part of their income for future plans (Marsh, 1991).

## Neighborhoods

For years, Mr. Rogers greeted preschool children singing, "It's a beautiful day in my neighborhood" and telling young viewers, "I've always wanted a neighbor just like you." Mr. Roger's neighborhood is indeed safe and nurturing, but not all children are so fortunate; their neighborhoods are neither safe nor nurturing. Do these differences in neighborhoods affect children's lives? We'll answer this question in the next few pages.

Before we consider how neighborhoods affect children, we need to decide what constitutes a neighborhood. Sometimes researchers define neighborhoods in terms of school districts or other government boundaries, but the most commonly accepted approach in the U.S. is to define neighborhoods in terms of census tracts. These usually include 3,000 to 8,000 people living in an area that has, according to local authorities, some identity based on physical features (e.g., streets, a commercial district, proximity to a school) or social features (e.g., most residents are members of the same racial or ethnic group). Using census-tract information, researchers have identified two features of neighborhoods that are particularly useful when it comes to understanding children's development: *socioeconomic status*, reflecting the income and education of the residents, and *stability*, typically defined as the percentage of residents who have lived in the neighborhood for several years (Leventhal & Brooks-Gunn, 2003).

Of course, defining neighborhoods in terms of these features of census tracts is not perfect; this approach ignores some potentially important features of neighborhoods. For example, they don't consider safety per se and they don't measure the presence of institutions like a church, temple, or school that can provide focus and vitality to a neighborhood. But the advantage is that census tracts are defined in a standard way across the United States and mountains of data concerning census tracts are available to researchers.

Do neighborhoods matter? Yes; all other things being equal, children benefit from living in a neighborhood where most of the adults are well educated and economically advantaged. These benefits are seen for both school achievement and psychological adjustment. In other words, when children live in economically advantaged neighborhoods, they tend to do better in school and are somewhat less likely to have behavioral and emotional problems (Gennetian & Miller, 2002; Ryan et al., 2002).

Researchers agree that neighborhoods per se do not influence children's behavior. Instead, the impact of neighborhoods is indirect, transmitted through people (parents and peers, primarily) and other social institutions. Several pathways of influence are possible (Leventhal & Brooks-Gunn, 2000). One concerns the availability of institutional resources: Economically advantaged neighborhoods more often have the kinds of resources that enhance children's development: libraries like the one in the photo, museums, quality day care, and good schools to foster children's cognitive development; medical services to provide for children's physical and mental health; and opportunities for adolescents to find work. In economically advantaged neighborhoods that tend to have these resources, children are more likely to have experiences that lead to school success, to good health, and to the ability to find part-time jobs as teenagers. In contrast, in economically disadvantaged neighborhoods that frequently lack these resources, children are often prepared inadequately for school, receive little medical care, and are unable to find jobs as teenagers, so they turn to delinquent or criminal behavior.

A second way in which neighborhoods affect children and adolescents is based

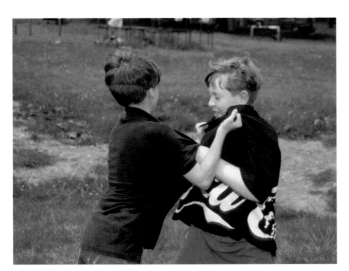

on the fact that, because economically advantaged neighborhoods are more likely to be stable, they are more cohesive and close-knit, which means residents take a greater interest in neighborhood goings-on, including those of children and adolescents (Leventhal & Brooks-Gunn, 2000). Suppose, for example, adults see the two boys in the photo slugging it out in the park. In a cohesive neighborhood, adults are more likely to intervene (e.g., break up the fight and scold the children for fighting) because they are committed to its residents; in a less cohesive neighborhood, adults might ignore the children because they don't want the hassle of getting involved. Thus, in cohesive neighborhoods, residents are much more likely to monitor the activities of neighborhood children, making it less likely that children get in trouble.

Finally, neighborhoods affect children through their impact on parenting behavior. Adults living in chronic poverty often experience much stress and are prone to depression, factors that typically reduce the quality of parenting. That is, when parents worry constantly about not having enough money to buy food or to pay rent, they are less warm to their children, praise them less frequently, and, instead, are often angry with them. When parents act this way consistently, their children are at risk for behavioral problems (Evans & English, 2002; Mistry et al., 2002).

Chronic poverty is particularly hard for parents because they usually have few social supports to help them cope with stress. When adults living in economically advantaged neighborhoods find life so stressful that they need help, they can turn to neighbors or health-care professionals. In contrast, adults living in poverty are less likely to turn to either a neighbor (because they don't know anyone well enough due to instability in the neighborhood) or a health-care professional (because one is not available nearby or they can't afford it). Thus, adults living in chronic poverty experience a "double whammy"—more stress and fewer resources to cope with stress—which contributes to less effective parenting.

Thus, children growing up in economically disadvantaged neighborhoods typically have access to fewer institutional resources, are monitored less often by neighbors, and experience less effective parenting brought on by chronic stress. At the

Children who grow up in poverty have access to fewer resources, are monitored less often by neighbors, and experience less effective parenting.

same time, the research suggests that an effective way to invest in poverty-ridden neighborhoods is by providing additional institutional resources (Leventhal & Brooks-Gunn, 2000). When neighborhoods have good child care and good schools, many opportunities for recreation, and effective health care, children benefit directly. They also benefit indirectly because when parents feel less stress they parent more effectively, and because residents are less likely to move, contributing to neighborhood cohesiveness.

Schools are such a salient resource for children that we need to know what makes them effective; that's our next topic.

# School

At age 5 or 6, most American children head off to kindergarten, starting an educational journey that lasts 13 years for most and more than 17 years for some. How do schools influence children's development? Answering this question is difficult because American education is a smorgasbord, reflecting local control by communities throughout the United States. Schools differ on many dimensions, including their emphasis on academic goals and parent involvement. Teachers, too, differ in many ways, such as how they run their classrooms and how they teach. These and other variables affect how much students learn, as you'll see in the next few pages. Let's begin with school-based influences.

**SCHOOL-BASED INFLUENCES ON STUDENT ACHIEVEMENT.**  Roosevelt High School, in the center of Detroit, has an enrollment of 3,500 students in grades 9 to 12. Opened in 1936, the building shows its age. The rooms are drafty, the desks are decorated with generations of graffiti, and new technology means an overhead projector. Nevertheless, attendance at Roosevelt is good, most students graduate, and many continue their education at community colleges and state universities. Southport High School, in Boston, has about the same enrollment as Roosevelt High and the building is about the same age. Yet truancy is commonplace at Southport, where fewer than half the students graduate and almost none go to college.

These schools are hypothetical, but accurately portray American education. Some schools are much more successful than others, regardless of whether success is defined in terms of the percentage of students who are literate, graduate, or go to college. Why are some schools successful and not others? Researchers (Good & Brophy, 2002; Stevenson & Stigler, 1992; Walberg, 1995; Wentzel, 2002) have identified a number of factors linked with successful schools:

- *Staff and students alike understand that academic excellence is the primary goal and standards are set accordingly.* The school day emphasizes instruction, and students are recognized publicly for their academic accomplishments.

- *The school climate is safe and nurturing.* Students know that they can devote their energy to learning (instead of worrying about being harmed in school), and they know the staff truly wants to see them succeed.

- *Parents are involved.* In some cases, this may be through formal arrangements, such as parent-teacher organizations. Or it may be informal. Parents may spend some time each week in school grading papers or, like the dad in the photo, tutoring a child. Such involvement signals both teachers and students that parents are committed to students' success.

- *Progress of students, teachers, and programs is monitored.* The only way to know if schools are succeeding is by measuring performance. Students, teachers, and programs need to be evaluated regularly, using objective measures that reflect academic goals. In schools that follow these guidelines, students usually succeed. In schools where the guidelines are ignored, students more often fail.

Of course, on a daily basis, individual teachers have the most potential for impact. Let's see how teachers can influence their students' achievement.

**TEACHER-BASED INFLUENCES.** Take a moment to recall your teachers in elementary school, junior high, and high school. Some you probably remember fondly, because they were enthusiastic and innovative and they made learning fun. You may remember others with bitterness. They seemed to have lost their love of teaching and children, making class a living hell. Your experience tells you that some teachers are better than others, but what exactly makes a good teacher? Personality and enthusiasm are not the key elements. Although you may enjoy warm and eager teachers, research (Good & Brophy, 2002; Stevenson & Stigler, 1992; Walberg, 1995) shows several other factors are critical when it comes to students' achievement. Students tend to learn the most when teachers

- *manage the classroom effectively so they can devote most of their time to instruction.* When teachers like the man in the photo spend a lot of time disciplining students, or when students do not move smoothly from one class activity to the next, instructional time is wasted, and students are apt to learn less.

- *believe they are responsible for their students' learning and that their students will learn when taught well.* When students don't understand a new topic, these teachers repeat the original instruction (in case the student missed something) or create new instruction (in case the student heard everything but just didn't "get it"). These teachers keep plugging away because they feel at fault if students don't learn.

- *pay careful attention to pacing.* They present material slowly enough that students can understand a new concept, but not so slowly that students get bored.

- *emphasize mastery of topics.* Teachers should introduce a topic, then give students many opportunities to understand, practice, and apply the topic. Just as you'd find it hard to go directly from driver's ed to driving a race car, students more often achieve when they grasp a new topic thoroughly, then gradually move on to other, more advanced topics.

- *teach actively.* They don't just talk or give students an endless stream of worksheets. Instead, they demonstrate topics concretely or have hands-on demonstrations for students. They also have students participate in class activities and encourage students to interact, generating ideas and solving problems together.

- *value tutoring.* They work with students individually or in small groups, so they can gear their instruction to each student's level and check each student's understanding. They also encourage peer tutoring, in which more capable students tutor less capable students. Children who are tutored by peers do learn, and so do the tutors, evidently because teaching helps tutors organize their knowledge.

- *teach children techniques for monitoring and managing their own learning.* Students are more likely to achieve when they are taught how to recognize the aims of school tasks and know effective strategies for achieving those aims (like those described on pages 217-218).

Thus, what makes for effective schools and teachers? No single element is crucial. Instead, many factors contribute to make some schools and teachers remarkably effective. Some of the essential ingredients include parents who are involved, teachers who care deeply about their students' learning and manage classrooms well, and a school that is safe, nurturing, and emphasizes achievement.

Of course, many schools are not very successful. However, as parents, teachers, and concerned citizens, we need to resist the idea that any single magic potion can cure a school's ills. As we have seen throughout this book, the outcome of development—in this case, academic achievement—is determined by many factors, including environmental forces (e.g., parents, teachers) as well as the contributions of children themselves. To foster academic success, we need to consider all these factors, not focus narrowly on one or two.

On a more general note, understanding why and how children succeed in school (and in other domains of life) is indeed a challenging puzzle. But, scientists are making remarkable progress in solving the child-development puzzle; as we end the book, I hope you've enjoyed learning about their discoveries. Thanks for reading.

## CHECK YOUR LEARNING

1. Parents need not worry about harmful effects of day care on their children as long as _____.

2. Older children and adolescents who care for themselves after school get along well as long as _____.

3. Adolescents who work extensively at part-time jobs during the school year often get lower grades, have behavior problems, and _____.

4. Part-time employment during the school year can be beneficial if adolescents limit the number of hours that they work and _____.

5. Children often fare better in economically advantaged neighborhoods because more institutional resources are available, because neighbors are more likely to monitor the behavior of children and adolescents, and because _____.

6. In successful schools, academic excellence is a priority, the school is safe and nurturant, progress of students and teachers is monitored, and _____.

7. Effective teachers manage classrooms well, believe they are responsible for their students' learning, _____, teach actively, pay attention to pacing, value tutoring, and show children how to monitor their own learning.

**CONNECTIONS**

In this module, we've seen that cultural institutions (e.g., schools) can affect a child's development. Describe how this influence illustrates connections in different domains of development.

**Answers:** (1) children are enrolled in high-quality day care, (2) they are at home rather than unsupervised and away from home (e.g., at a mall), (3) mistakenly think they are affluent, (4) hold jobs that allow them to use and develop skills, (5) their parents are not subject to the chronic stress associated with living in poverty, (6) parents are involved, (7) emphasize mastery of subjects

# Unifying Themes: Continuity

In this last chapter of the book, I want to remind you that *early development is related to later development but not perfectly.* Children who are rejected by their peers are, over time, more likely to do poorly in school, have lower self-esteem, and have behavioral problems. Of course, not all rejected children suffer this fate. Some do well in school, have high self-esteem, and avoid behavioral problems. Positive outcomes are more likely to occur when children learn effective skills for interacting with others. As we've seen many times in previous chapters, early experiences often point children toward a particular developmental path, but later experiences can cause them to change course.

## See for Yourself

The best way to understand the differences between good and bad teaching is to visit some actual school classrooms. Try to visit three or four classes in at least two different schools. (You can usually arrange this by speaking with the school's principal.) Take along the principles of good teaching that are listed on page 492. Start by watching how the teachers and children interact. Then, decide how much the teacher relies on each of the principles. You'll probably see that most teachers use some but not all of these principles. And you'll also see that, in today's classroom, consistently following all the principles is very challenging. See for yourself!

## Resources

For more information about...

what makes some schools more effective than others, read Edward Fiske's *Smart Schools, Smart Kids* (Simon and Schuster, 1991), which examines some exceptional U.S. schools to discover the key ingredients to a successful school.

the impact of child care on children's development, visit the Web site of The NICHD Study of Early Child Care and Youth Development, **http://secc.rti.org/**

## Key Terms

clique 472
cooperative play 463
crowd 472
dominance hierarchy 473
friendship 467

latchkey children 486
nonsocial play 462
parallel play 462
rough-and-tumble play 466
simple social play 463

## 16.1 Peers

### Development of Peer Interactions
Children's first real social interactions, at about 12 to 15 months, take the form of parallel play, in which infants play alone while watching each other. A few months later, simple social play emerges, in which toddlers engage in similar activities and interact with one another. At about 2 years, cooperative play organized around a theme becomes common.

Make-believe play is also common and, in addition to being fun, promotes cognitive development and lets children examine frightening topics in a nonthreatening way. Most forms of solitary play are harmless. Parents foster children's play by acting as skilled playmates, mediating disputes, and coaching social skills.

Beyond preschool, peer relations improve and emphasize talking and being together, as well as rough-and-tumble play.

### Friendship
Friendships among preschoolers are based on common interests and getting along well. As children grow, loyalty, trust, and intimacy become more important features in their friendships. Friends are usually similar in age, sex, race, and attitudes. Children with friends are more skilled socially and better adjusted.

### Romantic Relationships
Romantic relationships emerge in adolescence, beginning with mixed-group activities. For younger adolescents, romantic relationships offer companionship and the possibility of sexual exploration; for older adolescents, they provide trust and support.

By the time they finish high school, most adolescents have had sex. Pregnancy is common because many adolescents engage in unprotected sex. Comprehensive sex education is effective in reducing teenage sexual activity.

Adolescents often wonder about their sexual orientation but only a small percentage report having homosexual experiences. Research has discredited many explanations of the origins of homosexual orientations but suggests some sort of biological influences.

### Groups
Older children and adolescents often form cliques—small groups of like-minded individuals that become part of a crowd. Some crowds have higher status than others, and members of higher-status crowds often have higher self-esteem than members of lower-status crowds.

Most groups have a dominance hierarchy, a well-defined structure with a leader at the top. Physical power often determines the dominance hierarchy, particularly among younger boys. With older children and adolescents, dominance hierarchies are more often based on skills that are important to group functioning.

Peers are particularly influential when standards of behavior are unclear, such as for taste in music or clothing, or concerning drinking, using drugs, and sex.

### Popularity and Rejection
Popular children are socially skilled. They generally share, cooperate, and help others; they are unlikely to behave antisocially (fight or whine).

Some children are rejected by their peers because they are too aggressive. These children are often unsuccessful in school and have behavioral problems. Their aggressive style of interacting can often be traced to parents who are belligerent or inconsistent in their discipline.

## 16.2 Electronic Media

### Television
Many popular criticisms about TV as a medium (e.g., it shortens children's attention span) are not supported by research. However, the content of TV programs can affect children's attitudes and social behavior, their consumer behavior, and their cognitive development. Youngsters who frequently watch prosocial TV become more skilled socially, and preschoolers who watch *Sesame Street* improve their academic skills and adjust more readily to school.

### Computers
At home, children use computers to play games (and are influenced by the contents of the games they play) and to access the Internet. Computers are used in school as tutors, to provide experiential learning, and as a multipurpose tool to achieve traditional academic goals.

## 16.3 Institutional Influences

### Day Care
Many U.S. children are cared for at home by a father or other relative, in a day-care provider's home, or in a day-care center. Infants and young children are not harmed by such arrangements as long as the care is high quality and parents remain responsive to their children. Children can care for themselves after school if they are mature enough, live in a safe neighborhood, and are supervised by an adult.

### Part-Time Employment
Most adolescents in the United States have part-time jobs. Adolescents who are employed more than 15 hours per week during the school year typically do poorly in school, often have lowered self-esteem and increased anxiety, and have problems interacting with others. Employed adolescents save relatively little of their income. Instead, they spend most of it on clothing, food, and entertainment for themselves, which can give misleading expectations about how to allocate income.

Part-time employment can be beneficial if adolescents work relatively few hours, if the work allows them to use existing skills or acquire new ones, and if teens save some of their earnings. Summer employment, because it does not conflict with the demands of school, can also be beneficial.

### Neighborhoods
Children are more likely to thrive when they grow up in a neighborhood that is economically advantaged (the adults are well educated and have higher incomes) and that is stable. These neighborhoods are better for children because more institutional resources (e.g., schools, libraries, health care) are available, because residents are more likely to monitor the behavior of children and adolescents living in the neighborhood, and because parents are not living in chronic stress associated with poverty.

### School
Schools influence students' achievement in many ways. Students are most likely to achieve when their school emphasizes academic excellence, has a safe and nurturing environment, monitors pupils' and teachers' progress, and encourages parents to be involved.

Students achieve at higher levels when their teachers manage classrooms effectively, take responsibility for their students' learning, teach mastery of material, pace material well, value tutoring, and show children how to monitor their own learning.

# GLOSSARY

## A

**accommodation** According to Piaget, changing existing knowledge based on new knowledge.

**achievement status** The identity status in Marcia's theory in which adolescents have explored alternative identities and are now secure in their chosen identities.

**active gene-environment relation** The phenomenon in which individuals actively seek environments related to their genetic makeup.

**active–passive child issue** The issue of whether children are simply at the mercy of the environment (passive child) or actively influence their own development through their own unique individual characteristics (active child).

**adolescent egocentrism** The self-absorption that is characteristic of teenagers as they search for identity.

**African American English** A dialect of standard English spoken by some African Americans that has slightly different grammatical rules than standard English.

**age of viability** The age at which a fetus can survive because most of its bodily systems function adequately, typically at 7 months after conception.

**aggression** Behavior meant to harm others.

**allele** A variation of a specific gene.

**altruism** Prosocial behavior, such as helping and sharing, in which the individual does not benefit directly from his or her behavior.

**amniocentesis** A prenatal diagnostic technique that involves withdrawing a sample of amniotic fluid through the abdomen using a syringe.

**amnion** An inner sac in which the developing child will rest.

**amniotic fluid** Fluid in the amnion that cushions the embryo and maintains a constant temperature.

**androgens** Hormones secreted by the testes that influence aggressive behavior.

**androgynous** Having a combination of gender-role traits that includes both instrumental and expressive behaviors.

**animism** Crediting inanimate objects with life and lifelike properties such as feelings.

**anorexia nervosa** A persistent refusal to eat, accompanied by an irrational fear of being overweight.

**anoxia** Lack of oxygen during delivery, typically because the umbilical cord becomes pinched or tangled during delivery.

**Apgar score** A measure to evaluate the newborn's condition, based on breathing, heart rate, muscle tone, presence of reflexes, and skin tone.

**applied developmental science** A scientific discipline that uses child-development research to promote healthy development, particularly for vulnerable children and families.

**assimilation** According to Piaget, taking in information that is compatible with what one already knows.

**attachment** The affectionate, reciprocal relationship that is formed at about 6 or 7 months between an infant and his or her primary caregiver, usually the mother.

**attention** Processes that determine which information will be processed further by an individual.

**attributions** An individual's personal explanation for success or failure.

**auditory threshold** The quietest sound that a person can hear.

**authoritarian parenting** A style of parenting that combines high levels of control and low levels of warmth toward children.

**authoritative parenting** A style of parenting that combines a moderate degree of control with being warm and responsive toward children.

**autobiographical memory** A person's memory of the significant events and experiences of his or her own life.

**automatic processes** Cognitive activities that require virtually no effort.

**autosomes** The first 22 pairs of chromosomes.

**avoidant attachment** A relationship in which infants turn away from their mothers when they are reunited following a brief separation.

**axon** A tubelike structure that emerges from the cell body and transmits information to other neurons.

## B

**babbling** Speechlike sounds that consist of vowel-consonant combinations.

**baby biographies** Detailed, systematic observations of individual children, often by famous scientists, that helped to pave the wave for objective research on children.

**basal metabolic rate** The speed with which the body consumes calories.

**basic cry** A cry that starts softly and gradually becomes more intense; often heard when babies are hungry or tired.

**basic emotions** Emotions that are experienced by people worldwide and that consist of a subjective feeling, a physiological change, and an overt behavior; examples include happiness, anger, and fear.

**behavioral genetics** The branch of genetics that deals with inheritance of behavioral and psychological traits.

**blastocyst** The fertilized egg 4 days after conception; consists of about 100 cells and resembles a hollow ball.

**blended family** A family consisting of a biological parent, a stepparent, and children.

**body mass index (BMI)** An adjusted ratio of weight to height used to define overweight.

**breech presentation** A birth in which the feet or bottom are delivered first, before the head.

**bulimia nervosa** An eating disorder in which individuals alternate between bingeing (when they eat uncontrollably) and purging through self-induced vomiting or with laxatives.

**bullying** Aggression that is unprovoked and seems to have as its sole goal to intimidate, harass, or humiliate another child; the most common form of aggression.

## C

**cardinality principle** The counting principle that the last number name denotes the number of objects being counted.

**cell body** The center of the neuron that keeps the neuron alive.

**centration** Narrowly focused thought characteristic of Piaget's preoperational stage.

**cerebral cortex** The wrinkled surface of the brain that regulates many functions that are distinctly human.

**cesarean section (C-section)** A surgical procedure in which an incision is made in the abdomen to remove the baby from the uterus.

**chorionic villus sampling (CVS)** A prenatal diagnostic technique that involves taking a sample of tissue from the chorion.

**chromosomes** Threadlike structures in the nucleus of the cell that contain genetic material.

**clique** Small groups of friends who are similar in age, sex, race, and interests.

**cognitive-developmental theory** An approach to development that focuses on how children think and on how their thinking changes over time.

**cognitive self-regulation** Skill at identifying goals, selecting effective strategies, and accurate monitoring; a characteristic of successful students.

**componential subtheory** In Sternberg's triarchic theory, the idea that intelligence depends on basic cognitive processes.

**components** Basic cognitive processes that, in Sternberg's componential subtheory, are the basis of intelligence.

**comprehension** The process of extracting meaning from a sequence of words.

**concrete operational stage** The third of Piaget's stages, from 7 to 11 years, in which children first use mental operations to solve problems and to reason.

**cones** Specialized neurons in the back of the eye that detect wavelength of light and, therefore, color.

**congenital adrenal hyperplasia (CAH)** A genetic disorder in which girls are masculinized because the adrenal glands secrete large amounts of androgen during prenatal development.

**constricting** An interaction style, common among boys, in which one child tries to emerge as the victor by threatening or contradicting the others, by exaggerating, and so on.

**constructivism** The view, associated with Piaget, that children are active participants in their own development who systematically construct ever more sophisticated understandings of their worlds.

**contextual subtheory** In Sternberg's triarchic theory, the idea that intelligent behavior involves adapting to an environment to achieve one's goals.

**continuity–discontinuity issue** An issue concerned with whether a developmental phenomenon follows a smooth progression throughout the life span or a series of abrupt shifts.

**conventional level** The second level of reasoning in Kohlberg's theory, where moral reasoning is based on society's norms.

**convergent thinking** Using information to arrive at one standard, correct answer.

**cooing** Early vowel-like sounds that babies produce.

**cooperative play** Play that is organized around a theme, with each child taking on a different role; begins at about 2 years of age.

**core knowledge hypothesis** The view that infants are born with rudimentary knowledge of the world that is elaborated based on children's experiences.

**corpus callosum** A thick bundle of neurons that connects the two cerebral hemispheres.

**correlation coefficient** A statistic that reveals the strength and direction of the relation between two variables.

**correlational study** A research design in which investigators look at relations between variables as they exist naturally in the world.

**cortex** The wrinkled outer surface of the brain that regulates many important human behaviors.

**counterimitation** A type of observational learning in which the child observes and learns what should not be done.

**critical period** A time in development when a specific type of learning can take place; before or after the critical period, the same learning is difficult or even impossible.

**cross-sectional study** A research design in which people of different ages are compared at the same point in time.

**crowd** A large group that includes many cliques with similar attitudes and values.

**crowning** The appearance of the top of the baby's head during labor.

**crystallization** The first phase in Super's theory of career development, in which adolescents use their emerging identities for ideas about careers.

**crystallized intelligence** A person's culturally influenced accumulated knowledge and skills, including understanding printed language, comprehending language, and knowing vocabulary.

**culture** The knowledge, attitudes, and behavior associated with a group of people.

**culture-fair intelligence tests** Tests designed to reduce the impact of different experiences by including items based on experiences common to many cultures.

# D

**deductive reasoning** Drawing conclusions from facts; characteristic of formal operational thought.

**dendrite** The end of the neuron that receives information; it looks like a tree with many branches.

**deoxyribonucleic acid (DNA)** A molecule composed of four nucleotide bases that is the biochemical basis of heredity.

**dependent variable** The behavior that is observed after other variables are manipulated.

**depression** A disorder characterized by pervasive feelings of sadness, irritability, and low self-esteem.

**differentiation** Distinguishing and mastering individual motions.

**diffusion status** The identity status in Marcia's theory in which adolescents do not have an identity and are doing nothing to achieve one.

**direct instruction** A parental behavior in which adults try to influence their children's behavior by telling them what to do, when, and why.

**dismissive attachment representation** A representation of parent–child relations in which adults describe childhood experiences in very general terms and often idealize their parents.

**disorganized (disoriented) attachment** A relationship in which infants don't seem to understand what's happening when they are separated and later reunited with their mothers.

**dispensing-family-wisdom grandparents** Grandparents who assume an authoritarian position and dispense information and advice to parents and child alike.

**display rules** Culturally specific standards for appropriate expressions of emotion in a particular setting or with a particular person or persons.

**dispositional praise** Praise that links a child's altruistic behavior to an underlying altruistic disposition.

**distant grandparents** Grandparents who have little contact except on holidays, birthdays, or other family celebrations.

**divergent thinking** Thinking in novel and unusual directions.

**dizygotic (fraternal) twins** Twins that are the result of the fertilization of two separate eggs by two sperm.

**dominance hierarchy** An ordering of individuals within a group in which group members with lower status defer to those with greater status.

**dominant** The form of an allele whose chemical instructions are followed.

**doula** A person familiar with childbirth who provides emotional and physical support throughout labor and delivery.

**Down syndrome** A disorder, caused by an extra chromosome, in which individuals are mentally retarded and have a distinctive appearance.

**dynamic systems theory** A theory that views motor development as involving many distinct skills that are organized and reorganized over time to meet demands of specific tasks.

**dynamic testing** An approach to intelligence testing that measures a child's learning potential by having the child learn something new in the presence of the examiner and with the examiner's help.

# E

**ectoderm** The outer layer of the embryo, which will become the hair, outer layer of skin, and nervous system.

**ego** According to Freud, the rational component of the personality; develops during the first few years of life.

**egocentrism** Difficulty in seeing the world from another's point of view; typical of children in Piaget's preoperational stage.

**elaboration**  A memory strategy in which information is embellished in order to make it more memorable.

**electroencephalogram (EEG)**  A pattern of brain waves recorded from electrodes that are placed on the scalp.

**embryo**  The name given to the developing baby once the zygote is completely embedded in the uterine wall.

**emotional intelligence**  The ability to use one's own and others' emotions effectively for solving problems and living happily.

**empathic orientation**  According to Eisenberg, a level of prosocial reasoning common in some children and many adolescents in which their thinking considers the injured child's perspective and how their own actions would make the child feel.

**empathy**  Experiencing another person's feelings.

**enabling**  An interaction style, common among girls, in which children's actions and remarks tend to support others and to sustain the interaction.

**endoderm**  The inner layer of the embryo, which will become the lungs and the digestive system.

**epiphyses**  Ends of bone tissue, which are formed first before the center is formed.

**equilibration**  According to Piaget, the process by which children reorganize their schemes and, in the process, move to the next developmental stage.

**ethnic identity**  The feeling that one is part of an ethnic group and the understanding of special customs and traditions of the group's culture and heritage.

**ethological theory**  A theory in which development is seen from an evolutionary perspective and behaviors are examined for their survival value.

**evocative gene-environment relation**  The phenomenon in which different genotypes evoke different responses from the environment.

**evolutionary psychology**  The theoretical view that many human behaviors represent successful adaptation to the environment.

**executive functioning**  A mechanism of growth that includes inhibitory processes, planning, and cognitive flexibility.

**exosystem**  According to Bronfenbrenner, social settings that influence one's development even though one does not experience them firsthand.

**experiential subtheory**  In Sternberg's triarchic theory, the idea that intelligence is revealed on both novel and familiar tasks.

**experiment**  A systematic way of manipulating factors that a researcher thinks cause a particular behavior.

**expressive style**  A style of language learning that describes children whose vocabularies include many social phrases that are used like one word.

**expressive traits**  Psychological characteristics that describe a person who is focused on emotions and interpersonal relationships.

# F

**familial mental retardation**  A form of mental retardation that does not involve biological damage but represents the low end of the normal distribution of intelligence.

**family policy**  Laws and regulations that directly or indirectly affect families with children.

**fast mapping**  The fact that children make connections between new words and referents so quickly that they can't be considering all possible meanings.

**fetal alcohol syndrome (FAS)**  A disorder affecting babies whose mothers consumed large amounts of alcohol while they were pregnant.

**fetal medicine**  The branch of medicine that deals with treating prenatal problems.

**field experiment**  A type of experiment in which the researcher manipulates independent variables in a natural setting so that the results are more likely to be representative of behavior in real-world settings.

**fine-motor skills**  Motor skills associated with grasping, holding, and manipulating objects.

**fluid intelligence**  The ability to perceive relations among stimuli.

**foreclosure status**  The identity status in Marcia's theory in which adolescents have an identity that was chosen based on advice from adults, rather than one that was a result of personal exploration of alternatives.

**formal grandparents**  Grandparents who see their role in traditional terms, expressing a strong interest in the grandchild but maintaining a hands-off attitude toward child rearing.

**formal operational stage**  The fourth of Piaget's stages, from roughly age 11 into adulthood, in which children and adolescents can apply mental operations to abstract entities, allowing them to think hypothetically and reason deductively.

**friendship**  A voluntary relationship between two people involving mutual liking.

**frontal cortex**  A brain region that regulates personality and goal-directed behavior.

**functional magnetic resonance imaging (F-MRI)**  A technique for measuring brain activity that uses magnetic fields to track the flow of blood in the brain.

**fun-seeking grandparents**  Grandparents who see themselves as a primary source of fun for their grandchildren and who avoid more serious interactions.

# G

**gender consistency**  The understanding, usually acquired between ages 4 and 7 years, that maleness and femaleness do not change over situations or according to personal wishes.

**gender constancy**  A stage in which children have mastered gender labels, gender stability, and gender consistency.

**gender identity**  The perception of oneself as either male or female.

**gender labeling**  Children's understanding, by 2 or 3 years, that they are either boys or girls, and their use of these words to label themselves.

**gender role**  Culturally prescribed behaviors considered appropriate for males and females.

**gender-schema theory**  A theory that children learn gender roles by first deciding if an object, activity, or behavior is female or male, then using this information to decide whether they should learn more about the object, activity, or behavior.

**gender stability**  Children's understanding, during the preschool years, that gender does not change: Boys become men and girls become women.

**gender stereotypes**  Beliefs and images about males and females that are not necessarily true.

**gene**  A group of nucleotide bases that provide a specific set of biochemical instructions.

**genetic engineering**  A branch of fetal medicine in which defective genes are replaced with synthetic normal genes.

**genotype**  A person's hereditary makeup.

**germ disc**  A small cluster of cells near the center of the zygote that develops into the baby.

**gifted**  Traditionally, individuals with intelligence test scores of at least 130.

**grammar**  A language's rules for combining words to create sentences.

**grammatical morphemes**  Words or endings of words that make a sentence grammatical.

**growth hormone**  A hormone, secreted by the pituitary gland during sleep, that regulates growth by triggering the release of other hormones that cause muscles and bones to grow.

# H

**habituation**  Becoming unresponsive to a stimulus that is presented repeatedly.

**hedonistic orientation**  According to Eisenberg, a level of prosocial reasoning common in preschool and elementary-school children in which they emphasize pursuing their own pleasure.

**hemispheres**  The right and left halves of the cortex.

**heterozygous** When the genes for any hereditary characteristic differ from each other.

**homozygous** When the genes for any hereditary characteristic are the same.

**Huntington's disease** A type of dementia caused by a dominant allele; characterized by degeneration of the nervous system.

# I

**id** According to Freud, the element of personality that wants immediate gratification of bodily wants and needs; present at birth.

**illusion of invulnerability** The belief, common among adolescents, that misfortune only happens to others.

**imaginary audience** Adolescents' feeling that their behavior is constantly being watched by their peers.

**imitation (observational learning)** Learning that takes place simply by observing others.

**immanent justice** A characteristic of the stage of moral realism in which children believe that breaking a rule always leads to punishment.

**implantation** The process in which the zygote burrows into the uterine wall and establishes connections with a woman's blood vessels.

**implementation** The third phase in Super's theory of career development, in which individuals enter the workforce.

**imprinting** Learning that occurs during a critical period soon after birth or hatching, as demonstrated by chicks creating an emotional bond with the first moving object they see.

**incomplete dominance** The situation in which one allele does not dominate another completely.

**independent variable** The factor that is manipulated by the researcher in an experiment.

**indifferent-uninvolved parenting** A style of parenting that provides neither warmth nor control and that minimizes the amount of time parents spend with children.

**indulgent-permissive parenting** A style of parenting that offers warmth and caring but little parental control over children.

**infant-directed speech** Speech that adults use with babies that is slow and loud and has exaggerated changes in pitch.

**infant mortality** The number of infants out of 1,000 births who die before their first birthday.

**infantile amnesia** The inability to remember events from early in one's life.

**information-processing theory** A view that human cognition consists of mental hardware and software.

**inhibitory processes** Processes that prevent task-irrelevant information from entering working memory.

**inner speech** Vygotsky's term for thought.

**instrumental aggression** Aggression used to achieve an explicit goal.

**instrumental traits** Psychological characteristics that describe a person who acts on and influences the world.

**integration** Linking individual motions into a coherent, coordinated whole.

**intelligence quotient (IQ)** A ratio of mental age to chronological age, multiplied by 100.

**internal working model** An infant's understanding of how responsive and dependable the mother is; thought to influence close relationships throughout the child's life.

**interposition** A perceptual cue to depth based on the fact that nearby objects partially obscure more distant objects.

**intersensory redundancy** Information that is presented simultaneously to different sensory modes, such as rhythm.

**intonation** A pattern of rising and falling pitch in speech or babbling that often indicates whether the utterance is a statement, question, or command.

**in vitro fertilization** The technique of fertilizing eggs with sperm in a petri dish and then transferring several of the fertilized eggs to the mother's uterus, where they might implant in the lining of the uterine wall.

# J

**joint custody** When both parents retain legal custody of their children following a divorce.

**Just Communities** Special groups of students and teachers within public high schools created by Kohlberg to foster discussion and expose students to more advanced moral thinking.

# K

**knowledge-telling strategy** A strategy for writing, often used by younger writers, in which information is written in sequence as it is retrieved from memory.

**knowledge-transforming strategy** A strategy for writing, often used by older writers, in which they decide what information to include and how best to organize it for the point they wish to convey to their reader.

# L

**language** Any rule-based system for expressing ideas.

**latchkey children** Children who care for themselves after school.

**learning disability** When a child with normal intelligence has difficulty mastering at least one academic subject.

**linear perspective** A cue to depth perception based on the fact that parallel lines come together at a single point in the distance.

**locomotion** The ability to move around in the world.

**longitudinal study** A research design in which a single cohort is studied over multiple times of measurement.

**long-term memory** A permanent storehouse for memories that has unlimited capacity.

# M

**macrosystem** According to Bronfenbrenner, the cultural and subcultural settings in which the microsystems, mesosystems, and exosystems are embedded.

**mad cry** A more intense version of a basic cry.

**malnutrition** Being small for one's age because of inadequate nutrition.

**maturational theory** The view that child development reflects a specific and prearranged scheme or plan within the body.

**memory strategies** Activities that improve remembering.

**menarche** The onset of menstruation.

**mental age (MA)** In intelligence testing, a measure of children's performance corresponding to the chronological age of those whose performance equals the child's.

**mental operations** Cognitive actions that can be performed on objects or ideas.

**mental retardation** A disorder in which, before 18 years of age, individuals have substantially below-average intelligence and problems adapting to an environment.

**mental rotation** One aspect of spatial ability involving the ability to imagine how an object will look after it has been moved in space.

**mesoderm** The middle layer of the embryo, which will become the muscles, bones, and circulatory system.

**mesosystem** According to Bronfenbrenner, the interrelations between different microsystems.

**meta-analysis** A tool that allows researchers to synthesize the results of many studies to estimate relations between variables.

**metacognitive knowledge** A person's knowledge and awareness of cognitive processes.

**metamemory** A person's informal understanding of memory; includes the ability to diagnose memory problems accurately and to monitor the effectiveness of memory strategies.

**microgenetic study** A special type of longitudinal study in which children are tested repeatedly over a span of days or weeks, with the aim of observing change directly as it occurs.

**microsystem** According to Bronfenbrenner, the people and objects that are present in one's immediate environment.

**monozygotic (identical) twins** Twins that result when a single fertilized egg splits to form two new individuals.

**moral realism** A stage described by Piaget that begins at about 5 years and continues through age 7, in which children believe that rules are created by wise adults and therefore must be followed and cannot be changed.

**moral relativism** A stage described by Piaget that begins at about age 8, in which children understand that rules are created by people to help them get along.

**moratorium status** The identity status in Marcia's theory in which adolescents are still examining different alternatives and have yet to find a satisfactory identity.

**motor skills** Coordinated movements of the muscles and limbs.

**myelin** A fatty sheath that surrounds neurons in the central nervous system and allows them to transmit information more rapidly.

# N

**naming explosion** A period, beginning at about age 18 months, in which children learn new words very rapidly.

**naturalistic observation** A method of observation in which children are observed as they behave spontaneously in a real-life situation.

**nature–nurture issue** An issue concerning the manner in which genetic and environmental factors influence development.

**needs-oriented orientation** According to Eisenberg, a level of prosocial reasoning common in some preschool and many elementary-school children in which they are concerned about others' needs and want to help.

**negative reinforcement trap** A situation in which parents often unwittingly reinforce the very behaviors they want to discourage; particularly likely between mothers and sons.

**neo-Piagetian theories** Theories that share Piaget's basic assumptions about cognitive development.

**neural plate** A flat group of cells present in prenatal development that becomes the brain and spinal cord.

**neuron** A cell that is the basic unit of the brain and nervous system; specializes in receiving and transmitting information.

**neurotransmitters** Chemicals released by terminal buttons that carry information to nearby neurons.

**niche picking** The process of deliberately seeking environments that are compatible with one's genetic makeup.

**non-REM (regular) sleep** Sleep in which heart rate, breathing, and brain activity are steady.

**nonshared environmental influences** Forces within a family that make children different from one another.

**nonsocial play** An early form of play, identified by Parten (1932), in which children play alone or watch others play but do not play themselves.

**norepinephrine** A neurotransmitter that helps regulate brain centers that allow people to experience pleasure; below-normal levels of norepinephrine may contribute to depression.

# O

**object permanence** The understanding, acquired in infancy, that objects exist independently of oneself.

**one-to-one principle** The counting principle that states that there must be one and only one number name for each object counted.

**operant conditioning** A view of learning, proposed by Skinner, that emphasizes reward and punishment.

**ordinality** The fact that numbers can differ in magnitude; some values are greater than others.

**organic mental retardation** Mental retardation that can be traced to a specific biological or physical problem.

**organization** A memory strategy in which information to be remembered is structured so that related information is placed together.

**orienting response** The response to an unfamiliar or unusual stimulus in which a person startles, fixates the eyes on the stimulus, and shows changes in heart rate and brain-wave patterns.

**osteoporosis** A disease, common among women over age 50, in which a person's bones become thin and brittle, and, as a consequence, sometimes break.

**overextension** When children define words more broadly than adults do.

**overregularization** Children's application of rules to words that are exceptions to the rule; used as evidence that children master grammar by learning rules.

# P

**pain cry** A cry that begins with a sudden, long burst, followed by a long pause and gasping.

**parallel play** When children play alone but are aware of and interested in what another child is doing; occurs soon after the first birthday.

**passive gene-environment relation** The phenomenon in which parents pass on genotypes to their children and provide much of the early environment for their young children.

**period of the fetus** The longest period of prenatal development, extending from the ninth week after conception until birth.

**personal domain** The domain of decisions concerning one's body (e.g., what to eat and wear) and choices of friends or activities.

**personal fable** The feeling of many adolescents that their feelings and experiences are unique and have never been experienced by anyone else before.

**phenotype** The physical, behavioral, and psychological features that are the result of the interaction between one's genes and the environment.

**phonemes** Unique speech sounds that can be used to create words.

**phonological awareness** The ability to hear the distinctive sounds associated with specific letters.

**phonology** The sounds of a language.

**placenta** The structure through which nutrients and wastes are exchanged between the mother and the developing child.

**plasticity** In the context of neural development, the extent to which brain organization is flexible.

**polygenic inheritance** When phenotypes are the result of the combined activity of many separate genes.

**population** A broad group of children that are the usual focus of research in child development.

**positron emission tomography (PET) scan** A procedure that shows the amount of activity in various regions of the brain by monitoring levels of radioactive glucose.

**postconventional level** The third level of reasoning in Kohlberg's theory, in which morality is based on a personal moral code.

**postpartum depression** A condition affecting 10 to 15 percent of new mothers in which irritability continues for months and is often accompanied by feelings of low self-worth, disturbed sleep, poor appetite, and apathy.

**pragmatics** How people use language to communicate effectively.

**preconventional level** The first level of reasoning in Kohlberg's theory, where moral reasoning is based on external forces.

**prejudice** A view of other people, usually negative, that is based on their membership in a specific group.

**premature infant** A baby born before the 38th week after conception.

**prenatal development** The many changes that turn a fertilized egg into a newborn human.

**preoccupied attachment representation** A representation of parent–child relations in which adults describe childhood experiences emotionally and often express anger or confusion regarding relationships with their parents.

**preoperational stage** The second of Piaget's stages, from 2 to 7 years, in which children first use symbols to represent objects and events.

**primary circular reaction** According to Piaget, when infants accidentally produce pleasant events that are centered on the body and then try to recreate the events.

**primary sex characteristics** Changes in bodily organs directly involved in reproduction (i.e., the ovaries, uterus, and vagina in girls and the scrotum, testes, and penis in boys) that are signs of physical maturity.

**private speech** Comments that are not intended for others but that help children regulate their own behavior.

**propositions** Ideas created during reading by combining words.

**prosocial behavior** Any behavior that benefits another person.

**psychodynamic theory** A view first formulated by Sigmund Freud in which development is largely determined by how well people resolve conflicts they face at different ages.

**psychometricians** Psychologists who specialize in the measurement of psychological characteristics such as intelligence and personality.

**psychosocial theory** A theory proposed by Erik Erikson in which personality development is the result of the interaction of maturation and societal demands.

**puberty** A collection of physical changes that marks the onset of adolescence, such as the growth spurt and the growth of breasts or testes.

**punishment** Applying an aversive stimulus (e.g., a spanking) or removing an attractive stimulus (e.g., TV viewing); an action that discourages the reoccurrence of the response that it follows.

# Q

**quasi-experimental design** A research design in which statistical methods are used to make nonrandom groups comparable.

# R

**rapid-eye-movement (REM) sleep (irregular sleep)** Irregular sleep in which an infant's eyes dart rapidly beneath the eyelids, while the body is quite active.

**reaction range** The phenomenon that a particular genotype can interact with various environments to produce a range of phenotypes.

**reactive aggression** Aggression prompted by another child's behavior.

**recessive** An allele whose instructions are ignored when it is combined with a dominant allele.

**referential style** A style of language learning that describes children whose vocabularies are dominated by names of objects, persons, or actions.

**reflexes** Unlearned responses that are triggered by specific stimulation.

**rehearsal** A memory strategy that involves repetitively naming information that is to be remembered.

**reinforcement** A consequence that increases the likelihood that a behavior will be repeated in the future.

**relational aggression** A form of verbal aggression in which children try to hurt others by undermining their social relationships.

**relative size** A perceptual cue to depth based on the fact that nearby objects look substantially larger than objects in the distance.

**reliability** As applied to tests, how consistent test scores are from one testing time to another.

**resistant attachment** A relationship in which, after a brief separation, infants want to be held but are difficult to console.

**retinal disparity** A perceptual cue to depth based on the fact that, when a person views an object, the retinal images in the left and right eyes differ.

**rough-and-tumble play** A form of play common during the elementary-school years in which children playfully chase, punch, kick, shove, fight, and wrestle with peers.

# S

**sample** A group of children drawn from a population that participates in research.

**savants** Individuals with mental retardation who are quite talented in one domain.

**scaffolding** A teaching style in which adults adjust the amount of assistance that they offer, based on the learner's needs.

**scheme** According to Piaget, a mental structure that organizes information and regulates behavior.

**school phobia** An overwhelming fear of going to school and active resistance to attending school.

**script** The means by which people remember common events consisting of sequences of activities.

**secondary circular reaction** According to Piaget, when infants accidentally produce interesting events with objects and then try to repeat those events.

**secondary sex characteristics** Physical signs of maturity in body parts not linked directly to the reproductive organs (e.g., growth of breasts in girls, the appearance of facial hair in boys, the appearance of body hair in both boys and girls).

**secular growth trends** Changes in physical development from one generation to the next; for example, the fact that people in industrialized societies are larger and are maturing earlier than in previous generations.

**secure attachment** A relationship in which infants have come to trust and depend on their mothers.

**secure attachment representation** A representation of parent–child relations in which adults describe childhood experiences objectively and mention both positive and negative aspects of their parents.

**self-concept** Attitudes, behaviors, and values that a person believes make him or her a unique individual.

**self-conscious emotions** Emotions, such as pride, guide, or embarrassment, that involve feelings of success when one's standards or expectations are met and feelings of failure when they aren't; emerge between 18 to 24 months of age.

**self-control** The ability to rise above immediate pressures and not give in to impulse.

**self-efficacy** The belief that one is capable of performing a certain task.

**self-esteem** A person's judgment and feelings about his or her own worth.

**self reports** Children's answers to questions about specific topics.

**semantic bootstrapping hypothesis** A view that children rely on their knowledge of word meanings to discover grammatical rules.

**semantics** The study of words and their meaning.

**sensorimotor stage** The first of Piaget's four stages of cognitive development, which lasts from birth to approximately 2 years, in which infants progress from responding reflexively to using symbols.

**sensory and perceptual processes** The means by which the nervous system receives, selects, modifies, and organizes stimulation from the world.

**sensory memory** A type of memory in which information is held in raw, unanalyzed form very briefly (no longer than a few seconds).

**serotonin**   A neurotransmitter that helps regulate brain centers that allow people to experience pleasure; below-normal levels of serotonin may contribute to depression.

**sex chromosomes**   The 23rd pair of chromosomes; these determine the sex of the child.

**short-term storage space**   In Case's neo-Piagetian theory, a memory used to store schemes; its capacity increases with age.

**sickle cell trait**   A disorder in which individuals show signs of mild anemia only when they are seriously deprived of oxygen; occurs in individuals who have one dominant allele for normal blood cells and one recessive sickle cell allele.

**simple social play**   Play that begins at about 15 to 18 months; toddlers engage in similar activities as well as talk and smile at each other and offer each other toys.

**size constancy**   The realization that an object's actual size remains the same despite changes in the size of its retinal image.

**small-for-date infants**   Newborns who are substantially smaller than would be expected based on the length of time since conception.

**sociability**   The dimension of temperament defined by preference for being with other people.

**social-cognitive flexibility**   A person's skill in solving social problems with relevant social knowledge; an aspect of interpersonal intelligence.

**social cognitive theory**   A theory developed by Albert Bandura in which children use reward, punishment, and imitation to try to understand what goes on in their world.

**social conventions**   Arbitrary standards of behavior agreed to by a cultural group to help coordinate interactions of individuals within the group.

**social referencing**   A phenomenon in which infants in an unfamiliar or ambiguous environment look at their mother or father, as if searching for cues to help them interpret the situation.

**social role**   A set of cultural guidelines about how one should behave, especially with other people.

**social smiles**   Smiles that first appear at about 2 months of age, when infants see another human face.

**specification**   The second phase in Super's theory of career development, in which adolescents learn more about specific lines of work and begin training.

**spermarche**   The first spontaneous ejaculation of sperm-laden fluid; typically occurs at age 13.

**spina bifida**   A disorder in which the embryo's neural tube does not close properly during the first month of pregnancy.

**stable-order principle**   The counting principle that states that number names must always be counted in the same order.

**stereotyped, approval-focused orientation**   According to Eisenberg, a level of prosocial reasoning common in many elementary-school children and adolescents in which they behave as they think society would expect "good people" to behave.

**stereotype threat**   The self-fulfilling prophecy in which knowledge of stereotypes leads to anxiety and reduced performance consistent with the original stereotype.

**stranger wariness**   An infant's apparent concern or anxiety in the presence of an unfamiliar adult, typically observed at about 6 months of age.

**stress**   A person's physical and psychological responses to threatening or challenging situations.

**structured observation**   A method in which the researcher creates a setting to elicit the behavior of interest.

**sudden infant death syndrome (SIDS)**   A disorder in which a healthy baby dies suddenly, for no apparent reason, typically occurring between 2 and 4 months of age.

**superego**   According to Freud, the moral component of the personality that has incorporated adult standards of right and wrong.

**surrogate-parent grandparents**   Grandparents who assume many of the normal roles of parents.

**synapse**   The gap between one neuron and the next.

**synaptic pruning**   Gradual loss of unused synapses, beginning in infancy and continuing into early adolescence.

**syntax**   Rules that specify how words are combined to form sentences.

**systematic desensitization**   A therapeutic technique that associates deep relaxation with progressively more anxiety-provoking situations.

**systematic observation**   A method of observation in which investigators watch children and carefully record what they do or say.

# T

**telegraphic speech**   A style of speaking common in 1-year-olds that includes only words directly relevant to meaning.

**temperament**   A consistent style or pattern of behavior.

**teratogen**   An agent that causes abnormal prenatal development.

**terminal buttons**   Small knobs at the end of an axon that release neurotransmitters.

**tertiary circular reaction**   According to Piaget, repeating old schemes with new objects.

**texture gradient**   A perceptual cue to depth based on the fact that the texture of objects changes from coarse but distinct for nearby objects to finer and less distinct for distant objects.

**theory**   An organized set of ideas that is designed to explain development.

**theory of mind**   An intuitive understanding of the connections among thoughts, beliefs, intentions, and behavior; develops rapidly in the preschool years.

**time-out**   Punishment that involves removing a child who is misbehaving to a quiet, unstimulating environment.

**toddlers**   Young children who have just learned to walk.

**triarchic theory**   A theory of intelligence proposed by Sternberg that includes componential, experiential, and contextual subtheories.

# U

**ultrasound**   A prenatal diagnostic technique that involves bouncing sound waves off the fetus to generate an image of the fetus.

**umbilical cord**   A structure containing veins and arteries that connects the developing child to the placenta.

**underextension**   When children define words more narrowly than adults do.

# V

**validity**   As applied to tests, the extent to which the test measures what it is supposed to measure.

**variable**   Any factor subject to change.

**vernix**   A thick, greasy substance that covers the fetus and protects it during prenatal development.

**villi**   Finger-like projections from the umbilical blood vessels that are close to the mother's blood vessels and thus allow nutrients, oxygen, vitamins, and waste products to be exchanged between mother and embryo.

**visual acuity**   The smallest pattern that one can distinguish reliably.

**visual cliff**   A glass-covered platform that appears to have a "shallow" side and "deep" side; used to study infants' depth perception.

# W

**word recognition**   The process of identifying a unique pattern of letters.

**working memory**   A type of memory in which a small number of items can be stored briefly.

# Z

**zone of proximal development**   The difference between what children can do with assistance and what they can do alone.

**zygote**   The fertilized egg.

Ablow, J. C., & Measelle, J. R. (1993). *Berkeley puppet interview: Administration and scoring system manuals*. Berkeley: University of California.

Aboud, F. E. (1993). The developmental psychology of racial prejudice. *Transcultural Psychiatric Research Review, 30,* 229–242.

Achenbach, T. M., Phases, V., Howell, C. T., Rauh, V. A., & Nurcombe, B. (1990). Seven-year outcome of the Vermont intervention program for low-birthweight infants. *Child Development, 61,* 1672–1681.

Ackerman, B. P. (1993). Children's understanding of the speaker's meaning in referential communication. *Journal of Experimental Child Psychology, 55,* 56–86.

Adams, J. (1999). On neurodevelopmental disorders: Perspectives from neurobehavioral teratology. In H. Tager-Flusberg (Ed.), *Neurodevelopmental disorders* (pp. 451–468). Cambridge, MA: MIT.

Adams, M. J., Treiman, R., & Pressley, M. (1998). Reading, writing, and literacy. In W. Damon (Ed.), *Handbook of child psychology* (Vol. 4). New York: Wiley.

Adams, R. J., & Courage, M. L. (1995). Development of chromatic discrimination in early infancy. *Behavioral Brain Research, 67,* 99–101.

Adler, N. (1994). *Adolescent sexual behavior looks irrational—But looks are deceiving*. Washington, DC: Federation of Behavioral, Psychological, and Cognitive Sciences.

Administration on Children, Youth, and Families. (April, 2002). *National Child Abuse and Neglect Data System: Summary of key findings from calendar year 2000.* www.calib.com/nccanch/pubs/factsheets/canstats.cfm

Adolph, K. (2003). Learning to keep balance. In R. V. Kail (Ed.), *Advances in child development and behavior,* Vol. 30. Orlando. FL: Academic Press.

Adolph, K. E. (1997). Learning in the development of infant locomotion. *Monographs of the Society for Research in Child Development, 62,* 1–140.

Adolph, K. E. (2000). Specificity of learning: Why infants fall over a veritable cliff. *Psychological Science, 11,* 290–295.

Adolph, K. E., Eppler, M. A., & Gibson, E. J. (1993). Crawling versus walking infants' perception of affordances for locomotion over sloping surfaces. *Child Development, 64,* 1158–1174.

Adolph, K. E., Vereijken, B., & Denny, M. A. (1998). Learning to crawl. *Child Development, 69,* 1299–1312.

Aguiar, A., & Baillargeon, R. (2002). Developments in young infants' reasoning about occluded objects. *Cognitive Psychology, 45,* 267–336.

Ainsworth, M. D. S. (1978). The development of infant-mother attachment. In B. M. Caldwell & H. N. Ricciuti (Eds.), *Review of child development research* (Vol. 3). Chicago: University of Chicago Press.

Ainsworth, M. S. (1993). Attachment as related to mother-infant interaction. *Advances in Infancy Research, 8,* 1–50.

Akhtar, N., Jipson, J., & Callanan, M. (2001). Learning words through overhearing. *Child Development, 72,* 416–430.

Alibali, M. W. (1999). How children change their minds: Strategy change can be gradual or abrupt. *Developmental Psychology, 35,* 127–145.

Allen, L., Cipielewski, J., & Stanovich, K. E. (1992). Multiple indicators of children's reading habits and attitudes: Construct validity and cognitive correlates. *Journal of Educational Psychology, 84,* 489–503.

Aman, C. J., Roberts, R. J., & Pennington, B. F. (1998). A neuropsychological examination of the underlying deficit in attention deficit hyperactivity disorder: Frontal lobe versus right parietal lobe theories. *Developmental Psychology, 34,* 956–969.

Amato, P. R. (2001). Children of divorce in the 1990s: An update of the Amato and Keith (1991) meta-analysis. *Journal of Family Psychology, 15,* 355–370.

Amato, P. R., & Keith, B. (1991). Parental divorce and the well-being of children: A meta-analysis. *Psychological Bulletin, 110,* 26–46.

American Academy of Pediatrics (AAP). (1992, Spring). Bedtime doesn't have to be a struggle. *Healthy Kids,* pp. 4–10.

American Psychiatric Association. (1994). *Diagnostic and statistical manual of mental disorders* (4th ed.). Washington, DC: Author.

Anand, K. J., & Hickey, P. R. (1987). Pain and its effect in the human neonate and fetus. *New England Journal of Medicine, 31,* 1321–1329.

Anastasi, A. (1988). *Psychological testing* (6th ed.). New York: Macmillan.

Andersen, A. M. N., Wohlfahrt, J., Christens, P., Olsen, J., & Melbye, M. (2000). Maternal age and fetal loss: Population based register linkage study. *British Medical Journal, 320,* 1708–1712.

Anderson, C. A., & Bushman, B. J. (2001). Effects of violent video games on aggressive behavior, aggressive cognition, aggressive affect, physiological arousal, and prosocial behavior: A meta-analytic review of the scientific literature. *Psychological Science, 12,* 353–359.

Anderson, D. R., Huston, A. C., Schmitt, K. L., Linebarger, D. L., & Wright, J. C. (2001). Early childhood television viewing and adolescent behavior. *Monographs of the Society for Research in Child Development, 66* (Serial No. 264).

Anderson, E. R., Greene, S. M., Hetherington, E. M., & Clingempeel, W. G. (1999). The dynamics of parental remarriage: Adolescent, parent, and sibling. In E. M. Hetherington (Ed.), *Coping with divorce, single parenting, and remarriage: A risk and resiliency perspective.* Mahwah, NJ: Erlbaum.

Anderson, S. W., Damasio, H., Tranel, D., & Damasio, A. R. (2001). Long-term sequelae of prefrontal cortex damage acquired in early childhood. *Developmental Neuropsychology, 18,* 281–296.

Anglin, J. M. (1993). Vocabulary development: A morphological analysis. *Monographs of the Society for Research in Child Development, 58* (10, Serial No. 238).

Antonarakis, S. E., & the Down Syndrome Collaborative Group. (1991). Parental origin of the extra chromosome in trisomy 21 as indicated by analysis of DNA polymorphisms. *New England Journal of Medicine, 324,* 872–876.

Apgar, V. (1953). A proposal for a new method of evaluation of the newborn infant. *Current Researches in Anesthesia and Analgesia, 32,* 260–267.

Archer, N., & Bryant, P. (2001). Investigating the role of context in learning to read: A direct test of Goodman's model. *British Journal of Psychology, 92,* 579–591.

Arseneault, L., Tremblay, R. E., Boulerice, B., & Saucier, J. F. (2002). Obstetrical complications and violent delinquency: Testing two developmental pathways. *Child Development, 73,* 496–508.

Ashcraft, M. H. (1982). The development of mental arithmetic: A chronometric approach. *Developmental Review, 2,* 212–236.

Aslin, R. N. (1987). Visual and auditory discrimination in infancy. In J. D. Osofsky (Ed.), *Handbook of infant development* (2nd ed.). New York: Wiley.

Aslin, R. N., Jusczyk, P. W., & Pisoni, D. B. (1998). Speech and auditory processing during infancy: Constraints on and precursors to language. In W. Damon (Ed.), *Handbook of child psychology* (Vol. 2). New York: Wiley.

Aslin, R. N., Saffran, J. R., & Newport, W. L. (1998). Computation of conditional probability statistics by 8-month-old infants. *Psychological Science, 9,* 321–324.

Au, T. K., & Glusman, M. (1990). The principle of mutual exclusivity in word learning: To honor or not to honor? *Child Development, 61,* 1474–1490.

Avenevoli, S., & Steinberg, L. (2001). The continuity of depression across the adolescent transition. *Advances in Child Development and Behavior, 28,* 139–173.

Averill, J. A. (1980). A constructivist view of emotion. In R. Plutchik & H. Kellerman (Eds.), *Emotion: Theory, research, and experience* (Vol. 1): *Theories of emotion.* New York: Academic Press.

Ayduk, O., Mendoza-Denton, R., Mischel, W., Downey, G., Peake, P. K., & Rodriguez, M. (2000). Regulating the interpersonal self: Strategic self-regulation for coping with rejection sensitivity. *Journal of Personality and Social Psychology, 79,* 776–792.

Bachman, J. (1983, Summer). Premature affluence: Do high school students earn too much? *Economic Outlook USA,* 64–67.

Bachman, J. G., & Schulenberg, J. (1993). How part-time work intensity relates to drug use, problem behavior, time use, and satisfaction among high school seniors: Are these consequences or merely correlates? *Developmental Psychology, 29,* 229–230.

Backscheider, A. G., Shatz, M., & Gelman, S. A. (1993). Preschoolers' ability to distinguish living kinds as a function of regrowth. *Child Development, 64,* 1242–1257.

Baddeley, A. (1996). Exploring the central executive. *Quarterly Journal of Experimental Psychology: Human Experimental Psychology, 49,* 5–28.

Baenninger, M., & Newcombe, N. (1995). Environmental input to the development of sex-related differences in spatial and mathematical ability. *Learning & Individual Differences, 7,* 363–379.

Baer, D. M., & Wolf, M. M. (1968). The reinforcement contingency in preschool and remedial education. In R. D. Hess & R. M. Baer (Eds.), *Early education.* Chicago: Aldine.

Bagwell, C. L., Newcomb, A. F., & Bukowski, W. M. (1998). Preadolescent friendship and peer rejection as predictors of adult adjustment. *Child Development, 69,* 140–153.

Bahrick, L. E., & Lickliter, R. (2000). Intersensory redundancy guides attentional selectivity and perceptual learning in infancy. *Developmental Psychology, 36,* 190–201.

Bahrick, L. E., & Lickliter, R. (2002). Intersensory redundancy guides early perceptual and cognitive development. In R. V. Kail (Ed.), *Advances in child development and behavior* (Vol. 30). Orlando, FL: Academic Press.

Bailey, D. A., & Rasmussen, R. L. (1996). Sport and the child: Physiological and skeletal issues. In F. L. Smoll & R. E. Smith (Eds.), *Children and youth in sport: A biopsychological perspective* (pp. 187–199). Dubuque, IA: Brown & Benchmark.

Bailey, J. M., Bobrow, D., Wolfe, M., & Mikach, S. (1995). Sexual orientation of adult sons of gay fathers. *Developmental Psychology, 31,* 124–129.

Bailey, J. M., Dunne, M. P., & Martin, N. G. (2000). Genetic and environmental influences on sexual orientation and its correlates in an Austrian twin sample. *Journal of Personality and Social Psychology, 78,* 524–436.

Baillargeon, R. (1987). Object permanence in $3\frac{1}{2}$- and $4\frac{1}{2}$-month-old infants. *Developmental Psychology, 23,* 655–664.

Baillargeon, R. (1994). How do infants learn about the physical world? *Current Directions in Psychological Science, 3,* 133–140.

Baillargeon, R. (1998). Infants' understanding of the physical world. *Advances in Psychological Science, 2,* 503–529.

Baker, C. (1993). *Foundations of bilingual education and bilingualism.* Clevedon, England: Multilingual Matters.

Baker, L. (1994). Fostering metacognitive development. In H. W. Reese (Ed.), *Advances in child development and behavior* (Vol. 25). San Diego: Academic Press.

Baker, L., & Brown, A. L. (1984). Metacognitive skills and reading. In P. D. Pearson (Ed.), *Handbook of reading research, Part 2.* New York: Longman.

Baker, L., Fernandez-Fein, S., Scher, D., & Williams, H. (1998). Home experiences related to the development of word recognition. In J. L. Metsala & L. C. Ehri (Eds.), *Word recognition in beginning literacy* (pp. 263–287). Mahwah, NJ: Erlbaum.

Baldwin, D. A., Markman, E. M, Bill, B., Desjardins, R. N., & Irwin, J. M. (1996). Infants' reliance on a social criterion for establishing word-object relations. *Child Development, 67,* 3135–3153.

Bancroft, J., Axworthy, D., & Ratcliffe, S. (1982). The personality and psycho-sexual development of boys with 47–XXY chromosome constitution. *Journal of Child Psychology and Psychiatry, 23,* 169180.

Bandura, A. (1977). *Social learning theory.* Englewood Cliffs, NJ: Prentice-Hall.

Bandura, A. (1986). *Social foundations of thought and action: A social-cognitive theory.* Englewood Cliffs, NJ: Prentice-Hall.

Bandura, A. (1997). *Self-efficacy: The exercise of control.* New York: W. H. Freeman.

Bandura, A., & Mischel, W. (1965). Modification of self-imposed delay of reward through exposure to live and symbolic models. *Journal of Personality and Social Psychology, 2,* 698–705.

Bandura, A., Ross, D., & Ross, S. A. (1963). Imitation of film-mediated aggressive models. *Journal of Abnormal and Social Psychology, 66,* 3–11.

Bardwell, J. R., Cochran, S. W., & Walker, S. (1986). Relationship of parental education, race, and gender to sex role stereotyping in five-year-old kindergartners. *Sex Roles, 15,* 275–281.

Barenboim, C. (1981). The development of person perception in childhood and adolescence: From behavioral comparisons to psychological constructs to psychological comparisons. *Child Development, 52,* 129–144.

Barinaga, M. (1997). Researchers find signals that guide young brain neurons. *Science, 278,* 385–386.

Barkley, R. A. (1990). Attention deficit disorders: History, definition, and diagnosis. In M. Lewis & S. M. Miller (Eds.), *Handbook of developmental psychopathology.* New York: Plenum.

Barkley, R. A. (1994). Impaired delayed responding: A unified theory of attention-deficit hyperactivity disorder. In R. A. Barkley (Ed.), *Disruptive behavior disorders in childhood.* New York: Plenum.

Barton, M. E., & Tomasello, M. (1991). Joint attention and conversation in mother-infant-sibling triads. *Child Development, 62,* 517–529.

Bartsch, K., & Wellman, H. M. (1995). *Children talk about the mind.* New York: Oxford University Press.

Baskett, L. M. (1985). Sibling status effects: Adult expectations. *Developmental Psychology, 21,* 441–445.

Bates, E., Benigni, L., Bretherton, I., Camaioni, L., & Volterra, V. (1979). *The emergence of symbols: Cognition and communication in infancy.* New York: Academic Press.

Bates, E., Bretherton, I., & Snyder, L. (1988). *From first words to grammar: Individual differences and dissociable mechanisms.* New York: Cambridge University Press.

Bates, J. E., Pettit, G. S., Dodge, K. A., & Ridge, B. (1998). Interaction of temperamental resistance to control and restrictive parenting in the development of externalizing behavior. *Developmental Psychology, 34,* 982–995.

Bates, J. E., Viken, R. J., Alexander, D. B., Beyers, J., & Stockton, L. (2002). Sleep and adjustment in preschool children: Sleep diary reports by mothers relate to behavioral reports by teachers. *Child Development, 73,* 62–74.

Bauer, P. J., Burch, M. M., & Kleinknecht, E. F. (2002). Developments in early recall memory: Normative trends and individual differences. In R. V. Kail (Ed.), *Advances in child development and behavior* (Vol. 30, pp. 103–15). San Diego: Academic Press.

Baumrind, D. (1975). *Early socialization and the discipline controversy.* Morristown, NJ: General Learning Press.

Baumrind, D. (1991). Parenting styles and adolescent development. In R. M. Lerner, A. C. Petersen, & J. Brooks-Gunn (Eds.), *Encyclopedia of adolescence.* New York: Garland.

Bauserman, R. (2002). Child adjustment in joint-custody versus sole-custody arrangements: A meta-analytic review. *Journal of Family Psychology, 16,* 91–102.

Bayley, N. (1970). Development of mental abilities. In P. H. Mussen (Ed.), *Carmichael's manual of child psychology.* New York: Wiley.

Bayley, N. (1993). *Bayley scales of infant development: Birth to two years* (2nd ed.). San Antonio, TX: Psychological Corporation.

Beal, C. R. (1996). The role of comprehension monitoring in children's revision. *Educational Psychology Review, 8,* 219–238.

Beal, C. R., & Belgrad, S. L. (1990). The development of message evaluation skills in young children. *Child Development, 61,* 705–712.

Becker, B. J. (1986). Influence again: An examination of reviews and studies of gender differences in social influence. In J. S. Hyde & M. C. Linn (Eds.), *The psychology of gender differences. Advances through meta-analysis.* Baltimore, MD: Johns Hopkins University Press.

Behnke, M., & Eyler, F. D. (1993). The consequences of prenatal substance use for the developing fetus, newborn, and young child. *International Journal of the Addictions, 28,* 1341–1391.

Bell, A. P., Weinberg, M. S., & Hammersmith, S. K. (1981). *Sexual preference: Its development in men and women.* New York: Simon & Schuster.

Beller, M., & Gafni, N. (1996). The 1991 international assessment of educational progress in mathematics and sciences: The gender differences perspective. *Journal of Educational Psychology, 88,* 365–377.

Belsky, J. (1993). Etiology of child maltreatment: A developmental-ecological analysis. *Psychological Bulletin, 114,* 413–434.

Belsky, J., Fish, M., & Isabella, R. A. (1991). Continuity and discontinuity in infant negative and positive emotionality: Family antecedents and attachment consequences. *Developmental Psychology, 27,* 421–431.

Belsky, J., Steinberg, L., & Draper, P. (1991). Childhood experience, interpersonal development, and reproductive strategy: An evolutionary theory of socialization. *Child Development, 62,* 647–670.

Belsky, J., Woodworth, S., & Crnic, K. (1996). Trouble in the second year: Three questions about family interaction. *Child Development, 67,* 556–578.

Bem, D. J. (1996). Exotic becomes erotic: A developmental theory of sexual orientation. *Psychological Review, 103,* 320–335.

Bem, S. L. (1984). Androgyny and gender schema theory: A conceptual and empirical integration. In T. B. Sonderegger (Ed.), *Nebraska symposium on motivation: Psychology and gender.* Lincoln, NE: University of Nebraska Press.

Bem, S. L. (1989). Genital knowledge and gender constancy in preschool children. *Child Development, 60,* 649–662.

Benton, S. L., Corkill, A. J., Sharp, J. M., Downey, R. G., et al. (1995). Knowledge, interest, and narrative writing. *Journal of Educational Psychology, 87,* 66–79.

Bereiter, C., & Scardamalia, M. (1987). *The psychology of written composition.* Hillsdale, NJ: Erlbaum.

Berenbaum, S. A., Duck, S. C., & Bryk, K. (2000). Behavioral effects of prenatal vs. postnatal androgen excess in children with 21-hydroxylase-deficient congenital adrenal hyperplasia. *Journal of Clinical Endocrinology and Metabolism, 85,* 727–733.

Berenbaum, S. A., & Snyder, E. (1995). Early hormonal influences on childhood sex-typed activity and playmate preferences: Implications for the development of sexual orientation. *Developmental Psychology, 31,* 31–42.

Berk, L. E. (1992). Children's private speech: An overview of theory and the status of research. In R. M. Diaz & L. E. Berk (Eds.), *Private speech: From social interaction to self-regulation.* Hillsdale, NJ: Erlbaum.

Berk, L. E. (1994). Vygotsky's theory: The importance of make believe play. *Young Children, 50,* 30–38.

Berko, J. (1958). The child's learning of English morphology. *Word, 14,* 150–177.

Berkowitz, L. (1989). Frustration-aggression hypothesis: Examination and reformulation. *Psychological Bulletin, 106,* 59–73.

Berkowitz, M. W., & Gibbs, J. C. (1985). The process of moral conflict resolution and moral development. In M. W. Berkowitz (Ed.), *Peer conflict and psychological growth* (pp. 71–84). San Francisco: Jossey-Bass.

Berndt, T. J., & Keefe, K. (1995). Friends' influence on adolescents' adjustment to school. *Child Development, 66,* 1312–1329.

Berndt, T. J., & Murphy, L. M. (2002). Influences of friends and friendships: Myths, truths, and research recommendations. *Advances in Child Development and Behavior, 30,* 275–310.

Berndt, T. J., & Perry, T. B. (1990). Distinctive features and effects of adolescent friendships. In R. Montemeyer, G. R. Adams, & T. P. Gullotta (Eds.), *From childhood to adolescence: A transition period?* London: Sage.

Berry, J. W. (1993). Ethnic identities in plural societies. In M. E. Bernal & G. P. Knight (Eds.), *Ethnic identity: Formation and transmission among Hispanics and other minorities.* New York: State University of New York Press.

Bertenthal, B. H., & Clifton, R. K. (1998). Perception and action. In W. Damon (Ed.), *Handbook of child psychology* (Vol. 2). New York: Wiley.

Berthier, N. E. (1996). Learning to reach: A mathematical model. *Developmental Psychology, 32,* 811–823.

Besharov, D. J., & Gardiner, K. N. (1997). Trends in teen sexual behavior. *Children and Youth Services Review, 19,* 341–367.

Best, C. T. (1995). Learning to perceive the sound pattern of English. In C. Rovee-Collier (Ed.), *Advances in infancy research.* Norwood, NJ: Ablex.

Best, D. L. (2001). Gender concepts: Convergence in cross-cultural research and methodologies. *Cross-Cultural Research: The Journal of Comparative Social Science, 35,* 23–43.

Best, D. L., Williams, J. E., Cloud, J. M., Davis, S. W., Robertson, L. S., Edwards, J. R., Giles, H., & Fowles, J. (1977). Development of sex-trait stereotypes among young children in the United States, England, and Ireland. *Child Development, 48,* 1375–1384.

Bettencourt, B. A., & Miller, N. (1996). Gender differences in aggression as a function of provocation: A meta-analysis. *Psychological Bulletin, 119,* 422–447.

Bialystok, E. (1988). Levels of bilingualism and levels of linguistic awareness. *Developmental Psychology, 24,* 560–567.

Bialystok, E. (1997). Effects of bilingualism and biliteracy on children's emerging concepts of print. *Developmental Psychology, 33,* 429–440.

Bialystok, E., Shenfield, T., & Codd, J. (2000). Languages, scripts, and the environment: Factors in developing concepts of print. *Developmental Psychology, 36,* 66–76.

Bigler, R., Brown, C., & Markell, M. (2001). When groups are not created equal: Effects of group status on the formation of intergroup attitudes in children. *Child Development, 72,* 1151–1162.

Bigler, R. S. (1995). The role of classification skill in moderating environmental influences on children's gender stereotyping: A study of the functional use of gender in the classroom. *Child Development, 66,* 1072–1087.

Bigler, R. S., Jones, L. C., & Lobliner, D. B. (1997). Social categorization and the formation of intergroup attitudes in children. *Child Development, 68,* 530–543.

Bigler, R. S., & Liben L. S. (1990). The role of attitudes and interventions in gender-schematic processing. *Child Development, 61,* 1440–1452.

Bigler, R. S., & Liben, L. S. (1992). Cognitive mechanisms in children's gender stereotyping: Theoretical and educational implications of a cognitive-based intervention. *Child Development, 63,* 1351–1363.

Bigner, J. J., & Jacobsen, R. B. (1989). Parenting behavior of homosexual and heterosexual fathers. *Journal of Homosexuality, 18,* 173–186.

Birch, L. L. (1991). Obesity and eating disorders: A developmental perspective. *Bulletin of the Psychonomic Society, 29,* 265–272.

Birch, L. L., & Fisher, J. A. (1995). Appetite and eating behavior in children. *Pediatric Clinics of North America, 42,* 931–953.

Birch, S. A. J., & Bloom, P. (2002). Preschoolers are sensitive to the speaker's knowledge when learning proper names. *Child Development, 73,* 434–444.

Birnholz, J. C., & Benacerraf, B. R. (1983). The development of human fetal hearing. *Science, 222,* 516–518.

Bjorklund, D. F., & Pellegrini, A. D. (2000). Child development and evolutionary psychology. *Child Development, 71,* 1687–1708.

Bjorklund, D. F., Yunger, J. L., & Pellegrini, A. D. (2002). The evolution of parenting and evolutionary approaches to childrearing. In M. H. Bornstein (Ed.), *Handbook of parenting, vol. 2: Biology and ecology of parenting* (pp. 3–30). Mahwah, NJ: Erlbaum.

Black-Gutman, D., & Hickson, F. (1996). The relationship between racial attitudes and social-cognitive development in children: An Australian study. *Developmental Psychology, 32,* 448–456.

Blake, J., O'Rourke, P., & Borzellino, G. (1994). Form and function in the development of pointing and reaching gestures. *Infant Behavior & Development, 17,* 195–203.

Blamey, P., Barry, J., Bow, C., Sarant, J., Paatsch, L., & Wales, R. (2001). The development of speech production following cochlear implantation. *Clinical Linguistics & Phonetics, 15,* 363–382.

Blanchard, R. (1997). Birth order and sibling sex ratio in homosexual versus heterosexual males and females. *Annual Review of Sex Research, 8,* 27–67.

Blanchard, R., Zucker, K. J., Siegelman, M., Dickey, R., & Klassen, P. (1998). The relation of birth order to sexual orientation in men and women. *Journal of Biosocial Science, 30,* 511–519.

Block, J. (1976). Debatable conclusions about sex differences. *Contemporary Psychology, 21,* 517–522.

Block, J. H. (1978). Another look at sex differentiation in the socialization behaviors of mothers and fathers. In J. Sherman & F. L. Denmark (Eds.), *Psychology of women: Future directions for research* (pp. 29–87). New York: Psychological Dimensions.

Bloom, L., Margulis, C., Tinker, E., & Fujita, N. (1996). Early conversations and word learning: Contributions from child and adult. *Child Development, 67,* 3154–3175.

Bloom, L., Rocissano, L., & Hood, L. (1976). Adult-child discourse: Developmental interaction between information processing and linguistic knowledge. *Cognitive Psychology, 8,* 521–552.

Bloom, L., & Tinker, E. (2001). The intentionality model and language acquisition. *Monographs of the Society for Research in Child Development, 66,* Serial No. 267.

Bogatz, G. A., & Ball, S. (1972). *The second year of "Sesame Street": A continuing evaluation.* Princeton, NJ: Educational Testing Service.

Boivin, M., Vitaro, F., & Gagnon, C. (1992). A reassessment of the self-perception profile for children: Factor structure, reliability, and convergent validity of a French version among second through sixth grade children. *International Journal of Behavioral Development, 15,* 275–290.

Bolger, K. E., & Patterson, C. J. (2001). Developmental pathways from child maltreatment to peer rejection. *Child Development, 72,* 549–568.

Bornstein, M. H. (1981). Psychological studies of color perception in human infants: Habituation, discrimination and categorization, recognition, and conceptualization. *Advances in Infancy Research, 1,* 1–40.

Bornstein, M. H. (1997). Stability in mental development from early life: Methods, measures, models, meanings, and myths. In G. E. Butterworth & F. Simion (Eds.), *The development of sensory, motor, and cognitive capacities in early infancy: From sensation to perception.* Hove, England: Psychology Press.

Bornstein, M. H., Haynes, O. M., O'Reilly, A. W., & Painter, K. M. (1996). Solitary and collaborative pretense play in early childhood: Sources of individual variation in the development of representational competence. *Child Development, 67,* 2910–2929.

Bornstein, M. H., Haynes, O. M., Pascual, L., Painter, K. M., & Galperin, C. (1999). Play in two societies: Pervasiveness of process, specificity of structure. *Child Development, 70,* 317–331.

Bowlby, J. (1969). *Attachment and loss* (Vol. 1). New York: Basic Books.

Bowlby, J. (1991). Ethological light on psychoanalytical problems. In P. Bateson et al. (Eds.), *The development and integration of behaviour: Essays in honour of Robert Hinde.* Cambridge, England: Cambridge University Press.

Bradley, L., & Bryant, P. E. (1983). Categorising sounds and learning to read—a causal connection. *Nature, 301,* 419–421.

Bradley, R. H., Caldwell, B. M., Rock, S. L., Ramey, C. T., Barnard, K. E., Gray, C., Hammond, M. A., Mitchell, S., Gottfried, A. W., Siegel, L., & Johnson, D. L. (1989). Home environment and cognitive development in the first 3 years of life: A collaborative study involving six sites and three ethnic groups in North America. *Developmental Psychology, 25,* 217–235.

Bradley, R. H., Corwyn, R. F., Burchinal, M., McAdoo, H. P., & Coll, C. G. (2001). The home environments of children in the United States Part II: Relations with behavioral development through age thirteen. *Child Development, 72,* 1868–1886.

Braet, C., Mervielde, I., & Vandereycken, W. (1997). Psychological aspects of childhood obesity: A controlled study in a clinical and nonclinical sample. *Journal of Pediatric Psychology, 22,* 59–71.

Brainerd, C. J. (1996). Piaget: A centennial celebration. *Psychological Science, 7,* 191–203.

Brainerd, C. J., & Reyna, V. F. (2002). Recollection rejection: How children edit their false memories. *Developmental Psychology, 38,* 156–172.

Brand, E., Clingempeel, W. G., & Bowen-Woodward, D. (1988). Family relationships and children's psychological adjustment in stepmother and stepfather families. In E. M. Hetherington & J. D. Arasten (Eds.), *Impact of divorce, single parenting and step parenting on children* (pp. 299–324). Hillsdale, NJ: Erlbaum.

Braungart, J. M., Plomin, R., DeFries, J. C., & Fulker, D. W. (1992). Genetic influence on tester-rated infant temperament as assessed by Bayley's Infant Behavior Record: Nonadoptive and adoptive siblings and twins. *Developmental Psychology, 28,* 40–47.

Brazelton, T. B. (1984). *Brazelton Behavior Assessment Scale* (rev. ed.). Philadelphia: Lippincott.

Brazelton, T. B., Nugent, J. K., & Lester, B. M. (1987). Neonatal behavioral assessment scale. In J. D. Osofsky (Ed.), *Handbook of infant development* (2nd ed.). New York: Wiley.

Brendgen, M., Vitaro, F., Bukowski, W. M., Doyle, A. B., & Markiewicz, D. (2001). Developmental profiles of peer social preference over the course of elementary school: Associations with trajectories of externalizing and internalizing behavior. *Developmental Psychology, 37,* 308–320.

Brennan, P. A., Grekin, E. R., Mortensen, E. L., & Mednick, S. A. (2002). Relationship of maternal smoking during pregnancy with criminal arrest and hospitalization for substance abuse in male and female adult offspring. *American Journal of Psychiatry, 159,* 48–54.

Brennan, P. A., Hammen, C., Andersen, M. J., Bor, W., Najman, J. M., & Williams, G. M. (2000). Chronicity, severity, and timing of maternal depressive symptoms: Relationships with child outcomes at age 5. *Developmental Psychology, 36,* 759–766.

Bretherton, I. (1992). The origins of attachment theory: John Bowlby and Mary Ainsworth. *Developmental Psychology, 28,* 759–775.

Brockington, I. (1996). *Motherhood and mental health.* Oxford, England: Oxford University Press.

Brody, G. H. (1998). Sibling relationship quality: Its causes and consequences. *Annual Review of Psychology, 49,* 1–24.

Brody, G. H., & Flor, D. L. (1998). Maternal resources, parenting practices, and child competence in rural, single-parent African American families. *Child Development, 69,* 803–816.

Brody, G. H., Stoneman, Z., & McCoy, J. K. (1994). Forecasting sibling relationships in early adolescence from child temperaments and family processes in middle childhood. *Child Development, 65,* 771–784.

Brodzinsky, D. M., & Pinderhughes, E. (2002). Parenting and child development in adoptive families. In M. H. Bornstein (Ed.), *Handbook of parenting, vol. 1: Children and parenting* (pp. 279–311). Mahwah, NJ: Erlbaum.

Bronfenbrenner, U. (1979). *The ecology of human development.* Cambridge: Harvard University Press.

Bronfenbrenner, U. (1995). Developmental ecology through space and time: A future perspective. In P. Moen, G. H. Elder, Jr., & K. Luscher (Eds.), *Examining lives in context: Perspectives on the ecology of human development.* Washington, DC: American Psychological Association.

Brooks-Gunn, J., Klebanov, P. K., & Duncan, G. J. (1996). Ethnic differences in children's intelligence test scores: Role of economic deprivation, home environment, and maternal characteristics. *Child Development, 67,* 396–408.

Brown, B. B., & Lohr, M. J. (1987). Peer-group affiliation and adolescent self-esteem: An integration of ego-identity and symbolic-interaction theories. *Journal of Personality and Social Psychology, 52,* 47–55.

Brown, B. B., Lohr, M. J., & McClenahan, E. L. (1986). Early adolescents' perceptions of peer pressure. *Journal of Early Adolescence, 6,* 139–154.

Brown, B. B., Mounts, N., Lamborn, S. D., & Steinberg, L. (1993). Parenting practices and peer group affiliation in adolescence. *Developmental Psychology, 64,* 467–482.

Brown, B. B. & Theobald, W. (1999). How peers matter: A research synthesis of peer influences on adolescent pregnancy. In P. Bearman,

H. Bruckner, B. B. Brown, W. Theobald, & S. Philliber (Eds.), *Peer potential: Making the most of how teens influence each other.* Washington DC: National Campaign to Prevent Teen Pregnancy.

Brown, C. S., & Bigler, R. S. (2002). Effects of minority status in the classroom on children's intergroup attitudes. *Journal of Experimental Child Psychology, 83,* 77–110.

Brown, J. R., & Dunn, J. (1992). Talk with your mother or your sibling? Developmental changes in early family conversations about feelings. *Child Development, 63,* 336–349.

Brown, J. R., & Dunn, J. (1996). Continuities in emotion understanding from three to six years. *Child Development, 67,* 789–802.

Brown, R. (1973). *A first language: The early stages.* Cambridge, MA: Harvard University Press.

Brown, R., Pressley, M., Van Meter, P., & Schuder, T. (1996). A quasi-experimental validation of transactional strategies instruction with low-achieving second-grade readers. *Journal of Educational Psychology, 88,* 18–37.

Bryant, B. K. (1992). Conflict resolution strategies in relation to children's peer relations. *Journal of Applied Developmental Psychology, 13,* 35–50.

Bryant, B. K., & Crockenberg, S. B. (1980). Correlates and dimensions of prosocial behavior: A study of female siblings with their mothers. *Child Development, 51,* 529–554.

Buchanan, C. M., Eccles, J. S., & Becker, J. B. (1992). Are adolescents the victims of raging hormones? Evidence for activational effects of hormones on moods and behavior at adolescence? *Psychological Bulletin, 111,* 62–107.

Buchholz, M., Karl, H. W., Pomietto, M., & Lynn, A. (1998). Pain scores in infants: A modified infant pain scale versus visual analogue. *Journal of Pain & Symptom Management, 15,* 117–124.

Buhrmester, D., & Furman, W. (1987). The development of companionship and intimacy. *Child Development, 58,* 1101–1113.

Buhrmester, D., & Furman, W. (1990). Perceptions of sibling relationships during middle childhood and adolescence. *Child Development, 61,* 1387–1398.

Buhs, E. S., & Ladd, G. W. (2001). Peer rejection as antecedent of young children's school adjustment: An examination of mediating processes. *Developmental Psychology, 37,* 550–560.

Bullock, M., & Lütkenhaus, P. (1990). Who am I? The development of self-understanding in toddlers. *Merrill-Palmer Quarterly, 36,* 217–238.

Burks, V. S., Dodge, K. A., Price, J. M., & Laird, R. D. (1999). Internal representational models of peers: Implications for the development of problematic behavior. *Developmental Psychology, 35,* 802–810.

Buss, K. A., & Goldsmith, H. H. (1998). Fear and anger regulation in infancy: Effects on the temporal dynamics of affective expression. *Child Development, 69,* 359–374.

Butler, R. (1992). What young people want to know when: The effects of mastery and ability on social information seeking. *Journal of Personality and Social Psychology, 62,* 934–943.

Button, E. J., Sonuga-Burke, E. J. S., Davis, J., & Thompson, M. (1996). A prospective study of self-esteem in the prediction of eating problems in schoolgirls: Questionnaire findings. *British Journal of Clinical Psychology, 35,* 193–203.

Byrne, B. M., & Gavin, D. A. W. (1996). The Shavelson model revisited: Testing for the structure of academic self-concept across pre-, early, and late adolescents. *Journal of Educational Psychology, 88,* 215–228.

Byrnes, J. P., Miller, D. C., & Schafer, W. D. (1999). Gender differences in risk taking: A meta-analysis. *Psychological Bulletin, 125,* 367–383.

Cain, K. (1999). Ways of reading: How knowledge and use of strategies are related to reading comprehension. *British Journal of Developmental Psychology, 17,* 293–312.

Cairns, R. B., Cairns, B. D., Neckerman, H. J., Ferguson, L. L., & Gariépy, J-L. (1989). Growth and aggression: 1. Childhood to early adolescence. *Developmental Psychology, 25,* 320–330.

Cairns, R. B., Leung, M. C., Buchannan, L., & Cairns, B. D. (1995). Friendships and social networks in childhood and adolescence: Fluidity, reliability, and interrelations. *Child Development, 66,* 1330–1345.

Call, K. T. (1996). Adolescent work as an "arena of comfort" under conditions of family discomfort. In J. T. Mortimer & M. D. Finch (Eds.), *Adolescents, work, and family: An intergenerational developmental analysis.* Thousand Oaks, CA: Sage.

Callahan, C. M. (2000). Intelligence and giftedness. In R. J. Sternberg (Ed.), *Handbook of intelligence* (pp. 159–175). Cambridge, England: Cambridge University Press.

Cameron, C. A., Edmunds, G., Wigmore, B., Hunt, A. K., & Linton, M. J. (1997). Children's revision of textual flaws. *International Journal of Behavioral Development, 20,* 667–680.

Campbell, F. A., Pungello, E. P., Miller-Johnson, S., Burchinal, M., & Ramey, C. T. (2001). The development of cognitive and acade-

mic abilities: Growth curves from an early childhood educational experiment. *Developmental Psychology, 37,* 231–242.

Campbell, F. A., & Ramey, C. T. (1994). Effects of early intervention on intellectual and academic achievement: A follow-up study of children from low-income families. *Child Development, 65,* 684–698.

Campbell, R., & Sais, E. (1995). Accelerated metalinguistic (phonological) awareness in bilingual children. *British Journal of Developmental Psychology, 13,* 61–68.

Campbell, S. B., Cohn, J. F., Flanagan, C., Popper, S., & Meyers, T. (1992). Course and correlates of postpartum depression during the transition to parenthood. *Development and Psychopathology, 4,* 29–47.

Campos, J. J., Hiatt, S., Ramsay, D., Henderson, C., & Svejda, M. (1978). The emergence of fear on the visual cliff. In M. Lewis & L. Rosenblum (Eds.), *The origins of affect.* New York: Plenum.

Camras, L. A., Oster, H., Campos, J., Campos, R., Ujiie, T., Miyake, K., Wang, L., & Meng. Z. (1998). Production of emotional facial expressions in European, American, Japanese, and Chinese infants. *Developmental Psychology, 34,* 616–628.

Canfield, R. L., & Smith, E. G. (1996). Number-based expectations and sequential enumeration by 5-month-old infants. *Developmental Psychology, 32,* 269–279.

Cannon, T. D., Rosso, I. M., Hollister, J. M., Bearden, C. E., Sanchez, L. E., & Hadley, T. (2000). A prospective cohort study of genetic and perinatal influences in the etiology of schizophrenia. *Schizophrenia Bulletin, 26,* 351–366.

Capaldi, D. M., & Patterson, G. R. (1991). Relation of parental transitions to boys' adjustment problems: I. A linear hypothesis. II. Mothers at risk for transitions and unskilled parenting. *Developmental Psychology, 27,* 489–504.

Capelli, C. A., Nakagawa, N., & Madden, C. M. (1990). How children understand sarcasm: The role of context and intonation. *Child Development, 61,* 1824–1841.

Carey, S. (1992). Becoming a face expert. In V. Bruce, A. Cowey, A. W. Ellis, & D. I. Perrett (Eds.), *Processing the facial image.* Oxford: Clarendon Press.

Carey, S., & Spelke, E. S. (1994). Domain-specific knowledge and conceptual change. In L. A. Hirschfeld & S. A. Gelman (Eds.), *Mapping the mind* (pp. 169–200). Cambridge UK: Cambridge University Press.

Carlo, G., Koller, S. H., Eisenberg, N., Da Silva, M. S., & Frohlich, C. B. (1996). A cross-national study on the relations among prosocial moral reasoning, gender role orientations, and prosocial behaviors. *Developmental Psychology, 32,* 231–240.

Carlson, E. A. (1998). A prospective longitudinal study of attachment disorganization/disorientation. *Child Development, 69,* 1107–1128.

Carpenter, P. A., & Daneman, M. (1981). Lexical retrieval and error recovery in reading: A model based on eye fixations. *Journal of Verbal Learning and Verbal Behavior, 20,* 137–160.

Carrere, S., & Gottman, J. M. (1999). Predicting the future of marriages. In E. M. Hetherington (Ed.), *Coping with divorce, single parenting, and remarriage: A risk and resiliency perspective.* Mahwah, NJ: Erlbaum.

Carroll, J. B. (1993). *Human cognitive abilities: A survey of factor-analytic studies.* New York: Cambridge University Press.

Carroll, J. B. (1996). A three-stratum theory of intelligence: Spearman's contribution. In I. Dennis & P. Tapsfield (Eds.), *Human abilities: Their nature and measurement.* Mahwah, NJ: Erlbaum.

Carroll, J. L., & Loughlin, G. M. (1994). Sudden infant death syndrome. In F. A. Oski, C. D. DeAngelis, R. D. Feigin, J. A. McMillan, & J. B. Warshaw (Eds.), *Principles and practice of pediatrics.* Philadelphia: Lippincott.

Carver, L. J., & Bauer, P. J. (2001). The dawning of a past: The emergence of long-term explicit memory in infancy. *Journal of Experimental Psychology: General, 130,* 726–745.

Casaer, P. (1993). Old and new facts about perinatal brain development. *Journal of Child Psychology and Psychiatry, 34,* 101–109.

Case, R. (1992). *The mind's staircase: Exploring the conceptual underpinnings of children's thought and knowledge.* Hillsdale, NJ: Erlbaum.

Case, R. (1998). The development of conceptual structures. In W. Damon (Ed.), *Handbook of child psychology* (Vol. 2). New York: Wiley.

Casey, B. J., Trainor, R. J., Orendi, J. L., Schubert, A. B., Nystrom, L. E., Giedd, J. N., Castellanos, F. X., Haxby, J. V., Noll, Douglas C., Cohen, J. D., Forman, S. D., Dahl, R. E., & Rapoport, J. L. (1997). A developmental functional MRI study of prefrontal activation during performance of a Go-No-Go task. *Journal of Cognitive Neuroscience, 9,* 835–847.

Casiglia, A. C., Coco, A. L., & Zappulla, C. (1998). Aspects of social reputation and peer relationships in Italian children: A cross-cultural perspective. *Developmental Psychology, 34,* 723–730.

Caspi, A. (1998). Personality development across the life course. In N. Eisenberg (Ed.), *Handbook of child psychology, Vol. 3: Social, emotional, and personality development* (5th ed., pp. 311–388). New York: Wiley.

Caspi, A., & Silva, P. A. (1995). Temperamental qualities at age three predict personality traits in young adulthood: Longitudinal evidence from a birth cohort. *Child Development, 66,* 485–498.

Cassidy, J. (1994). Emotion regulation: Influences of attachment relationships. *Monographs of the Society for Research in Child Development, 59,* 228–283.

Cattell, R. B. (1965). *The scientific analysis of personality.* Baltimore: Penguin.

Ceci, S. J., & Bruck, M. (1995). *Jeopardy in the courtroom: A scientific analysis of children's testimony.* Washington, DC: American Psychological Association.

Ceci, S. J., & Bruck, M. (1998). Children's testimony: Applied and basic issues. In W. Damon (Ed.), *Handbook of child psychology* (Vol. 4). New York: Wiley.

Center for Disease Control and Prevention. (2000). *Childhood injury fact sheet.* http://www.cdc.gov/ncipc/factsheets/childh.htm

Cerella, J., & Hale, S. (1994). The rise and fall in information-processing rates over the life span. *Acta Psychologica, 86,* 109–197.

Cervantes, C. A., & Callanan, M. A. (1998). Labels and explanations in mother-child emotion talk: Age and gender differentiation. *Developmental Psychology, 34,* 88–98.

Chan, R. W., Raboy, B., & Patterson, C. J. (1998). Psychosocial adjustment among children conceived via donor insemination by lesbian and heterosexual mothers. *Child Development, 69,* 443–457.

Chandler, M., & Moran, T. (1990). Psychopathy and moral development: A comparative study of delinquent and nondelinquent youth. *Development and Psychopathology, 2,* 227–246.

Chanquoy, L. (2001). How to make it easier for children to revise their writing: A study of text revision from 3rd to 5th grades. *British Journal of Educational Psychology, 71,* 15–41.

Chao, R. K. (1994). Beyond parental control and authoritarian parenting style: Understanding Chinese parenting through the cultural notion of training. *Child Development, 65,* 1111–1119.

Chapman, P. D. (1988). *Schools as sorters: Lewis M. Terman, applied psychology, and the intelligence testing movement, 1890–1930.* New York: New York University Press.

Chase-Lansdale, P. L., Brooks-Gunn, J., & Zamsky, E. S. (1994). Young African-American multigenerational families in poverty: Quality of mothering and grandmothering. *Child Development, 65,* 373–393.

Chase-Lansdale, P. L., Cherlin, A. J., & Kiernan, K. E. (1995). The long-term effects of parental divorce on the mental health of young adults: A developmental perspective. *Child Development, 66,* 1614–1634.

Chase-Lansdale, P. L., & Hetherington, E. M. (1990). The impact of divorce on life-span development: Short and long term effects. In P. B. Baltes, B. L. Featherman, & R. M. Lerner (Eds.), *Life-span development and behavior* (Vol. 10). Hillsdale, NJ: Erlbaum.

Chase-Lansale, P. L., Moffitt, R. A., Lohman, B. J., Cherlin, A. J., Coley, R. L., Pittman, L. D., Roff, J., & Votruba-Drzal, E. (2003). Mothers' transitions from welfare to work and the well-being of preschoolers and adolescents. *Science, 299,* 1548–1552.

Chen, X., Rubin, K. H., & Li, Z. (1995). Social functioning and adjustment in Chinese children. *Developmental Psychology, 31,* 531–539.

Chi, M. T. H. (1978). Knowledge structures and memory development. In R. Siegler (Ed.), *Children's thinking: What develops?* Hillsdale, NJ: Erlbaum.

Children's Defense Fund. (1996). *The state of America's children yearbook, 1996.* Washington, DC: Author.

Chilman, C. S. (1983). *Adolescent sexuality in a changing American society* (2nd ed.). New York: Wiley.

Chomitz, V. R., Cheung, L. W. Y., & Lieberman, E. (1995). The role of lifestyle in preventing low birth weight. *The Future of Children, 5,* 121–138.

Chomsky, N. (1957). *Syntactic structures.* The Hague: Mouton.

Chomsky, N. (1995). *The minimalist program.* Cambridge: MIT Press.

Chorpita, B. F., & Barlow, D. H. (1998). The development of anxiety: The role of control in the early environment. *Psychological Bulletin, 124,* 3–21.

Christensen, A., & Heavey, C. L. (1999). Intervention for couples. *Annual Review of Psychology, 50,* 165–190.

Cicchetti, D., Toth, S. L., & Maughan, A. (2000). An ecological-transactional model of child maltreatment. In A. J. Sameroff, M. Lewis, & S. M. Miller (Eds.), *Handbook of developmental psychopathology* (2nd ed., pp. 689–722). New York, NY: Kluwer Academic/Plenum Publishers.

Cipani, E. (1991). Educational classification and placement. In J. L. Matson & J. A. Mulick (Eds.), *Handbook of mental retardation* (2nd ed.). New York: Pergamon.

Clark, K. B. (1945). A brown girl in a speckled world. *The Journal of Social Issues, 1,* 10–15.

Clark, K. B. & Clark, M. K. (1940). Skin color as a factor in racial identification of Negro preschool children. *The Journal of Social Psychology, 11,* 159–169.

Clifton, R., Perris, E., & Bullinger, A. (1991). Infants' perception of auditory space. *Developmental Psychology, 27,* 187–197.

Cocking, R. R. (2001). Editor's introduction to the special issue: Children in the digital age. *Journal of Applied Developmental Psychology, 22,* 1–2.

Cohen, S., & Williamson, G. M. (1991). Stress and infectious disease in humans. *Psychological Bulletin, 109,* 5–24.

Coie, J. D., & Dodge, K. A. (1998). Aggression and antisocial behavior. In W. Damon (Ed.), *Handbook of child psychology* (Vol. 3). New York: Wiley.

Coie, J. D., Dodge, K. A., Terry, R., & Wright, V. (1991). The role of aggression in peer relations: An analysis of aggression episodes in boys' play groups. *Child Development, 62,* 812–826.

Colby, A., Kohlberg, L., Gibbs, J. C., & Lieberman, M. (1983). A longitudinal study of moral development. *Monographs of the Society for Research in Child Development, 48* (Whole #200).

Cole, D. A. (1991). Change in self-perceived competence as a function of peer and teacher evaluation. *Developmental Psychology, 27,* 682–688.

Cole, D. A., Maxwell, S. E., Martin, J. M., Peeke, L. G., Seroczynski, A. D., Tram, J. M., Hoffman, K. B., Ruiz, M. D., Jacquez, F., & Maschman, T. (2001). The development of multiple domains of child and adolescent self-concept: A cohort sequential longitudinal design. *Child Development, 72,* 1723–1746.

Collaer, M. L., & Hines, M. (1995). Human behavioral sex differences: A role for gonadal hormones during early development? *Psychological Bulletin, 118,* 55–107.

Coltheart, M., Curtis, B., Atkins, P., & Haller, M. (1993). Models of reading aloud: Dual-route and parallel-distributed-processing approaches. *Psychological Review, 100,* 589–608.

Committee on Genetics. (1996). Newborn screening fact sheet. *Pediatrics, 98,* 473–501.

Condry, J. C., & Ross, D. F. (1985). Sex and aggression: The influence of gender label on the perception of aggression in children. *Child Development, 56,* 225–233.

Conger, R. D., Patterson, G. R., & Ge, X. (1995). It takes two to replicate: A mediational model for the impact of parents' stress on adolescent adjustment. *Child Development, 66,* 80–97.

Conway, M. A., & Pleydell-Pearce, C. W. (2000). The construction of autobiographical memories in the self-memory system. *Psychological Review, 107,* 261–288.

Coopersmith, S. (1967). *The antecedents of self-esteem.* San Francisco: W. H. Freeman.

Coplan, R. J., Gavinski-Molina, M. H., Lagace-Seguin, D. G., & Wichmann, C. (2001). When girls versus boys play alone: Nonsocial play and adjustment in kindergarten. *Developmental Psychology, 37,* 464–474.

Copper, R. L., Goldenberg, R. L., Das, A., Elder, N., et al. (1996). The preterm prediction study: Maternal stress is associated with spontaneous preterm birth at less than thirty-five weeks' gestation. *American Journal of Obstetrics & Gynecology, 175,* 1286–1292.

Corballis, M. C. (1997). The genetics and evolution of handedness. *Psychological Review, 104,* 714–727.

Corballis, M. C. (2001). Is the handedness gene on the X chromosome? Comment on Jones and Martin (2000). *Psychological Review, 108,* 805–810.

Corbin, C. B., & Pangrazi, R. P. (1992). Are American children and youth fit? *Research Quarterly for Exercise and Sport, 63,* 96–106.

Cornelius, M., Taylor, P., Geva, D., & Day, N. (1995). Prenatal tobacco exposure and marijuana use among adolescents: Effects on offspring gestational age, growth, and morphology. *Pediatrics, 95,* 738–743.

Cornwell, K. S., Harris, L. J., & Fitzgerald, H. E. (1991). Task effects in the development of hand preference in 9-, 13-, and 20-month-old infant girls. *Developmental Neuropsychology, 7,* 19–34.

Cosmides, L., & Tooby, J. (2000). Evolutionary psychology and the emotions. In M. Lewis & J. Haviland-Jones (Eds.), *Handbook of emotions* (2nd ed., pp. 91–115). New York: Guilford Press.

Costa, P. T., & McRae, R. R. (2001). A theoretical context for adult temperament. In T. D. Wachs & G. A. Kohnstamm (Eds.), *Temperament in context* (pp. 1–21). Mahwah, NJ: Erlbaum.

Costin, S. E., & Jones, D. C. (1992). Friendship as a facilitator of emotional responsiveness and prosocial interventions among young children. *Developmental Psychology, 28,* 941–947.

Cox, M. J., Owen, M. T., Henderson, V. K., & Margand, N. A. (1992). Prediction of infant-father and infant-mother attachment. *Developmental Psychology, 28,* 474–483.

Craig, K. D., Whitfield, M. F., Grunau, R. V. E., Linton, J., & Hadjistavropoulos, H. D. (1993). Pain in the preterm neonate: Behavioural and physiological indices. *Pain, 52,* 238–299.

Creusere, M. A. (1999). Theories of adults' understanding and use of irony and sarcasm: Applications to and evidence from research with children. *Developmental Review, 19,* 213–262.

Crick, N. R., Casas, J. F., & Nelson, D. A. (2002). Toward a more comprehensive understanding of peer maltreatment: Studies of relational victimization. *Current Directions in Psychological Science, 11,* 98–101.

Crick, N. R., & Dodge, K. A. (1994). A review and reformulation of social information-processing mechanisms in children's social adjustment. *Psychological Bulletin, 115,* 74–101.

Crick, N. R., & Grotpeter, J. K. (1995). Relational aggression, gender, and social-psychological adjustment. *Child Development, 66,* 710–722.

Crick, N. R., Grotpeter, J. K., & Bigbee, M. A. (2002). Relationally and physically aggressive children's intent attributions and feelings of distress for relational and instrumental peer provocations. *Child Development, 73,* 1134–1142.

Crick, N. R., & Werner, N. E. (1998). Response decision processes in relational and overt aggression. *Child Development, 69,* 1630–1639.

Crowder, R. G., & Wagner, R. K. (1992). *The psychology of reading: An introduction* (2nd ed.). New York: Oxford University Press.

Cuellar, I., Nyberg, B., Maldonado, R. E., & Roberts, R. E. (1997). Ethnic identity and acculturation in a young adult Mexican-origin population. *Journal of Community Psychology, 25,* 535–549.

Cummings, E. M., Iannotti, R. J., & Zahn-Waxler, C. (1989). Aggression between peers in early childhood: Individual continuity and developmental change. *Child Development, 60,* 887–895.

Cunningham, A. E., Perry, K. E., Stanovich, K. E., & Share, D. L. (2002). Orthographic learning during reading: Examining the role of self-teaching. *Journal of Experimental Child Psychology, 82,* 185–199.

Curtain, S. C., & Park, M. M. (1999). Trends in the attendant, place, and timing of births and in the use of obstetric interventions: United States, 1989–1997. *National Vital Statistics Report, 47,* 1–12.

Curtiss, S. (1989). The independence and task-specificity of language. In M. H. Bornstein & J. S. Bruner (Eds.), *Interaction in human development* (pp. 105–137). Hillsdale, NJ: Erlbaum.

Daley, T. C., Whaley, S. E., Sigman, M. D., Espinosa, M. P., & Neumann, C. (2003). IQ on the rise: The Flynn effect in rural Kenyan children. *Psychological Science, 14,* 215–219.

Daly, M., & Wilson, M. (1996). Violence against stepchildren. *Current Directions in Psychological Science, 5,* 77–81.

Damon, W., & Hart, D. (1988). *Self-understanding in childhood and adolescence.* New York: Cambridge University Press.

Dannemiller, J. L. (1998). Color constancy and color vision during infancy: Methodological and empirical issues. In V. Walsh & J. Kulikowski (Eds.), *Perceptual constancy: Why things look as they do.* New York: Cambridge University Press.

D'Augelli, A. R. (1996). Lesbian, gay, and bisexual development during adolescence and young adulthood. In R. P. Cabaj & T. S. Stein (Eds.), *Textbook of homosexuality and mental health.* Washington, DC: American Psychiatric Press.

Davidson, F. H., & Davidson, M. M. (1994). *Changing childhood prejudice: The caring work of the schools.* Westport, CT: Bergin & Garvey/Greenwood.

Davidson, K. M., Richards, D. S., Schatz, D. A., & Fisher, D. A. (1991). Successful in utero treatment of fetal goiter and hypothyroidism. *New England Journal of Medicine, 324,* 543–546.

Davies, P. T., & Cummings, E. M. (1998). Exploring children's emotional security as a mediator of the link between marital relations and child adjustment. *Child Development, 69,* 124–139.

Davis, B. L., MacNeilage, P. F., Matyear, C. L., & Powell, J. K. (2000). Prosodic correlates of stress in babbling: An acoustical study. *Child Development, 71,* 1258–1270.

Day, J. D., Engelhardt, S. E., Maxwell, S. E., & Bolig, E. E. (1997). Comparison of static and dynamic assessment procedures and their relation to independent performance. *Journal of Educational Psychology, 89,* 358–368.

Deater-Deckard, K., & Plomin, R. (1999). An adoption study of the etiology of teacher and parent reports of externalizing behavior problems in middle childhood. *Child Development, 70,* 144–154.

De Beni, R., & Palladino, P. (2000). Intrusion errors in working memory tasks: Are they related to reading comprehension ability? *Learning & Individual Differences, 12,* 131–143.

DeCasper, A. J., & Spence, M. J. (1986). Prenatal maternal speech influences newborns' perception of speech sounds. *Infant Behavior and Development, 9,* 133–150.

de Castro, B. O., Veerman, J. W., Koops, W., Bosch, J. D., & Monshouwer, H. J. (2002). Hostile attribution of intent and aggressive behavior: A meta-analysis. *Child Development, 73,* 916–934.

de Jong, P. F., & Leseman, P. P. M. (2001). Lasting effects of home literacy on reading achievement in school. *Journal of School Psychology, 39,* 389–414.

Dekovic, M., & Janssens, J. M. (1992). Parents' child-rearing style and child's sociometric status. *Developmental Psychology, 28,* 925–932.

Dellas, M., & Jernigan, L. P. (1990). Affective personality characteristics associated with undergraduate ego identity formation. *Journal of Adolescent Research, 5,* 306–324.

DeLoache, J. S. (1984). Oh where, oh where: Memory-based searching by very young children. In C. Sophian (Ed.), *Origins of cognitive skills.* Hillsdale, NJ: Erlbaum.

DeLoache, J. S. (1995). Early understanding and use of models: The modal model. *Current Directions in Psychological Science, 4,* 109–113.

DeLoache, J. S. (2000). Dual representation and young children's use of scale models. *Child Development, 71,* 329–338.

DeLoache, J. S., Miller, K. F., & Rosengren, K. S. (1997). The credible shrinking room: Very young children's performance with symbolic and nonsymbolic relations. *Psychological Science, 8,* 308–313.

Dempster, F. N. (1995). Interference and inhibition in cognition: An historical perspective. In F. N. Dempster & C. J. Brainerd (Eds.), *Interference and inhibition in cognition.* San Diego, CA: Academic Press.

DeRosier, M. E., Kupersmidt, J. B., & Patterson, C. J. (1995). Children's academic and behavioral adjustment as a function of the chronicity and proximity of peer rejection. *Child Development, 65,* 1799–1813.

Detterman, D. K., Gabriel, L. T., & Ruthsatz, J. M. (2000). Intelligence and giftedness. In R. J. Sternberg (Ed.), *Handbook of intelligence* (pp. 141–158). Cambridge, England: Cambridge University Press.

deVilliers, J. G., & deVilliers, P. A. (1985). The acquisition of English. In D. I. Slobin (Ed.), *The cross-linguistic study of language acquisition.* Hillsdale, NJ: Erlbaum.

DeWolff, M. S., & van IJzendoorn, M. H. (1997). Sensitivity and attachment: A meta-analysis on parental antecedents of infant attachment. *Child Development, 68,* 571–591.

Dews, S., Winner, E., Kaplan, J., Rosenblatt, E., Hunt, M., Lim, K., McGovern, A., Qualter, A., & Smarsh, B. (1996). Children's understanding of the meaning and functions of verbal irony. *Child Development, 67,* 3071–3085.

Diamond, M., Johnson, R., Young, D., & Singh, S. (1983). Age-related morphologic differences in the rat cerebral cortex and hippocampus: Male-female; right-left. *Experimental Neurology, 81,* 1–13.

Dick, D. M., & Rose, R. J. (2002). Behavior genetics: What's new? What's next? *Current Directions in Psychological Science, 11,* 70–74.

Dick, D. M., Rose, R. J., Viken, R. J., & Kaprio, J. (2000). Pubertal timing and substance abuse: Associations between and within families across late adolescence. *Developmental Psychology, 36,* 180–189.

Dickens, W. T., & Flynn, J. R. (2001). Heritability estimates versus large environmental effects: The IQ paradox resolved. *Psychological Review, 108,* 346–369.

Dick-Read, G. (1959). *Childbirth without fear.* New York: Harper and Brothers.

DiPietro, J. A., Hodgson, D. M., Costigan, K. A., & Hilton, S. C. (1996). Fetal neurobehavioral development. *Child Development, 67,* 2553–2567.

DiPietro, J. A., Hodgson, D. M., Costigan, K. A., & Johnson, T. R. B. (1996). Fetal antecedents of infant temperament. *Child Development, 67,* 2568–2583.

Dishion, T. J. (1990). The family ecology of boys' peer relations in middle childhood. *Child Development, 61,* 874–892.

Dockrell, J., & McShane, J. (1993). *Children's learning difficulties: A cognitive approach.* Cambridge: Blackwell Publishers.

Dodge, K. A., Bates, J. E., & Pettit, G. S. (1990). Mechanisms in the cycle of violence. *Science, 250,* 1678–1683.

Dodge, K. A., & Crick, N. R. (1990). Social information-processing bases of aggressive behavior in children. *Personality and Social Psychology Bulletin, 16,* 8–22.

Donkin, A. J. M., Neale, R. J., & Tilston, C. (1993). Children's food purchase requests. *Appetite, 21,* 291–294.

Donovan, W. L., Leavitt, L. A., & Walsh, R. O. (2000). Maternal illusory control predicts socialization strategies and toddler compliance. *Developmental Psychology, 36,* 402–411.

Downey, G., Lebolt, A., Rincon, C., & Freitas, A. L. (1998). Rejection sensitivity and children's interpersonal difficulties. *Child Development, 69,* 1074–1091.

Drabman, R. S., & Thomas, M. H. (1976). Does watching violence on television cause apathy? *Pediatrics, 52,* 329–331.

Draghi-Lorenz, R., Reddy, V., & Costall, A. (2001). Rethinking the development of "nonbasic" emotions: A critical review of existing theories. *Developmental Review, 21,* 263–304.

DuBois, D. L., & Hirsch, B. J. (1990). School and neighborhood friendship patterns of black and whites in early adolescence. *Child Development, 61,* 524–536.

Dumas, J. E., LaFreniere, P. J., & Serketich, W. J. (1995). "Balance of power": A transactional analysis of control in mother-child dyads involving socially competent, aggressive, and anxious children. *Journal of Abnormal Psychology, 104,* 104–113.

Duncan, G. J., & Brooks-Gunn, J. (2000). Family poverty, welfare reform, and child development. *Child Development, 71,* 188–196.

Dunham, P. J., Dunham, F., & Curwin, A. (1993). Joint-attentional states and lexical acquisition at 18 months. *Developmental Psychology, 29,* 827–831.

Dunn, J., & Kendrick, C. (1981). Social behavior of young siblings in the family context: Differences between same-sex and different-sex dyads. *Child Development, 52,* 1265–1273.

Dunn, J., & Plomin, R. (1990). *Separate lives: Why siblings are so different.* New York: Basic Books.

Dunn, J., Slomkowski, C., & Beardsall, L. (1994). Sibling relationships from the preschool period through middle childhood and early adolescence. *Developmental Psychology, 30,* 315–324.

Dunson, D. B., Colombo, B., & Baird, D. D. (2002). Changes in age in the level and duration of fertility in the menstrual cycle. *Human Reproduction, 17,* 1399–1403.

Durik, A. M., Hyde, J. S., & Clark, R. (2000). Sequelae of cesarean and vaginal deliveries: Psychosocial outcomes for mothers and infants. *Developmental Psychology, 36,* 251–260.

Eacott, M. J. (1999). Memory for the events of early childhood. *Current Directions in Psychological Science, 8,* 46–49.

Eagly, A. H. (1995). The science and politics of comparing women and men. *American Psychologist, 50,* 145–158.

Eagly, A. H., Karau, S. J., & Makhijani, M. G. (1995). Gender and the effectiveness of leaders: A meta-analysis. *Psychological Bulletin, 117,* 125–145.

Easterbrook, M. A., Kisilevsky, B. S., Hains, S. M. J., & Muir, D. W. (1999). Faceness or complexity: Evidence from newborn visual tracking of facelike stimuli. *Infant Behavior & Development, 22,* 17–35.

Eaton, W. O., Chipperfield, J. G., & Singbeil, C. E. (1989). Birth order and activity level in children. *Developmental Psychology, 25,* 668–672.

Eaton, W. O., & Enns, L. R. (1986). Sex differences in human motor activity level. *Psychological Bulletin, 100,* 19–28.

Eccles, J. S., & Harold, R. D. (1991). Gender differences in sport involvement: Applying the Eccles' expectancy-value model. *Journal of Applied Sports Psychology, 3,* 7–35.

Eccles, J. S., Jacobs, J. E., & Harold, R. D. (1990). Gender role stereotypes, expectancy effects, and parents' socialization of gender differences. *Journal of Social Issues, 46,* 183–201.

Edelbrock, C., Rende, R., Plomin, R., & Thompson, L. A. (1995). A twin study of competence and problem behavior in childhood and early adolescence. *Journal of Child Psychology and Psychiatry, 36,* 775–785.

Edwards, C. A. (1994). Leadership in groups of school-age girls. *Developmental Psychology, 30,* 920–927.

Egan, S. K., Monson, T. C., & Perry, D. G. (1998). Social-cognitive influences on change in aggression over time. *Developmental Psychology, 34,* 996–1006.

Egan, S. K., & Perry, D. G. (1998). Does low self-regard invite victimization? *Developmental Psychology, 34,* 299–309.

Eisenberg, N. (1982). The development of reasoning regarding prosocial behavior. In N. Eisenberg (Ed.), *The development of prosocial behavior.* New York: Academic Press.

Eisenberg, N. (1986). *Altruistic emotion, cognition, and behavior.* Hillsdale, NJ: Erlbaum.

Eisenberg, N. (1988). The development of prosocial and aggressive behavior. In M. H. Bornstein & M. E. Lamb (Eds.), *Developmental psychology: An advanced textbook* (2nd ed.). Hillsdale, NJ: Erlbaum.

Eisenberg, N., Carlo, G., Murphy, B., & Van Court, P. (1995). Prosocial development in late adolescence: A longitudinal study. *Child Development, 66,* 1179–1197.

Eisenberg, N., Cumberland, A., Spinrad, T. L., Fabes, R. A., Shepard, S. A., Reiser, M., Murphy, B. C., Losoya, S. H., & Guthrie, I. K. (2001). The relations of regulation and emotionality to children's externalizing and internalizing problem behavior. *Child Development, 72,* 1112–1134.

Eisenberg, N., Fabes, R. A., Schaller, M., Carlo, G., & Miller, P. A. (1991). The relations of parental characteristics and practices to children's vicarious emotional responding. *Child Development, 62,* 1393–1408.

Eisenberg, N., & Morris, A. S. (2002). Children's emotion-related regulation. *Advances in Child Development and Behavior, 30,* 189–229.

Eisenberg, N., & Shell, R. (1986). Prosocial moral judgment and behavior in children: The mediating role of cost. *Personality and Social Psychology Bulletin, 12,* 426–433.

Eisenberg, N., Shepard, S. A., Fabes, R. A., Murphy, B. C., & Guthrie, I. K. (1998). Shyness and children's emotionality, regulation, and coping: Contemporaneous, longitudinal, and across-context relations. *Child Development, 69,* 767–790.

Eisenberg, N., Zhou, Q., & Koller, S. (2001). Brazilian adolescents' prosocial moral judgment and behavior: Relations to sympathy, perspective taking, gender-role orientation, and demographic characteristics. *Child Development, 72,* 518–534.

Eizenman, D. R., & Bertenthal, B. I. (1998). Infants' perception of object unity in translating and rotating displays. *Developmental Psychology, 34,* 426–434.

Elkind, D. (1978). *The child's reality: Three developmental themes.* Hillsdale, NJ: Erlbaum.

Elkind, D., & Bowen, R. (1979). Imaginary audience behavior in children and adolescents. *Developmental Psychology, 15,* 38–44.

Ellis, B. J., & Garber, J. (2000). Psychosocial antecedents of variation in girls' pubertal timing: Maternal depression, stepfather presence, and marital and family stress. *Child Development, 71,* 485–501.

Ellis, W. K., & Rusch, F. R. (1991). Supported employment: Current practices and future directions. In J. L. Matson & J. A. Mulick (Eds.), *Handbook of mental retardation* (2nd ed.). New York: Pergamon.

Elmer-DeWitt, P. (1994, January 17). The genetic revolution. *Time,* 46–53.

Enns, J. T. (1990). Relations between components of visual attention. In J. T. Enns (Ed.), *The development of attention.* Amsterdam: North Holland.

Epstein, L. H., & Cluss, P. A. (1986). Behavioral genetics of childhood obesity. *Behavior Therapy, 17,* 324–334.

Epstein, L. H., Valoski, A. M., Vara, L. S., McCurley, J., et al. (1995). Effects of decreasing sedentary behavior and increasing activity on weight change in obese children. *Health Psychology, 14,* 109–108.

Erel, O., & Burman, B. (1995). Interrelatedness of marital relations and parent-child relations: A meta-analytic review. *Psychological Bulletin, 118,* 108–132.

Erel, O., Margolin, G., & John, R. S. (1998). Observed sibling interaction: Links with the marital and the mother-child relationship. *Developmental Psychology, 34,* 288–298.

Erikson, E. H. (1968). *Identity: Youth and crisis.* New York: Norton.

Eskritt, M., & Lee, K. (2002). Remember when you last saw that card?: Children's production of external symbols as a memory aid. *Developmental Psychology, 38,* 254–266.

Etaugh, C., & Liss, M. B. (1992). Home, school, and playroom: Training grounds for adult gender roles. *Sex Roles, 26,* 129–147.

Evans, G. W., & English, K. (2002). The environment of poverty: Multiple stressor exposure, psychophysiological stress, and socioemotional adjustment. *Child Development, 73,* 1238–1248.

Eyer, D. E. (1992). *Mother-infant bonding: A scientific fiction.* New Haven, CT: Yale University Press.

Fabes, R. A., Eisenberg, N., Jones, S., Smith, M., Guthrie, I., Poulin, R., Shepard, S., & Friedman, J. (1999). Regulation, emotionality, and preschoolers' socially competent peer interactions. *Child Development, 70,* 432–442.

Fabes, R. A., Eisenberg, N., Smith, M. C., & Murphy, B. C. (1996). Getting angry at peers: Associations with liking of the provocateur. *Child Development, 67,* 942–956.

Fagot, B. I. (1985). Changes in thinking about early sex role development. *Developmental Review, 5,* 83–98.

Falbo, T., & Polit, D. F. (1986). Quantitative review of the only child literature: Research evidence and theory development. *Psychological Bulletin, 100,* 176–186.

Farrant, K., & Reese, E. (2000). Maternal style and children's participation in reminiscing: Stepping stones in children's autobiographical memory development. *Journal of Cognition & Development, 1,* 193–225.

Farrar, M. J., & Boyer-Pennington, M. (1999). Remembering specific episodes of a scripted event. *Journal of Experimental Child Psychology, 73,* 266–288.

Farver, J. M., & Branstetter, W. H. (1994). Preschoolers' prosocial responses to their peers' distress. *Developmental Psychology, 30,* 334–341.

Farver, J. M., & Shin, Y. L. (1997). Social pretend play in Korean- and Anglo-American preschoolers. *Child Development, 68,* 544–556.

Fasig, L. (2002). Calling all researchers… *SRCD Developments, 45,* 3–5.

Fasig, L. G. (2000). Toddlers' understanding of ownership: Implications for self-concept development. *Social Development, 9,* 370–382.

Federal Interagency Forum on Child and Family Statistics. (2000). *America's Children: Key National Indicators of Well-Being, 2000.* Federal Interagency Forum on Child and Family Statistics. Washington, DC: U.S. Government Printing Office.

Feigenson, L., Carey, S., & Hauser, M. (2002). The representations underlying infants' choice of more: Object files versus analog magnitudes. *Psychological Science, 13,* 150–156.

Feldhusen, J. F. (1996). Motivating academically able youth with enriched and accelerated learning experiences. In C. P. Benbow & D. J. Lubinski (Eds.), *Intellectual talent: Psychometric and social issues.* Baltimore: Johns Hopkins Press.

Feldman, H. M., Dollaghan, C. A., Campbell, T. F., Kurs-Lasky, M., Janosky, J. E., & Paradise, J. L. (2000). Measurement properties of the MacArthur Communicative Development Inventories at ages one and two years. *Child Development, 71,* 310–322.

Feldman, S. S., & Wentzel, K. R. (1990). The relationship between parental styles, sons' self-restraint, and peer relations in early adolescence. *Journal of Early Adolescence, 10,* 439–454.

Fenson, L., Dale, P. S., Reznick, J. S., Bates, E., et al. (1994). Variability in early communicative development. *Monographs of the Society for Research in Child Development, 59,* Whole No. 173.

Fergusson, D. M., Horwood, L. J., & Shannon, F. T. (1987). Breast-feeding and subsequent social adjustment in six- to eight-year-old children. *Journal of Child Psychology and Psychiatry and Allied Disciplines, 28,* 379–386.

Fergusson, D. M., & Woodward, L. J. (2000). Teenage pregnancy and female educational underachievement: A prospective study of a New Zealand birth cohort. *Journal of Marriage & the Family, 62,* 147–161.

Field, T. M. (1990). *Infancy.* Cambridge, MA: Harvard University Press.

Field, T. M., & Widmayer, S. M. (1982). Motherhood. In B. J. Wolman (Ed.), *Handbook of developmental psychology.* Englewood Cliffs, NJ: Prentice Hall.

Fincham, F. (1998). Child development and marital relations. *Child Development, 69,* 543–574.

Finley, G. E. (1999). Children of adoptive families. In W. K. Silverman & T. H. Ollendick (Eds.), *Developmental issues in the clinical treatment of children* (pp. 358–370). Boston: Allyn and Bacon.

Finn-Stevenson, M., Desimone, L., & Chung. A. (1998). Linking child care and support services with the school: Pilot evaluation of the School of the 21st Century. *Children and Youth Services Review, 20,* 177–205.

Fisch, S., & McCann, S. K. (1993). Making broadcast television participative: Eliciting mathematical behavior through Square One TV. *Educational Technology Research and Development, 41,* 103–109.

Fisch, S., Truglio, R. T., & Cole, C. F. (1999). The impact of *Sesame Street* on preschool children: A review and synthesis of 30 years' research. *Media Psychology, 1,* 165–190.

Fischer, K. W., & Granott, N. (1995). Beyond one-dimensional change: Parallel, concurrent, socially distributed processes in learning and development. *Human Development, 38,* 302–314.

Fischer, M., Barkley, R. A., Fletcher, K. E., & Smallish, L. (1993). The adolescent outcome of hyperactive children: Predictors of psychiatric, academic, social, and emotional adjustment. *Journal of the American Academy of Child and Adolescent Psychiatry, 32,* 324–332.

Fisher, C. (1996). Structural limits on verb mapping: The role of analogy in children's interpretations of sentences. *Cognitive Psychology, 31,* 41–81.

Fitzgerald, J. (1987). Research on revision in writing. *Review of Educational Research, 57,* 481–506.

Flavell, J. H. (1985). *Cognitive development* (2nd ed.). Englewood Cliffs, NJ: Prentice-Hall.

Flavell, J. H. (1996). Piaget's legacy. *Psychological Science, 7,* 200–203.

Flavell, J. H. (1999). Cognitive development: Children's knowledge about the mind. *Annual Review of Psychology, 50,* 21–45.

Flavell, J. H. (2000). Development of children's knowledge about the mental world. *International Journal of Behavioral Development, 24,* 15–23.

Flavell, J. H., Flavell, E. R., & Green, F. L. (2001). Development of children's understanding of connections between thinking and feeling. *Psychological Science, 12,* 430–432.

Flynn, J. R. (1998). IQ gains over time: Toward finding the causes. In U. Neisser (Ed.), *The rising curve: Long-term gains in IQ and related measures* (pp. 25–66). Washington, DC: American Psychological Association.

Flynn, J. R. (1999). Searching for justice: The discovery of IQ gains over time. *American Psychologist, 54,* 5–20.

Fonzi, A., Schneider, B. H., Tani, F., & Tomada, G. (1997). Predicting children's friendship status from their dynamic interaction in structured situations of potential conflict. *Child Development, 68,* 496–506.

Foreyt, J. P., & Goodrick, G. K. (1995). Obesity. In R. T. Ammerman & M. Hersen (Eds.), *Handbook of child behavior therapy in the psychiatric setting.* New York: Wiley.

Foster, S. H. (1986). Learning discourse topic management in the preschool years. *Journal of Child Language, 13,* 231–250.

Fox, N. A., Kimmerly, N. L., & Schafer, W. D. (1991). Attachment to mother/attachment to father: A meta-analysis. *Child Development, 62,* 210–225.

Frank, D. A., Augustyn, M., Knight, W. G., Pell, T., & Zuckerman, B. (2001). Growth, development, and behavior in early childhood following prenatal cocaine exposure: A systematic review. *Journal of the American Medical Association, 285,* 1613–1625.

Franquart-Declercq, C., & Gineste, M. (2001). Metaphor comprehension in children. *Annee Psychologique, 101,* 723–752.

French, D. C. (1988). Heterogeneity of peer-rejected boys: Aggressive and nonaggressive subtypes. *Child Development, 53,* 976–985.

French, D. C. (1990). Heterogeneity of peer-rejected girls. *Child Development, 61,* 2028–2031.

French, D. C., Jansen, E. A., & Pidada, S. (2002). United States and Indonesian children's and adolescents' reports of relational aggression by disliked peers. *Child Development, 73,* 1143–1150.

Fried, P. A., O'Connell, C. M., & Watkinson, B. (1992). 60- and 72-month follow-up of children prenatally exposed to marijuana, cigarettes, and alcohol: Cognitive and language assessment. *Journal of Developmental & Behavioral Pediatrics, 13,* 383–391.

Friedman, J. M., & Polifka, J. E. (1996). *The effects of drugs on the fetus and nursing infant: A handbook for health care professionals.* Baltimore: Johns Hopkins University Press.

Frye, D. (1993). Causes and precursors of children's theories of mind. In D. F. Hay & A. Angold (Eds.), *Precursors and causes in development and psychopathology.* Chichester, England: Wiley.

Furman, W. (2002). The emerging field of adolescent romantic relationships. *Current Directions in Psychological Science, 11,* 177–180.

Furstenberg, F. F. (1993). How families manage risk and opportunity in dangerous neighborhoods. In W. J. Wilson (Ed.), *Sociology and the public agenda.* Newbury Park, CA: Sage.

Furstenburg, F. F., & Teitler, J. O. (1994). Reconsidering the effects of marital disruption: What happens to children of divorce in early adulthood? *Journal of Family Issues, 15,* 173–190.

Gable, S., & Isabella, R. A. (1992). Maternal contributions to infant regulation of arousal. *Infant Behavior and Development, 15,* 95–107.

Galambos, N. L., & Maggs, J. L. (1991). Out-of-school care of young adolescents and self-reported behavior. *Developmental Psychology, 27,* 644–655.

Galler, J. R., & Ramsey, F. (1989). A follow-up study of the influence of early malnutrition on development: Behavior at home and at school. *Journal of the American Academy of Child and Adolescent Psychiatry, 28,* 254–261.

Galler, J. R., Ramsey, F., & Forde, V. (1986). A follow-up study of the influence of early malnutrition on subsequent development: IV. Intellectual performance during adolescence. *Nutrition and Behavior, 3,* 211–222.

Garbarino, J., & Kostelny, K. (1992). Child maltreatment as a community problem. *Child Abuse and Neglect, 16,* 455–464.

Garber, J., Robinson, N. S., & Valentiner, D. (1997). The relation between parenting and adolescent depression: Self-worth as a mediator. *Journal of Adolescent Research, 12,* 12–33.

Garcia, M. M., Shaw, D. S., Winslow, E. B., & Yaggi, K. E. (2000). Destructive sibling conflict and the development of conduct problems in young boys. *Developmental Psychology, 36,* 44–53.

Gardner, H. (1983). *Frames of mind: The theory of multiple intelligences.* New York: Basic Books.

Gardner, H. (1993). *Multiple intelligences: The theory in practice.* New York: Basic Books.

Gardner, H. (1995). Reflections on multiple intelligences: Myths and messages. *Phi Delta Kappan, 77,* 200–203, 206–209.

Gardner, H. (1999). *Intelligence reframed: Multiple intelligences for the 21st century.* New York: Basic Books.

Gardner, H. (2002). *MI millennium: Multiple intelligences for the new millennium* [video recording]. Los Angeles: Into the Classroom Media.

Garner, P. W., Jones, D. C., & Palmer, D. J. (1994). Social cognitive correlates of preschool children's sibling caregiving behavior. *Developmental Psychology, 30,* 905–911.

Garvey, C., & Berninger, G. (1981). Timing and turn taking in children's conversations. *Discourse Processes, 4,* 27–59.

Gash, H., & Morgan, M. (1993). School-based modifications of children's gender-related beliefs. *Journal of Applied Developmental Psychology, 14,* 277–287.

Gaulin, S. J. C., & McBurney, D. H. (2001). *Psychology: An evolutionary approach.* Upper Saddle River, NJ: Prentice-Hall.

Gauvain, M. (1998). Cognitive development in social and cultural context. *Current Directions in Psychological Science, 7,* 188–192.

Gavin, L. A., & Furman, W. (1996). Adolescent girls' relationships with mothers and best friends. *Child Development, 67,* 375–386.

Ge, X., Conger, R. D., Cadoret, R. J., Neiderhiser, J. M., et al. (1996). The developmental interface between nature and nurture: A mutual influence model of child antisocial behavior and parent behaviors. *Developmental Psychology, 32,* 574–589.

Ge, X., Conger, R. D., & Elder, G. H. (1996). Coming of age too early: Pubertal influences on girls' vulnerability to psychological distress. *Child Development, 67,* 3386–3400.

Ge, X., Conger, R. D., & Elder, G. H. (2001). Pubertal transition, stressful life events, and the emergence of gender differences in adolescent depressive symptoms. *Developmental Psychology, 37,* 404–417.

Geary, D. C. (2002). Sexual selection and human life history. In R. V. Kail (Ed.), *Advances in child development and behavior* (Vol. 30, pp. 41–102). San Diego, CA: Academic Press.

Geisel, T. (1960). *Green eggs and ham, by Dr. Seuss.* New York: Beginner.

Gelman, R. (1969). Conservation acquisition: A problem of learning to attend to relevant attributes. *Journal of Experimental Child Psychology, 7,* 167–187.

Gelman, R., & Meck, E. (1986). The notion of principle: The case of counting. In J. Hiebert (Ed.), *Conceptual and procedural knowledge: The case of mathematics.* Hillsdale, NJ: Erlbaum.

Gelman, S. A., & Gottfried, G. M. (1996). Children's casual explanations of animate and inanimate motion. *Child Development, 67,* 1970–1987.

Gennetian, L. A., & Miller, C. (2002). Children and welfare reform: A view from an experimental welfare program in Minnesota. *Child Development, 73,* 601–620.

George, C., Kaplan, N., & Main, M. (1985). *The adult attachment interview.* Unpublished manuscript, University of California, Department of Psychology, Berkeley.

Gibbs, J. C., Clark, P. M., Joseph, J. A., Green, J. L., Goodrick, T. S., & Makowski, D. (1986). Relations between moral judgment, moral courage, and field independence. *Child Development, 57,* 185–193.

Giberson, P. K., & Weinberg, J. (1992). Fetal alcohol syndrome and functioning of the immune system. *Alcohol Health and Research World, 16,* 29–38.

Gibson, E. J., Riccio, G., Schmuckler, M. A., Stoffregen, T. A., Rosenberg, D., & Taormina, J. (1987). Detection of the traversability of surfaces by crawling and walking infants. *Journal of Experimental Psychology: Human Perception & Performance, 13,* 533–544.

Gibson, E. J., & Walk, R. D. (1960). The "visual cliff." *Scientific American, 202,* 64–71.

Gilligan, C. (1982). *In a different voice: Psychological theory and women's development.* Cambridge, MA: Harvard University Press.

Gilligan, C., & Attanucci, J. (1988). Two moral orientations: Gender differences and similarities. *Merrill-Palmer Quarterly, 34,* 223–237.

Gleason, T. R., Sebanc, A. M., & Hartup, W. W. (2000). Imaginary companions of preschool children. *Developmental Psychology, 36,* 419–428.

Glick, P. C. (1989). The family life cycle and social change. *Family Relations, 38,* 123–129.

Glick, P. C., & Lin, S. (1986). Recent changes in divorce and remarriage. *Journal of Marriage and the Family, 48,* 737–747.

Goldenberg, R. L., & Klerman, L. V. (1995). Adolescent pregnancy—Another look. *New England Journal of Medicine, 332,* 1161–1162.

Goldman, L. S., Genel, M., Bezman, R. J., & Slanetz, P. J. (1998). Diagnosis and treatment of attention-deficit/hyperactivity disorder in children and adolescents. *Journal of the American Medical Association, 279,* 1100–1107.

Goldsmith, H. H., Buss, K. A., & Lemery, K. S. (1997). Toddler and childhood temperament: Expanded content, stronger genetic evidence, new evidence for the importance of environment. *Developmental Psychology, 33,* 891–905.

Goldsmith, H. H., & Harman, C. (1994). Temperament and attachment: Individuals and relationships. *Current Directions in Psychological Science, 3,* 53–57.

Goleman, D. (1995). *Emotional intelligence: Why it can matter more than IQ.* New York: Bantam.

Goleman, D. (1998). *Working with emotional intelligence.* New York: Bantam.

Goleman, D., Bayatzis, R., & McKee, A. (2002). *Primal leadership: Realizing the power of emotional intelligence.* Boston: Harvard Business Press.

Golinkoff, R. M. (1993). When is communication a "meeting of minds"? *Journal of Child Language, 20,* 199–207.

Golombok, S., MacCallum, F., & Goodman, E. (2001). The "test-tube" generation: Parent-child relationships and the psychological well-being of in vitro fertilization children at adolescence. *Child Development, 72,* 599–608.

Golombok, S., & Tasker, F. (1996). Do parents influence the sexual orientation of their children? Findings from a longitudinal study of lesbian families. *Developmental Psychology, 32,* 3–11.

Good, T. L., & Brophy, J. E. (1996). *Looking in classrooms* (7th ed.). New York: Addison-Wesley.

Good, T. L., & Brophy, J. E. (2002). *Looking in classrooms* (9th ed.). Boston: Allyn & Bacon.

Goodman, G. S., Emery, R. E., & Haugaard, J. J. (1998). Developmental psychology and law: Divorce, child maltreatment, foster care, and adoption. In W. Damon (Ed.), *Handbook of child psychology* (Vol. 4). New York: Wiley.

Goodnow, J. J. (1992). *Parental belief systems: The psychological consequences for children.* Hillsdale, NJ: Erlbaum.

Goodwyn, S. W., & Acredolo, L. P. (1993). Symbolic gesture versus word: Is there a modality advantage for onset of symbol use? *Child Development, 64,* 688–701.

Gordon, B. N., Baker-Ward, L., & Ornstein, P. A. (2001). Children's testimony: A review of research on memory for past experiences. *Clinical Child & Family Psychology Review, 4,* 157–181.

Gordon, C. P. (1996). Adolescent decision making: A broadly based theory and its application to the prevention of early pregnancy. *Adolescence, 31,* 561–584.

Gottfredson, L. S. (1997). Why g matters: The complexity of everyday life. *Intelligence, 24,* 79–132.

Gottlieb, L. N., & Mendelson, M. J. (1990). Parental support and firstborn girls' adaptation to the birth of a sibling. *Journal of Applied Developmental Psychology, 11,* 29–48.

Gottman, J. M. (1986). The world of coordinated play: Same- and cross-sex friendships in children. In J. M. Gottman & J. G. Parker (Eds.), *Conversations of friends.* New York: Cambridge University Press.

Gottman, J. M., Katz, L. F., & Hooven, C. (1996). Parental meta-emotion philosophy and the emotional life of families: Theoretical models and preliminary data. *Journal of Family Psychology, 10,* 243–268.

Goubet, N., Clifton, R. K., & Shah, B. (2001). Learning about pain in preterm newborns. *Journal of Developmental and Behavioral Pediatrics, 22,* 418–424.

Governor's Task Force on Children's Justice. (1998). *Forensic interviewing protocol.* Author.

Govier, E., & Salisbury, G. (2000). Age-related sex differences in performance on a side-naming spatial task. *Psychology, Evolution, & Gender, 2,* 209–222.

Graber, J. A., Brooks-Gunn, J., & Warren, W. P. (1995). The antecedents of menarcheal age: Heredity, family environment, and stressful life events. *Child Development, 66,* 346–359.

Graesser, A. C., Singer, M., & Trabasso, T. (1994). Constructing inferences during narrative text comprehension. *Psychological Review, 101,* 371–395.

Graham, S., Berninger, V. W., Abbott, R. D., Abbott, S. P., & Whitaker, D. (1997). Role of mechanics in composing of elementary school students: A new methodological approach. *Journal of Educational Psychology, 89,* 170–182.

Graham, S., Harris, K. R., & Fink, B. (2000). Is handwriting causally related to learning to write? Treatment of handwriting problems in beginning writers. *Journal of Educational Psychology, 92,* 620–633.

Graham, S., & Juvonen, J. (1998). Self-blame and peer victimization in middle school: An attributional analysis. *Developmental Psychology, 34,* 587–599.

Granrud, C. E. (1986). Binocular vision and spatial perception in 4- and 5-month-old infants. *Journal of Experimental Psychology: Human Perception and Performance, 12,* 36–49.

Grantham-McGregor, S., Ani, C., & Fernald, L. (2001). The role of nutrition in intellectual development. In R. J. Sternberg & E. L. Grigorenko (Eds.), *Environmental effects on cognitive abilities* (pp. 119–155). Mahwah, NJ: Erlbaum.

Gray, S. W., & Klaus, R. A. (1965). An experimental preschool program for culturally deprived children. *Child Development, 36,* 887–898.

Greenberg, B. S., Fazel, S., & Weber, M. (1986). *Children's view on advertising.* New York: Independent Broadcasting Authority Research Report.

Greenberg, M. T., & Crnic, K. A. (1988). Longitudinal predictors of developmental status and social interaction in premature and full-term infants at age two. *Child Development, 59,* 554–570.

Greenfield, P. M. (1998). The cultural evolution of IQ. In U. Neisser (Ed.), *The rising curve: Long-term gains in IQ and related measures* (pp. 81–123). Washington DC: American Psychological Association.

Greenhoot, A. F. (2000). Remembering and understanding: The effects of changes in underlying knowledge on children's recollections. *Child Development, 71,* 1309–1328.

Grigorenko, E. L., & Sternberg, R. J. (1998). Dynamic testing. *Psychological Bulletin, 124,* 75–111.

Groen, G. J., & Resnick, L. B. (1977). Can preschool children invent addition algorithms? *Journal of Educational Psychology, 69,* 645–652.

Grusec, J. E., Goodnow, J. J., & Cohen, L. (1996). Household work and the development of concern for others. *Developmental Psychology, 32,* 999–1007.

Guerra, N. G., & Slaby, R. G. (1990). Cognitive mediators of aggression in adolescent offenders: 2. Intervention. *Developmental Psychology, 26,* 269–277.

Guillemin, J. (1993). Cesarean birth: Social and political aspects. In B. K. Rothman (Ed.), *Encyclopedia of childbearing.* Phoenix, AZ: Oryx Press.

Gunnar, M. R., Bruce, J., & Grotevant, H. D. (2000). International adoption of institutionally reared children: Research and policy. *Development and Psychopathology, 12,* 677–693.

Gurucharri, C., & Selman, F. L. (1982). The development of interpersonal understanding during childhood, preadolescence, and adolescence: A longitudinal follow-up study. *Child Development, 53,* 924–927.

Guttmacher, A. F., & Kaiser, I. H. (1986). *Pregnancy, birth, and family planning.* New York: New American Library.

Halford, G. S. (1993). *Children's understanding: The development of mental models.* Hillsdale, NJ: Erlbaum.

Hall, D. G., Lee, S. C., & Belanger, J. (2001). Young children's use of syntactic cues to learn proper names and count nouns. *Developmental Psychology, 37,* 298–307.

Hall, G. S. (1904). *Adolescence, I.* New York: Appleton.

Hall, J. A., & Halberstadt, A. G. (1981). Sex roles and nonverbal communication skills. *Sex Roles, 7,* 273–287.

Hallinan, M. T., & Teixeira, R. A. (1987). Opportunities and constraints: Black-white differences in the formation of interracial friendships. *Child Development, 58,* 1358–1371.

Halpern, D. F. (2000). *Sex differences in cognitive abilities* (3rd ed.). Mahwah, NJ: Erlbaum.

Halpern, L. F., MacLean, W. E., & Baumeister, A. A. (1995). Infant sleep-wake characteristics: Relation to neurological status and the prediction of developmental outcome. *Developmental Review, 15,* 255– 291.

Hamilton, C. E. (2000). Continuity and discontinuity of attachment from infancy through adolescence. *Child Development, 71,* 690–694.

Hamm, J. V. (2000). Do birds of a feather flock together? The variable bases for African American, Asian American, and European American adolescents' selection of similar friends. *Developmental Psychology, 36,* 209–219.

Hammill, D. D. (1990). On defining learning disabilities: An emerging consensus. *Journal of Learning Disabilities, 23,* 74–84.

Hankin, B. L., & Abramson, L. Y. (2001). Development of gender differences in depression: An elaborated cognitive vulnerability-transactional stress theory. *Psychological Bulletin, 127,* 773–796.

Hansen, M., Kurinczuk, J. J., Bower, C., & Webb, S. (2002). The risk of major birth defects after intracytoplasmic sperm injection and in vitro fertilization. *New England Journal of Medicine, 346,* 725–730.

Harley, K., & Reese, E. (1999). Origins of autobiographical memory. *Developmental Psychology, 35,* 1338–1348.

Harris, B., Lovett, L., Newcombe, R. G., Read, G. F., Walker, R., & Riad-Fahmy, D. (1994). Maternity blues and major endocrine changes: Cardiff puerperal mood and hormone study II. *British Medical Journal, 308,* 949–953.

Harris, L. J. (1983). Laterality of function in the infant: Historical and contemporary trends in theory and research. In G. Young, S. J. Segalowitz, C. M. Corter, & S. E. Trehub (Eds.), *Manual specialization and the developing brain.* New York: Academic Press.

Harris, P. L., Brown, E., Marriot, C., Whithall, S., & Harmer, S. (1991). Monsters, ghosts, and witches: Testing the limits of the fantasy-reality distinction in young children. *British Journal of Developmental Psychology, 9,* 105–123.

Harris, P. L., & Kavanaugh, R. D. (1993). Young children's understanding of pretense. *Monographs of the Society for Research in Child Development, 58,* Serial No. 231.

Harrist, A. W., Zaia, A. F., Bates, J. E., Dodge, K. A., & Pettit, G. S. (1997). Subtypes of social withdrawal in early childhood: Sociometric status and social-cognitive differences across four years. *Child Development, 68,* 278–294.

Hart, C. H., Nelson, D. A., Robinson, C. C., Olsen, S. F., & McNeilly-Choque, M. K. (1998). Overt and relational aggression in Russian nursery-school-age children: Parenting style and marital linkages. *Developmental Psychology, 34,* 687–697.

Harter, S. (1985). *Manual for the self-perception profile for children.* Denver, CO: University of Denver.

Harter, S. (1988). Developmental processes in the construction of the self. In T. D. Yawkey & J. E. Johnson (Eds.), *Integrative processes and socialization: Early to middle childhood.* Hillsdale, NJ: Erlbaum.

Harter, S. (1990). Self and identity development. In S. S. Feldman & G. R. Elliott (Eds.), *At the threshold: The developing adolescent.* Cambridge, MA: Harvard University Press.

Harter, S. (1994). Developmental changes in self-understanding across the 5 to 7 shift. In A. Sameroff & M. M. Haith (Eds.), *Reason and responsibility: The passage through childhood.* Chicago: University of Chicago Press.

Harter, S. (1999). *The construction of the self: A developmental perspective.* New York: Guilford.

Harter, S., & Monsour, A. (1992). Developmental analysis of conflict caused by opposing attributes in the adolescent self-portrait. *Developmental Psychology, 28,* 251–260.

Harter, S., & Pike, R. (1984). The pictorial scale of perceived competence and social acceptance for young children. *Child Development, 55,* 1969–1982.

Harter, S., Waters, P., & Whitesell, N. R. (1998). Relational self-worth: Differences in perceived worth as a person across interpersonal contexts among adolescents. *Child Development, 69,* 756–766.

Harter, S., Waters, P. L., Whitesell, N. R., & Kastelic, D. (1998). Level of voice among female and male high school students: Relational context, support, and gender orientation. *Developmental Psychology, 34,* 892–901.

Harter, S., Whitesell, N. R., & Kowalski, P. S. (1992). Individual differences in the effects of educational transitions on young adolescents' perceptions of competence and motivational orientation. *American Educational Research Journal, 29,* 777–807.

Hartup, W. W. (1983). Peer relations. In P. H. Mussen (Ed.), *Handbook of child psychology* (Vol. 4). New York: Wiley.

Hartup, W. W. (1992a). Peer relations in early and middle childhood. In V. B. Van Hasselt & M. Hersen (Eds.), *Handbook of social development: A lifespan perspective.* New York: Plenum.

Hartup, W. W. (1992b). Friendships and their developmental significance. In H. McGurk (Ed.), *Contemporary issues in childhood social development.* London: Routledge.

Hartup, W. W., & Stevens, N. (1999). Friendships and adaptation across the life span. *Current Directions in Psychological Science, 8,* 76–79.

Haselager, G. J. T., Hartup, W. W., van Lieshout, C. F. M., & Riksen-Walraven, J. M. A. (1998). Similarities between friends and nonfriends in middle childhood. *Child Development, 69,* 1198–1208.

Hastings, P. D., & Rubin, K. H. (1999). Predicting mothers' beliefs about preschool-aged children's social behavior: Evidence for maternal attitudes moderating child effects. *Child Development, 70,* 722–741.

Haviland, J. M., & Lelwica, M. (1987). The induced affect response: 10-week-old infants' responses to three emotion expressions. *Developmental Psychology, 23,* 97–104.

Hayes, D. P. (1988). Speaking and writing: Distinct patterns of word choice. *Journal of Memory and Language, 27,* 572–585.

Hedges, L. V., & Nowell, A. (1995). Sex differences in mental test scores, variability, and numbers of high-scoring individuals. *Science, 269,* 41–45.

Herrnstein, R. J., & Murray, C. (1994). *The bell curve: Intelligence and class structure in American life.* New York: Free Press.

Hespos, S. J., & Baillargeon, R. (2001). Infants' knowledge about occlusion and containment events: A surprising discrepancy. *Psychological Science, 121,* 141–147.

Hess, U., & Kirouac, G. (2000). Emotion expression in groups. In M. Lewis & J. Haviland-Jones (Eds.), *Handbook of emotions* (2nd ed., pp. 368–381). New York: Guilford Press.

Hetherington, E. M. (1988). Family relations six years after divorce. In K. Pasley & M. Ihinger-Tallman (Eds.), *Remarriage and stepparenting: Current research and theory.* New York: Guilford Press.

Hetherington, E. M. (1989). Coping with family transitions: Winners, losers and survivors. *Child Development, 60,* 1–14.

Hetherington, E. M. (1993). An overview of the Virginia Longitudinal Study of Divorce and Remarriage with a focus on early adolescence. *Journal of Family Psychology, 7,* 39–56.

Hetherington, E. M. (1999). Social capital and the development of youth from nondivorced, divorced, and remarried families. In W. A. Collins & B. Laursen (Eds.), *Minnesota Symposia on Child Psychology.* Mahwah, NJ: Erlbaum.

Hetherington, E. M., & Kelly, J. (2002). *For better or for worse: Divorce reconsidered.* New York: W. W. Norton.

Hetherington, E. M., & Stanley-Hagan, M. (2002). Parenting in divorced and remarried families. In M. H. Bornstein (Ed.), *Handbook of parenting: Vol. 3. Status and social conditions of parenting* (2nd ed., pp. 287–315). Mahwah, NJ: Erlbaum.

Hetherington, S. E. (1990). A controlled study of the effect of prepared childbirth classes on obstetric outcomes. *Birth, 17,* 86–90.

Heyman, G. D., & Gelman, S. A. (1999). The use of trait labels in making psychological inferences. *Child Development, 70,* 604–619.

Higgins, A. (1991). The Just Community approach to moral education: Evolution of the idea and recent findings. In W. M. Kurtines & J. L. Gewirtz (Eds.), *Handbook of moral behavior and development* (Vol. 3). Hillsdale, NJ: Erlbaum.

Hill, N. E., Bush, K. R., & Roosa, M. W. (2003). Parenting and family socialization strategies and children's mental health: Low income, Mexican-American and Euro-American mothers and children. *Child Development, 74,* 189–204.

Ho, C. S., & Fuson, K. C. (1998). Children's knowledge of teen quantities as tens and ones: Comparisons of Chinese, British, and American kindergartners. *Journal of Educational Psychology, 90,* 536–544.

Hodges, E. V. E., Malone, M. J., & Perry, D. G. (1997). Individual risk and social risk as interacting determinants of victimization in the peer group. *Developmental Psychology, 33,* 1032–1039.

Hoff, E. (2001). *Language development* (2nd ed.). Belmont, CA: Wadsworth.

Hoff, E., & Naigles, L. (2002). How children use input to acquire a lexicon. *Child Development, 73,* 418–433.

Hoffman, M. L. (1988). Moral development. In M. H. Bornstein & M. E. Lamb (Eds.), *Developmental psychology: An advanced textbook* (2nd ed.). Hillsdale, NJ: Erlbaum.

Hoffman, M. L. (1994). Discipline and internalization. *Developmental Psychology, 30,* 26–28.

Hoge, D. D., Smit, E. K., & Hanson, S. L. (1990). School experiences predicting changes in self-esteem of sixth- and seventh-grade students. *Journal of Educational Psychology, 82,* 117–127.

Hogge, W. A. (1990). Teratology. In I. R. Merkatz & J. E. Thompson (Eds.), *New perspectives on prenatal care.* New York: Elsevier.

Holden, G. W., & Miller, P. C. (1999). Enduring and different: A meta-analysis of the similarity in parents' child rearing. *Psychological Bulletin, 125,* 223–254.

Hollich, G. J., Hirsh-Pasek, K., & Golinkoff, R. M. (2000). Breaking the language barrier: An emergentist coalition model for the origins of word learning. *Monographs of the Society for Research in Child Development, 65,* Serial No. 262.

Hollon, S. D., Haman, K. I., & Brown, L. L. (2002). Cognitive-behavioral treatment of depression. In I. H. Gotlib & C. L. Hammen (Eds.), *Handbook of depression* (pp. 383–403). New York: Guilford.

Hood, B., Carey, S., & Prasada, S. (2000). Predicting the outcomes of physical events: Two-year-olds fail to reveal knowledge of solidity and support. *Child Development, 71,* 1540–1554.

Horowitz, F. D., & O'Brien, M. (1986). Gifted and talented children: State of knowledge and directions for research. *American Psychologist, 41,* 1147–1152.

Howe, M. L., & Courage, M. L. (1997). The emergence and early development of autobiographical memory. *Psychological Review, 104,* 499–523.

Howe, N., Petrakos, H., & Rinaldi, C. M. (1998). "All the sheeps are dead. He murdered them": Sibling pretense, negotiation, internal state language, and relationship quality. *Child Development, 69,* 182–191.

Howe, N., & Ross, H. S. (1990). Socialization perspective taking and the sibling relationship. *Developmental Psychology, 26,* 160–165.

Howes, C., & Matheson, C. C. (1992). Sequences in the development of competent play with peers: Social and social pretend play. *Developmental Psychology, 28,* 961–974.

Howes, C., Unger, O., & Seidner, L. B. (1990). Social pretend play in toddlers: Parallels with social play and with solitary pretend. *Child Development, 60,* 77–84.

Hudson, J. (1988). Children's memory for atypical actions in script-based stories: Evidence for a disruption effect. *Journal of Experimental Child Psychology, 46,* 159–173.

Hudson, J. A. (2001). The anticipated self: Mother-child talk about future events. In C. Moore & K. Lemmon (Eds.), *The self in time: Developmental perspectives* (pp. 53–74). Mahwah, NJ: Erlbaum.

Huesmann, L. R. (1986). Psychological processes promoting the relation between exposure to media violence and aggressive behavior by the viewer. *Journal of Social Issues, 42,* 125–139.

Hulit, L. M., & Howard, M. R. (2002). *Born to talk: An introduction to speech and language development* (3rd ed.). Boston: Allyn and Bacon.

Hulme, C., Hatcher, P. J., Nation, K., Brown, A., Adams, J., & Stuart, G. (2002). Phoneme awareness is a better predictor of early reading skill than onset-rime awareness. *Journal of Experimental Child Psychology, 82,* 2–28.

Huston, A. C. (1983). Sex typing. In P. H. Mussen (Ed.), *Handbook of child psychology* (Vol. 4). New York: Wiley.

Huston, A. C., Donnerstein, E., Fairchild, H., Feshbach, N. D., Katz, P. A., Murray, J. P., Rubinstein, E. A., Wilcox, B. L., & Zuckerman, D. (1992). *Big world, small screen: The role of television in American society.* Lincoln: University of Nebraska Press.

Huston, A. C., Watkins, B. A., & Kunkel, D. (1989). Public policy and children's television. *American Psychologist, 44,* 424–433.

Huston, A. C., & Wright, J. C. (1998). Mass media and children's development. In W. Damon (Ed.), *Handbook of child psychology* (Vol. 4). New York: Wiley.

Hutchins, E. (1983). Understanding Micronesian navigation. In D. A. Gentner & A. Stevens (Eds.), *Mental models.* Hillsdale, NJ: Erlbaum.

Huttenlocher, J., Haight, W., Bryk, A., Seltzer, M., & Lyons, T. (1991). Early vocabulary growth: Relation to language input and gender. *Developmental Psychology, 27,* 236–248.

Hyde, J. S., Fennema, E., & Lamon, S. J. (1990). Gender differences in mathematics performance: A meta-analysis. *Psychological Bulletin, 107,* 139–155.

IFICF. (2000). *Starting solids: A guide for parents and child care providers.* Washington, DC: Author.

Inhelder, B., & Piaget, J. (1958). *The growth of logical thinking from childhood to adolescence.* New York: Basic Books.

Institute of Medicine. (1990). *Nutrition during pregnancy.* Washington, DC: National Academy Press.

Israel, A. C., Guile, C. A., Baker, J. E., & Silverman, W. K. (1994). An evaluation of enhanced self-regulation training in the treatment of childhood obesity. *Journal of Pediatric Psychology, 19,* 737–749.

Izard, C. E. (1991). *The psychology of emotions.* New York: Plenum.

Izard, C. E., & Ackerman, B. P. (2000). Motivational, organizational, and regulatory functions of discrete emotions. In M. Lewis & J. Haviland-Jones (Eds.), *Handbook of emotions* (2nd ed., pp. 253–264). New York: Guilford Press.

Izard, C. E., Fantauzzo, C. A., Castle, J. M., Haynes, O. M., Rayias, M. F., & Putnam, P. H. (1995). The ontogeny and significance of infants' facial expressions in the first 9 months of life. *Developmental Psychology, 31,* 997–1013.

Jacklin, C. N. (1989). Female and male: Issues of gender. *American Psychologist, 44,* 127–133.

Jacklin, C. N., & Maccoby, E. E. (1978). Social behavior at thirty-three months in same-sex and mixed-sex dyads. *Child Development, 49,* 557–569.

Jacobs, J. E., & Klaczynski, P. A. (2002). The development of judgment and decision making during childhood and adolescence. *Current Directions in Psychological Science, 11,* 145–149.

Jacobson, J. L., & Jacobson, S. W. (1996). Intellectual impairment in children exposed to polychlorinated biphenyls in utero. *The New England Journal of Medicine, 335,* 783–789.

Jacobson, J. L., Jacobson, S. W., Sokol, R. J., & Ager, J. W. (1998). Relation of maternal age and pattern of pregnancy drinking to functionally significant cognitive deficit in infancy. *Alcoholism: Clinical and Experimental Research, 22,* 345–351.

Jacobson, S. W., & Jacobson, J. L. (2000). Teratogenic insult and neurobehavioral function in infancy and childhood. In C. A. Nelson (Ed.), *The Minnesota symposium on child psychology, Vol. 31: The effects of early adversity on neurobehavioral development* (pp. 61–112). Mahwah, NJ: Erlbaum.

Jaffe, J., Beatrice, B., Stanley, F., Crown, C. L., & Jasnow, M. D. (2001). Rhythms of dialogue in infancy: Coordinated timing in development. *Monographs of the Society for Research in Child Development, 66,* Serial No. 265.

Jaffee, S., & Hyde, J. S. (2000). Gender differences in moral orientation: A meta-analysis. *Psychological Bulletin, 126,* 703–726.

Jensen, P. S., Hinshaw, S. P., Swanson, J. M., Greenhill, L. L., Conners, C. K., Arnold, L. E., et al. (2001). Findings from the NIMH Multimodal Treatment Study of ADHD (MTA): Implications and applications for primary care providers. *Journal of Developmental and Behavioral Pediatrics, 22,* 60–73.

Jiao, S., Ji, G., & Jing, Q. (1996). Cognitive development of Chinese urban only children and children with siblings. *Child Development, 67,* 387–395.

Jiao, Z. (1999, April). *Which students keep old friends and which become new friends across a school transition?* Paper presented at the 1999 meeting of the Society for Research in Child Development, Albuquerque, New Mexico.

Johanson, R. B., Rice, C., Coyle, M., Arthur, J., Anyanwu, L., Ibrahim, J., Warwick, A., Redman, C. W. E., & O'Brien, P. M. S. (1993). A randomized prospective study comparing the new vacuum extractor policy with forceps delivery. *British Journal of Obstetrics and Gynecology, 100,* 524–530.

Johnson, J. G., Cohen, P., Smailes, E. M., Kasen, S., & Brook, J. S. (2002). Television viewing and aggressive behavior during adolescence and adulthood. *Science, 295,* 2468–2471.

Johnson, M. H. (1998). The neural basis of cognitive development. In W. Damon (Ed.), *Handbook of child psychology* (Vol. 2). New York: Wiley.

Johnson, M. H. (2000). Functional brain development in infants: Elements of an interactive specialization framework. *Child Development, 71,* 75–81.

Johnson, S. P. (2001). Visual development in human infants: Binding features, surfaces, and objects. *Visual Cognition, 8,* 565–578.

Johnson, S. P., & Aslin, R. N. (1995). Perception of object unity in 2-month-old infants. *Developmental Psychology, 31,* 739–745.

Johnstone, B., Frame, C. L., & Bouman, D. (1992). Physical attractiveness and athletic and academic ability in controversial-aggressive and rejected-aggressive children. *Journal of Social and Clinical Psychology, 11,* 71–79.

Jones, D., & Christensen, C. A. (1999). Relationship between automaticity in handwriting and students' ability to generate written text. *Journal of Educational Psychology, 91,* 44–49.

Joseph, R. (2000). Fetal brain behavior and cognitive development. *Developmental Review, 20,* 81–98.

Jusczyk, P. W. (1995). Language acquisition: Speech sounds and phonological development. In J. L. Miller & P. D. Eimas (Eds.), *Handbook of perception and cognition: Vol. 11. Speech, language, and communication.* Orlando, FL: Academic Press.

Jusczyk, P. W. (2002). How infants adapt speech-processing capacities to native-language structure. *Current Directions in Psychological Science, 11,* 15–18.

Jusczyk, P. W., & Aslin, R. N. (1995). Infants' detection of the sound patterns of words in fluent speech. *Cognitive Psychology, 29,* 1–23.

Kagan, J. (1989). Temperamental contributions to social behavior. *American Psychologist, 44,* 668–674.

Kagan, J., Arcus, D., Snidman, N., Feng, W. Y., Hendler, J., & Greene, S. (1994). Reactivity in infants: A cross-national comparison. *Developmental Psychology, 30,* 342–345.

Kagan, J., & Moss, H. A. (1962). *Birth to maturity: A study in psychological development.* New York: Wiley.

Kaijura, H., Cowart B. J., & Beauchamp, G. K. (1992). Early developmental change in bitter taste responses in human infants. *Developmental Psychobiology, 25,* 375–386.

Kail, R. (1990). *The development of memory in children* (3rd ed.). New York: W. H. Freeman.

Kail, R. (1995). Processing speed, memory, and cognition. In F. E. Weinert & W. Schneider (Eds.), *Memory performance and competencies.* Mahwah, NJ: Erlbaum.

Kail, R. (2000). Speed of information processing: Developmental change and links to intelligence. *Journal of School Psychology, 38,* 51–61.

Kail, R. V. (2002). Developmental change in proactive interference. *Child Development, 73,* 1703–1714.

Kail, R., & Bisanz, J. (1992). The information processing perspective on cognitive development in childhood and adolescence. In R. J. Sternberg & C. A. Berg (Eds.), *Intellectual development.* New York: Cambridge University Press.

Kail, R., & Park, Y. (1990). Impact of practice on speed of mental rotation. *Journal of Experimental Child Psychology, 49,* 227–244.

Kako, E. (1999). Elements of syntax in the systems of three language-trained animals. *Animal Learning and Behavior, 27,* 1–14.

Kamerman, S. B. (1993). International perspectives on child care policies and programs. *Pediatrics, 91,* 248–252.

Kandel, E., & Mednick, S. A. (1991). Perinatal complications predict violent offending. *Criminology, 29,* 519–529.

Kaplan, P. S., Goldstein, M. H., Huckeby, E. R., & Cooper, R. P. (1995). Habituation, sensitization, and infants' responses to motherese speech. *Developmental Psychobiology, 28,* 45–57.

Karniol, R. (1989). The role of manual manipulative states in the infant's acquisition of perceived control over objects. *Developmental Review, 9,* 205–233.

Katz, L. F., & Woodin, E. M. (2002). Hostility, hostile detachment, and conflict engagement in marriages: Effects on child and family functioning. *Child Development, 73,* 636–652.

Keane, S. P., Brown, K. P., & Crenshaw, T. M. (1990). Children's intention-cue detection as a function of maternal social behavior: Pathways to social rejection. *Developmental Psychology, 26,* 1004–1009.

Kearney, C. A., & Silverman, W. K. (1995). Family environment of youngsters with school refusal behavior: A synopsis with implications for assessment and treatment. *American Journal of Family Therapy, 23,* 59–72.

Keller, M., Edelstein, W., Schmid, S., Fang, F., & Fang, G. (1998). Reasoning about responsibilities and obligations in close relationships: A comparison across two cultures. *Developmental Psychology, 34,* 731–741.

Kelley, M. L., Power, T. G., & Wimbush, D. D. (1992). Determinants of disciplinary practices in low-income Black mothers. *Child Development, 63,* 573–582.

Kellman, P. J., & Banks, M. S. (1998). Infant visual perception. In W. Damon (Ed.), *Handbook of child psychology* (Vol. 2). New York: Wiley.

Kilgore, K., Snyder, J., & Lentz, C. (2000). The contribution of parental discipline, parental monitoring, and school risk to early-onset conduct problems in African American boys and girls. *Developmental Psychology, 36,* 835–845.

Kim, K. J., Conger, R. D., Lorenz, F. O., & Elder, G. H. Jr. (2001). Parent-adolescent reciprocity in negative affect and its relation to early adult social development. *Developmental Psychology, 37,* 775–790.

Kim, Y. H., & Goetz, E. T. (1994). Context effects on word recognition and reading comprehension of good and poor readers: A test of the interactive compensatory hypothesis. *Reading Research Quarterly, 29,* 178–188.

Kimball, M. M. (1986). Television and sex-role attitudes. In T. M. Williams (Ed.), *The impact of television* (pp. 265–301). New York: Academic Press.

Kimball, M. M. (1989). A new perspective on women's math achievement. *Psychological Bulletin, 105,* 198–214.

King, V., Elder, G. H., & Whitbeck, L. B. (1997). Religious involvement among rural youth: An ecological and life-course perspective. *Journal of Research on Adolescence, 7,* 431–456.

Kirby, D. (2001). *Emerging answers: Research findings on programs to reduce teen pregnancy (summary).* Washington, DC: National Campaign to Prevent Teen Pregnancy.

Kirby, D. (2002). *Do abstinence-only programs delay the initiation of sex among young people and reduce teen pregnancy?* Washington, DC: National Campaign to Prevent Teen Pregnancy.

Kisilevsky, B. S., & Low, J. A. (1998). Human fetal behavior: 100 years of study. *Developmental Review, 18,* 1–29.

Klaczynski, P. A. (2000). Motivated scientific reasoning biases, epistemological beliefs, and theory polarization. *Child Development, 71,* 1347–1366.

Klaczynski, P. A., & Narasimham, G. (1998). Development of scientific reasoning biases: Cognitive versus ego-protective explanations. *Developmental Psychology, 34,* 175–187.

Klahr, D., & MacWhinney, B. (1998). Information processing. In W. Damon (Ed.), *Handbook of child psychology* (Vol. 2). New York: Wiley.

Klapper, J. T. (1968). The impact of viewing "aggression": Studies and problems of extrapolation. In O. N. Larsen (Ed.), *Violence and the mass media.* New York: Harper & Row.

Klatzky, R. L. (1980). *Human memory* (2nd ed.). San Francisco: Freeman.

Klaus, M., & Kennell, H. H. (1976). *Mother-infant bonding.* St. Louis: Mosby.

Knight, G. P., Fabes, R. A., & Higgins, D. A. (1996). Concerns about drawing causal inferences from meta-analyses: An example in the study of gender differences in aggression. *Psychological Bulletin, 119,* 410–421.

Kochanska, G. (1991). Socialization and temperament in the development of guilt and conscience. *Child Development, 62,* 1379–1392.

Kochanska, G. (1993). Toward a synthesis of parental socialization and child temperament in early development of conscience. *Child Development, 64,* 325–347.

Kochanska, G. (1995). Children's temperament, mothers' discipline, and security of attachment: Multiple pathways to emerging internalization. *Child Development, 66,* 597–615.

Kochanska, G. (1997a). Multiple pathways to conscience for children with different temperaments: From toddlerhood to age 5. *Developmental Psychology, 33,* 228–240.

Kochanska, G. (1997b). Mutually responsive orientation between mothers and their young children: Implications for early socialization. *Child Development, 68,* 94–112.

Kochanska, G., Coy, K. C., & Murray, K. T. (2001). The development of self-regulation in the first four years of life. *Child Development, 72,* 1091–1111.

Kochanska, G., DeVet, K., Goldman, M., Murray, K., et al. (1994). Maternal reports of conscience development and temperament in young children. *Child Development, 65,* 852–868.

Kochanska, G., Gross, J. N., Lin, M., & Nichols, K. E. (2002). Guilt in young children: Development, determinants, and relations with a broader system of standards. *Child Development, 73,* 461–482.

Kochanska, G., Murray, K. T., & Harlan, E. T. (2000). Effortful control in early childhood: Continuity and change, antecedents, and implications for social development. *Developmental Psychology, 36,* 220–232.

Kochanska, G., Padavich, D. L., & Koenig, A. L. (1996). Children's narratives about hypothetical moral dilemmas and objective measures of their conscience: Mutual relations and socialization antecedents. *Child Development, 67,* 1420–1436.

Kochanska, G., & Radke-Yarrow, M. (1992). Inhibition in toddlerhood and the dynamics of the child's interaction with an unfamiliar peer at age five. *Child Development, 63,* 325–335.

Kochenderfer, B. J., & Ladd, G. W. (1996). Peer victimization: Cause or consequence of school maladjustment? *Child Development, 67,* 1305–1317.

Kochenderfer-Ladd, B., & Skinner, K. (2002). Children's coping strategies: Moderators of the effects of peer victimization? *Developmental Psychology, 38,* 267–278.

Kochenderfer-Ladd, B., & Wardrop, J. L. (2001). Chronicity and instability of children's peer victimization experiences as predictors of loneliness and social satisfaction trajectories. *Child Development, 72,* 134–151.

Kogan, N. (1983). Stylistic variation in childhood and adolescence: Creativity, metaphor, and cognitive style. In P. H. Mussen (Ed.), *Handbook of child psychology* (Vol. 3). New York: Wiley.

Kohlberg, L. (1966). A cognitive-developmental analysis of children's sex-role concepts and attitudes. In E. E. Maccoby (Ed.), *The development of sex differences.* Stanford: Stanford University Press.

Kohlberg, L. (1969). Stage and sequence: The cognitive-developmental approach to socialization. In D. Goslin (Ed.), *Handbook of socialization theory and research* (pp. 347–480). Chicago: Rand McNally.

Kohlberg, L., & Ullian, D. Z. (1974). Stages in the development of psychosexual concepts and attitudes. In R. C. Friedman, R. M. Richart, & R. L. Van Wiele (Eds.), *Sex differences in behavior.* New York: Wiley.

Kojima, Y. (2000). Maternal regulation of sibling interactions in the preschool years: Observational study in Japanese families. *Child Development, 71,* 1640–1647.

Kokko, K., & Pulkkinen, L. (2000). Aggression in childhood and long-term unemployment in adulthood: A cycle of maladaptation and some protective factors. *Developmental Psychology, 36,* 463–472.

Kolb, B. (1989). Brain development, plasticity, and behavior. *American Psychologist, 44,* 1203–1212.

Kolb, B., & Whishaw, I. Q. (1998). Brain plasticity and behavior. *Annual Review of Psychology, 49,* 43–64.

Kolberg, K. J. S. (1999). Environmental influences on prenatal development and health. In T. L. Whitman & T. V. Merluzzi (Eds.), *Life-span perspectives on health and illness* (pp. 87–103). Mahwah, NJ: Erlbaum.

Kopp, C. B. (1987). The growth of self-regulation: Caregivers and children. In N. Eisenberg (Ed.), *Contemporary topics in developmental psychology.* New York: Wiley.

Kopp, C. B. (1997). Young children: Emotion management, instrumental control, and plans. In S. L. Friedman & E. K. Scholnick (Eds.), *The developmental psychology of planning: Why, how, and when do we plan?* (pp. 103–124). Mahwah, NJ: Erlbaum.

Kopp, C. B., & McCall, R. B. (1982). Predicting later mental performance for normal, at-risk, and handicapped infants. In P. B. Baltes & O. G. Brim (Eds.), *Life-span development and behavior* (Vol. 4). New York: Academic Press.

Korbin, J. E. (1987). Child abuse and neglect: The cultural context. In R. E. Helfer & R. S. Kempe (Eds.), *The battered child* (4th ed., pp. 23–41). Chicago: University of Chicago Press.

Kotovsky, L., & Baillargeon, R. (1998). The development of calibration-based reasoning about collision events in young infants. *Cognition, 67,* 311–351.

Kovacs, D. M., Parker, J. G., & Hoffman, L. W. (1996). Behavioral, affective, and social correlates of involvement in cross-sex friendship in elementary school. *Child Development, 67,* 2269–2286.

Kowal, A., & Kramer, L. (1997). Children's understanding of parental differential treatment. *Child Development, 68,* 113–126.

Krebs, D., & Gillmore, J. (1982). The relationship among the first stages of cognitive development, role-taking abilities, and moral development. *Child Development, 53,* 877–886.

Krispin, O., Sternberg, K. J., & Lamb, M. E. (1992). The dimensions of peer evaluation in Israel: A cross-cultural perspective. *International Journal of Behavioral Development, 15,* 299–314.

Kroger, J. (2000). *Identity development: Adolescence through adulthood.* Thousand Oaks CA: Sage.

Kroger, J., & Green, K. E. (1996). Events associated with identity status change. *Journal of Adolescence, 19,* 477–490.

Kuebli, J., Butler, S., & Fivush, R. (1995). Mother-child talk about past emotions: Relations of maternal language and child gender over time. *Cognition & Emotion, 9,* 265–283.

Kuhl, P. K., Andruski, J. E., Chistovich, I. A., Chistovich, L. A., Kozhevnikova, E. V., Ryskina, V. L., Stolyarova, E. I., Sundberg, U., & Lacerda, F. (1997). Cross-language analysis of phonetic units in language addressed to infants. *Science, 277,* 684–686.

Kuhn, D. (2000). Metacognitive development. *Current Directions in Psychological Science, 9,* 178–181.

Kunzig, R. (1998). Climbing through the brain. *Discover, 19,* 60–69.

Ladd, G. W. (1998). Peer relationships and social competence during early and middle childhood. *Annual Review of Psychology, 50,* 333–359.

Ladd, G. W. (2003). Probing the adaptive significance of children's behavior and relationships in the school context: A child by environment perspective. In R. V. Kail (Ed.), *Advances in child development and behavior* (Vol. 31). San Diego, CA: Academic Press.

Ladd, G. W., & Ladd, B. K. (1998). Parenting behaviors and parent-child relationships: Correlates of peer victimization in kindergarten? *Developmental Psychology, 34,* 1450–1458.

Ladd, G. W., & Le Sieur, K. D. (1995). Parents and children's peer relationships. In M. H. Bornstein (Ed.), *Handbook of parenting, Vol. 4. Applied and practical parenting* (pp. 377–410). Mahwah, NJ: Erlbaum.

LaFreniere, P., Strayer, F. F., & Gauthier, R. (1984). The emergence of same-sex affiliative preferences among preschool peers: A developmental/ethnological perspective. *Child Development, 55,* 1958–1965.

Lagattuta, K. H., Wellman, H. M., & Flavell, J. H. (1997). Preschoolers' understanding of the link between thinking and feeling: Cognitive cuing and emotional change. *Child Development, 68,* 1081–1104.

LaGreca, A. M. (1993). Social skills training with children: Where do we go from here? *Journal of Clinical Child Psychology, 22,* 288–298.

Laible, D. J., & Thompson, R. A. (1998). Attachment and emotional understanding in preschool children. *Developmental Psychology, 34,* 1038–1045.

Lalumière, M. L., Blanchard, R., & Zucker, K. J. (2000). Sexual orientation and handedness in men and women: A meta-analysis. *Psychological Bulletin, 126,* 575–592.

Lamaze, F. (1958). *Painless childbirth.* London: Burke.

Lamb, M. E. (1999). Nonparental child care. In M. E. Lamb (Ed.), *Parenting and child development in "nontraditional" families.* Mahwah, NJ: Erlbaum.

Lamb, M. E., Sternberg, K. J., & Esplin, P. W. (2000). Effects of age and delay on the amount of information provided by alleged sex abuse victims in investigative interviews. *Child Development, 71,* 1586–1596.

Lampinen, J. M., & Smith, V. L. (1995). The incredible (and sometimes incredulous) child witness: Child eyewitnesses' sensitivity to source credibility cues. *Journal of Applied Psychology, 80,* 621–627.

Lane H., & Bahan, B. (1998). Ethics of cochlear implantation in young children: A review and reply from a DEAF-WORLD perspective. *Otolaryngology—Head and Neck Surgery, 119,* 293–313.

Lane, H. L. (1992). *The mask of benevolence: Disabling the deaf community.* New York: Knopf.

Langlois, J. H., & Downs, A. C. (1980). Mothers, fathers, and peers as socialization agents of sex-typed play behaviors in young children. *Child Development, 51,* 1237–1247.

Lanza, E. (1992). Can bilingual two-year-olds code-switch? *Journal of Child Language, 19,* 633–658.

Larson, R. W. (1997). The emergence of solitude as a constructive domain of experience in early adolescence. *Child Development, 68,* 80–93.

Larson, R. W. (2000). Toward a psychology of positive youth development. *American Psychologist, 55,* 170–183.

Larson, R. W. (2001). How US children and adolescents spend time: What it does (and doesn't) tell us about their development. *Current Directions in Psychological Science, 10,* 160–164.

Lau, S. (1989). Sex role orientation and domains of self-esteem. *Sex Roles, 21,* 415–422.

Laursen, B., & Collins, W. A. (1994). Interpersonal conflict during adolescence. *Psychological Bulletin, 115,* 197–209.

Laursen, B., Finkelstein, B. D., & Betts, N. T. (2001). A developmental meta-analysis of peer conflict resolution. *Developmental Review, 21,* 423–449.

Lazar, I., & Darlington, R. (1982). Lasting effects of early education: A report from the Consortium for Longitudinal Studies. *Monographs of the Society for Research in Child Development, 47,* (2–3, Serial No. 195).

Lazarus, R. S. (1991). *Emotion and adaptation.* New York: Oxford University Press.

Leach, P. (1991). *Your baby and child: From birth to age five* (2nd ed.). New York: Knopf.

Leaper, C., Anderson, K. J., & Sanders, P. (1998). Moderators of gender effects on parents' talk to their children: A meta-analysis. *Developmental Psychology, 34,* 3–27.

Leichtman, M. D., & Ceci, S. L. (1995). The effects of stereotypes and suggestions on preschoolers' reports. *Developmental Psychology, 31,* 568–578.

LeMare, L. J., & Rubin, K. H. (1987). Perspective taking and peer interaction: Structural and developmental analyses. *Child Development, 58,* 306–315.

Lengua, L. J. (2002). The contribution of emotionality and self-regulation to the understanding of children's response to multiple risk. *Child Development, 73,* 144–161.

Lengua, L. J., Sandler, I. N., West, S. G., Wolchik, S. A., & Curran, P. J. (1999). Emotionality and self-regulation, threat appraisal, and coping in children of divorce. *Development & Psychopathology, 11,* 15–37.

Lengua, L. J., West, S. G., & Sandler, I. N. (1998). Temperament as a predictor of symptomatology in children: Addressing contamination of measures. *Child Development, 69,* 164–181.

Lepper, M. R., & Gurtner, J. (1989). Children and computers. *American Psychologist, 44,* 170–178.

Lerner, R. M., Fisher, C. B., & Weinberg, R. A. (2000). Toward a science for and of the people: Promoting civil society through the application of developmental science. *Child Development, 71,* 11–20.

Leventhal, T., & Brooks-Gunn, J. (2000). The neighborhoods they live in: The effects of neighborhood residence on child and adolescent outcomes. *Psychological Bulletin, 126,* 309–337.

Leventhal, T., & Brooks-Gunn, J. (2003). Children and youth in neighborhood contexts. *Current Directions in Psychological Science, 12,* 27–31.

Levine, L. E. (1983). Mine: Self-definition in 2-year-old boys. *Developmental Psychology, 19,* 544–549.

Levine, L. J. (1995). Young children's understanding of the causes of anger and sadness. *Child Development, 66,* 697–709.

Levitt, A. G., & Utman, J. A. (1992). From babbling towards the sound systems of English and French: A longitudinal two-case study. *Journal of Child Language, 19,* 19–49.

Levitt, M. J., Guacci-Franco, N., & Levitt, J. L. (1993). Convoys of social support in childhood and early adolescence: Structure and function. *Developmental Psychology, 29,* 811–818.

Levy, G. D., & Boston, M. B. (1994). Preschoolers' recall of own-sex and other-sex gender scripts. *Journal of Genetic Psychology, 155,* 367–371.

Levy, G. D., Taylor, M. G., & Gelman, S. A. (1995). Traditional and evaluative aspects of flexibility in gender roles, social conventions, moral rules, and physical laws. *Child Development, 66,* 515–531.

Levy, J. (1976). A review of evidence for a genetic component in the determination of handedness. *Behavior Genetics, 6,* 429–453.

Lewis, M. (1987). Social development in infancy and early childhood. In J. D. Osofsky (Ed.), *Handbook of infant development.* New York: Wiley.

Lewis, M. (1997). The self in self-conscious emotions. In J. G. Snodgrass & R. L. Thompson (Eds.), *The self across psychology: Self-awareness, self-recognition, and the self-concept* (pp. 119–142). New York: New York Academy of Sciences.

Lewis, M. (2000). The emergence of human emotions. In M. Lewis & J. Haviland-Jones (Eds.), *Handbook of emotions* (2nd ed., pp. 265–280). New York: Guilford Press.

Lewis, M., Ramsay, D. S., & Kawakami, K. (1993). Differences between Japanese infants and Caucasian American infants in behavioral and cortisol response to inoculation. *Child Development, 64,* 1722–1731.

Lewis, M. D., Koroshegyi, C., Douglas, L., & Kampe, K. (1997). Age-specific associations between emotional responses to separation and cognitive performance in infancy. *Developmental Psychology, 33,* 32–42.

Lewkowicz, D. J. (2000a). Infants' perception of the audible, visible, and bimodal attributes of multimodal syllables. *Child Development, 71,* 1241–1257.

Lewkowicz, D. J. (2000b). The development of intersensory perception: An epigenetic systems/limitations view. *Psychological Bulletin, 126,* 281–308.

Liben, L. S., & Bigler, R. S. (2002). The developmental course of gender differentiation. *Monographs of the Society for Research in Child Development, 67,* Serial No. 269.

Liben, L. S., Bigler, R. S., & Krogh, H. R. (2001). Pink and blue collar jobs: Children's judgments of job status and job aspirations in relation to sex of worker. *Journal of Experimental Child Psychology, 79,* 346–363.

Liben, L. S., & Signorella, M. L. (1993). Gender-schematic processing in children: The role of initial interpretations of stimuli. *Developmental Psychology, 29,* 141–149.

Lieberman, M., Doyle, A., & Markiewicz, D. (1999). Developmental patterns in security of attachment to mother and father in late childhood and early adolescence: Associations with peer relations. *Child Development, 70,* 202–213.

Liebert, R. M., & Sprafkin, J. (1988). *The early window: Effects of television on children and youth.* New York: Pergamon.

Lillard, A. (1999). Developing a cultural theory of mind: The CIAO approach. *Current Directions in Psychological Science, 8,* 57–61.

Lillard, A. (2001). Pretend play as twin Earth: A social-cognitive analysis. *Developmental Review, 21,* 495–531.

Lin, C. C., & Fu, V. R. (1990). A comparison of childrearing practices among Chinese, immigrant Chinese, and Caucasian-American parents. *Child Development, 61,* 429–433.

Linden, M. G., Bender, B. G., Harmon, R. J., Mrazek, D. A., & Robinson, A. (1988). 47–XXX: What is the prognosis? *Pediatrics, 82,* 619–630.

Livesley, W. J., & Bromley, D. B. (1973). *Person perception in childhood and adolescence.* New York: Wiley.

Loehlin, J. C. (2000). Group differences in intelligence. In R. J. Sternberg (Ed.), *Handbook of intelligence* (pp. 176–193). New York: Cambridge University Press.

Looney, M. A., & Plowman, S. A. (1990). Passing rates of American children and youth on the FITNESSGRAM criterion-referenced physical fitness standards. *Research Quarterly of Exercise and Sport, 61,* 215–223.

Lord, S. E., Eccles, J. S., & McCarthy, K. A. (1994). Surviving the junior high transition: Family processes and self-perception as protective and risk factors. *Journal of Early Adolescence, 14,* 162–199.

Lowry, R., Wechsler, H., Kann, L., & Collins, J. L. (2001). Recent trends in participation in physical education among US high school students. *Journal of School Health, 71,* 145–152.

Ludemann, P. M. (1991). Generalized discrimination of positive facial expressions by seven- and ten-month-old infants. *Child Development, 62,* 55–67.

Luecke-Aleksa, D., Anderson, D. R., Collins, P. A., & Schmitt, K. L. (1995). Gender constancy and television viewing. *Developmental Psychology, 31,* 773–780.

Lueptow, L. B., Garovich-Szabo, L., & Lueptow, M. B. (2001). Social change and the persistence of sex typing: 1974–1997. *Social Forces, 80,* 1–36.

Luthar, S. S., Zigler, E., & Goldstein, D. (1992). Psychosocial adjustment among intellectually gifted adolescents: The role of cognitive-developmental and experiential factors. *Journal of Child Psychology and Psychiatry and Allied Disciplines, 33,* 361–373.

Lutz, S. E., & Ruble, D. N. (1995). Children and gender prejudice: Context, motivation, and the development of gender conception. In R. Vasta (Ed.), *Annals of child development* (Vol. 10, pp. 131–166). London: Jessica Kingsley.

Lyon, G. R. (1996). Learning disabilities. In E. J. Mash & R. A. Barkley (Eds.), *Child psychopathology.* New York: Guilford.

Lytton, H., & Romney, D. M. (1991). Parents' differential socialization of boys and girls: A meta-analysis. *Psychological Bulletin, 109,* 267–296.

Maccoby, E. E. (1984). Socialization and developmental change. *Child Development, 55,* 317–328.

Maccoby, E. E. (1988). Gender as a social category. *Developmental Psychology, 24,* 755–765.

Maccoby, E. E. (1990). Gender and relationships: A developmental account. *American Psychologist, 45,* 513–520.

Maccoby, E. E. (1998). *The two sexes: Growing up apart, coming together.* Cambridge, MA: Belknap Press.

Maccoby, E. E., Buchanan, C. M., Mnookin, R. H., & Dornbusch, S. M. (1993). Postdivorce roles of mothers and fathers in the lives of their children. *Journal of Family Psychology, 7,* 24–38.

Maccoby, E. E., & Jacklin, C. N. (1974). *The psychology of sex differences.* Stanford, CA: Stanford University Press.

Maccoby, E. E., & Jacklin, C. N. (1980). Sex differences in aggression: A rejoinder and reprise. *Child Development, 51,* 964–980.

Maccoby, E. E., & Martin, J. A. (1983). Socialization in the context of the family: Parent-child interaction. In P. H. Mussen (Ed.), *Handbook of child psychology* (Vol. 4). New York: Wiley.

MacKinnon-Lewis, C., Rabiner, D., & Starnes, R. (1999). Predicting boys' social acceptance and aggression: The role of mother-child interactions and boys' beliefs about peers. *Developmental Psychology, 35,* 632–639.

MacWhinney, B. (1998). Models of the emergence of language. *Annual Review of Psychology, 49,* 199–227.

Main, M., & Cassidy, J. (1988). Categories of response to reunion with the parent at age 6: Predictable from infant attachment classifications and stable over a 1-month-period. *Developmental Psychology, 24,* 415–426.

Malinosky-Rummell, R., & Hansen, D. J. (1993). Long-term consequences of childhood physical abuse. *Psychological Bulletin, 114,* 68–79.

Mandel, D. R., Jusczyk, P. W., & Pisoni, D. B. (1995). Infants' recognition of the sound patterns of their own names. *Psychological Science, 6,* 314–317.

Mangelsdorf, S., Gunnar, M., Kestenbaum, R., Lang, S., & Andreas, D. (1990). Infant proneness-to-distress temperament, maternal personality, and mother-infant attachment: Associations and goodness of fit. *Child Development, 61,* 820–831.

Mangelsdorf, S. C. (1992). Developmental changes in infant-stranger interaction. *Infant Behavior and Development, 15,* 191–208.

Mangelsdorf, S. C., Shapiro, J. R., & Marzolf, D. (1995). Developmental and temperamental differences in emotional regulation in infancy. *Child Development, 66,* 1817–1828.

Maratsos, M. (1998). The acquisition of grammar. In W. Damon (Ed.), *Handbook of child psychology* (Vol. 2). New York: Wiley.

Marcia, J. E. (1980). Identity in adolescence. In J. Adelson (Ed.), *Handbook of adolescent psychology.* New York: Wiley.

Marcia, J. E. (1991). Identity and self-development. In R. M. Lerner, A. C. Petersen, & J. Brooks-Gunn (Eds.), *Encyclopedia of adolescence* (Vol. 1). New York: Garland.

Marcus, G. F., Pinker, S., Ullman, M., Hollander, M., Rosen, T. J., & Xu, F. (1992). Overregularization in language acquisition. *Monographs of the Society for Research in Child Development, 58* (4, Serial No. 228).

Marcus, J., Maccoby, E. E., Jacklin, C. N., & Doering, C. H. (1985). Individual differences in mood in early childhood: Their relation to gender and neonatal sex steroids. *Developmental Psychobiology, 18,* 327–340.

Markovits, H., & Vachon, R. (1989). Reasoning with contrary-to-fact propositions. *Journal of Experimental Child Psychology, 47,* 398–412.

Markstrom-Adams, A. (1989). Androgyny and its relation to adolescent well-being: A review of the literature. *Sex Roles, 21,* 325–340.

Marsh, H. W. (1991). Employment during high school: Character building or a subversion of academic goals? *Sociology of Education, 64,* 172–189.

Marsh, H. W., Chessor, D., Craven, R., & Roche, L. (1995). The effects of gifted and talented programs on academic self-concept: The big fish strikes again. *American Educational Research Journal, 32,* 285–319.

Marsh, H. W., & Yeung, A. S. (1997). Causal effects of academic self-concept on academic achievement: Structural equation models of longitudinal data. *Journal of Educational Psychology, 89,* 41–54.

Marshall, E. (1995). Gene therapy's growing pains. *Science, 269,* 1050–1052.

Marshall-Baker, A., Lickliter, R., & Cooper, R. P. (1998). Prolonged exposure to a visual pattern may promote behavioral organization in preterm infants. *Journal of Perinatal and Neonatal Nursing, 12,* 50–62.

Martin, C. L. (1989). Children's use of gender-related information in making social judgments. *Developmental Psychology, 25,* 80–88.

Martin, C. L., Eisenbud, L., & Rose, H. (1995). Children's gender-based reasoning about toys. *Child Development, 66,* 1453–1471.

Martin, C. L., & Fabes, R. A. (2001). The stability and consequences of young children's same-sex peer interactions. *Developmental Psychology, 37,* 431–446.

Martin, C. L., Fabes, R. A., Evans, S. M., & Wyman, H. (1999). Social cognition on the playground: Children's beliefs about playing with girls versus boys and their relations to sex segregated play. *Journal of Social and Personal Relationships, 16,* 751–772.

Martin, C. L., & Halverson, C. F. (1981). A schematic processing model of sex typing and stereotyping in children. *Child Development, 52,* 1119–1134.

Martin, C. L., & Halverson, C. F. (1987). The roles of cognition in sex roles and sex typing. In D. B. Carter (Ed.), *Current conceptions of sex roles and sex typing: Theory and research.* New York: Praeger.

Martin, C. L., & Little, J. K. (1990). The relation of gender understandings to children's sex-typed preferences and gender stereotypes. *Child Development, 61,* 1427–1439.

Martin, J. A., Hamilton, B. E., Ventura, S. J., Menacker, F., & Park, M. M. (2002). Births: Final data for 2000. *National Vital Statistics Reports, 50,* 1–5.

Martin, R. P., Olejnik, S., & Gaddis, L. (1994). Is temperament an important contributor to schooling outcomes in elementary school? Modeling effects of temperament and scholastic ability on academic achievement. In W. B. Casey & S. C. McDevitt (Eds.), *Prevention and early intervention.* New York: Brunner/Mazel.

Masur, E. F. (1995). Infants' early verbal imitation and their later lexical development. *Merrill-Palmer Quarterly, 41,* 286–306.

Mattys, S. L., & Jusczyk, P. W. (2001). Phonotactic cues for segmentation of fluent speech by infants. *Cognition, 78*, 91–121.

Mattys, S. L., Jusczyk, P. W., Luce, P. A., & Morgan, J. L. (1999). Phonotactic and prosodic effects on word segmentation in infants. *Cognitive Psychology, 38*, 465–494.

Matusov, E., Bell, N., & Rogoff, B. (2002). Schooling as cultural process: Working together and guidance by children from schools differing in collaborative practices. In R. V. Kail & H. W. Reese (Eds.), *Advances in child development and behavior* (Vol. 29, pp. 129–160). San Diego, CA: Academic Press.

Maughan, A., & Cicchetti, D. (2002). Impact of child maltreatment and interadult violence on children's emotion regulation abilities and socioemotional adjustment. *Child Development, 73*, 1525–1542.

Mayer, J. D., Caruso, D. R., & Salovey, P. (1999). Emotional intelligence meets traditional standards for an intelligence. *Intelligence, 27*, 267–298.

Mayer, J. D., Salovey, P., & Caruso, D. R. (2000). Selecting a measure of emotional intelligence: The case for ability scales. In R. Bar-On & J. D. A. Parker (Eds.), *Handbook of emotional intelligence* (pp. 320–342). San Francisco: Jossey-Bass.

Maynard, A. E. (2002). Cultural teaching: The development of teaching skills in Maya sibling interactions. *Child Development, 73*, 969–982.

Mazur, E., Wolchik, S. A., Virdin, L., Sandler, I. N., & West, S. G. (1999). Cognitive moderators of children's adjustment to stressful divorce events: The role of negative cognitive errors and positive illusions. *Child Development, 70*, 231–245.

McBride-Chang, C., & Kail, R. V. (2002). Cross-cultural similarities in the predictors of reading acquisition. *Child Development, 73*, 1392–1407.

McCall, R. B. (1989). Commentary. *Human Development, 32*, 177–186.

McCall, R. B., Applebaum, M. I., & Hogarty, P. S. (1973). Developmental changes in mental performance. *Monographs of the Society for Research in Child Development, 38*(Whole No. 150).

McCall, R. B., & Groark, C. J. (2000). The future of applied child development research and public policy. *Child Development, 71*, 197–204.

McCarty, M. E., & Ashmead, D. H. (1999). Visual control of reaching and grasping in infants. *Developmental Psychology, 35*, 620–631.

McCarty, M. E., Clifton, R. K., Ashmead, D. H., Lee, P., & Goubet, N. (2001). How infants use vision for grasping objects. *Child Development, 72*, 973–987.

McClure, E. B. (2000). A meta-analytic review of sex differences in facial expression processing and their development in infants, children, and adolescents. *Psychological Bulletin, 126*, 424–453.

McCormick, C. (2000). Twin miracles: Mashpee mother has groundbreaking surgery to save her two fetuses. *Cape Code Times*, August 26, 2000. Retrieved May 10, 2002 from http://www.capecodonline.com/cctimes/archives/2000/aug/26/twinmiracles26.htm

McCormick, C. B., & Pressley, M. (1997). *Educational psychology*. New York: Longman.

McCutchen, D., Covill, A., Hoyne, S. H, & Mildes, K. (1994). Individual differences in writing: Implications of translating fluency. *Journal of Educational Psychology, 86*, 256–266.

McCutchen, D., Francis, M., & Kerr, S. (1997). Revising for meaning: Effects of knowledge and strategy. *Journal of Educational Psychology, 89*, 667–676.

McGee, R., Williams, S., & Feehan, M. (1992). Attention deficit disorder and age of onset of problem behaviors. *Journal of Abnormal Child Psychology, 20*, 487–502.

McGraw, M. B. (1935). *Growth: A study of Johnny and Jimmy*. East Norwalk, CT: Appleton-Century-Crofts.

McHale, S. M., Bartko, W. T., Crouter, A. C., & Perry-Jenkins, M. (1990). Children's housework and psychosocial functioning: The mediating effects of parents' sex-role behaviors and attitudes. *Child Development, 61*, 1413–1426.

McKusick, V. A. (1995). *Mendelian inheritance in man: Catalogs of autosomal dominant, autosomal recessive, and X-linked phenotypes* (10th ed.). Baltimore: Johns Hopkins University Press.

McManus, I. C., Sik, G., Cole, D. R., Kloss, J., Mellon, A. F., & Wong, J. (1988). The development of handedness in children. *British Journal of Developmental Psychology, 6*, 257–273.

McNally, S., Eisenberg, N., & Harris, J. D. (1991). Consistency and change in maternal child-rearing practices and values: A longitudinal study. *Child Development, 62*, 190–198.

McNaughton, S., & Leyland, J. (1990). The shifting focus of maternal tutoring across different difficulty levels on a problem solving task. *British Journal of Developmental Psychology, 8*, 147–155.

Measelle, J. R., Ablow, J. C., Cowan, P. A., & Cowan, C. P. (1998). Assessing young children's views of their academic, social, and emotional lives: An evaluation of the self-perception scales of the Berkeley puppet interview. *Child Development, 69*, 1556–1576.

Mennella, J. A., & Beauchamp, G. K. (1996). The human infant's response to vanilla flavors in mother's milk and formula. *Infant Behavior and Development, 19*, 13–19.

Mennella, J., & Beauchamp, G. K. (1997). The ontogeny of human flavor perception. In G. K. Beauchamp & L. Bartoshuk (Eds.), *Tasting and smelling. Handbook of perception and cognition*. San Diego, CA: Academic Press.

Messinger, D. S. (2002). Positive and negative: Infant facial expressions and emotions. *Current Directions in Psychological Science, 11*, 1–6.

Meyer, D. R., & Garasky, S. (1993). Custodial fathers: Myths, realities, and child support policy. *Journal of Marriage and the Family, 55*, 73–79.

Miller, B. C., Benson, B., & Galbraith, K. A. (2001). Family relationships and adolescent pregnancy risk: A research synthesis. *Developmental Review, 21*, 1–38.

Miller, B. C., Fan, X., Christensen, M., Grotevant, H. D., & van Dulmen, M. (2000). Comparisons of adopted and nonadopted adolescents in a large, nationally representative sample. *Child Development, 71*, 1458–1473.

Miller, J. G., & Bersoff, D. M. (1992). Culture and moral judgment: How are conflicts between justice and interpersonal responsibilities resolved? *Journal of Personality and Social Psychology, 62*, 541–554.

Miller, K. F., Smith, C. M., Zhu, J., & Zhang, H. (1995). Preschool origins of cross-national differences in mathematical competence: The role of number-naming systems. *Psychological Science, 6*, 56–60.

Miller, P. A., Eisenberg, N., Fabes, R. A., & Shell, R. (1996). Relations of moral reasoning and vicarious emotion to young children's prosocial behavior toward peers and adults. *Developmental Psychology, 32*, 210–219.

Miller, P. M., Danaher, D. L., & Forbes, D. (1986). Sex-related strategies of coping with interpersonal conflict in children aged five to seven. *Developmental Psychology, 22*, 543–548.

Miller, S. A., & Brownell, C. A. (1975). Peers, persuasion, and Piaget: Dyadic interaction between conservers and nonconservers. *Child Development, 46*, 992–997.

Mills, R. S. L., & Grusec, J. E. (1989). Cognitive, affective, and behavioral consequences of praising altruism. *Merrill-Palmer Quarterly, 35*, 299–326.

Miringoff, M. L., Miringoff, M., & Opdycke, S. (1996). Monitoring the nation's social performance: The Index of Social Health. In E. F. Zigler, S. L. Kagan, & N. W. Hall (Eds.), *Children, families, and government: Preparing for the twenty-first century*. New York: Cambridge University Press.

Mischel, W. (1970). Sex-typing and socialization. In P. H. Mussen (Ed.), *Carmichaels' manual of child psychology* (Vol. 2). New York: Wiley.

Mischel, W., Cantor, N., & Feldman, S. (1996). Principles of self-regulation: The nature of willpower and self-control. In E. T. Higgins & A. W. Kruglanski (Eds.), *Social psychology: Handbook of basic principles* (pp. 329–360). New York: Guilford Press.

Mischel, W., & Ebbesen, E. (1970). Attention in delay of gratification. *Journal of Personality and Social Psychology, 16*, 329–337.

Mistry, R. S., Vandewater, E. A., Huston, A. C., & McLoyd V. C. (2002). Economic well-being and children's social adjustment: The role of family process in an ethnically diverse low-income sample. *Child Development, 73*, 935–951.

Mize, J., & Ladd, G. W. (1990). A cognitive social-learning approach to social skill training with low-status preschool children. *Developmental Psychology, 26*, 388–397.

Mize, J., & Pettit, G. S. (1997). Mothers' social coaching, mother-child relationship style, and children's peer competence: Is the medium the message? *Child Development, 68*, 312–332.

Mize, J., Pettit, G. S., & Brown, E. G. (1995). Mothers' supervision of their children's peer play: Relations with beliefs, perceptions, and knowledge. *Developmental Psychology, 31*, 311–321.

Mizes, J., Scott, P., & Tonya, M. (1995). Eating disorders. In M. Hersen & R. T. Ammerman (Eds.), *Handbook of prevention and treatment with children and adolescents: Intervention in the real world context*. New York: Wiley.

Moats, L. C., & Lyon, G. R. (1993). Learning disabilities in the United States: Advocacy, science, and the future of the field. *Journal of Learning Disabilities, 26*, 282–294.

Moffitt, T. E., Caspi, A., Belsky, J., & Silva, P. A. (1992). Childhood experience and the onset of menarche: A test of a sociobiological model. *Child Development, 63*, 47–58.

Molfese, D. L., & Burger-Judisch, L. M. (1991). Dynamic temporal-spatial allocation of resources in the human brain: An alternative to the static view of hemisphere differences. In F. L. Ketterle (Ed.), *Cerebral laterality: Theory and research. The Toledo symposium*. Hillsdale, NJ: Erlbaum.

Monk, C., Fifer, W. P., Myers, M. M., Sloan, R. P., Trien, L., & Hurtado, A. (2000). Maternal stress responses and anxiety during pregnancy: Effects on fetal heart rate. *Developmental Psychobiology, 36*, 67–77.

Montague, D. P., & Walker-Andrews, A. S. (2001). Peekaboo: A new look at infants' perception of emotion expressions. *Developmental Psychology, 37*, 826–838.

Moore, B. S., Underwood, B., & Rosenhan, D. L. (1973). Affect and altruism. *Developmental Psychology, 8*, 99–104.

Moore, K. L., & Persaud, T. V. N. (1993). *Before we are born* (4th ed.). Philadelphia: W. B. Saunders.

Moore, M. R., & Brooks-Gunn, J. (2002). Adolescent parenthood. In M. H. Bornstein (Ed.), *Handbook of parenting: Vol. 3: Being and becoming a parent* (2nd ed., pp. 173–214). Mahwah, NJ: Erlbaum.

Morgan, B., & Gibson, K. R. (1991). Nutritional and environmental interactions in brain development. In K. R. Gibson & A. C. Peterson (Eds.), *Brain maturation and cognitive development: Comparative and cross-cultural perspectives*. New York: Aldine De Gruyter.

Morgane, P. J., Austin-LaFrance, R., Bronzino, J. D., Tonkiss, J., Diaz-Cintra, S., Cintra, L., Kemper, T., & Galler, J. R. (1993). Prenatal malnutrition and development of the brain. *Neuroscience and Biobehavioral Reviews, 17*, 91–128.

Morison, R., & Masten, A. S. (1991). Peer reputation in middle childhood as a predictor of adaptation in adolescence: A seven-year follow-up. *Child Development, 62*, 991–1007.

Morris, P. A., (2002). The effect of welfare reform policies on children. *Social Policy Report, 16*, 4–18.

Morris, S. C., Taplin, J. E., & Gelman, S. A. (2000). Vitalism in naïve biological thinking. *Developmental Psychology, 36*, 582–595.

Mortimer, J. T. (1991). Employment. In R. M. Lerner, A. C. Petersen, & J. Brooks-Gunn (Eds.), *Encyclopedia of adolescence* (Vol. 1). New York: Garland.

Mortimer, J. T., Finch, M. D., Rye, S., Shanahan, M. J., & Call, K. T. (1996). The effects of work intensity on adolescent mental health, achievement, and behavioral adjustment: New evidence from a prospective study. *Child Development, 67*, 1243–1261.

Mortimer, J. T., Harley, C., & Staff, J. (2002). The quality of work and youth mental health. *Work & Occupations, 29*, 166–197.

Morton, J., & Johnson, M. H. (1991). CONSPEC and CONLERN: A two-process theory of infant face recognition. *Psychological Review, 98*, 164–181.

Moses, L. J., Baldwin, D. A., Rosicky, J. G., & Tidball, G. (2001). Evidence for referential understanding in the emotions domain at twelve and eighteen months. *Child Development, 72*, 718–735.

Moss, E., Rousseau, D., Parent, S., St-Laurent, D., & Saintonge, J. (1998). Correlates of attachment at school age: Maternal reported stress, mother-child interaction, and behavior problems. *Child Development, 69*, 1390–1405.

Mumme, D. L., Fernald, A., & Herrera, C. (1996). Infants' responses to facial and vocal emotional signals in a social referencing paradigm. *Child Development, 67*, 3219–3237.

Murphy, N., & Messer, D. (2000). Differential benefits from scaffolding and children working alone. *Educational Psychology, 20*, 17–31.

Murray, L., Fiori-Cowley, A., Hooper, R., & Cooper, P. (1996). The impact of postnatal depression and associated adversity on early mother-infant interactions and later infant outcomes. *Child Development, 67*, 2512–2526.

Nadig, A. S., & Sedivy, J. C. (2002). Evidence of perspective-taking constraints in children's on-line reference resolution. *Psychological Science, 13*, 329–336.

Naigles, L. G., & Gelman, S. A. (1995). Overextensions in comprehension and production revisited: Preferential-looking in a study of dog, cat, and cow. *Journal of Child Language, 22*, 19–46.

Nation, K., Adams, J. W., Bowyer-Crane, C. A., & Snowling, M. J. (1999). Working memory deficits in poor comprehenders reflect underlying language impairments. *Journal of Experimental Child Psychology, 73*, 139–158.

National Center for Education Statistics. (2000). *Pursuing excellence: Comparisons of international eighth-grade mathematics and science achievement from a U.S. perspective, 1995 and 1999: Initial findings from the Third International Mathematics and Science Study – Repeat*. Washington, DC: U.S. Department of Education.

National High Blood Pressure Education Program Working Group on Hypertension Control in Children and Adolescents. (1996). Update on the 1987 task force report on high blood pressure in children and adolescents: A working group report from the National High Blood Pressure Education Program. *Pediatrics, 98*, 649–658.

National Institutes of Health. (2000). *To reduce SIDS risk, doctor's advice most important in choice of placing infants to sleep on their backs*. Washington, DC: Author.

National Research Council. (1989). *Recommended dietary allowances* (10th ed.). Washington, DC: National Academy Press.

Neisser, U., Boodoo, G., Bouchard, T. J., Boykin, A. W., Brody, N., Ceci, S. J., Halpern, D. F., Loehlin, J. C., Perloff, R., Sternberg, R. J., & Urbina, S. (1996). Intelligence: Knowns and unknowns. *American Psychologist, 51,* 77–101.

Nelson, C. A. (1997). The neurobiological basis of early memory development. In N. Cowan (Ed.), *The development of memory in childhood: Studies in developmental psychology* (pp. 41–82). Hove, England: Psychology Press/Erlbaum (UK) Taylor & Francis.

Nelson, C. A. (1999). Neural plasticity and human development. *Current Directions in Psychological Science, 8,* 42–45.

Nelson, K. (1973). Structure and strategy in learning to talk. *Monographs of the Society for Research in Child Development, 38* (No. 149).

Nelson, K. (1993). Explaining the emergence of autobiographical memory in early childhood. In A. F. Collins & S. E. Gathercole (Eds.), *Theories of memory.* Hove, England: Erlbaum.

Nelson, K. (2001). Language and the self: From the "Experiencing I" to the "Continuing Me". In C. Moore & K. Lemmon (Eds.), *The self in time: Developmental perspectives* (pp. 15–33). Mahwah, NJ: Erlbaum.

Nesdale, D., & Flesser, D. (2001). Social identity and the development of children's group attitudes. *Child Development, 72,* 506–517.

Neugarten, B. L., & Weinstein, K. K. (1964). The changing American grandparent. *Journal of Marriage and the Family, 26,* 299–304.

Nevid, J. S., Rathus, S. A., & Greene, B. (2003). *Abnormal psychology in a changing world* (5th ed.). Upper Saddle River NJ: Prentice-Hall.

Newcomb, A. F., & Bagwell, C. L. (1995). Children's friendship relations: A meta-analytic review. *Psychological Bulletin, 117,* 306–347.

Newcomb, A. F., Bukowski, W. M., & Pattee, L. (1993). Children's peer relations: A meta-analytic review of popular, rejected, neglected, controversial, and average sociometric status. *Psychological Bulletin, 113,* 99–123.

Newman, L. S., Cooper, J., & Ruble, D. N. (1995). Gender and computers: II. Interactive effects of knowledge and constancy on gender-stereotyped attitudes. *Sex Roles, 33,* 325–351.

Newport, E. L. (1991). Contrasting conceptions of the critical period for language. In S. Carey & R. Gelman (Eds.), *The epigenesis of mind: Essays on biology and cognition* (pp. 111–130). Hillsdale, NJ: Erlbaum.

NICHD Early Child Care Research Network. (1997). The effects of infant child care on infant-mother attachment security: Results of the NICHD Study of Early Child Care. *Child Development, 68,* 860–879.

NICHD Early Child Care Research Network. (1998). Early child care and self-control, compliance, and problem behavior at twenty-four and thirty-six months. *Child Development, 69,* 1145–1170.

NICHD Early Child Care Research Network. (2000). The relation of child care to cognitive and language development. *Child Development, 71,* 960–980.

NICHD Early Child Care Research Network. (2001). Child-care and family predictors of preschool attachment and stability from infancy. *Developmental Psychology, 37,* 847–862.

NICHD Early Child Care Research Network. (2002). Child-care structure-process-outcome: Direct and indirect effects of child-care quality on young children's development *Psychological Science, 13,* 199–206.

Nielson, A. C. (1990). *Annual Nielsen report on television: 1990.* New York: Nielson Media Research.

Nolen-Hoeksema, S., & Girgus, J. S. (1994). The emergence of gender differences in depression during adolescence. *Psychological Bulletin, 115,* 424–443.

Nosek, B. A., Banaji, M. R., & Greenwald, A. G. (2002). Math = male, me = female, therefore math not = me. *Journal of Personality and Social Psychology, 83,* 44–59.

Notaro, P. C., Gelman, S. A., & Zimmerman, M. A. (2001). Children's understanding of psychogenic bodily reactions. *Child Development, 72,* 444–459.

Nucci, L., & Weber, E. (1995). Social interactions in the home and the development of young children's conception of the personal. *Child Development, 66,* 1438–1452.

Nurmi, J., Poole, M. E., & Kalakoski, V. (1996). Age differences in adolescent identity exploration and commitment in urban and rural environments. *Journal of Adolescence, 19,* 443–452.

Oates, C., Blades, M., & Gunter, B. (2002). Children and television advertising: When do they understand persuasive intent? *Journal of Consumer Behaviour, 1,* 238–245.

Ochs, E. (1988). *Culture and language development.* Cambridge: Cambridge University Press.

Offer, D., Ostrov, E., Howard, K. I., & Atkinson, R. (1988). *The teenage world: Adolescents' self-image in ten countries.* New York: Plenum.

Okagaki, L., & Frensch, P. A. (1994). Effects of video game playing on measures of spatial performance: Gender effects in late adolescence. *Journal of Applied Developmental Psychology, 15,* 33–58.

Okagaki, L., & Sternberg, R. J. (1993). Parental beliefs and children's school performance. *Child Development, 64,* 36–56.

Okie, S. (2000, April 12). Over the tiniest patients, big ethical questions: Fetal surgery's growing reach raises issues of need and risks. *Washington Post,* pp. A1, A16.

Olsen, O. (1997). Meta-analysis of the safety of home birth. *Birth—Issues in Perinatal Care, 24,* 4–13.

Olweus, D. (1978). *Aggression in the schools: Bullies and whipping boys.* Washington, DC: Hemisphere.

Olweus, D. (1994). Bullying at school: Basic facts and effects of school based intervention program. *Journal of Child Psychology and Psychiatry, 35,* 1171–1190.

O'Moore, M., & Kirkham, C. (2001). Self-esteem and its relationship to bullying behavior. *Aggressive Behavior, 27,* 269–283.

O'Neill, D. K. (1996). Two-year-old children's sensitivity to a parent's knowledge state when making requests. *Child Development, 67,* 659–677.

Paarlberg, K. M., Vingerhoets, A. J. J. M., Passchier, J., Dekker, G. A., et al. (1995). Psychosocial factors and pregnancy outcome: A review with emphasis on methodological issues. *Journal of Psychosomatic Research, 39,* 563–595.

Padilla, A. M., Lindholm, K. J., Chen, A., Duran, R., Hakuta, K., Lambert, W., & Tucker, G. R. (1991). The English-only movement. Myths, reality, and implications for psychology. *American Psychologist, 46,* 120–130.

Parault, S. J., & Schwanenflugel, P. J. (2000). The development of conceptual categories of attention during the elementary school years. *Journal of Experimental Child Psychology, 75,* 245–262.

Parazzini, F., Luchini, L., La Vecchia, C., & Crosignani, P. G. (1993). Video display terminal use during pregnancy and reproductive outcome—A meta-analysis. *Journal of Epidemiology and Community Health, 47,* 265–268.

Parke, R. D. (1977). Punishment in children: Effects, side effects and alternative strategies. In H. L. Hom, Jr. & A. Robinson (Eds.), *Psychological processes in early education.* New York: Academic.

Parke, R. D. (2002). Fathers and families. In M. H. Bornstein (Ed.), *Handbook of parenting, Vol. 3: Being and becoming a parent* (pp. 27–73). Mahwah, NJ: Erlbaum.

Parke, R. D., & Bahvnagri, N. P. (1989). Parents as managers of children's peer relationships. In D. Belle (Ed.), *Children's social networks and social supports.* New York: Wiley.

Parke, R. D., & Buriel, R. (1998). Socialization in the family: Ethnic and ecological perspectives. In W. Damon (Ed.), *Handbook of child psychology* (Vol. 3). New York: Wiley.

Parker, J. G., & Seal, J. (1996). Forming, losing, renewing, and replacing friendships: Applying temporal parameters to the assessment of children's friendship experiences. *Child Development, 67,* 2248–2268.

Parritz, R. H. (1996). A descriptive analysis of toddler coping in challenging circumstances. *Infant Behavior and Development, 19,* 171–180.

Parten, M. (1932). Social participation among preschool children. *Journal of Abnormal and Social Psychology, 27,* 243–269.

Pascalis, O., de Haan, M., & Nelson, C. A. (2002). Is face processing species-specific during the first year of life? *Science, 296,* 1321–1323.

Pascual-Leone, J. (1970). A mathematical model for the transition rule in Piaget's developmental stages. *Acta Psychologica, 32,* 301–345.

Passler, M. A., Isaac, W., & Hynd, G. W. (1985). Neuropsychological development of behavior attributed to frontal lobe functioning in children. *Developmental Neuropsychology, 1,* 349–370.

Patterson, C. J. (1992). Children of lesbian and gay parents. *Child Development, 63,* 1025–1042.

Patterson, C. J. (2002). Lesbian and gay parenthood. In M. H. Bornstein (Ed.), *Handbook of parenting: Vol. 3. Status and social conditions of parenting* (2nd ed., pp. 317–338). Mahwah, NJ: Erlbaum.

Patterson, G. R. (1980). Mothers: The unacknowledged victims. *Monographs of the Society for Research in Child Development, 45*(5, Serial No. 186).

Patterson, G. R. (1984). Microsocial process: A view from the boundary. In J. C. Masters & K. Yarkin-Levin (Eds.), *Boundary areas in social and developmental psychology.* New York: Academic Press.

Pearlman, M., & Ross, H. S. (1997). The benefits of parent intervention in children's disputes: An examination of concurrent changes in children's fighting styles. *Child Development, 68,* 690–700.

Pearson, J. L., Hunter, A. G., Ensminger, M. E., & Kellam, S. G. (1990). Black grandmothers in multigenerational households: Diversity in family structure and parenting involvement in the Woodlawn community. *Child Development, 61,* 434–442.

Pederson, D. R., Gleason, K. E., Moran, G., & Bento, S. (1998). Maternal attachment representations, maternal sensitivity, and the infant-mother attachment relationship. *Developmental Psychology, 34,* 925–933.

Pellegrini, A. D., & Smith, P. K. (1998). Physical activity play: The nature and function of a neglected aspect of play. *Child Development, 69,* 577–598.

Pellegrino, J. W., & Kail, R. V. (1982). Process analysis of spatial aptitude. In R. J. Sternberg (Ed.), *Advances in the psychology of human intelligence* (Vol. 1). Hillsdale, NJ: Erlbaum.

Pennington, B. F., Groisser, D., & Welsh, M. C. (1993). Contrasting cognitive deficits in attention deficit hyperactivity disorder versus reading disability. *Developmental Psychology, 29,* 511–523.

Perfetti, C. A., & Curtis, M. E. (1986). Reading. In R. F. Dillon & R. J. Sternberg (Eds.), *Cognition and instructon.* Orlando, FL: Academic Press.

Perry, M. (2000). Explanations of mathematical concepts in Japanese, Chinese, and U.S. first- and fifth-grade classrooms. *Cognition & Instruction, 18,* 181–207.

Peterson, C. (1996). *The psychology of abnormality.* Fort Worth TX: Harcourt Brace.

Peterson, C., & Rideout, R. (1998). Memory for medical emergencies experienced by 1- and 2-year-olds. *Developmental Psychology, 34,* 1059–1072.

Peterson, L. (1983). Role of donor competence, donor age, and peer presence on helping in an emergency. *Developmental Psychology, 19,* 873–880.

Peterson, L. (1989). Latchkey children's preparation for self-care: Overestimated, under rehearsed and unsafe. *Journal of Child Clinical Psychology, 18,* 36–43.

Petrie, R. H. (1991). Intrapartum fetal evaluation. In S. G. Gabbe, J. R. Niebyl, & J. L. Simpson (Eds.), *Obstetrics: Normal & problem pregnancies* (2nd ed.). New York: Churchill Livingstone.

Pettit, G. S., Bakshi, A., Dodge, K. A., & Coie, J. D. (1990). The emergence of social dominance in young boys' play groups: Developmental differences and behavioral correlates. *Developmental Psychology, 26,* 1017–1025.

Pettit, G. S., Bates, J. E., & Dodge, K. A. (1997). Supportive parenting, ecological context, and children's adjustment: A seven-year longitudinal study. *Child Development, 68,* 908–923.

Pettit, G. S., Bates, J. E., Dodge, K. A., & Meece, D. W. (1999). The impact of after-school peer contact on early adolescent externalizing problems is moderated by parental monitoring, perceived neighborhood safety, and prior adjustment. *Child Development, 70,* 768–778.

Phinney, J. (1989). Stage of ethnic identity in minority group adolescents. *Journal of Early Adolescence, 9,* 34–49.

Phinney, J. (1990). Ethnic identity in adolescents and adults. *Psychological Bulletin, 108,* 499–514.

Phinney, J. S. (1996). When we talk about American ethnic groups, what do we mean? *American Psychologist, 51,* 918–927.

Phinney, J. S., & Chavira, V. (1992). Ethnic identity and self-esteem: An exploratory longitudinal study. *Journal of Adolescence, 15,* 271–281.

Phinney, J. S., Ong, A., & Madden, T. (2000). Cultural values and intergenerational value discrepancies in immigrant and non-immigrant families. *Child Development, 71,* 528–539.

Piaget, J. (1929). *The child's conception of the world.* New York: Harcourt, Brace.

Piaget, J., & Inhelder, B. (1956). *The child's conception of space.* Boston: Routledge & Kegan Paul.

Pierce, S. H., & Lange, G. (2000). Relationships among metamemory, motivation, and memory performance in young school-age children. *British Journal of Developmental Psychology, 18,* 121–135.

Plomin, R., & Crabbe, J. (2000). DNA. *Psychological Bulletin, 126,* 806–828.

Plomin, R., DeFries, J. C., McClearn, G. E., & McGuffin, P. (2001). *Behavioral genetics* (4th ed.). New York: Freeman.

Plomin, R., Fulker, D. W., Corley, R., & DeFries, J. C. (1997). Nature, nurture, and cognitive development from 1 to 16 years: A parent-offspring adoption study. *Psychological Science, 8,* 442–447.

Plomin, R., & Petrill, S. A. (1997). Genetics and intelligence: What's new? *Intelligence, 24,* 53–77.

Plumert, J. M., & Nichols-Whitehead, P. (1996). Parental scaffolding of young children's spatial communication. *Developmental Psychology, 32*, 523–532.

Pollitt, E. (1994). Poverty and child development: Relevance of research in developing countries to the United States. *Child Development, 65*, 283–295.

Poole, D. A., & Lamb, M. E. (1998). *Investigative interviews of children: A guide for helping professionals.* Washington, DC: American Psychological Association.

Porter, R. H., & Winberg, J. (1999). Unique salience of maternal breast odors for newborn infants. *Neuroscience & Biobehavioral Reviews, 23*, 439–449.

Poulin, F., & Boivin, M. (2000). The role of proactive and reactive aggression in the formation and development of boys' friendships. *Developmental Psychology, 36*, 233–240.

Poulin-Dubois, D., & Forbes, J. N. (2002). Toddlers' attention to intentions-in-action in learning novel action words. *Developmental Psychology, 38*, 104–114.

Poulson, C. L., Kymissis, E., Reeve, K. F., Andreatos, M., & Reeve, L. (1991). Generalized vocal imitation in infants. *Journal of Experimental Child Psychology, 51*, 267–279.

Power, F. C., Higgins, A., & Kohlberg, L. (1989). *Lawrence Kohlberg's approach to moral education.* New York: Columbia University Press.

Powers, S. W., & Roberts, M. W. (1995). Simulation training with parents of oppositional children: Preliminary findings. *Journal of Clinical Child Psychology, 24*, 89–97.

Powlishta, K., Serbin, L. A., Doyle, A., & White, D. R. (1994). Gender, ethnic, and body type biases: The generality of prejudice in childhood. *Developmental Psychology, 30*, 526–536.

Priel, B., & deSchonen, S. (1986). Self-recognition: A study of a population without mirrors. *Journal of Experimental Child Psychology, 41*, 237–250.

Principe, G. F., & Ceci, S. J. (2002). I saw it with my own ears: The effects of peer conversations on preschoolers' reports of nonexperienced events. *Journal of Experimental Child Psychology, 83*, 1–25.

Project Zero. (1999). *Project SUMIT: Schools Using Multiple Intelligence Theory.* Retrieved from the World Wide Web: http://pzweb.harvard.edu/SUMIT/OUTCOMES.HTM

Quas, J. A., Goodman, G. S., Bidrose, S., Pipe, M., Craw, S., & Ablin, D. S. (1999). Emotion and memory: Children's long-term remembering, forgetting, and suggestibility. *Journal of Experimental Child Psychology, 72*, 235–270.

Rakic, P. (1995). Corticogenesis in human and nonhuman primates. In M. S. Gazzaniga (Ed.), *The cognitive neurosciences.* Cambridge, MA: MIT Press.

Rakison, D. H., & Poulin-Dubois, D. (2001). Developmental origin of the animate-inanimate distinction. *Psychological Bulletin, 127*, 209–228.

Ramey, C. T., & Campbell, F. A. (1991). Poverty, early childhood education, and academic competence: The Abecedarian experiment. In A. Huston (Ed.), *Children reared in poverty.* New York: Cambridge University Press.

Ramsey, P. G. (1995). Growing up with the contradictions of race and class. *Young Children, 50*, 18–22.

Ransjoe-Arvidson, A. B., Matthiesen, A. S., Lilja, G., Nissen, E., Widstroem, A. M., & Uvnaes-Moberg, K. (2001). Maternal analgesia during labor disturbs newborn behavior: Effects on breastfeeding, temperature, and crying. *Birth-Issues in Perinatal Care, 28*, 5–12.

Rapport, M. D. (1995). Attention-deficit hyperactivity disorder. In M. Hersen & R. T. Ammerman (Eds.), *Advanced abnormal child psychology.* Hillsdale, NJ: Erlbaum.

Rathunde, K. R., & Csikszentmihalyi, M. (1993). Undivided interest and the growth of talent: A longitudinal study of adolescents. *Journal of Youth and Adolescence, 22*, 385–405.

Reese, E., & Cox, A. (1999). Quality of adult book reading affects children's emergent literacy. *Developmental Psychology, 35*, 20–28.

Reich, P. A. (1986). *Language development.* Englewood Cliffs, NJ: Prentice-Hall.

Reid, D. H., Wilson, P. G., & Faw, G. D. (1991). Teaching self-help skills. In J. L. Matson & J. A. Mulick (Eds.), *Handbook of mental retardation* (2nd ed.). New York: Pergamon.

Reimer, M. S. (1996). "Sinking into the ground": The development and consequences of shame in adolescence. *Developmental Review, 16*, 321–363.

Repacholi, B. M. (1998). Infants' use of attentional cues to identify the referent of another person's emotional expression. *Developmental Psychology, 34*, 1017–1025.

Reynolds, A. J., & Robertson, D. L. (2003). School-based early intervention and later child maltreatment in the Chicago Longitudinal Study. *Child Development, 74*, 3–26.

Ricciuti, H. N. (1993). Nutrition and mental development. *Current Directions in Psychological Science, 2*, 43–46.

Rice, M. L., Huston, A. C., Truglio, R., & Wright, J. (1990). Words from "Sesame Street": Learning vocabulary while viewing. *Developmental Psychology, 26*, 421–428.

Richardson, G. A. (1998). Prenatal cocaine exposure. A longitudinal study of development. *Annals of the New York Academy of Sciences, 846*, 144–152.

Richters, J. E., Arnold, L. E., Jensen, P. S., Abikoff, H., Conners, C. K., & Greenhill, L. L., et al. (1995). NIMH collaborative multisite multimodal treatment study of children with ADHD: I. Background and rationale. *Journal of the American Academy of Child and Adolescent Psychiatry, 34*, 987–1000.

Rittle-Johnson, B., & Siegler, R. S. (1999). Learning to spell: Variability, choice, and change in children's strategy use. *Child Development, 70*, 332–348.

Roberts, D. F., Foehr, U. G., Rideout, V. J., & Brodie, M. (1999). *Kids & media @ the new millennium.* Menlo Park, CA: Kaiser Family Foundation.

Roberts, J. E., Burchinal, M., & Durham, M. (1999). Parents' report of vocabulary and grammatical development of African American preschoolers: Child and environmental associations. *Child Development, 70*, 92–106.

Roberts, R. E., Phinney, J. S., Masse, L. C., Chen, Y. R., Roberts, C. R., & Romero, A. (1999). The structure of ethnic identity of young adolescents from diverse ethnocultural groups. *Journal of Early Adolescence, 19*, 301–322.

Roberts, R. J., & Pennington, B. F. (1996). An interactive framework for examining prefrontal cognitive processes. *Developmental Neuropsychology, 12*, 105–126.

Roberts, W., & Strayer, J. (1996). Empathy, emotional expressiveness, and prosocial behavior. *Child Development, 67*, 449–470.

Robinson, A., & Clinkenbeard, P. R. (1998). Giftedness: An exceptionality examined. *Annual Review of Psychology, 49*, 117–139.

Robinson, B. E., Rowland, B. H., & Coleman, M. (1986). *Latchkey kids: Unlocking doors for children and their families.* Lexington MA: Lexington Books, Heath.

Robinson, E. J., Champion, H., & Mitchell, P. (1999). Children's ability to infer utterance veracity from speaker informedness. *Developmental Psychology, 35*, 535–546.

Rochat, P. (2001). Origins of self-concept. In G. Bremner & A. Fogel (Eds.), *Blackwell handbook of infant development* (pp. 191–212). Malden, MA: Blackwell.

Rochelle, J. M., Pea, R. D., Hoadley, C. M., Gordin, D. N., & Means, B. M. (2000). Changing how and what children learn in school with computer-based technologies. *Future of Children, 10*, 76–101.

Rodkin, P. C., Farmer, T. W., Pearl, R., & Van Acker, R. (2000). Heterogeneity of popular boys: Antisocial and prosocial configurations. *Developmental Psychology, 36*, 14–24.

Roffwarg, H. P., Muzio, J. N., & Dement, W. C. (1966). Ontogenetic development of the human sleep-dream cycle. *Science, 152*, 604–619.

Rogoff, B., Mistry, J., Goncu, A., & Mosier, C. (1993). Guided participation in cultural activity by toddlers and caregivers. *Monographs of the Society for Research in Child Development, 58* (Serial No. 236).

Rose, A. J., & Asher, S. R. (1999). Children's goals and strategies in response to conflicts within a friendship. *Developmental Psychology, 35*, 69–79.

Rose, S. A., Feldman, J. F., Futterweit, L. R., & Jankowski, J. J. (1997). Continuity in visual recognition memory: Infancy to 11 years. *Intelligence, 24*, 381–392.

Rose, S. A., Feldman, J. F., & Jankowski, J. J. (2001). Visual short-term memory in the first year of life: Capacity and recency effects. *Developmental Psychology, 37*, 539–549.

Rosengren, K. S., Gelman, S. A., Kalish, C., & McCormick, M. (1991). As time goes by: Children's early understanding of growth in animals. *Child Development, 62*, 1302–1320.

Rosenthal, D. A., & Feldman, S. S. (1992). The relationship between parenting behaviour and ethnic identity in Chinese-American and Chinese-Australian adolescents. *International Journal of Psychology, 27*, 19–31.

Rosenthal, R., Rosnow, R. L., & Rubin, D. B. (2000). *Contrasts and effect sizes in behavioral research: A correlational approach.* Cambridge, U.K.: Cambridge University Press.

Rosenthal, R., & Vandell, D. L. (1996). Quality of care at school-aged child-care programs: Regulatable features, observed experiences, child perspectives, and parent perspectives. *Child Development, 67*, 2434–2445.

Rostenstein, D., & Oster, H. (1997). Differential facial responses to four basic tastes in newborns. In P. Ekman & E. L. Rosenberg (Eds.), *What the face reveals: Basic and applied studies of spontaneous expression using the Facial Action Coding System (FACS).* New York: Oxford University Press.

Rotenberg, K. J., & Mayer, E. V. (1990). Delay of gratification in native and white children: A cross-cultural comparison. *International Journal of Behavioral Development, 13*, 23–30.

Rothbart, M. K., & Bates, J. E. (1998). Temperament. In N. Eisenberg (Ed.), *Handbook of child psychology, Vol. 3: Social, emotional, and personality development* (5th ed., pp. 105–176). New York: Wiley.

Rothbaum, F., & Weisz, J. R. (1994). Parental caregiving and child externalizing behavior in nonclinical samples: A meta-analysis. *Psychological Bulletin, 116*, 55–74.

Rothbaum, F., Weisz, J., Pott, M., Miyake, K., & Morelli, G. (2000). Attachment and culture: Security in the United States and Japan. *American Psychologist, 55*, 1093–1104.

Rotto, P. C., & Kratochwill, T. R. (1994). Behavioral consultation with parents: Using competency-based training to modify child noncompliance. *School Psychology Review, 23*, 669–693.

Rovee-Collier, C. (1987). Learning and memory in infancy. In J. D. Osofsky (Ed.), *Handbook of infant development* (2nd ed.). New York: Wiley.

Rovee-Collier, C. (1997). Dissociations in infant memory: Rethinking the development of implicit and explicit memory. *Psychological Review, 104*, 467–498.

Rovee-Collier, C. (1999). The development of infant memory. *Current Directions in Psychological Science, 8*, 80–85.

Rowe, D. C., Almeida, D. M., & Jacobson, K. C. (1999). School context and genetic influences on aggression in adolescence. *Psychological Science, 10*, 277–280.

Rubin, K. H., Bukowski, W., & Parker, J. G. (1998). Peer interactions, relationships, and groups. In W. Damon (Ed.), *Handbook of child psychology* (Vol. 3). New York: Wiley.

Rubin, K. H., Burgess, K. B., & Hastings, P. D. (2002). Stability and social-behavioral consequences of toddlers' inhibited temperament and parenting behaviors. *Child Development, 73*, 483–495.

Ruble, D. N., Boggiano, A. D., Feldman, N. S., & Loebl, N. H. (1980). Developmental analysis of the role of social comparison in self-evaluation. *Developmental Psychology, 16*, 105–115.

Ruble, D. N., & Martin, C. L. (1998). Gender development. In W. Damon (Ed.), *Handbook of child psychology: Vol. 3: Social, emotional, and personality development* (5th ed., pp. 933–1016). New York: Wiley.

Ruff, H. A., Capozzoli, M., & Weissberg, R. (1998). Age, individuality, and context as factors in sustained visual attention during the preschool years. *Developmental Psychology, 34*, 454–464.

Rutter, M. (2002). Nature, nurture, and development: From evangelism through science toward policy and practice. *Child Development, 73*, 1–21.

Ryan, C. S., McCall, R. B., Robinson, D. R., Groark, C. J., Mulvey, L., & Plemons, B. W. (2002). Benefits of the comprehensive child development program as a function of AFDC Receipt and SES. *Child Development, 73*, 315–328.

Rymer, R. (1993). *Genie.* New York: HarperCollins.

Sabbagh, M. A., & Baldwin, D. A. (2001). Learning words from knowledgeable versus ignorant speakers: Links between preschoolers' theory of mind and semantic development. *Child Development, 72*, 1054–1070.

Sadeh, A., Gruber, R., & Raviv, A. (2002). Sleep, neurobehavioral functioning, and behavior problems in school-age children. *Child Development, 73*, 405–417.

Sadeh, A., Raviv, A., & Gruber, R. (2000). Sleep patterns and sleep disruptions in school-age children. *Developmental Psychology, 36*, 291301.

Saffran, J. R., Aslin, R. N., & Newport, E. L. (1996). Statistical learning by 8-month-old infants. *Science, 274*, 1926–1928.

Sagi, A., Koren-Karie, N., Gini, M., Ziv, Y., & Joels, T. (2002). Shedding further light on the effects of various types and quality of early child care on infant-mother attachment relationship: The Haifa study of early child care. *Child Development, 73*, 1166–1186.

Sagi, A., van IJzendoorn, M. H., Aviezer, O., Donnell, F., & Mayseless, O. (1994). Sleeping out of home in a kibbutz communal arrangement: It makes a difference for infant-mother attachment. *Child Development, 65*, 992–1004.

Sanders, M. R., Montgomery, D. T., & Brechman-Toussaint, M. L. (2000). The mass media and the prevention of child behavior problems: The evaluation of a television series to promote positive outcome for parents and their children. *Journal of Child Psychology & Psychiatry & Allied Disciplines, 41*, 939–948.

Sandler, I. N., Tein, J.-Y., Mehta, P., Wolchik, S., & Ayers, T. (2000). Coping efficacy and psychological problems of children of divorce. *Child Development, 71*, 1099–1118.

Savage-Rumbaugh, E. S., Murphy, J., Sevcik, R. A., Brakke, K. E., Williams, S. L., & Rumbaugh, D. M. (1993). Language comprehension in ape and child. *Monographs of the Society for Research in Child Development, 58*(34, Serial No. 233).

Saxe, G. B. (1988). Candy selling and math learning. *Educational Researcher, 17,* 14–21.

Scarr, S. (1992). Developmental theories for the 1990s: Development and individual differences. *Child Development, 63,* 1–19.

Scarr, S., & McCartney, K. (1983). How people make their own environments: A theory of genotype-environment effects. *Child Development, 54,* 424–435.

Schaal, B., Marlier, L., & Soussignan, R. (1998). Olfactory function in the human fetus: Evidence from selective neonatal responsiveness to the odor of amniotic fluid. *Behavioral Neuroscience, 112,* 1438–1449.

Schmidt, F. L., & Hunter, J. E. (1998). The validity and utility of selection methods in personnel psychology: Practical and theoretical implications of 85 years of research findings. *Psychological Bulletin, 124,* 262–274.

Schneider, B. H., Atkinson, L., & Tardif, C. (2001). Child-parent attachment and children's peer relations: A quantitative review. *Developmental Psychology, 37,* 86–100.

Schneider, M. L. (1992). The effect of mild stress during pregnancy on birthweight and neuromotor maturation in rhesus monkey infants (Macaca mulatta). *Infant Behavior and Development, 15,* 389–403.

Schneider, W., & Bjorklund, D. F. (1998). Memory. In W. Damon (Ed.), *Handbook of child psychology* (Vol. 2). New York: Wiley.

Schnorr, T. M., Grajewski, B. A., Hornung, R. W., Thun, M. J., Egeland, G. M., Murray, W. E., Conover, D. L., & Halperin, W. E. (1991). Video display terminals and the risk of spontaneous abortion. *New England Journal of Medicine, 324,* 727–733.

Schramm, W., Lyle, J., & Parker, E. B. (1961). *Television in the lives of our children.* Stanford, CA: Stanford University Press.

Schwartz, D., Chang, L., & Farver, J. M. (2001). Correlates of victimization in Chinese children's peer groups. *Developmental Psychology, 37,* 520–532.

Schwartz, D., Dodge, K. A., Pettit, G. S., & Bates, J. E. (1997). The early socialization of aggressive victims of bullying. *Child Development, 68,* 665–675.

Schwartz, D., Dodge, K. A., Pettit, G. S., Bates, J. E., & The Conduct Problems Prevention Research Group. (2000). Friendship as a moderating factor in the pathway between early harsh home environment and later victimization in the peer group. *Developmental Psychology, 36,* 646–662.

Scott, W. A., Scott, R., & McCabe, M. (1991). Family relationships and children's personality: A cross-cultural, cross-source comparison. *British Journal of Social Psychology, 30,* 1–20.

Secada, W. G., Fennema, E., & Adajian, L. B. (Eds.). (1995). *New directions for equity in mathematics education.* New York: Cambridge University Press.

Seidenberg, M. S., & McClelland, J. L. (1989). A distributed, developmental model of word recognition and naming. *Psychological Review, 96,* 523–568.

Seifer, R., Schiller, M., Sameroff, A. J., Resnick, S., & Riordan, K. (1996). Attachment, maternal sensitivity, and infant temperament during the first year of life. *Developmental Psychology, 32,* 12–25.

Selman, R. L. (1980). *The growth of interpersonal understanding: Developmental and clinical analyses.* New York: Academic Press.

Selman, R. L. (1981). The child as a friendship philosopher: A case study in the growth of interpersonal understanding. In S. R. Asher & J. M. Gottman (Eds.), *The development of children's friendships.* Cambridge, England: Cambridge University Press.

Selman, R. L., & Byrne, D F. (1974). A structural-developmental analysis of levels of role-taking in middle childhood. *Child Development, 45,* 803–806.

Sénéchal, M., & LeFevre, J. (2002). Parental involvement in the development of children's reading skill: A five-year longitudinal study. *Child Development, 73,* 445–460.

Sénéchal, M., Thomas, E., & Monker, J. (1995). Individual differences in 4-year-old children's acquisition of vocabulary during storybook reading. *Journal of Educational Psychology, 87,* 218–229.

Serbin, L. A., Powlishta, K. K., & Gulko, J. (1993). The development of sex typing in middle childhood. *Monographs of the Society for Research in Child Development, 58*(Serial No. 232).

Serdula, M. K., Ivery, D., Coates, R. J., Freedman, D. S., Williamson, D. F., & Byers, T. (1993). Do obese children become obese adults? A review of the literature. *Preventive Medicine, 22,* 167–177.

Seyfarth, R., & Cheney, D. (1996). Inside the mind of a monkey. In M. Bekoff & D. Jamieson (Eds.), *Readings in animal cognition.* Cambridge, MA: MIT Press.

Shanahan, M. J., Elder, G. H., Burchinal, M., & Conger, R. D. (1996a). Adolescent earnings and relationships with parents: The work-family nexus in urban and rural ecologies. In J. T. Mortimer & M. D. Finch (Eds.), *Adolescents, work, and family: An intergenerational developmental analysis.* Thousand Oaks, CA: Sage.

Shanahan, M. J., Elder, G. H., Burchinal, M., & Conger, R. D. (1996b). Adolescent paid labor and relationships with parents: Early work-family linkages. *Child Development, 67,* 2183–2200.

Share, D. L. (1999). Phonological recoding and orthographic learning: A direct test of the self-teaching hypothesis. *Journal of Experimental Child Psychology, 72,* 95–129.

Sharpe, R. M., & Skakkebaek, N. E. (1993). Are oestrogens involved in falling sperm counts and disorders of the male reproductive tract? *Lancet, 341,* 1392–1395.

Shatz, M. (1983). Communication. In P. H. Mussen (Ed.), *Handbook of child psychology* (Vol. 3). New York: Wiley.

Shatz, M., & Gelman, R. (1973). The development of communication skills: Modifications in the speech of young children as a function of listener. *Monographs of the Society for Research in Child Development, 38*(5, Serial No. 152).

Shaw, D. S., Winslow, E. B., & Flanagan, C. (1999). A prospective study of the effects of marital status and family relations on young children's adjustment among African American and European American families. *Child Development, 70,* 742–755.

Shaw, G. M. (2001). Adverse human reproductive outcomes and electromagnetic fields: A brief summary of the epidemiologic literature. *Bioelectromagnetics, 5,* S5–18.

Shaw, G. M., Schaffer, D., Velie, E. M., Morland, K., & Harris, J. A. (1995). Periconceptional vitamin use, dietary folate, and the occurrence of neural tube defects. *Epidemiology, 6,* 219–226.

Shelov, S. P. (1993). *Caring for your baby and young child: Birth to age 5.* New York: Bantam.

Sherrod, K. B., O'Connor, S., Vietze, P. M., & Altemeier, W. A. III (1984). Child health and maltreatment. *Child Development, 55,* 1174–1183.

Sherry, J. L. (2001). The effects of violent video games on aggression: A meta-analysis. *Human Communication Research, 27,* 409–431.

Shi, R., & Werker, J. F. (2001). Six-month old infants' preference for lexical words. *Psychological Science, 12,* 70–75.

Shields, A., Ryan, R. M., & Cicchetti, D. (2001). Narrative representations of caregivers and emotion dysregulation as predictors of maltreated children's rejection by peers. *Developmental Psychology, 37,* 321–337.

Shih, M., Pittinsky, T. L., & Ambady, N. (1999). Stereotype susceptibility: Identity salience and shifts in quantitative performance. *Psychological Science, 10,* 80–83.

Shiwach, R. (1994). Psychopathology in Huntington's disease patients. *Acta Psychiatrica Scandinavica, 90,* 241–246.

Shoda, Y., Mischel, W., & Peake, P. K. (1990). Predicting adolescent cognitive and self-regulatory competencies from preschool delay of gratification: Identifying diagnostic conditions. *Developmental Psychology, 26,* 978–986.

Shonk, S. M., & Cicchetti, D. (2001). Maltreatment, competency deficits, and risk for academic and behavioral maladjustment. *Developmental Psychology, 37,* 3–17.

Shrager, J., & Siegler, R. S. (1998). SCADS: A model of children's strategy choices and strategy discoveries. *Psychological Science, 9,* 405–410.

Shulman, S., & Kipnis, O. (2001). Adolescent romantic relationships: A look from the future. *Journal of Adolescence, 24,* 337–351.

Shuter-Dyson, R. (1982). Musical ability. In D. Deutsch (Ed.), *The psychology of music.* New York: Academic Press.

Shwe, H. I., & Markman, E. M. (1997). Young children's appreciation of the mental impact of their communicative signals. *Developmental Psychology, 33,* 630–636.

Siddiqui, A. (1995). Object size as a determinant of grasping in infancy. *Journal of Genetic Psychology, 156,* 345–358.

Siegler, R. S. (1981). Developmental sequences within and between concepts. *Monographs of the Society for Research in Child Development, 46*(Serial No. 189).

Siegler, R. S. (1986). Unities in strategy choices across domains. In M. Perlmutter (Ed.), *Minnesota symposia on child development* (Vol. 19). Hillsdale, NJ: Erlbaum.

Siegler, R. S. (1989). Mechanisms of cognitive development. *Annual Review of Psychology, 40,* 353–379.

Siegler, R. S. (1996). *Emerging minds: The process of change in children's thinking.* New York: Oxford.

Siegler, R. S. (1998). *Children's thinking* (3rd ed.). Upper Saddle River, NJ: Prentice-Hall.

Siegler, R. S., & Ellis, S. (1996). Piaget on childhood. *Psychological Science, 7,* 211–215.

Siegler, R. S., & Jenkins, E. (1989). *How children discover new strategies.* Hillsdale, NJ: Erlbaum.

Siegler, R. S., & Robinson, M. (1982). The development of numerical understandings. In H. W. Reese & L. P. Lipsitt (Eds.), *Advances in child development and behavior* (Vol. 16). New York: Academic Press.

Siegler, R. S., & Shrager, J. (1984). Strategy choices in addition and subtraction: How do children know what to do? In C. Sophian (Ed.), *Origins of cognitive skills.* Hillsdale, NJ: Erlbaum.

Signorella, M. L., Bigler, R. S., & Liben, L. S. (1993). Developmental differences in children's gender schemata about others: A meta-analytic review. Early gender-role development. *Developmental Review, 13,* 147–183.

Signorielli, N., & Lears, M. (1992). Children, television, and conceptions about chores: Attitudes and behaviors. *Sex Roles, 27,* 157–170.

Silverman, I. W., & Ragusa, D. M. (1990). Child and maternal correlates of impulse control in 24-month-old children. *Genetic, Social, and General Psychology Monographs, 116,* 435–473.

Silverman, W. K., La Greca, A. M., & Wasserstein, S. (1995). What do children worry about? Worries and their relations to anxiety. *Child Development, 66,* 671–686.

Simmons, R., & Blyth, D. (1987). *Moving into adolescence.* New York: Aldine de Gruyter.

Simons, D. J., & Keil, F. C. (1995). An abstract to concrete shift in the development of biological thought: The insides story. *Cognition, 56,* 129–163.

Simons-Morton, B. G., McKenzie, T. J., Stone, E., Mitchell, P., Osganian, V., Strikmiller, P. K., Ehlinger, S., Cribb, P., & Nader, P. R. (1997). Physical activity in the multiethnic population of third graders in four states. *American Journal of Public Health, 87,* 45–50.

Simpson, E. L. (1974). Moral development research: A case study of scientific cultural bias. *Human Development, 17,* 81–106.

Singer, J. D., Fuller, B., Keiley, M. K., & Wolf, A. (1998). Early childcare selection: Variation by geographic location, maternal characteristics, and family structure. *Developmental Psychology, 34,* 1129–1144.

Singer, L. T., Arendt, R., Minnes, S., Farkas, K., Salvator, A., Kirchner, H. L., & Kliegman, R. (2002). Cognitive and motor outcomes of cocaine-exposed infants. *Journal of the American Medical Association, 287,* 1952–1960.

Skinner, B. F. (1957). *Verbal behavior.* New York: Appleton-Century-Crofts.

Slobin, D. I. (1985). Cross-linguistic evidence for the language-making capacity. In D. I. Slobin (Ed.), *The cross-linguistic study of language acquisition: Vol. 2: Theoretical issues.* Hillsdale, NJ: Erlbaum.

Smetana, J. G. (2002). Culture, autonomy, and personal jurisdiction in adolescent-parent relationships. *Advances in Child Development and Behavior, 29,* 52–87.

Smetana, J. G., Schlagman, N., & Adams, P. W. (1993). Preschool children's judgments about hypothetical and actual transgressions. *Child Development, 64,* 202–214.

Smith, E. R., & Mackie, D. M. (2000). *Social psychology* (2nd ed.). Philadelphia: Psychology Press.

Smith, L. B., Quittner, A. L. Osberger, M. J., & Miyamoto, R. (1998). Audition and visual attention: The developmental trajectory in deaf and hearing populations. *Developmental Psychology, 34,* 840–850.

Smith, L. B., Thelen, E., Titzer, R., & McLin, D. (1999). Knowing in the context of acting: The task dynamics of the A-not-B error. *Psychological Review, 106,* 235–260.

Smith, P. K., & Drew, L. M. (2002). Grandparenthood. In M. H. Bornstein (Ed.), *Handbook of parenting: Vol. 3. Status and social conditions of parenting* (2nd ed., pp. 141–172). Mahwah, NJ: Erlbaum.

Smith, R. (1999, March). The timing of birth. *Scientific American,* 68–75.

Smith, R. E., & Smoll, F. L. (1997). Coaching the coaches: Youth sports as a scientific and applied behavioral setting. *Current Directions in Psychological Science, 6,* 16–21.

Smock, T. K. (1999). *Physiological psychology: A neuroscience approach.* Upper Saddle River, NJ: Prentice-Hall.

Smoll, F. L., & Schutz, R. W. (1990). Quantifying gender differences in physical performance: A developmental perspective. *Developmental Psychology, 26,* 360–369.

Smoll, F. L., Smith, R. E., Barnett, N. P., & Everett, J. J. (1993). Enhancement of children's self-esteem through social support training for youth sport coaches. *Journal of Applied Psychology, 78,* 602–610.

Snedeker, B. (1982). *Hard knocks: Preparing youth for work.* Baltimore, MD: Johns Hopkins University Press.

Snow, C. W. (1998). *Infant development* (2nd ed.). Upper Saddle River, NJ: Prentice-Hall.

Snow, M. E., Jacklin, C. N., & Maccoby, E. E. (1983). Sex-of-child differences in father-child interaction at one year of age. *Child Development, 54,* 227–232.

Solomon, G. E. A., Johnson, S. C., Zaitchik, D., & Carey, S. (1996). Like father, like son: Young children's understanding of how and why offspring resemble their parents. *Child Development, 67,* 151–171.

Sophian, C., & Wellman, H. M. (1987). The development of indirect search strategies. *British Journal of Developmental Psychology, 5,* 9–18.

Spearman, C. (1904). "General intelligence" objectively determined and measured. *American Journal of Psychology, 15,* 201–293.

Spelke, E. S. (1994). Initial knowledge: Six suggestions. *Cognition, 50,* 431–445.

Spence, J. T. (1985). Achievement American style: The rewards and costs of individualism. *American Psychologist, 40,* 1285–1295.

Sporkin, E., Wagner, J., & Tomashof, C. (1992, February). A terrible hunger. *People,* 92–98.

Springer, K., & Keil, F. C. (1991). Early differentiation of causal mechanisms appropriate to biological and nonbiological kinds. *Child Development, 62,* 767–781.

Sroufe, L. A., & Waters, E. (1976). The ontogenesis of smiling and laughter: A perspective on the organization of development in infancy. *Psychological Review, 83,* 173–189.

St. George, I. M., Williams, S., & Silva, P. A. (1994). Body size and the menarche: The Dunedin study. *Journal of Adolescent Health, 15,* 573–576.

St. James-Roberts, I., & Plewis, I. (1996). Individual differences, daily fluctuations, and developmental changes in amounts of infant waking, fussing, crying, feeding, and sleeping. *Child Development, 67,* 2527–2450.

Stalikas, A., & Gavaki, E. (1995). The importance of ethnic identity: Self-esteem and academic achievement of second-generation Greeks in secondary school. *Canadian Journal of School Psychology, 11,* 1–9.

Stanovich, K. E. (1993). Dysrationalia: A new specific learning disability. *Journal of Learning Disabilities, 26,* 501–515.

Stattin, H., & Magnusson, D. (1989). The role of early aggressive behavior in the frequency, seriousness, and types of later crime. *Journal of Consulting and Clinical Psychology, 57,* 710–718.

Steele, C. M. (1997). A threat in the air: How stereotypes shape intellectual identity and performance. *American Psychologist, 52,* 613–629.

Steele, C. M., & Aronson, J. (1995). Stereotype threat and the intellectual test performance of African Americans. *Journal of Personality and Social Psychology, 69,* 797–811.

Steelman, J. D. (1994). Revision strategies employed by middle level students using computers. *Journal of Educational Computing Research, 11,* 141–152.

Steinberg, L. (1990). Autonomy, conflict, and harmony in the family relationship. In S. S. Feldman & G. R. Elliott (Eds.), *At the threshold: The developing adolescent.* Cambridge, MA: Harvard University Press.

Steinberg, L. (1990). Interdependence in the family: Autonomy, conflict, and harmony in the parent-adolescent relationship. In S. S. Feldman & G. R. Elliott (Eds.), *At the threshold: The developing adolescent* (pp. 255–275). Cambridge MA: Harvard University Press.

Steinberg, L., & Dornbusch, S. M. (1991). Negative correlates of part-time employment during adolescence: Replication and elaboration. *Developmental Psychology, 27,* 304–313.

Steinberg, L., Fegley, S., & Dornbusch, S. M. (1993). Negative impact of part-time work on adolescent adjustment: Evidence from a longitudinal study. *Developmental Psychology, 29,* 171–180.

Steinberg, L., Lamborn, S. D., Dornbusch, S. M., & Darling, N. (1992). Impact of parenting practices on adolescent achievement: Authoritative parenting, school involvement, and encouragement to succeed. *Child Development, 63,* 1266–1281.

Steinberg, L. D. (1999). *Adolescence* (5th ed.). Boston, MA: McGraw-Hill.

Steiner, J. E., Glaser, D., Hawilo, M. E., & Berridge, K. C. (2001). Comparative expression of hedonic impact: Affective reactions to taste by human infants and other primates. *Neuroscience & Biobehavioral Reviews, 25,* 53–74.

Stern, M., & Karraker, K. H. (1989). Sex stereotyping of infants: A review of gender labeling studies. *Sex Roles, 20,* 501–522.

Sternberg, C. R., & Campos, J. (1990). The development of anger expressions in infancy. In N. Stein, B. Leventhal, & T. Trabasso (Eds.), *Psychological and biological approaches to emotion.* Hillsdale, NJ: Erlbaum.

Sternberg, R. J. (1977). *Intelligence, information processing, and analogical reasoning.* Hillsdale, NJ: Erlbaum.

Sternberg, R. J. (1985). *Beyond IQ: A triarchic theory of human intelligence.* Cambridge: Cambridge University Press.

Sternberg, R. J. (1997). *Successful intelligence.* New York: Plume.

Sternberg, R. J., & Grigorenko, E. L. (2002). *Dynamic testing: The nature and measurement of learning potential.* New York: Cambridge University Press.

Sternberg, R. J., & Kaufman J. C. (1998). Human abilities. *Annual Review of Psychology, 49,* 479–502.

Stevahn, L., Johnson, D. W., Johnson, R. T., Oberle, K., & Wahl, L. (2000). Effects of conflict resolution training integrated into a kindergarten curriculum. *Child Development, 71,* 772–784.

Stevenson, H. W., & Lee, S. (1990). Contexts of achievement. *Monographs of the Society for Research in Child Development, 55*(Serial No. 221).

Stevenson, H. W., & Stigler, J. W. (1992). *The learning gap.* New York: Summit Books.

Stewart, L., & Pascual-Leone, J. (1992). Mental capacity constraints and the development of moral reasoning. *Journal of Experimental Child Psychology, 54,* 251–287.

Stewart, R. B., Mobley, L. A., Van Tuyl, S. S., & Salvador, W. A. (1987). The firstborns' adjustment to the birth of a sibling: A longitudinal assessment. *Child Development, 58,* 341–355.

Stice, E. (2001). Risk factors for eating pathology: Recent advances and future directions. In R. H. Striegel-Moore & L. Smolak (Eds.), *Eating disorders: Innovative directions in research and practice* (pp. 51–73). Washington, DC: American Psychological Association.

Stice, E., Presnell, K., & Bearman, S. K. (2001). Relation of early menarche to depression, eating disorders, substance abuse, and comorbid psychopathology among adolescent girls. *Developmental Psychology, 37,* 608–619.

Stifter, C. A., & Fox, N. A. (1990). Infant reactivity: Physiological correlates of newborn and 5-month temperament. *Developmental Psychology, 26,* 582–588.

Stifter, C. A., Spinrad, T. L., & Braungart-Rieker, J. M. (1999). Toward a developmental model of child compliance: The role of emotion regulation in infancy. *Child Development, 70,* 21–32.

Stigler, J. W., Gallimore, R., & Hiebert, J. (2000). Using video surveys to compare classrooms and teaching across cultures: Examples and lessons from the TIMSS video studies. *Educational Psychologist, 35,* 87–100.

Stiles, J. (2001). Neural plasticity and cognitive development. *Developmental Neuropsychology, 18,* 237–272.

Stiles, J., Stern, C., Trauner, D., & Nass, R. (1996). Developmental change in spatial grouping activity among children with early focal brain injury: Evidence from a modeling task. *Brain and Cognition, 31,* 46–62.

Stoolmiller, M. (2001). Synergistic interaction of child manageability problems and parent-discipline tactics in predicting future growth in externalizing behavior for boys. *Developmental Psychology, 37,* 814–825.

Stormshak, E. A., Bellanti, C. J., Bierman, K. L., & the Conduct Problems Prevention Research Group. (1996). The quality of sibling relationships and the development of social competence and behavioral control in aggressive children. *Developmental Psychology, 32,* 79–89.

Stormshak, E. A., Bierman, K. L., Bruschi, C., Dodge, K. A., Coie, J. D., & the Conduct Problems Prevention Research Group. (1999). The relation between behavior problems and peer preference in different classroom contexts. *Child Development, 70,* 169–182.

Strauss, M. S., & Curtis, L. E. (1984). Development of numerical concepts in infancy. In C. Sophian (Ed.), *Origins of cognitive skills.* Hillsdale, NJ: Erlbaum.

Strayer, J., & Schroeder, M. (1989). Children's helping strategies: Influences of emotion, empathy, and age. In N. Eisenberg (Ed.), *New directions for child development: Empathy and related emotional responses* (Vol. 44). San Francisco: Jossey-Bass.

Strough, J., & Berg, C. A. (2000). Goals as a mediator of gender differences in high-affiliation dyadic conversations. *Developmental Psychology, 36,* 117–125.

Stunkard, A. J., Sorensen, T. I. A., Hanis, C., Teasdale, T. W., Chakraborty, R., Schull, W. J., & Schulsinger, F. (1986). An adoption study of human obesity. *New England Journal of Medicine, 314,* 193–198.

Subrahmanyam, K., Greenfield, P., Kraut, R., & Gross, E. (2001). The impact of computer use on children's and adolescents' development. *Journal of Applied Developmental Psychology, 22,* 7–30.

Sullivan, L. W. (1987). The risks of the sickle-cell trait: Caution and common sense. *New England Journal of Medicine, 317,* 830–831.

Sullivan, S. A., & Birch, L. L. (1990). Pass the sugar, pass the salt: Experience dictates preference. *Developmental Psychology, 26,* 546–551.

Super, C. M. (1981). Cross-cultural research on infancy. In H. C. Triandis & A. Heron (Eds.), *Handbook of cross-cultural psychology, Vol. 4: Developmental psychology.* Boston: Allyn & Bacon.

Super, C. M., Herrera, M. G., & Mora, J. O. (1990). Long-term effects of food supplementation and psychosocial intervention on the physical growth of Colombian infants at risk of malnutrition. *Child Development, 61,* 29–49.

Super, D. E. (1976). *Career education and the meanings of work.* Washington, DC: U.S. Offices of Education.

Super, D. E. (1980). A life span, life space approach to career development. *Journal of Vocational Behavior, 16,* 282–298.

Svirsky, M. A., Robbins, A. M., Kirk, K. I., Pisoni, D. B., & Miyamoto, R. T. (2000). Language development in profoundly deaf children with cochlear implants. *Psychological Science, 11,* 153–158.

Szagun, G. (2001). Language acquisition in young German-speaking children with cochlear implants: Individual differences and implications for conceptions of a "sensitive phase"? *Audiology & Neuro-Otology, 6,* 288–297.

Szkrybalo, J., & Ruble, D. N. (1999). "God made me a girl": Sex-category constancy judgments and explanations revisited. *Developmental Psychology, 35,* 392–402.

Tager-Flusberg, H. (1993). Putting words together: Morphology and syntax in the preschool years. In J. Berko Gleason (Ed.), *The development of language* (3rd ed.). New York: Macmillan.

Tamis-LeMonda, C. S., & Bornstein, M. H. (1996). Variation in children's exploratory, nonsymbolic, and symbolic play: An explanatory multidimensional framework. In C. Rovee-Collier & L. P. Lipsitt (Eds.), *Advances in infancy research* (Vol. 10). Norwood, NJ: Ablex.

Tamis-LeMonda, C. S., & Bornstein, M. H. (2002). Maternal responsiveness and early language acquisition. In R. V. Kail & H. W. Reese (Eds.), *Advances in child development and behavior* (Vol. 29, pp. 90–127). San Diego, CA: Academic Press.

Tanner, J. M. (1970). Physical growth. In P. H. Mussen (Ed.), *Carmichael's manual of child psychology* (3rd ed.). New York: Wiley.

Tanner, J. M. (1990). *Fetus into man: Physical growth from conception to maturity* (2nd ed.) Cambridge, MA: Harvard University Press.

Taylor, H. G., Klein, N., Minich, N. M., & Hack, M. (2000). Middle-school-age outcomes in children with very low birthweight. *Child Development, 71,* 1495–1511.

Taylor, M., Cartwright, B. S., & Carlson, S. M. (1993). A developmental investigation of children's imaginary companions. *Developmental Psychology, 29,* 276–285.

Taylor, M. G. (1996). The development of children's beliefs about social and biological aspects of gender differences. *Child Development, 67,* 1555–1571.

Taylor, R., Casten, R., Flickinger, S. M., Roberts, D., & Fulmore, C. D. (1994). Explaining the school performance of African-American adolescents. *Journal of Research on Adolescence, 4,* 21–44.

Taylor, R. D., & Roberts, D. (1995). Kinship support and maternal and adolescent well-being in economically disadvantaged African-American families. *Child Development, 66,* 1585–1597.

Teichman, Y. (2001). The development of Israeli children's images of Jews and Arabs and their expression in human figure drawings. *Developmental Psychology, 37,* 749–761.

Thelen, E., & Smith, L. B. (1998). Dynamic systems theories. In W. Damon (Ed.), *Handbook of child psychology* (Vol. 1). New York: Wiley.

Thelen, E., & Ulrich, B. D. (1991). Hidden skills. *Monographs of the Society for Research in Child Development, 56* (Serial No. 223).

Thelen, E., Ulrich, B. D., & Jensen, J. L. (1989). The developmental origins of locomotion. In M. H. Woollacott & A. Shumway-Cook (Eds.), *Development of posture and gait across the life span.* Columbia: University of South Carolina Press.

Thomas, A., Chess, S., & Birch, H. G. (1968). *Temperament and behavior disorders in children.* New York: New York University Press.

Thomas, H., & Kail, R. (1991). Sex differences in the speed of mental rotation and the X-linked genetic hypothesis. *Intelligence, 15,* 17–32.

Thomas, J. R., & French, K. E. (1985). Gender differences across age in motor performance: A meta-analysis. *Psychological Bulletin, 98,* 260–282.

Thompson, G. G. (1952). *Child psychology.* Boston: Houghton Mifflin.

Thompson, R. A. (1998). Early socio-personality development. In N. Eisenberg (Ed.), *Handbook of child psychology, Vol. 3: Social, emotional, and personality development* (5th ed., pp. 25–104). New York: Wiley.

Thompson, R. A. (2000). The legacy of early attachments. *Child Development, 71,* 145–152.

Thompson, R. A., Laible, D. J., & Ontai, L. L. (2003). Early understandings of emotion, morality, and self: Developing a working model. *Advances in Child Development and Behavior, 31,* 137–172.

Thompson, R. A., & Limber, S. (1991). "Social anxiety" in infancy: Stranger wariness and separation distress. In H. Leitenberg (Ed.), *Handbook of social and evaluation anxiety.* New York: Plenum.

Thorne, B. (1993). *Gender play: Girls and boys in school.* New Brunswick, NJ: Rutgers University Press.

Thurstone, L. L., & Thurstone, T. G. (1941). Factorial studies of intelligence. *Psychometric Monograph*, No. 2.

Tincoff, R., & Jusczyk, P. W. (1999). Some beginnings of word comprehension in 6-month-olds. *Psychological Science, 10*, 172–175.

Tisak, M. (1993). Preschool children's judgements of moral and personal events involving physical harm and property damage. *Merrill-Palmer Quarterly, 39*, 375–390.

Toda, S., & Fogel, A. (1993). Infant response to the still-face situation at 3 and 6 months. *Developmental Psychology, 29*, 532–538.

Trainor, L. J., Austin, C. M., & Desjardins, R. N. (2000). Is infant-directed speech prosody a result of the vocal expression of emotion? *Psychological Science, 11*, 188–195.

Treiman, R. (2000). The foundations of literacy. *Current Directions in Psychological Science, 9*, 89–92.

Treiman, R., & Kessler, B. (2003). The role of letter names in the acquisition of literacy. *Advances in Child Development and Behavior, 31*, 105–135.

Tudge, J. R. H., Winterhoff, P. A., & Hogan, D. M. (1996). The cognitive consequences of collaborative problem solving with and without feedback. *Child Development, 67*, 2892–2909.

Turiel, E. (1997). Beyond particular and universal ways: Contexts for morality. In H. D. Saltzstein (Ed.), *Culture as a context for moral development: New perspectives on the particular and the universal: New directions for child development, No. 76* (pp. 87–105). San Francisco: Jossey-Bass.

Turiel, E. (1998). The development of morality. In W. Damon (Ed.), *Handbook of child psychology, Vol. 3: Social, emotional, and personality development* (pp. 863–932). New York: Wiley.

Turiel, E., & Neff, K. (2000). Religion, culture, and beliefs about reality in moral reasoning. In K. S. Rosengren, C. N. Johnson, & P. L. Harris (Eds.), *Imagining the impossible: Magical, scientific, and religious thinking in children* (pp. 269–304). New York: Cambridge University Press.

Turkheimer, E., & Waldron, M. (2000). Nonshared environment: A theoretical, methodological, and quantitative review. *Psychological Bulletin, 126*, 78–108.

Twenge, J. M., & Campbell, W. K. (2001). Age and birth cohort differences in self-esteem: A cross-temporal meta-analysis. *Personality & Social Psychology Review, 5*, 321–344.

Tyrka, A. R., Graber, J. A., & Brooks-Gunn, J. (2000). The development of disordered eating: Correlates and predictors of eating problems in the context of adolescence. In A. J. Sameroff, M. Lewis, & S. M. Miller (Eds.), *Handbook of developmental psychopathology* (2nd ed., pp. 607–624). New York, NY: Kluwer Academic/Plenum Publishers.

U. S. Bureau of the Census. (1994). *Marital status and living arrangements: March 1993.* Washington, DC: U. S. Government Printing Office.

U. S. Bureau of the Census. (1995). *Statistical abstract of the United States* (115th ed.). Washington, DC: U. S. Government Printing Office.

U. S. Department of Health and Human Services. (2001). *The Surgeon General's call to action to prevent and decrease overweight and obesity.* Rockville MD: Author.

U. S. Department of State. (2002). *Country reports on human rights practices, 2001.* Retrieved from the World Wide Web November 15, 2002: http://www.state.gov/g/drl/rls/hrrpt/2001/

Umbel, V. M., Pearson, B. Z., Fernandez, M. C., & Oller, D. K. (1992). Measuring bilingual children's receptive vocabularies. *Child Development, 63*, 1012–1020.

Unger, R., & Crawford, M. (1996). *Women and gender: A feminist psychology* (2nd ed.). New York: McGraw-Hill.

Urberg, K. A., Değirmencioğlu, S. M., & Pilgrim, C. (1997). Close friend and group influence in the context of adolescent cigarette smoking and alcohol use. *Developmental Psychology, 33*, 834–844.

Valkenburg, P. M., & van der Voort, T. H. A. (1994). Influence of TV on daydreaming and creative imagination: A review of research. *Psychological Bulletin, 116*, 316–339.

Valkenburg, P. M., & van der Voort, T. H. A. (1995). The influence of television on children's daydreaming styles: A 1-year-panel study. *Communication Research, 22*, 267–287.

van den Boom, D. C. (1994). The influence of temperament and mothering on attachment and exploration: An experimental manipulation of sensitive responsiveness among lower-class mothers with irritable infants. *Child Development, 65*, 1457–1477.

van den Boom, D. C. (1995). Do first-year intervention effects endure? Follow-up during toddlerhood of a sample of Dutch irritable infants. *Child Development, 66*, 1798–1816.

van IJzendoorn, M. (1995). Adult attachment representations, parental responsiveness, and infant attachment: A meta-analysis on the predictive validity of the Adult Attachment Interview. *Psychological Bulletin, 117*, 387–403.

van IJzendoorn, M. H., & Kroonenberg, P. M. (1988). Cross-cultural patterns of attachment: A meta-analysis of the Strange Situation. *Child Development, 59*, 147–156.

van IJzendoorn, M., H., Moran, G., Belsky, J., Pederson, D., Bakermans-Kranenburg, M. J., & Kneppers, K. (2000). The similarity of siblings' attachments to their mother. *Child Development, 71*, 1086–1098.

van IJzendoorn, M. H., & Sagi, A. (1999). Cross-cultural patterns of attachment. In J. Cassidy & P. R. Shaver (Eds.), *Handbook of attachment: Theory, research, and clinical applications* (pp. 713–734). New York: Guilford.

Vandell, D. L., & Ramanan, J. (1991). Children of the National Longitudinal Survey of Youth: Choices in after-school care and child development. *Developmental Psychology, 27*, 637–643.

Vandell, D. L., & Shumow, L. (1999). After-school child care programs. *Future of Children, 9*, 64–80.

Vander Wal, J. S., & Thelen, M. H. (2000). Eating and body image concerns among obese and average-weight children. *Addictive Behaviors, 25*, 775–778.

Verma, I. M. (1990). Gene therapy. *Scientific American, 263*, 68–84.

Verschueren, K., Buyck, P., & Marceon, A. (2001). Self-representations and socioemotional competence in young children: A 3-year longitudinal study. *Developmental Psychology, 37*, 126–134.

Volling, B. L., & Belsky, J. (1992). The contribution of mother-child and father-child relationships to the quality of sibling interaction: A longitudinal study. *Child Development, 63*, 1209–1222.

von Hofsten, C., Vishton, P., Spelke, E. S., Feng, Q., & Rosander, K. (1998). Predictive action in infancy: Tracking and reaching for moving objects. *Cognition, 67*, 255–285.

Vorhees, C. V., & Mollnow, E. (1987). Behavior teratogenesis: Long-term influences on behavior. In J. D. Osofsky (Ed.), *Handbook of infant development* (2nd ed.). New York: Wiley.

Voyer, D., Voyer, S., & Bryden, M. P. (1995). Magnitude of sex differences in spatial abilities: A meta-analysis and consideration of critical variables. *Psychological Bulletin, 117*, 250–270.

Vurpillot, E. (1968). The development of scanning strategies and their relation to visual differentiation. *Journal of Experimental Child Psychology, 6*, 632–650.

Vygotsky, L. S. (1934/1986). *Thought and language* (A. Kozulin, Trans.). Cambridge, MA: MIT Press. (Original work published in 1934.)

Vygotsky, L. S. (1978). *Mind in society: The development of higher psychological processes* (M. Cole, V. John-Steiner, S. Scribner, & E. Soubermen, Eds.). Cambridge, MA: Harvard University Press.

Waber, D. P. (1977). Sex differences in mental abilities, hemispheric lateralization, and rate of physical growth at adolescence. *Developmental Psychology, 13*, 29–38.

Wachs, T. D. (1983). The use and abuse of environment in behavior-genetic research. *Child Development, 54*, 396–407.

Wachs, T. D., & Bates, J. E. (2001). Temperament. In G. Bremner & A. Fogel (Eds.), *Blackwell handbook of infant development* (pp. 465–501). Malden, MA: Blackwell.

Wagner, R. K., Torgesen, J. K., Rashotte, C. A., Hecht, S. A., Barker, T. A., Burgess, S. R., Donahue, J., & Garon, T. (1999). Changing relations between phonological processing abilities and word-level reading as children develop from beginning to skilled readers: A 5-year longitudinal study. *Developmental Psychology, 33*, 468–479.

Walberg, H. J. (1995). General practices. In G. Cawelti (Ed.), *Handbook of research on improving student achievement.* Arlington, VA: Educational Research Service.

Walker, L. J. (1980). Cognitive and perspective-taking prerequisites for moral development. *Child Development, 51*, 131–139.

Walker, L. J. (1995). Sexism in Kohlberg's moral psychology? In W. M. Kurtines & J. L. Gewirtz (Eds.), *Moral development: An introduction.* Boston: Allyn & Bacon.

Walker, L. J., Hennig, K. H., & Krettenauer, T. (2000). Parent and peer contexts for children's moral reasoning development. *Child Development, 71*, 1033–1048.

Walker, L. J., & Taylor, J. H. (1991). Family interactions and the development of moral reasoning. *Child Development, 62*, 264–283.

Ward, S. L., & Overton, W. F. (1990). Semantic familiarity, relevance, and the development of deductive reasoning. *Developmental Psychology, 26*, 288–493.

Warren, A. R., & McCloskey, L. A. (1993). Pragmatics: Language in social contexts. In J. Berko Gleason (Ed.), *The development of language* (3rd ed., pp. 195–238). New York: Macmillan.

Warren-Leubecker, A., & Bohannon, J. N. (1989). Pragmatics: Language in social contexts. In J. Berko Gleason (Ed.), *The development of language* (2nd ed., pp. 327–368). Columbus, OH: Merrill.

Waters, E., & Cummings, E. M. (2000). A secure base from which to explore close relationships. *Child Development, 71*, 164–172.

Waters, E., Merrick, S., Treboux, D., Crowell, J., & Albersheim, L. (2000). Attachment security in infancy and early adulthood: A twenty-year longitudinal study. *Child Development, 71*, 684–689.

Waters, H. F. (1993, July 12). Networks under the gun. *Newsweek*, 64–66.

Waters, H. S. (1980). "Class news": A single-subject longitudinal study of prose production and schema formation during childhood. *Journal of Verbal Learning and Verbal Behavior, 19*, 152–167.

Watson, J. B. (1925). *Behaviorism.* New York: Norton.

Webb, S. J., Monk, C. S., & Nelson, C. A. (2001). Mechanisms of postnatal neurobiological development: Implications for human development. *Developmental Neuropsychology, 19*, 147–171.

Wechsler, D. (1991). *Manual for the Wechsler Intelligence Test for Children – III.* New York: The Psychological Corporation.

Wegman, M. E. (1994). Annual summary of vital statistics-1993. *Pediatrics, 95*, 792–803.

Weinberg, M. K., & Tronick, E. Z. (1994). Beyond the face: An empirical study of infant affective configurations of facial, vocal, gestural, and regulatory behaviors. *Child Development, 65*, 1503–1515.

Weinberg, M. K., Tronick, E. Z., Cohn, J. F., & Olson, K. L. (1999). Gender differences in emotional expressivity and self-regulation during early infancy. *Developmental Psychology, 35*, 175–188.

Weisner, T. S., & Wilson-Mitchell, J. E. (1990). Nonconventional family lifestyles and sex typing in six-year-olds. *Child Development, 61*, 1915–1933.

Weissman, M. D., & Kalish, C. W. (1999). The inheritance of desired characteristics: Children's view of the role of intention in parent-offspring resemblance. *Journal of Experimental Child Psychology, 73*, 245–265.

Weizman, Z. O., & Snow, C. E. (2001). Lexical output as related to children's vocabulary acquisition: Effects of sophisticated exposure and support for meaning. *Developmental Psychology, 37*, 265–279.

Wellman, H. M. (1992). *The child's theory of mind.* Cambridge, MA: MIT Press.

Wellman, H. M. (1993). Early understanding of mind: The normal case. In S. Baron-Cohen, H. Tager-Flusberg, & D. J. Cohen (Eds.), *Understanding other minds: Perspectives from autism.* Oxford, England: Oxford University Press.

Wellman, H. M. (2002). Understanding the psychological world: Developing a theory of mind. In U. Goswami (Ed.), *Blackwell handbook of childhood cognitive development* (pp. 167–187). Malden, MA: Blackwell.

Wellman, H. M., Cross, D., & Bartsch, K. (1986). Infant search and object permanence: A meta-analysis of the A not B error. *Monographs of the Society for Research in Child Development, 51*(Serial No. 214).

Wellman, H. M., Cross, D., & Watson, J. (2001). Meta-analysis of theory-of-mind development: The truth about false belief. *Child Development, 72*, 655–684.

Wellman, H. M., & Gelman, S. A. (1998). Knowledge acquisition in foundational domains. In W. Damon (Ed.), *Handbook of child psychology* (Vol. 2). New York: Wiley.

Wendland-Carro, J., Piccinini, C. A., & Millar, W. S. (1999). The role of an early intervention on enhancing the quality of mother-infant interaction. *Child Development, 70,* 713–721.

Wentworth, N., Benson, J. B., & Haith, M. M. (2000). The development of infants' reaches for stationary and moving targets. *Child Development, 71,* 576–601.

Wentzel, K. R. (2002). Are effective teachers like good parents? Teaching styles and student adjustment in early adolescence. *Child Development, 73,* 287–301.

Werker, J. F., & Tees, R. C. (1999). Influences on infant speech processing: Toward a new synthesis. *Annual Review of Psychology, 50,* 509–535.

Werner, E. E. (1995). Resilience in development. *Current Directions in Psychological Science, 4,* 81–85.

Werner, H. (1948). *Comparative psychology of mental development.* Chicago: Follet.

Wertsch, J. V., & Tulviste, P. (1992). L. S. Vygotsky and contemporary developmental psychology. *Developmental Psychology, 28,* 548–557.

West, S. G., Biesanz, J. C., & Pitts, S. C. (2000). Causal inference and generalization in field settings: Experimental and quasi-experimental designs. In H. T. Reis & C. M. Judd (Eds.), *Handbook of research methods in social and personality psychology* (pp. 40–84). New York: Cambridge University Press.

Whitaker, R. C., Wright, J. A., Pepe, M. S., Seidel, K. D., & Dietz, W. H. (1997). Predicting obesity in young adulthood from childhood and parental obesity. *New England Journal of Medicine, 337,* 869–873.

White, S. H. (1996). The relationships of developmental psychology to social policy. Health. In E. F. Zigler, S. L. Kagan, & N. W. Hall (Eds.), *Children, families, and government: Preparing for the twenty-first century.* New York: Cambridge University Press.

Whitehead, J. R., & Corbin, C. B. (1997). Self-esteem in children and youth: The role of sport and physical education. In K. R. Fox, et al. (Eds.), *The physical self: From motivation to well-being.* Champaign, IL: Human Kinetics.

Whitehurst, G. J., & Vasta, R. (1975). Is language acquired through imitation? *Journal of Psycholinguistic Research, 4,* 37–59.

Whitehurst, G. J., & Vasta, R. (1977). *Child behavior.* Boston: Houghton Mifflin.

Whitesell, N. R., & Harter, S. (1996). The interpersonal context of emotion: Anger with close friends and classmates. *Child Development, 67,* 1345–1359.

Whiting, J. W. M., & Child, I. L. (1953). *Child training and personality: A cross-cultural study.* New Haven: Yale University Press.

Whitney, E. N., & Hamilton, E. M. N. (1987). *Understanding nutrition* (4th ed.). St. Paul: West.

Wicks-Nelson, R., & Israel, A. C. (1991). *Behavior disorders of childhood* (2nd ed.). Englewood Cliffs, NJ: Prentice-Hall.

Wiegers, T. A., van der Zee, J., & Keirse, M. J. (1998). Maternity care in The Netherlands: The changing home birth rate. *Birth, 25,* 190–197.

Williams, J. E., & Best, D. L. (1990). *Measuring sex stereotypes: A thirty-nation study* (rev. ed.). Newbury Park, CA: Sage.

Williams, J. M. (1997). *Style: Ten lessons in clarity and grace* (5th ed.). New York: Longman.

Willinger, M. (1995). Sleep position and sudden infant death syndrome. *Journal of the American Medical Association, 273,* 818–819.

Wills, T. A., Sandy, J. M., Yaeger, A., & Shinar, O. (2001). Family risk factors and adolescent substance use: Moderation effects for temperament dimensions. *Developmental Psychology, 37,* 283–297.

Wilson, B. J., Smith, S. L., Potter, W. J., Kunkel, D., Linz, D., Colvin, C. M., & Donnerstein, E. (2002). Violence in children's television programming: Assessing the risks. *Journal of Communication, 52,* 5–35.

Wilson, C. C., Piazza, C. C., & Nagle, R. (1990). Investigation of the effect of consistent and inconsistent behavioral example upon children's donation behavior. *Journal of Genetic Psychology, 151,* 361–376.

Wilson, G. T., Heffernan, K., & Black, C. M. D. (1996). Eating disorders. In E. J. Marsh & R. A. Barkley (Eds.), *Child psychopathology.* New York: Guilford.

Wilson, M. (1989). Child development in the context of the black extended family. *American Psychologist, 44,* 380–383.

Wilson, R. D. (2000). Amniocentesis and chorionic villus sampling. *Current Opinion in Obstetrics & Gynecology, 12,* 81–86.

Wilson, R. S. (1983). The Louisville Twin Study: Developmental synchronies in behavior. *Child Development, 54,* 298–316.

Winer, G. A., Craig, R. K., & Weinbaum, E. (1992). Adults' failure on misleading weight-conservation tests: A developmental analysis. *Developmental Psychology, 28,* 109–120.

Winner, E. (2000). Giftedness: Current theory and research. *Current Directions in Psychological Science, 9,* 153–156.

Winter, C. (1997). *The fertility race: Part 3, the fertility industry* [Radio series]. Minneapolis: Minnesota Public Radio. Retrieved May 6, 2002, from http://news.mpr.org/features/199711/20_smiths_fertility/part3/

Wintre, M. G., & Vallance, D. D. (1994). A developmental sequence in the comprehension of emotions: Intensity, multiple emotions, and valence. *Developmental Psychology, 30,* 509–514.

Wise, B. W., Ring, J., & Olson, R. K. (1999). Training phonological awareness with and without explicit attention to articulation. *Journal of Experimental Child Psychology, 72,* 271–304.

Wolfe, D. A. (1985). Child-abusive parents: An empirical review and analysis. *Psychological Bulletin, 97,* 462–482.

Wolff, P. H. (1987). *The development of behavioral states and the expression of emotions in early infancy.* Chicago: University of Chicago Press.

Wolfson, A. R., & Carskadon, M. A. (1998). Sleep schedules and daytime functioning in adolescents. *Child Development, 69,* 875–887.

Wolraich, M. L., Lindgren, S. D., Stumbo, P. J., Stegink, L. D., Appelbaum, M. I., & Kiritsy, M. C. (1994). Effects of diets high in sucrose or aspartame on the behavior and cognitive performance of children. *New England Journal of Medicine, 330,* 301–307.

Wong-Fillmore, L., Ammon, P., McLaughlin, B., & Ammon, M. S. (1985). *Learning English through bilingual instruction.* Rosslyn, VA: National Clearinghouse for Bilingual Education.

Woodward, A. L., & Markman, E. M. (1998). Early word learning. In W. Damon (Ed.), *Handbook of child psychology* (Vol. 2). New York: Wiley.

Woollacott, M. H., Shumway-Cook, A., & Williams, H. (1989). The development of balance and locomotion in children. In M. H. Woollacott & A. Shumway-Cook (Eds.), *Development of posture and gait across the life span.* Columbia: University of South Carolina Press.

World Health Organization. (1997). Integrated management of childhood Illness: A WHO/UNICEF initiative. *Bulletin of the World Health Organization, 75,* Supplement 1.

World Health Organization. (1999). *Removing obstacles to healthy development.* World Health Organization.

Wright, J. C., Huston, A. C., Vandewater, E. A., Bickham, D. S., Scantlin, R. M., Kotler, J. A., Caplovitz, A. G., Lee, J. H., Hofferth, S., & Finkelstein, J. (2001). American children's use of electronic media in 1997: A national survey. *Journal of Applied Developmental Psychology, 22,* 31–47.

Wynn, K. (1996). Infants' individuation and enumeration of actions. *Psychological Science, 7,* 164–169.

Xiaohe, X., & Whyte, M. K. (1990). Love matches and arranged marriages. *Journal of Marriage and the Family, 52,* 709–722.

Yang, B., Ollendick, T. H., Dong, Q., Xia, Y., & Lin, L. (1995). Only children and children with siblings in the People's Republic of China: Levels of fear, anxiety, and depression. *Child Development, 66,* 1301–1311.

Yang, Q., Rasmussen, S. A., & Friedman, J. M. (2002). Mortality associated with Down's syndrome in the USA from 1983 to 1997: A population-based study. *The Lancet, 359,* 1019–1025.

Yates, M., & Youniss, J. (1996). Community service and political-moral identity in adolescents. *Journal of Research on Adolescence, 6,* 271–284.

Yeung, W. J., Sandberg, J. F., Davis-Kean, P. E., & Hofferth, S. L. (2001). Children's time with fathers in intact families. *Journal of Marriage and Family, 63,* 136–154.

Yonas, A., & Owsley, C. (1987). Development of visual space perception. In P. Salapatek & L. Cohen (Eds.), *Handbook of infant perception* (Vol. 2). Orlando, FL: Academic Press.

Young, S. K., Fox, N. A., & Zahn-Waxler, C. (1999). The relations between temperament and empathy in 2-year-olds. *Developmental Psychology, 35,* 1189–1197.

Youngblade, L. M., & Dunn, J. (1995). Individual differences in young children's pretend play with mother and sibling: Links to relationships and understanding of other people's feelings and beliefs. *Child Development, 66,* 1472–1492.

Yuill, N., & Pearson, A. (1998). The development of bases for trait attribution: Children's understanding of traits as causal mechanisms based on desire. *Developmental Psychology, 34,* 574–586.

Zahn-Waxler, C., Cole, P. M., & Barrett, K. C. (1991). Guilt and empathy: Sex differences and implications for the development of depression. In J. Garber & K. Dodge (Eds.), *The development of emotion regulation and dysregulation* (pp. 243–272). Cambridge: Cambridge University Press.

Zahn-Waxler, C., Friedman, R. J., Cole, P. M., Mizuta, I., & Hiruma, N. (1996). Japanese and United States preschool children's responses to conflict and distress. *Child Development, 67,* 2462–2477.

Zahn-Waxler, C., Radke-Yarrow, M., Wagner, E., & Chapman, M. (1992). Development of concern for others. *Developmental Psychology, 28,* 126–136.

Zarbatany, L., Hartmann, D. P., & Rankin, D. B. (1990). The psychological functions of preadolescent peer activities. *Child Development, 61,* 1067–1080.

Zelazo, N. A., Zelazo, P. R., Cohen, K. M., & Zelazo, P. D. (1993). Specificity of practice effects on elementary neuromotor patterns. *Developmental Psychology, 29,* 686–691.

Zelazo, P. D., Carter, A., Reznick, J. S., & Frye, D. (1997). Early development of executive function: A problem-solving framework. *Review of General Psychology, 1,* 1–29.

Zelazo, P. R. (1983). The development of walking: New findings and old assumptions. *Journal of Motor Behavior, 15,* 99–137.

Zelazo, P. R., Weiss, M. J., Papageorgiou, A. N., & Laplante, D. P. (1989). Recovery and dishabituation of sound localization among normal-, moderate-, and high-risk newborns: Discriminant validity. *Infant Behavior and Development, 12,* 321–340.

Zeman, J., & Garber, J. (1996). Display rules for anger, sadness, and pain: It depends on who is watching. *Child Development, 67,* 957–973.

Zeman, J., & Shipman, K. (1997). Social-contextual influences on expectancies for managing anger and sadness: The transition from middle childhood to adolescence. *Developmental Psychology, 33,* 917–924.

Zhou, Q., Eisenberg, N., Losoya, S. H., Fabes, R. A., Reiser, M., Guthrie, I. K., Murphy, B. C., Cumberland, A. J., & Shepard, S. A. (2002). The relations of parental warmth and positive expressiveness to children's empathy-related responding and social functioning: A longitudinal study. *Child Development, 73,* 893–915.

Zigler, E. (1998). A place of value for applied and policy studies. *Child Development, 69,* 532–542.

Zigler, E. F., & Gilman, E. (1996). Not just any care: Shaping a coherent child care policy. In E. F. Zigler, S. L. Kagan, & N. W. Hall (Eds.), *Children, families, and government: Preparing for the twenty-first century.* New York: Cambridge University Press.

Zigler, E., & Finn-Stevenson, M. (1992). Applied developmental psychology. In M. H. Bornstein & M. E. Lamb (Eds.), *Developmental psychology: An advanced textbook.* Hillsdale, NJ: Erlbaum.

Zigler, E., & Styfco, S. J. (1994). Head Start: Criticisms in a constructive context. *American Psychologist, 49,* 127–132.

Zigler, E. F., & Muenchow, S. (1992). *Head Start: Inside story of America's most successful educational experiment.* New York: Basic Books.

Zimiles, H., & Lee, V. E. (1991). Adolescent family structure and educational progress. *Developmental Psychology, 27,* 314–320.

Zimmerman, B. J. (2001). Theories of self-regulated learning and academic achievement: An overview and analysis. In B. J. Zimmerman & D. H. Schunk (Eds.), *Self-regulated learning and academic achievement: Theoretical perspectives* (2nd ed., pp. 1–37). Mahwah, NJ: Erlbaum.

Zinar, S. (2000). The relative contributions of word identification skill and comprehension-monitoring behavior to reading comprehension ability. *Contemporary Educational Psychology, 25,* 363–377.

Zukow-Goldring, P. (2002). Sibling caregiving. In M. H. Bornstein (Ed.), *Handbook of parenting: Vol. 3. Status and social conditions of parenting* (2nd ed., pp. 253–286). Mahwah, NJ: Erlbaum.

# ACKNOWLEDGMENTS

## Photographs

**About the Author** Page xxiii, Courtesy of Robert V. Kail.

**Chapter 1** Page 11 Nina Leen, Time Life Pictures/Getty Images. Page 12 (top)Yang Liu, Corbis. Page 12 (bottom) Alan Carey, The Image Works. Page 14 Bob Daemmrich, The Image Works. Page 15 (top) AP/Wide World Photos. Page 15 (bottom) Laura Dwight, PhotoEdit. Page 17 Lawrence Migdale, Stock Boston. Page 18 Bill Varie, Corbis. Page 23 David Young-Wolff, PhotoEdit.

**Chapter 2** Page 29 (top) Lawrence Migdale, Stock Boston. Page 29 (bottom) Jan Mueller, Jan Mueller Photography. Page 31(top) Tony Freeman, PhotoEdit. Page 31(bottom) Pamela Johnson Meyer, Photo Researchers, Inc. Page 35(bottom) Robert V. Kail. Page 35 (top) Ogust, The Image Works. Page 36 (top left) Dennis MacDonald, PhotoEdit. Page 36 (bottom left) Myrleen F. Cate, PhotoEdit. Page 36 (top middle) Michael Newman, PhotoEdit. Page 36 (bottom middle) Jan Mueller Photography. Page 36 (top right) Michael Newman, PhotoEdit. Page 36 (bottom right) David Young-Wolff, PhotoEdit. Page 39 Will and Deni McIntyre/Science Source, Photo Researchers, Inc. Page 39 (top left) David Young-Wolff, PhotoEdit. Page 39 (bottom left) David Young-Wolff, PhotoEdit. Page 39 (top right) David Young-Wolff, PhotoEdit. Page 39 (bottom right) Francelle Carapetyan. Page 43 Jonathan Nourok, PhotoEdit. Page 45 (top) Tom Grill, Corbis RF. Page 45 (bottom) Lisa Murena.

**Chapter 3** Page 52 (top left) Dr. Gopal Murti/Science Photo Library, Custom Medical Stock Photo, Inc. Page 52 (top right) Francis Leroy/Biocosmos/Science Photo Library, Photo Researchers, Inc. Page 52 (bottom) David Phillips, Photo Researchers, Inc. Page 53 (top) Alexander Tsiaras/Science Source, Photo Researchers, Inc. Page 53 (bottom) Biophoto Associates, Photo Researchers, Inc. Page 58 Spencer Grant, Stock Boston. Page 64 Aaron Haupt, David R. Frazier Photolibrary, Inc. Page 69 Jeff Greenberg, PhotoEdit.

**Chapter 4** Page 77 Photo Lennart Nilsson/Albert Bonniers Forlag. Page 78 (left) Photo Lennart Nilsson/Albert Bonniers Forlag. Page 78 (right) Petit Format/Nestle/Science Source, Photo Researchers, Inc. Page 80 (top) Photo Lennart Nilsson/Albert Bonniers Forlag AB. Page 80 (bottom) Beaura Kathy Ringrose, Michael Tobin. Page 83 Amy C. Etra, PhotoEdit. Page 85 David Young-Wolff, PhotoEdit. Page 86 Streissguth, A.P., Clarren, S.K., & Jones, K.L. (1985). Natural History of the Fetal Alcohol Syndrome: A 10-year follow-up of eleven patients. "The Lancet", "2", 85-91. Page 92 (top) Brownie Harris, Corbis/Stock Market. Page 92 (bottom) Science Source, Photo Researchers, Inc. Page 97 Lawrence Migdale, Photo Researchers, Inc. Page 98 Margaret Miller, Photo Researchers, Inc. Page 100 Tom Stewart, Corbis/Stock Market. Page 103 Robert V. Kail. Page 106 (top) Jennie Woodcock; Reflections Photolibrary, Corbis. Page 106 (bottom) Stephen R. Swinburne, Stock Boston.

**Chapter 5** Page 119 (top) Francis Dean, The Image Works. Page 119 (bottom) Stock Boston. Page 121 Bob Daemmrich, Stock Boston. Page 123 Bill Gillette, Stock Boston. Page 124 Myrleen Ferguson Cate, PhotoEdit. Page 125 (top) Robert V. Kail. Page 125 (bottom) Michael Newman, PhotoEdit. Page 127 Kilkullen/Trocaire, Corbis/Sygma. Page 128 Richard T. Nowitz, Corbis. Page 129 Philip Gould, Corbis. Page 130 © Nazima Kowall/Corbis. Page 131 (top) Rhoda Sidney, Stock Boston. Page 131(bottom) Lawrence Migdale, Stock Boston. Page 133 (top) Getty Images, Inc. – Photodisc. Page 133 (middle) Ed Reschke, Ed Reschke. Page 133 (bottom) Don W. Fawcett/Komuro/Science Source, Photo Researchers, Inc. Page 135 Alexander Tsiaras, Stock Boston. Page 136 Richard T. Nowitz, Corbis.

**Chapter 6** Page 145 (top) Dion Ogust, The Image Works. Page 145 (bottom) Michael Tamborrino, Medichrome/The Stock Shop, Inc. Page 147 Corbis. Page 148 Jose Luis Pelaez, Corbis. Page 152 (left) Michael Agliolo Productions, ImageState/International Stock Photography Ltd. Page 152 (right) Jan Mueller, Jan Mueller Photography. Page 154, Innervisions. Page 155 (top left) Joe Sohm/Chromosohm, The Image Works. Page 155 (top right) Tadao Kimura, Tadao Kimura. Page 155 (bottom left) Bob Daemmrich, Stock Boston. Page 155(bottom right) John William Banagan, Getty Images Inc. - Image Bank. Page 157 Laima Druskis, Pearson Education/PH College. Page 159 Coco McCoy, Rainbow. Page 161(top) © Kevin R. Morris/Corbis. Page 161 (bottom) © Greg Flume/Corbis. Page 163 Dexter Gormley. Page 164 Mitch Reardon, Photo Researchers, Inc. Page 165 Alan Carey, The Image Works. Page 166 (top) Felicia Martinez, PhotoEdit. Page 166 (bottom) David R. Frasier, David R. Frazier Photolibrary, Inc. Page 167 Elizabeth Crews, The Image Works. Page 168 (top) Bill Bachmann, The Image Works. Page 168 (middle) Lori Adamski Peek, Getty Images Inc. - Stone Allstock. Page 168 (bottom) ImageState/International Stock Photography Ltd.

**Chapter 7** Page 175 Elizabeth Crews, The Image Works. Page 178 Laura Dwight, Laura Dwight Photography. Page 179 (top) Jan Mueller, Jan Mueller Photography. Page 179 (bottom) Julian Hirshowitz, Corbis. Page 181 Tony Freeman, PhotoEdit. Page 182 Tony Freeman, PhotoEdit. Page 183 Courtesy of Judy DeLoache. Page 186 Richard Hutchings, Photo Researchers, Inc. Page 192 Beaura Kathy Ringrose, Michael Tobin. Page 200 (top) Tom & Dee Ann McCarthy, Corbis. Page 200 (bottom) Jose Luis Pelaez, Corbis. Page 202 Eric A. Wessman, Stock Boston.

**Chapter 8** Page 212 Bob Daemmrich, Stock Boston. Page 216 Courtesy of Carolyn Rovee-Collier. Page 217 Robert V. Kail. Page 220 Gail Zucker, Stock Boston. Page 221 Robert V. Kail. Page 222 L. O'Shaughnessy, Visuals Unlimited. Page 228 Ellen Senisi, The Image Works. Page 229 Laura Dwight, Laura Dwight Photography. Page 232 Jennie Woodcock; Reflections Photolibrary, Corbis. Page 235 Alan Oddie, PhotoEdit. Page 237 Audrey Gottlieb, Audrey Gottlieb.

**Chapter 9** Page 246 Paul L. Merideth, Paul L. Merideth. Page 248 (left) Macduff Everton, Macduff Everton. Page 248 (right) Anna E. Zuckerman, PhotoEdit. Page 253 Laura Dwight, Laura Dwight Photography. Page 256 Corbis. Page 258 Bob Daemmrich, Stock Boston. Page 262 Okoniewski, Getty Images, Inc – Liaison. Page 264 Lawrence Migdale, Stock Boston. Page 265 SuperStock, Inc.

**Chapter 10** Page 275 Bob Daemmrich, Bob Daemmrich Photography, Inc. Page 279 Stefanie Felix, Susie Fitzhugh. Page 280 David Young-Wolf, PhotoEdit. Page 281 Jeff Persons, Stock Boston. Page 283 Tom Prettyman, PhotoEdit. Page 284 Elena Rooraid, PhotoEdit. Page 289 Susan Kuklin/Science Source, Photo Researchers, Inc. Page 290 Jan Mueller, Jan Mueller Photography. Page 293 Tony Freeman, PhotoEdit. Page 294 Beaura Kathy Ringrose, Michael Tobin.

**Chapter 11** Page 305 (left) Laura Dwight, Laura Dwight Photography. Page 305 (middle) Michael Newman, PhotoEdit. Page 305 (right) Comstock Images. Page 306 (top)© Elizabeth Hathon/Corbis Stock Market. Page 306 (bottom) Robert V. Kail. Page 307 Myrleen Ferguson Cate, PhotoEdit. Page 308 Bob Daemmrich, Stock Boston. Page 310 SuperStock, Inc. Page 314 Myrleen Ferguson, PhotoEdit. Page 315 Innervisions. Page 320 (top) Mark Richards, PhotoEdit. Page 320 (bottom) Don Boroughs, The Image Works. Page 321 (left) Courtesy of David Corcoran and Everett Waters. Page 321 (middle) Courtesy of David Corcoran and Everett Waters. Page 321 (right) Courtesy of David Corcoran and Everett Waters. Page 322 Laura Dwight, Laura Dwight Photography. Page 323 Harriet Gans, The Image Works.

**Chapter 12** Page 332 PT Santana, Getty Images Inc. - Stone Allstock. Page 333 Comstock Images. Page 335 (top) Kirk Condyles, The Image Works. Page 335 (bottom) Beaura Kathy Ringrose, Michael Tobin. Page 337 (bottom) Stock Boston. Page 338 Michael Newman, PhotoEdit. Page 345 Bob Daemmrich, Stock Boston. Page 348 D&I MacDonald, Index Stock Imagery, Inc. Page 355 Robert V. Kail. Page 356 Bob Daemmrich, Stock Boston. Page 357 © Robert Maass/Corbis.

**Chapter 13** Page 363 Elizabeth Hathon, Corbis/Stock Market. Page 368 Laura Dwight, Laura Dwight Photography. Page 370 Tony Freeman, PhotoEdit. Page 373 The Image Works. Page 374 David R. Frazier, David R. Frazier Photolibrary, Inc. Page 375 Skjold, The Image Works. Page 376 Michael Newman, PhotoEdit. Page 378 © Bob Daemmrich/Stock Boston. Page 380 (top) Lawrence Migdale/Pix. Page 380 (bottom) AP/Wide World Photos. Page 383 Bill Lai, Index Stock Imagery, Inc. Page 385 Laura Dwight, Laura Dwight Photography. Page 387 Bill Aron, PhotoEdit. Page 389 John Coletti, Index Stock Imagery, Inc. Page 393 © Jennie Woodcock/Corbis.

**Chapter 14** Page 401 D. Young-Wolff, PhotoEdit. Page 406 (top) Mark Downey, Mark Downey/Lucid Images. Page 406 (middle) Bernard Wolf, Bernard Wolf. Page 406 (bottom) Myrleen Cate, Index Stock Imagery, Inc. Page 408 (top) Kirk Anderson, ImageState/International Stock Photography Ltd. Page 408 (bottom) Bob Daemmrich, Stock Boston. Page 409 (left) Bob Daemmrich, Stock Boston. Page 410 (right) © Bob Daemmrich/Stock Boston. Page 412 (top) C.W. McKeen, The Image Works. Page 412 (bottom) PhotoEdit. Page 416 (top) Corbis. Page 416 (middle) Tony Freeman, PhotoEdit. Page 416 (bottom) George Goodwin, George Goodwin. Page 420 Elizabeth Crews, Elizabeth Crews Photography. Page 421 John Burke, Index Stock Imagery, Inc. Page 422 Nancy Sheehan, PhotoEdit.

**Chapter 15** Page 432 (top) Jean Hangarter, Index Stock Imagery, Inc. Page 432 (bottom) Phyllis Picardi, Stock Boston. Page 434 Michael Newman, PhotoEdit. Page 435 James Shaffer, PhotoEdit. Page 436 Charles Thatcher, Getty Images Inc. - Stone Allstock. Page 438 Pam Francis, Getty Images, Inc – Liaison. Page 441(bottom) Bachmann, PhotoEdit. Page 442 (top) A. Ramey, Woodfin Camp & Associates. Page 442 (bottom) Peter Chen, The Image Works. Page 443 Cindy Charles, PhotoEdit. Page 445 Cathlyn Melloan, Getty Images Inc. - Stone Allstock. Page 447 © Reed Kaestner/Corbis. Page 451 PhotoEdit. Page 453 Copyright by the San Francisco Child Abuse Council. Reprinted with permission. Page 454 Jan Mueller, Jan Mueller Photography.

**Chapter 16** Page 463 (top) David M. Grossman, David M. Grossman. Page 463 (bottom) Laura Dwight, Laura Dwight Photography. Page 465 © Rob Crandall/Stock Boston. Page 468 D. Young-Wolff, PhotoEdit. Page 470 © Tim O'Hara/Corbis. Page 471 Barbara Penoya, Getty Images, Inc. Page 474 Rolf Bruderer, Corbis. Page 476 Bob Daemmrich, Stock Boston. Page 480 Tony Freeman, PhotoEdit. Page 481 R. Termine/CTW, Everett Collection, Inc. Page 486 © Jeff Dunn/Stock Boston/PNI. Page 487 (top) Boulton-Wilson, Jeroboam, Inc. Page 487 (middle) David Young-Wolff, PhotoEdit. Page 487 (bottom) Billy E. Barnes, Stock Boston. Page 489 Tony Freeman, PhotoEdit. Page 490 Ellen Senisi, The Image Works. Page 491 Jose L. Pelaez, Corbis/Stock Market. Page 492 Photo Researchers, Inc.

## Cartoons, Figures, and Tables

**Chapter 1** Page 21 *Hi and Lois* © 1993. Reprinted with special permission of King Features Syndicate.

**Chapter 3** Fig. 3–5 Reprinted figure 1 in Plomin, R. et al. Nature, nurture, and cognitive development from 1 to 15 years: A parent-offspring adoption study. *Psychological Science, 8,* 442–447. Reprinted with permission from Blackwell Publishers.

**Chapter 4** Figs. 4–4 and 4–7 Reprinted figures 7–1 and 9–12 from Moore and Persaud (1993) *Before we are born* with permission from Elsevier Science.

**Chapter 5** Fig. 5–6 from J.M. Tanner (1989). *Fetus into man.* Cambridge, MA: Harvard University Press. Reprinted by permission of the publishers. © 1978, 1989 by J. M. Tanner.

**Chapter 7** Fig. 7–8 From U. Frith (1989). *Autism: Explaining the enigma.* Oxford, UK: Blackwell Publishers. © Axel Scheffler, Illustrator. Reprinted with permission.

**Chapter 8** Fig. 8–7 From R. V. Kail (1990). *The development of memory in children,* 3rd ed. New York: Freeman. © by W. H Freeman. Reprinted with permission.

**Chapter 9** Fig 9–1 From John B. Carroll (1993). *Human cognitive abilities.* New York: Cambridge University Press. Reprinted with the permission of Cambridge University Press. Fig. 9–3 Simulated items similar to those in the Wechsler Intelligence Scales for Adults and Children. © 1948, 1974, 1981, 1997 by The Psychological Corporation. Reproduced by permission. All Rights Reserved. Fig. 9–4 From B. Bloom (1974). *Stability and change in human characteristics.* New York: John Wiley & Sons. Copyright by Benjamin Bloom. Reprinted with permission. Fig. 9–6 Figure 1, page 236 from *Developmental Psychology, 37.* © 2001 by the American Psychological Association. Reprinted with permission. Fig. 9–8 © by Scholastic Testing Service, Inc., Bensonville, IL. Reprinted with permission. (Test completed by Laura Kail.)

**Chapter 10** Page 277 Reprinted by permission of Johnny Hart and Creators Syndicate, Inc.

**Chapter 12** Page 337 Reprinted by permission of Bunny Hoest, Wm. Hoest Enterprises, Inc. Fig. 12–3 Adapted from Fig. 1 in S. Hunter & R. Pike, (1984). The pictorial scale of perceived competence and social acceptance for young children. *Child Development, 55,* 1973. © Society for Research in Child Development, Inc. Reprinted with permission.

**Chapter 13** Page 362 Calvin and Hobbs © 1993 Watterson. Distributed by Universal Press Syndicate. Reprinted with permission. All Rights Reserved. Table 13-1 From Shoda et al. (1990). Predicting adolescent cognitive and self-regulatory competencies from preschool delay of gratification: Identifying diagnostic conditions. *Developmental Psychology, 26,* 978-986. © 1990 by the American Psychological Association. Reprinted with permission. Fig. 13–3 Fig. 1 in A. Colby, L. Kohlberg, J. C. Gibbs, & M. Lieberman (1983). A longitudinal study of moral development. *Monographs of the Society for Research in Child Development, 48.* © Society for Research in Child Development, Inc. Reprinted with permission. Fig. 13–6 From N.R. Crick & K. A. Dodge (1994). A review and reformulation of social information-processing mechanisms in children's social adjustment. *Psychological Bulletin, 115,* 74–101. © 1994 by the American Psychological Association. Fig. 13–7 Adapted from Figure 1 in L. Steven, et al. (2000) Effect of conflict resolution training integrated into a kindergarten curriculum. *Child Development, 71,* 772–784. © Society for Research in Child Development, Inc. Reprinted with permission.

**Chapter 14** Fig 14–3 From J. W. Pellegrino & R. V. Kail (1982). Process analysis of spatial aptitude, In R. Sternberg (Ed.), *Advances in the psychology of human intelligence, Vol. 1.* Hillsdale, NJ: Lawrence Erlbaum Associates. Reprinted with permission. Fig. 14–7 Adapted from C.L. Martin & C.F. Halvorsen, Jr. (1981). A schematic processing model of sex typing and stereotyping in children. *Child Development, 52,* 1121. © Society for Research in Child Development, Inc. Reprinted with permission.

**Chapter 15** Page 441 PEANUTS © 1993 United Features Syndicate. Reprinted by permission.

**Chapter 16** Table 16–1 Adapted from Morrison & A.S. Masten (1991). Peer reputation in middle childhood as a predictor of adaptation in adolescence: A seven year follow-up. *Child Development, 62,* 1001. © Society for Research in Child Development, Inc. Reprinted with permission. Page 478 © by Martha F. Campbell. Reprinted with permission.

# NAME INDEX

Brown, C.S., 356
Brown, E.G., 465
Brown, J.R., 310, 443
Brown, K.P., 476
Brown, L.L., 340
Brown, R., 231, 286
Brownell, C.A., 193
Bruce, J., 442
Bruck, M., 225
Bryant, B.K., 383, 475
Bryant, P.E., 229
Bryden, M.P., 407
Bryk, K., 420
Buchanan, C.M., 412
Bucholz, M., 145
Buhrmester, D., 444, 468
Buhs, E.S., 475
Bukowski, W.M., 387, 462, 469, 474
Bullinger, A., 146
Bullock, M., 333
Burch, M.M., 216
Burchinal, M., 282
Burger-Judisch, L.M., 136
Burgess, K.B., 315
Buriel, R., 431
Burks, V.S., 391
Burman, B., 448
Bush, K.R., 432
Bushman, B.J., 389
Buss, K.A., 311, 314
Butler, R., 348, 411
Button, E.J., 350
Buyck, P., 350
Byrne, B.M., 347
Byrne, D.F., 354
Byrnes, J.P., 406
Cain, K., 231
Cairns, R.B., 386, 410, 472
Call, K.T., 487
Callahan, C.M., 262
Callanan, M.A., 280, 310
Cameron, C.A., 232
Campbell, F.A., 258
Campbell, R., 284
Campbell, S.B., 99
Campbell, W.K., 345
Campos, J.J., 154, 306
Camras, L.A., 308
Canfield, R.L., 233
Cannon, T.D., 100
Cantor, N., 368
Capaldi, D.M., 452
Capelli, C.A., 298
Capozzoli, M., 157
Carey, S., 156, 195, 196, 234
Carlo, G., 374
Carlson, E.A., 323
Carlson, S.M., 464
Carpenter, P.A., 230
Carrerre, S., 437
Carroll, J., 245
Carroll, J.L., 107
Carskadon, M.A., 340
Cartwright, B.S., 464
Caruso, D.R., 247

Carver, L., 216
Casaer, P., 134
Casas, J.F., 392
Case, R., 194, 211
Casey, B.J., 136, 409
Casiglia, A.C., 475
Caspi, A., 313, 315
Cassidy, J., 321, 324
Cattell, R.B., 244
Ceci, S.J., 222, 225
Cerella, J., 213
Cervantes, C.A., 310
Champion, H., 297
Chan, R.W., 439
Chandler, M., 373
Chang, L., 393
Chanquoy, L., 233
Chao, R.K., 437
Chapman, P.D., 250, 251
Chase-Lansdale, P.L., 438, 448
Chavira, V., 338
Chen, X., 475
Cheney, D., 289
Cherlin, A.J., 448
Chess, S., 313, 316
Cheung, L.W.Y., 100
Chi, M.T.H., 219
Chilman, C.S., 123
Chipperfield, J.G., 441
Chomitz, V.R., 100
Chomsky, N., 288
Chorpita, B.F., 308
Christensen, A., 437
Chung, A., 46
Cicchetti, D., 453, 454
Cipani, E., 264
Cipielewski, J., 283
Clark, K.B., 100
Clark, M.K., 357
Clifton, R.K., 146, 163, 165
Clingempeel, W.G., 451
Clinkenbeard, P.R., 262
Cluss, P.A., 129
Cochran, S.W., 403
Cocking, R.R., 482
Coco, A.L., 475
Codd, J., 284
Cohen, L., 383
Cohen, S., 84
Coie, J.D., 385, 392
Colby, A., 373
Cole, C.F., 481
Cole, D.A., 345, 348
Cole, P.M., 411
Coleman, M., 486
Collaer, M.L., 409, 420
Collins, W.A., 340
Coltheart, M., 228
Condry, J.C., 410
Conger, R.D., 125, 432
Conway, M.A., 221
Cooper, J., 418
Cooper, R.P., 101
Coopersmith, S., 348
Coplan, R.J., 465

Copper, R.L., 84
Corballis, M.C., 167
Corbin, C.B., 167, 168
Cornelius, M., 86
Cornwell, K.S., 166
Cosmides, L., 304
Costa, P.T., 315
Costall, A., 305
Costin, S.E., 381
Courage, M.L., 148, 222
Cowart, B.J., 145
Cox, A., 283
Cox, M.J., 324
Coy, K.C., 366
Crabbe, J., 60
Craig, R.K., 190
Crawford, M., 125
Crenshaw, T.M., 476
Creusere, M.A., 298
Crick, N.R., 386, 390, 391, 392, 410–11
Crnic, K.A., 100, 437
Crockenberg, S.B., 383
Cross, D., 190
Crowder, R.G., 230
Csikszentmihalyi, M., 262
Cuellar, I., 339
Cummings, E.M., 323, 385, 448
Cunningham, A.E., 229
Curtain, S.C., 98
Curtis, L.E., 234
Curtis, M.E., 230
Curtiss, S., 290
Curwin, A., 282
Daly, M., 455
Damon, W., 334
Danaher, D.L., 412
Daneman, M., 230
Dannemiller, J.L., 148, 154
Darlington, R., 258
Darwin, C., 9
D'Augelli, 471, 472
Davidson, F.H., 356
Davidson, K.M., 93
Davidson, M.M., 356
Davies, P.T., 448
Davis, B.L., 276
Day, J.D., 256
Deater-Deckard, K., 388
De Beni, R., 230
DeCaspar, A.J., 80
de Castro, B.O., 391
Degirmencioglu, S.M., 474
de Haan, M., 156
de Jong, P.F., 228
Dekovic, M., 477
Dellas, M., 336
DeLoache, J., 182–84, 217
Dement, W.C., 107
Dempster, F.N., 212
Denny, M.A., 164
DeRosier, M.E., 475
deSchonen, N., 333
Desimone, L., 46
Desjardins, R.N., 275
Detterman, D.K., 263